RESPONSIBLE GRACE:

JOHN WESLEY'S PRACTICAL THEOLOGY

Responsible Grace:
John Wesley's Practical Theology

Randy L. Maddox

Kingswood Books
An Imprint of Abingdon Press
Nashville, Tennessee

RESPONSIBLE GRACE:
JOHN WESLEY'S PRACTICAL THEOLOGY

09 — 16

Library of Congress Cataloging-in-Publication Data

Maddox, Randy L.
Responsible grace : John Wesley's practical theology / by Randy L. Maddox.
p. cm.
Includes bibliographical references and index.
ISBN 0-687-00334-2 (alk. paper)
1. Wesley, John. 1703–1791. 2. Theology, Practical. I. Title.
BX8495.W5M284 1994
230 ' .7 ' 092—dc20 94-28926
CIP

ISBN 13: 978-0-687-00334-1

Printed in the United States of America
on recycled, acid-free paper

For

Thane Eugene & Velma Lou Maddox

and

E. Lloyd & Timeylee Chadwick

CONTENTS

Acknowledgments 13

Introduction 15

Chapter 1: Human Knowledge of the God of Responsible Grace 26

The Fount of Knowledge—God's Gracious Self-Revelation . . 26

Excursus: Wesley's Epistemology 27
The Gracious Character of *All* Revelation 28
Initial Universal Revelation 29
Definitive Christian Revelation 30
Excursus: The Possibility of Extra-Christian Salvation 32
Excursus: The Possibility and Purpose of a Natural Theology 34

Sources/Criteria of Christian Doctrine 36

The "Wesleyan Quadrilateral" 36
Scripture 36
Reason 40
"Tradition" 42
Experience 44
Wesley's "Method"? 46

Chapter 2: The God of Responsible Grace 48

The Problem of God-Knowledge 48

Sources of Human Knowledge of God 48
Nature of Human "God-Language" 49
Reflexive Nature of Knowledge of God 50

The Nature of God 50

God's Natural Attributes 51
God's Moral Attributes 53
Crucial Concern: God's Sovereignty 54
Excursus: Wesley on Predestination 55

The Work of God/Father 58

God/Father as Creator and Sustainer 58

God/Father as Provider 60
God/Father as Governor or Judge. 61
God/Father as Physician. 62
Summary: God as Father. 63

Chapter 3: Humanity's Need and God's Initial Restoring Grace. . . . 65

General Character of Wesley's Anthropology 65

Humanity as God's Gracious Creation. 67
The Image of God in Humanity. 68
Wesley's Relational Anthropology 68
Wesley's Holistic Psychology. 69
Wesley's Holistic Anthropology? 70
Humanity as Male and Female 72

Humanity as Fallen: Debilitated and Depraved, but Guilty? 73
The Two Dimensions of Sin 73
Original Sin or Inbeing Sin? 74
The Source of Inbeing Sin 75
The Nature of Inbeing Sin 81
The Extent of Inbeing Sin—Total Depravity 82
Pause for Perspective. 82

Humanity as Nascently Restored 83
The Prevenience of Restoring Grace. 83
The Character of Restoring Grace. 84
Prevenient Grace as the Beginning of Restoration. 87
Excursus: Wesley's "Synergism"? 91
The Resulting Actual Human Situation 92

Chapter 4: Christ—The Initiative of Responsible Grace 94

General Character of Wesley's Christology 94

Christ—An Atonement for Sin 96
Atonement as Liberation? 97
Excursus: Wesley on the Nature and Uses of the Law 98
Atonement as Pardon 101
Atonement as Display of God's Love 106
The Point of the Atonement 109

The Three Offices of Christ 109
Christ as Priest. 110
Christ as Prophet. 111
Christ as King/Physician. 112
"Preaching Christ In All His Offices". 113

The Nature of Christ 114
Stress on Christ's Divinity 115
Discomfort with Accenting Christ's Humanity 115
Practical Monophysitism? 116
Wesley's Concern? 117

Chapter 5: Holy Spirit—The Presence of Responsible Grace 119
The Holy Spirit as God's Restored Presence 119
The Holy Spirit as Inspiring Physician 121
The Dimensions of the Spirit's Inspiration 123
The Universal Restoring Presence of the Spirit 123
The Witness of the Spirit 124
Excursus: Wesley on the Assurance of Faith 124
Excursus: Wesley on the Nature of Faith 127
Excursus: Wesley on the Perceptibility of Grace 128
Summary and Evaluation 129
The Fruit of the Spirit 131
The Guidance of the Spirit 133
The Gifts of the Spirit 133
Excursus: Wesley the Charismatic? 134
Spirit, Son, and Father: Wesley on the Trinity 136
The Spirit and the Son: The Filioque? 137
Unity or Distinction of the Divine Persons 137
Doctrine of the Trinity as a Grammar of Responsible Grace 139

Chapter 6: Grace and Response—The Nature of Human Salvation 141
The Three Dimensions of Salvation 143
The Therapeutic Focus of Salvation 144
The Holistic Scope of Salvation 145
Excursus: Wesley on Physical Health and Healing 146
The Co-Operant Character of Salvation 147
Excursus: Wesley on Justification by Faith Alone 148
The Possibility of Apostasy 151
The Gradual Process of Salvation 151
The Place of Instantaneous Transitions in Christian Life . . . 153
The Individual Variability of Salvation 155

Chapter 7: The Way of Salvation—Grace Upon Grace 157

Regeneration 159

Awakening 160

Repentance 161
- Repentance *prior* to Justification/New Birth 162
- Excursus: Wesley on Sin in Believers 163
- Repentance within the Christian Life 165

Justification 166
- Pardoned by the Merits of Christ 166
- Pardoned *in order* to Participate (Adoption) 168
- Justification and Sanctification 169
  - First Justification and the New Birth 170
  - Final Justification and Sanctification Proper 171
  - The Dynamic Tension 172

Faith 172
- Faith and Justification 173
- Faith and Repentance 173
- Faith Working By Love 174

Sanctification 176
- New Birth 176
- "Growth in Grace" 177
- Christian Perfection 179
  - Chronological Perspectives 180
  - Central Themes 187
- Summary 189

Glorification 190

Chapter 8: The Means of Grace and Response 192

The Role of the Means of Grace in Christian Life 192
- The Mediation of Grace 193
- Ordinary and Extraordinary Means of Grace 193
- Effective Means and Requisite Response 195
- Guarantees of Pardon or Means of Healing? 197
- Nurturing Grace and Patterning Exercises 200

Means of Sanctifying Grace 201
- The Lord's Supper 202
- Corporate Worship 205
  - Formal Prayers 206
  - Scripture Lectionary 207

Church Year 207
Hymns 208
Sermon 208
Communal Support 209
Love Feasts 210
Watch-Night Services 210
Covenant Renewal 210
Accountability 211
The General Rules 211
Spiritual Directors 212
Accountability Groups 212
Private Exercises 213
Study of Scripture 214
Devotional/Catechetical Readings 214
Private Prayers 214
Works of Mercy 215
Love of God and Love of Others 215
Formative Effect of Works of Mercy 215
The Place of Self-Denial 215

Means of Justifying Grace 216
Historical Perspectives on Wesley's Pastoral Challenge 216
Wesley's Pastoral Response 218
Call to Renewed Responsiveness 218
Methodist Society as Catechumenate 219
Excursus: The Lord's Supper as a Converting Ordinance 219
Practical-Theological Implications for Baptism 221
Adult Baptism as a Means of Responsible Grace 222
The Benefits of Infant Baptism 223
Practical-Theological Implications for Confirmation 225
The Importance of Childhood Catechesis 225
The Rite of Confirmation 227
Communion of Children 227

Means of Prevenient Grace? 228

Chapter 9: The Triumph of Responsible Grace 230

The Historical Context of Wesley's Eschatology 231

Responsible Grace's Triumph in Process 235
Wesley's Millennialism? 236
The Kingdom of Grace and the Kingdom of Glory 239
The Reign of Grace in and through the Church 241
Wesley's Eschatological Ethics 242
Personal Ethics 243

Social Ethics 243
Ecological Ethics 246

Responsible Grace's Triumphant Goal 247
Death, Immortality, Resurrection 248
Intermediate States 249
Judgment 251
The New Creation 252

Concluding Reflections 254

Notes 257

Selected Bibliography 375

Index of Selected Names 409

Index of Selected Subjects 415

ACKNOWLEDGMENTS

As this project draws to a close, I am profoundly aware that it would have been impossible without support. To begin with, I want to express gratitude to Sioux Falls College, and particularly its president Thomas Johnson, for the variety of ways that institutional support has been given to my work. One form of this support was a full-year sabbatical (1988-89) to begin the concentrated research and writing, a year made possible in part by a much appreciated supplementary grant from the General Board of Higher Education and Ministry of the United Methodist Church. I also would like to recognize publicly my specific debt to the interlibrary-loan offices of Sioux Falls College and the University of Iowa for their prompt and courteous handling of my seemingly endless stream of requests for that "Wesley stuff." Less institutional, but even more indispensable, has been the help that I have received through conversations with, letters from, and suggestions of Wesley scholars too numerous to mention here. I have tried to reflect this contribution in my notes. I trust that they will consider this study a small payment on my debt, and I look forward to reaping the dividend of their critical appraisal. I am equally indebted to student assistants Anita Bieber and Shane Thomas for their cheerful participation in many of the mundane tasks of scholarly writing, and to faculty colleagues Michael Cosby, Michael Hagan, Benjamin Leslie, and Richard Mayer for the hours that they put in reading drafts of selected chapters for accuracy and style. Finally, I consider it a pleasure and privilege to have worked with Rex Matthews of Abingdon Press as editorial advisor throughout this project.

Professional debts are one thing, personal debts are another. As I have labored to come to terms with my Wesleyan heritage, I have become immensely more sensitive to the contribution of our predecessors to our faith and self-understanding. The dedication of this book to my parents (by birth and by marriage) is intended as an expression of gratitude for their contribution to my life and that of my family. As for debts to my immediate family for their support and patience throughout this much-too-prolonged project, words alone cannot even begin to repay them (vacations, bike rides, and long talks are more in order).

Finally, there is my debt to Wesley himself. It struck me as very fitting that the bicentenary of Wesley's death (3 March 1991) occurred in the midst of my work on this project. Over the past few years the "whole Wesley" has become an important dialogue partner for me. During these dialogues there have been flashes of deep insight as well as periods of consternation. There have been areas of profound agreement as well as issues of perennial argument. Whatever the case, it is my sincere conviction that Wesley has shown me something of what it means to bring theological reflection into the service of nurturing Christian life and witness. May this lesson not be soon forgotten!

INTRODUCTION

A book of this length on John Wesley's theology might seem odd to some readers. It has become commonplace for critics to dismiss both Wesley and the movement that he founded as having no serious theological concern.[1] More important, even sympathetic Methodist analyses of Wesley's theological convictions have traditionally begun with some type of apology that he was not a "real" theologian![2]

Increasingly, however, Wesley scholars are challenging the conventional ease with which Wesley is devalued as theologian. To begin with, they remind us that Wesley was a serious student of theology, indeed one of the better trained students of his day: he completed nearly all the requirements for Oxford University's Bachelor of Divinity degree (considerably more demanding than the present Master of Divinity);[3] he was elected a Fellow of Lincoln College, Oxford; and throughout his career he was a voracious reader of theological and other works.[4] Of course, studying theology is one thing, engaging in theological reflection and debate is another. There is increasing scholarly recognition—directly contesting a common earlier assumption—that Wesley also participated actively in the full range of doctrinal discussion.[5] As the subsequent chapters will demonstrate, Wesley touched on every major area of Christian doctrine at one time or other in his pastoral career. Moreover, he did not limit himself to doctrines whose implications for Christian life (or evangelism) were immediately evident. He found it necessary to take up some quite technical debates, such as the question of whether Christ's death was the *formal* or *meritorious* cause of justifying faith. He also dealt with such speculative issues as the nature of animals in Heaven, the nature of the torments in Hell, and how God will deal with those who have never heard of Christ.

Perhaps the most surprising aspect of recent studies of Wesley, however, is the positive attention that his *model* of theological activity is beginning to receive.[6] No one can represent better, or has contributed more to, the changing evaluation of Wesley's model of theological activity than Albert Outler. In 1961, moving very much against the stream, he began to argue that Wesley should be valued as a major theologian.[7] To make this case, he found it necessary to distinguish between academic theology (with its normative standard of a Systematic Theology) and Wesley's "folk theology," arguing that Wesley's value as a major theologian lay in his ability to simplify, synthesize, and communicate the essential teachings of the Christian gospel to laity, not in his contributions to speculative academic theology.[8] Although this characterization of Wesley as a "folk theologian" remained constant throughout Outler's studies, the relative valuation of such folk theology in comparison with academic theology underwent a very important shift. In the early 1960s Outler simply assumed that folk theologians did not belong in the front rank with speculative theologians. By the mid-1980s he was arguing that Wesley's theological model was an authentic and creative form in its own right, and no longer needed to be compared negatively with academic theology.[9]

In retrospect, it is clear that Outler's reevaluation of Wesley's model of theological activity was not motivated solely by new insights into Wesley. It also reflects a growing uneasiness with the reigning academic model of theology against which Wesley was previously being measured and found wanting. In contemporary academic theological circles there has been a mounting call for recovering an understanding and practice of serious theological activity that is more closely connected to Christian life and worship.[10] As Outler seemed to realize, such an agenda involves far more than simply valuing "folk theology" alongside academic theology; it calls for recasting the dominant model of theology itself.

It was in this context that I argued in an earlier essay for a renewed appreciation of Wesley as a "practical theologian." My major contention was that Wesley's theological activity could only be adequately understood and assessed in terms of the approach to theology as a practical discipline (*scientia practica*) which characterized the pre-university Christian setting and remained influential in eighteenth-century Anglicanism.[11] This earlier approach to theological activity reflected a multi-layered understanding of the nature of theology. At the most basic level, theology was the (usually implicit) basic worldview that frames the temperament and practice of believers' lives. This worldview is not simply bestowed with conversion, it must be developed. This need gave rise to the next major dimension of theology: the disciplined concern to form and norm the Christian worldview in believers. Given the communal nature of Christian discipleship, this concern took most direct expression in such "first-order" theological activities as pastoral shepherding and the production of catechisms, liturgies, and spiritual discipline manuals. These activities in turn frequently sparked "second-order" theological reflection on such issues as the grounding for, or interrelationships and consistency of, various theological commitments. But even at this second-order level theology remained a practical discipline, ultimately basing the most metaphysical reflections about God on the life of faith and drawing from these reflections ethical and soteriological implications.

Thus, as Wesley understood and practiced theology, the defining task of "real" theologians was neither developing an elaborate System of Christian truth-claims nor defending these claims to their "cultured despisers;" it was nurturing and shaping the worldview that frames the temperament and practice of believers' lives in the world. Theologians may well engage in apologetic dialogues or in reflection on doctrinal consistency, but ideally because—and to the extent that—these are in service to their more central task. In keeping with its defining task, the primary (or first-order) literary forms of "real" theological activity for Wesley were not Systematic Theologies or Apologetics; they were carefully-crafted liturgies, catechisms, hymns, sermons, and the like. And finally, the quintessential practitioner of theology was not the detached academic theologian; it was the pastor/theologian who was actively shepherding Christian disciples in the world.[12]

It occurred to me that current efforts to reform academic theology were calling for something like Wesley's model of practical-theological activity; or, at least, that our contemporary efforts could benefit from serious consideration of Wesley's example.[13] That is how this study began. I dug into the breadth of Wesley's practical-theological materials (which, besides his well-known sermons, included letters, controversial essays and tracts, conferences, disciplinary guides for Christian life, spiritual biographies and autobiography, and a range of editorial work on creeds, liturgies, prayerbooks, bible study aids, hymnals, catechisms, and devotional guides) to gain a sense of how specific doctrinal convictions take shape in practical-theological activity. Sharing some of the results of this search is one of the goals of this book.

As I worked with Wesley's materials I was frequently reminded that the greatest concern expressed in recent discussion of proposed models of theology as a practical discipline relates to its occasional and contextual nature. In particular, there is the legitimate worry that the demands of the situation will so dominate theological reflection that there will be no congruity between the various situation-related theological judgments. But, what type of congruity should be desired, and how might it be achieved? Given its Hegelian influence, modern Systematic Theology has tended to seek more than a lack of contradiction between theological claims (consistency), it has called for their logical co-entailment (coherence). Experience has shown that such coherence can usually be attained only at the expense of exegetical and/or contextual considerations.

Accordingly, those seeking to relate theology more integrally to Christian life and practice have tended instead to take consistency as a sufficient goal. But how can even this be obtained without overriding contextual authenticity?

I have come to believe that help in answering this question can be found in the related argument that what gives consistency (*if* there is any) to particular theological traditions within a religion are not unchanging doctrinal summaries, or a theoretical Idea from which all truth is deduced or given order in a System; it is instead a basic orienting perspective or metaphor that guides their various particular theological activities.[14] Perhaps—by analogy—what provides consistency to situation-related theological judgments is that the changing specific situations are addressed in light of a common "orienting concern."[15]

This suggestion needs explication. First, I am designating this proposed factor in maintaining consistency in theological activity an orienting *concern* because I want to make clear that it is not simply one theological concept or metaphor among others. It is a perspective within which one construes (or a "worry" which one brings to) all of the various types of theological concepts.[16] Second, in keeping with its meta-conceptual nature, an orienting concern is not an architectonic Idea from which all other theological affirmations would be deduced, or under which they must be subsumed. Its role is not to be the fountain from which doctrines spring or the pattern into which they must fit, but the abiding interest which influences the selection, interpretation, relative emphasis, and interweaving of theological affirmations and practices. Third, an orienting concern is often implicit, having been imbibed with one's theological nurture. It functions in theological reflection as a way of thinking that seems so natural and inevitable that it is seldom directly scrutinized. Instead, it is the light in which all else is scrutinized.[17] Fourth, one need not have a comprehensive summary of the claims consistent with a particular orienting concern prior to engaging in theological reflection. In fact, it is precisely the search for consistent expressions in relation to new issues that enlivens a theological tradition.[18] Fifth, it is probably possible to operate with more than one orienting concern. However, if Peter Slater is correct that religious traditions seek related clusters of primary symbols and that it is typically a central symbol which provides this relation, then the relative primacy of one orienting concern within an individual's practical-theological activity is likely.[19] And finally, given Christianity's salvific emphasis, Christian orienting concerns will characteristically focus on the general issue of how God interacts with humanity.[20]

My interest in the potential function of an "orienting concern" for providing appropriate consistency to situation-related theological reflection grew as I continued to work through Wesley's writings. I became increasingly persuaded that there was such a phenomenon discernable in his various situation-related theological reflection. More specifically, I discerned in Wesley's work an abiding concern to preserve the vital tension between two truths that he viewed as co-definitive of Christianity: without God's grace, we *cannot* be saved; while without our (grace-empowered, but uncoerced) participation, God's grace *will not* save. I have chosen to designate this as a concern about "responsible grace." The formulation of this designation is quite specific. It focuses Wesley's distinctive concern on the nature of God and God's actions, rather than on humanity. It makes clear that God's indispensable gift of gracious forgiveness and empowerment is fundamental, while capturing Wesley's characteristic qualification of such empowerment as enabling rather than overriding human responsibility.[21]

A major goal of this book is to demonstrate the presence and function of this concern for "responsible grace" through the range of Wesley's work. One contribution of this demonstration will be to the broader contemporary discussion about the possibility of consistency in situation-related theological activity. Another contribution will be to the more specific debate in the field of Wesley Studies about consistency in Wesley's doctrinal convictions.

There are actually three different dimensions in which the issue of consistency in Wesley's practical-theological work arises. The first dimension concerns whether there is a demonstrable consistency among his judgments concerning a doctrinal area or issue *within differing contexts.* The second dimension turns to whether there is an acceptable congruence among his affirmations in *related doctrinal areas.* The final dimension raises questions about whether there was consistency *over time* in Wesley's doctrinal convictions. I will address all three of these dimensions in the following analysis, but will devote particular attention to the third dimension. Some historical perspective on the debates in this area might help explain this focus.

Wesley frequently responded to accusations of inconsistencies in his writings. In these responses he willingly admitted that there had been a significant alteration in his doctrinal convictions between his earliest publications (1725) and the beginning of the Methodist revival (1738); namely, he had acquired a deeper appreciation for the doctrine of justification by grace and for the experience of faith as a conscious pardon from sin. However, Wesley typically insisted that he had remained thoroughly consistent in his doctrinal convictions since this earlier alteration.

As he put it in 1789, "I defy any [one][22] living to prove that I have contradicted myself at all in any of the writings which I have published from the year 1738 to the year 1788."[23] To be sure, there were a few times when he quietly admitted changes on issues even after 1738 (such as whether one must have a *clear* sense of pardon to be justified).[24] But he was usually more willing to qualify overstatements later than to acknowledge them as being overstatements in the first place, or to admit any inconsistency between earlier and later remarks.[25]

Wesley's apologetic stance on the question of change and continuity in his thought was given an ironic twist in Methodist struggles of the nineteenth century over the Catholic[26] elements of his theology. The most typical strategy for negating Wesley's early training in—and obvious sympathy for—his Anglican tradition (with its Catholic elements) was to construe Aldersgate as a radical theological reversal to low-Church Protestant convictions. Such an approach has been carried over into many of the more recent "Protestant" readings of Wesley, which stress the contrast before and following 1738 while minimizing any variations thereafter.[27] In response, those who champion a more "Catholic" reading of Wesley have typically argued that the Protestant deviation in 1738 was temporary, followed by a fundamental Catholic "retroversion."[28]

Current Wesley scholarship has sought to mediate these earlier positions. It has become increasingly common for studies of his theological convictions to distinguish between the "early Wesley" (1733–38), the "middle Wesley" (1738–65), and the "late Wesley" (1765–91). While emphases differ, these designations are typically correlated to transitions in Wesley's general view of the Christian life from (1) a dominant emphasis on the importance of moral rectitude or conformity to the likeness of God (or, at least, sincere attempts[29]); to (2) a deeper appropriation of Protestant emphases concerning salvation by grace, creating some initial tensions within his thought; and climaxing in (3) a mature integration of the primacy of grace into his enduring concern for Christian holiness.

Those proposing this threefold model of Wesley's theological transitions have usually argued that there was both greater continuity between the early Wesley and the middle Wesley, and more significant development from the middle Wesley to the late Wesley, than has been acknowledged in prior scholarship.[30] For example, it is now widely agreed that the early Wesley did not have a total lack of appreciation for the role of grace and faith in the Christian life. After all, the doctrine of justification by faith is present in the Thirty-Nine Articles of the Anglican tradition. While Wesley undeniably gave this doctrine more orienting influence following 1738, this transition was neither *de novo* nor a total reversal of his concern for Christian holiness.[31] Likewise, as will be detailed in subsequent chapters, Wesley progressively revised or nuanced several of the assumptions about salvation by grace that accompanied the transition to his middle period, integrating them more fully into his continuing interest in holy living.[32] The result, however, was not simply a "Catholic Retroversion." I hope to demonstrate that it is better seen as an "upward spiralling" that wove his deepened conviction of the graciousness of salvation into his consistent emphasis on God's desire for our holiness in heart and life.[33]

However they are interrelated, the existence of transitions in Wesley's theological convictions has obvious methodological implications for interpreting any particular piece of his work. As Frederick Maser has put it, one must always be prepared to ask:

> "At what time of his life did Wesley believe this, and how does it compare with what he believed earlier or later?" and "How much of this is the result of Wesley's matured thought and how much a hasty abridgment of something that temporarily appealed to him?"[34]

I have tried in this study to bring such contextual and developmental perspective to each of the areas of Wesley's doctrinal convictions.

The transitions in Wesley's thought also raise questions about which phase should be considered most definitive of his position. Such questions take on a distinctive importance in many of the traditions descended from Wesley's ministry due to their ascription of normative status to certain of his works (most dating from the middle Wesley).[35] Fortunately, my interest is not in settling such ecclesiastical issues, but simply in the most adequate understanding of Wesley's doctrinal convictions as they find expression in his practical-theological activity. For this purpose it seems appropriate to value the "wisdom" that Wesley acquired through the full course of his life, particularly given the important role that he assigned to life-experience in theological reflection (see Chapter One). This leads me to agree with Albert Outler that the broadened and nuanced perspective that was characteristic of the late Wesley should be given more weight in defining his theological convictions than has been the case in most previous studies.[36] However, I hasten to add that this does not mean that earlier phases (or materials produced therein) should be neglected. Wesley's "mature" position on many issues coalesced long before 1765.[37] Moreover, the dynamic theological consistency that I will argue unites the phases of Wesley's life and ministry is often most evident in his very process of nuancing issues. As such, consideration of the *whole* Wesley is necessary to understand his mature position adequately.

Hints of another debate in Wesley Studies have emerged in the preceding discussion—namely, disagreement over which Christian theological traditions were most influential in forming his doctrinal convictions, or to which tradition(s) he bears the greatest similarity. There is more room for debate on this issue than one might expect, precisely because Wesley grew up and took his theological training in an Anglican context. Eighteenth-century Anglicanism was the most diverse theological arena of its time, due to its unique history. The original split from Rome had been more over jurisdictional matters than theological ones. As a result, the English church has never lacked influential voices sympathetic to Catholic concerns. At the same time, there were powerful currents within the newly autonomous church that urged it to complete its reformation by casting off the theology of Rome along with Roman jurisdictional authority. A few of these advocates turned to the Lutheran tradition for a model of a fully Protestant church, while most were attracted to the Reformed tradition as a guide for purging Anglicanism of its remaining Catholic elements. Ultimately, neither Protestant alternative carried the day. Instead, Anglicanism gravitated toward an understanding of itself as a *via media* (middle way) between the Roman Catholic and Protestant traditions.

Given this Anglican setting, it is not surprising that there have been debates over Wesley's theological place, or that these debates quickly focused on whether he was more "Protestant" or "Catholic."[38] Neither is it surprising that attempts to champion either reading of Wesley one-sidedly have eventually proven inadequate. Indeed, the course of the debate over Wesley's theological place has returned full circle to the argument of Richard Urlin (in perhaps the first book devoted to this question) that Wesley was essentially an "Anglican in Earnest."[39] And yet, this very point raises other questions. Eighteenth-century Anglicans were a diverse group with competing and sometimes conflicting elements. Which of these elements were most influential on or attractive to Wesley?

One strand of his context with which Wesley clearly resonated was a renewed appreciation of *early* Christian theology and practice. When Anglicans moved toward becoming a *via media* in the sixteenth century, it was not by direct mediation between contemporary Protestant traditions and Roman Catholicism. Rather, influential voices called for a recovery of the faith and practice of the first four centuries of the church.[40] Since this early tradition antedated the later divisions, they believed that its recovery would provide a more authentic mediating position. As the discussion of Wesley's view of tradition in Chapter One will demonstrate, he readily adopted this esteem for "primitive" (i.e., pristine) Christian theology and practice. Moreover, this was hardly a casual attitude of respect. He devoted considerable attention to the scholarship that was being produced by the Anglican patristics renaissance. This has led some to suggest that Wesley's differences from the various Protestant and Roman Catholic voices of his day (and his distinctive type of Anglicanism) result primarily from his commitment to recovering the theological balance of the Early Church.[41]

The general importance of the Early Church to Wesley's understanding of Christian life and doctrine has come to be widely recognized by Wesley scholars. Recently, some have drawn attention to a specific aspect of Anglican patristics scholarship—it devoted particular emphasis to Greek authors who had receded from Western consciousness following the fourth century of the Church's existence. Wesley not only became aware of many of these Greek authors through his study, he seems to have imbibed a marked preference for them over the Latin writers! A growing group of Wesley scholars is suggesting the importance of the influence of these early Greek authors (whether directly or through summaries in Anglican patristic scholars) on Wesley's theology. The background to this importance is that early Latin and Greek theologians tended toward different understandings of the relation of creation, sin, and salvation. These differences developed further in the progressively separated Western (Latin) and Eastern (Greek) Christian traditions, with the eventual result that the soteriology of the main strands of Western Christianity (both Protestant and Roman Catholic) came to be characterized by a dominant *juridical* emphasis on guilt and absolution, while Eastern Orthodox soteriology typically emphasized more the *therapeutic* concern for healing our sin-diseased nature. The point is that these scholars have become convinced that the defining emphasis of Wesley's understanding of sin and Christian life is also therapeutic, and they see his exposure to early Greek theologians as part of the explanation for this.[42]

My ongoing dialogue with Wesley convinced me that he is indeed best understood as one fundamentally committed to the therapeutic view of Christian life. Demonstrating this primacy, and reflecting on how Wesley integrated the juridical convictions of Western Christianity into his more basic therapeutic viewpoint, has become another major goal of this book. I have also highlighted parallels with characteristic Eastern Christian theological perspectives throughout the work. In noting these parallels I have purposefully avoided attempts to demonstrate Wesley's specific dependance upon early Greek theologians for the point in question. Strong historical demonstration of such reliance would be extremely difficult, particularly since Wesley was equally aware of minority voices in Western Christianity that inclined toward a more developmental and therapeutic model of Christian life (e.g., some mystics, many Pietists, and the Anglican "holy living" divines).[43] I have been content simply to provide a counterpart to the many comparisons of Wesley to the various Western Christian traditions already available in Wesley scholarship.

The current state of Wesley scholarship itself actually provided the final motivation that convinced me to undertake this specific book. When I looked for secondary sources to aid my consideration of Wesley's practical-theological activity I found that Colin Williams' *John Wesley's Theology Today* was still the standard survey text on Wesley's theology, even though it was published in 1960.[44] This situation is quite lamentable, given how much has happened in the field of Wesley Studies since 1960.

To begin with, the same year that Williams published his text witnessed the inception of the first truly critical edition of Wesley's writings: *The Bicentennial Edition of the Works of John Wesley*. Williams had to labor without the benefits of the critically-determined text or the scholarly notes provided in this edition. While the *Bicentennial Edition* is presently only about one-third complete, the volumes already published are some of the most crucial, providing significant materials that were previously unavailable.[45]

The *Bicentennial Edition* is just one indication of the fact that during the last thirty years Wesley scholarship has blossomed dramatically. Due to the leadership of tireless advocates like Frank Baker and Albert Outler, the study of Wesley has grown from an occasional avocation of a few scholars to an academic subject in its own right, with scholarly societies, research specializations, and so on.[46] A welcome result of this maturation is the exponential increase in specialized secondary studies of Wesley. A glance through my Select Bibliography will show that there have been over 100 book-length studies since 1960 on aspects of Wesley's theology.

Unfortunately, the benefits of this recent Wesley scholarship have not been adequately accessible to this point. Part of the reason is that many of the works are unpublished dissertations. Likewise, the essays are often widely scattered in professional journals and monograph collections. Finally, the growth in Wesley Studies has become truly international—a fact which, while laudable, has increased the problem of linguistic barriers (at least for mono-linguistic North Americans). My final goal in this book is to provide a guide to this secondary scholarship that can orient readers to the basic aspects of Wesley's theology and enable them to pursue further the available works relevant to subjects of their interest. I have quite consciously sought to make this survey an *orientation* to Wesley's theological materials, not a compend of them. It would be the height of irony to argue for the importance of Wesley's practical forms of theological reflection and then provide a systematic *replacement* for studying his theology. That is why I provide numerous references but few extended quotations. My hope is to encourage and enable readers to get into Wesley for themselves.

It remains only to explain the organization of the following survey of Wesley's doctrinal convictions. Let me start by insisting that there is no uniquely correct organization, because Wesley's theology simply is not "systematic" in the Hegelian sense of being derived from or subsumable under a single Idea or structure.[47] But while there is no requisite pattern for presenting Wesley's theological convictions, some may well be more appropriate than others. I have opted for an organization reflecting the Christian experience of salvation as the recovery of holiness. This pattern seems particularly appropriate to Wesley's therapeutic soteriology.[48] It also preserves the creation/re-creation parameters that distinguish his theology from much of the later Wesleyan traditions.

Chapter One is prefatory in nature, detailing Wesley's meta-theological convictions concerning revelation (How do we obtain knowledge of God and of ourselves in light of God?) and theological authorities (What are the sources or criteria of authentically Christian claims?). The survey of Wesley's theological worldview begins in Chapter Two, which sketches his convictions about God as the Source of all existence and value and as the Paradigm of authentic human life. Chapter Three turns to Wesley's anthropology, highlighting the human problem resulting from sin and God's gracious response. Attention then switches to God's provisions for needy humanity: God's gracious initiative in Jesus Christ to redeem us (Chapter Four); and Divine grace active in the Holy Spirit to heal and empower us (Chapter Five). Chapters Six and Seven trace the interweaving of God's gracious initiative and humanity's (uncoerced, but essential) response throughout the process of salvation. Wesley was persuaded that this process of developing Christian character must be nurtured by the means of grace, which are surveyed in Chapter Eight. Chapter Nine then climaxes the theme of recovered holiness by sketching Wesley's eschatology, both as the final goal and as a present dimension of all God's gracious actions.

CHAPTER 1

Human Knowledge of the God of Responsible Grace

Whenever Christians articulate, inculcate, reformulate, or defend primary theological convictions, they operate (implicitly or explicitly) with assumptions about where one can obtain reliable input regarding these issues and how one should draw upon this input to insure truly Christian convictions. That is, they operate with assumptions about the manner of revelation and the criteria of doctrinal decisions. This chapter will assess Wesley's assumptions about these "meta-theological" issues.

An initial caveat is in order. I have chosen to discuss these issues prior to consideration of Wesley's theological worldview only because it provides a helpful context for understanding some of his doctrinal decisions. I am not meaning to imply that Wesley developed explicit stances on these issues *prior to* engaging in doctrinal reflection. He was not subject to the "paralysis of analysis" that plagues modern theologians, leaving them hesitant to engage in actual doctrinal reflection until they have solved all methodological puzzles. Indeed, Wesley seldom provided extended articulations of his methodological assumptions. He postulated them in passing, or exemplified them in the process of actual theological activity. I will be gathering these scattered insights, while watching for any developments or tensions.

The Fount of Knowledge—God's Gracious Self-Revelation

One set of meta-theological assumptions concerns the sources of theological knowledge. How and where can we have access to knowledge about God and God's will for us? The best way to approach Wesley's answer to this question is in light of his general epistemological commitments.

Excursus: Wesley's Epistemology

Discussions of epistemology, which inquires into the sources of human knowledge, had divided into two major camps in the Western intellectual traditions by Wesley's time. The rationalist camp (hailing back to Plato) stressed the role of reason in providing the most important knowledge, particularly through innate ideas—ideas resident in our minds prior to any experience. By contrast, empiricists (championing Aristotle) denied that there were innate ideas, arguing that experience was the source of all foundational human knowledge. Where did Wesley fit in this debate?

The issue of Wesley's epistemological commitments has attracted considerable scholarly interest recently.[1] What has become clear through this study is that Wesley self-consciously sided with the empiricist denial of innate ideas. He frequently quoted the slogan *nihil est in intellectu quod non fuit prius in sensu,* "nothing is in the mind that is not first in the senses".[2] He embraced the Aristotelian logical tradition at Oxford.[3] He commented favorably on John Locke's *Essay on Human Understanding,*[4] and he appended an abridgement of Peter Browne's *The Procedure, Extent, and Limits of Human Understanding* to his compendium of natural philosophy.[5]

This is not to say that Wesley agreed totally with (then current) Lockean empiricism. He dissented from this tradition in two significant ways. In the first place, Wesley was epistemologically more optimistic than Locke. He considered Locke much too prone to believe that our senses could mislead us, or that the abstractions which our minds form based on our experience might not correspond to the way things really are.[6]

Wesley's second divergence from contemporary empiricists dealt specifically with the issue of knowledge of God. Most contemporary empiricists assumed that knowledge of God was available only by inference from our experience of the world or by assent to the external testimony of Scripture.[7] While Wesley allowed a role for such indirect knowledge of God, he desired more direct knowledge as well. Yet, since he agreed with empiricists that direct knowledge must come through the senses, he postulated (in conscious contrast with Locke and Browne) that God provided humans with *spiritual senses* to sense spiritual realities, just as our physical senses sense physical realities.[8]

Where could Wesley have found such a notion of spiritual senses? One possible source was his reading of John Norris, who espoused a form of Malebranchean Platonism that included an important role for spiritual senses as the means of our perception of God.[9] Another likely source was his study of early Eastern Christian writers. In particular, this theme was common in the Macarian Homilies.[10] The theme can also be found in Western spiritualist, Pietist, and Puritan writers.[11]

Whatever its source, Wesley called upon this notion of spiritual senses in two distinct contexts. Sometimes he was primarily concerned to explain how Christians could have an *assurance* that they are accepted by God.[12] At other times he further credited the spiritual senses with providing immediate perceptual *access* to such spiritual realities as the existence of our soul, angels, and the afterlife.[13] It is the latter appeal that will be of most interest as we turn now to considering how Wesley's basic epistemological commitments found expression in his understanding of the nature of revelation.

The Gracious Character of All *Revelation*

There has been an ongoing debate in recent Wesley scholarship over whether Wesley believed that human beings could have knowledge of God apart from God's definitive revelation in Jesus Christ. This debate appears to result more from an inappropriate framing of the question than from ambiguities in Wesley. The debate has typically been framed in terms of whether Wesley affirmed a "natural revelation" or a "natural theology."[14] Behind such designations is the assumption that any universal knowledge of God available through consideration of the world and human life would necessarily be "natural" knowledge *rather than* "gracious" knowledge.

It is not surprising that the question is frequently framed this way, because the polarization of nature and grace increasingly characterized Western theology, becoming definitive of much of Protestantism.[15] Thus when Wesley is read in a Protestant paradigm (as is most common), he is forced toward one or the other of opposing alternatives: either he is assumed to affirm that humans can have some knowledge of God apart from grace, or he is read to deny the existence of any significant knowledge outside of definitive Christian revelation.

By contrast with later Western theology, early Greek theologians and the continuing Eastern Orthodox tradition have rejected such polarization. They make no absolute separation between general and Christian revelation, but they see both as based in God's grace, with God's revelation in Christ establishing and completing divine revelation in creation.[16]

Wesley's convictions about revelation appear to be more in line with early Greek perspectives than with later Western theology. He too wanted to affirm that there is an initial universal knowledge of God available to those who have not heard of Christ, while insisting that this knowledge was itself an expression of God's gracious activity epitomized in the revelation of Christ.[17]

To be sure, Wesley achieved this result in a different manner than was typical of early Greek theologians. They usually assumed that there was a continuing (weakened) influence of the grace of *creation* even after the Fall. Through his distinctive wedding of total depravity with universal Prevenient Grace, Wesley grounded the knowledge of God available to those who have not heard of Christ in an initial expression of the grace of *restoration.*

In other words, Wesley was convinced that no one had access to God apart from the gracious restoration of Divine self-revelation. However, he also believed that this restoration took place in a continuum of progressively more definitive expressions, beginning with a basic knowledge that was universally available and reaching definitive expression in Christ.[18]

Initial Universal Revelation

In keeping with his epistemological commitments, Wesley denied that humans have an innate idea of God stamped on our souls. All knowledge of God must come either through inference from creation or by direct sensation through our spiritual senses. The major source that Wesley consistently identified for the universally-restored initial revelation of God was inference from creation.[19] Beyond this constant, his precise convictions about the content and effectiveness of God's restored initial self-revelation fluctuated somewhat through time.

The early Wesley apparently romanticized the situation of native peoples (who would have no revelation of Christ) as being free from the distorting sophistication and ambitions of much Christian culture. He assumed that they were innocent, humble, willing to learn, and eager to do the will of God. He even claimed that one of his main reasons for undertaking the mission to Georgia was to present his understanding of the gospel to the Native Americans, for they would immediately discern if his doctrines were authentic or not![20] Needless to say, his actual encounters with Native Americans failed to live up to such unrealistic expectations. In reaction, Wesley was soon castigating the religion of those who had no revelation of Christ as being demonic.[21]

Wesley's disillusionment in Georgia coincided with his heightened appreciation for the Protestant emphasis on distinctively Christian grace. As a result, the period shortly following Aldersgate evidenced his most negative evaluations of any universal revelation of God. He did not deny it, but he saw it as nearly empty. Consideration of God's creation might convince us of God's existence, but it could tell us nothing of God's nature.[22]

As time passed, Wesley's estimation of the contribution of restored universal revelation appears to have increased. In 1748 we find him suggesting that God's basic attributes of omnipresence, omnipotence, and wisdom can be deduced from creation.[23] By 1754 he included at least a vague awareness of the general lines of good and evil in the religious knowledge that was universally available.[24]

This is not to say that Wesley now considered this initial restored revelation to be self-sufficient. Indeed, in 1757 he wrote a lengthy polemic against Bishop John Taylor's deistic claim that "heathens" (i.e., those lacking the revelation of Christ) have sufficient knowledge and power to know God and obey God's will. Given the situational nature of this piece, it is not surprising that it one-sidedly emphasized the limitations of universal revelation. However, even here Wesley did not deny that some restored knowledge was available to all, only that it was effective in producing virtuous (i.e., holy) lives.[25]

By the 1780s Wesley had nuanced even this assumption. He now claimed that initial universal revelation enabled people to infer not only that there was a powerful, wise, just, and merciful Creator, but also that there would be a future state of punishment or reward for present actions. More importantly, he suggested that God may have taught some heathen all the essentials of true religion (i.e., holiness) by an inward voice.[26] That is, he raised the possibility that Prevenient Grace might involve more than simply strengthening our human faculties and testifying to us through creation; it might also provide actual overtures to our spiritual senses![27] With such provisions, some people would surely pursue virtuous lives, and Wesley appeared willing to acknowledge some attainment. However, he was quick to add that such cases would be less pure and far less common than in the Christian dispensation, and he was convinced that these persons would not have the *assurance* that is available to Christians through the Spirit.[28]

Definitive Christian Revelation

Wesley's acknowledgement and understanding of an initial universal revelation would have been largely acceptable to the emerging deistic temper of his day, that is, until he raised the suggestion of direct spiritual sensation! Here was the crucial parting of the roads between Wesley and contemporary Deism (in both its rationalist and empiricist forms). Deists limited all credible revelation to that either grounded in or conformable with general human knowledge.[29] Wesley, by contrast, assumed that the most definitive and important knowledge of God was not universally available, nor derived by mere inference. It must be obtained directly from God.[30]

How do we receive such direct revelation from God? Wesley's notion of spiritual senses immediately comes to mind, and rightly so. However, one must be careful in developing this. Wesley's own occasional unguarded comments in this area left him open to accusations that he taught a religious "enthusiasm," encouraging people to make their individual inward impulses the guides of their actions and beliefs.[31] Wesley's consistent response to such accusations was that all present inward revelations must be tested by Scripture.[32] As Charles once put it, "Whate'er his Spirit speaks in me, must with the written Word agree."[33]

In other words, Wesley ultimately focused definitive revelation in Scripture.[34] But what makes an external entity like Scripture normative over immediate personal experience? Is not definitive revelation supposed to come directly from God? While Wesley gives no elaborate discussion of this question, his answer is quite clear: he sees Scripture itself as being directly from God. His most typical way of expressing this is to describe Scripture as the direct words or teaching of God,[35] and yet he is well aware that this Divine Word comes through human words. In what sense then is it immediate revelation from God?

Wesley sees it as so in a two-fold sense. First, the original inspiration of the writers of Scripture would have been through immediate contact of the Holy Spirit with their spiritual senses, for their knowledge transcended what could be known by empirical experience or inference alone. So God's revelation was direct to them, but what about us? One of Wesley's more characteristic claims is that God's presence can be communicated through means and still be immediate.[36] In particular, the definitive revelation of God may come to us through Scripture but still be immediate because the Spirit who originally addressed the spiritual senses of the writers will also open our spiritual senses to perceive and attest to the truth they expressed.[37]

This latter claim distances Wesley from even the "benevolent Deists" of his day. These were folk like Peter Browne who were willing to allow definitive Christian revelation to provide knowledge beyond that generally available, *as long as* there was universally-available empirical or rational evidence that Scripture was indeed divine. In other words, their assent to Scripture was based on inference or rational proof. The typical evidences invoked to provide such proof were the miracles of Christ and the apostles, the fulfillment of prophecies in history, Scripture's endorsement of general revelation, and its internal consistency of teaching.[38]

Wesley once offered a similar attempt to demonstrate the divine origin of Scripture.[39] It is far from convincing. More important, it was highly uncharacteristic. His more typical course was to appeal to the immediate "internal witness of the Spirit" (through the spiritual senses) and the transformation of present Christian lives (i.e., the "external witness of the Spirit") as the strongest evidences of the truth of biblical revelation.[40] That is, he based the authority of Scripture on its sufficiency for effecting saving relationship with God, rather than vice versa.[41] While this approach raises more epistemological ambiguities than Wesley was aware of, it holds promise as an alternative to the frequent modern polarity of extreme fideism versus hard rationalism.[42]

Thus for Wesley, definitive Christian revelation finds normative expression in Scripture, a status that is personally attested by the internal witness of the Spirit. The other major way in which it differs from initial universal revelation is in its transforming content. Wesley considered two major elements of the Christian worldview to be known only in the definitive Christian revelation: the free forgiveness of God offered through Christ and the renewing power of God present in the Holy Spirit.[43] As will be shown in later chapters, these two are inherently interrelated. One of Wesley's most fundamental convictions was that authentic Christian life flows out of love, and that genuine human love can only exist in *response* to an awareness of God's pardoning love to us. It is in Christ's atoning work that the divine pardoning love is clearly revealed to humanity and it is through the witness of the Spirit that this love is "shed abroad in our hearts," empowering our loving response. Herein lies the rationale for Wesley's assumption, noted earlier, that Christians have available a greater potential for recovering holiness of life than do those with only the initial restored revelation.

Excursus: The Possibility of Extra-Christian Salvation[44]

This brings up, of course, the perennial Christian perplexity about how God will deal with those who are never exposed to definitive Christian revelation. It must be noted at the outset that Wesley rejected one possible solution to this problem that has had advocates through the history of the Church—namely, the notion of God might provide another chance after death for those who do not receive the full revelation in this life, so that they might be made aware of it and respond (positively or negatively). He specifically rejected the Roman Catholic notion of limbo for patriarchs,[45] and he even opposed the idea that Christ descended into Hell between his death and resurrection.[46] In both cases his concern seems to have been avoiding any suggestion of a second chance for those who resist repentance in this life.[47]

Then how does Wesley believe that God will deal with the unevangelized? Will they be "saved"? Given his understanding of salvation as recovered holiness (not merely forgiveness), this issue has two dimensions for Wesley. At its most abstract level, it was simply the question whether those who lack Christian revelation will be summarily excluded from eternal blessing. At a more concrete level, it was the question whether such persons can—or must—develop holiness *in this life,* which (for Wesley) is the Christian foretaste and condition of final salvation.

Wesley's answer to the first question is fairly clear and apparently consistent throughout his life. His conviction of the unfailing justice and universal love of God made it impossible for him to believe that people who lacked knowledge of Christ through no fault of their own (invincible ignorance) would be automatically excluded from heaven.[48] Accordingly, he repeatedly prefaced claims about the qualifications for eternal salvation with an exemption from consideration of those who received only initial revelation. He argued that Scripture gave no authority for anyone to make definitive claims about them. Their fate must be left to the mercy of God, who is the God of heathens as well as of Christians.[49] This conviction took its most formal expression when he deleted the Anglican Article XVIII ("Of Obtaining Eternal Salvation Only by the Name of Christ") from the Articles of Religion that he sent to the American Methodists.[50]

At times, Wesley ventured beyond this mere refusal to condemn those who had available only initial restored revelation. When he did so, the second dimension of the issue—the connection of present salvation (holiness, in some degree) to future salvation—came into play. Given his assumption that God's self-revelation in Christ and the Spirit empowered humans to recover a level of holiness unattainable through initial restored revelation, Wesley's unique dilemma was why God allowed some to be born in areas where the development of requisite holiness was not possible (he rejected the suggestion that it was punishment for pre-existent disobedience[51]). This situation struck at the heart of Wesley's theological concern, because a God of truly "responsible grace" could neither summarily condemn such people for lacking holiness nor indiscriminately affirm them all (i.e., universalism, which denies them the freedom to refuse divine grace).

The late Wesley (with his more positive estimate of initial revelation) turned to a solution for this problem that had also recommended itself to many Christians before him: God will judge the unevangelized with some discrimination after all; not directly in terms of their appropriation or rejection of Christ, but in terms of how they respond to the gracious revelation (light) that they do receive.[52] This assumes, of course, that some degree of true spirituality or holiness can emerge in response to God's graciously restored initial revelation—something that we have seen the late Wesley was willing to admit. To be sure, this holiness may still fall short of Christian standards for final salvation, but the lack will be supplied by divine indulgence.[53]

In other words, there is a stronger suggestion in Wesley's mature thought than has usually been recognized of the possibility that some who have not heard of Christ may enter into saving relationship with God.[54] Of course, while such salvation might be possible without explicit acquaintance with Christ, Wesley would always maintain that it too was "through Christ," since any human response to God was possible only because of the universal Prevenient Grace of God, which is rooted in the atoning work of Christ.[55] Likewise, Wesley would not see this possibility of salvation among the unevangelized in any way lessening the urgency of their evangelization, or even less suggesting that they are better left without the added responsibility for definitive Christian revelation.[56] For him the good news of God's pardoning love manifest in Christ does not add extra *content* to the task of obedience, it brings a renewing *power* for the life of obedience.

Excursus: The Possibility and Purpose of a Natural Theology

There is one other issue that merits discussion under the topic of revelation: "natural theology," in the sense of the inquiry into God's existence and nature on the basis of creation (rather than Scripture).

It is generally recognized that Wesley questioned the adequacy of traditional metaphysical arguments for the existence of God. For example, while he personally appreciated Joseph Butler's *Analogy of Religion,* he judged its argumentation to be too complex to convince its potential audience.[57] This is not to say—as is sometimes implied—that Wesley totally rejected the study of metaphysics.[58] Nor did he totally avoid rational arguments for accepting God's existence. He simply favored approaches that were more accessible to a general audience. For example, he once offered a version of Pascal's Wager (the argument that it is more prudent to base one's life on the bet that God exists than vice versa, because one risks only a temporal loss for a possible eternal gain).[59]

Wesley's greatest interest, however, was in the possible support for Christian belief to be derived from the emerging scientific awareness of the intricate complexities of creation. As he once put it, in response to a complex rational argument for God's existence by Andrew Ramsay, "the meanest plant is a stronger proof hereof than all his demonstrations."[60] In this retort, Wesley joined the growing ranks of his contemporaries who favored "scientific" evidence about God, arguing that the evident order in creation required a Designer (i.e., a teleological argument for God).[61]

Wesley's interest in such a use of emerging scientific knowledge led to one of his edited publications: *A Survey of the Wisdom of God in Creation.*[62] The basis of the original edition of this work was a Latin summary of the current state of natural science by Johann Franz Buddeus. Wesley articulated his agenda for translating and editing Buddeus in the Preface to the third edition of *Survey*:

> I wished to see this short, full, plain account of the visible creation directed to its right end: not barely to entertain an idle, barren curiosity; but to display the invisible things of God, his power, wisdom and goodness.[63]

For his theological commentary on Buddeus, Wesley drew upon several previous English examples of the nascent genre of natural theology.[64] The final product of merging these various sources was a progressive description of the levels of creation, from the molecular to the stellar, with periodic pauses to comment on the wisdom and goodness of God as the only possible explanation for such intricacy and apparently purposeful design.[65] Throughout it is obvious that Wesley's interest in natural science was hardly fascination with nature itself. Indeed, he specifically warned against getting wrapped up in "things" rather than focusing on how they teach us of the nature and existence of God.[66]

Clearly then, Wesley endorsed a type of natural theology, but what did he see as its purpose? While he occasionally maintained that any reasonable person who considered such evidence would be compelled to believe in God, this must be seen as rhetorical. He elsewhere explicitly denied that reason alone could ever conclusively prove this—or any other—theological claim.[67] The witness of the Spirit was also necessary. In this light I would suggest that Wesley's natural theology is best understood in terms of the less ambitious (but probably more important) task of *strengthening* one's religious convictions by showing how they "make sense" of broadly-accepted human knowledge. As he once put it, a Christian's happiness may be increased by taking knowledge of God's eternal power and wisdom in the things that are seen.[68]

Sources/Criteria of Christian Doctrine

The second major set of meta-theological assumptions deal with identifying the sources or criteria of doctrinal decisions. What specific vehicles of God's gracious revelation do we turn to for determining whether a particular claim or action is authentically Christian, and how do we draw upon these sources? Consideration of such questions has been a particular interest of the Anglican tradition. It should be no surprise that they surface frequently (albeit, usually in passing) in Wesley's works.

The "Wesleyan Quadrilateral"

What sources or criteria did Wesley invoke in deliberating or defending doctrinal convictions? Contemporary discussions of this question quickly focus on the "Wesleyan quadrilateral;" i.e., Scripture, reason, tradition, and experience.[69] This move can be misleading, for Wesley himself never used the term, nor explicitly conjoined its four components in any description of his theological method. Rather, the term was coined by Albert Outler to emphasize that Wesley relied more on "standards of doctrine" in his theological approach than on theological Systems or juridical Confessions of Faith.[70]

While not directly derived from Wesley, a conjoined consideration of Scripture, reason, experience, and "tradition" (in the sense specified later) as criteria in his theological judgments is not entirely inappropriate.[71] He does appeal to each of these individually in various settings. He also often appeals to two or three of them jointly. His most common conjunction in certifying a position as authentically Christian is to argue that it is both scriptural and rational.[72] Examples can also be found of joint appeals to Scripture and "tradition,"[73] or Scripture and experience.[74] Finally, there are examples of appeals linking Scripture, reason, and "tradition";[75] or Scripture, reason, and experience.[76]

Thus, it is reasonably warranted to focus on these four areas in discussing Wesley's process of theological judgment. The issue then becomes how Wesley construed these elements and how he drew upon them as criteria in his theological activity.

Scripture[77]

Given his correlation of definitive revelation with Scripture, it is no surprise that Wesley consistently identified the Bible as the most basic authority for determining Christian belief and practice. Indeed, at times he declared it the *sole* or only authority.[78] These declarations must be balanced by his equally emphatic statement that anyone who says that they need no book but the Bible is a rank enthusiast.[79] In reality, Wesley interpreted the Protestant *sola Scriptura* (in good Anglican fashion[80]) to mean that Scripture is the *primary*, rather than exclusive, Christian authority.

Authority for what? Wesley's response was nearly all-inclusive. As he once put it, Scripture should be the "constant rule of all our tempers, all our words, and all our actions."[81] As the rule of our tempers, Wesley considered the Bible to be the most effective means to awaken people to their spiritual corruption and the most reliable guide for their spiritual transformation.[82] As the rule of our words, Wesley meant more than avoiding profanity. He believed that Christians should adopt the very language of Scripture, as far as possible, in all their conversation.[83] As the rule of our actions, Wesley turned to Scripture not only on moral issues, but also for testing supposed leadings of the Spirit, for deciding questions of worship practice, and so on.[84]

For present purposes, it is also important to note that Wesley clearly valued Scripture for determining doctrinal issues. He considered the Bible to be a "solid and precious system of Divine Truth."[85] He was concerned to regulate his own theological opinions thereby, and argued that no pastor could be a good divine (i.e., theologian) without being a good textuary.[86] The best evidence of his seriousness about this matter is the profusion of biblical references and allusions in his sermons and theological tracts.

It would be a mistake to confuse Wesley's prolific use of Scripture in doctrinal materials with naive biblicism. He lived during the beginnings of the critical study of Scripture and was exposed to its methods and results during his training at Oxford. He was convinced of the value of reading Scripture in its original languages.[87] He understood the issues of textual criticism, using the best available Greek text (Johannes Bengel's) for his own translation of the New Testament (an update of the Authorized Version!).[88] And, he drew upon respected biblical scholarship in preparing both his *Explanatory Notes Upon the Old Testament* (*OT Notes*) and his *Explanatory Notes Upon the New Testament (NT Notes.)*[89]

Moreover, Wesley's various appeals to Scripture in his doctrinal works reflect a self-aware, contemporary approach to biblical exegesis.[90] He was solidly committed to the primacy of the literal meaning in interpreting Bible texts (a principle that the Reformers had emphasized to counter the fluidity of allegorical and spiritual exegesis, and a presupposition of the emerging historical-critical method).[91] In cases where two biblical texts appeared to contradict each other, he stressed that the more obscure text should be understood in light of the clearer one.[92] Likewise, he was aware of the importance of context in interpreting Scripture; both the specific context of any particular verse or phrase and the overall context of the Bible. In fact, one of Wesley's most frequent objections to opponents' exegetical claims was that they contradicted "the whole tenor and scope of Scripture."[93]

If Wesley was not simply a naive biblicist, neither was he an incipient fundamentalist. To begin with, his preference for the literal meaning of texts assumed inquiry into original languages. It was not simply an appeal to the meaning seen by the "common person," as was typical of emergent fundamentalism, and many of its present exponents.[94]

Likewise, while Wesley generally used dictation imagery in describing the inspiration of Scripture, he recognized the evidences of human deliberation and participation in the process.[95] As such, though he clearly considered Scripture to be an infallible, or totally reliable, guide for Christian life and belief, it is doubtful that he should be characterized as an inerrantist in the contemporary sense of the term.[96]

Most important, Wesley was sensitive to some of the problems with treating Scripture as a depository of "nuggets" of divine truth; i.e., isolated truths that could be extracted at will and organized as desired into doctrinal claims.[97] As a result, his continual appeal to Scripture only infrequently degenerated into proof-texting.

What helped Wesley avoid fragmentary proof-texting was another of his exegetical principles: that any particular Scripture must be interpreted according to the "analogy of faith."[98] For Wesley, this term referred to a "connected chain of Scripture truths." He highlighted four soteriological truths in particular: the corruption of sin, justification by faith, the new birth, and present inward and outward holiness.[99] He believed that it was the shared articulation of these truths that gave the diverse components of Scripture their unity. Accordingly, he required that all passages be read in light of these truths.

Obviously, such a thematically-controlled reading of Scripture has negative as well as positive possibilities. Both are evident in Wesley. On the one hand, it may impose too heavy a unity on Scripture, harmonizing all differences and "discovering" later orthodox Christian doctrines too easily in the text. This is particularly a danger in relation to the Hebrew Scriptures, which it might read (and Wesley often did) too directly as a Christian book.[100] On the other hand, it may provide an authentic insight into the shared convictions that make the many books of Scripture into one Book (*Biblos*).

The difference between these two outcomes will depend largely on whether interpreters remain open to the challenges that the text presents to their presuppositions about the analogy of faith. Perhaps the best way to evaluate Wesley in this regard is to see that his articulation of the analogy of faith is not simply a *set* of soteriological teachings. I would suggest that it is one way of expressing his orienting concern.[101] The doctrines that he lists focus on presenting humanity as totally dependent upon God's freely-offered *grace*, yet *responsible* for putting that grace to work in the transformation of their lives. It is this underlying concern, more than appeals to specific doctrines, that is manifest in actual examples of Wesley's theologically-sensitive exegesis. A classic instance is his response to the claim that predestination is a biblical doctrine:

> (The doctrine of predestination) destroys all [God's] attributes at once. It overturns both his justice, mercy and truth. Yea, it represents the most Holy God as worse than the devil . . . . But you say you will 'prove it by Scripture'. Hold! What will you prove by Scripture? That God is worse than the devil? It cannot be. Whatever that Scripture proves, it never can prove this. . . . There are many Scriptures the true sense whereof neither you or I shall know till death is swallowed up in victory. But this I know, better it were to say it had no sense at all than to say it had such a sense as this. . . . No Scripture can mean that God is not love, or that his mercy is not over all his works.[102]

The overall adequacy of Wesley's theological exegesis, then, would be a function of how well his orienting concern captured the central unifying convictions of Scripture.

There is one last debate concerning the use of Scripture in guiding theological decisions that merits our attention. While Protestants agreed that Scripture was the final authority of Christian belief and life, they divided in practice on the question of how to use Scripture in addressing cases not explicitly covered therein. In general, Luther took the more flexible stance that one could accept from tradition or experience anything not explicitly *condemned* in Scripture, while Zwingli urged the tighter principle of rejecting everything not explicitly *condoned* in Scripture. Wesley stood with Luther in this debate. He frequently argued that whatever Scripture neither forbids nor enjoins was of an indifferent nature; i.e., open to Christians to decide either way.[103] Of course, he was quick to add that Scripture might teach *principles* relevant to a specific decision even if it did not address it explicitly.[104]

To summarize, Wesley identified Scripture as the most basic authority for Christian faith and life; he approached Scripture in terms of the best scholarly principles of his day; he focused on the major soteriological themes of Scripture and sought to interpret all passages in their light; and, he was explicitly aware that Scripture did not definitively address every possible issue. While several of his specific appeals to Scripture may have been called into question by more recent scholarship, his general approach seems congenial to postmodern trends (such as canonical exegesis).

Reason[105]

Following Scripture, reason was the criterion that Wesley invoked most often in defending a belief or practice as authentically Christian.[106] In fact, it was more typical for him to refer to Scripture and reason conjoined than to Scripture alone.

To understand this emphasis on reason, we must recall Wesley's early-Enlightenment context. There were two major emphases of the Enlightenment relative to theological method: (1) the rejection of sole reliance on traditional authority in truth-claims, requiring some (present) rational or empirical justification for all knowledge; and (2) the scorning of all appeals to mystery or miracle, and to enthusiastic (i.e., nonrational) avenues to truth. In an extreme form, such commitments led to the rejection of special revelation, or to its reduction into a mere reiteration of the "eternal truths of reason."

Wesley was deeply influenced by the Enlightenment spirit, but also firmly committed to the possibility of special revelation. As such, he rejected both antirational Christian enthusiasm and antisupernatural Enlightenment rationalism; though, on balance, he appears to have been more worried about the rejection of reason than its exaltation.[107] He found an attractive alternative to both of these extremes in the Aristotelian logic of his Oxford training, and in the empirical strands of the Enlightenment tradition itself. Central to both of these influences was the denial that reason was the primal *source* of knowledge, whether through innate ideas (Plato) or by deduction from indubitable principles (Descartes). Experience was the source of knowledge. Reason, by contrast, was a processor (*organon*) of knowledge, organizing and drawing inferences from the input of experience. The mature Wesley concurred with this more limited epistemological role for reason. While there are occasional references in his early years to the "eternal reason" typical of the moderate rationalism of the Cambridge Platonists, his later writings present reason as a "faculty of the soul" that is limited to operations of simple apprehension, judgment, and discourse (in modern terms: perception, comparison, and inference).[108]

When reason is construed in this regulative sense, the polarization between it and revelation breaks down. Reason no longer presents independent knowledge claims that either contradict or surpass revelation. Rather, it is a faculty to be used (either well or poorly) to understand and respond to the claims of revelation.[109] Accordingly Wesley could claim that, far from bypassing or destroying reason, religious experience and belief actually provide reason with essential information (apprehension), clarify its judgment, and strengthen its inferential abilities (discourse).[110]

Against this background, Wesley's understanding of the role of reason in theological judgment should be clear. It was not another source of revelation supplementing that of creation or the Bible, it was "the candle of the Lord" given to help us appropriate revelation.[111] Its value lay in its ability to provide *responsible* (i.e., publicly-defensible) interpretations and applications of God's *gracious* revelation in nature and Scripture, as contrasted with "enthusiastic" assertions.

Reason's proper use clearly depended upon a recognition of the parameters of God's definitive revelation in Scripture. When it tried to move beyond these boundaries, or function as an independent norm, it became suspect.[112] Admittedly, Wesley did occasionally make claims such as "I am ready to give up every opinion which I cannot by calm, clear reason defend."[113] However, these are best understood on the proviso that Scripture be the main warrant to which reason appealed in building its case.[114]

If publicly defensible interpretation of God's self-revelation was the task of theological reasoning, what was its method? It was not highly technical. The logic that Wesley studied at Oxford (and handed on to his preachers) retained the imprint of Peter Ramus, who had placed primary emphasis on making clear distinctions, providing careful organization according to level of specificity (genus, species, etc.), and using a plain style of argumentation.[115] Several of Wesley's sermons exemplify such reasoning. Thus, he could appropriately describe them as "plain truth for plain people."[116]

It is also significant that Wesley often equated reason with "common sense."[117] He inherited this equation from seventeenth-century Anglicanism. In response to the growing awareness of the lack of absolute certainty in most human knowing, theologians like William Chillingsworth, John Tillotson, and Edward Stillingfleet began to argue that absolute certainty was not necessary. In its place they advocated a "common sense" approach of asking only for certainty beyond a reasonable doubt. This allowed them to defend theological claims as reasonable that were not amenable to strict deductive logic. Their approach proved attractive outside of theological circles, influencing the British scientific community and such philosophers as John Locke.[118] It also shaped Wesley, whose recognition of the limits of human understanding of revelation is evidenced by his designation of all individual theological views as "opinions."[119]

To summarize, Wesley characteristically restricted the role of reason in theology to organizing and drawing inferences from revelation. He showed little concern for providing a rational foundation for the claims of revelation, or for articulating any metaphysical framework (such as the "inner Trinity") supposedly underlying revelation.[120] Such a limited role for reason in theology must have seemed anemic to the rationalists of Wesley's day (and of ours). On the other hand, it is quite amenable with contemporary nonfoundationalism and the attempt to recover theology as a practical discipline.

"Tradition"[121]

The two doctrinal criteria beyond Scripture and reason that Wesley invoked are "tradition" and experience. These two were assigned a more restricted role in explicit descriptions of his norms.[122] "Tradition" will be considered first because it was invoked more often in formal contexts.[123] The topic of Wesley's use of tradition has sparked an amazing variety of responses among his modern interpreters. One finds everything from the worry that Wesley betrays a Roman Catholic tendency to supplement Scripture by tradition, to the opposing lament by a Roman Catholic scholar that Wesley never allowed tradition to correct his reading of Scripture.[124] This diversity highlights the need for clarifying Wesley's understanding and use of historical precedent in theological reflection.

The obvious place to begin with such clarification is to note that, while appeals to theological voices and decisions scattered through the range of Christian history can be found in Wesley's various theological materials, he did not formally ascribe authority to Christian tradition as a whole.[125] In explicit terms he affirmed only the Anglican standards of doctrine and the teachings and example of the Early Church to be normative for present Christian belief and life.[126]

Instances abound of Wesley's affirmation of the Anglican Articles, *Homilies,* and *Book of Common Prayer* as norms for his doctrinal commitments.[127] He also recommended these standards to his people. Indeed, his first published theological manifesto (1739) was an abridgment of the *Homilies.*[128] Thus began a life-long practice of appealing to the Anglican standards as warrant for his theological claims.[129] And yet, Wesley's adherence to these standards was not unquestioning. There were some aspects of them (most notably, questions of ecclesiastical structure and authority for ordination) that he came to reject[130] most often by appeal to the Early Church.[131]

Wesley's conception of this "Early Church" was fairly specific. He strongly favored the Ante-Nicene or pre-Constantinian period. Moreover, he tended to focus more on particular persons (with a preponderance of Greek writers) than on formal creeds.[132] This should not be taken as an indication that he dismissed the importance of the Early Church for determining matters of doctrine, however, for he could claim that "whatever doctrine is *new* must be *wrong*; for the *old* religion is the only *true* one; and no doctrine can be right unless it is the very same 'which was from the beginning'."[133] Likewise, his most commonly recommended textbook on Christian doctrine was a commentary on the Apostles' Creed by Bishop John Pearson.[134] His problem with many of the early creeds was not their basic teaching but some of their philosophical formulations and their polemic tone.[135]

At the same time, Wesley did not restrict the value of the Early Church to matters of Christian doctrine. Particularly from his middle period on, he was *more* concerned about the model provided there of "genuine religion"; i.e., the type of Christian spirituality and discipleship that he was trying to recover in the Methodist movement.[136] This concern also encouraged his focus more on individual authors than on official creeds—he was interested in the history of the Church as a "history of saints" to be emulated.[137]

When pressed to justify his appeal to the Ante-Nicene writers as authoritative for Christian doctrine and life, Wesley presented three major reasons: their proximity to Biblical times, their eminent character, and a special endowment of the Holy Spirit upon them.[138] By contrast, his reason for restricting authority to this period was his belief that Christian life degenerated rapidly after Constantine gave official status (and riches!) to the Church.[139]

Wesley's focus on the spiritual example of the pre-Constantinian period is reminiscent of the restorationist vision of many Pietists and Anabaptists. These folk believed that the primitive Church was a pristine period and hoped to return the present corrupt Church to that earlier ideal. Wesley's appeals to Christian Antiquity reveal a similar programmatic agenda.[140] However, he became increasingly aware that there were problems in both doctrine and life from almost the beginning of the Church.[141] Thus, his was not a totally naive primitivism.

Wesley's recognition of problems even in that Christian period which was most authoritative for him suggests his mature stance on the relationship between the doctrinal criteria of Scripture and "tradition." This issue had surfaced with particular force in 1738, gradually resolving itself in a clear affirmation of antiquity's subordinate status to Scripture.[142] The proper role of antiquity was to clarify those aspects of Scripture that were ambiguous and to provide specific implications of Scripture's general principles.[143] In this sense, later Christian teaching might legitimately go *beyond* Scripture. However, it should never go *against* Scripture.[144]

Understood in such terms, the interchange between Scripture and later Christian teachings is reciprocal.[145] These teachings aid in understanding and applying Scripture, while Scripture questions the legitimacy of traditional theological judgments, worship practices, and so on. As such, Wesley felt free to question some traditional decisions in light of the scriptural "analogy of faith" (i.e., his orienting concern). The most striking examples concern three men declared heretics: Montanus, Novatian, and Pelagius.[146] Wesley was inclined to believe that all three had been holy men whose teaching affirmed the *responsibility* of those who are forgiven and empowered by God's *grace* to grow in holiness. He took their condemnation to be a self-indictment of the antinomianism of their opponents. Whether one agrees with Wesley's particular judgment in any of these cases or not, they demonstrate that he was not an unquestioning traditionalist.

To summarize, Wesley valued tradition critically, as a "normed norm" that helped enlighten and apply Scripture. More precisely, he valued primarily the Early Church and the Anglican standards. This limitation apparently reflects a common assumption that tradition is helpful only when it is correct. Wesley's general commitments (and actual practice) do not require this assumption, however. They seem amenable to an approach that appeals to the breadth of Christian tradition, gaining practical "wisdom" from the Church's mistakes as well as from its most authentic moments—that is, an approach that views Christian history as an arena of context-specific expressions of practical-theological judgment.

Experience[147]

Most Anglican discussions of the sources of doctrinal judgment prior to Wesley dealt exclusively with Scripture, reason, and antiquity. Only a few gave notice to the possible role of experience. One of Wesley's contributions to such discussions was to make the consideration of experience more explicit.[148]

The importance of experience to Wesley has been noted by many of his later interpreters; indeed, they have become embroiled in debates concerning the topic. These debates have centered around two sets of interrelated issues. One set deals with the *type* of experience that Wesley appealed to: Was it his own inner spiritual experience, or his observation of the lives of his Methodist people? The second set of issues question the *purpose* of Wesley's appeal to experience: Was it to formulate doctrinal claims, or to confirm doctrines derived from Scripture?[149]

I would suggest that these disputes can be resolved by distinguishing carefully between two different contexts in which Wesley deals with experience: (1) when considering the source of personal assurance of salvation (the *experience* of the witness of the Spirit), and (2) when considering particular doctrinal claims (such as the *doctrine* of the witness of the Spirit).[150]

Concerning the first context, Chapter Five will make clear how essential Wesley believed it was that individuals have a personal assurance of God's acceptance. What is relevant in the present regard is that he believed the firmest ground for such assurance was an inward "sensation" of God's love. In other words, the experience of assurance which Wesley proclaimed to be available was a *personal* matter, meant to confirm *salvation.* But on what grounds did Wesley decide that such assurance was indeed available? This question moves into the second context where Wesley appealed to experience.

How did Wesley use "experience" in debating or defending doctrinal claims, such as his doctrine of the witness of the Spirit? To begin with this particular example, he clearly did not invoke experience as the sole, or even primary, evidence for the doctrine. He devoted his two classic sermons on the topic (Sermons 10 and 11) to a careful argument for its scriptural warrant. His explicit appeal to experience in relation to the doctrine was only to confirm what Scripture proclaimed.[151]

Did Wesley ever try to formulate a doctrinal claim working mainly with experience? His treatise *The Doctrine of Original Sin* is the most likely example of such a use.[152] The first part of this treatise is devoted to an historical and phenomenological survey of human behavior. It draws on Scripture, but only as a supposedly objective historical record. It concludes that the universality of sin should be obvious to "even the most careless, inaccurate observer."[153] This certainly sounds like an inductive formulation of doctrine from human experience! However, one must be careful of Wesley's rhetoric. He wrote *The Doctrine of Original Sin* in response to a deistic-inclined rejection of the doctrine. This constrained his defense to appeal to general human experience, for that is what deists considered normative. In reality, he did not merely provide an objective analysis of human behavior, he *interpreted* it from a biblical standpoint. That Wesley was not unaware of this is suggested by his sermonic distillation of the treatise, which begins with the biblical affirmations of universal human sinfulness and then argues that daily experience confirms this biblical account, though the natural (i.e., deistic) person does not discern it![154]

In other words, Wesley's discussions of Original Sin conform to the claim that he considered experience to be subordinate to Scripture in theological reflection. His typical way of expressing this was that experience "confirmed" Scripture. Actually, something more fundamental was taking place; experience was being used to *test* proposed *interpretations* of Scripture.[155] There is no better evidence for this than the fact that Wesley's most frequent appeals to experience were on issues where his distinctive interpretation of Scripture was being challenged—such as whether a sense of assurance is essential to justification, or whether believers continue to struggle with an inclination to sin.[156]

The other distinctive Wesleyan doctrinal debate that yields insight into his use of experience is the question whether God works entire sanctification gradually or instantaneously. Since Wesley believed that Scripture was silent on this issue, experience became (by default) his primary criterion for settling it.[157] As a result, we can see here more clearly the characteristic *type* of experience that Wesley appealed to in doctrinal reflection. As Frank Baker has insisted, it was not an individual's instinctive "feeling" about the matter, but an analysis of the objective realities of Christian life.[158] Wesley's concern was not that the Spirit directly assure him of this (or any other) doctrinal claim, but that the claim "prove true" in his life and the lives of his people over time.[159] The type of experience that he valued for doctrinal decisions was the *wisdom* acquired through living, not immediate spiritual sensations.[160]

To summarize, Wesley's appeal to experience in doctrinal decisions was typically to an external, long-term, communal reality: his observation of his life, the lives of his Methodist people, and human life in general.[161] Consideration of such experience served primarily to test understandings of Scripture. It took a more conscious constructive role only where he believed that Scripture was silent or inconclusive on an issue. Throughout, its subordination to Scripture was clear. Such a use of experience stands up well to modern methodological insights.[162] It also conforms to the desired model of a recovered practical theology, where reflection on current praxis would stimulate reconsideration of doctrinal understandings.

Wesley's "Method"?

The preceding discussion has shown that Scripture, reason, "tradition," and experience all played roles in Wesley's theological reflection. It should also have made clear that Scripture held a conscious primacy of place. Indeed, Wesley's so-called "quadrilateral" of theological authorities could more adequately be described as a unilateral *rule* of Scripture within a trilateral *hermeneutic* of reason, tradition, and experience.[163]

If these are the criteria with which Wesley worked in theological judgments, can we discern any distinctive pattern or process by which he drew upon them? Many have thought so. For example, Edward Sugden was persuaded that Wesley "first worked out his theology by strict logical deduction from the Scriptures; and then he corrected his conclusions by the test of actual experience."[164] More detailed is Paul Hoon's claim that Wesley's procedure for arriving at a doctrine was first, to derive it from and formulate it on the basis of Scripture; second, to test and modify it in accord with experience; third, to test it by reason; and fourth, to test it by tradition.[165]

Such crisp descriptions of Wesley's "method" imply first, that he started *de novo,* or without presuppositions, and second, that he proceeded methodically (i.e., "scientifically") in formulating his doctrines.[166] Neither of these assumptions stands up to examination.

Concerning the first, cognitive psychology and hermeneutic philosophy have demonstrated that all human knowing takes places within the tension between what is preunderstood and what is presented for integration into (or transformation of) one's existing beliefs. Moreover, our earliest patterns of preunderstandings are conveyed to us socially long before we begin conscious evaluation of them. As such, few of Wesley's theological convictions were initially "chosen" in an unbiased conscious manner; they were imbibed with his familial and ecclesial nurture.

In other words, "tradition" (socio-culturally defined) was the initial source of much of Wesley's theology. When experience called some aspect of this assumed theology into question, he then had to decide whether to retain, revise, or reject the conviction at issue. The mature Wesley consciously sought to guide such decisions by Scripture—as enlightened by reason, experience, and "tradition" (more narrowly defined, as a criterion of theological judgment). As such, if there was a process to Wesley's doctrinal reflection, it is best described as a "hermeneutic spiral" of becoming aware of and testing preunderstandings.[167]

This brings us to the second assumption. Given the dynamics of human life and his praxis-related style of theology, Wesley's reconsiderations of theological convictions were rarely methodical in the classic academic sense: he dealt with issues as they arose in his spiritual life or his ministry among his people; he dealt with them drawing on the sources and criteria most relevant to the particular situation or audience; and, he usually dealt only with the specific aspects of a doctrine at issue. These characteristics of his theological activity have been considered detriments in the past. By contrast, they are exactly what is expected of (and desired in) theology pursued as a practical discipline.

CHAPTER 2

The God of Responsible Grace

With his meta-theological assumptions in mind, the survey of Wesley's understanding of the basic Christian worldview can begin, starting with his characteristic emphases concerning the nature and activity of God. As is true of Christian tradition from its beginning, Wesley used the word "God" ambiguously—to refer to "The whole Godhead, but more eminently God the Father."[1] This overlap is almost inescapable, but must be distinguished. Claims about God's basic attributes relate to the entire Godhead, not simply God/Father. By contrast, claims about God's "work" often assume a primary application to God/Father. This distinction will structure the following analysis of Wesley's understanding of God.[2]

The Problem of God-Knowledge

It is impossible to pursue questions about the nature or work of God without coming face to face with two crucial issues: (1) Where do we obtain knowledge of God? and, (2) How can our finite minds and language ever be adequate to comprehend God? Wesley broached these issues repeatedly in the various contexts of his practical-theological activity.

Sources of Human Knowledge of God

Chapter One noted that Wesley believed that all human knowledge of God is derived from experience: our experience of God's restored initial revelation in nature, our experience of God's definitive revelation recorded in Scripture, and our experience of God's direct address to our spiritual senses. *Our* experience of God's direct address (as distinguished from God's address to the authors of Scripture) served primarily to confirm God's revelation through nature and Scripture. As such, it was to the latter two that Wesley typically turned for the "content" of our knowledge of God.

It was also suggested previously that Wesley was more interested in the evidence about God which he discerned in the budding scientific investigations of nature than that provided by classical metaphysical arguments.[3] That is why he collected this evidence in the *Survey of the Wisdom of God in the Creation.* What is important to develop in this context is that Wesley (and his sources) discerned in these scientific findings more than just evidence for God's existence; there was also evidence about God's nature. The periodic theological glosses in the *Survey* abound with claims that the scientific findings being presented confirm such attributes of God as goodness, power, wisdom, and love.[4]

As the word "confirm" implies, Wesley's primary source of evidence for claims about the nature of God was Scripture. Whenever he was involved in a dispute over an attribute, he turned to the Bible as definitive. Appeals to nature were used to reinforce scriptural teachings.

Nature of Human "God-Language"

Even if knowledge of God is graciously provided for us, how can our human minds comprehend it? Moreover, if our human language is derived from our finite experience (as Wesley assumed to be the case), how can we use it to describe God? These questions have perennially troubled Christian theologians, leading some to enjoin total silence, while others suggest that we can only know how God is *not* like us.

By contrast, some writers in Wesley's day were confident that our human reason and experience were quite sufficient for understanding God. Indeed, a few of them rejected any claim about God that appeared to transcend our reason or experience.

Wesley's sympathy lay with those who emphasized how little we humans are capable of knowing or comprehending about the being and attributes of God.[5] And yet, he was convinced that God had entered into meaningful communication with us. For this to happen, God must be willing to condescend to our limited capacities.[6] There must be some way that we can appropriately understand and speak about God.

What Wesley needed was a cautious alternative to both silence and presumption, an alternative classically offered in the doctrine of analogy. He found a congenial exposition of this understanding of God-language in the writings of Peter Browne.[7] Browne shared Wesley's assumption that humans have no innate idea of God. We form our understanding of God indirectly, based on our experience of the world and human life. Some resulting ideas, while informative, have no essential correspondence with

Divine reality (e.g., metaphors, such as the biblical image of God's "arm" delivering Israel). However, Browne insisted that there were also instances where our human language did express a significant correspondence to God's reality. These were "analogies," which could be rendered at least minimally adequate for describing God by removing all distortions of human imperfection (*via negativa*) and maximizing all that is true and valued in human existence (*via positiva*). The resulting conceptions were far from definitive of God. Even so, Browne contended that—used cautiously—they could be appropriate indicators of God's perfections.

As Wesley's republication of Browne's work implies, he shared Browne's sensitivity to the limitations of human God-language. He repeatedly commented that the anthropomorphic descriptions of God in Scripture were metaphors, conforming to human limitation.[8] When dealing with more central attributes like love and justice, he took up the language of analogy, for here there was a correspondence to human realities.[9] However, he also insisted on the difference in meaning when applied to Creator and creature, countering the possible error of reducing God to creaturely status.[10]

Wesley's conviction of the limitations, yet legitimacy, of human descriptions of God particularly surfaced when potential misunderstandings impinged on his distinctive concern. For example, when defending the unfailing mercy *(grace)* of God, he went to great lengths to contrast it with limited human mercy.[11] On the other hand, when confronted with dismissals of God's wrath as an anthropomorphic concept, he defended the analogical use of such language, fearing that its loss would undermine God's justice, and the correlated human *responsibility.*[12]

Reflexive Nature of Knowledge of God

Wesley's most characteristic emphasis related to God-knowledge goes beyond his defense of the legitimacy of applying human language to God. It focused on the implications of our knowledge of God for human life. For him, God was essentially a relational reality.[13] As such, every major attribute or action of God had implications for understanding what humans are to be and to do.[14] Clarifying such anthropological and soteriological implications often took center stage in his theological reflection, as it had in the Early Church. Examples of such clarifications will be noted throughout the following discussion.

The Nature of God

Viewed from a modern perspective, one of the striking things about Wesley's various discussions of God is that he devoted much more attention to God's *nature* than to God's *existence*. While he often warned his people against a "practical atheism" of ignoring God, he shared the contemporary Anglican doubt that actual intellectual rejection of God's existence was a serious threat.[15] He judged truly skeptical Enlightenment thought like that of David Hume to be incredible.[16] He was much more worried about the impact of false understandings of God on the Christian formation of his people; e.g., understandings that resulted from pernicious doctrines like divine reprobation and from the deistic implications of moderate Enlightenment thought. Interestingly, recent advocates of recovering a more practical theology agree with this implicit assessment that issues of God's character are more crucial to actual Christian praxis than the theoretical question of God's existence.[17]

Wesley's comments on God's character utilize the traditional language of God's attributes or perfections.[18] Perhaps following Peter Browne, he typically distinguished between God's natural and moral attributes.[19]

God's Natural Attributes

By "natural attributes," Wesley meant those characteristics that are definitive of the Divine nature; without these characteristics, God would not be God. Wesley became increasingly convinced of the formative (and *de*formative) influence of our understanding of these attributes toward the end of his ministry, publishing several sermons on them.[20] While these sermons contain no original solutions to doctrinal dilemmas, they provide several examples of him articulating the doxological and soteriological implications of God's nature.[21] They also reveal the impact of Wesley's orienting concern on understanding God.

To begin with, Wesley affirmed with Article I of his Anglican tradition that God is "spirit."[22] From this he drew the conclusions there stated that God has no corporeal body and is not divisible into parts. There is greater question, however, about his agreement with the third conclusion of Article I—that God has no "passions" such as humans possess. He did include this phrase in his edited version of the Articles, but appears to disagree elsewhere with some understandings of it. In particular, he retained a place for affections in God.[23] If "passions" is equivalent to "affections," then the American Methodists were not betraying Wesley when they deleted the phrase denying passions to God from the Articles of Religion which he sent them.[24]

Historically, of course, the claim that God is impassible was not primarily a denial of divine affections (like love). It was an assertion that God is not subject to unwanted change due to any external agent. This was affirmed partly as a protection of God's sovereignty. It was also reasoned that any change in God would either be for the worse, or (if for the better) would indicate that God had not been as perfect previously as God could be. The obvious implication is that, even if God had affections, they were not "affected" by anything external to God.

While Wesley was sensitive to this concern, he was also convinced that Scripture portrayed a God who took individual interest in us. This tension is evident in his argument that the scriptural claim that God experiences joy at a person's conversion was an appropriate "representation."[25] More to the point (and central to his orienting concern) was his defense of the possibility of persons culpably falling from grace, against the charge that this made God changeable. His basic argument was that a God who did not take into account the changing response of humanity would cease to be unchangeably just and gracious.[26]

Wesley's understanding of what it means for God to be eternal reflects a common Christian tension resulting from the merger of differing emphases. On the one hand, he preferred the more typically Hebraic definition of eternity as "everlasting time" or "boundless duration."[27] On the other hand, he occasionally described God's relation to the created world in terms of the more characteristically Greek conception of being nontemporal—i.e., comprehending all eternity at once.[28] The former emphasis was more fundamental, buttressing his assumptions of God's particular interest in individuals and God's action in the world.[29] The major connection in which the latter emphasis arose is when Wesley was trying to solve the problem of how God could know future events without determining them.[30]

The other major natural attributes of God are particular dimensions of being infinite (i.e., not subject to limitations). The first of these is omnipresence. Wesley's sermon on this topic complained about how little is written on it; or at least, how little that develops its plain implications for human life. Therefore, following a fairly standard affirmation of God's ability to work everywhere, he devoted a major section to developing these implications. Characteristically, his implications center on the point that in no situation are we ever separated from God's grace or from our accountability.[31]

Another dimension of God's infinitude is omniscience. As we have noted, Wesley assumed a very strong conception of this attribute, including the necessity of God knowing all future contingent events. He specifically rejected the suggestion that God may have voluntarily chosen not to know the future (in order to preserve human freedom). However, his reason for this was not philosophical, it was exegetical. Scripture claims that God's works are known to God from eternity (Acts 15:18), so Wesley was compelled to affirm this, even if he did not understand how it was consistent with human freedom.[32] If he had possessed a more nuanced hermeneutic for dealing with such passages, he might have decided that a "self-limiting God" was consistent with his general convictions about how God works.[33]

The final dimension of God's infinitude is omnipotence. If Wesley had a characteristic emphasis here, it was that we cannot properly understand God's power apart from God's moral attributes. Therefore, I will pause to consider the moral attributes before discussing God's sovereignty.

God's Moral Attributes

The importance of God's moral attributes is that they define God's character. Theoretically, a divine Being could be eternal, omnipresent, omniscient, and omnipotent, while being indifferent to humanity, or even maleficent. Central to Christian revelation is the claim that this is not the case! God's character is one more aptly defined by words like caring, pure, forgiving, holy, and gracious.

Wesley joined a long tradition of Christian theology in assuming that God's moral attributes converge in two central virtues: justice and goodness (or love).[34] For many in this tradition the term "holiness" is preferred to "justice." Wesley could use it as well, but his more typical use of "justice" suggests that what was at stake in this attribute, for him, was more God's *fairness* in dealing with sinful humanity than God's *glory* which warrants the condemnation of sin. This is not to suggest that he neglected the theme of judgment. He could defend the legitimacy of God's wrath against sin as vigorously as anyone.[35] However, he grounded such judgment in God's concern to preserve universal human responsibility, not simply God's moral superiority.

Consistent with his orienting concern, Wesley considered God's mercy to be more fundamental than even God's fairness. As he once put it, God is "a God of unblemished justice and truth: but above all is his mercy."[36] His more typical way of putting this was to describe love as God's "reigning attribute, the attribute that sheds an amiable glory on all his other perfections."[37]

The point of this comparative valuation of love was surely not to oppose love and justice. Rather, it was to ground justice itself in God's love, while defining God's love as a "holy love" which respects the worth and accountability of the one loved. There may be contextual reasons for laying more stress on God's love or justice in particular situations, but they must never be separated or counterposed.[38]

Crucial Concern: God's Sovereignty

No issue concerning God's nature received more attention from Wesley than that of Divine sovereignty. Central to his various discussions of this issue was the insistence that Divine sovereignty not be understood in isolation from God's other attributes. In particular, it must never be understood in abstraction from God's justice or love.[39] Involved here is a perennial debate concerning whether God's will defines what is right, or the right determines what God wills. While Wesley professed little patience with this debate, his consideration of it rejected the nominalists' suggestion that God's will can be considered apart from God's nature.[40]

Such emphasis on the unity of God's nature and will (i.e., God's simplicity) has far-reaching implications for understanding God's omnipotence. Wesley could define this attribute in fairly traditional terms, as the exclusion of any bounds to God's power.[41] Whenever he developed this point however, it became clear that his distinctive concern was that God's power not be defined or defended in any way that undercuts human responsibility.

Wesley discerned such a mistaken conception of Divine power in the claims of his predestinarian opponents that they preserved the glory of God better than he did. Their obvious assumption was that one could ascribe the full glory of salvation to God only if God alone effected salvation, without human concurrence. Wesley countered that affirming a place for (uncoerced) human response in salvation did not detract from God's glory, provided that it was God's grace which enabled humans to respond. Moreover, he charged, the biblical notion of the "glory of God" does not refer primarily to God's power, it refers to the manifestation of all God's attributes, and especially justice and love![42]

The importance of a proper understanding of God's power comes up as well in Wesley's discussion of Divine wisdom. He could never make up his mind where wisdom fit in the classification of God's attributes.[43] However, he was sure that its co-determination of God's power was crucial. As he once put it, were God to abolish sin and evil by overriding human freedom

> it would imply no wisdom at all, but barely a stroke of omnipotence. Whereas all the manifold wisdom of God (as well as all his power and goodness) is displayed in governing [humans] as [human]; not as a stock or a stone, but as an intelligent and free spirit.[44]

What then is the proper understanding of God's power or sovereignty? Wesley utilized a distinction between God's work as Creator and as Governor to answer this question. He allowed that it may be permissible to speak of God working alone and irresistibly when creating and sustaining nonpersonal nature, but not when governing human life—for this would eliminate human responsibility.[45] As Governor, God enables human obedience, but will not force it. As Wesley reminded his followers,

> You know how God wrought in *your own* soul when he first enabled you to say, "The life I now live, I live by faith in the Son of God, who loved me, and gave himself for me.' He did not take away your understanding, but enlightened and strengthened it. He did not destroy any of your affections; rather they were more vigorous than before. Least of all did he take away your liberty, your power of choosing good or evil; he did not *force* you; but being *assisted* by his grace you . . . *chose* the better part.[46]

Perhaps the best way to capture Wesley's conviction here is to say that he construed God's power or sovereignty fundamentally in terms of *empowerment*, rather than control or *overpowerment*. This is not to weaken God's power but to determine its character! As Wesley was fond of saying, God works "strongly and sweetly."[47] That is, God's *grace* works powerfully, but not irresistibly, in matters of human life and salvation; thereby empowering our *response-ability*, without overriding our *responsibility*.[48] While such an understanding of God's power may be less typical in the West, it is quite similar to central Eastern Orthodox emphases.[49]

Excursus: Wesley on Predestination

The preceding general reflections on God's sovereignty provide a good backdrop for considering the particular issue of predestination.[50] It might surprise some that I deal with this issue in the chapter on God instead of that on salvation. There is precedent for such an organization. Calvin discussed predestination in the section of the *Institutes* dealing with God's providence through the early editions, locating it in the section on salvation only in the final edition. Later Reformed scholastics returned the doctrine of predestination to the systematic locus of God the Father, though likely for different reasons than those of Calvin's early practice.[51]

Such a placement of the doctrine of predestination suggests an important perspective on the issue of the central difference between Wesley and his predestinarian opponents. The typical charge of Calvinist writers is that those who deny unconditional election to salvation do so primarily because of an inappropriate optimism about our innate human capacity to serve God, apart from God's prior restoring grace.[52] The discussion of Wesley's anthropology in the next chapter should make clear that this was definitely not the case for him. At this point my greater interest is in the countersuggestion that the fundamental difference between Wesley and his Calvinist opponents really lies more in their respective understanding of the nature of God than in their evaluation of the human situation.[53]

On investigation it becomes clear that Wesley's most characteristic complaint about predestination was its incompatibility with the nature of God.[54] In particular, he argued that unconditional election to salvation and damnation is inconsistent with the impartiality of Divine justice and mercy, that it casts doubt on God's sincerity (in light of the apparent suggestions of the universal availability of salvation in Scripture), and especially that it conflicts with the universal love and goodness of God.[55] Indeed, he contended that it was more reasonable to be an atheist than to affirm a God who was capable of unconditional reprobation.[56] As in other cases, John's various concerns were boiled down into a verse by Charles (which John endorsed by publication in the *Arminian Magazine*):

'Tis thus, O God, they picture Thee,
Thy Justice and Sincerity;
Thy Truth which never can remove,
Thy bowels of unbounded Love:
Thy freedom of Redeeming Grace,
'With-held from almost all the Race,
'Made for Apollyon to devour,
'In honour of thy Sovereign Power!'[57]

Note in this verse that the objection is to the way that the Calvinists "picture" God. This suggests that the Wesleys sensed their most basic disagreement with their opponents to lie in their respective defining models of God.[58] For the Calvinists, the defining model was a sovereign monarch (in the heat of controversy John put it much less graciously: an omnipresent almighty tyrant![59]). By contrast, Wesley more commonly employed the model of a loving parent.[60]

While a sovereign monarch might technically be free to dispose of subjects as he or she sees fit, a loving parent would not even consider withholding potential saving aid from any child (i.e., unconditional reprobation or limited atonement).[61] On the other hand, truly loving parents also respect the integrity of their children. Ultimately, they would not impose their assistance against the (mature) child's will. It is precisely from this perspective that Wesley considers the human dimension of the doctrine of predestination. He does not deny humanity's universal need for restoring grace if we are to love and serve God. He simply denies that this grace is any less universal than the need, or that it functions irresistibly. If it were to function irresistibly, God would contradict the very Divine design for humanity—that we live responsible lives of holy love for God and one another.[62]

As this suggests, there was an integral connection between Wesley's rejection of predestination and his emphasis on the life of holiness that Christians are to live in response to God's grace.[63] Indeed, whenever Wesley the practical theologian enumerated the deadly effects of teaching predestination, at the top of the list was the charge that it hinders the work of God in the soul and undercuts our holiness.[64] If one really believed that "The elect shall be saved, do what they will: The reprobate shall be damned, do what they can," the vital connection between God's gracious initiative and our response is severed.[65]

For all his problems with unconditional predestination, Wesley faced a major obstacle to any simple rejection of the doctrine. His respect for the authority of Scripture and the Thirty-Nine Articles was observed in the previous chapter; both of these mention predestination. How could he deal with these in a manner consistent with his concern?

To begin with the Articles, the Wesleys often found Article XVII ("Of Predestination and Election") used against them in arguments with their predestinarian opponents. Their typical response was to claim that this article had not originally been intended as a strong affirmation of unconditional election, but as a purposefully ambiguous statement that allowed a variety of acceptable interpretations, including their own (which based election on Divine foreknowledge).[66] Even granting such flexibility, this article was a problem and it is not surprising that John deleted it from the Articles of Religion for the American church.[67]

Unlike the creed, troublesome passages in Scripture could not simply be edited out. Here Wesley's theological activity took the form of explanatory notes on the passages central to the debates. One set of these passages were the explicit mentions of predestination in the New Testament. Wesley consistently interpreted these references as "popular representations" (i.e., metaphors) of God's eternal foreknowledge. God's election does not *cause* our sin or faith, it *recognizes* it.[68] The other passages that had become central to Protestant discussion of predestination were the various instances of God hardening hearts, particularly the case of Pharaoh.[69] Wesley admitted in the Preface to his *OT Notes* that his major reason for abridging Henry's comments was to remove suggestions of predestination.[70] Thus, throughout the account of Pharaoh and in other passages which suggest that God hardened a person's heart, Wesley added notes that render this action reciprocal—God's hardening only followed upon their (uncoerced) rejection of God and hardening of their own heart.[71]

The debate over predestination was a particularly distressful one for Wesley. On the one hand, the issue went to the center of his orienting concern. On the other hand, any open debate on it was likely to alienate some of his closest associates and split the Methodist movement. As a result of this tension, Wesley's various comments on predestination reveal more contextual variations than perhaps any other doctrine.[72] At times when he is most concerned about the damaging impact of the doctrine on his followers, he issued impassioned defenses of unlimited atonement such as his sermon on "Free Grace." At times when he is more troubled by the damage being done within the Methodist movement by the debate over the doctrine, he searched for any possible common ground he shared with his opponents and the most conciliatory ways that he could express his central claims.[73] Through all of these variations, however, his central affirmation of God's universal resistible grace remained consistent. Further aspects of this affirmation will be developed as appropriate.

The Work of God/Father

It has just been argued that Wesley's defining model of God was that of a loving parent. This claim conveniently turns our attention to Wesley's specific understanding of the first "Person" of the Trinity—God as Father. The best way to approach this issue is to investigate the distinctive work or roles that Wesley attributed to God/Father. His various discussions of God reveal four major aspects of this work: (1) the creation and sustaining of the universe; (2) the providential care for humanity; (3) the moral governance of the creation; and (4) the healing of the corruptions of sin.[74]

God/Father as Creator and Sustainer

The work that typically headed Wesley's discussions of God/Father is that of Creator and Sustainer. These two were usually listed together because Wesley shared the general assumptions of his time that (1) creation per se had occurred relatively instantaneously (i.e., in six days) about six thousand years earlier, and (2) there had been no origination or loss of matter since creation, only regulated fluctuations in its form.[75] As such, God's work as Creator (in the most proper sense) was completed at the origination of the universe with its laws for subsequent natural processes. Since then, God has been sustaining this created order. Apart from such sustaining work, the universe would immediately cease to exist.

A few Wesley scholars have suggested that he began to move beyond the assumptions of his time, prefiguring the later Darwinian idea of evolution or progressive creation.[76] This suggestion is an overreading of Wesley's adoption of the notion of the "Chain of Being" that was so popular in the eighteenth century.[77] The main claim of this notion is that creation demonstrates the perfection of its Creator by its organization into an exhaustively populated series of progressively more complex beings—from the simplest elements to the highest spiritual beings. Importantly, precisely because it was meant to demonstrate an immutable God, this chain of beings was considered static! The progressive description of beings as "higher" or "next" did not indicate their temporal succession. More precisely, there was no temporalization of the chain of being until late in the eighteenth century. While it was beginning to change during his time, Wesley's major sources for the notion (John Ray and Charles Bonnet) retained static understandings of the chain of being.[78] Likewise, he fervently defended the permanent boundaries between species.[79] There is no prescient advocate of biological evolution here.

Wesley's assumption of the general stability of creation was consistent with his eighteenth-century British Enlightenment setting. He also shared his setting's tendency to emphasize God's action through the laws of nature, minimizing appeal to special Divine intervention in the created order.[80] However, he did not deny the possibility of such intervention. Neither did he join the deistic tendency to separate creation from God, leaving it as an autonomous machine. Instead, he emphasized that God was the ultimate agent of all action in the material world, for the laws of nature were simply descriptions of how God normally worked in sustaining the material realm.[81]

Concerning the nature of the creation itself, Wesley's occasional cosmological comments reflect the transitional character of his times. For example, he could affirm earth, water, air, and fire as the four constituent parts of the universe on one occasion, while rejecting Newton's theory of gravitation in favor of a primal material ether in another, and suggesting that this ether was electricity in still another![82] Again, he could endorse Copernicus' model of the solar system, while incorporating the traditional distinction between three heavens—the residence of God, the realm of the stars, and the sublunary heaven of the earth's atmosphere.[83] If he had a characteristic concern in any of this, it was to affirm the reality of a spiritual realm that transcended this empirical world but could be experienced within it, via the spiritual senses.[84]

Wesley was also very concerned that the material creation not be seen as evil. He insisted that the biblical condemnations of the "world" related to non-Christian society, not physical reality per se.[85] He vigorously defended the doctrine of *creatio ex nihilo*, with its implication that God was the direct source of matter.[86] On this basis, he affirmed the goodness of the original creation and even speculated about its paradisiacal nature prior to sin.[87]

God/Father as Provider

The affirmation of the goodness of creation leads directly to the second aspect of the work of God/Father. As Wesley would put it, the God who created and sustains the entire universe is not a lazy, indolent, epicurean deity. Rather, God/Father is the Provider who is constantly concerned with what befalls creation.[88] As such, nothing happens in our world by chance, even though we cannot always understand its purpose.[89]

When Wesley developed his understanding of providence, it becomes clear that it related largely to human creation. Moreover, he suggested that, while God's providential care was universal, it manifested a special concern for "real Christians."[90]

His assumptions concerning the process of Divine providence shared much with his eighteenth-century Anglican setting. In particular, he accepted the role of subordinate means of providential care. He referred to angels on several occasions in this connection.[91] At least once he suggested a participation by the "souls of departed Christians" (saints?).[92] The major means of God's providence, however, was clearly the general order which God sustained in the universe.

The recognition of such a general providence was common in Wesley's time, acceptable to even the Deists. Where Wesley took a more distinct position within this context was in refusing to reduce providence to simply the maintenance of the general order of the universe. He was convinced that such a reduction ultimately eliminated belief in God's providential actions for particular individuals or situations.[93] Worse yet, it denied the possibility of miracles, a possibility that Wesley vigorously defended.[94]

Wesley's confidence in God's particular providence found expression in some unique ways. Surely the most quaint (and often notorious) was his occasional resort to bibliomancy or casting lots to discern God's will.[95] Another expression was his conviction that historical accounts should include demonstrations of God's providence in history.[96] More characteristic of his practical theology was the repeated articulation of devotional and affectional implications of God's providence: We should compose ourselves to a steady and grateful dependence upon Divine Providence.[97]

What is most characteristic in Wesley's reflections on divine providence is the evidence of his orienting concern! He desired to emphasize the universality of God's gracious providential action as much as possible. At the same time, he recognized a necessary limit to such emphasis. As he once put it, "We cannot impute too much to divine providence, unless we make it interfere with our free-agency."[98] While God's providence is often mysterious, we can be sure that it will hold together mercy (grace) and truth (responsibility).[99]

God/Father as Governor or Judge

The concern for truth leads into the third aspect of the work of God/Father. The basic claim in this case is clear, God is the Governor of creation in general, and humanity in particular, preserving order and justice. The immediate problem with such a claim is also obvious: Why then is there sin, suffering, and evil in the world? How do these realities correspond with our confession of God's power and goodness in governing creation?[100]

Wesley believed in the existence of Satan and lesser devils who inflict suffering on humans and tempt us to sin. However, he carefully avoided any dualistic solutions to the problem of sin and evil. He insisted that even Satan was once good, and that diabolic activity could go no further than God allowed, for God remains sovereign.[101]

Did this mean that God is the direct cause of suffering or sin? Regarding suffering, the early Wesley did occasionally assign events such as fires, earthquakes, and wars directly to God's agency. In his later years he was more careful to talk about God only "allowing" them.[102] Concerning sin, his view was less variable. He believed that a necessary correlate of God being a gracious and just Governor was the creation of humans with free-agency.[103] However, while God's gracious empowerment was the source of our resulting *ability* to sin, God is never the cause of our *choice* to sin.[104] Wesley was convinced that assigning God/Father any more of a role in either suffering or sin than this would undermine the unity of love and holiness that was definitive of God.[105] A further problem with emphasizing the role of either God or Satan in sin was that it lessened human responsibility. Ultimately, Wesley always laid the blame for sin at humanity's feet.[106]

Given his commitment to human responsibility, it is not surprising that Wesley also tied suffering and evil to human sin. He assumed that evil and suffering resulted from the Fall, as its punishment in some sense.[107] On the other hand, he became increasingly skeptical about connecting specific events of suffering with specific acts of sin.[108] Thus, while he favored a penal explanation of suffering, he was aware of some of its limitations.

The problem with a penal explanation of suffering is not simply that the innocent often suffer while the evil prosper. Nor is it merely that suffering often transcends any warranted punishment for our sins. The major problem is that it is solely punitive, lacking a redemptive dimension.

Wesley sensed the importance of a redemptive dimension in explaining suffering. One way that he invoked this dimension was to emphasize how suffering could be a stimulus for spiritual growth. Some of his particular comments in this regard, especially early ones, come dangerously close to making God the cause of the suffering. In more careful instances he talked only of how God's providence and wisdom allow God to derive spiritual benefits even from events that were caused by human sin.[109]

Ultimately, deriving good from the evil in our world was not enough. Wesley's strongest expressions of God's redemption of sin and suffering promise the rectification of all wrong and the healing of all evil. Thereby, he joined those who argue that what Christianity offers is not so much an *explanation* of evil (showing why it has to exist) as a *promise* of victory over evil. As he once put it, "It will not always be thus: these things are only permitted for a season by the great Governor of the world, that he may draw immense, eternal good out of this temporary evil."[110]

God/Father as Physician

This transition to the theme of overcoming evil highlights the fourth aspect of the work of God/Father. One of Wesley's common titles for God was the "Great Physician" or "Physician of souls."[111] Such titles focus on God/Father's work in healing the damage that has been done by sin.

As the discussion of Wesley's soteriology in Chapter Six will make clear, he did not limit either sin's damage or its healing to human "souls." He looked for the same holism in God's redemption that there had been in creation—there would be healing of human bodies as well as souls.

Going a step further, while Wesley believed that humans were uniquely related to God, he was equally convinced that God's mercy reached to all other sentient creatures. Therefore, if animals had suffered from the effects of sin (as he assumed to be the case), then they too will participate in God's healing work.[112]

Perhaps the most distinctive aspect of Wesley's confidence in God's healing work (again, with some analogy in Eastern Christian thought[113]) is that he believed it would go beyond merely restoring things to their pre-Fall condition. While God did not intend the Fall, divine grace is such that God will bring about an even *more* wonderful glory for creation than if sin had not entered the scene. Both humanity and all other animal life will have greater abilities and blessings in the redeemed creation than they had in the original creation. Wesley's major reason for asserting this was that it helped explain why God would chance allowing humans to sin. It also reiterated that God's justice must be understood in the more fundamental context of God's mercy.[114]

Summary: God as Father

For Wesley, then, the first "Person" of the Godhead relates to humanity as Creator/Sustainer, Provider, Governor/Judge, and Physician. The identification of these functions is hardly novel in the Christian tradition, although the fourth is less common than the others. If there is anything distinctive in Wesley's treatment, it is his interrelation of the four.[115]

It was suggested earlier that Wesley's defining model for understanding God was more that of a loving parent than of a sovereign monarch. This suggestion seems consistent with his convictions about the work of God/Father. The dimensions of God's work as Creator and Governor are easily appropriated within a defining model of sovereign monarch. When the dimensions of Provider and Physician are integrated with these, however, a beneficent tone is added which is more typical of familial settings than regal ones.

A parental model of God is particularly appropriate if, as I am inclined to think, Physician and Provider are the dimensions of God's work that Wesley valued most. As evidence I would point to his sermon on "God's Love to Fallen Man," where he argues that if humanity had not fallen, we would never have had the wound for whose healing Christ had to take our nature. He then concludes that without the Fall we would have known God as Creator, Preserver, and Governor; but not under the "nearest and dearest relation of delivering up his Son for us all."[116] That is, we would not have known God as the one *providing healing* for our wound.

The resulting focus of Wesley's understanding of God is perhaps best seen in his suggestion for how a parent can explain God to a child:

> God (though you cannot see him) is above the sky, and is a deal brighter than the sun! It is he, it is God, that made the sun, and you and me, and everything. It is he that makes the grass and the flowers grow; that makes the trees green, and the fruit to come upon them! Think what he can do! He can do whatever he pleases. He can strike me or you dead in a moment. But he loves you; he loves to do you good. He loves to make you happy. Should not you then love *him*! You love *me*, because I love you and do you good. But it is God that makes me love you. Therefore you should love him.[117]

Note how this explanation touches briefly on Creator and Governor dimensions of God, but moves to Provider and parental images in the main point.

Also evident in the preceding quotation are the numerous masculine pronouns for God. Wesley followed traditional Christian practice in calling the first "Person" of the Godhead "Father." However, his reasons were more than merely traditional. The claim that God was not a dispassionate, aloof Sovereign but a protecting, providing Father was central to his conception of the Christian faith. Of course, given his recognition of the analogical nature of God-language, the primary issue here was not God's sex, but God's personal and caring character; as he commented on the opening of the Lord's Prayer, "if [God] is a Father, then he is good, then he is loving to his children."[118]

It is suggestive in this regard that Wesley could also refer to God as "Parent."[119] All the same, there is little evidence that he used consciously maternal or female images for God—even though there was biblical warrant to do so.[120] Whatever his relative sensitivity to the inclusive nature of God, Wesley remained a man of his context.[121]

CHAPTER 3

Humanity's Need and God's Initial Restoring Grace

The survey of Wesley's understanding of the Christian worldview began with his convictions about God because, for him, God was the foundation and focus of both Christian life and belief. Given his assumption that God is a relational being, the obvious set of convictions to take up next are those concerning human nature and the human condition. Indeed, one could easily structure Wesley's overall theology around the dynamics of the Divine-human relationship.[1]

General Character of Wesley's Anthropology

Most previous discussions of Wesley's basic understanding of human nature, the problem of sin, and the resulting human situation have revolved around determining his place within the various Western Christian traditions. Was he more Lutheran, Calvinist, Arminian, or Roman Catholic? Or (heaven forbid!), was he Pelagian?[2] The arguments between these alternatives have largely stalemated one another. The most important reason for this is that some central elements of his anthropological convictions were not adequately considered, elements that have been more characteristic of Eastern Christianity.

For a variety of reasons, early Latin- and Greek-writing theologians tended toward different emphases concerning human nature and the human problem (with correlated implications for the nature of salvation, to be considered later).[3] The progressively isolated Western and Eastern Christian traditions developed these differences even further. The eventual dominant perspective in the Western traditions typically assumed that humans were created in a complete and perfect state—the epitome of what God intended them to be. God's original will was simply that they retain this perfection. However, humans were created in the Image of God, which included an ability for self-determination. Unexplainably, Adam and Eve used this self-determining power to turn away from God. Thus came the Fall with its devastating effects: the loss of self-determination (we are no longer free *not* to sin), and the inheritance of the guilt of this Original Sin by all human posterity. Since this fallen condition is universal, the West has tended to talk of it as the "natural" state of human existence; i.e., they have based their anthropology primarily on the Fall, emphasizing the guilt and powerlessness of fallen humans apart from God's grace.

Characteristic Eastern anthropology differs from the West on nearly every point. First, influential early Greek theologians assumed that humans were originally innocent, but not complete.[4] We were created with a dynamic nature destined to develop in communion with God. This conviction found expression in their distinction between the Image of God and the Likeness of God. "Image of God" denoted the universal human potential for life in God. "Likeness of God" was the progressive realization of that potentiality. Such realization (often called "deification") was only possible by "participation" in Divine life and grace through worship, sacraments, and the like. Moreover, it was neither inevitable nor automatic. The Image of God necessarily included the aspect of human freedom, though it centered in the larger human capacity for communion with God.

Like the West, Eastern theology from its beginnings saw the Fall as a result of the human preference to compete with God as God's equal, rather than accepting our need for participating in the Divine gifts.[5] However, they understood the results of the Fall differently. First, they rejected the idea of human posterity inheriting guilt from the Fall; we become guilty only when we imitate our Parents' sin. Second, they argued that the primary result of the Fall was the introduction of death and corruption into human life, and its subsequent dominion over humanity. Finally, while early Greek theologians clearly believed that the death and disease thus introduced have so weakened the human intellect and will that we can no longer hope to attain the Likeness of God on our own, they did not hold that the Fall deprived us of all grace, or of the accountability for responding to God's offer of restored communion in Christ. That is, a characteristic Eastern Christian affirmation of co-operation in divine/human interactions remains even after the Fall. In this sense, they base their anthropology more on Creation than on the Fall.

As a result of his exposure to the Anglican patristic revival, his acquaintance with several minority Western voices, and some direct reading of early Greek theologians, Wesley incorporated into his anthropology elements that had become typical of both Eastern and Western traditions. This is the reason for many of the puzzles and unresolved tensions over which his later interpreters have debated. Rather than rehearse these debates in any detail, I want to advance a proposal that I believe resolves many of them: Wesley's understanding of human nature and the human problem gives primacy of place to therapeutic concerns, like those more characteristic of Eastern Christianity, and integrates the more typically Western juridical concerns into this orientation.[6]

This proposal seems unlikely at first glance, because Wesley undeniably assumed (like the Western tradition) that humanity was created in an original state of complete perfection.[7] One should not read too much into this, however, because he apparently did not realize that there was an alternative developmental view of original humanity in earlier Christian tradition.[8] More to the point, whatever the state of original humanity, Wesley strongly emphasized the dynamic nature of *present* human spiritual development.[9]

This stress on spiritual transformation points toward a much more basic commonality between Wesley and the therapeutic emphasis characteristic of Eastern Orthodoxy. Like the later Western traditions, early Greek theologians affirmed the two consecutive states of humanity—before and after the Fall. However, their real interest was focused on a third state, the gracious and gradual restoration of humanity to God-likeness.[10] By contrast, the later Western juridical emphasis often reduced this third state to a momentary transaction: from guilty to forgiven. Wesley shared the early Greek understanding of this third state, as evidenced by his common definition of Christian salvation as "the renewal of our souls after the image of God."[11] He also joined them in focusing primarily on this third state when defining the actual human situation.[12]

In keeping with his own focus, the following analysis of Wesley's theological anthropology will be organized around the three themes of (1) Humanity as God's Gracious Creation, (2) Humanity as Fallen, and (3) Humanity as Nascently Restored.

Humanity as God's Gracious Creation[13]

Wesley's most fundamental conviction about human life was that we are created and dependent beings.[14] Our very existence and all of our faculties are gifts of God's grace.[15] When he enlarged upon this basic conviction in descriptions of human nature and existence, he typically framed his discussion in the biblical language of the Image of God.

The Image of God in Humanity

Wesley occasionally mentioned three dimensions of the Image of God in humanity: the natural image, the political image, and the moral image. More often, he distinguished between only the natural and moral images.[16] This latter distinction correlated with his differentiation between God's natural and moral attributes. That is, the natural Image of God in humanity referred to those characteristics or faculties definitive of being human, while the moral Image of God referred to the "character" of holiness and love that God intended for humanity.[17]

While using different terms, Wesley was affirming the same basic point expressed by the typical Eastern contrast between the Image and the Likeness of God: Humans were originally created capable of participating in God, and when they do so participate they embody God's moral character and find fulfillment. As he once put it,

> [Adam] was a creature capable of God, capable of knowing, loving and obeying his Creator. And in fact he did know God, did unfeignedly love and uniformly obey Him. . . . From this right state, and the right use of all his faculties, his happiness naturally flowed.[18]

Wesley's Relational Anthropology

As their stress on "participation" suggests, the characteristic Eastern Orthodox understanding of human nature and existence focuses consideration of our various faculties (such as mind and will) on their contribution to a more fundamental human reality—that we are capable of (and find our true meaning in) relationships.[19] Wesley also oriented consideration of the various human faculties around the basic capacity for relating to God. As such, his was a relational anthropology, making proper relationships central to true human existence.[20]

Wesley's anthropology recognized four basic human relationships: with God, with other humans, with lower animals, and with ourselves. A holy (and whole!) person is one in whom all of these relationships are properly expressed. The proper relationship to God is knowing, loving, obeying, and enjoying God eternally (i.e., participation).[21] The proper relationship to other humans is loving service.[22] The proper relationship to all other animals is loving protection.[23] When each of these relationships is properly expressed, we will also have a proper relationship to ourselves of self-acceptance.[24]

Wesley's Holistic Psychology

Obviously, the capacity for relationships (i.e., the Image of God) involves particular faculties. Wesley's characteristic enumeration of these faculties was that humans were endowed by God with understanding, will, and liberty.[25] Comparison reveals some differences between this list and the more common distinction in Wesley's time between intellect, desire, and will. His correlated conceptions of these differed even more! Put briefly, Wesley purposefully distanced himself from the intellectualist tradition that was gaining dominance in Western psychology. This stream concentrated on the need for reason to subordinate and control emotion in human actions. Wesley, by comparison, had a deeper appreciation for the positive contribution of the emotions to truly human life and action.[26]

To develop this point it is important to recognize that Wesley was not using "will" to designate the human faculty of rational self-determination, as is typical in current usage; rather, he equated the will with the affections.[27] These affections are not simply passive "feelings" for Wesley, they are motivating dispositions of the person.[28] In their ideal expression, they integrate the rational and emotional dimensions of human life into a holistic inclination toward particular choices or actions.[29] Thus, the primal example of an affection for Wesley is love of God and neighbor.[30]

It is equally important to note that Wesley assumed that these motivating affections were not simply transitory, but can (and should) be habituated into enduring dispositions.[31] To capture this potential Wesley traded on a slight—but significant—distinction between affections and tempers.[32] He was using "temper" in this connection in a characteristic eighteenth-century sense of an enduring or *habitual* disposition of a person.[33] His point could also be captured in terms of the Eastern distinction between the Image of God and the Likeness of God. The capacity for affections is part of the Image of God. The proper enduring orientation of these affections would constitute the Christian tempers (or inward holiness) which is the Likeness of God.[34] From the motivating disposition of these tempers would then flow holy words and actions.[35]

Wesley's language of holy actions "flowing" from holy tempers suggests that he appreciated the sense in which habituated affections bring "freedom" for human actions—the freedom that comes from disciplined practice (e.g., the "freedom" to play a Bach concerto).[36] Yet, Wesley was also aware that some thinkers presented the influence of our affections on our actions as invincible, thereby undermining human freedom. To avoid such implications he carefully distinguished "liberty" from will.[37] He understood liberty as our capacity to enact (or refuse to enact) our desires and inclinations.[38] This capacity is what allowed Wesley to affirm the contributions of habit, education, and argument to human action, without rendering such action totally determined. He repeatedly argued that if humans had not been *graced* with liberty, they would not have been capable of either virtue or guilt,[39] that is, they could not have been *responsible*.

There is one other human faculty essential to human morality that Wesley frequently mentioned—conscience. Indeed, conscience was so central to being human that Wesley could term it "our inmost soul."[40] His general understanding of conscience was fairly traditional: it is a faculty that continually assesses our tempers, thoughts, words, and actions against the moral standard by which we are supposed to live. It is a tribunal that can approve or accuse, but cannot itself institute change (that is the role of liberty). But where does conscience obtain the standard by which it judges? This question is particularly difficult to answer from our side of the Fall. Wesley maintained that its essential moral elements were graciously instilled within humanity as part of our creation and thus were self-evident. However, he immediately conceded that they are now at best dimly perceived, vary by education and circumstance, and need the external correction of God's definitive revelation.[41]

Wesley's Holistic Anthropology?

Another classic issue of Christian anthropology which Wesley addressed on various occasions was the relation of the physical dimension of human life to other dimensions. Several traditional tensions had developed over this issue, owing largely to the problems of integrating biblical faith with the Greco-Roman context of the developing Church. To begin with, Scripture sometimes distinguished three dimensions of human being (spirit, soul, and body) and other times mentioned only body and soul. The latter usage was particularly attractive to significant strands of Greek philosophical thought which construed the difference between body and soul as a metaphysical and ethical dualism. They understood the confinement of the immortal soul to the mortal body to be the cause of human faults and suffering, with escape from the body becoming the goal of salvation. This negative evaluation of the body made subtle inroads into many Christian anthropologies, despite the fact that it found little support in Scripture.

Wesley's various considerations of anthropological issues reflect these traditional tensions. When commenting on relevant biblical texts, he followed their precedent of distinguishing soul and spirit. In most other contexts he identified the two. When explicitly wrestling with this apparent problem toward the end of his life, he speculated that the soul was simply the "immediate clothing of the spirit," a type of ethereal vehicle in which the spirit resided, and from which it would never be separated.[42]

For all intents and purposes, then, Wesley assumed a two-dimensional anthropology: humans exist in this world as embodied souls/spirits.[43] He considered these two dimensions to be obvious from our experience. On the one hand, humans are more than merely physical because we are capable of self-initiation, which matter is not. On the other hand, our soul cannot experience sensation or exert any of its operations apart from union with bodily organs.[44]

Once one distinguishes these two dimensions of human life, of course, the question of how they interrelate becomes unavoidable. One way in which Wesley approached this issue was to inquire about the soul's location in the body. For some time he was content simply to adopt biblical language identifying the soul with the heart.[45] His reading of contemporary works in natural philosophy eventually led him to speculate that the soul resided in the brain, perhaps specifically in the pineal gland.[46]

These readings also exposed him to the debate about the relationship of the mind to the body (for Wesley, soul to brain). His basic response to this debate was to affirm that God preserved a parallelism between the functions of the soul and brain, even if we cannot understand how.[47] What is more striking, however, was his emphatic rejection of both a materialist reduction of this relationship and Malebranche's opposite reduction of all creaturely action to God's immediate causation. For Wesley, both of these extremes discount the divine gift of liberty present in the human soul, and undercut the *responsibility* correlated with that *gracious* gift.[48]

Wesley's parallelism of the actions of the soul and the body raises the question of whether he embraced a metaphysical dualism. The answer depends on the meaning of this term. If it means to affirm an immortal soul that preexisted its embodiment and is destined to return to a disembodied state, then Wesley does not fit the classification. He did indeed talk of an "immortal soul," but only in the sense that after it is created it cannot be destroyed. An individual's soul does not exist prior to the creation of the whole person.[49] Likewise, Wesley could often talk of the soul continuing to exist after the body had died. However, he always assumed that the ultimate destiny of humans was re-embodiment in incorruptible bodies.[50] So integral was the embodiment of the soul to him, in fact, that he occasionally advanced a distinction between "body" and "flesh and blood" which allowed him to assert that the soul was embodied by an "ethereal body" even in its intermediate state.[51] In short, while Wesley viewed the body and soul as distinct realities, he did not view them as inappropriately conjoined.[52]

This brings us to the ethical level of anthropological dualism. Some Greek portrayals of the body/soul relationship assigned the body a privative, if not actively antagonistic, impact on spiritual life. By contrast, the Bible presents the body as part of God's original good creation, and sin as a distortion of *every* dimension of human life. Wesley's direct comments on this point typically side with Scripture: he decried the philosophical contempt of the body; rejected any claim that matter was the source of evil; and argued that the biblical notion of sinful "flesh" did no refer to the body per se, but to the corruption of all dimensions of human nature.[53] On the other hand, Wesley undeniably imbibed some of the ethical dualism that had crept into Christian tradition. There is no better example than his ambivalence about sexuality, even in marriage.[54]

Overall, allowing for some dualistic influences, it seems fair to say that Wesley's two-dimensional anthropology did not degenerate into a strong metaphysical or ethical dualism.[55] His basic anthropological convictions sought to emulate the holism of biblical teachings. At the same time, it must be admitted that his valuation of bodiliness was not as positive, and his conception of the interrelationship of body and soul was not as integral and dynamic, as present theologians might desire.

Humanity as Male and Female

There is one further aspect of Wesley's anthropology that is of interest to modern theology, even if it was seldom a conscious focus of his own reflection; namely, the distinction between and relationship of male and female. Concerning the first point, Wesley clearly assumed that the differences between the sexes involved more than anatomy. He largely adopted contemporary stereotypes about these differences—describing women as more passionate, less intellectual, and less courageous than men.[56]

To be sure, Wesley did not understand any of this to deny the *spiritual* equality of men and women. Whatever their differences, they are equally capable of relationship with and obedience to God. But what about *social* equality? Wesley generally reflected the reigning assumption of his day that women should be subordinate to men in social structures, though his explanation of why changed over time.[57] In 1754 he invoked with no qualifications the common supposition that Eve's creation subsequent to Adam demonstrated that women were originally intended to be subordinate to men.[58] However, by 1765 he inclined more to the view that male and female were created by God to be equal in all ways, with women's subjection to men being one of the results of the Fall.[59] The purported justification for this subjection was that woman (Eve) had proven more prone to sin (Adam sinning only out of love for Eve!), thus in need of male protection. In other words, Wesley joined his contemporaries in *mis*reading Genesis 3 through the eyes of Milton![60] Ironically, this misreading created at least the possibility of advocating restoration of the social equality of women as one aspect of the Christian healing of the damage of the Fall.[61]

Humanity as Fallen: Debilitated and Depraved, but Guilty?

The consideration of Wesley's anthropology so far has focused on the ideal state of humanity created in God's Image and living in God's Likeness. Wesley was aware that this ideal is not what we actually experience in our present world. Indeed, he rarely passed up an opportunity to affirm the universal problem of human sinfulness. He considered any denial of this reality to be both contrary to general experience and a fundamental rejection of Christianity.[62]

In moving to a consideration of humanity as fallen, then, the task will not be to demonstrate that Wesley affirmed this reality but to investigate his understanding of the *nature* of human sinfulness. As with his larger anthropological convictions, his understanding of the human problem integrated Western juridical concerns into a broader therapeutic emphasis more characteristic of Eastern Christian thought.[63]

The Two Dimensions of Sin

When representative Western and Eastern Christian discussions of sin are compared, it eventually becomes clear that they accent different dimensions of the problem of sin. Western Christians typically place greatest emphasis on the dimension of the sinner's obligations to others (especially God), and the guilt that our sinful acts acquire from breaching these obligations. Eastern theology has focused attention more on the dimension of the sinner per se; in particular, the infirmity of our nature that results from (and becomes the source of) our actual sins.

These dimensions are certainly not mutually exclusive. However, both Christian traditions worry that the other pays insufficient attention to their favored dimension. When Wesley is read in this light, his recognition of the importance of both dimensions of sin is striking. Consider a representative quotation:

> [Our sins], considered in regard to ourselves, are chains of iron and fetters of brass. They are wounds wherewith the world, the flesh, and the devil, have gashed and mangled us all over. They are diseases that drink up our blood and spirits, that bring us down to the chambers of the grave. But

considered . . . with regard to God, they are debts, immense and numberless.[64]

As the preceding lines suggest, when dealing with the problem that sin creates between the human sinner and God, Wesley typically took up the juridical language of guilt and requisite forgiveness. As he put it in his *NT Notes* comment on 1 John 3:4, the sinner "transgresses the holy, just, and good law of God, and so sets his authority at nought." When attention turned to the sinner per se, his preference switched to therapeutic language, characterizing sin in terms like "loathsome leprosy."[65] Indeed, his writings abound with descriptions of the diseased human soul.[66] This very abundance appears to warrant Lindström's claim that Wesley was particularly concerned with the second dimension of sin—as an infirmity of our human nature.[67]

Original Sin or Inbeing Sin?

The differing accents of Eastern and Western understandings of sin become more pointed when we focus on the question of initial human guilt. Particularly in the West this question came to be debated under the topic of "Original Sin." This term was used to refer both to the event of Adam and Eve using their self-determining power to turn away from God, and to the effects of this "Fall" upon subsequent humanity.[68]

As was stated earlier, the dominant streams of Western Christianity eventually affirmed two major effects of the Fall upon subsequent humanity: (1) we inherit the guilt of the Original Sin; and (2) as one sign of God's judgment, our human faculties are depraved to the point that we are free to do little more than sin.[69] Eastern Christianity has vigorously denied both of these effects. They contend that the true significance of the Fall was our loss of the Spirit's immediate Presence, resulting in the introduction of mortality into human life. This mortality weakened our human faculties and effaced our moral Likeness of God. Thus, the Fall did render us prone to sin, but not incapable of co-operating with God's offer of healing. As a result, we only become guilty when we reject the offered grace of God, *like* Adam and Eve did.[70]

An initial compilation of Wesley's various comments relating to present human sinfulness and guilt reveals a bewildering variety of elements. To sort these out, one must consider (1) the time period of the comment within his theological development, (2) the occasion of the comment, and (3) the tensions arising from his integration of juridical and therapeutic concerns.

An excellent example is the question of whether Wesley agreed with the typical Western claim that humans inherit the guilt of the Original

Sin.[71] The early Wesley would have been familiar with this theme in his Anglican standards, but it was not prominent in his own work.[72] There is a notable increase in assertions of such guilt during his middle (most Protestant) period, particularly in contexts responding to Enlightenment optimism.[73] However, there is also a worry evident in these materials that emphasizing inherited guilt could impugn God's justice and mercy. The middle Wesley turned to the Reformed notion of Adam as the Federal Head of all humankind as one way to address this worry.[74] However, his reservations about this notion—as possibly diminishing individual responsibility—are evident in his conjoined insistence that no human will ever be condemned on account of the imputed guilt of Original Sin alone.[75] This insistence grew stronger in Wesley's late period. In his debates with the predestinarians about the universality of the atonement, he ultimately declared that any inherited human guilt was universally cancelled *at birth*, as one benefit of Christ's redemption.[76] In effect, his concession of inherited guilt was now annulled by the invocation of Prevenient Grace! This is likely why he pruned suggestions of inherited guilt from the Thirty-Nine Articles in preparing the Articles of Religion for the American Methodists.[77]

Wesley's growing uncomfortableness with the notion of inherited guilt was not due to any doubt about universal human sinfulness, but rather was an expression of his life-long conviction that God deals responsibly with each individual. This conviction led him to locate the issue of guilt in our own sins rather than the sin of our ancestors. More broadly, it inclined him to focus less on the origin of sin than on the fact of sin's present infection of our nature (and our resulting need for God's grace). Such a focus is reflected in his evident preference of the title "Inbeing Sin" over "Original Sin."[78] In scholastic terms, this alternative title concentrated the problem of inherited sin more on the aspect of *corruptio* (the present distortion of our nature) than on the aspect of *reatus* (guilt).[79]

The Source of Inbeing Sin

This brings up the question of what accounts for the present corruption of human nature.[80] For early Christians this question focused on how the depravity of Adam's nature resulting from the Fall was passed on to his descendants. A popular image which they invoked to explain this was that all subsequent humans were "in the loins of Adam."[81] This notion of our seminal connection with Adam has obvious biological connotations. Indeed, the early models that emerged to explain the propagation of Adam's corruption each included a biological component.

One of these models was named "Traducianism" because of its claim that the entire nature (body *and* soul) of human persons are transmitted (*traduce*) from their parents. On such terms, subsequent humans are "infected" by the corruption resulting from the Fall because our bodies and souls are derived from Adam's. The biblical warrant offered for this claim was Genesis 5:3, which states that Adam begat a son "in his own likeness." The earliest form of this model—developed by Tertullian—assumed that the soul was corporeal like the body, though of a more refined matter. Tertullian also gives the occasional impression that subsequent persons are simply fragments of Adam's nature. Such implications led his version of traducianism to be decisively rejected. Augustine initiated a revision of the basic traducian claim that would have longer influence. While tracing both the soul and body back to our biological parents, he preserved individuality—we are each a new person generated by procreation (hence this revision is sometimes called "Generationism"), not simply a comminution of our father. He also maintained the difference in nature between the soul and the body—with the parental body generating body, while the parental soul generates soul.

A major objection raised against traducian models was that Genesis 2:7 presents the origination of Adam's soul as a distinct act from that of his body. On analogy, many early theologians argued that only the body is produced by human procreation, with each soul being created and instilled directly by God (hence the name "Creationism"). But this leaves the problem of universal corruption. God would not have created our souls already corrupt, so how do they become so? The most common answer picked up on the negative use of "flesh" in Scripture—the soul is instantly corrupted by its incorporation into fallen human flesh. The corruption of the flesh itself was again traced biologically to our seminal connection with Adam.

During the fifth century the Roman Church rejected even Augustine's version of traducianism. As a result the creationist explanation of the transmission of corruption became standard for medieval Scholasticism.[82] This position carried over into early Reformed theology.[83] By contrast, Luther recovered the traducianism of his Augustinian heritage, and this view became standard in Lutheran scholasticism.[84]

In retrospect, Augustine's most influential contribution to Western discussion of human corruption was not his modified form of traducianism but his linkage of our corruption with the emphasis on inherited guilt. Given his juridical orientation, Augustine desired more than an *explanation* of present human corruption, he sought a *justification* for it. He derived his justification from Jerome's mistranslation of Romans 5:12 in the Vulgate, which suggested that death spread to all humanity because all sinned *in Adam*.[85] While Augustine never fully explained how we participated, this verse led him—and most later Western theology—to speak of our present corruption as deserved, due to our participation in Adam's sin!

This very point increasingly led Reformed scholasticism to question the traditional creationist position's biological explanation of depravity as resulting from the soul's incorporation into sinful flesh. While not doubting creationism, they argued that this explanation conflicted with the juridical justification of depravity. Drawing on some scattered precedents, they developed a purely juridical explanation of how all sinned *in Adam* (still assuming the mistranslation of Romans 5:12!). Adam was cast as the Federal Head or legal representative of all humanity when he accepted and broke God's original covenant. On such terms, Adam's guilt would be legally imputable to all who were represented by him. So would his penalty. The corruption of every subsequent human's soul *and* body results from the direct imposition (rather than biological inheritance) of that penalty.[86]

This Reformed "imputed depravity" model became an influential Western alternative to biological explanations of depravity.[87] In doing so, it intensified the very aspect of the earlier models that some other Western theologians found most questionable—the supposed corporate nature of Adam's sin. Under the banner of judicial fairness, a third variation of the creationist position found occasional voice in the West. This version argued that all human souls were originated simultaneously at the beginning of creation. We pre-existed our present embodiment, and participated jointly in the rebellion denoted by Original Sin. That is why we each deserve the judicially-imposed corruption of our faculties in our present existence.[88]

In contrast to the various developed Western positions, Eastern Christian reflection on the source of our present corruption has witnessed little concern to explain why we "deserve" this corruption. A major reason is that they did not share the West's reading of Romans 5:12. Continuing to use the Greek text, Eastern theologians read it either "death spread to all humanity because *all* sinned" or "because *death* spread to all humanity, all sinned." The second reading is grammatically less likely, but had wide influence due to its explanation for universal sinfulness. In essence, Eastern Christians came to identify the entry of mortality into human life as the inevitable consequence (rather than juridical punishment) of Adam's separation from God. Mortality then debilitated and corrupted Adam's nature, as it has the nature of every person since, accounting for our sinful inclinations.[89] The biological tone of this account is obvious. Some early Greek theologians who contributed to it offered explicit traducian accounts of human procreation (e.g., Gregory of Nyssa). However, in keeping with its characteristic hesitance to explain mysteries, Eastern Orthodoxy has not required the clarification of this matter. It has simply stressed that the cause of mortality is our separation from God's empowering Presence, and that the path to overcoming its effects begins with our renewed participation in God.[90]

In making a transition to Wesley, we need to consider the teachings of his Anglican tradition. The relevant line in the Thirty-Nine Articles says simply that the corruption of our basic nature is "naturally engendered" in the offspring of Adam. Most early Anglicans would have understood this in terms of the medieval creationism/sinful flesh model. However it is also capable (perhaps purposefully so) of being read in terms of Early Church or Lutheran traducianism. Given the date of their framing, there is no sign in the Thirty-Nine Articles of the "imputed depravity" model developed by Reformed scholasticism.[91]

The lack of concern for exact definition of this issue in the Anglican Articles rubbed off on Wesley. For some time, he saw little practical-theological reason to engage in the traditional debates. As he responded sarcastically in 1753 to an elaborate discussion of the possible ways that Original Sin is transmitted, "The fact I know, both by Scripture and by experience. I know it is transmitted: but *how* it is transmitted I neither know nor desire to know."[92] As was often the case in such contexts, Wesley was exaggerating. His scattered comments on the matter prior to this time reveal a change of emphasis that indicates some "desire to know."[93]

The early Wesley inclined toward a biological account of present human corruption. For example, in an unpublished 1730 sermon he speculated that the forbidden fruit which Adam and Eve ate had a juice containing particles that cleaved to and clogged their veins—rendering them mortal, causing numerous physical disorders, and impairing their human faculties.[94] The implication was that Adam and Eve passed this corrupting agent on to their descendants. This explanation fits within the Thirty-Nine Articles' description of corruption as "naturally engendered." It is also resonant with imagery in Wesley's favored early Greek theologians.[95] However, it would be dissatisfying to one influenced by the Reformed juridical concern. As such, it is no surprise that Wesley's explanations of corruption shortly following 1738 drastically distilled this speculation, and added the theme of Adam as Representative of humanity—to justify the passing of corruption to us.[96]

Further concerns about his early inclination toward a biological transmission of corruption were raised by a letter which Wesley received in 1755 from Richard Tompson, a former colleague who was now objecting to Wesley's affirmation of entire sanctification. One of Tompson's queries concerned how parents who were both freed from sin could then pass on a fallen nature to their children. Wesley's weak response was that such a situation of two entirely-sanctified persons marrying and having children would never occur. When Tompson challenged the adequacy of this response, Wesley ducked behind a plea of insufficient time to formulate a fuller answer.[97] He was clearly troubled by the suggestion that the biological transmission of corruption implied limits on the extent of God's gracious transformation of our lives.

But what alternatives were there? The dialogue with Tompson may have heightened Wesley's interest in the "imputed depravity" version of creationism as a possibility. Such interest is evident in *NT Notes*, which he finalized in the midst of their exchange.[98] Wesley drew heavily on Johann Bengel's *Gnomon Novi Testamenti* in preparing the *NT Notes*. One specific example of this dependence is Romans 5:12. Wesley's translation of the verse follows Bengel in returning to the Greek text that "death passed upon all [humanity], in that all sinned." But then his comments also follow Bengel in preserving the Western claim that all sinned *in Adam*, along with a designation of Adam as representative of humanity.[99] This typical continuity with Bengel makes Wesley's comment on Hebrews 12:9 all the more striking. Since this verse (which describes God as the "Father of spirits") was a frequent proof-text in Reformed attacks on traducianism, Bengel (a Lutheran) provided an interpretive note for a traducian reading.[100] This time, in a rare direct reversal, Wesley substituted a tentative (but clear) option for creationism.[101]

Wesley's inclination toward an "imputed depravity" creationism proved indeed to be tentative. About a year after finishing *NT Notes* he began drafting a long-planned response to John Taylor's critique of the doctrine of Original Sin.[102] In this response he had several opportunities to champion Reformed models of the transmission of corruption because Taylor's work included a dialogue with the Westminster Larger Catechism, which contains intermixed elements of the "imputed depravity" and the earlier "sinful body" models of creationism. While Wesley did defend elements of these models which Taylor had attacked, he hardly championed either model. Rather, he explicitly denied having a definitive explanation of the transmission of corruption.[103] More to the point, he proved unwilling to affirm that God actively wills our inheritance of Adam's depravity.[104] When this is conjoined with his progressive qualification of imputed guilt noted earlier, and his contemporaneous rejection of the imputation of Christ's active righteousness discussed in Chapter Four, it becomes evident that any interest that Wesley had in the "imputed depravity" approach was rapidly fading. While biological accounts might place limits on the transforming possibilities of God's *grace*, the emphasis on imputed sin (and obedience) raised serious questions about individual *responsibility*. In this light, the amount of energy that Wesley devoted to arguing with Taylor that the curse on Adam was not simply physical death, but a closely related spiritual death, takes on great interest.[105] It seems to signal renewed emphasis on "natural generation." This would explain why Wesley's comments on the transmission of corruption in subsequent sermons return to language of being "in the loins of Adam," or "begat in Adam's likeness," dropping reference to Adam as the Representative of humanity.[106] Similar language is found in his renewed attempt to answer Tompson's objection about the propagation of fallenness through entirely-sanctified parents.[107]

An even more interesting aspect of Wesley's response to Taylor is his repeated accusation that Taylor lacked sufficient appreciation of the distinction between primary and secondary causation. Wesley insisted that God can be the First Cause of human generation or corruption's transmission, while human beings or human nature are the efficient or natural causes.[108] This point could fit a "sinful body" version of creationism. However, it seems particularly appropriate for the refined form of traducianism! What Wesley needed was a convincing articulation of the latter approach. It was not long in coming. In January 1762 he read Henry Woolnor's *The True Original of the Soule*, which argued in detail that only a traducian approach could explain the transmission of Original Sin. Wesley was persuaded.[109] As one response, he immediately revised the *NT Notes* comment on Hebrews 12:9 to suggest that God created our souls "at the beginning of the world."[110] The point of this revision was that our souls were "in the loins of Adam" and passed to us (like our bodies) through our parents. Thus, when Wesley received a letter in 1763 raising standard Lutheran criticisms of the creationist stance in his original *NT Notes* comment, it was anachronistic.[111]

Wesley's affirmation of a traducian anthropology found its most explicit form in 1782.[112] This affirmation put him in a position to reappropriate his early emphasis on biological factors in the transmission of depravity. Thus, the same year, he published a rewrite of his early sermon on this theme. The published sermon repeats the general theme that the Fall introduced mortality into human life, which corrupts our faculties through the processes of aging and hardening of the arteries![113] What is also apparent in this sermon—and others of the time—is the late Wesley's greater willingness to acknowledge the *responsible* limits which the feebleness of the human body places on a person's *gracious* transformation.[114]

There is one other characteristic of the late Wesley's reflections on the Fall, corresponding to his annulment of inherited guilt noted above: his assessments of our present corruption treat it more as an inherited *consequence* of Adam's sin than as *punishment* for our participation in that sin. He thereby approached the Eastern reading of Romans 5:12 in spirit, if not in fact.[115] Far from an aberration, this move illustrates the dynamic consistency in Wesley's theology. In retrospect, the most basic and consistent claims running throughout his reflection on inherited corruption resonate with the Eastern theme of *lost participation*: Humans are creaturely beings who can develop spiritual wholeness only through dynamic relationship with God's empowering grace. The essence of the first sin was the severing of this relationship, the desire to be independent of God. When Adam and Eve separated from God's Presence the result was their spiritual death—their loss of the Likeness of God (moral Image of God) and the corruption of their basic human faculties (natural Image of God). All subsequent human beings come into the world already separate from God, hence spiritually dead.[116]

The Nature of Inbeing Sin

Earlier this century several scholars accused Wesley of viewing Inbeing Sin as a foreign substance or entity that caused sinful actions, based on his occasional references to it in terms such as "an evil root."[117] More recent scholars have generally argued that a relational understanding of the nature of sin was more characteristic of Wesley.[118] While there are ambiguities, the preceding section offers support for the relational reading. The most basic cause of our present infirmity for Wesley was not some "thing" that we inherit, but the distortion of our nature resulting from being born into this world already separated from the empowering Divine Presence. *Deprived* of this essential relationship, our various faculties inevitably become *debilitated*, leaving us morally *depraved*.[119]

Wesley often delineated the character of the depravity (Inbeing Sin) resulting from our separation from God. To locate such sketches, however, it is necessary to distinguish them from his equally common classifications of actual sin, namely his contrast between voluntary and involuntary sin, and his appropriation of Augustine's division of actual sins into three categories (following 1 John 2:16): the desires of the flesh, the desires of the eye, and the pride of life.[120] When dealing with Inbeing Sin, Wesley was seeking the source of such actual sins, not simply classifying them.

This very relation between Inbeing Sin and actual sins is expressed in another of Wesley's threefold divisions of sin: sinful nature or tempers, sinful words, and sinful actions.[121] The point of this division was to emphasize that our sinful actions and words *flow from* enduring corruptions of our affections (one of our human faculties). Inbeing Sin is precisely this corruption of our human faculties resulting from our separation from God's empowering Presence;[122] to enumerate, our understanding is darkened, our will is seized by wrong tempers, our liberty is lost, and our conscience is left without a standard.[123] From this spiritual corruption spring our actual sins, which affect all four relationships definitive of human life. We no longer consistently love and serve either God or other humans; we neglect or actively terrorize the "lower" animals; and, as a result, our own happiness and self-acceptance drain away.[124]

The Extent of Inbeing Sin—Total Depravity

How bad is this corruption of our faculties? In Reformed theology it became common to describe it as "total depravity." This phrase could easily be misunderstood to suggest that every human person is as evil as one could possibly be. Such was not its intent. Reformed theologians meant only to affirm that the corruption of sin decisively affects every faculty of the human person, leaving us incapable of living in God's likeness—or even truly desiring to—through our debilitated powers alone. Even construed in these more limited terms, the affirmation of total depravity was broadly rejected outside of Protestant circles. Not by Wesley (at least after 1738)! While not always using the specific term, he repeatedly affirmed the point that Inbeing Sin's corruption pervades every human faculty and power, leaving us utterly unable to save ourselves.[125] Fortunately, however, God the Great Physician can heal our diseased nature.[126]

Pause for Perspective

I suggested earlier that Wesley's understanding of the human problem gave primacy of place to therapeutic concerns like those characteristic of Eastern Christianity. This is verified by the relative stress that he placed on Inbeing Sin over inherited guilt, with its implication that our most fundamental need is not just forgiveness but the healing of our diseased nature. We need God's restoring grace!

I also argued that Wesley integrated into his therapeutic emphasis the juridical concerns more typical of Western Christianity. This integration was important to preserving human responsibility. In their rejection of the notion of inherited guilt, Eastern theologians have sometimes verged on construing fallen humanity as simply "victims" of mortality.[127] Wesley refused to dismiss our culpability for our present fallen condition. At the same time, as noted above, he became increasingly uncomfortable with attributing this culpability to our participation in the Original Sin. As will soon be shown, his eventual resolution of this quandary was to ground our culpability in our *present refusal* of God's gracious restoring work in our lives.

Grace has now been mentioned twice, which brings me to my final point. Wesley's convictions about fallen humanity must always be read in light of the larger creation/fall/restoration framework of his theology. He could emphasize the full extent of the problem of sin precisely because he did not see it as the defining truth about, or the final situation of, humanity.[128] As Jennings has insisted, the purpose of Wesley's reflections on fallen humanity was not to provide a justification *for* sin, but to demonstrate the necessity and scope of salvation *from* sin.[129]

Humanity as Nascently Restored

Attention must turn finally, therefore, to the crowning aspect of Wesley's anthropology—the *third* state of humanity, as recipients of God's restoring grace. The basic Christian confession is that God has graciously come to fallen humanity, seeking to restore our right standing, our faculties, and our moral character (Likeness of God). It is in Wesley's understanding of the initial aspect of this gracious restoring work that one finds the most distinctive anthropological elements of his interweaving of the various theological traditions that influenced him.

The Prevenience of Restoring Grace

Wesley's affirmation of total depravity left him in an awkward situation within his Western Christian context. On the one hand, the Protestant theologians who shared with him this affirmation drew from it implications about limited atonement and unconditional election with which he could hardly agree, given his conviction about *responsible* grace. On the other hand, the typical way that Roman Catholicism (and many Eastern theologians) avoided these implications was to insist that depravity was not total; some of the freedom graciously provided in creation remained in fallen humanity, preserving the basis for our response to God's offer of salvation.[130] For Wesley, this both underestimated the impact of Inbeing Sin and endangered the unmerited nature of God's restoring *grace*.

Thus his orienting concern drove Wesley to search for a way to affirm that *all* possibility of our restored spiritual health—including the earliest inclination and ability to respond to God's saving action—is dependent upon a renewing work of God's grace, *without* rendering our participation in this process automatic. In this search he turned to an emphasis on "prevenience;" i.e., that God's grace always pre-vents (comes before) and makes possible human response.[131]

It is important to note that Wesley used the characterization of grace as "prevenient" in both a broad and a narrower sense, reflecting different traditions upon which he drew.[132] In its broad sense, Wesley invoked the prevenience of grace to affirm that *every* salutary human action or virtue, from the earliest expression of faith to the highest degree of sanctification, is grounded in the prior empowering of God's grace. This affirmation permeates his writings, finding particularly frequent expression in the collected devotions and prayers (the practical-theological form that most directly leads us to place our lives in the context of God's grace).[133] This broad sense of prevenient grace goes back to the Early Church and is found in many classic Roman Catholic sources.[134] More important, it pervades the Anglican standards of doctrine, which were surely the most direct source for Wesley's own understanding.[135] If there was any distinctive element in his broad affirmation of grace's prevenience—in comparison with these Anglican precedents—it is that Wesley grounded the gratuity of grace (which prevenience insures) more in God's love than God's sovereignty.[136]

The narrower use of "prevenient grace" in Wesley's works is drawn from the Calvinist/Arminian debates of his Anglican setting. In this case, the term designates a specific Arminian doctrine about God's saving work in fallen humanity *prior to justification.* As Colin Williams has noted, Wesley appropriated the specific doctrine of Prevenient Grace[137] to counteract the logical necessity with which his affirmation of total depravity seemed to lead to the Calvinist doctrine of predestination.[138] And yet, simply affirming that God's saving grace preceded the human response of faith did not counteract Calvin; he stressed this too, in regards to the elect! If we are to understand adequately how Wesley's specific doctrine of Prevenient Grace provided a viable alternative to Calvin we must first consider his assumptions about the character of God's restoring grace in general.

The Character of Restoring Grace[139]

A theological tradition's appraisal of the human problem is largely reflected in its conception of the nature of God's restoring grace. This means that the differences between characteristic Eastern and Western emphases carry over into this area of doctrine. Wesley's distinctive integration of these emphases does as well.

Given their juridical focus, Western theologians have identified God's grace predominately as *pardon*, or the unmerited forgiveness of our guilt through Christ. By contrast, Eastern theologians construe grace primarily in terms of the *power* to heal our infirm nature that comes through participation in God. What do we find in Wesley? Robert Hillman has undertaken an extended consideration of Wesley's preaching in this regard, in comparison with that of John Calvin (a particularly revealing comparison because Calvin has one of the stronger doctrines of sanctification among Western theologians). He found that in Calvin grace almost exclusively means pardon or mercy (and is rarely connected to sanctification). By contrast, the meanings of pardon and power are almost evenly represented in Wesley.[140]

Considered temporally, there appears to have been some fluctuation in Wesley's emphasis on these two dimensions of grace. The early Wesley construed grace primarily in terms of the requisite power of God that heals our corrupted nature and enables us to grow in virtue.[141] With his deeper appropriation of the Protestant emphasis on forensic justification in 1738, the definition of grace as unmerited pardon jumped to the forefront.[142] In later conflicts with quietistic and enthusiastic misunderstandings of Christian life, definitions of grace as the merciful power of God that enables responsible Christian life returned to prominence.[143]

The point of this temporal consideration is not to force a choice between the two dimensions of Wesley's understanding of grace. Rather, it is to suggest that his overall concern was to integrate them. Consider perhaps his clearest explication:

> By 'the grace of God' is sometimes to be understood that free love, that unmerited mercy, by which I, a sinner, through the merits of Christ am now reconciled to God. But in this place it rather means that power of God the Holy Ghost which 'worketh in us both to will and to do of his good pleasure.' As soon as ever the grace of God (in the former sense, his pardoning love) is manifested to our soul, the grace of God (in the latter sense, the power of his Spirit) takes place therein. And now we can perform through God, what to [ourselves] was impossible . . . a recovery of the image of God, a renewal of soul after His likeness.[144]

As this quotation suggests, Wesley's integration of the two dimensions of grace was not merely a conjunctive one. The emphasis on pardon was incorporated into the larger theme of empowerment for healing.[145] Thereby, God's unmerited forgiveness became instrumental to the healing of our corrupt nature, in keeping with Wesley's deep sympathy with a therapeutic emphasis like that characteristic of Eastern Christianity. At the same time, the Christological basis of grace was made more evident than is typical of the East, integrating the legitimate juridical concern emphasized by the West.

Further insight into Wesley's understanding of grace is shed by his frequent equation of God's grace with God's love.[146] Since love is inherently a relationship between two persons, this identification suggests that

Wesley's conception of grace, like that of sin, is fundamentally relational in nature. The power that enables our recovery of Christ-likeness is not some metaphysical property bestowed upon us, but an expression of God's renewed presence in our life.[147]

The general relational character of his understanding of grace has been often noted in Wesley scholarship.[148] However, the distinctive nature of this has not always been recognized. One of the major debates between Eastern and Western theologians has been whether saving grace was "created" or "uncreated;" that is, whether it was a divinely-originated *product* bestowed upon humanity or the Divine energies per se present within us. Western theology has generally assumed that grace was created, and then debated over its exact nature—is it simply the imposition of an alien righteousness (most Protestants), or the infusion of an actual character (*habitus*) of Christian obedience (Roman Catholics)? Eastern theologians have insisted instead that saving grace is fundamentally uncreated; it is not a possession given to humanity to justify God's mercy, it is the accompanying effect of the Divine energies present in our life through the Holy Spirit.[149]

When read in terms of this debate, Wesley's overall understanding of grace resonates strongly with the Eastern notion of uncreated grace.[150] This is hardly surprising. While the technical notion itself postdates the early Greek writers that he valued, the basic theme permeates their work, particularly the homilies of Macarius.[151] For them, as for Wesley, grace *is* the Holy Spirit at work in our life, initiating and sustaining our recovery of Christ-likeness. If Wesley's adaptation of this theme has a distinctive element, it is his assumption that an integral part of the Spirit's initiatory work is assuring us of God's forgiveness. Indeed, Wesley apparently considered this transformation of our perception of God a central way that the Spirit empowers our spiritual recovery.[152]

So far it has been noted that Wesley understood grace essentially as God's loving personal Presence at work in our lives. In light of the discussion of God's sovereignty in the previous chapter, the next point should be clear: this grace *inspires* and *enables*, but does not *overpower*. Put in more technical terms, Wesley understood grace (in good Anglican form) to be resistible or co-operant.[153] Put in my suggested terms, he understood grace to be responsible—it empowers our response, but does not coerce that response.

This co-operant nature of grace was so central to Wesley that he would create a neologism, if necessary, to express it. In his 1748 sermon on "The Great Privilege of Those who are Born of God" Wesley argued that those in whom God's Spirit is acting must, by a spiritual re-action, return to God the grace which they receive, for God does not continue to act upon a soul unless the soul re-acts upon God.[154] This use of "re-action" was apparently novel.[155] It captured well his basic conviction that God's gracious influences "are not to supersede, but to encourage, our own efforts."[156]

A final observation on Wesley's general understanding of grace follows naturally from all that has been seen so far. If God's grace is a personal and co-operant merciful empowering, it is surely gradual. Like all personal relationships, it deepens (or weakens) over time, because God respects and awaits our progressive response. In this sense, Wesley can talk about degrees of grace and corresponding degrees of salvation.[157] His understanding of progressive salvation will be developed in later chapters. At this point, the issue is his convictions about the earliest degree of grace—Prevenient Grace.

Prevenient Grace as the Beginning of Restoration[158]

Wesley's distinctive conception of God's restoring grace, particularly his understanding of its co-operant nature, comes into sharpest focus in his doctrine of Prevenient Grace, because this doctrine deals with God's very first activity in fallen human lives. The characteristic Arminian claim in this regard, which Wesley affirmed with increasing clarity through his life, was that this initial restored activity of God's grace was universally available, yet resistible.[159] Beyond this general point, what was Wesley's mature conception of Prevenient Grace?

A good place to begin answering this question is to note the benefits that Wesley attributed to Prevenient Grace. As with restoring grace in general, he identified in it dimensions of both pardon and power. The dimension of pardon may be surprising, since Prevenient Grace precedes the forgiveness of actual sins. However, one must remember that Wesley imbibed the general Western belief of inherited guilt from Original Sin. His growing uneasiness with some of the implications of this was noted earlier. He eventually resolved the issue by insisting that inherited guilt is universally cancelled at birth by virtue of Christ's redemption. In effect, this made forgiveness of inherited guilt a benefit of Prevenient Grace.[160] Any present human culpability for our fallen condition results from our rejection of God's offered restoring work in our lives, not any continuing responsibility for the Original Sin.

In terms of power, Prevenient Grace effects a partial restoring of our sin-corrupted human faculties, sufficient that we might sense our need and God's offer of salvation, and respond to that offer.[161] To begin with, there is some restoration of our understanding. Wesley mentioned two distinct aspects in this regard. First is a renewed possibility of basic knowledge of "divine things" (e.g., God's existence and nature, and the possibility of future reward or punishment).[162] The second aspect is a rudimentary discernment of the difference between moral good and evil, providing a standard by which our conscience can assess our lives.[163] In both cases we are dealing particularly with the gracious provision of initial restored revelation, since Prevenient Grace is universally available.[164]

The second basic human faculty that Prevenient Grace partially restores is liberty. It is not enough to be graciously made aware of our need for God's forgiving and healing grace, we must be able to respond to this awareness in some way. As such, at least a minimal degree of liberty must be universally restored in Prevenient Grace; the only alternative, a very unacceptable one, is unconditional election and irresistible grace.[165]

The remaining human faculty in need of restoration from the corruptions of Inbeing Sin is the will—i.e., our affectional nature. Wesley consistently maintained that recovery of right affections required God's empowering presence.[166] At the same time, he could not deny that many who have not yet entered a saving relationship with Christ exhibit at least nascent virtuous tempers and actions. He attributed this possibility to God's Prevenient Grace.[167]

On reflection, the "power" benefits of Prevenient Grace mentioned so far might seem to contradict Wesley's general claim that all grace is resistible; for, he surely considered these to be enduring realities in human life.[168] Our rejection of God's overtures does not deprive us of these benefits. Indeed, our very act of rejection presupposes them. And yet, we noted above Wesley's warning that God will not compel grace upon those who reject God's activity in their life. How would this apply to Prevenient Grace?

To answer this question, one must note that Wesley did not limit the activity of Prevenient Grace to upholding our partially restored faculties. He also attributed to it God's initial *overtures* to individuals. As he once put it, Prevenient Grace includes "all the drawings of the Father . . . [and] all the convictions which his Spirit from time to time works in every [person]."[169] If we persist in ignoring or rejecting these overtures of Prevenient Grace, we may effectively shut them out (i.e., harden our hearts). The restored potential of our faculties to perceive and respond would theoretically remain upheld, but would be fruitless because unaddressed.[170] Put in other terms, we might silence the overtures of Prevenient Grace, but would not drive its very Presence from our lives. Therein lies our only hope of a later "awakening" to God's further overtures.[171]

Such are the potential benefits of Prevenient Grace. But, what is its exact status? This question has spawned a variety of answers among Wesley scholars. Thomas Langford has provided a helpful typology of this discussion.[172] He discerns four major competing interpretations. At one end of the spectrum is the evaluation of the benefits of Prevenient Grace as simply part of the human condition. This position verges on dismissing total depravity and attributing Prevenient Grace to creation rather than merciful restoration; i.e., humans are accountable determinators of their destiny simply by virtue of being human.[173] The impossibility of squaring this evaluation with either Wesley's emphasis on Inbeing Sin or his understanding of restoring grace should be obvious.

Diametrically opposed to the first position is the argument of Robert Cushman that Prevenient Grace simply awakens fallen humanity to our inability and drives us to despair. It does not communicate an ability to accept God's offer of salvation, for our proper human role is not an active one; we are simply to raise no resistance to the powerful work of God's saving grace.[174] Cushman's reading is an understandable reaction to the danger of aligning Wesley with those who reduce the Christian gospel to humanistic moralism. However, its ultimate sacrifice of Wesley's affirmation of the co-operant nature of responsible grace does not seem warranted.[175]

Most Wesley scholars have judged his true conception to lie between the previous two extremes. Langford senses two slightly differing emphases among these mediating positions. Some scholars stress the possibility of human participation in salvation that Prevenient Grace restores. Indeed, they are willing to talk of human "initiative" in renewing relationship with God, based on our graciously-restored faculties. Other scholars shy away from any such language of human initiative. They argue that the provisions of Prevenient Grace are simply preparatory to God's further initiative in salvation. Our graciously-restored faculties require igniting by a further degree of God's grace if we are to respond and move into saving relationship.[176]

These mediating readings are surely closer to Wesley. However, I would suggest that they both stumble by failing to distinguish between Prevenient Grace as the upholding of our partially-restored faculties and Prevenient Grace as God's earliest overtures via these faculties. On the one hand, it is always God who initiates renewed relationship through the overtures of Prevenient Grace. We either respond to, ignore, or resist these overtures. On the other hand, these overtures are themselves an expression of Prevenient Grace. It is *as* we respond to them that we experience further depths of God's forgiving and empowering grace, not before.

Langford identifies another basic problem that permeates the various interpretations of Prevenient Grace—they tend to assume that it is a human "possession." By contrast, he argues that Prevenient Grace should not be considered a gift *from* God, but the gift *of* God's activity in our lives, sensitizing and inviting us.[177] What he is defending, of course, is Wesley's consonance with the Eastern Orthodox notion of uncreated grace!

This raises the question of the source(s) of Wesley's doctrine of Prevenient Grace. Within the context of contemporary debates he identified himself as an Arminian. However, his actual reading in Arminius' works was limited. More important, his general conception of Prevenient Grace was not cast within assumptions dictated by hyper-Calvinism, as was the case with Arminius. Most of what Wesley termed "Arminianism" was more properly a native English tradition (reaching back long before Arminius) that affirmed a role for human co-operation in salvation.[178] In other words, Wesley imbibed the basic convictions of Prevenient Grace with his Anglican setting and training. One particular aspect of this was his encounter with influential articulations of the basic notion in early Greek theologians.[179]

Thus, Langford's description of Prevenient Grace in terms parallel to the Eastern Orthodox notion of uncreated grace is appropriate. In fact, Craig Blaising has demonstrated that many of the supposed contradictions in Wesley's claims about Prevenient Grace (when read with Western assumptions about created grace) are resolved by construing it in terms of uncreated grace. In particular, it allows Wesley's simultaneous affirmation of our inherent total depravity and our ability to respond to God's grace.[180] Seen in terms of uncreated grace, depravity is not the obliteration of our human faculties, but their debilitation when devoid of God's empowering Presence. Likewise, Prevenient Grace is not a new endowment given into human possession, it is an accompanying effect of God's initial move towards mercifully-restored Presence in our lives. With God's approach our faculties are increasingly empowered, to the point that we can recognize our need and God's offer of renewed relationship, and respond to it. The key point, of course, is that our response is made possible by grace, not something that we accomplish with our *inherent* (dis)abilities.[181]

To summarize, Wesley understood Prevenient Grace to be God's initial move toward restored relationship with fallen humanity. As a first dimension, this involved God's merciful removal of any inherited guilt, by virtue of Christ. A second dimension of God's initial move to restored Presence is a partial healing of our debilitated human faculties, sufficient for us to sense and respond to God. The final dimension is God's specific overtures to individuals, inviting closer relationship. If these overtures are welcomed, a grace-empowered relationship of co-operative and progressive transformation sets forth. Since God's grace is universal, so is the possibility of such relationship. Since God's grace is resistible, no individual's participation is inevitable.

Excursus: Wesley's "Synergism"?

With this understanding of Prevenient Grace in mind, we are in a good position to evaluate the ongoing debate among scholars about whether Wesley was a synergist. The basic issue goes all the way back to accusations Wesley faced that he taught "salvation by works."[182] It flared up in recent scholarship with George Cell's insistence that Wesley's understanding of grace and Christian life was strictly monergistic.[183] In response, William Cannon led a series of counterclaims that Wesley was most definitely a synergist.[184] Several scholars have been uncomfortable with either of these alternatives, suggesting mediating options such as evangelical synergist, mild synergist, covenantal synergist, conditional monergist, and even "synergist within a monergistic framework."[185]

On consideration it becomes clear that this debate is not so much a disagreement over Wesley as over the meaning of "monergist" and "synergist." If monergism is understood to teach that God (the *only* power) irresistibly performs our human acts of faith and virtue for us, then those who reject its application to Wesley are surely correct. However, all Cell directly attributed to the term was the claim that humans are totally dependent upon God for the energy by which we live in obedience to God's call.[186] This more restricted claim is clearly in line with Wesley's understanding of Prevenient Grace. Likewise, if synergism is taken to designate a position that assumes humans *initiate* the saving encounter or respond to God's initial offer of salvation out of their *own* power, then it hardly fits Wesley.[187] However, if synergism is understood as simply the preservation of a role for grace-empowered human co-operation in salvation, then it too reflects a concern of Wesley's understanding of Prevenient Grace.[188]

It would probably be best, however, to avoid either of these terms in describing Wesley, for their prototypical meanings are framed within debates between Continental Protestantism and Roman Catholicism. By contrast, the major sources of Wesley's basic understanding of Divine/human interaction were Anglican and Early Church (particularly Greek). There is no better expression of this than his classic statement of the relation between Divine grace and human response—a sermon on Philippians 2:12-13, entitled "On Working Out Our Own Salvation."[189] As Wesley prepared this sermon for publication in 1785, he surely bore in mind two previous sermons on this text that he had valued for years and recommended to others: one by the Anglican William Tilly, the other a homily of Macarius.[190]

This is not to say that Wesley's sermon on Philippians 2:12-13 merely repeated these predecessors. Both Tilly and Macarius had stressed that humans must co-operatively "put to work" the grace of God. Wesley agreed. However, comparatively, he made clearer than they did that the priority lies in God's empowering grace.[191] Indeed, he spends the first two-thirds of his sermon on the point that "It is God that worketh in us both to will and to do," before moving to the implications that (1) therefore we *can* work, for all are encountered by at least God's Prevenient Grace; and (2) therefore we *must* work, for if we do not re-act to God's gracious overtures, they will cease.

In short, Wesley did indeed affirm a role for meaningful human participation in salvation. However, he always maintained that this role was grounded in God's gracious empowering, not our inherent abilities. As he repeatedly insisted, we must hold in tension the two biblical teachings: "Without me you can do nothing," and "I can do all things through Christ strengthening me."[192] Pastoral situations might well demand a practical theologian to highlight one or the other aspect of this tension more heavily; but they must never be divorced, for this would foster either quietism or enthusiastic pride.[193]

What should one call such a position as this? A traditional possibility would be "co-operant grace."[194] I prefer "responsible grace," however, because it internalizes Wesley's conviction that our requisite co-operation is only possible in *response* to God's empowering. It also carries hints of the universality of Prevenient Grace—it is because God is graciously present to all humanity that all humanity are responsible.

The Resulting Actual Human Situation

This brings us to a final question: Just what is the "natural" situation of humanity (i.e., the situation prior to conversion), for Wesley? Does he agree with Calvin and Luther that humanity is incapable naturally of even desiring to please God? That is, does he really believe in total depravity? Or does he, in effect, side with Catholics (East and West) in assuming that fallen humans retain some "natural" ability to respond to God's offer of salvation?

Wesley's references to humanity's natural state fluctuated somewhat, then *moved beyond* these options with the transitions in his general theological convictions. In his early "gospel of moral rectitude," with its emphasis on encouraging humans to recover our original spiritual health, there are intimations of a slight residual created ability to do so.[195] The decisive rejection of any such natural ability was central to his deeper appropriation of the Protestant conviction of "grace alone" in 1738. From this point there are more consistent and frequent designations of humanity's fallen state as "natural." Humans, by nature, are wholly corrupt and incapable of any response to God apart from a new work of grace.[196] By his late period, Wesley had become uncomfortable with many of the ways that this emphasis on human inability was understood, particularly those that suggested quietism, limited atonement, or unconditional election. In response, he insisted that we are not excused from personal responsibility, even though we are dead in sin by nature, because no one actually exists in a state of "mere nature."[197] That is, he wed his affirmation of total depravity with his conviction of the universal initial restoring effects of Prevenient Grace.

Some have tried to capture Wesley's final position on this point with the claim that the "natural man" was a logical abstraction for him,[198] yet this is a misleading way of putting it. It could easily suggest that the late Wesley, in effect, relinquished the assumption of inherent human inability.[199] By contrast, I have argued that Wesley's mature understanding of (uncreated) Prevenient Grace actually *enhanced* his conviction of our inherent inability, while simultaneously allowing his strong insistence on universal responsibility. He did not base our ability to respond to God in any *inherent* strength that we possess, but in the gracious *restoration* of our faculties that God's Presence effects, by virtue of Christ.[200]

Why is this distinction so important? What practical difference does it make if our initial ability to respond to God is grounded in creation or restoration? After all, Wesley understood both creation and restoration to be works of God's grace. And, both options end up with humanity capable of responsibly co-operating with God's converting grace.[201]

One possible advantage of Wesley's formulation is that it intensifies our recognition of the role of God's grace in salvation. As he once put it, for the God of gracious creation to return in gracious restoring power to fallen humanity is "grace upon grace."[202] I would suggest that another advantage of Wesley's formulation is that it more clearly unites the pardon and power dimensions of God's grace: from our earliest encounter to our deepest appropriation, God's gracious Presence in our lives *both* assures us of forgiving love *and* empowers us for healing our sin-corrupted lives.

What then, for Wesley, is our actual human situation? We are creatures whose empowerment and fulfillment flow from relationship with God. We are creatures who have separated from that relationship, resulting in the debilitation of our faculties, the corruption of our moral nature, and the loss of our contentment. We are creatures totally dependent upon God's forgiving and restoring Presence if any of this is to change. Happily, we are each also recipients of this unmerited Presence in its initial degrees. For this reason alone, we are creatures capable of responding to and welcoming God's further transforming work in our lives; or, since God's grace is resistible, of culpably rejecting it.

CHAPTER 4

Christ—The Initiative of Responsible Grace

So far we have considered Wesley's basic understanding of God and his analysis of the human situation. This consideration made clear that, for Wesley, fallen humanity stands in definite need of both forgiveness and healing. God's initial gracious provision for this need was also noted. Before detailing the further dimensions of human transformation that Divine grace makes available, attention needs to return to God—who is both the Initiator and the Empowering Presence of this salvation.

When Wesley considered the Godhead specifically in light of the needs of fallen humanity, the second and third "Persons" of the Trinity moved to the forefront. They *both* come into consideration because of our twofold need: it is through the Incarnate God that we are graciously reconciled, and through the Indwelling God that we are graciously empowered for our healing.[1] Wesley's understanding of Christ's provision for our reconciliation will be elaborated in this chapter, while his conception of the Spirit's provision for our healing will occupy the next.

General Character of Wesley's Christology

When Wesley took up questions in Christology, his focus was definitely not on the "Jesus of history." Indeed, he was suspicious of anyone with interest in Jesus as a "mere man," and even of those (like the Moravians) who used intimate language to address Jesus. Such folk were being "too familiar with the great Lord of Heaven and earth."[2] On the other hand, his interest was not controlled by issues of explaining Christ's nature as God-Incarnate either. He agreed with Peter Browne that much of the historical debate over Christ's nature was simply unwarranted imposition of philosophical conceptions on the simply-expressed teachings of Scripture and the earliest Church.[3] So, where did his interest lie? It was in Jesus as the Christ, the Saviour of the world. Put in technical terms, his focal Christological concern was with the *work* of Christ.[4]

To be sure, Wesley was not unique in this regard. Despite what the typical structure of Scholastic-influenced textbooks suggests, most theological traditions define the nature of Christ in light of what they consider to be the central benefits or work of Christ. This was especially the case in the early debates over Christ's nature. Varying understandings of Christ emerged from differing conceptions of the basic human need and Christ's role in meeting that need.[5] In particular, the differences noted earlier between characteristic Eastern and Western Christian understandings of salvation had correlates in their emphases regarding the work of Christ (and the implied nature of Christ).

With the West's juridical focus—stressing the guilt of sin and our inability to atone for ourselves—Christological interest centered around Christ's death as the perfect Atonement. Thereby the death of Christ became the defining part of his mission. Indeed, if there had been no Fall (and resulting guilt to atone for), it was broadly assumed in the West that there would have been no Incarnation. Western Christians have gotten into debates over the precise explanation of how Christ's death atones for sin, but rarely over the focus on Atonement itself.

In comparison with this Western focus, early Greek and later Eastern Orthodox theologians have placed more emphasis on the importance of the Incarnation per se. This relates to their judgment that the essential human need is therapeutic: we need to recover the Likeness of God in our lives; if this is to happen, we need to be freed from our slavery to sin and empowered by the restored Presence of God; the Incarnation is the gracious act by which God freed us and reclaimed our human nature for its proper end. As Athanasius put it, in the Incarnation "God became like us so that we might become like God."[6]

Interestingly, Orthodox theologians have generally assumed that the Incarnation would have been necessary for our spiritual growth even if there had been no Fall. The Fall did accentuate this need radically by introducing mortality and corruption into human life. It also necessitated the death of Christ. However, this was not primarily a forensic need of dealing with guilt. Rather, Christ's death became integral to his total identification with our human nature, which now included mortality. By his death, then, Christ reclaimed fallen human nature, and through his resurrection and ascension he transformed and exalted it, providing for our spiritual healing and renewed growth. Since they view the latter as the defining goal of Christ's mission, Eastern Christians have typically placed more emphasis on the resurrected and ascended Lord than on the crucified Lamb.

The discussion of Wesley's anthropology in Chapter Three noted strong therapeutic concerns like those of Eastern Orthodoxy. As such, one might expect significant parallels between Wesley's Christological convictions and those of the East,—but will be largely disappointed! His central emphases about the work of Christ stand squarely within the Western focus on Christ's death, understood in terms of dealing with the guilt of sin.[7] Indeed, he specifically criticized a suggestion by William Law that Christ's death was not to atone for sin but to renew fallen human nature. For Wesley, such renewal might be a secondary benefit of Christ's death, but the primary purpose was to atone for sin.[8]

This is not to say that Wesley's Christology is thoroughly Western. In what remains the most thorough study, John Deschner made a valiant attempt to interpret Wesley's Christology within the Western categories of neo-Orthodoxy. He discovered that the central problem in this interpretation was doing justice to Wesley's concern for moral transformation of Christian life, a concern that Wesley maintained even after his deeper appropriation of the theme of forensic justification in 1738.[9] At crucial junctures Deschner found it necessary to suggest alternative formulations of Wesley's concern that imputed righteousness not supplant personal holiness, so that it might fit more typical neo-Orthodox categories.[10]

What Deschner is struggling with here, as he himself admits, is the presence of a deep therapeutic concern even in the materials from Wesley's most "Protestant" period (which Deschner had limited himself to).[11] Imagine how much more difficult it would be to provide a consistent Western reading of his Christology dealing with the whole Wesley! It would also be undesirable. A more appropriate agenda is to discern how Wesley's understanding of Christ fits within his concern to integrate the juridical emphasis typical of Western theology into his basic therapeutic view of Christian life. In particular, what role does the Atonement play in his overall understanding of salvation?

Christ—An Atonement for Sin

There can be little doubt of the importance of the Atonement to Wesley. His early complaint against William Law was that Law had failed to teach him the need for or truth of the Atonement.[12] The Atonement became central enough to his mature understanding of the meaning of Christ that he endorsed the typical Western conviction that the Son would not have become incarnate if Adam and Eve had not fallen, creating the problem of sin and guilt.[13] Indeed, he once even declared the Atonement the most significant Christian doctrine of all! His reason for this is revealing—it provided the distinguishing point between the Deism of his day and true Christianity.[14] In other words, it preserved Christianity's status as a religion of gracious salvation, rather than mere humanistic moralism.

It is one thing to value the Atonement; it is another to explain it. For all of his emphasis on the Atonement, Wesley never provided a prolonged or systematic summary of his understanding of it. His characteristic emphases and concerns must be observed in the various practical-theological contexts where he found consideration of the Atonement necessary.[15]

Atonement as Liberation?

In its most general sense, an atonement is simply an action or gift that helps reconcile parties estranged from one another. It need not be predominately forensic in nature, dealing with removal of guilt. This is important to remember in considering one conception of the Atonement common in the Early Church, particularly among Greek authors (and which has remained influential in Eastern Orthodoxy).[16]

Behind this conception of the Atonement is the assumption of early Greek theologians that our most basic human problem is our withdrawal from participation in God's Presence, resulting in our mortality and our enslavement to Satan and sin. The purpose of Christ's coming, in this case, is to reclaim human life, free us from our slavery, and restore our participation in God. Christ reclaims human life by joining the Divine nature with our human nature and "recapitulating" all the stages of human life (including death). But how does Christ liberate us from our slavery to the Satan, death, and sin? The basic answer is that Christ defeated Satan, thereby conquering death and restoring our relationship to God, which relationship empowers our deliverance from sin. This basic claim took two slightly different versions. One version construes Christ's incarnation and death as a ransom that he freely offered to Satan in exchange for our lives. Satan accepted the trade, but soon learned that he had been outwitted. In the resurrection Christ escaped Satan's hold, taking us with him. The other version describes our rescue from Satan in military terms, simply as a victory in which Christ triumphs over Satan (again, in the resurrection).

Given Wesley's appreciation for early Greek theologians, it is not surprising that we occasionally find echoes of these themes in his works. What *is* surprising is how few echoes we find, particularly since he shares their larger conviction that God's ultimate agenda is for us to recover the

Divine Likeness in our lives.[17] About the only place where the idea of Christ recapitulating the various stages of human life can be found is in his *NT Notes* comments on texts that simply demand such a reading.[18] The same is true of his even scarcer clear echoes of the military or ransom explanations of Christ's death and resurrection.[19] The paucity of ransom language in Wesley becomes even more striking when one compares him with the *Book of Common Prayer*, which he valued so highly. The ransom theme is much more prevalent in the latter.[20]

That Wesley would differ so markedly from such valued sources suggests that he is consciously avoiding use of the ransom model as a primary explanation of Christ's death. Why would he do so? Part of the answer might be that he understood fallen humanity to be enslaved less to Satan than to corrupt tempers.[21] The deeper reason was likely that the ransom model pays little attention to the problem of the guilt of sin.[22] Wesley was convinced that without an atonement first made for the guilt of sin, we could never be delivered from its enslaving power.[23] More precisely, he viewed Christ's Atonement for guilt as *itself* what truly liberates us from captivity to sin and Satan. As he commented on Col. 1:14 in *NT Notes*, "The voluntary passion of our Lord appeased the Father's wrath, obtained pardon and acceptance for us, and, *consequently*, dissolved the dominion and power which Satan had over us through our sins" (emphasis added).

In short, while Wesley believed that liberation may result from the Atonement, he assumed that its originating purpose was to absolve our guilt. He stands solidly with the West on this score. Of course, more than one way of explaining how human guilt is removed has developed in the West. As a prelude to placing Wesley within this variety, it would be helpful to gain an awareness of his theological assumptions regarding the basic moral law.

Excursus: Wesley on the Nature and Uses of the Law

Every forensic explanation of the Atonement makes general assumptions about the nature and purpose of God's law, and the specific relationship of law to Christian life. Fortunately Wesley's assumptions are not hard to find. His practical-theological task of forming the worldview and character of his people inevitably led him into conflict with alternative assumptions, forcing him to articulate and defend his views repeatedly.[24] Central to these defenses was a relatively consistent concern to affirm that the basic moral law is a gift of God's *grace* to which Christians remain *responsible*; indeed, we become more *response-able* through our relationship with Christ.[25]

Wesley's most fundamental conviction about the law was its integral relation to God. He emphatically rejected the nominalist suggestion that the law might be an arbitrary imposition of the Divine will.[26] It springs from and partakes of the holy nature of God.[27] This means that God may not simply ignore violations of the law. It also means that God will not arbitrarily apply the law to some persons while exempting others. Either of these actions would violate God's very nature.

To approach from the other direction, Wesley was convinced that the basic law of which humans are aware is not a human creation. It is an imperfect copy of a Divine original.[28] As a result, it is essentially good. It is a gracious gift that prescribes the way of life that is in our best interest.[29] This lies behind Wesley's repeated assertion that it is only when we are holy that we will be happy.[30]

Several claims about the "law" have been made already, without being very precise about what is involved. Perhaps the best way to clarify this is to trace the history of the giving of the law, as Wesley understood it. The "original" of the law is the basic moral sense that was extensively inscribed in the first humans at creation. This law demanded perfect obedience in all details, which was possible because of the original perfection of their human faculties. With the Fall this original detailed awareness of the moral law and the original perfection of our faculties were lost.[31]

Because of the continued corruption of our human faculties since the Fall, Wesley assumed that absolutely perfect obedience to the law is no longer possible, or demanded. Rather, what God now desires is that we avoid "voluntary transgressions of known laws."[32] And how do we even know God's law in our current state? To begin with, as was noted in the last chapter, there is a universal partial reinscription of the basic moral law through Prevenient Grace. This rudimentary restored knowledge is crucial to the preservation of universal moral accountability.[33] However, it remains vague at best, and tangled in cultural diversity.

For greater clarity in our knowledge of the law we are dependent upon God's definitive revelation. This revelation begins with Israel and the Mosaic law. Wesley assumed that the fundamental core of the Mosaic law was the moral code (epitomized by the Ten Commandments), and that this code recapitulated the original moral law.[34] More precisely, it presents the aspect of this moral law which is still applicable in our sin-diminished state, the law of love for God and neighbor.[35] As such, this moral code is "the heart of God" disclosed to humanity.[36]

Given such a high estimation of the Mosaic moral code, how does Wesley deal with Paul's claim that Christ is the end of the law? He interpreted "end" to mean fulfillment rather than discontinuation.[37] To be sure, this fulfillment distinguished between the Jewish ceremonial and civil codes and the basic moral code of love for God and neighbor. The former were set aside as having no continuing purpose, while the latter is reaffirmed as defining God's eternal relationship to and continuing will for humanity.[38] For Wesley, Christ's own articulation of this basic moral law is epitomized in the Sermon on the Mount, which explains why he devoted nearly one-fourth of his first collection of *Sermons* to expositions of this passage.[39]

Christ's fulfillment also set up a different relationship between humanity and the moral law. God's saving acceptance is no longer contingent upon our prior perfect execution of the law.[40] Instead, our obedience to the law becomes a growing reality, in *response* to our realization of God's prior *gracious* acceptance. Wesley repeatedly insisted that we cannot love either God or others (i.e., keep the basic law) unless it is in response to an awareness that God already loves us. By contrast, from such awareness our obedience will naturally flow.[41]

What makes us aware that God loves us? The objective evidence of this love is Christ's atoning death. The subjective means of its discernment is the Holy Spirit's present witness with our spirit, assuring us of God's love and renewed Presence in our lives.[42] As the discussion of uncreated grace in the previous chapter should have made clear, this Presence is precisely what empowers our response of loving God and others. This suggests Wesley's final point about Christ's fulfillment of the law: the liberty that Christ brings is not a liberty *from* the law, but a liberty *for* the law.[43] The crowning aspect of the Christian dispensation is the Gift of the Spirit which empowers us to live as God has always desired that we should, something not really possible before that bestowal.[44]

Given his understanding of the nature of the law, Wesley vigorously rejected any attempt to oppose the law with the gospel, or with faith. The gospel is not the overthrow of the law, but the proclamation of its fulfillment in Christ—in the senses just summarized. Likewise, faith in God's promise of unmerited love is not something that supersedes holy living, but what empowers such living.[45] The issue here, of course, is not just clarity. Wesley's practical-theological concern is for the spiritual well-being of the Christian community: improper contrasts of gospel with law are likely to stifle responsible Christian living.[46]

This brings us, finally, to Wesley's understanding of the "uses of the law" in fostering and forming Christian life. This issue had been subject to extended debates in Protestantism. Because of his pervading concern about works-righteousness, Luther had increasingly restricted the law to a negative role of demonstrating our total inability and driving us (in despair) to accept the Gospel of unmerited justification. Later Lutheran Orthodoxy and the Reformed tradition as a whole were uncomfortable with such a dualistic contrast of law and Gospel. While agreeing that *one* function of the law was the negative task of convincing us of our sin and our need for grace, they identified two further positive functions: to restrain wickedness so that fallen humanity will not self-destruct; and to teach believers a Christ-like way of life. In order to maintain the primacy of grace over law, the law involved in the third function was often identified as a specific Christian law of love—i.e., a less rigorous standard than the Mosaic law or even Christ's Sermon on the Mount.[47]

Considering Wesley's concern for responsible Christian living, it is not surprising that he joined those who affirmed a positive function for the law in Christian life. His understanding of this, however, is somewhat unique. The three functions of the law that he distinguished are (1) to awaken a conviction of sin, (2) to drive us to Christ for our pardon and conversion, and (3) to keep Christians alive and growing in the renewal of their nature.[48] Not only does Wesley's list vary slightly from the typical one, his understanding of the third function of the law is particularly distinct. He does not see Christ providing a different law for Christians from that found in the Mosaic moral code. Rather, Christ restores our relationship with God, thereby progressively empowering us to fulfill the basic moral law itself.[49]

Atonement as Pardon

Wesley's conception of the nature and uses of the law has many implications for Christian life, which will be elaborated in appropriate contexts. At this point I am interested in its ramifications for understanding the Atonement. To begin with, his very focusing of the Atonement on the problem of guilt is explained—a God of truly Holy Love, when seeking to restore relationship with us, may not simply ignore our accountability (guilt) for violating the divine law. Wesley's conception also lays outs some boundaries for an acceptable explanation of how God deals with this problem of guilt: (1) it must not be arbitrary in its application to humanity; (2) it should not undercut the role of responsible Christian growth in conformity to God's will; and (3) it needs to make clear that such growth is a response to God's acceptance, not a precondition of that acceptance.

Of course, Wesley did not set out with such guidelines in mind and construct an original explanation of how Christ's death absolved our guilt. Rather, he inherited a blend of traditional explanations which he reflected on as situations in his pastoral activity highlighted apparent implications. In this process he rejected some elements of these traditional explanations. These rejections led to occasional charges that he had given up the Atonement per se![50]

There were at least three identifiable variations of the forensic emphasis on the Atonement dominant in Western Christianity to which Wesley would have been exposed.[51] The first of these is the "Divine Satisfaction" explanation of Christ's death. This explanation was given its most detailed expression by St. Anselm, who formalized early-Medieval Latin tendencies to construe sin and forgiveness in the prevalent terms of honor, merit, and demerit. In such terms, the problem of sin is that it fractures the cosmic harmony God intended and affronts God's honor (as Overlord). If we want to set such an offense right we must offer a gift of merit equal to or greater than the demerit originally incurred, *or* we must suffer punishment. Herein lies our problem! Since God is infinite, so is the offense. It would take a gift of infinite merit to satisfy Divine honor (or a punishment of eternal death!). Obviously, we finite and guilty human beings have no such gift to offer. On the other hand, God is not prone to punish, because God's eternal intention for humanity is our blessedness. But God must also honorably uphold the order and balance of the universe.[52] That is why God the Son became human (*Cur Deus Homo*). As human, Christ could offer to God the meritorious gift of his voluntary passion. As divine, Christ's gift would have infinite merit. With this gift to offset the demerit of sin, God could honorably restore right relationship with the creation, removing our liability to punishment.

Anselm's Divine Satisfaction approach has maintained a continuing presence in later Western theology, especially Roman Catholic. Sometimes this presence has taken the form of a subtle translation—into a "Penalty Satisfaction" approach. Characteristic themes of this variation can be found in Thomas Aquinas. Influenced by Aristotle's recovered political and ethical writings, Thomas' understanding of God came to focus more on God as Sustainer of the Good than on God as Sovereign Overlord. By corollary, his construal of the Atonement came to focus more on expressing Divine righteousness than on satisfying Divine honor. On these terms, sins become violations of the Divine law that carry penalties. Since the laws broken are infinite, so are the penalties. We are again unable to satisfy such penalties ourselves. It is conceivable that God might simply forgive our sins, but satisfaction of the penalties would express more clearly God's righteousness and mercy. Therefore, God sent the Son as a penalty substitute for humanity. Through the incarnation Christ identified with humanity as a whole. Through his death (as the innocent, infinite one) Christ more than satisfied any penalty due human sin. Accordingly, God can now pardon us without infringing Divine righteousness.[53]

Obviously, the Divine Satisfaction and Penalty Satisfaction explanations of the Atonement are closely related. Their differences lie in emphasis, not kind. Penalty Satisfaction has tended to supersede Divine Satisfaction since the seventeenth century, though they are often found mingled together.[54] By contrast, the third variation of a forensic understanding of the Atonement emerged in Protestantism as a direct alternative to both previous accounts.

Luther and Calvin were bothered by two related features of the earlier views. First, these views focus more on God's provision for restoring the fallen order *as a whole* than on the issue of individual justification. They leave open (often intentionally) the possible role for humans to merit the benefits of Christ's atonement, even though we cannot merit salvation itself. Put in other terms, the previous views deal almost exclusively with the possibility of our *forgiveness* in Christ. They do not detail how we achieve the positive *righteousness* that merits eternal blessing. As before, they leave the possibility of our own contribution (merit) in this regard.

The Reformers emphatically rejected any such role for human merit in salvation. To protect against it they engendered an understanding of the Atonement that, in its developed form, might best be called "Substitutionary Justification." Central to this view is an emphasis on both Christ's passive and active obedience. His passive obedience is his suffering of the ultimate punishment for sin in death.[55] His active obedience is his positive fulfillment of God's moral law during his life. In each individual act of justification, God allows Christ to become the sinner's substitute, imputing the guilt of sin to Christ (who suffers its penalty) and the active righteousness of Christ to the justified person (who is now not merely pardoned, but warrants salvation as positively righteous). In this way, the Christian's entire salvation rests on the merits of Christ alone.

Given the eclectic nature of his Anglican context, Wesley was exposed to all three variations of the forensic understanding of the Atonement. As such, one encounters elements of each in the appraisals of Christ's significance for our salvation in his writings following the deeper appropriation of the emphasis on justification by grace in 1738. A good example comes from his 1742 delineation of *The Principles of a Methodist*:

> I believe three things must go together in our justification: upon God's part, his great mercy and grace; upon Christ's part, the satisfaction of God's justice by the offering his body and shedding his blood, 'and fulfilling the law of God perfectly'; and upon our part, true and living faith in the merits of Jesus Christ.[56]

This quotation contains reference to Christ's active as well as passive obedience.[57] There are also at least hints of the satisfaction of God's offended honor in the mention of "merits."[58] What is most evident, however, is the theme of Penalty Satisfaction: Christ's death fulfills the just penalty for our sins.

It is no accident that the Penalty Satisfaction motif was prominent in Wesley. It had emerged as the dominant theme in the Anglican standards upon which he drew and to which he appealed to defend his preaching of "free grace."[59] And yet—in comparison with those standards—over time Wesley appears to have refined the focus on the Penalty Satisfaction account of the Atonement even further.[60]

Wesley's deeper appropriation of the Protestant emphasis on justification by grace in 1738 placed him in conversation with the Substitutionary Justification understanding of Atonement. As he sought to shepherd his revival movement, he was soon struggling with possible implications of this understanding. In both the early disputes with the Moravian quietists and the later tensions with the Calvinist Methodists the concept of Christ's imputed active righteousness was used against Wesley as a defense for why Christians are *already* seen as perfect by God, so need not be constantly exhorted to "go on to perfection," as he was wont to do.[61] In response, Wesley eventually decided to reject publicly the imputation of Christ's active righteousness or obedience to believers. One of the earliest evidences of this resolve was a 1756 public letter questioning a defense of the Substitutionary Justification approach by James Hervey, an earlier associate of Wesley.[62] His most extended treatment of the issue was a 1765 sermon on "The Lord Our Righteousness," in which Wesley refused to separate between Christ's active and passive righteousness, such that one would apply to our forgiveness and the other account for our present righteousness. He insisted instead that all that they account for—*together*—is our initial and continuing merciful pardon by God. Any actual righteousness that we might display is a result of our response to the Holy Spirit's present work in our lives, not an imputation of Christ's obedience.[63]

Clearly, what was at issue here is Wesley's practical-theological concern that an improper understanding of the imputation of Christ's righteousness was undercutting the place for *responsible* Christian growth in response to God's *grace*. As he would put it, if Christ's personal obedience is mine from the moment I believe, what can possibly be added? Might not Christ's imputed righteousness become a cover for my continuing unrighteousness?[64] He was quick to add, of course, that he was not assuming that we must have a prior inherent righteousness to merit God's acceptance, only that the fruit of God's acceptance should be the development of actual righteousness in our lives.[65]

There was another aspect of the Substitutionary Justification understanding of the Atonement to which Wesley objected. Given its agenda of showing that Christ has done all that is necessary for our acceptance by God as righteous, its logic almost inevitably led to either universalism or a limited Atonement. Wesley consistently rejected both of these options—as inconsistent with Scripture, injurious of Divine justice, and conducive to antinomianism. Instead, he emphasized Christ's role as a "public person" whose atoning work is sufficient for the pardon of all humanity, though not irresistibly imposed upon any person.[66]

Unlike the case with Substitutionary Justification, Wesley did not so much reject a Divine Satisfaction understanding of the Atonement as subsume it into a Penalty Satisfaction emphasis. Given his integral correlation of God and the law, any offense that we might make against God would inevitably focus in the issue of Divine righteousness.[67] As a result, Wesley's central emphasis about the Atonement was that in Christ the issue of guilt due to our sins has been fully addressed; therefore God can mercifully offer us pardon without violating Divine justice.[68]

There are two potential distortions of such an understanding of Atonement that must be guarded against. Both flow from falsely separating God's love and God's justice. The first distortion would portray God as longing simply to forgive our sin, but somehow constrained to punish at least someone for it. Wesley would quickly remind us that justice is not a rigid external reality to which even God must (unwillingly) submit, it is the dynamic expression of God's nature as Holy Love.[69] Precisely for this reason, Wesley was willing to qualify a demand for exhaustive satisfaction of Divine justice, if necessary, in order to preserve the fundamental primacy of God's mercy.[70]

The other possible distortion of a Penalty Satisfaction understanding of the Atonement is more serious (and, unfortunately, more frequent in popular piety).[71] It portrays God/Father as unmerciful until after Christ propitiates the Divine wrath and constrains God to love us. It must be admitted that Wesley's language sometimes suggests this second distortion. A particularly striking example is his retort to a tract of William Law, "If God was never *angry* (as this tract asserts) he could never be *reconciled*. And consequently the whole Christian doctrine of *reconciliation by Christ* falls to the ground at once."[72] In his more careful moments, however, Wesley makes it clear that God's mercy is itself the cause of Christ coming to atone for our guilt. The problem is not that God/Father is unwilling to forgive, but that the (entire) Godhead of Holy Love is concerned to uphold the law—because of its value for human life—in the process of mercifully providing for the pardoning of our sin.[73]

This is to say that Renshaw's conclusions from his extended study of the teachings of both Wesleys concerning the Atonement seem valid: (1) their real concern was to stress that the integrity of God's character was not abrogated in the atoning work of Christ; and (2) their overriding emphasis was not on God's wrath, but on the love of God in initiating and effecting our salvation.[74] For the Wesleys, to preach the life, death, resurrection, and intercession of Christ was most fundamentally to preach "the love of God".[75]

Atonement as Display of God's Love

The recognition of his insistence that Christ's Atonement is an expression of the love of God raises the question of possible connections between Wesley's understanding of the Atonement and the major alternative accounts in Western Christianity. These alternative accounts are frequently designated "Subjective" or "Moral Influence" theories. Their chief objection to the dominant Western juridical understandings of the Atonement is that the latter focus exclusively on the objective issue of the remission of penalty, while lacking an adequate explanation for how Christ's death might actually inspire alienated humans to renewed discipleship.

The classic example of such an alternative account is Peter Abelard, who developed his approach in explicit contrast to Anselm. Abelard's central claim was that the problem which Christ addressed was not an offended God but a rebellious and fearful humanity. Christ's voluntary sacrifice was put forward by God as an exhibition of Divine forgiving love, in hope that this would remove our lingering fear of God's wrath and enkindle responsive love for God and others.[76] Implicit in this explanation of the Atonement are two assumptions: (1) that there is no substantial reason for fulfilling the penalty due human sin, and (2) that humans retain some inherent ability to respond to God's display of available forgiveness.

There is more resonance with Abelard's central theme in Wesley's reflections on the Atonement than is often admitted.[77] Even in his middle period one can find instances where his primary emphasis is on the fact that we should have no fear of returning to God because God's forgiving acceptance has been decisively demonstrated.[78] This emphasis became even more explicit in his later years. Some of the most striking (and formatively influential) expressions of it are in hymns of Charles that John selected for inclusion in the 1780 *Hymns.*[79] Consider just two examples:

1 O Love Divine! What hast thou done!
  Th'immortal God hath died for me!
The Father's co-eternal Son
  Bore all my sins upon the tree:
Th'immortal God for me hath died,
My Lord, my love is crucified.

. . . .

3 Is crucified for me and you,
  To bring us rebels back to God; . . .[80]

1 And can it be, that I should gain
  An interest in the Saviour's blood?
Died he for me, who caused his pain?
  For me? Who him to death pursued?
Amazing love! How can it be
That Thou, my God, shouldst die for me?

. . . .

5 No condemnation now I dread,
  Jesus, and all in him, is mine.
Alive in him, my living head,
  And clothed in righteousness divine,
Bold I approach th'eternal throne,
And claim the crown, through Christ my own.[81]

Note the integral connection in these hymns between Christ and God.[82] The Cross is not so much a sacrifice made *to* an offended Judge to obtain our acquittal, as the basis and offer of forgiveness *from* a loving God to us! Lest these hymns be considered instances of editorial oversight where John let through a theme of Charles with which he did not himself agree, consider the even clearer articulation of this basic emphasis in John's 1787 sermon "What is Man." The general theme of this sermon is the insignificance of humanity and the sheer graciousness of God's love. As one evidence of God's regard for us Wesley refers us to the fact that God sent the Son to bear our sins. He then concludes, "After this demonstration of his love is it possible to doubt any longer God's tender regard for [humanity]?"[83]

Despite all the resonance just noted, I am not suggesting that Wesley should be equated with Abelard. On the contrary, Wesley would reject both of Abelard's apparent assumptions. To begin with the second, Wesley always insisted that any ability that we have to respond to God—even to the demonstration of God's love in Christ—is contingent on the restored Presence of God in our lives. Likewise, Wesley consistently judged provision for the penalty of sin to be a necessary aspect of the Atonement, in addition to whatever exemplary purpose it might have.[84]

But why is it essential that God somehow address the penalty of sin, rather than simply remitting it? There has been one Western answer given to this question that is usually classified as more a Moral Influence than a forensic understanding of the Atonement. It is often designated the "Governmental" model, and was given its clearest early formulation by Hugo Grotius, an associate of Arminius.[85] Grotius, a legal scholar, was troubled by the assumption of both the Penalty Satisfaction and Substitutionary Justification accounts of the Atonement that it is consistent with God's justice to punish someone else (Christ) in our place. He was also uncomfortable with the anthropomorphic connotations of language about God's wrath. On the other hand, Grotius had a deep appreciation for the role of just punishment in deterring lawlessness and upholding order. He approached Christ's death in this light.

Grotius' most basic assumption was that the reason that God must uphold personal accountability is to preserve the moral order, which is a Divine provision of what is best for humanity. This means, of course, that the primary goal of punishment is not retribution but restored obedience. As such, it would be in keeping with the Divine purpose if some other creative means of accomplishing this goal were found. The self-sacrificial death of Christ is such a means. He suffered as a *representative* of humanity, dramatically portraying the seriousness and consequences of sin. That is, Christ did not *take our place* in punishment, his death *took the place of* our punishment, fulfilling its governmental purpose as a deterrent.[86] With this dramatic portrayal in place to reinforce the importance of obedience, God could mercifully restore repentant sinners without irresponsibly endangering the moral order of the universe.

Wesley was aware of the work of Grotius and occasionally appealed to the idea of Christ as Representative, perhaps drawing on him.[87] Beyond this, he never explicitly evaluated Grotius' explanation of the Atonement. This is not overly surprising, for Grotius' explanation has most often suffered the fate of being blended into other emphases, rather than defended as a distinct alternative. Even so, some later Methodist theologians have considered it particularly appropriate to Wesley's theology.[88]

There is indeed affinity between Wesley and Grotius, particularly *if* Grotius viewed God's concern for moral government as an expression of God's intrinsic nature as Holy Love, rather than a constraint to an external norm. There is also real question whether Grotius emphasized as clearly as Wesley that our ability to respond to God's offered forgiveness is itself an effect of Divine restoring grace. In any case, they certainly share the conviction that God's grace is the source of and upholds human responsibility.

The Point of the Atonement

However many the similarities, there appears to be a significant underlying difference between Grotius and Wesley. While Wesley could fully appreciate the need to uphold the moral order of the universe, he did not assume that our obedience to God's law can ultimately be grounded in fear, as Grotius' emphasis on deterrence could imply. Rather, he was convinced that our obedience must spring from our love of God and others, and that we can only have such love *in response* to our awareness of God's love for us.[89]

But how do we come to be convinced of God's love? *Through the Cross*! That is, Wesley understood Christ's role in his sacrificial death to be much more than the Representative of humanity; he was most fundamentally the Representative of *God*. In particular, he was the Representative of God's pardoning and restoring love. It is in light of Christ that we sing

> My God is reconciled,
> His pard'ning voice I hear;
> He owns me for his child,
> I can no longer fear:
> With confidence I now draw nigh,
> And Father, Abba, Father, cry![90]

In other words, the central point that Wesley consistently wanted to make about the significance of Christ is that there remains no reason for us to fear that the guilt of our sins bars renewed relationship with God. God has mercifully transcended that barrier in Christ. Christ is the pardoning Initiative of God's *responsible grace*.[91] If we will respond to this pardoning love of God and allow God's Presence deeper access to our lives, then we will be liberated from our captivity to sin and the process of our transformation into the fullness that God has always intended for us can begin. One is tempted to describe this as a Penalty Satisfaction *explanation* of the Atonement which has a Moral Influence *purpose*, and a Ransom *effect*![92]

The Three Offices of Christ

I have focused consideration of Wesley's Christology on the Atonement to this point, because this was his own relative emphasis. This could suggest that Wesley considered the work of Christ to be completed or that he restricted it to the past. This was surely not the case![93] There is no better evidence for this than Wesley's summary of the message that he wanted his preachers to proclaim: "Christ dying for us" *and* "Christ reigning in us."[94] Christ's Atonement was not the totality of Christ's work, it was the foundation for his *present* work!

When Wesley turned attention to this present work, he typically made use of the formula (which had become standard in the West) of the three "offices" of Christ: Prophet, Priest, and King.[95] This formula was clearly more than a traditional shibboleth for Wesley. In conferences with his ministers he repeatedly reminded them that preaching Christ in all three offices was the most effectual way to preach him.[96] This fact, combined with the very frequency of the triadic formula in Wesley's work led Deschner to suggest that it was a type of dogmatic shorthand for a complex of ideas codified in Wesley's mind.[97]

I will return to Deschner's suggestion, after first analyzing Wesley's characteristic understanding of each office. This analysis will vary from the traditional order slightly—beginning with Priest, then dealing with Prophet and King. The latter order better fits Wesley's understanding of the offices, because he did not use them primarily as an historical organization of Christ's work (i.e., life, death, and resurrected Lord), but as a means of coordinating Christ's present work.[98]

Christ as Priest

In a real sense, Wesley viewed Christ's role as Priest as the presupposition of all Christ's other work in our lives. This is to say more than just that Christ's death is the basis for our forgiveness, for Christ's work as Priest involved more than simply the original act of Atonement. The forgiveness that his death made possible historically must be mediated presently to individual lives. It is this present mediatorial work that is at focus in most of Wesley's considerations of Christ as Priest.[99]

The traditional language that Wesley had inherited for this present mediatorial work was that Christ is now making intercession to God for sinners. He could appropriate this language, but in comparison with contemporary standards like the *Book of Common Prayer* he seems to have been sparing in his use of it.[100] This may have been due to a concern about its potential for anthropomorphic misconceptions (such as that God must be repeatedly persuaded to forgive and accept us). For Wesley, Christ's present work as Priest was not aimed so much at changing God's mind about us, as our mind about God! He details this work, in one of his most extended considerations, as involving the destruction of our pride and self-will and the renewal of our faith, so that we guilty outcasts can be restored to God's favor, pardon, and peace.[101]

If Wesley had a characteristic concern about the work of Christ as Priest, it was to emphasize that Christians never outgrow our need of Christ in this office. We never reach a point where we surpass the need for Divine mercy. It was inevitable that Wesley had to stress this point, for his affirmation of the possibility of Christian perfection made him an easy target for accusations to the contrary. In response, he insisted that those who have experienced the greatest transformation of their lives are precisely the ones who are the most conscious of their continuing need for Christ as Priest, because they become ever more aware of their remaining defects. More important, they are convinced that whatever measure of Christ-Likeness they might have attained was possible only in and through Christ's continuing mediation.[102]

To summarize, when identifying Christ as Priest Wesley was emphasizing that it is in and through Christ that we are each assured of the pardon of our sin, a pardon that initiates our restored relationship with God and that maintains us in that relationship.

Christ as Prophet

In his discussions of Christ as Priest Wesley was typically quick to note that Christ not only offers pardon for sin, he also delivers his people from the power of sin.[103] When he enlarged upon this latter aspect of Christ's work, it was usually in the context of the other offices—Prophet and King.

How does Christ as Prophet help us in overcoming the power of sin? The specific contribution that Wesley identified with this office is the gracious restoration of our knowledge of God's will for human life (which had been lost in the Fall).[104] The paradigmatic expression of this work, for Wesley, was Jesus' Sermon on the Mount. Indeed, he characterized the Beatitudes as a picture of God in so far as God can be imitated by humanity—a picture drawn by God's own hand![105] It was also in this context that Wesley located the authentic purpose of Christ's active obedience to God's law. We noted above that he rejected the substitutionary imputation of this obedience to believers. Rather than taking the place of our obedience, Wesley valued Christ's exemplary life of service as one more means of Christ's gracious instruction of fallen humanity.[106]

Wesley's identification of Christ's Prophetic role as primarily the revelation of God's law might raise suspicions of works-righteousness.[107] If so, they would be unfounded. One must remember that Christ's work as Priest (restoring our relationship with God) is a presupposition of Christ's work as Prophet. It is only because of God's gracious Presence already at work in our lives that we have any ability to emulate God's law, breaking the power of sin.

On the other hand, Wesley was refusing to polarize God's grace and the law. He understood the law itself to be an expression of God's grace, which Christ came to "establish, illustrate, and explain," not to destroy.[108] If Christ's work as Priest is integral to the work of Prophet, Christ's work as Prophet is also essential to the work of Priest. After all, it is through the law that we become aware of our need for pardon (both initially and within the Christian walk). And, it is the law which provides the orientation or pattern for our continuing response to God's pardoning Presence in our lives.

To summarize, Christ as Prophet is the source of our restored awareness of God's law. Through this awareness we are awakened to our sin, directed to Christ as Priest for pardoning assurance, and guided in the renewal of our nature into Christ-Likeness.

Christ as King/Physician

The actual process of our renewal in Christ-Likeness falls within the purview of Christ as King. As Wesley put it in his most extended summary of this office, Christ's Kingship involves (1) giving laws to all those he has bought with his blood, (2) restoring those to the (moral) image of God whom he had first reinstated in his favor, and (3) reigning in all believing hearts until he has 'subdued all things to himself.'[109]

The overlap or integration of the offices of Christ are again evident in this description. Christ as King is the sanction of the law which Christ as Prophet reveals, and Christ as Priest ushers us into the renewing realm of Christ's regal work. Wesley's assumption of the ultimate cosmological and eschatological scope of Christ's work is also apparent.

Interestingly, the context in which Wesley most frequently appealed to Christ as King seems to have been his 1780 collection of *Hymns.* This may simply be an indication of Charles' interest in this office, but I am inclined to think that it is also because the weekly worship of the believing community is such an important practical-theological context for reinforcing the central point of Christ's Kingship; namely, that it is only through Christ's strength that we are able to live as his people.[110]

It is in the general context of Christ's restoring work as King that Wesley occasionally takes up the image of Christ as Physician. In one of the best examples Wesley exhorted his readers to conceive of Christ as the physician of our souls who is seeking to heal our wounds and make us partakers of his holiness.[111] While this image of Christ as Physician is much less common in the West than that of Christ as King, it was a favorite of many early Eastern Christians (particularly Syriac-speaking!).[112] Wesley specifically retained it in his abridgement of the *Homilies* of Macarius.[113] The image of Christ as Physician was also a favorite of Charles, and is found quite frequently in the 1780 *Hymns*.[114]

If anything, one is surprised by the fact that John does not use the image of Christ as Physician more. An explanation is not hard to find. When he turned detailed attention to the actual process of our spiritual healing it was the "Person" of the Holy Spirit that came into focus. Thus, the image of Holy Spirit as Physician complements that of Christ as Physician for Wesley.

To summarize, as King, Christ is the one who guides Christians in their process of renewal, thereby delivering them from the power of sin. And Christ as King will eventually deliver the whole creation from the very presence of sin, returning it to God/Father.[115]

"Preaching Christ In All His Offices"

We are now ready to return to the question of why Wesley stressed so frequently that his preachers should preach Christ "in all his offices." I noted above John Deschner's suggestion that this formula was a type of dogmatic shorthand for a complex of Christological ideas codified in Wesley's mind. The fact that Wesley's concern surfaced in relation to preaching suggests a preferable way of putting this point: the doctrine of the Three Offices served for Wesley as a "grammar" for norming practical-theological activities aimed at forming the beliefs, affections, and practices of his people.[116] In other words, Wesley's question was not whether the preachers had mastered or frequently repeated a set of ideas, but whether their ministry was inculcating the *pattern* of Christ's work in the Methodist people.[117]

What pattern were they to inculcate? The analysis of Wesley's understanding of each office should make this clear. They were to maintain the inherent connection between Christ's gracious provision of pardon for our sin and Christ's expectation of the renewal of our nature. They were to avoid any legalistic preaching of Christ as Prophet without Christ as Priest, or any antinomian preaching of Christ as Priest without Christ as King, and so on. In reality, Wesley's charge to preach Christ "in all his offices" was a methodological expression of his orienting concern. He wanted to insure that God's *grace* known in Christ as Priest was never separated from the *response* of discipleship that Christ modeled as Prophet and calls for from his followers as King.

Clearly Wesley's concern went beyond the use of specific titles. In practice, one could "preach Christ in his three offices" without ever mentioning them. After all, proper writing does not so much repeat grammatical rules as write in light of them! Thus, one way of preaching Christ in all his offices would be holding law and gospel in creative interrelation.[118] Again, it would mean avoiding any antithesis between justification and sanctification.[119] In its most general sense, it would mean carrying on Wesley's integration of the juridical and therapeutic dimensions of Christian truth.

Likewise, preaching is surely not the only practical-theological activity in which concern for maintaining the balance of Christ's offices should be exercised. Any activity that contributes to shaping Christian character would bear this charge. And what contributes more in this regard than worship materials? Thus, it was in keeping with his own exhortation that Wesley manifested a concern for maintaining the balance of the "total Christ" in his production of the 1780 collection of *Hymns*, as the perceptive study by Craig Gallaway has shown.[120]

The Nature of Christ

We come finally to Wesley's understanding of the nature of Christ. Any consideration of this topic must begin with the recognition that Wesley would have understood himself as simply affirming the traditional position of the historic Church. Indeed, his longest summary of these issues, in *A Letter to a Roman Catholic*, sounds nearly like a personal rendition of the Nicene-Constantinopolitan creed. In it he affirms that Christ was "the proper, natural Son of God, God of God, very God of very God"; and that he "was made man, joining human nature with the divine in one person."[121]

At the same time, the classic Christological creeds did not establish a detailed uniformity within the Church. Rather, they created boundaries for determining legitimate diversity—any proposed Christology must preserve both the reality of the two natures of Christ and their unity in one person. Within these boundaries there remained considerable room for varying emphases. For present purposes, the most significant difference is one that can be discerned between characteristic Western and Eastern Christologies. Most Western theologies have been quite concerned to maintain the distinctness of the two natures of Christ—in order to preserve contact with both parties in the Atonement, and to avoid any hint of "deification."[122] By contrast Eastern theologians, with their explicit emphasis on participation in God and on Christ's "deification" of human nature, have accented the interpenetration of Christ's two natures. To Western observers this has often appeared to reach the point of Monophysitism, with the Divine nature swallowing up the human nature.

Naturally the East denies this, countering that the West places inadequate stress on the co-inherence of the two.

Fortunately, it is not my task to settle this debate. Rather I want to consider Wesley in light of it. When one does so, a very interesting point emerges. While, as we have seen, Wesley's understanding of Christ's work stands largely within the Western focus on the Atonement, his characteristic emphases about Christ's nature sound strangely Eastern. Indeed, he has often been charged with being a "practical Monophysite," or even a Docetic (i.e., completely denying Christ's humanity).[123] It is the task of this section to determine the degree to which this might be true, and why.

Stress on Christ's Divinity

It is clear that whenever Wesley's attention turned to issues of Christ's nature his consistent concern was to affirm Christ's deity.[124] Indeed, the only Christological heresies that drew his explicit condemnation were those which he believed denied Christ's full divinity—Arianism and Socinianism. These two drew his attention repeatedly, for he believed that they "strike at the root of Christianity."[125]

Given his concern for affirming Christ's deity, one might expect Wesley to provide repeated defenses of it. Such was not the case. He was usually content simply to assert this truth and develop its implications. The most substantial apologetic that he did provide focused, interestingly, on the propriety of worshipping Christ.[126] Such practical-theological issues are exactly what spawned most early Christian apologetics for the divinity of Christ and the Holy Spirit. Whatever the situation that sparked it, when Wesley did offer a defense of Christ's deity his fear was explicit: to deny this deity would be to remove the foundation of all our hope.[127]

Discomfort with Accenting Christ's Humanity

The counterpart of Wesley's identification of the Christian hope with the deity of Christ was a discomfort, noticeable throughout his *NT Notes*, with those biblical accounts that highlight Jesus' humanity. A particularly instructive example is the account of Jesus raising Lazarus from the dead in John 11.[128] To the terse statement that Jesus wept (vs. 35) Wesley was compelled to add that this was only out of sympathy for those in tears around him, and from a sense of the misery that sin had brought upon human nature. He apparently considered the suggestion that Jesus actually sorrowed over the loss of a friend inappropriate. Indeed, two verses earlier (vs. 33) he had drawn from the common Greek idiom that Jesus "troubled himself" over Lazarus' death the edifying (?) reflection that Jesus' affections were not properly passions, but voluntary emotions which were wholly within his control![129] Then, when Jesus "lifted up his eyes" to pray (vs. 41), Wesley immediately added that it is not that Jesus needed assistance from the Father, he was merely thanking the Father for arranging this situation so that he could demonstrate his power!

There are further evidences of uncomfortableness with any stress on Jesus' humanity in Wesley's other theological work. For example, when he edited the Ignatian epistles for his *Christian Library*, he consistently omitted passages that described Jesus as born "of the race of David according to the flesh."[130] Likewise, his edited version of the Thirty-Nine Articles deleted the phrase that Christ's human nature was "of the substance" of Mary. He did not deny that Christ had a human nature, but apparently considered it a direct creation of God.[131]

The reason for Wesley's uncomfortableness with focused attention on Christ's human nature is not altogether clear. Deschner has suggested that it is a reflection of his concern that a stress on Christ's active obedience undercuts our own obedience.[132] This is possible. I wonder, however, if it is not more an expression of his distaste for being overly "familiar" with the Great Lord of Heaven.[133] One of the characteristics that Wesley found admirable in Jesus was his custom (so Wesley assumed!) of calling his mother simply "woman," showing that he did not relate to even her "after the flesh."[134] It would appear that Wesley went overboard in trying to pay the same (supposed) compliment to Jesus!

Practical Monophysitism?

For all of his reservations, Wesley had no intention of denying Christ's humanity. The question remains, however, whether his actual descriptions of Christ had the effect of annulling it. There is good reason to believe that they did.

To begin with, there is no suggestion at all in Wesley that the person of Christ came into being with the specific union of natures in the incarnation. Rather, he clearly assumed that the person of Christ was the Son, the second "Person" of the Trinity. The Son was simply taking on human nature, not becoming a human person.[135]

Moreover, Wesley did not depict the Son's act of taking on human nature as an act of *kenosis* (emptying), where the Son laid the Divine attributes aside. In his *NT Notes* comments on Phil. 2:6-7 (the verse usually appealed to in defending the notion of *kenosis*), Wesley maintained that Christ was simply veiling the divine attributes from sight, not renouncing them.[136] As such, they could "dart out" on occasions like the Transfiguration.[137] Of course, this left Wesley with the need to explain passages where Jesus' divine attributes were apparently denied. For instance, when Mark 13:32 asserted that the Son does not know the time of the Second Coming,

Wesley clarified that this applied only to his human nature; his divine nature would have known. Likewise, he maintained that the claim in Luke 2:52 that Jesus grew in wisdom applied only to his human nature.

To be sure, there was a classic way to maintain both natures within the one person of Christ, the doctrine of shared attributes (*communicatio idiomatum*). Wesley appealed to this doctrine one time, in his *NT Notes* comment on John 3:13, trying to explain how the Son can be both omnipresent and also embodied in Christ. However, as Deschner has shown, his use of this doctrine was inconsistent and one-sided.[138] He was quick to assume that divine properties are communicated to the human nature—so that, for example, the pre-Resurrection Jesus could become invisible.[139] But he showed little interest in the transfer of human properties to the divine nature. In effect, he allowed Christ's human nature to be subsumed within the divine from the very beginning of the Incarnation.

Wesley's Concern?

In light of the preceding evidence, it must be admitted that Wesley came right to the border of monophysitism, if not stepping over. I do not note this to charge him with heresy, or to defend him from it. Rather, I am interested in determining what concern pushed him in this direction.

Deschner has suggested that this aspect of Wesley's thought betrays a negative underlying attitude about human nature, such that he can allow the Son only to subjugate it, not affirm it.[140] I am not convinced. There are indeed dualistic residues in Wesley's anthropology, as was noted in the previous chapter. However, his dominating emphasis on humanity as created in the Image and Likeness of God, and destined to regain both in their fullness, can hardly be described as negative.

Another suggestion about Wesley's concern might be drawn from the fact that his focus on Christ's divine nature resembles characteristic Eastern Orthodox Christology. Is he, like they, drawn to Christ's divinized human nature as an expression of what all Christians can become through restored participation in God? While Wesley would not deny this basic claim, it was certainly not his focal Christological agenda. He was interested in Christ primarily as the locus of God's activity in our midst, rather than as an example of what the Divine power can effect in human nature.[141]

In other words, Wesley's consuming emphasis on the deity of Christ was an expression of his conviction that *God is the one who takes initiative in our salvation*: it is God who died in Christ to make possible our pardon;[142] it is God who awakens us to our need of grace in Christ the Prophet and drives us to Christ the Priest;[143] it is God who initiates our restored relationship in Christ the Priest; and, it is God who guides us as Christ the King, leading us into all holiness and happiness.[144]

One can surely wish that Wesley had paid more attention to other aspects of Christology. For example, liberation theologians have rightly lamented the paucity of interest in Jesus' model of liberating action and in the dimension of Prophet that challenges unjust political laws.[145] Likewise, he endangers crucial Christian concerns in his submersion of Christ's humanity. And yet, we should not fail to appreciate the coherence between his views on Christ's work and Christ's person. One should also recognize the basic consistency of his Christological convictions with his broader theological commitments. By emphasizing Christ as the pardoning Initiative of God in salvation, Wesley has underlined the prevenience of *grace* to our *response.*

CHAPTER 5

Holy Spirit—The Presence of Responsible Grace

The previous chapter developed Wesley's understanding of Christ as the Divine Initiative in restoring sinful and alienated humanity to relationship with God: we receive God's pardon through Christ the Priest, we behold the moral Image that God intends for us in Christ the Prophet, and we are led towards its recovery by Christ the King. This in itself is Good News. But Wesley understood the Gospel to involve much more. If fallen humanity were left to respond to God's Initiative from our own resources we would never overcome our spiritual infirmity, because our faculties are debilitated. For this reason God has graciously provided not only pardon but also a renewed empowering Presence in our lives. In the most proper sense, for Wesley, this Presence is the Holy Spirit.

The Holy Spirit as God's Restored Presence

Wesley penned few extended expositions of the doctrine of the Holy Spirit.[1] And yet issues related to the nature and work of the Spirit came up repeatedly in his controversial writings, because he placed the Spirit at the center of his understanding of Christian life.[2] The best way to understand this, in light of the earlier chapters, is to recognize that Wesley *equated* the Holy Spirit with God's gracious empowering Presence restored through Christ.[3]

In the discussion of the character of restoring grace in Chapter Three I suggested that Wesley purposefully incorporated the aspect of grace as pardon (more typical in the West) into his larger emphasis on grace as power (more characteristic of the East). I also observed that he equated the aspect of grace as power with the Holy Spirit. It is worth quoting again one of his clearest expressions of this point:

> By 'the grace of God' is sometimes to be understood that free love, that unmerited mercy, by which I, a sinner, through the merits of Christ am now reconciled to God. But in this place it rather means that power of God the Holy Ghost which 'worketh in us both to will and to do of His good pleasure'.[4]

The role of the Holy Spirit thus described was far from incidental to Wesley. Indeed, while he would always want to include both aspects, it seems fair to say that the aspect of grace as the power of the Holy Spirit was most definitive for him.[5] This is particularly evident in his most succinct or elementary definitions. For example, in *Instructions for Children* he defined grace simply as "the power of the Holy Ghost enabling us to believe and love and serve God."[6] Again, in his sermon on "The Good Steward" God's grace is identified as "the power of his Holy Spirit, which alone worketh in us all that is acceptable in his sight."[7]

Wesley's equation of the Holy Spirit with God's power should not be construed as suggesting that the Holy Spirit was only an attribute of God, or even a created agent of God. He was quite clear that the Holy Spirit was fully divine, "equal with the Father and the Son."[8] If he seldom tried to prove this, it was because he took it for granted.[9]

He was equally clear that the Holy Spirit should be seen as fully personal, not merely a force or energy in our lives.[10] This point was central to his understanding of grace. It was argued in Chapter Three that Wesley's conception of God's restoring grace resonated with the Eastern notion of uncreated grace. Grace, for him, was not simply a Divinely-originated product bestowed upon humanity, it was the activity of God's very Self in human life. As Daniel Luby has so aptly defined it, "Grace for Wesley [was] the pardoning, transforming love of God, present to us in the indwelling Person of the Holy Spirit."[11] The centrality of love to the Spirit's work will be developed later. At this point I want simply to note that if our experience of grace is epitomized in love, then the Holy Spirit must be fully personal, because love is something that exists in its truest sense only between persons.

There is an important implication of Wesley's stress on the personal and loving nature of the Holy Spirit. Eastern Orthodox theologians have often charged that it is because so much Western theology sees grace as an impersonal power, rather than as the personal Presence of the Holy Spirit, that it is prone to assume that God overrides human freedom.[12] This argument has real merit, *but* it does not apply to Wesley. His affirmation of the personal nature of God's work in our life (epitomized in the Holy Spirit) was consistently connected to a recognition of God's preservation of our integrity. As he once put it, "The God of love is willing to save all the souls he has made . . . but will not force them to accept of it."[13]

The Holy Spirit as Inspiring Physician

For Wesley, then, the Holy Spirit is the restored personal Presence of God in our lives, empowering us. This latter aspect needs to be developed further, in order to distinguish his characteristic pneumatology. Two particular issues come to mind: (1) What is the purpose of the Spirit's empowerment? and, (2) What is the manner of the Spirit's empowerment?

Wesley's assumption about the purpose of the Spirit's empowering Presence was explicit and consistent—the Holy Spirit's power enables us to become holy; in other words, to love and serve God as we were intended.[14] As should be expected by now, he often put this point in therapeutic language: the Holy Spirit is the Divine Physician whose Presence effects the healing of our sin-diseased nature.[15] Once again, such language was common in the early Eastern Christian writers that he read.[16] It was also present in Anglican devotional material that he treasured, and abridged for his followers.[17]

What is the specific manner by which the Spirit effects our healing? Wesley characteristically expressed this in terms of the "inspiration" of the Holy Spirit. As he once summarized the beliefs of his followers,

> You believe, farther, that both this faith and love are wrought in us by the Spirit of God; nay, that there cannot be in any [person] one good temper or desire, or so much as one good thought, unless it be produced by the almighty power of God, by the inspiration or influence of the Holy Ghost.[18]

It is important to clarify what Wesley intended by "inspiration" in this context. The word often functions in Western theology as a technical term designating a cognitive influence of the Holy Spirit, particularly upon the writers of Scripture. Wesley is not using the term in this sense here. He is intending something more like the basic meaning of the Latin original, *inspirare*: to breathe into, animate, excite, or inflame.[19] In fact, he defined "inspiration" in his *Dictionary* simply as the (restored) influence of the Holy Spirit that enables persons to love and serve God.

Why did Wesley choose the term "inspiration" to describe the Spirit's general empowering work, given the possible confusion with the more technical theological meaning? To begin with, such a general use of the term was common in Anglican liturgical materials—the best example being the Collect for Purity in the weekly eucharistic liturgy.[20] However, a deeper reason is that description of the Spirit's work as "inspiration" helped Wesley avoid two possible misunderstandings: (1) that the Spirit's restored Presence is a permanent endowment given to Christians, regardless of our response; or (2) that it goes beyond empowering us, irresistibly effecting our acts of obedience.[21] Concern to avoid these conjoined implications is central to his most explicit description of the Spirit's inspiration:

> [The life of God in the soul of a believer] immediately and necessarily implies the continual inspiration of God's Holy Spirit: God's breathing into the soul, and the soul's breathing back what it first receives from God; a continual action of God upon the soul, the re-action of the soul upon God. . . . And hence we may infer the absolute necessity of this re-action of the soul (whatsoever it be called) in order to the continuance of the divine life therein.[22]

In other words, Wesley found "inspiration" a congenial summary term for the Holy Spirit's work because it preserved the personal, responsive nature of God's Presence in human life. When we respond to the pardoning love of God offered in Christ, we experience a deepened participation of the Divine Presence in our lives through the inspiration of the Holy Spirit. As we continue to respond within this deepening participation we are progressively empowered and guided in transforming our sin-warped nature (i.e., sanctification).

For Wesley, then, the Spirit's work of sanctification was not merely a forensic declaration of how God will treat us (regardless of what we are in reality). Neither was it a matter of directly infusing virtues in Christian lives. It was a process of character-formation that is made possible by a restored participation of fallen humanity in the Divine life and power. This understanding of sanctification has significant parallels with the Eastern Orthodox theme of deification (*theosis*), a point that I will return to in Chapter Seven. But I would note here that it has begun to receive increased consideration in Western circles as an alternative to more typical ways of understanding sanctification. In particular, William Alston has recently presented a very sophisticated philosophical argument that the most appropriate way to understand how the Holy Spirit effects sanctification is by an actual "sharing" that allows human beings to participate (in a limited sense) in the life of God.[23] Unfortunately, he seems unaware that such an understanding is already available—in Eastern Orthodoxy and Wesley, among others.

The Dimensions of the Spirit's Inspiration

Having established that the Holy Spirit is God's gracious Presence in our lives and that the Spirit's general work is to empower our recovery of the holiness of life that God intended for us, it would be helpful now to detail what is involved in that work. An appropriate place to begin is with Wesley's most compact summary of his understanding of the Holy Spirit:

> I believe the infinite and eternal Spirit of God, equal with the Father and the Son, to be not only perfectly holy . . . . but the immediate cause of all holiness in us: enlightening our understandings, rectifying our wills and affections, renewing our natures, uniting our persons to Christ, assuring us of the adoption of sons, leading us in our actions, purifying and sanctifying our souls and bodies to a full and eternal enjoyment of God.[24]

This quotation makes it clear that, while there is a unifying goal to the Spirit's work, it involves several dimensions—corresponding to dimensions of human nature and human need. How might these various dimensions be organized? Wesley invoked two basic categorizations, the first being a distinction between the Spirit's work in relation to the "world" and in relation to believers.[25] The second (and more frequent) was a contrast between the ordinary operations and the extraordinary gifts of the Spirit.[26] If these two categorizations are overlapped, five major dimensions that Wesley discerned in the Spirit's work emerge: (1) a universal restoring Presence of the Spirit in the "world"; (2) the witness of the Spirit in those who respond to God's offer of restored relationship; (3) fruit of the Spirit that develop in believers' lives; (4) guidance which the Spirit offers believers; and (5) extraordinary gifts of the Spirit.[27]

The Universal Restoring Presence of the Spirit

Wesley's identification of the purpose of the Spirit's Presence in the "world" is to convince non-believers of sin.[28] In light of the discussion in Chapter Three, it should be evident that we are dealing here with his affirmation of Prevenient Grace. In other words, the most rudimentary expression of the Spirit's inspiration is the universal partial restoration of Divine Presence in human life, by virtue of Christ's Atonement. This Presence effects the partial healing of our debilitated human faculties, sufficient for us to be convinced of our sin and capable of responding to God's overtures for restored relationship. If we welcome these overtures, we open ourselves to further dimensions of the Spirit's inspiration.

The Witness of the Spirit[29]

Wesley designated the initial dimension of the Spirit's deeper Presence within those who welcomed God's overtures the Holy Spirit's "witness." Many scholars have recognized the particular importance of this dimension of the Spirit's work to Wesley. Indeed, Thomas Lessmann has characterized it as the heart piece of his theology.[30] To evaluate such a claim it is crucial to determine *why* Wesley valued the Spirit's witness to the believer. Was his fascination with this topic evidence of an inordinate desire for certainty in matters of religion? Or, was his primary interest in maintaining a place for emotions in religion, over against the dry formalism of so much religion in his day?[31] Or, was Wesley's emphasis on this dimension of the Spirit's work perhaps another expression of his orienting concern about *responsible grace*?

Without denying the other factors, I hope to demonstrate that the third consideration suggested played a larger role than is usually recognized. This is not an easy task, because so many aspects of Wesley's thought weave together around this issue. In particular, he recognized himself that the inspiration of the Holy Spirit, the assurance of faith, and the revelation of Christ in us were integrally connected.[32] Thus I will need to investigate several of these separate threads before reaching any conclusions. I will begin with his general assumption about the importance of the assurance of faith (i.e., certainty about our pardon from God) to Christian life.

Excursus: Wesley on the Assurance of Faith

Wesley's views on the importance of assurance and the ground of that assurance underwent several transitions over the course of his life and ministry. These transitions have recently been traced, documented, and analyzed in a masterful study by Richard Heitzenrater.[33] I will summarize his basic findings, providing representative documentation.

If the early Wesley was convinced of anything, it was the importance of being assured of one's salvation. In 1725 he wrote that "if we can never have any certainty of our being in a state of salvation, good reason it is that every moment should be spent, not in joy, but fear and trembling."[34] But how does one obtain such assurance? Wesley took for granted that it was connected with faith, a common Protestant assumption.[35] At this juncture, however, he identified faith primarily as assent to the truth of a proposition based on its rational credibility.[36] On such a view, conviction of God's pardon would be based on the rational credibility both of the Divine revelation promising it and of our conformity to the conditions of that promise.[37] It was not long before the problems with both aspects of this approach were brought home to Wesley. Dialogue with his parents persuaded him of the deistic dangers of subordinating assent to Divine revelation too narrowly to rational credibility.[38] And, his own spiritual struggles increasingly convinced him not only that he lacked moral perfection but that he was not even certain of the sincerity of his efforts in that direction.

But where could he then turn for assurance? In retrospect Wesley would realize that a suggestion from his father (on his deathbed) pointed the way forward: "The inward witness, son ... that is the proof, the strongest proof, of Christianity."[39] Shortly after his father's death Wesley embarked on his mission to Georgia. During this trip he made his first contact with some German Moravians, who helped him see that Christian faith was more a matter of *trust* than of mere *assent.*[40] They also pressed on him the claim that the Holy Spirit's inner witness to our spirit was the ultimate basis of this trust.

This Moravian influence was significant, but it would be superficial to conclude that Wesley's conception of assurance was simply borrowed from them.[41] Through the Moravians he was actually making contact with a clear emphasis of both Luther and Calvin.[42] More importantly, he would later recognize that the essential elements of this theme were already present in the Anglican standards that he had valued since youth.[43] It is also significant to note, for present interests, that the need for believers to *perceive* the presence of the Holy Spirit in their lives was a particular emphasis of Macarius (whom he was reading while in Georgia!), and common in other Eastern writers.[44]

As a result of these various influences, by early 1738 Wesley was convinced that assurance of salvation was a provision available to Christians through the activity of the Holy Spirit in their lives. He became equally convinced that he did not yet have this assurance. A major reason for this evaluation—which he would later nuance—was that he came under the influence of some English Moravians on his return from Georgia (particularly Peter Böhler) who convinced him that when real saving faith came to a person, it would be instantaneously complete. One who had it would be free from all sin, all fear, and all doubt. Wesley recognized that he fell short of such an absolute standard.[45]

The corollary of Wesley's diagnosis of his need in terms of Böhler's criteria was that, when he found himself trusting in God's pardon that night at Aldersgate, he emerged from the event with "great expectations" that he would now have continual peace and certainty. These expectations were quickly shattered. Wesley's lack of constant joy, peace, and certainty following Aldersgate left him with a quandary—if faith inherently included these, then he had no faith! On the other hand, he found himself unable to believe that he did not have at least a "degree" of faith.[46] Such questions were fueled by his visit with the German Moravians, where he found some support for the notion of lesser degrees of saving faith.[47] As a result, Wesley increasingly questioned the absolutist claims of Böhler and the other English Moravians, leading to his eventual parting of ways from them.

On close inspection, the years following Aldersgate reveal a growing tension between Wesley's public proclamation and his private reflection in this regard. In public he continued to define faith in the terms that he had learned from Böhler—as ultimately excluding all doubt, fear, sorrow, and the like. Anyone who did not possess such assurance and virtue was only an "almost Christian," not yet in saving relation to God.[48] By contrast, in private letters of pastoral advice and his manuscript journal reflections Wesley was distinguishing between saving faith and the full assurance of that faith. He was talking of *degrees* of faith, as well as *degrees* of assurance. In short, he was allowing that someone could be *truly* Christian (albeit, imperfect) who was not yet *fully* Christian.[49]

Why were such qualifications not making their way into his preaching? I do not believe that Wesley should be accused of duplicity here. His qualifications were still tentative and he appears to have been simply continuing with Böhler's earlier advice: "Preach faith *till* you have it, and then, *because* you have it, you *will* preach faith."[50] As long as it remained possible that *full* assurance of faith was God's provision and desire, he dare not cease urging others toward it simply because he had not yet found it,[51] unless, of course, such urging was itself harmful!

Given Wesley's practical-theological concern, he had to consider this latter possibility very seriously. Reflection on it surfaced repeatedly at conferences with his preachers in the mid-1740s, where it was debated whether they were expecting too great a uniformity in people's experiences of saving faith. Was their demand for certainty driving some to surrender true faith in despair? Wesley found himself publicly conceding the possibility of exceptional cases where full assurance did not accompany saving faith.[52] By July 1747 he admitted to Charles that he had rethought the entire issue of whether justifying faith must always be accompanied by a distinct, conscious assurance of pardon. He now maintained that such an awareness of pardon was possible, indeed the "common privilege of real Christians," but denied that its accompaniment was essential to justifying faith. His earlier publications that had conjoined these two in absolute terms were now judged to be contrary to both Scripture and experience.[53]

From this time on, Wesley was careful in public treatises to distinguish between justifying faith and a full assurance of that faith—insisting that one might have the former without yet enjoying the latter.[54] He also began to encourage publicly those whose despair over the absence of full assurance led them to doubt their justification, as earnestly as he had previously challenged those who presumed that no such assurance was available.[55] At the heart of this encouragement was his valuation of faith as justifying from its earliest degree—i.e., the mere inclination to "fear God and work righteousness." To be sure, such nascent faith was not yet the fullness of Christian faith, for the latter would include clear assurance. It was the faith of a "servant." But if one continued to respond to God in this beginning sense, it would develop into the confident faith of a "son."[56] This more positive evaluation of nascent faith became so important to Wesley that he added clarifying footnotes to his republication of earlier materials that contradicted it.[57]

In short, the mature Wesley rejected his immediate post-Aldersgate assumption of an absolute connection between being the recipient of God's pardoning grace and having a clear assurance of that pardon. He allowed for broader variability in the manner that the Holy Spirit effects justification in individuals.[58] But this is not to say that he rejected the importance of assurance itself. As he remarked toward the end of his life, "We preach assurance as we always did, as a common privilege of real Christians; but [now] we do not enforce it, under pain of damnation, denounced on all who enjoy it not."[59]

Excursus: Wesley on the Nature of Faith

The changes in Wesley's assumptions about the connection between faith and assurance were integrally related to shifts in his understanding of the nature of faith itself. Rex Matthews has provided an insightful analysis of this issue.[60] He demonstrates that there were temporal shifts between three distinct conceptions of faith in Wesley's works: faith as *assent* to truth claims, faith as *trust* in God's love, and faith as an actual *spiritual experience* of God's love. In the early Wesley, as we have seen, it was faith as assent that was typically in view. Central to his deeper appropriation of the theme of justification by faith in 1738 was a shift to understanding faith as more properly trust in God's acceptance.[61] By the mid-1740's the theme of faith as spiritual experience was emerging, to become predominant in the writings of the late Wesley.[62] The most important point in Matthews' study, however, goes beyond the shifting balance of the three definitions of faith. He argues persuasively that the understanding of faith as spiritual experience became *foundational* for the mature Wesley, with faith as trust and faith as assent being grounded in this "objective" experience.[63]

It is no accident that this transition took place at the very time when Wesley was severing the required connection between full assurance and the justifying efficacy of faith. He had come to realize that making a clear consciousness of pardon the condition of pardon threatened to reduce faith to merely a psychological reality, obscuring both the psychological and the theological primacy of God's pardon *extra nos.*[64] As a result, he became increasingly hesitant to use the word "assurance," emphasizing instead that our sense of God's love is based on Divinely-granted *evidence.*[65] One of his designations for this evidence of God's love was "faith as spiritual experience." As he understood it, this aspect of faith was not a human action or creation, but the passive reception of God's gracious pardoning overtures.[66] By making this aspect of faith foundational to the other aspects of trust and assent (which *are* human actions) he was reenforcing the point that the latter are only possible as *re*-actions to God's prior gracious action in our lives.[67]

Obviously, using "faith" to cover both the evidence of God's love and our re-action to that evidence stretches the term quite broadly. Wesley's reason for doing so is apparent. He was trying to make his point about God's prevenience in the language of his (primarily Calvinist) opponents—for whom faith was the central soteriological category. In contexts not as controlled by these debates Wesley more typically identified the evidence of God's love as the Holy Spirit's witness to our spirit.

Excursus: Wesley on the Perceptibility of Grace

For the Holy Spirit's witness to be the evidence of God's love, however, Wesley had to assume that the Spirit's inspiration (grace) was *perceptible* to the believer. Daniel Luby has shown that Wesley not only operated on this assumption, but that he became explicitly conscious of it and defended it, and that it became an important element in his overall theology.[68]

Wesley's explicit defense of the perceptibility of grace emerged out of debates early in the Methodist revival. The most important episode was a series of letters that he exchanged in the mid-1740's with the anonymous correspondent, "John Smith."[69] During their dialogue Wesley eventually concluded that one of the key areas where he and "Smith" remained at odds concerned perceptible inspiration. As he explained his position:

> [We affirm] that inspiration of God's Holy Spirit whereby he fills us with righteousness, peace, and joy, with love to him and to all [people]. And we believe it cannot be, in the nature of things, that a [person] should be filled with this peace and joy and love . . . without perceiving it. . . This is . . . the main doctrine of the Methodists.[70]

In the course of this and later debates Wesley made two important clarifications of this basic claim. First, he denied that he believed every instance of God's gracious work in our lives to be perceptible, only that some crucial instances typically are.[71] Second, he emphasized that he was not claiming that we perceive the Holy Spirit per se, we only perceive the effects of the Spirit's inspiration; e.g., peace, joy, and love.[72] Private correspondence also manifests his mature pastoral sensitivity about the danger of assuming that authentic Christian life would require a constant perceptibility of the Spirit's work.[73]

Given Wesley's empiricist epistemology, one might well ask how humans could perceive even the effects of the Spirit's inspiration, since these are internal or spiritual realities. His answer, of course, was that we have graciously restored spiritual senses that enable us to be sensible of Divinely-fostered peace, joy, and love.[74] Indeed, "faith as spiritual experience" is precisely such restored sensory capability.

Why was Wesley so concerned to defend the perceptibility of grace? His underlying question was how we can know that God has renewed relationship with us in pardoning love. Given his empiricist epistemology, he was not content with the common suggestion that we *deduce* this fact from our clear conscience or virtuous life. Such evidence was too indirect and, hence, fallible.[75] Rather, we must *experience* this love in some manner. For Wesley, the witness of the Holy Spirit is the divine communication of that experience.

Summary and Evaluation

We are now in a position to summarize Wesley's conception of the Holy Spirit's witness to our spirit.[76] His central claim is that the authentic basis for anyone's assurance of God's pardon is a direct activity of the Holy Spirit that inwardly impresses upon them that they are children of God. As he favored putting it (echoing Romans 5:5), the Spirit "sheds the love of God abroad in their hearts."[77] As this suggests, he did not construe the Spirit's witness to be an ethereal verbal communication, but an inward awareness of merciful love that evidences our restored relationship to God.[78] In essence, it is God sharing Godself with us to the point where we can sense Divine mercy and love in a manner analogous to our awareness of our own affections and tendencies.[79]

Wesley championed the importance of the Spirit's witness in conscious contrast to two alternatives more common in his day: (1) that the ultimate basis of our assurance is our clear conscience; and (2) that this basis is the presence of Christian virtues (the "fruit of the Spirit") in our lives. Wesley did allow these alternative factors a subsidiary role in assurance, confirming the Spirit's direct witness. Indeed, he assumed that their presence was crucial for distinguishing between the true witness of the Spirit and false "enthusiasm." However, he denied that they were more reliable than, or foundational to, the direct witness.[80] He argued that a clear conscience might be merely an unawakened conscience, while the presence of some virtues in an individual's life might simply indicate rote outward conformity without a true inward love for God.

There are two aspects of Wesley's most mature understanding of the Spirit's witness with our spirit that deserve particular note. First, he increasingly focused attention away from the human *experience* of the witness and toward its Divine *source.*[81] The most striking example of this is found in a comparison of his 1746 sermon on "The Witness of the Spirit" with that of 1767 on the same topic. In the latter sermon he quotes a section of the earlier one discussing the difficulty of explaining the meaning of the Spirit's witness. The quote is nearly word-for-word, *except* for one phrase: "what the children of God experience" is changed to "what the Spirit of God works in his children"![82]

The second aspect of Wesley's most mature understanding of the Spirit's witness is that it reflected the qualifications of the importance of certainty that were noted earlier. In the 1746 sermon Wesley was still claiming that the authentic witness must exclude all doubt in Christian life.[83] By contrast, the 1767 sermon has a section explicitly recognizing the possibility of times of darkness or doubt within restored relationship with God—something Wesley could testify to from his own experience.[84] Perhaps more important, the dispositions that this sermon holds up as characteristic of the Christian life are not static absolutes, but dynamic realities such as "sweet calm," "clear satisfaction," and "steady peace."[85]

Whatever the qualifications, the mature Wesley still considered the Spirit's witness a crucial Christian teaching and experience. Why was it so important to him? His concern clearly went beyond preserving the legitimate place of emotions in Christian life. Indeed, the explicit worry that he mentions concerning devaluation of the Spirit's witness with our spirit is that one thereby verges on works-righteousness![86] To understand this worry one has to recall Wesley's fundamental conviction that authentic Christian obedience flows out of love, and that genuine human love can only exist in *response* to the prior empowering manifestation of God's love to us. The Spirit's witness is precisely such a manifestation of God's love in individual hearts, enabling them to respond and grow in Christ-likeness.[87] For Wesley, any model of the Christian life which excludes this witness would suggest that humans grow in Christ-likeness through their own power!

In other words, Wesley emphasized the Spirit's witness with our spirit partly because it was another way for him to accent the prevenience of God's *grace* in our salvation, while simultaneously explaining our *response-ability* to that grace. Moreover, he clearly assumed our *responsibility* to respond, else God's *grace* would gradually cease to empower us.[88] The most common way that Wesley made this latter point was his repeated distinction that we can only have evidence of our present relationship to God, not a guarantee of final perseverance.[89]

In light of the centrality of these implications to his overall theology, Wesley's doctrine of the Spirit's witness can hardly be dismissed as an idiosyncrasy. On the contrary, it merits serious consideration by his current heirs and the larger Christian tradition. Such consideration, however, will need to move beyond some of the historical constraints of his specific formulation of the doctrine.

In particular, a major limitation of Wesley's explication of the Spirit's witness is his appropriation of eighteenth-century empiricist language of self-evidence and immediacy.[90] This language obscures the inescapable influence of preunderstandings (formed by one's socio-cultural setting and tradition) in perceiving and interpreting personal experience. Wesley's own experience of the Spirit had not been free from such preunderstandings, as his struggle with the great expectations following Aldersgate dramatically demonstrates. Likewise, his reflections on the inspiration of the Spirit often tacitly recognized the need for interpreting the experience.[91] Unfortunately, the "quest for certainty" that had captured modern Western philosophy deprived him of the philosophical tools that might have helped him to deal with these preunderstandings in a positive manner.[92]

From our post-modern perspective, the valid point of Wesley's emphasis on the Spirit's witness might be best expressed in terms of the way that such an experience could help strengthen (or its absence undermine!) the plausibility of one's assumed worldview.[93] In particular, if it served to convince us that the pardon proclaimed by Christ was truly ours, then it would indeed become the "evidence of God's love" to us—empowering us to love God and others.

The Fruit of the Spirit

The preceding discussion of the witness of the Spirit should have made clear that Wesley's interest in the Spirit's inspiration of Christians reached beyond the evidence of restored relationship itself to its effects in their lives. The biblical term that Wesley took up to describe these effects was the "fruit of the Spirit" (Gal. 5:22-3). As the title suggests, Wesley considered the primal effects of the Spirit's ordinary operation in Christian lives to be love, joy, and peace.[94] Why did he focus on entities like these? What makes such "emotions" so fundamental?

To answer this question one must recall Wesley's psychology, in particular his understanding of will. It was noted in Chapter Three that

Wesley did not use "will" to designate our human capacity for self-determination (as now is common) but our affections. Involved in this use of "will" is a basic assumption about human choice and action. Put briefly, Wesley took for granted a virtue psychology that emphasizes the role of habituated affections in motivating and guiding authentic human actions.[95] Thus for him, love, joy, and peace are not *mere* emotions. They are the holy tempers from which flow holy thoughts, words, and actions.[96] That is why he repeatedly insisted that the essence of sanctification was not mere outward conformity to law, but the renewal of our affections (heart) through participation in the Divine nature.[97]

It might be noted in passing that there appears to be some pattern to Wesley's understanding of the various holy tempers, or fruit of the Spirit. What is most clear is the primacy of love among the tempers. Parallel with his assumption that our awareness of God's love for us is the foundation of our Christian life, Wesley makes our love for God and others the focus of that life. All other tempers or fruit flow from and find their place in connection with this love.[98] Beyond this unifying connection and their symbiotic interrelationship, Wesley's various discussions of particular tempers appear to distinguish between those that are stable orienting dispositions and those that are responsive motivating affections: included among the former would be humility, meekness, and simplicity; among the latter would be joy, hope, gratitude, fear, holy mourning, and peace.[99]

While it is important for us today to recognize the nature of the fruit of the Spirit as tempers, Wesley's own concern was that his people recognize that these are truly *fruit* of the Spirit. That is, these dispositions to truly Christian action are not inherent human possessions. They emerge in conjunction with the empowering Presence of the Holy Spirit in our lives.[100]

The immediate question this raises is "What about 'heathen' virtues?" Wesley did not deny that such exist, but distinguished between them and the Christian tempers that are fruit of the Spirit's Presence in believers.[101] In keeping with his mature understanding of Prevenient Grace, it might best be explained that heathen virtues are the fledgling effects of the Holy Spirit's initial restored Presence among humanity, while Christian tempers are the more vigorous effects of the deepened Presence of the Spirit in those who welcome God's overtures.[102] In either case, the affections behind *responsible* human actions are gifts of *grace.*

It should also be noted that Wesley's rejection of the inherent nature of Christian tempers was not a denial that these tempers become part of the continuing character of the believer. However, he attributed this continuity to the faithfulness of the Spirit's Presence, not to some indelible character of the tempers themselves.[103] In fact, consistent with his overall theology and orienting concern, Wesley was quite clear that the gracious tempers which the Presence of the Spirit effects in believers will wither and die if we cease to nurture and respond to that Presence.[104]

The Guidance of the Spirit

Another dimension of the Holy Spirit's inspiration among believers that Wesley identified was the guidance of individual decisions and actions. Like the witness of the Spirit, his affirmation of this dimension drew accusations of enthusiasm. He consistently denied these charges, arguing that such guidance was one of the ordinary operations of the Spirit testified to in Scripture.[105]

At the same time, Wesley was himself fairly cautious about the possibility of being mistaken concerning instances of supposed guidance, a caution that increased with outbreaks of "enthusiasm" among his followers.[106] In response, he emphasized the need to test apparent leadings of the Spirit. For example, in a letter to a person who had recently joined the Quakers, he rejected their tendency to elevate the Spirit as the *rule* of Christian life; rather, the Spirit only *guides* us, and always in accordance with our rule—which is Scripture![107] Likewise, in his sermon specifically devoted to the topic of enthusiasm he reminded his people that any supposed leading of the Spirit should be tested by reason, which God has given to us as a guide.[108] Thus, while one could legitimately question his occasional use of bibliomancy and lots to decide "open" matters, Wesley's claim that he was generally led by reason and Scripture (as opposed to impressions) seems justified.[109] In other words, while he defended guidance as an ordinary *operation* of the Spirit, he did not assume that direct impressions were the ordinary *means* of the Spirit's guidance in his life! It is clear that he wished his followers to imitate him in this regard.

The Gifts of the Spirit

Wesley did not discuss the gifts of the Spirit very often, and when he did it was usually in response to charges that he overemphasized extraordinary gifts. His typical rebuttal was that he focused instead on the "ordinary" operations of the Spirit. It is important to recognize the specific contrast that he is drawing here; it was not a distinction between the spectacular and the common, but between the exceptional and the enduring.[110] Wesley was insisting that his revival centered on operations of the Spirit that are constitutive of, and have always been considered available to, Christian life.

This helps explain the differing ways that Wesley drew the contrast between ordinary and extraordinary operations of the Spirit. Most frequently it was a contrast between the gifts of the Spirit and the sanctifying work or fruit of the Spirit.[111] The fruit of the Spirit are ordinary (though not very common) because they have been potentially available to Christians throughout the history of the Church. On the other hand, the gifts are extraordinary because—as a group—they have not been present through the history of the Church, having ended with the apostolic age (or so Wesley and most in his day believed).

At the same time, Wesley recognized that not all of the gifts disappeared with the earliest Church, some have had a continuing presence and function. Accordingly, he could differentiate between gifts for "ordinary" offices like pastor and teacher (which are continually present) and those for "extraordinary" offices like prophet, apostle, and evangelist (which are not).[112] He also occasionally suggested a distinction between ordinary and extraordinary gifts per se. Among the former were perennial gifts like persuasive speech and knowledge. Among the latter were exceptional gifts like miraculous healing, foretelling the future, speaking in tongues never learned, and miraculous interpretation of tongues.[113]

Excursus: Wesley the Charismatic?

From the preceding it should be clear that Wesley's disavowal of emphasizing extraordinary gifts was not a total rejection of the gifts of the Spirit. Beyond this minimal point, some have made the more ambitious claim that Wesley was an important forerunner of, or even in fundamental agreement with, the recent Charismatic emphasis on the gifts of the Spirit.[114] What should one make of this claim?

It would be helpful first to place Wesley in historical context relative to the theme of gifts of the Spirit. The landmark event in Christian history in this regard was the claim of Montanus and some female associates (ca. 180 C.E.) that he was the Paraclete that Jesus had promised, and that their teachings were an exercise of the gift of prophesy. The problem was not that they claimed this Spirit-led gift (many had before), but that the teachings they offered under this sanction involved an ascetic dualism that contradicted the teaching and model of Christ. Unfortunately, the response of influential Church leaders (especially in the Latin arena) was not simply to exercise discernment about the teachings of the Montanists; they decided that the gifts per se should be restricted to the control of properly prepared (and male!) persons—namely, the clergy. In essence, the bestowal of the gifts of prophesy, preaching, teaching, and so on was identified with the event of ordination. Of course, this left the problem of the New Testament language about all believers having gifts. Two interlocking explanations of this language developed. First, it was suggested that the availability of every gift to all believers was only for the extraordinary situation of the earliest Church when there were not yet sufficient clergy to care for the Church. Second, the gifts that continue to apply to all believers were identified as the seven-fold list in Isaiah 11:2, not the lists in Romans, 1 Corinthians, Ephesians, or 1 Peter. Of course, this seven-fold list was really more analogous to Paul's fruit of the Spirit than to the New Testament gifts of the Spirit.[115]

Wesley inherited these two basic assumptions regarding gifts and lay Christians. While he seldom referred explicitly to the seven-fold gifts of Isaiah, he consistently identified the primary benefits of the Spirit available to all believers as the fruit of the Spirit.[116] Likewise, his earliest materials reflect an unquestioned assumption that most of the New Testament gifts were only intended for the Early Church.[117]

In this light it might be surprising that one of the characterizations made of Wesley and his revival was that it was "Montanism Revived."[118] How could this be? Was he claiming that the extraordinary gifts of the Spirit were being revived? Wesley's correspondence with the author of this charge makes it clear that the focal concern was really his encouragement of lay preachers who operated without episcopal oversight.[119] Even so, this very encouragement had to raise questions in Wesley's mind about consigning the gifts wholly to the past or only to ordained persons.

Thus, by 1744 Wesley was raising the question in passing of whether the gifts might have been originally designed to remain in the Church for all ages, or whether they might be restored at the approach of the "restitution of all things."[120] The latter suggestion is particularly intriguing, because Wesley came to regard his revival as a sign of this approaching restitution.[121] Accordingly, one of his defenses of using women and lay male preachers was that his revival was an "extraordinary" event.[122]

Over time Wesley came to favor the position that the gifts had actually been intended to remain in the Church throughout its history. Their demise had not been part of God's design, but a result of the growing worldliness of Christians.[123] Wesley found himself now ready to defend Montanus as a holy man who had been condemned by dry, formal, orthodox men who had no gifts themselves![124] Since Wesley believed that his Methodist movement was recovering the holiness of the Early Church, it seems reasonable to suggest that he was open to renewed manifestations of even the extraordinary gifts among his followers, at least more open than was typical of Anglicans in his day.[125]

Beyond this narrow point, Howard Snyder has discerned four broader correlations between Wesley's understanding of Christian life and that characteristic of the Charismatic and Pentecostal movements: (1) their stress on God's grace in the life and experience of the Church; (2) the heightened role of the Holy Spirit in their respective theologies; (3) their heavy emphasis on the Church as community; and (4) the tension of their theology of the Church with institutional expressions of the Church.[126]

Part of the explanation of these correlations can be found in studies that trace the emergence of the Pentecostal movement (early twentieth century) and Charismatic movement (mid-twentieth century) back—via the American holiness movement—to Wesley's Methodist revival.[127] However, these studies also reveal some aspects of Pentecostal and Charismatic theology with which Wesley would have had serious questions. For example, while he certainly did not ban emotional expression or extravagant behavior from his revival meetings, he remained skeptical of it, always wanting to submit it to the test of Scripture.[128] Likewise, he apparently considered the gift of tongues to be an instantaneous knowledge of a language for purposes of evangelism—not the sign of the Spirit's filling, nor an ecstatic prayer language.[129] Again, Wesley had a much higher appreciation of sacraments than most Pentecostals and Protestant Charismatics. Most important, he rejected the idea that the "baptism of the Holy Spirit" was to be distinguished as a subsequent event to Christian conversion.[130]

In short, while there are indeed some parallels and precedents in Wesley for later emphases of the Pentecostal and Charismatic movements, there are also significant differences. These differences may be fewer with the Roman Catholic Charismatic movement than with Pentecostalism or Protestant Charismatics.[131] In either case, however, his *distinctive* concern was always more on the fruit of the Spirit (which are the embodiment of responsible grace) than on the gifts of the Spirit, particularly more than on the gift of tongues.[132]

Spirit, Son, and Father: Wesley on the Trinity[133]

The discussion in this chapter so far should help explain why several of the critical responses to Wesley focused on the doctrine of the Holy Spirit. Folk judged him to be attributing undue attention to the work of the Spirit.[134] Western Christianity prior to Wesley had developed a marked hesitance about devoting any direct consideration to the Spirit. Roman Catholicism had essentially identified the Spirit with the Church and its means of grace, sometimes proclaiming the holy Trinity of "Father, Son, and Church"! Meanwhile Magisterial Protestantism had largely restricted the work of the Spirit to the subjective application of Christ's salvation, typically discussing the Spirit in a brief subsection of the doctrine of salvation.[135] While Wesley also connected the work of the Spirit to the means of grace and appropriation of salvation, he did not reduce the Spirit to these dimensions; comparatively, he focused more direct attention on the Spirit per se.[136] To be sure, Wesley's increased interest in the Spirit did not emerge *de novo* in his Anglican context. The doctrine of the Holy Spirit had already begun to receive more focused attention among some radical seventeenth-century Puritans and the early Quakers.[137] Of course, such compatriots simply made Wesley's interest more suspect to most Anglicans.

The Spirit and the Son: The Filioque?

What Wesley's detractors feared was that his increased attention to the Spirit would become *independent* consideration of the Spirit. Western theologians have always been very concerned to stress the connection between the Spirit and the Word (both Christ and Scripture). Indeed, Eastern theologians—who are more comfortable with direct considerations of the Spirit—have charged that the West has largely subordinated the Spirit to the Word. The result, they contend, is that the Spirit is depersonalized and the Spirit's work unduly restricted. The symbol of this move, which they vigorously contest, is the *filioque* clause that was unilaterally added to the (previously) Ecumenical Creed by the West.[138]

We have seen that Wesley stressed the personal nature of the Spirit and I have argued that he attributed more to the Spirit's work than was typical in the West. Does this mean that he rejected the *filioque*? He certainly did not do so explicitly. He retained it in his edited Articles of Religion and made passing reference to it elsewhere.[139] Moreover, he clearly was concerned that the work of the Spirit not supersede or contradict the work of Christ—a danger that the West argued the *filioque* was designed to prevent.[140]

On the other hand, Wesley also shared the Eastern concern not to subordinate the Spirit's work unduly to that of Christ. In this regard, it is striking that his summary of his understanding of the Spirit (drawn from Bishop Pearson) in *A Letter to a Roman Catholic* omits the *filioque*. In its place, there is an affirmation of the equality of the Spirit with the Father and the Son.[141] On this basis, one could argue that Wesley's ascription to the *filioque* was simply routine, reflecting the limited contact (and debate) between East and West in his day.[142] Indeed a very plausible case could be made that Wesley's deepest sympathies would lie with those who are seeking an alternative to the *filioque* in current debates.[143]

Unity or Distinction of the Divine Persons

If attention is shifted to the question of the relationship of the Spirit with God/Father, Wesley's integral connection of the two is clear: the

Spirit's inspiration *is* the restored Presence of God/Father.[144] Does this mean that the two are identical? This question raises the perennial theological issue of the unity and distinction between the "Persons" of the Godhead. Once again, there has been a significant difference of emphasis between Eastern and Western Christianity on this issue, correlated to their concern about the status of the Spirit. Though both stand within creedal boundaries, the East has placed more emphasis on the *distinctness* of the "Persons" of the Godhead, while the West has stressed their *unity*. Thereby, the besetting danger in the East has been tritheism, while the West has more typically verged on Unitarianism or Sabellianism.[145]

These differing emphases on the Trinity can be discerned in retrospect in the early Latin and Greek theologians whom Wesley read, though the emphases were not directly opposed to one another. It was later East/West debates that widened the contrast. The typical eighteenth-century Anglican assumption was that the resulting differences between Eastern and Western theologians on the Trinity were only a matter of expression. Thus, it is not surprising that Wesley did not debate this contrast per se, and indeed, it is not clear that he even thought of them as contrasting alternatives, for his affirmations about the Trinity reveal elements of both.

On the one hand, he was influenced by the typical Western practice of first considering "The One God" (usually identified with the Father!), and then treating the distinction of the three "Persons" as (only?) a revelatory qualification of this One God. Indeed, he retained a prime example of this approach in his published extract of Peter Browne's *The Procedure, Extent, and Limits of Human Understanding.*[146] As such, it was only natural that he began his own summary of beliefs in *A Letter to a Roman Catholic*: "As I am assured that there is an infinite and independent Being and that it is impossible that there should be more than one, so I believe that this one God is the Father of all things."[147]

On the other hand, Wesley argued vigorously that we should view the Father, Son, and Spirit as distinct "Persons," not just different "offices" of God—in direct contrast to Browne.[148] While he does not define "person" in this context, some connotation of an individual center of consciousness is apparent in a parallel setting where his expressed concern is that the Son be able to provide a distinct witness to believers from that of the Father.[149] When this is correlated with his emphasis on the personal nature of the Spirit's witness, Wesley's major reason for emphasizing the distinct "personhood" of each of the Godhead would appear to be preservation of the *relational* character of our experience of Divine grace in all its dimensions.[150] The natural affinity between such a relational view of God and his relational anthropology is obvious, whether intended or not.[151]

On balance, it seems that Wesley's dominant concern was to preserve the distinctness of the Divine "Persons," much like Eastern Orthodoxy.[152] I hasten to add, however, that distinctness does not imply separation or opposition! To protect against such connotations of distinguishing the "Persons" of the Trinity, Eastern Orthodox theology eventually developed a doctrine of the thorough coinherence (*perichoresis*) of Father, Son, and Spirit. Similarly, Wesley would affirm that the three Divine "Persons" are "one in essence, in knowledge, in will, and in their testimony."[153] The reference to unity of essence here may seem to override any distinction between the "Persons." However, Wesley was likely referring to equal possession of full Divine power, not undifferentiated identity of being.[154] As such, one might say that Wesley adopted the notion of *perichoresis*, even though he never explicitly referred to it (and likely did not know it in any exact terms).[155]

Doctrine of the Trinity as a Grammar of Responsible Grace

So far I have been analyzing how Wesley conceived of the Trinity, concluding that his characteristic emphases resonate more with the Eastern Orthodox stress on the full coinherence of the three distinct and equal Divine "Persons" than with the Western tendency toward One God who is revealed to be Father, Son, and (often, subtly subordinate) Spirit. I turn now to the question of what importance for Christian life Wesley attributed to belief in the Trinity.

Since Wesley neglected many of the finer distinctions of Trinitarian doctrine and rarely engaged in protracted debates over the topic, one might think that he would join Schleiermacher in confining it to an appendix of Christian doctrine. Quite the contrary! He actually argued that the truth of the Trinity "enters into the very heart of Christianity; it lies at the root of all vital religion."[156] Of course, he immediately added that it was belief in the *fact* of the Trinity that was involved here, not adherence to any specific philosophical explication of the Trinity.[157]

Wesley's practical-theological activity bears out the importance to him of affirming the Trinity. While he published only one sermon devoted to the doctrine, it was apparently a favorite topic of his actual preaching.[158] Likewise, he repeatedly introduced Trinitarian reflections into his *NT Notes* comments, often in surprising contexts.[159] Finally, he greatly valued Charles' *Hymns on the Trinity* (1767) for their explication of the spiritual and ethical dimensions of the doctrine.[160]

But, *why* did Wesley consider affirmation of the Trinity to be so central to Christian life? Undeniably he was committed to the full divinity of the Son and the Spirit that was affirmed thereby. However, his explicit reasons were more practical-theological in nature. The implication about Christ that he stressed related to Christian worship—it is appropriate for Christians to honor the Son in the same way that we honor God/Father. The implication he highlighted about the Holy Spirit was that the assurance bestowed by the Spirit's witness makes no sense apart from the claims of the Trinity.[161] On reflection, these two implications coalesce, in line with Wesley's mature assumption about the formative role of doctrinal convictions: proper worship helps structure the formation of Christian character, while openness to the Spirit's witness provides access to the empowerment for this formation.[162]

Building on Wesley's explicit recognition of these formative implications of affirming the Trinity, I would suggest that it served implicitly as another "grammar" of his theological convictions.[163] While he never literally instructed his preachers to "proclaim God in all Three Persons," his very emphasis on the importance of the doctrine for Christian life suggests that he saw it as more than simply an affirmation about God. Reflexively, it portrayed the pattern that he expected in Christian life: we are to become "Transcripts of the Trinity."[164]

In other words, just as he had warned his followers against "practical atheism," Wesley was concerned that they avoid "practical unitarianism."[165] To develop this concern, we need to note that his characteristic way of distinguishing the "Persons" of the Trinity was in terms of their most defining work: creation/providence, redemption, and sanctification.[166] On such terms, a "unitarianism of the Father" would approach Christian life on the basis of created abilities, failing to recognize our fallenness and need for grace; a "unitarianism of the Son" might focus exclusively on Christ's provision of forgiveness, neglecting the Father's continuing will for our obedience and the Spirit's empowerment for such; and, a "unitarianism of the Spirit" could become enamored with the Spirit's power per se, forgetting its purpose of effecting our recovery of the moral Image that the Father intended for us and Christ displayed to us.

By contrast with all such unitarianisms, the Wesleys sought to form in their Methodist followers a truly trinitarian balance of (1) reverence for the God of Holy Love and for God/Father's original design for human life, (2) gratitude for the unmerited Divine Initiative in Christ that frees us from the guilt and enslavement of our sin, and (3) responsiveness to the Presence of the Holy Spirit that empowers our recovery of the Divine Image in our lives.[167] There can be no better expression of Wesley's theology of *responsible grace* than Christians who preserve such a trinitarian balance as they proceed along the Way of Salvation.

CHAPTER 6

Grace and Response—The Nature of Human Salvation

It is time to return attention to Wesley's understanding of the human dimensions and dynamics of salvation. This topic has been the common focus (indeed, often the exclusive focus) of previous expositions of Wesley's theology, reflecting its relative prominence in his own writings. This very prominence has sparked occasional accusations that Wesley's theology is plagued by an inordinate fixation on humanity and the psychological dynamics of our salvation, neglecting the Divine basis and empowerment of that salvation.[1] The discussions of his emphasis on the Divine Initiative expressed in Christ and the Divine Empowerment available through the Holy Spirit in the preceding two chapters, along with earlier considerations of his conceptions of Prevenient Grace and the nature of God/Father, should constitute a sufficient rejoinder to such accusations. Wesley was firmly convinced of the primacy of Divine *grace* in the work of salvation. At the same time, he frequently found it important in his practical-theological activity to clarify the role of *responsible* human participation in this gracious work.

This characteristic concern to maintain a dynamic relation between Divine grace and our response has sparked a variety of critical reactions within Wesley's Western context. As a result, most prior studies of his understanding of salvation have been largely concerned to locate and champion his "place" within the ongoing soteriological debates dividing Western Christianity (particularly Roman Catholic vs. Protestant, and Lutheran vs. Reformed). While these works have identified many areas of Wesley's indebtedness to Western traditions, they also reveal—by their very diversity and their unresolved issues—the limitations of interpreting his soteriological convictions within Western categories alone.[2]

A major claim running through the discussion of Wesley's conception of human nature and the human problem in Chapter Three was that he integrated the juridical concerns central to the Western Christian traditions within a larger therapeutic emphasis like that characteristic of Eastern Orthodoxy. Thus, it should come as no surprise if concurrence is now expressed with Albert Outler's proposal that Wesley's mature soteriological convictions manifested a blending of juridical and therapeutic elements, and that this blending most adequately defines his distinctive theological contribution.[3] Indeed, the purpose of the present chapter is to provide further warrant for this proposal by detailing the *characteristics* of Wesley's understanding of salvation. Chapter Seven will then take up the more common topic of the constituent elements of human salvation (*via salutis*), developing some implications of this proposal.

As background for the present task it would be helpful to sketch the basic soteriological convictions characteristic of Western and Eastern Christianity. In keeping with its primary understanding of sin, Western soteriology has tended to highlight the problem of remitting guilt. Its most central images are juridical. By comparison, early Greek theologians and the later Eastern Orthodox traditions have focused more on the problem of healing the corruption that results from sin. Their most central images are therapeutic. While these two approaches are not mutually exclusive, the emphases are determinative. Each tradition tends to subsume the concern of the other under its own dominant approach.[4]

The Western juridical focus inevitably vaulted the doctrine of justification onto center stage. This is not to say that Western traditions ignore growth in Christ-likeness (sanctification), only that such growth is construed in light of their concern for justification. Consider the example of the debate over the Council of Trent's claim that an infusion of holiness (i.e., created grace) must precede justification. Protestants (and some Roman Catholics) worry that this claim invalidates the doctrine of justification by grace. Perhaps so, but its original purpose was merely to explain *how* a gracious God could justly declare sinners justified.[5] As this case suggests, the major disagreements in Western soteriology have not been over the centrality of the issue of justification, but over how best to understand the conditions, process, and implications of justification.

Eastern Christianity's response to the question of how God could justly restore relationship with sinful humanity is simple—through merciful love. They have not felt it necessary to elaborate this point. Rather, they have concentrated on the question of how sin-diseased humans can recover their spiritual health and the Likeness of God.[6] Their characteristic answer to this question has centered on the necessity of human participation in the Divine life, through the means that God has graciously provided. Western observers (particularly Protestants) have usually construed this answer as a form of works-righteousness.[7] However, Eastern theologians insist that the question of meriting God's acceptance is not at issue.[8] They are simply recognizing that God's freely-bestowed grace functions co-operantly, empowering the spiritual renewal of those who responsively participate in it.

With these initial comparisons in mind the question of whether and how Wesley's soteriology might provide a distinctive integration of juridical and therapeutic elements can be taken up.

The Three Dimensions of Salvation

Wesley's classic mature articulation of his soteriology is the 1765 sermon "The Scripture Way of Salvation." He opened this sermon with a clarification that is central to his overall perspective:

> "What is *salvation*? The salvation which is here spoken of is not what is frequently understood by that word, the going to heaven, eternal happiness. . . . It is not a blessing which lies on the other side of death . . . it is a present thing . . . [it] might be extended to the entire work of God, from the first dawning of grace in the soul till it is consummated in glory.[9]

In denying here that human salvation is only a future hope, Wesley is also denying that it is solely juridical in nature. Salvation involves much more than a momentary legal transaction that guarantees eventual eternal blessedness (as a simplistic form of the juridical emphasis would suggest).

In contrast to such a truncated misunderstanding of salvation that he perceived in some "gospel preachers," Wesley called upon his preachers to "preach the whole gospel, even justification and sanctification, preparatory to glory."[10] This call suggests again Wesley's practical-theological concern for the proper formation of his people. Also evident is a distinction between three dimensions of human salvation. Wesley's most explicit delineation of these three dimensions was pardon—salvation begun, holiness—salvation continued, and heaven—salvation finished.[11] Some other common threefold formulations were justification, sanctification, and consummation; or pardon, grace, and glory.[12] To suggest an alliteration, Wesley understood human salvation in its fullest sense to include deliverance (1) immediately from the *penalty* of sin, (2) progressively from the *plague* of sin, and (3) eschatologically from the very *presence* of sin and its effects.

The Therapeutic Focus of Salvation

Throughout his various considerations of human salvation Wesley's focal interest remained on the middle dimension of deliverance from the plague of sin, albeit always in integral relation with the other two dimensions. To begin with the eschatological dimension, the central point of the passage quoted above from "The Scripture Way of Salvation" was that salvation must be seen as more than a future hope—it has a present reality. In other contexts Wesley insisted that the salvation which is perfected in heaven begins on earth and that this present experience of salvation is our "taste" of the heaven to which we are going; more precisely, it is the qualification for, the forerunner to, and the pledge of eternal salvation.[13] It is this insistence that has led some Wesley scholars to talk of his "inaugurated eschatology," a point that will be developed in Chapter Nine.

The juridical dimension of deliverance from the penalty of sin was also integrated by Wesley into his focal interest of deliverance from the plague of sin. This point can best be demonstrated by considering the most "Protestant" moment of his theological development—Aldersgate.

Wesley's famous description of the Aldersgate event culminates in the claim that then he sensed that Christ had "taken away *my* sins, even *mine*, and saved *me* from the law of sin and death."[14] It is sometimes assumed that Wesley was making here only a juridical claim that he was aware of God's pardon of the *penalty* of his sin.[15] He was actually claiming more than this, because he had come to Aldersgate Street on the evening of May 24 *expecting* much more than this!

The driving passion of Wesley's life prior to 1738 had been to conquer the *plague* of sin and be conformed to the model of Christ. Peter Böhler had recently persuaded him that this deliverance could happen instantaneously by simple faith, in conjunction with his assurance of God's forgiveness.[16] On the morning of May 24 he found his attention drawn to two Scripture verses: 2 Peter 1:4, which he took as a direct promise that he could *be* a partaker of the Divine nature; and Mark 12:34, which raised his expectation that this would happen very soon.[17] In worship that afternoon he was struck by the words of the anthem which called for trust in God to provide mercy *and* redemption from all one's sins.[18] Finally, the reading from Luther at Aldersgate Street that night placed as much stress on God's grace giving us a new heart that would incessantly do good works as it did on forgiveness.[19] Against this background, what Wesley hoped for—and initially claimed—at Aldersgate was *full* salvation from *both* the penalty and the plague of sin!

To be sure, Wesley's initial expectations at Aldersgate were soon disappointed and he had to admit "my wound was not fully healed."[20] But this realization did not lead him to downplay the concern for deliverance from the plague of sin. Instead, he eventually distinguished carefully between the instantaneous restoration of our responsive participation in God (the New Birth) and the resulting gradual therapeutic transformation of our lives (sanctification proper).[21] Thereby, the mature Wesley retained his focal interest in the deliverance from the plague of sin, while integrating into it a crucial contribution by our deliverance from the penalty of sin.[22]

As the example of Aldersgate should corroborate, Wesley's focus on the middle dimension of human salvation was hardly accidental; it was a natural corollary of his understanding of the human problem. If the crucial problem of sin is not just guilt but the spiritual debilitation and affliction of the human person, then salvation must involve more than pardon; it must also bring healing. This need accounts for the prominence of therapeutic language (resonating with early Greek practice) in Wesley's various comments on human salvation.[23] Indeed, Wesley characterized the very essence of religion as a θεραπεία ψυκάς—a therapy by which the Great Physician heals our sin-diseased souls, restoring the vitality of life that God intended for us.[24]

The Holistic Scope of Salvation

Wesley's description of Christian salvation as a therapy of the soul might suggest that he limited human salvation to an internal spiritual sphere of life. Given his understanding of the role of the affections or tempers in human action, he certainly assumed that this is where authentic salvation or holiness is grounded. Yet (like the early Greek theologians) Wesley insisted throughout his life that salvation must involve not only inner holiness but also the recovery of actual moral righteousness in our outward lives. To cite another classic excerpt:

> By salvation I mean, not barely (according to the vulgar notion) deliverance from hell, or going to heaven, but a present deliverance from sin, a restoration of the soul to its primitive health, its original purity; a recovery of the divine nature; the renewal of our souls after the image of God in righteousness and true holiness, in justice, mercy, and truth. This implies all holy and heavenly tempers, and *by consequence* all holiness of conversation.[25]

Wesley was using "conversation" in this quotation in the common eighteenth-century (though now archaic) sense of *all* types of human conduct.[26] Just as the corruption of sin distorts all four relationships that are constitutive of human life (Chapter Three), so the rejuvenation of humanity involves transformation of all four. As God's saving work progresses in our lives we experience a renewed active love for God and other humans, and a reawakened concern for the "lower" animals.[27] In conjunction with these progressive changes we also recover our own happiness (i.e., proper esteem for self).[28]

Such transformation obviously has ethical dimensions, which will be developed in Chapter Nine. What is worthy of note at this point is the balance involved in the aspects of holistic salvation discussed so far. Inner holiness of our tempers is balanced with outer holiness in our relationships; and renewed relationships with our various "others" nurtures healed relationship with our "selves." Albert Outler has captured this balance nicely in his characterization of Wesley's understanding of salvation as a journey from the *barely* human, to the *truly* human, to the *fully* human.[29]

Excursus: Wesley on Physical Health and Healing

For many Eastern Christian theologians (early and later) holistic Christian salvation has also included the possibility of initial therapeutic transformation of the mortal human *body* during this life.[30] While Wesley shows little knowledge of this specific idea, a somewhat analogous conviction can be found in his interest in physical health and healing.

Few non-specialists realize that the Wesley publication that has gone through the most editions and reissues is his *Primitive Physick.*[31] This historically influential work is a collection of folk remedies for various diseases and physical problems. Many of Wesley's recommended treatments (such as "tar water" and mild electrical shocks) will strike modern readers as bizarre. However, they were comparatively sane and effective for his time.[32] More important, they were inexpensive! Wesley's major stated reason for publishing this collection was that contemporary medicine was becoming too elitist and too costly. He wanted to make available to the poor the best time-tested home remedies.[33]

Interwoven with this practical purpose one can also discern theological convictions behind the publication of *Primitive Physick.* In particular, Wesley stressed the interrelation between physical health or disease and spiritual wholeness. To begin with the negative side, his Preface opened with the assertion that all bodily disease, weakness, and death are a result of the Fall. God did not desire any of these for humanity. And yet, "the seeds of weakness and pain, of sickness and death, are now lodged in our inmost substance." His collection of remedies was meant to provide means for lessening those inconveniences which cannot be wholly removed, softening the evils of life, and preventing in part the sickness and pain to which we are continually exposed.[34] That is, these remedies were providential gifts that help heal some of the ailing effects of sin in this life!

At the same time, Wesley specifically refused to restrict the means of restoring or preserving bodily health to pharmaceutical treatments (either folk or professional).[35] A survey of his various comments on health and healing reveals at least three other dimensions. The dimension that may be the most surprising (to those who assume that Wellness is a new idea) is his strong emphasis on the importance of hygiene, diet, and exercise for recovering or maintaining health.[36] Less surprising is his affirmation of the importance of prayer, both as a direct means of healing and in support of medical treatments.[37] The dimension that warrants particular attention, however, is his recognition of interconnections between emotional well-being and physical wellness. He insisted that the mind can be disordered by the body, *and* the body can be disordered by the mind (i.e., distorted passions or tempers).[38] This being the case, emotional or spiritual healing could itself contribute to physical health. Indeed, the Preface to *Primitive Physick* culminated with a section on this very point, which argued that the most effective prevention of the bodily disorders caused by distorted passions is the nurturing of a responsive love for God, for this keeps the passions in balance.[39]

In other words, Wesley's understanding of human salvation was holistic in a broader sense than simply his affirmation of the inward healing of our affections and the outward healing of the four relational dimensions of our lives. He was convinced that the Great Physician is committed to the ultimate healing of *both* body and soul, and that some degree of physical recovery is available even in this life—if we will allow it to begin.[40]

The Co-Operant Character of Salvation

The use of "allow" in the previous sentence hints at the next characteristic in Wesley's understanding of the nature of human salvation. His writings abound with affirmations of the prevenience and indispensability of God's pardoning/empowering grace for human salvation, particularly following 1738.[41] But even in their strongest formulation, such affirmations were tied to a recognition that humans may (regrettably) resist God's gracious salvific overtures, for God's restoring grace is co-operant.[42]

The co-operant nature of grace entails that (if it is to achieve its intended effect) we must "put it to work," as Wesley phrased it in his classic articulation of the co-operant nature of salvation: the 1785 sermon on Philippians 2:12-13, "On Working Out Our Own Salvation."[43] It is important to recall that the reason for our requisite—but uncoerced—participation in the process of salvation is not a deficiency in God's grace (needing the supplement of our efforts), but a quality of God's character: the God we know in Christ is a God of love who respects our integrity and will not force salvation upon us.[44] As even St. Augustine could put it in his own sermon on Philippians 2:12-13 (and one of Wesley's few appreciative quotations from Augustine), "[God] who made us without ourselves, will not save us without ourselves."[45] Put in slightly different terms, Wesley was convinced that, while we *can* not attain holiness (and wholeness) apart from God's grace, God *will* not effect holiness apart from our responsive participation.

Note that the sermon referenced to epitomize his commitment to the co-operant nature of salvation is from the late Wesley. This is no accident, as his views on this issue underwent some temporal development. As one would expect, given his Western Christian context, this development focused around the issue of justification.

Excursus: Wesley on Justification by Faith Alone

In keeping with its juridical focus, the doctrine of justification has been a classic locus of debate in Western theology. This debate has tended to polarize over the question of whether our justification is by faith *alone* or if it has some connection to our requisite personal holiness. In general terms Roman Catholics were more likely to contend for a connection to holy living while Protestants insisted that our justification was not dependent on any human work. Given their self-understanding, this debate took a particularly intense form among Anglicans, with strong voices on both sides and the majority seeking a mediating position. The result was that the language of justification by faith alone was incorporated into the Anglican standards (e.g., Article XI), while many influential Anglican divines insisted that some evidence of holy resolve (i.e., repentance and 'works meet for repentance') should precede justification.[46]

Wesley's convictions on the issues involved in this debate reflect the general transitions already noted in other aspects of his theology.[47] The early Wesley was influenced by several of the "holy living" divines and showed great discomfort with strong emphases on faith alone.[48] He tended toward a position which required a measure of responsible holiness (or at least sincere effort) to precede justification. To be sure, he would affirm that we are dependent upon the Spirit's empowerment for our sufficiency to this task.[49] But, while he thereby retained the technical primacy of Divine grace, his emphasis was clearly on our responsibility.

With the transition of 1738 Wesley became a vigorous champion of "justification by faith alone," defending the doctrine by appeal to the Anglican standards and calling it the fundamental doctrine of the Anglican Church![50] In order to accentuate our absolute dependence upon God's grace, he now sharply rejected any suggestion of requisite good works or holiness prior to justification, characterizing all human efforts prior to saving acceptance by God as sin.[51]

It was not long, however, before he became uncomfortable with implications that some drew from this theme of faith *alone*. The first issue to become a focus of concern was the "quietist" suggestion of the Moravians that one should await God's justifying work in total passivity, because any spiritual disciplines or other work would be an abandonment of faith.[52] This suggestion posed Divine grace and human responsibility as antipodes, something Wesley's most fundamental convictions could not allow. Hence, talk of prior repentance and works meet for repentance (if there be time)—as responsible "conditions" of God's justifying grace—resurfaced in his pastoral clarifications of the nature of salvation in the early 1740's.[53] As one might imagine, such talk quickly spawned accusations of a return to "works-righteousness."[54]

While the early quietist controversy had heavy Lutheran overtones of emphasis on *faith alone*, it was intermixed with more typically Reformed concerns about *God alone* working to effect salvation and this salvation being for the *elect alone*. These Reformed issues moved to the forefront in the middle years of the revival, with the increasing conflict between Calvinist and Wesleyan Methodists. As they did, Wesley's fundamental convictions again led him to resist any counterpoising of God's grace and our response. For example, he strongly rejected any suggestion that faith was simply "God believing through us," insisting that while faith was a gift of God we must "put it to work."[55] Likewise, his conviction of God's *universal* graciousness led him to a more positive evaluation of the "good works" of the unevangelized than the traditional Reformed view that works prior to justification were simply "splendid sins."[56] To the charge that these positions implied salvation by works, his response was that he preferred salvation by works, *if* the only alternative was unconditional predestination![57]

The focus so far has been on the implications of *faith alone* for works *prior* to justification. Some noticeable shifts in Wesley's perspective on this issue have been noted. What about works *after* justification? On this topic Wesley remained thoroughly consistent: one who enjoys God's gracious justifying Presence will naturally respond in good works and holiness.[58]

While Wesley initially assumed that this perspective was definitive of Protestantism, he soon found that there were some (distorted) understandings of justification by faith that worked against it—distortions that he was constrained by his fundamental convictions to contest. One distortion that he frequently challenged construed the Lutheran emphasis on faith *alone* to mean that expectations of good works should be avoided even within the Christian life, because these works might mislead folk to trust in their own "merits."[59] For Wesley this simply did not follow, for we are always aware that any good works we are capable of spring from God's empowering grace.[60] The other major threat to good works following justification that Wesley found need to contest was a distortion of the Reformed emphasis on the imputed righteousness of Christ. In this case some argued that since Christ had already fulfilled all holiness (for the elect) there was nothing left for them to do. Wesley's response was to remind them that justification was inherently connected to the New Birth.[61]

As debates over works following justification heated up an added emphasis gained prominence in Wesley's comments. He not only continued to claim that good works would naturally flow from justification, he increasingly emphasized that such works were necessary for the progress—indeed, even the very continuance—of our Christian life.[62] That is, he insisted on a dynamic interrelationship between our *response* and God's *grace*.[63]

As these various qualifications and clarifications accumulated, it is understandable that some would suggest that Wesley had redefined the notion of "justification by faith alone" to the point that it no longer meant what was intended by most Protestants.[64] Through his middle period Wesley reacted to such suggestions with a strong avowal of standing firmly with the Reformers.[65] The late Wesley was notably less insistent on this point.[66] While he had no intention of rejecting the doctrine, he now seemed willing to concede that his emphases concerning it were different than those of the Reformers.

Just what were the abiding emphases of Wesley's understanding of justification by faith? The central one is unquestionably that our salvation is never something that we merit or earn, it is a gift of God. His most consistent claim in the various debates over this issue was that justification by faith was an equivalent way of affirming "justification by the merits of Christ alone."[67] Sometimes he enlarged on this point, noting that just as all merit of salvation is in Christ, all power is from the Holy Spirit.[68] In light of the discussion in Chapters Four and Five, this would suggest that Wesley's most basic reason for defending justification *by faith* was to preserve the nature of salvation as fundamentally *by grace*.[69]

If the preceding suggestion is correct, then one would expect to find Wesley quick to qualify the affirmation of justification by faith any time that it seemed to endanger his distinctive understanding of the nature of God's salvific grace. Such qualification is exactly what is found in the characteristic claim of the mature Wesley that, while we are justified by *faith alone*, it is by such a faith as is *not alone*.[70] The fact that God is the ultimate source of all power for salvation does not mean that God effects salvation unilaterally. Rather, God has chosen to allow a place for our participation, both before and after our justification—not as a means of meriting salvation, but as a "condition" that upholds our integrity within the relational process of saving grace.[71]

To summarize, while there were indeed temporal modulations in Wesley's perspective on "justification by faith," their pattern was a spiraling that integrated his deeper appreciation of the graciousness of our justification in 1738 into his prior and broader conviction of God's desire for our therapeutic recovery of holiness.[72] This spiraling process was not accidental; it was propelled and guided by his orienting concern of *responsible grace*. It is ultimately this concern that finds expression in his distinctive resolution of the antinomy between "faith alone" and "holy living"—a resolution that Albert Outler has argued makes Wesley the most important Anglican theologian of the eighteenth century.[73]

The Possibility of Apostasy

As was hinted at above, one other major implication of the co-operant nature of grace is Wesley's concession of the possibility of Christians becoming apostate, in direct contrast to his predestinarian opponents.[74] Just as God's empowering grace does not work irresistibly in initiating our Christian life, so we may resist or slight God's gracious work *within* the Christian life, gradually weakening and ultimately dissolving our responsive relationship with God. Admittedly, Wesley held out hope for a while that there might be a state of Christian transformation available in this life from which believers could not finally fall away—Christian Perfection. However further consideration of Scripture and the lives of his people convinced him that God's saving grace remained co-operant and resistible in *every* degree of its transforming effect.[75]

The Gradual Process of Salvation

Perhaps a good image (even if traditionally un-Wesleyan) to capture salvation's co-operant nature is that of a *dance* in which God always takes the first step but we must participate responsively, lest the dance stumble or end. Besides highlighting the Divine prevenience in salvation, this image conveys that such responsive interaction takes place over time. In other words, human salvation—viewed in Wesley's terms—would be fundamentally *gradual* in process.

This is admittedly a controversial claim, precisely because it involves again differing comparative emphases of Eastern and Western Christianity. Given their identification of salvation with the therapeutic transformation of sin-distorted human life, most early Greek and later Orthodox theologians have considered gradualness to be essential to its nature—we are progressively *being* saved.[76] Western understandings of salvation have focused more on the legal act of pardon, which can be a momentary transaction. While many of these traditions have allowed a place for gradual sanctification in the Christian life, they have typically been careful to subsume this growth to the act of justification—either as a subsequent effect (Calvin) or as a prerequisite (Tridentine Catholicism).[77] The moment of justification itself is considered when we most properly *are* saved (that is, qualified for eschatological salvation).

Wesley was influenced by both of these understandings of salvation, but his most fundamental convictions lean toward the therapeutic emphasis. As evidence of this, consider his use of the term "conversion." For many Western Christians (particularly Protestants), conversion is identified with the moment of justification. Wesley's use of the term immediately following Aldersgate also reflected such an identification.[78] However he soon became uncomfortable with this usage because it implied that justification provided all the transformation that a person needed, obscuring the importance of further growth in holiness.[79] As a result he increasingly avoided the word "conversion," and when he did use it he was careful to define it in a way synonymous with sanctification: "a thorough change of heart and life from sin to holiness."[80] Such transformation of a person's tempers or character would seem to entail a gradual process, provided that God was amenable to working in a gradual manner.

In Wesley's opinion, God's *typical* manner of working in all areas of providence and grace was gradual. He appealed to the (relatively) gradual process of creation as the earliest expression of this fact.[81] As such, he was not hesitant to affirm the "gradual process of the work of God in the soul," or to speak of salvation gradually increasing in one's soul.[82] Likewise, he readily appropriated the analogical comparison (in 1 John) of Christian life with human maturing—passing progressively from new-born babes, to young adulthood, to full maturity.[83] The centrality of gradual process to Wesley's understanding of salvation is most evident in his ascription of it even to those who have attained "perfect love," insisting that this perfection too remains open to continual increase.[84] Indeed, he suggested at least once that gradual growth in grace would continue eschatologically.[85]

Not only did Wesley view growth in the Christian life as a continual possibility, it was his normative expectation. On analogy with natural life, he diagnosed stalled spiritual growth as a sign of potentially fatal disease.[86] His pastoral letters frequently admonish correspondents that they cannot stand still in their Christian walk, they must either press forward or they will regress.[87] As this point reminds us, while Wesley understood growth in holiness to be gradual, it was not automatic—we must nurture a continuing responsiveness to God's progressive empowering grace. Wesley's pastoral advice also makes clear that he did not view Christian apostasy as typically a sudden total rebellion. The process of straining and rupturing our relationship with God's restored empowering Presence is as gradual as the process of commencing and nurturing this relationship.[88]

The Place of Instantaneous Transitions in Christian Life

The preceding survey of Wesley's convictions about the gradual nature of salvation provides a good backdrop for considering his comments on two aspects of God's saving work: (1) entrance into justifying relationship with God and (2) attaining Christian perfection. During the early years of the revival Wesley defended the instantaneous character of justification vigorously. Similar avowals of the instantaneous attainment of entire sanctification became common in the 1760's. "Protestant" readings of Wesley have often seized on these affirmations as evidence that his soteriology was fundamentally Western—focusing on momentary transitions in juridical status. I would contend instead that this is another area where Wesley integrated characteristic Western concerns into his more central therapeutic understanding of salvation. To make this case, it is important to consider *why* Wesley stressed the instantaneous nature of these two aspects of the Christian life.

It was noted previously that Wesley was encouraged by the English Moravians to consider conversion an instantaneous and complete deliverance from all sin, fear, and doubt. His own experience, and consultation with other theological sources, soon persuaded him that full spiritual transformation was not instantaneously provided. However, he remained convinced of the importance of an instantaneous beginning of the Christian life. As he struggled to defend this conviction in controversial dialogue he ultimately admitted that his concern was not with matters of *circumstance* but of *substance*; that is, he was not so much defending a psychological *model* of conversion as a theological *evaluation* of it.[89] It also appears to have been concern for theological implications, more than psychological dynamics, that motivated his defense of the instantaneous nature of entire sanctification. This is most evident in his argument for entire sanctification being instantaneous even when not perceived so by the person involved (based on the questionable analogy that there is always a "moment" of death, however gradual the prior deterioration of vitality).[90]

What theological issue did Wesley consider to be at stake in these two contexts? A good indicator is his differentiation of repentance and faith from justification on the grounds that the former are co-operant (and gradual) while the latter is God's "mere gift" (and instantaneous).[91] Even clearer is his claim that "perfection is received by simple faith in God's gift, *consequently* in an instant."[92] In each case instantaneousness is seen as an implication of the status of justification or entire sanctification as unmerited gifts of God, rather than human achievements. In other words, Wesley stressed the instantaneous nature of these two aspects of salvation as assumed implications of God's gracious *prevenience* in human salvation.[93] In this light it was not accidental that the mature Wesley's growing openness to the possibility that some experience God's renewing work in a gradual manner was contemporaneous with the increasing emphasis in his later writings on universal Prevenient Grace—which establishes God's prevenience even prior to the gracious actions of justification and the New Birth!

However strong his stress on God's gracious prevenience in justification and Christian perfection, Wesley was quick to affirm an integral place for our responsive growth *following* these initiatory events, since we are dealing with a God of *responsible grace.*[94] Moreover, a second reason that he frequently invoked for stressing the instantaneous nature of entire sanctification in particular related to its impact on gradual responsive growth *prior* to this event. He became convinced by observation of his people that maintaining a high expectation of the immediate possibility of entire sanctification fostered the present gradual work of God in their souls, as they sought this experience.[95] He assumed an analogous benefit from encouraging those with only the "faith of a servant" to expect the witness of assurance at any moment.[96]

Thus, while Wesley indeed allowed for momentary transitions in the Christian life, he integrally related these transitions to gradual growth in response to God's grace, both preceding and following the transitions.[97] Thereby the overall dynamics of salvation retained a gradual nature, and more important, the fundamental goal of salvation remained therapeutic transformation, not simply a changed forensic situation.

The Individual Variability of Salvation

There was one other common argument that Wesley used for affirming the instantaneous character of justification and entire sanctification: the examples that he witnessed in his revival movement.[98] The crucial point that must be noted in this regard is that long-term observation of the lives of his Methodist people led him to revise some of his early assumptions about how humans experience God's saving work.[99]

Wesley began his revival movement shortly after Aldersgate, still strongly influenced by the model of conversion that had been recommended to him by Peter Böhler and the English Moravians. This was a classic "twice-born" model.[100] By conjoining justification with immediate deliverance from sin and doubt it implied that conversion would be a dramatic (if not traumatic) experience. Moreover, this model made such an experience normative for all cases—one was not a "real" Christian unless one could identify the specific time when one *experienced* conversion. Wesley's initial revival efforts reflected these "twice-born" assumptions. He doubted the reality of anyone's conversion who could not identify the exact time that they experienced God's justifying love.[101]

As was detailed in Chapter Five, Wesley revised his assumptions in the years following Aldersgate: first allowing that there were degrees of justifying assurance short of full assurance; then granting that there might be a few exceptional cases (due to bodily disorder or ignorance) where persons exercise justifying faith while lacking conscious assurance; and finally coming to value the nascent faith of the "servant of God" as justifying faith. With each of these concessions it became more difficult to assert an exclusive twice-born model where all believers would be able to date their "conversion experience."

This is not to say that Wesley rejected or came to impugn the twice-born model. It remained his favored model—as most expressive of the common Christian *privilege* of assurance, but he no longer considered it exclusively *normative*. His observation of the lives of his Methodist people convinced him that some Christians receive the renewing work of the Spirit in a gradual, almost imperceptible, manner. Indeed, the clarifying footnotes that he added in 1774 to his original account of Aldersgate suggest that Wesley had gravitated toward such a gradualist reading of his own spiritual journey. He now viewed the transitions in his spiritual life as more incremental in nature, and God's justifying acceptance as present prior to Aldersgate (he was *already* a "servant of God").

The key point is that practical-theological engagement with his revival movement eventually led to the kind of pastoral sensitivity evident in the late Wesley's advice to Mary Cooke:

> There is an irreconcilable variability in the operations of the Holy Spirit on [human] souls, more especially as to the manner of justification. Many find Him rushing in upon them like a torrent, while they experience "The o'erwhelming power of saving grace." . . . But in others He works in a very different way: "He deigns His influence to infuse; Sweet, refreshing, as the silent dews." It has pleased Him to work the latter way in you from the beginning . . . in a gentle and almost insensible manner. Let Him take His own way : He is wiser than you; He will do all things well.[102]

While this specific advice deals with justification, similar comments can be found regarding entire sanctification.[103] In both cases it is crucial to note that the issue is not whether some persons need spiritual renewal while other do not. All persons stand in need of the Spirit's renewing work in the New Birth. However, the Spirit can choose—in Divine Wisdom—to effect this renewing work in manners other than that characteristic of the "twice-born" model.

This mature recognition of individual variability in the dynamics (not the goal!) of salvation is quite consistent with Wesley's understanding of *responsible grace.* Recall that he identified grace as the personal Presence of the Holy Spirit in our lives, not some standardized commodity bestowed upon us. Likewise he assumed that our uncoerced response was integral to the God's progressive saving work in our lives. Responsiveness would surely vary among individuals.

Some other characteristics of Wesley's understanding of salvation, such as its corporate and sacramental nature will be developed in Chapter Eight. The characteristics sketched so far provide sufficient context for turning consideration now to the constituent elements of human salvation.

CHAPTER 7

The Way of Salvation—Grace Upon Grace

The preceding chapter sketched the general characteristics of Wesley's understanding of human salvation. Here attention turns to the constituent elements of this salvation. Previous studies have usually surveyed these elements under the rubric of the *ordo salutis* (Order of Salvation). This organization of soteriology, and the eventual designation itself, developed in Protestant Scholasticism and was particularly attractive to English Puritans. Its dominant feature is a depiction of salvation as a standard progressive sequence of God's works in the soul.[1]

Several scholars have argued recently that the label "*ordo salutis*" and its implied soteriological emphases are inappropriate for dealing with Wesley. They advocate instead some such designation as "*via salutis*," arguing that the word "way" better conveys the gradual dynamics of Wesley's understanding of salvation.[2] They note that Wesley himself used "way" to describe Christian life in the titles of such major sermons as "The Way to the Kingdom" (1746), "The Scripture Way of Salvation" (1765), and "The More Excellent Way" (1787).[3]

I would concur that Wesley's soteriology is more appropriately described under the rubric of the Way of Salvation than the Order of Salvation. Three connotations of the Reformed version of the *ordo salutis* in particular lead to this conclusion. In the first place, the Reformed scholastics' juridical focus inclined them to construe the *ordo salutis* as a series of discrete states. Persons moved *from* one state *to* another (e.g., from preparatory grace to regenerating grace), because these stages are "riveted together like the links of a chain."[4] On such terms, the Christian life becomes more a standard set of abrupt transitions in status than a developing responsive relationship with God. Early in his middle period Wesley did issue some accounts of Christian salvation that suggest such a series of standard transitions.[5] His later descriptions, however, lay much more emphasis on the gradual nature of salvation and the interrelationship of its different facets.[6] On these mature terms, he saw Christian life as a continuing journey into increasing depths of "grace upon grace."[7]

A second connotation of the Reformed version of the *ordo salutis* that limits the appropriateness of this term for expressing Wesley's soteriology results from their doctrine of perseverance: the possibility of regression is played down. In particular, Reformed scholastics argue that a person's justification is instantaneously complete and irreversible, it cannot be endangered by lack of subsequent growth in holiness.[8] Wesley's contrary conviction comes through clearly in the practical-theological context of the 1770 conference with his preachers:

> Does not talking, without proper caution, of a justified or sanctified state, tend to mislead [people]; almost naturally leading them to trust in what was done in one moment? Whereas we are every moment pleasing or displeasing to God, according to our works; according to the whole of our present inward tempers and outward behavior.[9]

The third problem with "Order of Salvation" for denoting Wesley's soteriology is precisely its scholastic overtones. The Protestant scholastics were concerned to produce a definitive description of the Christian faith that carefully distinguished and rationally organized its various component parts. While Wesley scholars agree (and some lament) that he produced no such account of the whole of Christian theology, many suggest that a more limited version of this project lies behind his numerous clarifications concerning the area of soteriology. Accordingly, they consolidate—and debate organizations of—these scattered reflections, in order to systematize the Wesleyan *ordo salutis* and defend it against its Western alternatives.[10] These projects have evoked some vigorous critiques recently, which argue that they are misreading Wesley's situation-related pastoral distinctions as technical scholastic distinctions.[11] There is much truth to this charge. While Wesley did argue for several fairly specific distinctions regarding human salvation, most of his considerations of these issues were sparked by, and sought to address, the pastoral needs of his revival movement, not the expectations of scholastic method. Talk of a Wesleyan *ordo salutis* connotes the contrary.

Thus, the topic of this chapter is Wesley's *via salutis.* For him the following aspects of human salvation were not an ordered series of discrete states, they are intertwined facets of an overarching purpose—our gradual recovery of the holiness that God has always intended for us.

Regeneration

There are few places where the typical Reformed *ordo salutis* differs more from Wesley's understanding of the Way of Salvation than the issue of regeneration. Reformed Scholastics equated regeneration in the most proper sense with the New Birth, which is God's gracious gift that instantaneously and irresistibly transforms sinners from their fallen state—in which they are incapable of good works, faith, or even repentance—to a new life where repentance and faith are natural. Some of them also used "regeneration" in a secondary sense to refer to the recovery of actual holiness within this New Life. The crucial point (on which all agreed) was that the New Birth must take place before humans can respond to God in any way, and that folk like Wesley who talk of repentance prior to the New Birth are rejecting God's gracious prevenience.[12]

Obviously, Wesley would want to refute this charge. To discern how he might do so, one must consider his understanding of regeneration. His typical definition of being "born again" or regenerated was quite broad: "being inwardly changed by the almighty operation of the Spirit of God; changed from sin to holiness; renewed in the image of him who created us."[13] This definition makes regeneration nearly synonymous with Wesley's therapeutic understanding of salvation per se. While one might appreciate such a synoptic perspective, it is ambiguous. For example, if taken in its strongest sense, it could equate the New Birth and entire sanctification!

Actually, Charles Wesley did tend to identify the New Birth with entire sanctification.[14] By contrast, John's own experience following Aldersgate and his practical-theological involvement in the early revival soon convinced him of the need to distinguish between the New Birth and sanctification—the first being the rejuvenation of our human faculties that accompanies the restored pardoning Presence of God in our lives, while the second is the gradual renewal of our moral nature that is then possible. In other words, the New Birth is only the gate or beginning to sanctification proper.[15] So which of these—New Birth or sanctification—should most properly be identified as "regeneration"? Wesley was convinced that *both* should be, as increasing *degrees* of a larger reality.[16]

The affirmation of degrees of regeneration is central to Wesley's mature soteriology, and to his rejoinder to accusations that he undervalues God's prevenience in salvation. This is because Wesley came to emphasize that there was a crucial degree of regeneration *prior* to the New Birth: the universal nascent regenerating effect of Prevenient Grace.[17] It is only through the benefits of this expression of God's gracious prevenience that anyone can turn to God in repentance and receive the more extensive renewal that comes from a restored pardoning relationship with God. In other words, Wesley affirmed the prevenience of God's regenerating grace as strongly as any Reformed scholastic. His difference from them was that he did not limit this initial grace to the elect, and he stressed that it works co-operantly, for God's grace is *responsible grace.*[18]

To summarize, the mature Wesley became convinced that regeneration is more than simply an initial stage in the "order" of Christian life. It is the crucial facet of God's prevenient empowering realized in intensifying degrees throughout human salvation as a whole. God's rejuvenating work in our lives is a process, even if one that incorporates certain transitions of "grace upon grace."

Awakening

Since salvation is co-operant, if we are even to begin the journey of renewal that God intends for us, we must first become aware of our need for it. Wesley was convinced that most people are not sufficiently conscious of this need. They have repressed the initial overtures of Prevenient Grace to the point that their spiritual senses are asleep (cf. Chapter Three). As such, the initial step for them in any potential healing would be an awakening to their need; for, "none will come to the Physician but they that are sick, and are thoroughly sensible of it."[19] How would such an awakening be effected? Among the common means that Wesley lists are tragedies and natural disasters (awful providences), awakening sermons and conversations, or perhaps a direct conviction by the Holy Spirit.[20] What does this awakening involve? Central to it is removal of one's apathy. We must be convinced of the sinfulness of our words, deeds, and tempers, and of our own helplessness to transform any of these.[21]

On all of these points Wesley remained consistent throughout his life. However, the emphasis he placed on—and purpose he attributed to—awakening underwent a shift which parallels the change noted in Chapter Five concerning assurance.[22] In the early years of the revival John (much more so than Charles) assumed a need to intensify and prolong the anxiety or feeling of helplessness in anyone who did not have a clear assurance of God's personal forgiving Presence.[23] These early methods of preaching for awakening have invited strong criticisms, some of which compare Wesley's techniques to brain-washing and specifically charge that he used fear of damnation as the main motive for conversion.[24] Wesley's defenders have responded that he did not preach on damnation as much as this caricature suggests, or use fear of punishment and reward of heaven as the main motives for conversion.[25]

Wesley's defenders have a point, *if* it is placed in temporal perspective. During the first years of the revival Wesley did indeed stress fear of punishment and reward of heaven as primary motives for salvation.[26] Of course, he also assumed at that time that conversion brought immediate deliverance from all fear. As he increasingly recognized the possibility of justifying relationship with God prior to full assurance, fear ceased to be merely a goad to salvation. Those who feared God and sought to work righteousness (i.e., "servants of God") were seen as already making the initial transition to restored pardoning relationship with God. On such terms the prolonging of despair became irresponsible and John curtailed it.[27] This is not to say that he stopped preaching awakening sermons, or on the subjects of death and hell. He could still do so on occasion, when he encountered an audience that he believed needed to be awakened, but no longer with the same severity or the consuming purpose of driving them to despair.[28] Moreover, the late Wesley placed increasing value on the more subtle *positive* ways that the overtures of Prevenient Grace awaken sinners.[29]

It might be noted in passing that a side-effect of Wesley's early form of awakening sermons were several instances of such extraordinary behavior as outcries, convulsions, and trances—particularly between 1739-44.[30] These caused some personal consternation to the typically staid Rev. Wesley and opened him to accusations of "enthusiasm." He defended himself in a variety of ways: by stressing that God can act as God pleases, by arguing that God often chooses to use such symptoms in the early stages of revivals, and sometimes by suggesting that Satan might be mimicking true phenomena to discredit his movement.[31]

The other point that should be observed about the facet of awakening is that there is a sense in which the mature Wesley broadened its application to the whole of Christian life, similar to what we noted earlier on regeneration. This point is best seen by considering a transition in his comments on the relative place of preaching the law and preaching the gospel. During the first decade of the revival his operating assumption was that the unconverted should be addressed primarily with the law while the gospel of God's loving acceptance would dominate sermons for believers.[32] With the growing conflict with antinomian understandings of the Christian life he placed more stress on the importance of the third use of the law *in* Christian life. He made more explicit the need to preach *both* law and gospel all along the Way of Salvation.[33] The result of this adjustment was a contextualized model of proclamation that recognized the need for continual awakenings to remaining sin within the Christian life, not simply an initial awakening to begin this life.[34]

Repentance

The facet of awakening is closely connected to that of repentance in Wesley's understanding of salvation. This is most obvious in his common equation of repentance with "knowing oneself as a sinner."[35] In essence, repentance is our personal *acknowledgement* of our spiritual need, as we are awakened to it by the Spirit. Of course, such simple definitions do not fare well in the intricacies of Western soteriological debate. More important, they do not adequately cover the numerous situational differences of human life. That is why Wesley found it necessary in the practical-theological shepherding of his Methodist movement to suggest distinctions within the general facet of repentance. Two overlapping distinctions emerged in particular, focusing on different issues: the status of repentance *prior* to justifying faith, and the need for repentance *within* the Christian life.[36]

Repentance prior *to Justification/New Birth*

Wesley's first suggested distinction regarding repentance grew out of his struggle in the early revival period to strike an authentic balance between the divergent emphases of "faith alone" and "holy living." On the one hand, as was discussed in Chapter Six, his retrieval of the theme of repentance prior to justifying faith brought charges from some elements of the revival that he was basing salvation on human works rather than faith *alone*. On the other hand, Anglican opponents of the revival accused Wesley of siding with the quietists—by unduly restricting repentance merely to conviction of sin, as contrasted with the broader meaning that is common in Scripture and Anglican liturgy of an actual change of life.[37]

Caught in this bind, Wesley groped for a way to preserve the characteristic tension of his orienting concern. He turned to a distinction between two aspects of repentance, reflected in the bi-part definition in his *Dictionary*: "a thorough conviction of sin, an entire change of heart and life." The first aspect of repentance was carefully defined in purely passive terms—as simple recognition of our sinfulness and helplessness. Moreover, Wesley stressed that this conviction was a *gift* of God. The key point is that it was only this aspect of repentance that he placed prior to faith in Christ. In this way he hoped to make clear that repentance prior to justification was not a human initiative but a response to God's gracious prevenience in awakening.[38] Of course, Wesley would not see this response as automatic. We must receive God's awakening overtures through a sincere desire to cease doing evil and to allow God's transforming work in our lives. As we do so, the second aspect of repentance begins—namely, repentance in the broader biblical and liturgical sense of an entire change of heart and life.[39]

It does not appear that this proposed distinction satisfied many of Wesley's evangelical critics that his conception of repentance prior to justifying faith escaped works-righteousness.[40] Even so, the debate shifted more toward the second aspect of repentance as the Methodist revival moved into its third decade. In Wesley's terms this second aspect was essentially equivalent with the progressive transformation of our life through the Christian journey. As he became increasingly aware, many in the Reformed tradition preferred to confine repentance (in its most proper sense) to the inception of the Christian life. They were uncomfortable with the apparent implication of Wesley's second aspect that there was a continuing necessity of repentance *within* the Christian life. They held that one's justification atoned for both past and future sins, hence there was technically no further need for "saving" repentance.[41]

Given Wesley's bi-part definition, one might expect that he placed great emphasis on repentance within the Christian life. In reality, it was not a prominent theme in the earliest years of the revival. To understand why, we need to trace his fluctuating assumptions about the place of sin in the lives of believers.

Excursus: Wesley on Sin in Believers

There are few issues on which Wesley's views underwent more revisions than that of the residual presence of sin in a Christian's life. This ongoing process of revision was not due to fickleness but to Wesley's persistent practical-theological reflection on the possibilities and dynamics of God's *responsible grace.*

The early Wesley never tired of encouraging believers to undertake the spiritual disciplines that would lead them unto "perfection." At the same time, when pressed about this possibility his response was that Christians should ultimately hope for sincerity, not absolute perfection—for even the Apostle Paul had perfection, at best, only in the sense of victory over voluntary breaches of known laws, and likely only over *habitual* breaches of such laws (trusting God's forgiveness for occasional transgressions).[42]

As was suggested in Chapter Six, Wesley appropriated a near reversal of this early qualification in the events surrounding Aldersgate. From this point on he would reject any proposed contrast between habitual sinning and occasional transgressions, considering them mere attempts to rationalize continued sinning in the Christian life.[43] His statements immediately following Aldersgate went much further—not only would there be no habitual sins or individual acts of willful sin in real believers following the New Birth, there would not even be sinful desires! The most he would allow was that there might remain some involuntary infirmities, but these were not properly "sins."[44]

As one might imagine, this exacting expectation quickly became a center of debate within the Methodist movement.[45] In response, Wesley soon narrowed his original claim to assert only the absence of "outward sins"—whether habitual or sporadic—from the lives of new believers, now conceding that sinful thoughts and tempers (i.e. "inward sin") would remain.[46] His practical-theological concern led to increasing insistence on this point in the context of the perfectionist controversy of the early 1760's. The hasty unwarranted claims of some to perfection drove him to issue the sermon "On Sin in Believers," which vigorously rejected the suggestion that inward sin (i.e., distorted passions, affections, or tempers) is immediately removed from believers at justification, declaring it contrary to Scripture, Christian experience, and tradition. New believers may indeed be delivered from the guilt and controlling power of sin, but not its being (inclination).[47]

Of course, this limitation of claimed deliverance to only outward sins was not a sufficient response to Wesley's critics. An accusation raised against the very sermon which introduced it was that he presented the "miracle-working power of the Spirit" as rendering new Christians *incapable* of outward sin. Given his assumption of the co-operant nature of grace this was not likely what Wesley intended. In dialogue with his accusers it became clear that he was simply maintaining that God's saving grace is sufficient that believers *need* not sin, *if* they remain responsive to it.[48] Subsequent sermons were more careful to make explicit this connection between a new believer's freedom from outward sin and his or her continuance in God's grace.[49]

The assumed possibility of falling is evident in the middle Wesley's claim that new believers are not guilty for *feeling* the inclinations of inward sin that remains in them, only for *yielding* to it.[50] What is not clear is how he could separate so neatly between inward sin and outward sin during this period. This is particularly puzzling in light of the role that he attributed to tempers in motivating and orienting human action. How could those who have not yet been delivered from evil tempers prevent any of these from finding expression in their outward actions? The response that Wesley would likely offer is that they are given "power to keep down all inward sin."[51] Yet, a more troubling connotation lurks within some of his discussions from this period; namely, that there are no cases of Christians who allow their inner sin to find expression in their actions, because they *cease* to be Christian at that instant. That is, in his concern to avoid antinomianism, Wesley was verging on Donatism![52]

The wisdom of the classic sermon on "The Scripture Way of Salvation" (which epitomizes the mature Wesley) shines through at precisely this point. In this sermon Wesley warns how easily those who experience the

New Birth can be temporarily misled into believing that all sin is gone. They soon come to realize that this is not the case, that sin remains in their hearts. Moreover, precisely because it remains in their hearts it cleaves *as well* to their words and actions (i.e., outer sin), such that even the best of these is a mixture of good and evil. Lest this recognition of remaining sin drive the believer to despair, Wesley now emphasizes that repentance and forgiveness of sin can take place *within* the Christian life as well as at its beginning. Characteristically, he adds that this recognition of remaining sin can be a positive thing if it keeps us from resting content until we attain the full promise of God: Christian Perfection.[53]

Wesley's understanding of Christian Perfection will be detailed below. For now I would simply note that he relocated here the major benefit which he had removed from the New Birth—namely, deliverance from the sinful inclinations that lead to outward sin. As shall be shown however, he nuanced even this claim by amplifying his distinction between sins and infirmities. While those who enjoy Christian Perfection may find freedom from sin "properly so-called," they will struggle with the human infirmities resulting from the Fall until their Glorification.

Repentance within the Christian Life

Given his fundamental convictions, Wesley's progressive acknowledgement of sin remaining in believer's lives and cleaving to their actions after the New Birth inclined him to place increasing emphasis on the proper, indeed *essential*, place for repentance within the Christian life. The discomfort of many evangelical friends with this theme required that he offer an explanation of how this repentance differed from initial justifying repentance.

The earlier distinction between repentance as our acknowledgment of need and as our subsequent transformation of life was not sufficient for the present purpose, because it was precisely our lack of (or failures in) subsequent transformation that called for repentance within the Christian life. Accordingly, Wesley's direct comparisons of initial justifying repentance with repentance within the Christian life define *both* primarily in terms of the acknowledgement of our sins and our inherent helplessness to change. Their difference lies not in this focus on conviction but in the presence or absence of a contemporaneous awareness of God's pardon. Repentance prior to justifying faith is characterized as a conviction that is not initially mitigated by a sense of forgiveness. By contrast, repentance within the Christian life retains the confidence of one's renewed pardoning relationship with God, even as it acknowledges continuing sin and need.[54] Through this integral connection between our recognition of need and our awareness of God's pardoning *grace*, repentance within the Christian life revitalizes our continuing *responsible* growth in holiness.

This explains the role for repentance after the New Birth. What about following entire sanctification? Even here Wesley defended a continuing place for repentance. While he did not consider the infirmities that remain in the entirely sanctified person to be sins "properly so-called," he still insisted that they stood under the benefit of Christ's atonement and should be included in the prayer of the liturgy "Forgive us our trespasses."[55] In addition, with his eventual surrender of the hope that Christian Perfection was irremissible, Wesley admitted the possibility of even sin "properly so-called" by one who had been entirely sanctified—and the resultant need for repentance if one was to be restored. Thus, no matter how much transformation we may experience along our Christian journey, we never outgrow our need for the facet of repentance as part of the Way of Salvation.

Justification[56]

If repentance is acknowledgement of our profound spiritual need, justification is one facet of God's gracious provision for that need. In his *Dictionary*, which was geared to simple definitions, Wesley defined justification in one word: forgiveness. His most common definition in other works was not much more extensive, equating justification with being pardoned and received into God's favor.[57]

The simplicity of such definitions can be misleading, suggesting a dearth of careful consideration behind them. This was hardly the case! Wesley was being very purposeful in what he *omitted* from his definition. For example, from shortly after Aldersgate he was mindful to circumscribe justification from sanctification, in order to preclude expectations of immediate recovery of full Christ-likeness such as the English Moravians had earlier inclined him toward.[58] Likewise, he was deliberately omitting from his typical definition of justification an aspect that was standard in other Protestant definitions—the imputation of Christ's active righteousness to the believer—because he was convinced that this aspect encouraged antinomianism. The best way to enlighten Wesley's understanding of justification, then, is to consider the practical-theological debates lying beneath his carefully restricted definition.

Pardoned by the Merits of Christ

Consider first the debate over the relationship of Christ's Atonement to our justification. This issue had become a hotly contested line of demarcation in Western soteriology by Wesley's day.[59] In responding to the Reformers the Council of Trent had analyzed justification in terms of the scholastic principle of levels of causation, contending that (1) the Final Cause (purpose/goal) of justification was the glory of God, (2) the Efficient Cause (stimulus) was God's gracious mercy, (3) the Meritorious Cause (i.e., "price" of atonement) was Christ's passion and death, (4) the Instrumental Cause (our means of appropriation) was baptism, and (5) the Formal Cause was the justice that God infused in believers. It was on the issue of Formal Cause that subsequent debate focused. A Formal Cause is basically a regular principle that explains the occurrence of the effect under consideration (for example, the "laws of nature" that became the subject of attention in the early modern period are a slight transmutation of Formal Cause). In identifying "infused righteousness" as the Formal Cause of justification then, Trent was trying to explain how God could justly accept sinners. Their solution was that God actively infused righteousness into believers, so that they could then be declared righteous without violating the principle of justice.

Reformed theologians, particularly Puritans like William Perkins, quickly (and incorrectly[60]) charged Trent with basing justification on inherent human righteousness. They insisted that Christ's death was the *Formal* (rather than Meritorious) Cause of our justification. For them, Christ's death epitomized his perfect active and passive righteousness which are both imputed to us in justification. Christ's death does not "earn" our salvation, it *is* our salvation—by imputation. A clear consequence of such a switch, of course, is the affirmation of predestination and limited atonement (or Universalism); Formal Causes apply consistently to all relevant cases, so all for whom Christ died would necessarily be justified.

Given its unique situation, Anglicanism witnessed advocates for both positions in this debate, and several variations between them. If a dominant position emerged from this interaction it was a *via media* that identified the Formal Cause of justification as God's covenantal principle to have mercy on all who believe. This allowed them to retain the role of Christ's death as a Meritorious Cause. Of course, it also left room for some suggestion that the act of believing was a human "work."[61]

The early Wesley was aware of this mediating Anglican position and appears to have endorsed it.[62] While he tried to avoid disputing the topic with his Calvinist associates in the earliest years of the revival, he eventually found it necessary to do so. His practical-theological problem was that the idea of Christ's imputed righteousness could so easily be understood in an antinomian sense—exempting us from any expectation of obedience in the Christian life. Thus by 1746, in a sermon on justification by faith, Wesley was explicitly criticizing the idea that God is *deceived* into considering sinners innocent because of the (imputed) innocence of Christ.[63]

As was noted in Chapter Four, he became progressively more public in his rejection of the Substitutionary Justification understanding of the Atonement, with its imputation of Christ's active righteousness or obedience to believers.

In contrast with the substitutionary understanding of justification, Wesley emphasized simply the merciful grace of God (the Formal Cause) that pardons us by virtue of the merits of Christ (the Meritorious Cause).[64] Thereby he could insist that we never "earn" or "deserve" God's pardoning favor, without calling into question our *responsibility* to respond to God's *gracious* acceptance.[65]

Pardoned in order *to Participate (Adoption)*

The mention of responsibility in the previous sentence could conjure fears of self-reliance in responding to God's pardon, until one remembers that Wesley always understood Divine grace to convey both *pardon* and *power.* In this regard, the most significant rejoinder that he ever made to claims about the imputation of Christ's righteousness to believers was his insistence that the Bible much more clearly affirms that believers recover a capacity of spiritual life, are reunited with God, and made partakers of the Divine Nature.[66] As Outler has nicely phrased it, Wesley's characteristic emphasis was that we are pardoned *in order to participate.*[67] In light of the discussion of uncreated grace in Chapter Three, it should be obvious that the result of such restored participation would be our empowerment for the recovery of the Likeness of God. Thus, we have here another expression of Wesley's distinctive integration of the central Western juridical concern into his more basic therapeutic emphasis (most characteristic of Eastern Orthodoxy).[68]

This may be the best place to consider the topic of adoption. Wesley did not explicitly invoke the category of "adoption" often.[69] When he did, it was usually more in connection with faith than with justification per se. The reason for this is (as was shown in Chapter Five) that he came to define faith as a divine evidence or assurance of God's pardoning love for us. On these terms, to enjoy faith is to receive the Spirit of Adoption.[70] Accordingly, "adoption" is one of Wesley's designations for restored participation in God. It is the initiation of Christianity's central goal: "restoring the due relations between God and [humanity], by uniting for ever the tender Father and the grateful, obedient [child]."[71] The importance of this is that our grateful perception of our reconciling Father is precisely what invites and empowers us to be obedient children.[72]

Justification and Sanctification

Wesley's connection between pardon and participation just noted lands us within another arena of Western soteriological debates—the relationship between justification and sanctification. In essence, Trent's emphasis on infused righteousness as the Formal Cause of justification made sanctification (our actual moral transformation) the prerequisite of justification (our acceptance by God as righteous). Luther and his descendants argued that any level of sanctification we might enjoy must instead follow and grow out of our justification. At the same time, the Lutheran scholastics' openness to the possibility that a regenerated person might not persevere allowed some connection between subsequent sanctification and continued justification.[73] By contrast, Calvin and the later Reformed scholastics not only insisted that sanctification followed our justification as a response to God's gift, they also kept it fundamentally distinct from justification—such that lack of growth in personal holiness could not endanger the justification of the elect.[74]

Once again, within all its diversity, Anglicanism sought a *via media* between these options. This is evident already in the Articles where the affirmation that we are justified by faith rather than our works (Article XI) is followed immediately by a stress that works which spring from faith are pleasing to God (Article XII). In 1690 George Bull (later a bishop) proposed in his *Harmonia Apostolica* a way of maintaining this mediating position that became very influential. He distinguished between our initial justification, which is *not* dependent upon prior holiness of life, and our final justification, which *is* dependent upon our justifying faith bearing fruit in sanctification.

The early Wesley found that the competing views in his Anglican training left him confused concerning the relation of justification and sanctification. However, following his stronger appropriation of justification by faith alone in 1738 he became convinced of the error of Trent's suggestion that sanctification must precede our justification.[75] Indeed, in the early years of the revival (his most "Reformed" phase) he vigorously rejected even Bull's attempt to create a more subtle connection between our sanctification and our justification.[76] As was detailed in Chapter Six, the middle Wesley became increasingly uncomfortable with those who played off justification against sanctification. Ironically, in seeking an adequate way to protect against this he ended up reclaiming something like Bull's distinction between initial and final justification, now—thirty years later—calling Bull a "Great Light of the Christian Church."[77]

First Justification and the New Birth

From 1739 Wesley was careful to distinguish justification from sanctification. His distinctions had levels of precision, depending on the situation at issue. For example, his most general distinction was between justification as a *relative* (i.e., relational) change in which God declares us forgiven by virtue of Christ, and sanctification as a *real* change in which the Spirit renews our fallen nature. His usual point in making this distinction was to insist that Christian salvation involves more than simply imputed righteousness, God's deepest desire is our actual moral renovation.[78]

When the temporal connection of justification and sanctification became the specific issue more precise definitions were called for. For example, his general definition often affirmed justification and sanctification to be contemporaneous. The intent of this affirmation was to protect against any suggestion of works-righteousness, where we would be expected to renovate our character *prior* to God's pardoning and empowering acceptance. But this affirmation could also suggest that our spiritual renewal will take place instantaneously at the moment of our justification. It was shown in the previous chapter that Wesley had to work through such a false expectation himself in the events surrounding Aldersgate. We also noted above that his eventual resolution of the turmoil this created came with the clarification of a difference between the momentary restoration of our responsive participation in God's pardoning grace (the New Birth) and the subsequent gradual therapeutic transformation of our lives (sanctification proper). With this distinction Wesley could stress that it is not entire sanctification that is contemporaneous with our justification, it is only the New Birth—the gate to the further regenerating work of the Spirit in our lives.[79]

While Wesley believed that justification and the New Birth occur at the same time, he often attributed logical (or *theo*logical) priority to justification.[80] Though this might seem a small point, it is central to his co-operant view of salvation. When the New Birth is given priority, whether temporal or logical, the implication (as Reformed theology has always understood) is unconditional election—only those who are previously reborn can exercise justifying faith. For Wesley it was instead our responsiveness to God's offer of restored pardoning relationship (Justification) that induces the gracious further regeneration of our human faculties in the New Birth. Of course, this response itself is co-operant because it is enabled by the prior rudimentary regeneration of Prevenient Grace. As we respond, the New Birth commences further co-operant transformation of our lives, empowered by sanctifying grace.

Final Justification and Sanctification Proper

It is possible to stress the theological priority of justification in a way that renders sanctification unnecessary, rather than empowering it. Given the dynamics of the evangelical movement in eighteenth-century England, Wesley frequently encountered such one-sided emphases on justification as imputed righteousness in his pastoral shepherding of his Methodist people. His orienting concern naturally constrained him to resist these positions. It was in this effort that he reclaimed the distinction between initial and final justification.[81]

Initial justification accompanies our earliest acknowledgement of God's pardoning love for us. Wesley assumed that this justification is immediately salvific in the sense that if we were to die directly thereafter we would enjoy eternal salvation.[82] However, he emphasized that in normal situations our initial justifying faith is intended to be salvific in the broader sense of activating our deliverance from the power as well as the guilt of sin.[83] It is in this connection that he once responded to the claim that our justification is complete from the first moment we believe by arguing instead that "there may be as many degrees in the favour as in the image of God."[84] His apparent point in this obscure aphorism is that, while initial justification constitutes the crucial base line of our entry into pardoning Divine acceptance, God desires and smiles upon our subsequent recovery of the Likeness of God. Indeed, if we *purposefully* neglect such transformation of our sinful lives following our initial justification, Wesley was convinced that we would eventually forfeit pardoning relationship with God. Unless we later returned to responsive relationship, we would not enjoy God's eschatological pardoning acceptance (i.e. final justification).[85] In this sense, while initial justification is not contingent upon prior sanctification, final justification is![86]

Surely the strongest form that Wesley ever put this point was in the infamous *Minutes* of the 1770 Conference.[87] Here he argued—in direct rebuttal to antinomian uses of the idea of imputed righteousness—that both inner and outer good works are required in our Christian life "as a condition" of final salvation. These *Minutes* created an immediate furor of accusations about a return to works-righteousness and led to a final split between the Calvinist and Wesleyan branches of the Methodist revival. They have caused consternation to Wesley scholars ever since.[88] Yet, while the specific terms chosen might be questioned, the general point in the 1770 *Minutes* is surely consistent with Wesley's larger theological convictions. He was not asserting that we must "merit" final salvation, or that our works are a *pre*requisite to God's acceptance. He was simply insisting that God's *gracious* empowering acceptance enhances rather than replaces our responsive and *responsible* growth in holiness.[89]

The Dynamic Tension

What can we conclude from the preceding discussion about the place of justification in Wesley's soteriology? To begin with, while he highly valued God's justifying grace, Wesley did not allow justification to dominate his understanding of salvation to the degree that is common among so many Western Christians, particularly Protestants.[90] For him the greatest value of justification was precisely its contribution to the higher goal of sanctification—our recovery of the Likeness of God. In this way, as Míguez Bonino has put it, Wesley actually transposed the Protestant theme of "justification by grace through faith" into one of "sanctification by grace through faith."[91]

But while the late Wesley could thus boast that Methodists "do not think or speak of justification so as to supersede sanctification," he was quick to add that "neither do they think or speak of sanctification so as to supersede justification."[92] As the earlier discussion of sin in believers noted, however extensive our spiritual transformation might be in this life, we still stand in need of God's gracious pardon. Therefore even our final justification will always be by grace.

In short, Wesley's understanding of the relation of justification and sanctification expressed structurally his fundamental conviction about the inherent relation of *grace* and *responsibility*: our very capacity for growth in Christ-likeness (New Birth) is contingent upon God's gracious pardoning prevenience (initial justification), while the continuance of God's acceptance (final justification) becomes contingent upon our responsive growth in Christ-likeness (sanctification). Justification is not a stage that we leave behind to enter sanctification, it is a facet of God's saving grace permeating the entire Way of Salvation.

Faith

In moving to the topic of faith we touch a juncture where the *ordo salutis* in Lutheran and Reformed Scholasticism often diverged. The specific issue at question was the relation between justification and faith. In the developed Lutheran *ordo salutis* discussion of faith was placed before justification, because faith was seen as the means of justification—those who have faith will be justified and those who do not, will not. Implicit in this order is the possible assumption of contingency in the matter of who will exercise faith. Reformed scholastics, of course, desired no room for such assumptions! They placed God's sovereign declaration of justification first—so that it effects faith (in the elect), rather than faith effecting justification.[93]

Wesley's understanding of the Way of Salvation is difficult to place within this Protestant debate, because his focal concern was different. His most fundamental question was not juridical in nature but therapeutic; that is, his central question was neither "What is the (contingent) means to justification?" nor "Who can be justified?" but "How can we recover the moral Image of God in our lives?" He became increasingly convinced of the crucial role that justification played in this recovery, restoring our participation in God's gracious empowering Presence. In this sense he was inclined to view justification as effecting faith, more than vice versa.

Faith and Justification

The topic of faith was covered in some detail in Chapter Five; only the main conclusions need to be recapped here. The mature Wesley came to understand faith as more than the "subjective" aspects of assent to spiritual truths or trust in God's love. In the most primal sense it was the "objective" *evidence* of God's pardoning love for us—i.e., the Spirit's Witness of our justification and adoption. It is this Witness that evokes within us, in response, a personal trust and confidence in God's specific gracious forgiveness and acceptance.[94]

Thus, faith is not portrayed by Wesley as an inherent human ability which we exercise in order to attain justified status. It is much more properly a "gift" that is graciously evoked in our lives by the pardoning overtures of God. And yet, since we are dealing with a God of *responsible grace,* faith is not evoked irresistibly by the Witness of the Spirit. We may refuse or neglect the gift. It is in precisely this sense—and this sense only—that subjective faith (i.e., our responsive trust of God's gift) was identified by Wesley as a necessary "condition" of our justification.[95]

The other major conclusion from Chapter Five that needs to be reiterated here is Wesley's eventual judgment that God's pardoning grace is effectual in our lives from the most nascent degree of our responsiveness, even the mere inclination to fear God and work righteousness (i.e., the faith of a servant). It is an initial response to God's pardoning overtures that is the necessary condition of our justification, not subjective certainty of that pardon.

Faith and Repentance

The discussion of faith so far should have suggested some parallels to repentance. Just as repentance is essentially our co-operant response to God's gracious prevenience in conviction or Awakening, faith is our response to God's prevenience in the Witness of the Spirit. Beyond these parallels in their nature, Wesley believed that there was an inherent connection between faith and repentance in the Way of Salvation. One early way that he tried to express this point was the suggestion that repentance is itself a "low species of faith" that is naturally followed by justifying faith.[96] This suggestion is problematic, and fortunately does not recur in Wesley's later works.[97] As it stands, it applies only to initial justification and implies that repentance is a "stage" of faith that we move *beyond* in justifying faith!

As was shown above, the mature Wesley became increasingly convinced of the importance of repentance within the Christian life. In this context he also came to a much more dynamic understanding of the relationship of repentance and faith. He now saw them as "answering one another" throughout our Christian journey: in repentance we repeatedly acknowledge our failure and inherent helplessness, while in faith we progressively receive God's gracious forgiveness and empowerment. Repentance forces us to confess that apart from God's grace we can do nothing, while faith assures us that, "I can do all things through Christ strengthening me."[98] In this dialogue is echoed the dynamic tension of God's *responsible grace.*

Faith Working By Love

So much for the relationship of the facet of faith to those of justification and repentance, what about its relationship to sanctification? In its most basic sense Wesley understood sanctification to be "such a love of God and [others] as produces all inward and outward holiness." He was convinced that this type of love could only spring "from a conviction wrought in us by the Holy Ghost of the pardoning love of God."[99] Indeed, there is no theme more common or central to Wesley's theology than that the only thing which can enable us to love God and others is an assurance that God loves us.[100] He specifically added that whereas he once thought that we *should* love God solely because of God's inherent perfections, he became convinced that we *can* love God only in response to our awareness of God's salvific love for us.[101]

What this entails is that faith (understood "objectively" as the evidence of God's pardoning love for us) is the motivating power of our sanctification. Importantly, this connection of faith to sanctification also implies that faith is not the epitome of Christian religion, as many Protestants are inclined to claim. For Wesley faith is the handmaid of love.[102] Indeed, he devoted an entire sermon (on 1 Corinthians 13:1-3) to the argument that love is more excellent than faith or hope, concluding that "If I have not the faith that worketh by love, that produces love to God and all [humankind], I am not in the narrow way which leadeth to life."[103]

When this orientation of faith to love is connected with Wesley's insistence that true Christian love rejoices to obey God's commands,[104] we are led directly into the perennial Western debate over the relationship of faith and good works. Protestants have constantly worried that Roman Catholics elevate good works at the expense of faith, while Roman Catholics have feared that the Protestant emphasis on "faith alone" undercuts good works rather than being productive of them. Wesley's mature comments touching on this issue reflect sensitivity to the concerns of both groups:

> We are doubtless 'justified by faith'. This is the corner-stone of the whole Christian building. . . . But [the works of the law] are an immediate fruit of that faith whereby we are justified. So that if good works do not follow our faith, even all inward and outward holiness, it is plain our faith is nothing worth; we are yet in our sins.[105]

Perhaps the most constructive contribution that Wesley has to offer to this characteristic Western debate lies in the way his nuanced understanding of faith allows him to avoid both horns of the supposed dilemma. This is best seen by considering his favorite text for preaching on faith and good works: "faith working by love" (Galatians 5:6).[106] This phrase itself became a focus of exegetical debate in Western soteriology. Roman Catholic theology continued the majority practice of the Early Church in translating ἐνεργουμένη as a passive participle, with the implication that our faith is generated (worked) through our repeated acts of love or virtue. Protestant exegetes argued instead that the participle was active in voice, insisting that Paul's point was that faith is the energizing source of any acts of real love. While Wesley endorsed the Protestant exegesis of this specific text, his broader perspective on the relation of faith and love integrated aspects of both interpretive traditions. On the one hand, he affirmed that Christian faith (understood subjectively) is evoked in us by an act of love; though it was God's ultimate act of love for us, not our acts of love. On the other hand, he was equally convinced that faith (understood "objectively" as the Witness of the Spirit) is the energizing source of our dispositions and acts of love for God and others.

Thus for Wesley, faith both "is worked" by love and "works" by love. One might question whether he stretched the meaning of faith too broadly in making this point; however, his basic intention is clear. It is also biblical—he was trying to preserve the inherent connection of faith and works that is embodied in the canonical dialogue between James and Paul. He consistently refused to play these two off against each other, arguing that the faith which Paul affirms is one that truly effects new lives of love while the faith which James condemns is one that does not.[107]

On reflection it should be clear that Wesley's orienting concern is emerging again in this debate—it is God's *gracious* prevenience that effects faith in us, while our co-operant *responsibility* takes expression in loving deeds. On comparison one will also find broad parallels between Wesley's interconnection of faith and love and Eastern Christian understandings of the relation of grace and works.[108]

Sanctification

We come now to the facet of the Way of Salvation known as sanctification. For Wesley this facet is an inseparable compliment to justification; namely, our present deliverance by God from the *plague* of sin, not just from its *penalty.*[109]

Wesley's actual use of the term "sanctification" fluctuated. In the early years of the revival it was often used to denote the ideal that he would later call "Christian Perfection." Eventually he recognized that the Bible usually used the term in a broader sense covering the entire therapeutic transformation of our lives following the New Birth, leading him to add qualifiers like "entire" when referring specifically to his conception of the ideal expression of sanctification in this life.[110] By corollary, as Lindström has argued, it is a significant distortion of Wesley's understanding of sanctification to confine discussion to this more specific aspect, as many have done.[111] Therefore Christian Perfection (i.e., *entire* sanctification) will be considered here within the broader context of the other dimensions of sanctification.

New Birth

The foundational dimension of the facet of sanctification for Wesley is the New Birth. This dimension addresses the question of our *ability* for recovering any holiness in our sin-distorted lives. We have touched on this dimension frequently in previous discussions, so I need only summarize the crucial points.

The most crucial point is Wesley's insistence that any such ability is *graciously restored.* If we strive after holiness with only our own fallen (dis)abilities, we will find ourselves crying out with Paul "Oh wretched one that I am! Who will deliver me from this body of death?"[112] If instead we welcome and embrace the initial overtures of Divine grace we will not only find pardon for our failures, we will experience a deeper[113] rejuvenation of our human faculties through the restored Presence of the Holy Spirit, such that we can proceed in the responsive journey of the Way of Salvation.

It is necessary to touch on an issue concerning Christian Perfection at this point. One common description of entire sanctification in early Methodist circles—that found scattered reference in John's correspondence and in one sermon—was the "Second Blessing" or the second time that God speaks to a Christian's soul.[114] The obvious question that such language raises is the nature of our "First Blessing" and its relation to this subsequent event. Some of Wesley's prominent associates turned to the situation of Jesus' disciples before and after Pentecost for an analogy in this regard: the disciples were already blessed with pardoning relationship to Jesus (i.e., justification), but they received the further blessing of the empowering Presence of the Holy Spirit only at Pentecost. On this model justified Christians awaiting entire sanctification would be lacking the "baptism of the Holy Spirit" in their lives![115] Such a conception is full of exegetical and theological difficulties. The important point to see is that Wesley was aware of these and specifically rejected this identification of entire sanctification with the baptism of the Holy Spirit.[116] For him the "baptism" of the Spirit's renewed Presence comes at the beginning of our Christian life, and provides the indispensable empowerment for our growth in holiness all along the Way of Salvation—including the potential attainment of Christian Perfection. Of course, this raises another issue that Wesley scholars have hotly debated: What relationship did Wesley assume between the New Birth and baptism? I will reserve that issue for Chapter Eight.

The other point that bears reiteration concerning Wesley's understanding of the New Birth is that he became intensely aware following Aldersgate that this rejuvenation is indeed only our *birth* as Christians. What it brings is a new vitality and responsiveness to God, not completed transformation of our sin-distorted character into the likeness of God. Such transformation is realized by our subsequent responsible participation in God's sanctifying grace.

"Growth in Grace"

The second dimension of sanctification evident in Wesley's mature descriptions is precisely our gradual spiritual recovery of the likeness of God following the New Birth. As was noted earlier, Wesley recognized that this gradual transformation was the primary referent of biblical uses of "sanctification." Among his own common terms for this process were "growth in grace" and "going on from grace to grace."

When experience disabused him of the English Moravians' suggestion that absolute perfection is bestowed with the New Birth, Wesley opted for a conception of Christian life (common in early Greek writers) on analogy with human maturation—from New Birth, through childhood, and on to adulthood.[117] An obvious assumption of this conception is the centrality of growth to the Christian life. Indeed now, drawing on Macarius, Wesley argued against the claim that new believers are immediately delivered from all sin on the specific grounds that this suggestion undercuts our acknowledgement of remaining *need*, which is prerequisite to our growth in sanctifying grace.[118]

It is important to recognize how integral this emphasis on growth is to Wesley's overall conception of sanctification. To understand why it is so integral one must recall his steadfast refusal to confine the holiness that God desires to restore in our lives to external matters such as avoiding evil or doing good. Indeed, Wesley's chief complaint against the models of Christian life which he discerned among his fellow Anglican clergy was that too many of them restricted themselves to such outward matters, neglecting the affectional dimension of human life.[119] By contrast, his own typical definition of sanctification consistently placed primary emphasis on this "inward" dimension, described in such terms as "the life of God in the [human] soul, a participation of the divine nature, the mind that was in Christ, or the renewal of our heart after the image of [God who] created us."[120]

The discussion in Chapter Three of the central role of the tempers in Wesley's understanding of human actions should make clear that his focus on this inward dimension of sanctification was not intended as a devaluation of external acts of obedience, but an explanation of their possibility! Far from dismissing the importance of holiness in our actions, Wesley framed his General Rules for continuance in the Methodist societies around the threefold exhortation to do no harm, to do all the good one could, and to attend the ordinances of grace.[121] At the same time, he recognized that such holy actions do not occur "naturally" or by simple desire—they are motivated and patterned by holy tempers.[122] That is why he identified the essential goal of all true religion as the recovery of holy tempers.[123] From these recovered tempers would flow holiness of thought, word, and action.

Wesley's appreciation for the holy tempers as the ground of holy actions lies behind his identification of love as the sum of Christian sanctification.[124] He considered love to be the central temper from which all other tempers (and eventual actions) follow. As he once put it, "From the true love of God and [other humans] directly flows every Christian grace, every holy and happy temper. And from these springs uniform holiness of conversation."[125] Thus, he could summarize God's desire for our sanctification as a desire for love to become the constant ruling temper of our soul.[126]

Another way that Wesley expressed his conviction of the vital contribution of tempers to actions was that holiness must become a "habitual disposition of the heart" if it is to be manifest in our lives.[127] Such language warrants the recent claim of several Wesley scholars that his model of Christian life is best portrayed in terms of a "character ethic" or "virtue ethic," where meaningful moral actions are grounded in nurtured inclinations (character dispositions).[128] The crucial implication of this claim is that Wesley's "holy tempers" would not be simply infused by God's sanctifying grace in instantaneous completeness; they would be developing realities, strengthened and shaped by our *responsible* participation in the empowering *grace* of God. The dimension of a gradual "growth in grace" would be integral to sanctification.

I share the conviction that the gradual, graciously-empowered formation of Christ-like character is at the center of Wesley's conception of sanctification. Indeed this assumption is basic to Chapter Eight, in which Wesley's understanding of and emphasis on the means of grace is probed—to illuminate *how* one responsibly grows in grace. This makes it important to consider the apparent counterevidence that Wesley argued on at least two occasions for God's ability to infuse holy habits or tempers instantaneously! The context in both cases was a defense of the possibility of Adam's creation with consummate moral character, against "deist" objectors. One could speculate what Wesley's response might have been if he had been aware of Irenaeus' alternative to this typical Western position (cf. Chapter Three). Even so, his actual counterarguments are revealing. In one case it becomes clear that his real concern was to insist that holy tempers are not simply the product of human efforts—they are effected by God's Spirit at work in us![129] Given his understanding of the co-operant nature of the Spirit's work, this point could be preserved without insisting that holy tempers are infused instantaneously mature. In the other case his rejoinder related to the possibility of Christian Perfection, which concerns the fulfillment of holy tempers in the Christian life rather than their nascent appearance.[130] As such, it would appear that Wesley's more characteristic position is the one found in noncontroversial settings, where he speaks of God implanting in believers only the "seed" of every virtue (i.e., that restored ability to develop holy tempers which the New Birth conveys).[131] These seeds then develop as we "grow in grace."[132]

Christian Perfection

With Wesley's therapeutic focus it is natural that a central question for him should become "How much deliverance from the plague of sin can we hope for in this life?" His distinctive answer—for which he is most widely known (and often criticized)—was that there is a possibility of *entire* sanctification, or Christian Perfection, in this life. Indeed, he claimed near the end of his life that propagation of this very teaching was the chief reason for which God had raised up the Methodists.[133]

Whether or not the propagation of Christian Perfection was the providential purpose of the early Methodists, it was certainly the cause of some of their most vigorous debates, both between themselves and with opponents. Among the charges made against Wesley were that his various claims on this topic were confusing, erratic, or simply incompatible. He responded in 1766 with *A Plain Account of Christian Perfection, as Believed and Taught by the Rev. Mr. John Wesley, From the Year 1725 to the Year 1765*, in which he quoted extensively from earlier works, arguing that his views had been entirely consistent (at least since 1738).[134] As in other cases we have seen, this claim must be taken with some reserve. There was indeed much more continuity in Wesley's teaching than his opponents allowed. However, there had also been more fluctuation of emphasis and nuancing of certain assertions than he was prone to admit overtly in the midst of controversy. Gaining chronological perspective on these moves should help to clarify the unifying themes of Wesley's doctrine of Christian Perfection.

Chronological Perspectives[135]

Wesley read avidly in "spiritual" writers through his university years. His scope was ecumenically broad, ranging among early Greek monastics, Roman Catholic mystics, Pietists, Puritans, and Anglican "holy living" divines. From this diverse group came such varying emphases concerning personal Christian holiness as the importance of spiritual disciplines, the primacy of proper intentions, the role of the affections, and the necessity of participation in God.[136] Much deeper than variation on such specifics, assumptions about any "perfection" in holiness among these writers tended to separate into alternative camps: (1) a dynamic conception of perfection as ever-increasing maturity (like the goal τελειότης in early Greek writers), and (2) a static conception of perfection as unsurpassable attainment (epitomized in the Latin model of Adam as perfectus est).[137] When a word is used in such different ways within the same arena ambiguity is inevitable.

This ambiguity is reflected in the early Wesley's own writings. On the one side, he championed pursuit of recovered holiness through spiritual disciplines, typically describing the goal to which one aspired via these means as "perfection" or "perfect love."[138] On the other side, he simultaneously issued denials of any "perfect" holiness in this life.[139] It is also clear in Wesley's early writings that his aspirations toward holiness were driven by a desire for assurance that he was in a state of acceptance with God (i.e., justification).[140] These two characteristics set the stage for the subsequent developments in his understanding of Christian Perfection.

The events of 1738 convinced Wesley that justification precedes and graciously empowers sanctification, rather than being based upon it. At the same time he was initially led to expect (and to proclaim) that justifying faith would bring instantaneous moral perfection, manifest in consummate affections and sinless actions (although involuntary "infirmities" would remain).[141] Personal experience soon persuaded Wesley that such transformation did not automatically accompany justification. His initial adjustment (in the notorious preface to the 1740 collection of *Hymns and Sacred Poems*) was to distinguish the New Birth from a subsequent time when Christians are born of God "in the full sense;" i.e., an event in which God's grace instantaneously frees us from all sin—not only sinful actions, but also corrupt tempers, evil thoughts, and even temptation![142]

Criticism of this preface was immediate and strong, prompting Wesley to publish a didactic sermon on Christian Perfection in 1741.[143] The central concern of this sermon was to sort out the ambiguity about the meaning of "perfection" noted earlier—by stressing the ways in which Christians can never be perfect in this life, while specifying the sense in which he believed that they may be. On the negative side Wesley stipulated that Christians, however mature they might become in this life, do not approach the absolute perfections of omniscience, infallibility, or omnipotence. Their understanding remains limited, their judgment subject to error (in matters not essential for salvation), and their actions limited by the (nonmoral) infirmities of the present human condition. As a tacit correction of the 1740 preface, Wesley also now conceded that no Christian should expect to be wholly free from temptation in this life.[144] Finally, he argued that the holiness properly called Christian Perfection was open to continual increase, specifically rejecting any notion of a static or absolute perfection in holiness.

There was little controversial in Wesley's disclaimers. The same cannot be said for his positive explication of Christian Perfection. He built this explication around a newly emphasized distinction between new-born and adult or "mature" Christians. His central claim was that even new-born Christians are perfect in the sense of being free from the necessity of committing any outward sin, while only mature Christians are perfect in the further sense of being free from evil thoughts and tempers. He recognized that some Scripture passages appear to contradict his claim about new-born Christians, and he devoted a large portion of his sermon to "clarifying" interpretations of these texts. His exegesis is not always convincing. More important—given his assumption that our moral actions flow from our tempers—he did not explain how a new-born Christian could avoid all outward sin while retaining evil tempers.[145] Whatever its difficulties, the claim that the New Birth brings freedom from the necessity of outward sin while Christian Perfection provides the further deliverance from all inward sin (i.e., sinful tempers) characterized Wesley's comments through the next two decades.[146] Another characteristic claim of this period related to the question of when Christian Perfection might be realized. The early Wesley had primarily stressed aspiring for holiness, whether it came before death or not. With the affirmation of God's prevenience throughout the Way of Salvation in 1738, the question of attaining Christian Perfection became one of the sufficiency of Divine grace rather than the ability of human effort.[147] On such terms, even though he might concede that the majority of Christians do not in fact attain entire sanctification until the point of death, the middle Wesley became a strong proponent of the possibility of such attainment *during* this life.[148]

This is not to say that he encouraged expectation that one's passage from the New Birth to Perfection would be brief or effortless. Quite the contrary, he specifically deleted such possible suggestions from works that he reprinted.[149] Given his strong conception of Christian Perfection (which included at this point the assumption that no one entirely sanctified would thereafter fall again into sin) Wesley proved rather leery of claims to attainment through the early years of the revival.[150] He worried that the claimants might be settling for something less than full renewal in the image of God.[151] He also feared that encouraging expectation of quick passage might induce some to discount God's existing gracious work in their lives, out of disappointment over their lack of full deliverance. His characteristic pastoral advice in the latter regard was to "buy up every opportunity of growing in grace" while waiting for God's good time in providing the full deliverance from sinful inclinations.[152]

Built into this pastoral advice is a strong positive valuation of growth in grace. Indeed, the middle Wesley specifically protested the accusation that the Methodists viewed gradual growth in grace as a "low or imperfect" way of Christian conversion, insisting that any form of Christian experience that leads to true renewal is to be highly valued.[153] Drawing on this point, I would suggest that while the middle Wesley always defended the present possibility of Christian Perfection, during the first two decades of the revival he actually placed primary emphasis on "pressing toward the goal" in anticipation of God's further gracious work.[154]

Toward the end of that second decade a subtle—but significant—shift in this emphasis emerged. One of the signal evidences is a 1757 letter in which Wesley now maintained that it was *un*common for God to withhold perfect love until just before death, and urged his correspondent to seek it earnestly so that she might find it speedily![155] The topic of Christian Perfection was central to the next two conferences with his preachers, with Wesley answering objections to the possibility of *immediate* attainment and urging his preachers to proclaim it more explicitly.[156] Over the next few years it became characteristic for Wesley to qualify discussions of gradual growth with an insistence that God could "cut short the work" (because time is relative to God), and sometimes to issue mild rebukes to suggestions that he emphasize the gradual work of grace more.[157] Whenever he came across apparent examples of a Divine "short-cut," they were highlighted in his *Journal*.[158] He was much less suspicious of such claims than in the first two decades of the revival, even of claims to being justified and sanctified simultaneously![159] His suspicion turned instead toward the negative effect of any suggestion that people could expect entire sanctification only at the point of death.[160]

How should we account for this increased emphasis on seeking Christian Perfection *now*? It is conceivable that it was simply a natural result of the maturing of the Methodist movement; i.e., in the early decades the focus was on converting unbelievers, now the consuming need was challenging these converts unto the fullest realization of salvation.[161] It is also likely that a surge in apocalyptic expectation in the latter half of the 1750's heightened the concern to attain Christian Perfection prior to Christ's return.[162] But might there have been more involved? It is significant that shortly before the shift becomes evident Wesley was responding to a charge that his earlier descriptions of Christian Perfection were "setting the mark too high" and causing needless fears.[163] While he argued at the time that it was better to chance this than risk setting his standard too low, the charge must have sparked some serious reflection on Wesley's part. Within a few years *he* was the one criticizing the danger of defining Christian Perfection in such exalted terms that one effectively renounced its possible attainment.[164] It would appear that Wesley became convinced around 1760 that he had been operating for the past several years with some assumptions about Christian Perfection that were too exacting, and that these were hindering his people from experiencing the blessing which he believed Scripture promised them. Therefore he began to modify these earlier assumptions.

One such modification of earlier assumptions about Christian Perfection is very clear: between 1757 and 1761 Wesley reversed his previous claim that one entirely sanctified could not fall again into sin.[165] This reversal correlated directly with his greater willingness to entertain claims of having attained Christian Perfection. Previously he had been hesitant to encourage or validate such claims lest a subsequent return to sin prove that they had not been true in the first place. Now he could accept them at face value, attributing later disappointments to a regrettable loss of the authentic blessing.[166] Likewise, earlier reticence could ease sufficiently for him to encourage those who had attained it to declare it freely to other believers who had not, as an incitement for them to seek after the same blessing.[167]

The other possible relevant modification of assumptions is admittedly less obvious. I see it signaled in Wesley's introduction at the 1759 conference of the sophisticated distinction between sin "properly-so-called" as "voluntary transgressions of a known law," and infirmities as "involuntary transgressions of a divine law, known or unknown." While Wesley had long been aware of such definitions and had presented major elements of them in earlier works, this detailed articulation in the specific context of entire sanctification was new and appears to be connected with a subtle change of emphasis from earlier discussions.[168]

We noted that Wesley turned to a distinction between outward sin and inward sin to specify the deliverance which awaited entire sanctification. In the same context he differentiated inward sin from "infirmities," which he characterized as inward or outward imperfections of human obedience that were not of a moral nature.[169] To understand this second differentiation one needs to recall Wesley's identification of "will" and "affections" (see Chapter Three). Potential imperfections of obedience flowing from wrong affections would be "voluntary" because they are effected by the will and subject to our liberty; hence, they would be sinful.[170] By contrast, infirmities are nonmoral because they are involuntary; i.e., they are not subject to our concurrence (liberty).[171] But what qualifies as an infirmity? Prior to 1759 Wesley spent more time criticizing suggested criteria than offering his own. Significantly, some of the earlier rejected possibilities bear strong resemblance to his own later sophisticated distinction!

For example, in 1741 Wesley vigorously protested the use of "infirmities" to classify any action that was known to be sinful through God's revelation in Scripture, without ever invoking the qualification that this revelation be "known" *to* the individual. He could do so because he assumed that Christians simply would not lack knowledge of any obedience necessary for salvation.[172] By 1756 this assumption had faded and he now readily concurred with the qualification that we are only accountable for violations of laws that are personally known to us (or for culpable ignorance).[173] The clearer concession of this qualification would obviously have made it easier to affirm deliverance from sin "properly-so-called."

In this very same 1756 context, however, Wesley refused to limit our culpability to only "willful" sin. This is not the first time he had made this point. Indeed, in 1746 he had argued that we are as accountable for our unwilling sins as for willing ones.[174] It is not entirely clear what he deemed so unacceptable in these earlier suggestions of restricting our culpability to "willful sin," though he probably understood this phrase to imply more than simply voluntary sin. Perhaps he was rejecting the suggestion that acts are sinful only if they are assertive or obstinate. Or, maybe he feared that emphasis on willful sin too easily allowed "pious intentions" to disallow culpability for our actions.[175] Whatever the case, it is significant that criticisms of restriction to willful sin disappear following the 1759 conference. Instead, Wesley now repeatedly insists—particularly in pastoral contexts—that the freedom bestowed in Christian Perfection is limited not only to breaches of *known* laws of God, but to specifically *voluntary* violations of those laws.[176] In response to concerns that this delimitation of sin "properly-so-called" was not explicit in biblical law codes, Wesley also elaborated a distinction between the absolute perfection required of Adam before the debilitating effects of sin and the more limited post-Fall expectations of fulfilling the law of love.[177] Whatever one thinks of the exegetical basis for these moves, it seems fair to say that the period following 1759 shows an increase in Wesley's concern to qualify the type of sin from which Christian Perfection brings deliverance.

As such qualifications concerning Christian Perfection began finding their way into the Methodist societies, there was a dramatic increase in instances of people claiming entire sanctification, as witnessed in Wesley's *Journal*.[178] With all of this increased interest in the present attainment of Christian Perfection there was also increased possibility of abuse or "enthusiasm." This possibility became a sad reality in the early 1760's, particularly in the London society under the influence of Thomas Maxfield and George Bell. In essence, Maxfield and Bell separated Wesley's increased emphasis on present attainment from his earlier teachings about sanctification. They proclaimed a perfection that was instantaneously attained by the simple affirmation "I believe," forfeiting any role for responsible growth prior to this event. They portrayed this perfection as "angelic" or absolute, such that there was no need for growth after the event, or for the continuing atoning work of Christ. Finally, they suggested that only those who are entirely sanctified enjoy eschatological salvation—effectively debasing justification.[179] Wesley reacted quickly to each of these points. He reiterated the central role of responsible growth to sanctification as a whole.[180] He vigorously denied any doctrine of "angelic" perfection, repeating his earlier teachings on the limiting impact of infirmities on our holiness and the continual place for growth in holiness during this life.[181] Finally, he insisted that Christian Perfection is not a required qualification for salvation, only a desirable blessing that God makes available for Christians in this life.[182]

In effect, Wesley's practical-theological response to the perfectionist controversy was to integrate his recently increased emphasis on the possibility of present attainment of Christian Perfection into his earlier stress on the responsibility of gradual growth in sanctification.[183] That is, he worked to establish a much closer connection between the potential of God's sanctifying *grace* and the place of our *responsible* participation in that grace. Once again the balance of his mature perspective is captured in the 1765 sermon "The Scripture Way of Salvation." On the one hand he continued to insist here that Christian Perfection is a present possibility because it is God's gift, not our accomplishment. On the other hand he emphasized that the way to "wait" for this gift is by repentance and growth through the means of grace, so there is no danger of antinomianism or enthusiasm should the gift not come immediately.[184]

Not all of Wesley's associates were convinced that he had found the proper balance of emphases, even in his most mature thought. The most interesting dissenter—and surely the most personally painful for John—was his brother Charles.[185] Charles refused to adopt the modified assumptions about entire sanctification which had made it possible for John to stress its present attainment. Indeed, in reaction to John's modifications and the subsequent perfectionist controversy, Charles moved towards a progressively *more* exacting expectation of what Christian Perfection involved. A predictable result was that Charles remained profoundly (at times, despairingly) aware of his lack of the perfection he desired. He became increasingly convinced that it could be attained only at death. By corollary, he was progressively more critical of John's heightened emphasis on expecting present attainment. Charles worried that urging novices on too fast caused pride and the loss of their real grace. We should instead lead them in "the usual course of saving grace, which step by step by grace proceeds."[186]

John never succeeded in convincing Charles to place more emphasis on the immediate possibility of entire sanctification, nor did Charles persuade John to surrender this possibility.[187] John did quietly reappropriate the earlier assumption that entire sanctification was "generally" attained only at death, but he refused to restrict it to that moment.[188] Despite his many concerns about enthusiastic and antinomian misuses, he remained convinced that Scripture presented Christian Perfection as available in this life.[189] Thus, to the end of his ministry he would exhort his followers to "go on to perfection," as something that they could attain *now*.[190]

Such were the changing emphases and occasional clarifications in Wesley's discussions of Christian Perfection. Hopefully it has become clear that they were not simply random. There is a pattern to them, even if not the spiraling integration that was suggested concerning justification by faith in Chapter Six. Here the movement was more dialectical, as Wesley's shepherding of the revival tested the tension in his orienting concern. His confidence in God's *grace* as the empowering source of our sanctification pushed him to emphasize the possibilities of our transformation; yet, his conviction that God's grace empowers us co-operantly, preserving our *responsibility*, constrained him to uphold a realism about these possibilities.

Central Themes

With these chronological perspectives in mind we are in a good position to summarize the central themes in Wesley's understanding of Christian Perfection, those unifying threads that provided consistency through the various emphases and clarifications.

One of Wesley's most characteristic descriptions of those who have attained Christian Perfection was that they are now adult—or *mature*—Christians.[191] From this developmental language we can sense that his basic conception of "perfection" in the Christian life was dynamic in nature. Indeed, he once defined the adjective "entire" applied to perfection as enjoying "as high a degree of holiness as is consistent with [one's] present state of pilgrimage."[192] As this definition suggests, Wesley assumed that growth in holiness would continue *within* Christian Perfection and not just before it. Several Eastern Orthodox theologians have found this dynamic conception of perfection reminiscent of their understanding of *theosis*.[193] By contrast, it has puzzled many of Wesley's Western colleagues, who operate out of the alternative static conception of perfection.[194]

For Wesley then, Christian Perfection was that dynamic level of maturity within the process of sanctification characteristic of "adult" Christian life. We noted earlier that he considered love to be the essence of Christian life. Thus, when he wanted to be more specific he would define Christian Perfection as "the humble, gentle, patient love of God, and our neighbor, ruling our tempers, words, and actions."[195] It is important to note that love is not only said to be present, it is *ruling*. God's love is shed abroad in the lives of all Christians, awakening their responsive love for God and others. But this love is weak, sporadic, and offset by contrary affections in new believers. In the lives of the entirely sanctified Wesley maintained that it rules "to the point that there is no mixture of any contrary affections—all is peace and harmony."[196]

Affections contrary to love would, of course, be "inward sin." Wesley believed that this inward sin was overcome in entire sanctification. In a few instances he described this overcoming as a "rooting out" or "destruction" of inward sin.[197] He may have taken such language from Macarius.[198] Whatever its source, it was problematic.[199] The particular problem that Wesley became quite sensitive to was that talk of the "destruction" of sinful affections could connote the impossibility of their return. By contrast, as we have seen, he came to recognize the sad reality that sinful affections (and resulting outward sins) may reemerge in lives that had been ruled by love. How could one express the benefits of Christian Perfection without obscuring this fact? When Wesley was pressed directly on this point he offered the alternative account that in the soul of an entirely sanctified person holy tempers (i.e., enduring affections) are *presently* reigning to the point of "driving out" opposing tempers (although these may return).[200] As Umphrey Lee has put it, this alternative distills the central claim of Wesley's conception of Christian Perfection to "the expulsive power of a new affection."[201]

It is important to remember that Wesley's focus on affections in describing Christian Perfection was not intended as an alternative to actions. He understood that acts of love flow from a heart of love. Yet, he also recognized that ignorance, mistakes, and other human frailties often distort the passage from affection to action.[202] It was in this sense that he tired of the debate over whether Christian Perfection was "sinless."[203] He did indeed believe that it consisted in holy tempers, but not that it was characterized by infallible expression of those affections in actions.

Perhaps the best way to summarize what we have seen so far is to say that Wesley was convinced that the Christian life did not have to remain a life of continual struggle. He believed that both Scripture and Christian tradition attested that God's loving grace can transform our lives to the point where our own love for God and others becomes a "natural" response.[204] Christians can aspire to take on the disposition of Christ, and live out that disposition within the constraints of our human infirmities.[205] To deny this possibility would be to deny the sufficiency of God's empowering grace—to make the power of sin greater than that of grace.[206]

Wesley was hardly the first to affirm such a possible degree of transformation in Christian life. So where did the real controversy about his doctrine of Christian Perfection lie? It was in his further claim that the specific transition to this dynamic level of Christian life is an instantaneous one, however much gradual growth there may be before or after it. Why did Wesley insist on this point? In the course of debates over the issue he conceded that Scripture did not explicitly affirm that the transition to Christian Perfection was instantaneous. On the other hand, it did not deny it. On Wesley's methodological assumptions (see Chapter One), when Scripture was not explicit on a matter experience plays a more important role in deciding the issue. Thus he defended his claim most often by appeal to examples among his Methodist people.[207] And yet, when he was pressed it becomes clear that these examples were not the original basis for his claim. He was preaching the possibility of instantaneous attainment before there were many examples and considered the emergence of these examples as confirmation for his preaching.[208] So what motivated the earlier preaching itself? As was argued in Chapter Six, I believe that the answer is to be found in his frequent conjunction of affirmation of the instantaneous nature of entire sanctification with reminders that it is a gift of God's grace. Wesley apparently assumed that an instantaneous transition at some point was a logical implication of Christian Perfection's status as effected by Divine grace, not simply a human achievement.

This brings us finally to the question of how one would know that one had experienced the transition to Christian Perfection. Wesley's early comments on this deal with it from a third-party perspective, stressing the need to evaluate the claimant's tempers, words, and actions over a period of at least two or three years![209] Eventually he postulated that there was a distinct Witness of the Spirit which convinces us of our entire sanctification, parallel to the provision for justification.[210] There is little biblical warrant for this postulate, and it has been debated in Methodist circles from Wesley's day to the present.[211] Its importance to Wesley might best be understood by recalling how the Witness of the Spirit to justification functioned to preserve the prevenience of God in salvation. I would suggest that the Spirit's Witness to our entire sanctification was another counter for Wesley to any suggestion of self-salvation. This Witness would have signified yet a deeper level of participation in God's uncreated grace, empowering us for the continuing life of growth in holiness within Christian Perfection. Importantly, the parallel between the Spirit's Witness to justification and to entire sanctification carries over even to Wesley's eventual concession that psychological certainty is not a prerequisite to the Spirit's work in sanctification.[212]

Summary

If I have devoted more attention to Christian Perfection than to the other dimensions of sanctification, it is because this dimension has been subject to so much debate. To balance this I would conclude by adding my voice to those who argue that Wesley's most fundamental concern lay on the theme of gradual growth in holiness.[213] To put it in the form of a thesis, while the affirmation of the possibility of entire sanctification may have been *distinctive* of Wesley, the conception of sanctification (as a whole) as the progressive journey in responsive co-operation with God's empowering grace was most *characteristic* of Wesley. Once again we are dealing more with a facet of the Way of Salvation than a step in the Order of Salvation.

The best evidence for this claim is the way in which Wesley surrounded the gracious possibility of Christian Perfection with the theme of responsible growth. To those who are acutely aware that they do not yet enjoy the full deliverance from inward sin that he has proclaimed is available, his admonition is that they not let the thought of receiving more grace tomorrow detract them from growing in grace today.[214] To any who may have attained it, he immediately gives the warning not to rest there but to continue growing in grace.[215] And to his preachers who are hesitant to proclaim the possibility of Christian Perfection, the mature Wesley's most consistent justification was that a sincere conviction of this possibility will nurture growth in grace among their hearers, whether they ever attain it or not![216]

If conviction of the further *possibilities* of God's grace is conducive to growth, so is a recognition of our continuing *need* for growth. In this regard it is extremely important that both of Wesley's early manifestos on Christian Perfection were prefaced by the maxim "not as though I had already attained."[217] While his focal goal in these pieces was to qualify the type of Christian Perfection which he believed *could* be attained, his qualifications also insured that it was a Perfection that would always have more *to be* attained. "Not as Though I had already Attained" is an appropriate motto indeed for all who are seeking and claiming the type of Christian Perfection that Wesley believed could be attained. His clear concern was to preserve a dynamic tension that could celebrate whatever God's *grace* has already made possible in our lives, without relinquishing our *responsibility* to put that grace to work in the new areas that God continually brings to our attention. Perhaps it was this very concern that kept Wesley from ever claiming to have "attained" Christian Perfection himself![218]

Glorification

There is one further dimension to salvation that must be touched on briefly, our deliverance from the very *presence* of sin in the facet of the Way of Salvation known as Glorification.[219] This dimension finds its fullest reality in the eschatological recreation of all things. However, Wesley joined most of the Christian tradition in assuming a conscious intermediate state (paradise) in which we enjoy a penultimate expression of its blessings.

Consistent with his therapeutic emphasis, Wesley stressed the need for Christians to recover the holiness of heart and life which God intends for us before we enter the ultimate state of freedom from the very presence of sin.[220] This does not mean, however, that he limited final justification to those who were entirely sanctified prior to their death. Rather, he was convinced that God would insure that all who are sincerely growing in grace would somehow attain Christian Perfection prior to the eschaton.[221] His most common suggestion was that it would be bestowed at the moment of death on those who had not attained it before.[222] His most interesting suggestion was that those who needed to would continue to "ripen" in paradise while they awaited the final eschaton.[223]

This latter suggestion is intriguing precisely because it brings the gradual dynamic so characteristic of Wesley into the third dimension of salvation. While most Western Christian traditions see paradise as a place of blessed rest where we simply wait for the ultimate state of the New Heavens and the New Earth, Wesley hints that it will be a place for growth in grace. Indeed, he once even suggested that the perfect would grow in grace to all eternity (i.e., beyond paradise)![224] To be sure, this suggestion raises more questions than Wesley ever adequately answered. Would the growth be in greater "moral" conformity to God? How could we need such growth if we are already free from the presence of sin? Might it be instead growth in overcoming the infirmities resulting from sin, so that our holy tempers could find undistorted expression? Or might our future growth involve transformation of our human faculties to a level beyond their original created state?

I will return to questions like these in the discussion of eschatology in Chapter Nine. First we need to consider in a little more detail how Wesley believed growth in grace in *this* life was nurtured and guided.

CHAPTER 8

The Means of Grace and Response

The preceding chapters have emphasized that Wesley considered present human salvation to be fundamentally a gradual therapeutic process that grows out of our responsive participation in God's forgiving and empowering grace. In its most normative sense, salvation appears neither unilaterally nor spontaneously in our lives; it must be progressively empowered and responsibly nurtured along the Way of Salvation. This point leads directly into Wesley's understanding of the "means of grace." The reason for this—as Henry Knight has argued—is that Wesley's vision of the sanctified life was not a universalized or abstract vision, it assumed the specific liturgical, communal, and devotional contexts within which he framed it.[1]

The Role of the Means of Grace in Christian Life

Wesley's interest in the means of grace spanned his life and pervades his writings. He discussed them in a number of contexts, with slightly differing lists in nearly every case. The items included in these lists range from such universal Christian practices as fasting, prayer, eucharist, and devotional readings to more distinctively Methodist practices like class meetings, love feasts, and special rules of holy living.[2]

While some of the specific means of grace that Wesley championed might raise questions, the issue of greater initial interest is his understanding of the role or function of the means of grace in general for Christian life.[3] This issue has been subject to significant debate between the various Christian traditions. The debate has been carried out most vigorously concerning the topic of the sacraments, but the differences apply by analogy to any area where human performances are related to God's gracious work.

The Mediation of Grace

Three major questions intertwine in Western debates over the relationship of sacramental rites to personal salvation, creating differences within Protestantism as well as between Protestants and Roman Catholics. The first of these questions concerns the ability of a spiritual reality like grace to be mediated through physical means or human actions. The classic focus of this question has been the eucharist.[4]

Luther retained and adamantly defended the Early Church (and continuing Roman Catholic) claim that the benefits of Christ are truly present to believers within the physical elements of the eucharist. Zwingli countered just as strongly that this was impossible, for "the flesh profiteth nothing!" He agreed that we should observe the *ordinance* of the Lord's Supper out of obedience to Christ's command, but denied that it mediated grace to the recipient. God provides grace *im*mediately, in response to faith in the Word.[5] While Zwingli's position would have a significant influence on the Radical Reformation, Calvin's mediating alternative was destined to have more impact on subsequent Reformed theology. At the heart of Calvin's alternative was an emphasis on the work of the Spirit.[6] He held that the Spirit indeed conveyed the benefits of Christ through the eucharist, but they were conveyed "spiritually" in the *act* of faithful communing, not "locally" within the elements of communion.

It will be shown later that, in these Western terms, Wesley is most adequately compared to Calvin's position of a "spiritual" mediation of grace through the act of communing. The crucial point to note at this juncture is that Wesley explicitly rejected attempts to substitute a purely spiritual or unmediated communion with Christ for the mediated communion of the Lord's Supper.[7] He insisted that while Christ is the meritorious cause of grace being provided to humanity he is not the efficient cause by which it is conveyed. This efficient cause (or power), in the most proper sense, is the Holy Spirit's Presence.[8] Precisely because of its "uncreated" nature, this Presence is *im*mediately effective even when mediated through means.[9] Thus Wesley had no reservations about encouraging his people to seek God's grace through the various outward signs, words, and actions that God has ordained as "ordinary" channels for conveying saving grace to humanity.[10]

Ordinary and Extraordinary Means of Grace

It is significant that Wesley called the means of grace the *ordinary* channels for conveying grace. This qualifier suggests his position on a second question threaded through the Western debates: How restrictive are the means of grace?

There are two closely related dimensions to this question. The first dimension concerns whether there is an exclusive set of means through which Divine grace is provided. During the medieval period Western Christianity developed a definitive list of seven sacraments, often suggesting that only these official actions were means of grace. An initial aspect of the Reformation period was the criticism and reduction of this official list (largely because of its clerical control of salvation). Before long the Reformers' attention turned in the other direction, arguing that many unofficial human activities (that is, actions not requiring ordination) such as study of Scripture and prayer were also vital means through which God ministers grace to believers.[11]

Wesley was convinced of the effective communication of God's grace through the sacraments of baptism and eucharist, and through means like liturgy and formal prayers that had come to be emphasized in Anglicanism. Yet, like the Reformers (and Eastern Christianity), he refused to confine grace to such official channels.[12] Indeed, one of the central features of the Methodist revival was Wesley's expectation that his people would avail themselves of *both* the traditional means of grace present in Anglican worship and such distinctive means as class meetings, love feasts, and covenant renewal services.

Henry Knight has argued that this dual expectation reflects Wesley's bi-focal concern that his people experience not only the Presence of God (which empowers them) but also the identity or character of God (which provides the pattern for their lives). In Knight's view, Wesley adopted the distinctive Methodist means because these were typically more effective in awakening an openness to God's Presence than the traditional Anglican means, while he relied on those traditional means to provide "objective" descriptions of God's character as a counterbalance to antinomian appropriations of God's Presence.[13] The resonance of this specific balancing of the means of grace with Wesley's larger tension of *responsible grace* should be obvious.

The second dimension involved in the possible restrictive nature of the means of grace concerns their exclusivity as sources of Divine grace: Is grace available *only* through specified means (however broadly identified)? Moreover, is it available only through proper execution of these means? The lines of division on this issue are often surprising. For all its emphasis on the connection between Divine grace and sacramental rites, Roman Catholicism officially concedes that grace can be conveyed apart from means in extraordinary situations (e.g., the "baptism of desire"). By contrast, some groups which deny that "ordinances" actually convey grace to believers give the distinct impression that salvation is strictly limited to those who have submitted to a proper administration of the ordinance of baptism!

Ironically, Wesley's stance on this issue is best captured by comparing two comments that he made about Quakers—who push a Zwinglian perspective to the conclusion of rejecting the practice of physical sacraments. He once exclaimed that he valued the sacraments so highly that he would as soon be a Deist as a Quaker. Yet shortly thereafter he responded to the suggestion that baptism was only salvific when performed in a certain mode by denying that the physical act of baptism itself was absolutely necessary, else "every Quaker must be damned, which I can in no wise believe."[14]

In short, Wesley refused to confine God's grace in *either* direction—whether by excluding it from all created means or by restricting it to certain authorized means.[15] This stance is clearly in keeping with his larger understanding of grace. If grace is the uncreated personal Presence of the Holy Spirit, then while it surely can be mediated through created means (for these are products of God's gracious activity in creation), it need not be confined to such means. Indeed, if Divine *grace* is *responsible*, it must be active in at least its initial universal dimension among those who have no access to specific means like Christian baptism or the study of Scripture.

Effective Means and Requisite Response

This brings us to the third, and most heated, question in the Western debates: What is the relationship between the effectiveness of the means of grace and the presence of human responsiveness (faith)? Protestants have commonly charged that Roman Catholics emphasize the effective power of the sacraments so much that the external rites become intrinsically salvific, apart from the responsive faith of the recipient (a charge most often based on a *mis*understanding of the Roman Catholic teaching that sacraments are effective *ex opere operato*[16]). By contrast Roman Catholics have worried that Protestants stress the contingency of the effectiveness of the rites upon the recipient's faith to the point where the physical sacraments (and perhaps grace itself!) become superfluous to salvation—hinting that groups like the Quakers reveal the logical implication of the Protestant position.

The Anglican attempt to preserve a *via media* resulted again in Western debate being internalized, this time into a tension between "high-church" and "low-church" (or sacramentalist and evangelical) poles. One of the longest-standing Methodist debates is where Wesley fits within this Anglican spectrum. While it is broadly accepted that the early Wesley belonged on the high-church side of the continuum, some scholars contend that his disillusionment leading up to Aldersgate marked a dramatic shift to a low-church position.[17] This argument has proven difficult to carry through, since Wesley's emphasis on the importance of the eucharist and other means of grace reappears within months of Aldersgate in direct response to the extreme stress on "faith alone" among the English Moravians.[18] A few Wesley interpreters have tried to account for these subsequent expressions as mere sacramentalist residue that was inadequately incorporated into his altered evangelical position. Most recent scholars have suggested instead that the mature Wesley integrated sacramentalist and evangelical emphases.[19]

Wesley did indeed develop a creative alternative to the common Western antinomy between (1) the dependence of human responsiveness upon the Divine gracious empowerment conveyed in sacraments, and (2) the prerequisite of human responsiveness to the effectiveness of sacraments. This alternative exemplifies the co-operant tension of *responsible grace.*[20] On the one hand, Wesley rejected as strongly as anyone the (supposed) implication of *ex opere operato* that sacramental rites are effective intrinsically, apart from the responsiveness of the recipient.[21] He constantly reminded folk that rote performance of such actions as regular worship and prayer are not salvific unless one recognizes and responds to God's gracious prevenience expressed through them.[22] On the other hand, while God's grace offered in the sacraments must be responsively received, Wesley was equally convinced that our response-ability is progressively nurtured by this very grace. Thus he repeatedly denounced the folly of those who desire "the end without the means"—i.e., those who expect growth in faith and holiness without regular participation in the means through which God has chosen to convey grace.[23]

Further insight into this co-operant character of sacramental grace may be provided by Wesley's account of the benefits of adult baptism. His discussions of baptism are framed in terms of the definition of a sacrament that he appropriated from the catechism in the *Book of Common Prayer*—the outward and visible sign of an inward and spiritual grace, and a means whereby we receive the same.[24] Among the benefits that Wesley attributed to the inward grace conveyed to adults through the outward sign of baptism are pardon, death to sin, new life unto righteousness, and *faith.*[25] I have highlighted the final benefit because Wesley was equally prone to stress that faith was essential to the due reception of the sacrament of baptism—apart from faith the outward sign would not convey the inward grace.[26] How could faith be both a prerequisite and a benefit of effective baptism for adults? This only makes sense on Wesley's assumption that the grace being offered through baptism (or any other means) itself empowers our responsive reception, without compelling that reception.[27]

Guarantees of Pardon or Means of Healing?

We have been considering Wesley so far in terms of Western debates over the means of grace. It is also instructive to consider him in terms of the concerns that Eastern Orthodoxy raises about Western accounts of the sacraments in general.[28] Basically, Eastern Christians argue that the dominating concern with our need for justification has inclined Western theologians to reduce the sacraments to merely certifications of juridical pardon. They believe that this explains why questions of "validity" have preoccupied Western sacramental theology. Whether it be the initial bestowal of justified status in baptism, or the repeated certification of continued justified status in admission to communion, Western debates have raged over who is qualified to receive the sacrament, who is qualified to bestow it, and what specific procedures are necessary to make it effective. The (in the East's view, inevitable) besetting danger of these debates has been a static and mechanical understanding of sacramental grace.

Of course, the Eastern soteriological focus has equally shaped their understanding of the sacraments. This shape is evident already in Ignatius of Antioch's designation of the eucharist as "the medicine of immortality." As this title suggests, Eastern Christians value the sacraments as central means by which the deifying presence of the Holy Spirit is conveyed for the healing of our sin-diseased nature. Indeed, it is characteristic for discussions of deification to be organized in terms of the sacraments.[29] Yet, since deifying grace *is* the Holy Spirit, Eastern Christians have not been inclined to limit it exclusively to the sacraments. The Spirit can work wherever the Spirit wills. This identification has also allowed the East to be less concerned than the West with defining formal conditions for the efficacy of the sacraments. The Spirit can easily accommodate imperfect human efforts. The failure of healing to accompany participation in the sacraments calls into question not God's efficacious Presence but our sincere response, for grace is co-operant. Moreover, since deification is a process of healing rather than a juridical change in status, the full benefit of the sacraments (and other means of grace) is realized gradually and cumulatively.

One issue of debate between East and West concerning the eucharist can illustrate these differences.[30] Early Christian liturgies for the eucharist reveal a variety of regional emphases. The recitation of the narrative of institution (*anamnesis*), which culminates in "this is my body - this is my blood," was nearly universal. Another common element, particularly in Syriac and Greek liturgies, was the invocation of the Spirit (*epiclesis*) upon the elements and the gathered community. There is little evidence of conflict between these elements in the early sources. By contrast, when medieval Western Christianity moved to an understanding of the mass as a periodic re-presentation of Christ's sacrifice that effects the remission of penalty for sins occurring within the Christian life, the *anamnesis* came to dominate the consecratory prayer (*anaphora*), widely eliminating the *epiclesis*. In particular, the *anamnesis* was identified as the moment of the transformation of the eucharistic elements into the body and blood of Christ, establishing their juridical value as the sacrifice for our recurrent sins. This move reenforced the narrowing of the purpose of eucharistic grace to renewing justification and the conception of this grace as a static "created" reality. Participation in the Lord's Supper became more a matter of having one's pardoned status recertified than of being nourished for Christian growth and living. The correlated pastoral task became insuring that recipients of communion were "worthy" of recertification.

In contrast with these medieval Western developments, Eastern Christian traditions not only retained the *epiclesis* in their eucharistic liturgy, it gradually gained primacy of emphasis (without disparaging the *anamnesis*). This move was in keeping with their valuation of the eucharist as a major Divinely-provided means for conveying "uncreated" deifying grace. Since the Holy Spirit *is* this grace, the invocation of the Spirit's Presence upon the elements and congregation is constitutive of the eucharist's effective power. The stronger emphasis on the Spirit's role also made clear that the purpose of the eucharist was more than just reception of Christ's pardoning benefits, it is intended to empower our gradual recovery of the Likeness of God. On such terms, the fundamental question becomes not whether we are "worthy" to receive this gracious empowerment, but whether we co-operantly receive—or squander—its healing potential.

One indicator of Wesley's sympathies in the differing emphases that we have been considering is his interest in the *epiclesis*, which was a debated topic in Anglicanism of his day.[31] Since none of the continental Reformers had done so, it was an innovation when Thomas Cranmer (in pursuit of a more "primitive" liturgy) added a brief *epiclesis* for the elements to the eucharistic prayer in the first edition (1549) of the *Book of Common Prayer*. Within three years he was forced to remove it, due to a charge that it implied transubstantiation. In time however, the Puritans began to show interest in the *epiclesis*, because of its patristic warrant and its resonance with their Reformed understanding of the sacrament. This may explain why the Prayerbook proposed in 1637 for a possible union of the Churches of England and Scotland restored the 1549 *epiclesis*. It surely explains why the 1644 *Westminster Directory* retained traces of an invocation of the Spirit, and why Richard Baxter's proposed *Reformation of the Liturgy* (1661) included a brief invocation for the elements and an extended invocation of the Spirit upon the recipients. Baxter's proposal was ignored and the 1662 restoration of the *Book of Common Prayer* (which remained in effect through Wesley's life) went back to the 1552 liturgy without the *epiclesis.*

Both John and Charles were influenced during their Oxford days by Puritans like Baxter and by the Manchester Non-Jurors, for whom the restoration of the 1549 *epiclesis* was a vocal cause. The Wesleys' support for this cause became evident in their joint-publication of *Hymns on the Lord's Supper,* which included several hymns of invocation for the Spirit upon the elements and upon the congregation.[32] These hymns were intended to accompany and supplement the Anglican liturgy. It was likely because he could assume their presence that John felt no need to take the controversial step of reinserting an explicit *epiclesis* in the eucharistic prayer when he revised the *Book of Common Prayer* for the American Methodists.[33]

It is important to note that Wesley's support for the *epiclesis* was not arbitrary. It resonates with some of his central theological convictions. For example, while all three "Persons" of the Trinity participate in every Divine work, certain works are more distinctive of each "Person's" economic role.[34] As Chapter Five detailed, Wesley considered the Holy Spirit's distinctive role to be the empowering Presence of Divine grace in our corrupted lives. His practical-theological incorporation of *epiclesis* hymns into the eucharistic setting is thoroughly consistent with this assumption.

This incorporation is also consistent with his conviction that grace (i.e., the Holy Spirit's Presence) bestows *both* pardon and power for healing through all of its manifestations. It was noted that the West's increasing focus on Christ's institution of the Lord's Supper tended to correlate with a narrowing of its benefits to justification. Wesley could never accept such a narrowing. Thus, practical-theological judgment is evident in his selection of Daniel Brevint's *On the Christian Sacrament and Sacrifice* to abridge and include as the preface to *Hymns on the Lord's Supper,* Brevint emphasized that the Lord's Supper bestows both "mercy and the strength to keep mercy," or (as Charles put it to verse) both pardon and grace.[35]

To take the argument one step further, Wesley's interest in the sacraments not only *included* their therapeutic dimension of empowering our recovery of holiness, this dimension was his *dominant* concern—as compared with the more common Western interest in their role as certifications of God's pardon.[36] This relative emphasis is evident in Wesley's mature definition of a sacrament. It was noted previously that he appropriated the definition of a sacrament as "an outward and visible sign of an inward and spiritual grace, and a means whereby we receive the same" from the Anglican catechism. There is one further phrase in the catechism's definition: "and a pledge to assure us thereof." In his 1745 abridgement of Brevint Wesley retained such a claim that the Lord's Supper was an infallible pledge of eschatological salvation.[37] However, he was rapidly becoming uncomfortable with how the slightest suggestion of a juridical guarantee of salvation denied the co-operant nature of grace (and often undercut Christian discipleship).[38] Thus, in subsequent allusions to the catechism's definition of a sacrament he consistently omitted the element of a pledge or guarantee of salvation.[39] He also removed suggestions of this notion when he prepared the Articles of Religion.[40] While Wesley affirmed that sacraments convey present pardon and power, he denied that their mere reception was a guarantee of our eschatological pardon. This latter dimension of salvation is contingent upon our *responsible* participation in the healing process which the Divine *grace* conveyed through the sacraments makes possible.

Nurturing Grace and Patterning Exercises

Wesley's therapeutic focus comes through clearly in his invitation for his people to meditate regularly on the affirmation that Christ "sealed His love with sacraments of grace, to breed and nourish up in us the life of love."[41] The obvious issue that this affirmation raises concerns *how* the sacraments—or means of grace in general—breed and nourish the life of love.[42] There are two major contrasting approaches to explaining this. For some the emphasis is placed on the human dimension of the various means of grace, viewing them as "exercises" that gradually develop Christ-like character. Others focus almost exclusively on the Divine dimension of the means of grace, stressing that they convey the "gift" of God's character-changing power, sometimes with the implication that the change is instantaneous.

The early Wesley's comments on the means of grace place greatest stress on their nature as exercises designed to develop the life of love that God desires from us.[43] Part of the transition to the middle Wesley was the deepened conviction that our love for God and others is possible only in response to God's gracious love for us. The corollary of this conviction was a rejection of any efficacy in the means of grace considered purely from a human dimension. While this corollary inclined some to reject the means of grace entirely, Wesley was not among them. Instead he shifted emphasis to how the means convey God's gracious empowering love to us.[44]

It was not long, however, before Wesley found himself arguing that all who sense a need for further empowering by God's *grace* should wait for it *responsibly*, by faithful participation in the means of grace.[45] As this suggests, his mature perspective on the means of grace integrally connected the two dimensions that we have been considering. On the one hand, he made it quite clear that the main reason for participating in the means of grace was not obedience to Divine command, or the human attempt to craft holy virtues, but the simple fact that we receive through them the forgiving and empowering Presence of God's grace.[46] On the other hand, the mature Wesley also affirmed the value of the means of grace as exercises that nourish the grace given to us. Perhaps the best expression of this is his advice in a 1766 pastoral letter:

> The spark of faith which you have received is of more value than all the world. O cherish it with all your might! Continually stir up the gift that is in you, not only by continuing to hear [God's] word at all opportunities, but by reading, by meditation, and above all by private prayer. Though sometimes it should be a grievous cross, yet bear your cross and it will bear you. . . . Surely His grace is sufficient for you.[47]

This balance which the mature Wesley established between (1) the insistence that empowerment for holiness is an undeserved gift of God's grace conveyed by various means, and (2) the recommendation of these same means as exercises for co-operantly nurturing that holiness, has rightly been identified as the genius of Methodist spirituality.[48] However, it has also proven to be a hard balance for his heirs to maintain. The major reason for this would seem to be that later Methodists have abandoned his holistic psychology. For Wesley Christian holiness was fundamentally a matter of purified and strengthened tempers. As such it was dependent upon God's grace which empowers and purifies one's affections, but it was also integrally related to disciplines which nurture and reshape those affections. When the role of tempers is dropped out (as happened widely in the nineteenth century with the triumph of a "decisionistic" psychology), holiness reduces to either an instantaneous gift of grace or an unreachable human ideal. In either case the value of regular participation in the means of grace becomes questionable—being justified mainly as a matter of duty, if at all.[49]

Means of Sanctifying Grace

It has been argued so far that Wesley understood the means of grace to be practices through which God's pardoning and empowering Presence is truly communicated to us for the healing of our sin-diseased nature, as well as exercises that co-operantly nurture this healing. This point can now be developed further by surveying his distinctive combination and utilization of the various means of grace. In keeping with one of his suggestions, the following survey is organized around the three dimensions of present saving grace: Prevenient Grace, justifying grace, and sanctifying grace.[50]

Since the majority of his pastoral attention was devoted to nurturing growth in holiness among his followers, Wesley's considerations of the means of grace focused predominately on their contribution to sanctification (in the broad sense). When one understands sanctification on Wesley's terms, as a life-long process of healing our sin-distorted affections, there is an obvious need for continually renewing the empowerment for this healing. The other essential requirement is a persistent deepening of our awareness of the deceptive motivations and prejudices remaining in our life, because co-operant healing entails some discernment of that which still needs to be healed.[51] Wesley understood the means of grace to provide for both of these needs. Clarifying how they do so will be central to the following discussion.

The Lord's Supper[52]

Wesley's discussions of the various means of grace reveal no consistent hierarchy. They each play valuable roles in the overall task of nurturing Christian holiness.[53] This admitted, he clearly had a particular appreciation for the contribution of the Lord's Supper to this end. He referred to it as the "grand channel" whereby the grace of the Spirit is conveyed to human souls, and identified partaking communion as the first step in working out our salvation.[54] His personal practice conformed to this valuation. He communed every week if possible (a rarity in his day), and often communed daily in the octave of Easter and the twelve festival days of Christmas. As a result he averaged communing about once every five days through his adult life.[55] This helps explain why he encouraged the American Methodists in 1784 to celebrate the Lord's Supper weekly, and published a sermon for all his people in 1787 on "The Duty of Constant Communion."[56]

Wesley's original assumption was that his Methodists would commune as he did—at the local Anglican church. He firmly believed that the Lord's Supper should be officiated by an ordained elder. Likewise, he understood his movement to be a renewal within Anglicanism, not a competitor to it. Over time this original assumption became problematic. Many came to Methodist societies from non-conformist traditions that did not offer communion as frequently as Wesley recommended. In addition, tensions developed between several societies and local Anglican priests, leading to the Methodists' absence (voluntary or otherwise) from Sunday worship. Precisely because of his valuation of this means of grace, Wesley's response was an increasing acceptance of celebrating the Lord's Supper in society meetings (whenever he or another ordained Methodist preacher was available).[57]

It was to resource these celebrations that John and Charles published *Hymns on the Lord's Supper* in 1745. This introduction of hymns into the communion service was a novelty, which surely enhanced the dimension of joy in the celebration. At the same time, the hymns maintain the general theology and structure of the Anglican liturgy.[58] Part of the reason for this continuity is that the hymns were correlated with Daniel Brevint's *On the Christian Sacrament and Sacrifice,* which John abridged as a preface to the collection. As this case illustrates, Wesley wrote little original on the theology of the eucharist. He was comfortable endorsing the basic Anglican position—as expressed in its standards, by expositors like Brevint, and in his brother's hymns.[59] The conscious level of his endorsement has inclined most Wesley scholars to consider these materials reliable indicators of his convictions about the eucharist.[60] I will draw on them as such in considering his position on several traditional issues.

A good place to start is with the medieval Western suggestion that the mass is a repeated sacrifice for recurrent sin. Wesley appropriated Protestant rejections of this notion, describing the Lord's Supper instead as a commemoration of Christ's sacrifice.[61] However, he meant more by "commemoration" than merely a reminder or memorial. As was noted in Chapter Four, the point of the Atonement for Wesley was that in Christ's sacrifice we are *convinced* of the love of God for us. Celebration of the Lord's Supper is a primary way in which this conviction is initially sparked and recurrently nurtured. To use language which eucharistic theology has favored in recent years, the communion service "re-presents" Christ's once-for-all sacrifice in dramatic display, conveying its salvific power.[62]

The mention of saving power brings us to a second traditional issue: What does reception of the eucharist do for the believer? On this issue the Wesleys stood firmly with their Anglican tradition, insisting that the Lord's Supper was truly a *sacrament* that conveys to believers the gracious gift of Christ. To quote Charles, "Ah, tell us no more the spirit and power of Jesus our God is not to be found in this life-giving food."[63] As we have noted repeatedly, this "life-giving food" would provide not only pardon but also empowerment for our growth in Christian holiness.

But how is this grace conveyed? In *Hymns on the Lord's Supper* the brothers appropriated Brevint's language of the "Real Presence" of Christ in the sacrament.[64] This must be read very carefully. In Roman Catholic and Lutheran settings this language is connected to an affirmation of a change in the "substance" of the eucharistic elements. For Luther it also implied the ubiquity of the body of the risen Christ. Wesley denied both of these notions.[65] Partly he objected to their presumption of deciphering a mystery, but he also feared that they fostered a misplaced interest in the elements per se.[66] In response to similar concerns the initial framers of the Anglican Articles had adopted a "Zwinglian" denial of the Real Presence. In the 1563 revision of the Articles, however, this was purposefully moderated to more characteristically Calvinist language that Christ is present in the Lord's Supper "only after a heavenly and spiritual manner." The mature Wesley's retention of this latter language in his Articles of Religion provides the most reliable context for interpreting any mention that he made of Christ's Real Presence.[67]

The brief phrase in the Anglican Articles was developed by Richard Hooker into a position often called "receptionism," because it relates the Real Presence to the communicant more than to the eucharistic elements. Basically, Hooker held that when one partakes of the sacrament faithfully one participates directly in the Presence of Christ with all of its pardoning and transforming benefits.[68] This position dominated Anglican theology during Wesley's Oxford training. The early Wesley had it reinforced by a recommendation from his mother! With such incentive, is it any wonder that Wesley scholars generally agree that he assumed a "receptionist" understanding of the Presence of Christ in the Lord's Supper?[69]

Actually, the more important contribution that Wesley's mother may have made was to suggest an emphasis on the agency of Holy Spirit as the means by which Christ is present to faithful communicants.[70] At the time, the early Wesley was content simply to affirm that Christ's divinity is united with believers in communion.[71] As his equation of grace with the Presence of the Holy Spirit (and correlated support of the *epiclesis*) matured, he more frequently specified that it was through the Spirit that Christ's benefits are present to faithful participants in the communion service. Thereby he reinforced the "uncreated" nature of sacramental grace—what we encounter in communion is not the static presence of a "benefit" but the pardoning and empowering Presence of a "Person."

A direct implication of the personal quality of eucharistic grace is its co-operant nature—the Spirit (i.e., grace) is always present in the means, but we must responsively welcome this Presence for it to be effective in healing our lives.[72] Full response in such a personal setting is rarely instantaneous, it grows through continuing relationship. Likewise, the healing which our sin-distorted lives require is a long-term project. This is precisely why Wesley encouraged frequent communion! Believers find in each new meal a fresh and deeper encounter with God's empowering love.[73]

We have noted the integral connection between the commemoration of Christ's past sacrifice and its present empowering effect in our lives. The recognition that this present effect is a gradual one provides a ready transition to the future dimension of the Lord's Supper.[74] Not only did the Wesleys recognize this future dimension, it has been argued that they gave more prominence to the eucharist as a celebration of Christ's resurrection and an anticipation of messianic banquet than had been common in the West since the beginning of the Middle Ages![75] Such anticipation of our future full salvation surely provides hope to sustain us within the struggles and disappointments of our present imperfect setting and lives. However, the Wesleys characteristically emphasized an additional function of the anticipatory dimension of the eucharist. The recurrent reminder of full salvation was viewed as an empowering stimulus for further progress along the Way of Salvation. And, the resurrected Christ was seen as the King who guides our journey.[76]

Attention has been focused to this point on how the Lord's Supper conveys *power* for transforming our sin-distorted lives. It also plays an important role in *shaping* that transformation. To understand this role we need simply to note that communion is not an isolated act, it takes place within a liturgical framework. A central aspect of this liturgy is guided reflection on and confession of our sins. The value of this repeated exercise for deepening our awareness of motivations, prejudices, and practices that remain in need of healing should be obvious.[77] The shaping takes the form of a positive role model as well. The closing prayer of the communion service moves from a thanksgiving for Christ's gift in our behalf to an offering of ourselves in grateful response. Wesley's conviction that the demonstration of God's love for us is what enables us to love God and others has been noted several times. In light of this conviction, it was natural that he would give special prominence to this theme of our responsive sacrifice of ourselves.[78] In the Lord's Supper we do not merely accept *gracious* forgiveness from Christ as Priest, we renew our *responsive* allegiance to Christ as King.

Corporate Worship[79]

The reminder of the specific liturgical framework of the Lord's Supper moves us naturally into the larger liturgical setting of corporate Christian worship. Wesley's valuation of this means of grace is expressed most clearly in his response to his followers' questions about the need for attending parish worship in addition to society worship. He struggled to convince them that it was not a matter of duty but of sustenance; liturgical worship provided spiritual nurture that they would abandon at their grave loss.[80]

That this was no opportunistic argument is evidenced by the frequent mention in Wesley's *Journal* of the benefit that he derived from the daily prayer services and the Sunday liturgy.[81]

This argument also makes clear that Wesley's advocacy of parish worship was based more on soteriological than ecclesiastical concerns. Accordingly, as his ability to convince his followers to remain in parish churches waned, his concern to compensate for their loss grew. He progressively introduced components of liturgical worship into meetings of the society. When he did so he had opportunity to institute some changes from traditional Anglican practice (like lay preachers and extemporaneous prayers). A wide variety of such changes were being championed by the various non-Conformist groups of his day. Wesley tended to adopt only those that had proven "edifying" in practice, *and* for which he believed he could find scriptural and "primitive" warrant.[82] The eventual result was a form of worship that bridged between official Anglicanism and the non-Conformists of the eighteenth century.[83] The fact that Wesley had no desire to depart from the enduring Christian liturgical tradition embodied in the Anglican *Book of Common Prayer* is evidenced by his decision simply to adapt this resource when providing a worship guide for the American Methodists after their total severing from Anglican worship.[84]

The *Sunday Service*, then, presents Wesley's mature pattern for weekly liturgical worship. The most striking thing about this pattern is a key change that he made in the Lord's Day liturgy from the *Book of Common Prayer*. To make room for his desired weekly Eucharist, he deleted the extended penitential litany from Sunday prayers (while retaining it for the corporate Wednesday and Friday prayers[85]). This had the laudable practical-theological effect of making Sunday worship more a eucharistic celebration of Christ's resurrection than a solemn time of penance.[86] To be sure, the element of repentance remained in the service, but it was cast more clearly in *response* to the grace of God celebrated in eucharist.

Formal Prayers

With its weekly pattern in mind, attention can turn to Wesley's valuation of the major components of liturgical worship. One component found in every type of Anglican worship was formal prayers. These prayers also occupied most dissenting groups' lists of objections, charging that formal prayers were "dead" prayers. The alternative widely urged by the dissenters was prayer from our spirit and led by the Spirit—i.e., extemporaneous prayer.[87] The early Wesley was shocked by his first encounter with extemporaneous prayer (among some Scottish Presbyterians). However, he soon became convinced that it could have a beneficial role to play as a *supplement* to formal prayers in worship.[88]

I have emphasized "supplement" because the mature Wesley rejected the exclusive use of extemporaneous prayer on practical-theological grounds. Experience had taught him that formal prayers (when personally appropriated) were "substantial food for any who are alive to God." The benefit which he most stressed was their provision for corporate confession, petition, intercession, and thanksgiving.[89] In other words, Wesley feared that use of extemporaneous prayer alone meant forfeiting the "objective" interrogation of our motivations and prejudices that is so crucial for continuing responsible growth in grace.

Scripture Lectionary

Another universal component of liturgical worship is the public reading of Scripture. This component developed of necessity in the Early Church, to insure that Scripture was available to all. The Western reformers—with their stress on Scripture over tradition—enlarged the place of public Scripture reading in services, while stripping it of some traditional associations. The *Book of Common Prayer* is a good example. Its schedule of Scripture readings was detached from the church year and set up on a cycle of continuous readings that provided for one covering of the Old Testament and three of the New Testament (except Revelation) each year. Wesley retained the basic Anglican lectionary guide for Lord's Day worship in the *Sunday Service*.[90] This retention is significant, in light of the frequent criticism of the lectionary by dissenters as stifling the leading of the Spirit in choosing texts for worship. While he never explicitly argued the case, Wesley's alternative concern appears to have been that his people benefit from the empowering and patterning potential of the *whole* of Scripture. To insure this, he continued the systematic cycle of readings.

Church Year

The most evident change that Wesley made from Anglican precedent in the *Sunday Service* was a drastic reduction of "holy days." In particular, he removed all days devoted to saints. He even removed direct mention of Epiphany and Lent (though retaining the corresponding lessons). Part of his agenda was simplicity, structuring the church year around seasons tied directly to Christ—Advent, Easter, and Ascension/Pentecost. As Casto has suggested, another likely practical-theological concern was to maintain that the entire year (like all of life) was to be holy, not just certain designated days.[91] He also may have judged that saint-days fostered a wrong understanding of the contribution of saints to our present Christian life. After all, he had nothing against remembering or giving thanks for the saints per se. Indeed, All-Saints day was one that he observed with personal fondness.[92] But his perspective on the day is clearly expressed in the "Office of the Saints" in *Devotions for Every Day,* which ends in a prayer for God to grant us grace "to imitate them here, and to rejoice with them in Thy kingdom hereafter."[93] Wesley valued the saints as honored exemplars, not intercessors.[94]

Hymns

In many of the dissenting traditions hymns came to replace the liturgy. Wesley was favorably impressed with their use by the Moravians during the voyage to Georgia. Upon arrival he published a *Collection of Psalms and Hymns* for his own congregation's worship.[95] Since current Anglican practice utilized only metrical psalms in worship, this was an innovation on Wesley's part.[96] Once introduced, hymns became integral to Methodist worship, opening and closing every major gathering.[97]

Some have characterized the purpose of this use of hymns as "romantic;" i.e., to allow expression of intense feelings. This claim need not be totally disavowed, since such expression can be an empowering event. However, most scholars of Charles' hymns have argued that he was more concerned to *direct* and *instruct* faith in others than to express his own.[98] A similar concern for instructive impact is evident in John's use of hymns in worship. For example, while he had a high appreciation for organ accompaniment in settings like serving communion, he preferred to sing accapella, lest the meaning of the words be obscured. He rejected complex anthems with overlapping vocals for the same reason.[99]

Wesley's assumption that hymns both empower and shape Christian discipleship is particularly evident in the 1780 *Hymns,* which he structured around the various dimensions of the Way of Salvation. To be sure, this structure could spark a rebuttal that one should organize around the liturgical year rather than the life of the believer, to provide an objective pattern for Christian life. The actual content of the hymns should allay this fear. Moreover, one must remember that this was only *one* collection of hymns, designed specifically for society worship. The Wesleys kept several other collections in publication related to the Christian seasons and liturgical worship.[100]

Sermon

In keeping with Reformation emphases, the sermon had become an integral component of the Anglican liturgy. If anything, Wesley would make it more so. To understand the role of the sermon within worship, however, one must observe his distinction between field preaching and pastoral preaching.[101] This distinction involves more than setting. Field preaching is characterized by a dominant evangelistic purpose of awakening general audiences to their spiritual need. Pastoral preaching was focused more on worship settings of the society, providing encouragement and guidance for their growth in saving relationship to God.

It was primarily concerning pastoral preaching that Wesley instructed his preachers to follow a general method of inviting, convincing, offering Christ, and building up—each in some measure in every sermon.[102] This advice reflects the mature Wesley's contextual integration of law and gospel. The role of the sermon as a means of grace in worship is to communicate Christ in all three offices: assuring us of God's pardoning love (Priest), while simultaneously revealing our remaining need (Prophet), and leading our further growth in Christ-likeness (King).[103]

Communal Support[104]

Such were the elements of liturgical worship that Wesley valued so highly as means of grace that he incorporated them into the society meetings when this became necessary. But what were the distinctive contributions provided by the Methodist society itself, that Wesley found to be lacking in the typical parish member's experience of church? Insight into this question is provided by accounts of the emergence of the Fetter Lane Society in 1738. The Wesley brothers had awakened some in London to the pursuit of more serious Christian discipleship. These folk then came under ridicule from others who did not share this vision. The "cognitive dissonance" of such a situation is intense—without the support of a community that shares one's view of reality it is difficult to continue following or affirming it. Therefore, the brothers encouraged their early followers to gather together often for mutual encouragement and support.[105]

Time would thoroughly substantiate this assumption that the gathering of their followers around a common vision of the Christian life would be a significant "spiritual help."[106] Indeed, Wesley would soon draw the broader conclusion of the inappropriateness of any model of spirituality that relied on the individual pursuit of holiness. As he once put it, "The gospel of Christ knows no religion, but social; no holiness but social holiness." And as he further clarified, "I mean not only that it cannot subsist so well, but that it cannot subsist at all without society, without living and conversing with [others]."[107]

Part of the contribution of society to holiness is mutual accountability, which will be developed shortly. Of interest at the moment is the element of basic communal support reflected in a hymnic prayer that Wesley designated for the society meetings:

> Help us to help each other, Lord,
> Each other's cross to bear;

Let each his friendly aid afford,
And feel his brother's care.
Help us to build each other up,
Our little stock improve;
Increase our faith, confirm our hope,
And perfect us in love.[108]

Love Feasts

One well-known expression of this communal support in Methodism was a service that Wesley called the "love feast," because he considered it to be a continuation of the early Christian *agape* meal.[109] Wesley had actually adapted the service (in which participants share non-consecrated bread and water with one another) from the Moravians. For them it had been a service of praise and fellowship. This element was primary in Wesley's practice as well, particularly at first when the love feast was an occasional service in the bands (i.e., convinced Christians). Over time the love feast became a monthly service open to the whole society, as well as a few serious outsiders. With this shift Wesley elevated the role of testimonies by believers.[110] His hope was that these shared stories would model and encourage progress along the Way of Salvation. They were to be one means through which God worked in the love feast to "nourish us with social grace."[111]

Watch-Night Services

A second distinctive Methodist service may have grown out of a particularly intense (and prolonged) love feast. Or, it may have been a practical-theological adaptation of a surrogate for revelry that emerged among the colliers' children at Kingswood.[112] Whatever its origin, the watch-night became an integral part of Methodist life. It was originally a monthly celebration, gradually shifted to a quarterly basis, and finally became a New Year's Eve tradition. As evidenced by the hymns that John selected for the service, its purpose was to provide a periodic time of reflection—both to awaken us to remaining sin and to convince us of God's support in our renewed obedient response.[113] The community setting of the service reflects Wesley's pastoral wisdom, providing both an incentive for personal honesty and a context of mutual support (compare his frequent description of the service as having been solemn *and* comforting).[114]

Covenant Renewal

Yet another distinctive Methodist service was the Covenant Renewal. In this case Wesley's major source was the Puritan Richard Alleine.[115] He had abridged Alleine's *Vindiciae Pietatis*, which suggested a periodic renewal of one's commitment to God, for the *Christian Library*. Two years later he led his first covenant renewal service, drawing on this abridgement.[116] This service eventually became a New Year's Day tradition. It's purpose was to provide a setting for (1) recurrent recognition and confession of our failures to live responsibly within our restored relationship to God, (2) an affirmation of God's faithfulness and forgiveness, and (3) the renewal of our commitment, based on God's gracious empowering.[117] The covenant service has occasionally been accused of fostering an individualistic understanding of the Christian life. Such criticism overlooks the communal context of the renewal, a context given eventual liturgical expression in a closing communion service. Moreover, as Rupert Davies has argued, the ritual places primary emphasis on God's holy love and grace, casting our human responsibility in its light.[118]

Accountability

In the discussion of watch-night services and covenant renewal the element of mutual accountability, which was integrally linked to communal support for Wesley, has already begun to surface.[119] It can now be brought into focal view. To talk of accountability is to suggest that some form of discipline is involved in Christian living. Wesley surely believed so. He frequently quoted the maxim "The soul and body make a [human]; but spirit and discipline make a Christian."[120] More to the point, he saw discipline as one of the crucial contributions provided to the Methodist people, which could guarantee their continued spiritual health if it were maintained.[121]

The General Rules

What was the nature of Methodist discipline? Wesley encapsulated it in the three-fold injunction of the General Rules: avoid all known sin, do as much good as one can, and attend all the ordinances of God. Anyone who joined a Methodist society became subject to the guidance of these rules, being examined quarterly by a Methodist preacher. If they persistently slighted the rules, the examiner would quietly revoke their ticket for society gatherings (disciplinary action being declared publicly only if there was danger of public scandal).[122]

Whenever a set of rules such as this is suggested for Christian living there is the fear of legalism, judgmentalism, or works-righteousness. Concerning the charge of legalism, it must be admitted that some of Wesley's specific applications of the General Rules could verge in this direction. However, it should also be noted that the late Wesley toned down many of his earlier suggestions. His professed goal was to capture the wisdom of common sense and Scripture, not to create a moral straitjacket.[123]

Concerns of judgmentalism would likely focus on Wesley's practice of removing from the society those who neglected or rebuked the discipline of the General Rules. When forced to justify this practice, he could note that Methodism was a voluntary society within the Church, so removal was not the equivalent of excommunication.[124] More important, his justifications reveal that his primary concern was not punitive but therapeutic; he was trying to preserve the spiritual health of the society and, he hoped, reawaken the spiritual responsiveness of the person involved.[125]

This brings us to the charge of works-righteousness. Here one must remember Wesley's assumptions about the co-operant nature of grace and the role of tempers in human actions. The purpose of the General Rules was not to enable people to "earn God's favor," but to nurture the reshaping of their character into Christ-likeness. Moreover, the very presence of an encouragement to attend the means of grace in the rules reinforces that their observation is undergirded by God's grace.[126]

Spiritual Directors

Given the subtleness and deceitfulness of sin, Wesley was convinced that every Christian needed spiritual direction to provide accountability for their growth in holiness.[127] This conviction lies behind his insistence that the task of Methodist preachers involves far more than preaching sermons or bringing people to repentance; they are in the business of "caring for souls," which necessarily includes supervising spiritual discipline in their charges.[128] Wesley's conviction also explains his development of substructures in the society to aid in this task.

Accountability Groups

I have in mind here the various forms of "Christian Conference" that Wesley treasured as means of grace—namely, the class meetings, bands, penitent bands, and select societies.[129] The primary purpose of these substructures of the Methodist societies was to support members' *responsible* participation in the transforming work of God's *grace.*[130] The different forms emerged gradually, as practical-theological responses to the changing needs and contexts of the growing movement.[131] As they emerged, Wesley wove them into a creative set of overlapping levels of accountability.[132]

The most basic substructure was the class meeting. Every person joining a Methodist society was assigned to a class of around a dozen members. Since the only requirement for joining was an awareness of one's spiritual need and a desire for God's help (not an assurance of God's pardoning acceptance) there was a potential wide range of spiritual need in the class. A spiritually-mature (lay) leader was designated for each class to help meet this need. The leader was responsible for visiting weekly with every member and inquiring into their spiritual responsiveness and growth, providing comfort, encouragement, advice, or reproof as appropriate.

By contrast with the classes, participation in the bands was voluntary for Methodists and intended only for those with some assurance of God's pardoning Presence.[133] Since some spiritual maturity and insight could be assumed in each member, the band operated with mutual accountability rather than designated leaders. One result of this was that many class leaders looked to the bands as a setting for their own accountability (along with the leaders' meeting). To enable open sharing (and circumvent conflicts of marital authority) Wesley established separate bands for men and women. He also offered specific guidance on providing accountability without violating confidence.[134]

Wesley visited the bands whenever he passed through, to encourage them and to handle any disciplinary action that might need taken. On occasion he became aware of some for whom the mutual accountability of the band had proven to be inadequate, as evidenced by their return to known, wilful sin. As an option to removal from the society, Wesley offered them a situation of more intense spiritual direction in a penitent band.[135] This was a temporary situation designed to restore their obedient responsiveness to God's grace.

The final substructure was the select society. As the name implies, this group was for the most committed of the Methodists. To be specific, it was created for those who were actively pressing after the experience of entire sanctification, to provide more serious mutual support and accountability for their quest. This need for accountability was even greater for those who claimed the experience, since it was open to continuing growth and (experience proved) capable of being lost.[136] Wesley demanded particular confidentiality within this group, partly because it was an arena in which *he* hoped to find mutual accountability.[137] He also expected them to model a pattern of holiness and love for the larger society. For example, he hoped (fruitlessly!) that the select societies would lead the other Methodists into "holding all things in common," like the early Church![138]

Private Exercises[139]

We turn next to a traditional group of means of grace that are geared to private use. The importance that Wesley attached to these is best seen in a letter where, after telling his correspondent that he needed to grow in grace, he encouraged him to fix some part of every day for private exercises of reading and prayer because "It is for your life; there is no other way: Do justice to your own soul: give it time and means to grow."[140] This advice makes clear that Wesley understood God to work through these exercises, renewing our energy for growth in holiness. I believe that he also sensed the formative contribution of the exercises.[141] To put it in an aphorism, "You become like those with whom you spend time." To become Christ-like, spend time with Christ through study of Scripture, devotional reading, and prayer.

Study of Scripture

Regular personal study of Scripture was at the top of Wesley's list of private exercises. Doubt has occasionally been expressed about this claim because of his deletion of the lectionary table (except for Sundays) from the *Sunday Service.*[142] However one explains this, Wesley's expectation of daily reading is clear and challenging. He specifically encouraged his people to read a portion of both the Old and New Testaments each morning and evening, and to meditate on them.[143]

Devotional/Catechetical Readings

The Puritans placed a special emphasis on the reading of devotional materials. This was one of the areas where they deeply influenced Wesley. A large number of Puritan devotional writings were among the "practical divinity" that he distilled in the *Christian Library* and elsewhere for circulation among his followers. In keeping with Wesley's conviction of the practical-theological connection between one's basic worldview and one's devotion or action, these publications also included several catechetical materials for adults. Wesley commended regular reading of this literature to all who desired to grow in grace.[144]

Private Prayers

The other major traditional private exercise is prayer (whether individual or as families). Wesley once called private prayer the "grand means of drawing near to God."[145] He made particular mention of its contribution to our empowerment by creating in us a disposition to receive God's grace and blessing.[146] Private prayer can also be a means of shaping Christian character, particularly if it is guided prayer. The concern to maximize this formative dimension is evident in Wesley's collections of prayers for individuals and families, which he selected and organized in terms of the various aspects of Christian belief and life.[147]

Works of Mercy

The other major category of means of sanctifying grace that Wesley consistently recommended was "works of mercy." This designation covers the range of possible contributions to the welfare of others—from clothing and shelter, to healthcare and education, to basic friendship. Wesley was aware that such actions were not typically identified as means of grace. In his mature opinion, they not only qualified as such, they could be valued as highly as any of the other means.[148] Behind this high valuation lies his conviction of the connection between love of God and love of others.

Love of God and Love of Others

Wesley's assumption that we can only love God or others in response to God's gracious love for us has been noted several times. What needs to be developed here is the connection that he drew between our responsive love for God and our love for others. This connection was dialectical. On the one hand he would insist (in contrast with deism) that we can truly love other humans only in conjunction with love for God.[149] On the other hand, he denied that anyone who failed to love their neighbor could truly love God.[150] On such terms, works of piety like worship—which express responsive love for God—would deepen our love for others, while works of mercy would deepen our love for God.[151]

Formative Effect of Works of Mercy

In his praise of works of mercy as means of grace Wesley contended that they "exercise all holy tempers," and thereby improve them.[152] As with all exercise, the improvement that one could expect would involve both strengthening and shaping. Given the reciprocal relationship of love for others and love for God, works of mercy would deepen one's relationship with God's empowering Presence. Given the ability for tempers to be patterned, imitation of Christ's model of servanthood would help reshape our moral nature into the image of Christ.

The Place of Self-Denial

Wesley's emphasis on works of mercy provides a helpful backdrop for understanding his insistence that "self-denial" is indispensable to the Christian life. One practice on which he laid particular emphasis (due to assumed primitive precedent) was regular fasting.[153] He also frequently called for the avoidance of frivolous pleasures like horse races and expensive clothes.[154] On the other hand, he was quick to criticize any suggestion of a positive contribution of physical suffering to spiritual formation.[155] For Wesley, self-denial had nothing to do with physical abuse of oneself, but was rather a willingness to embrace God's will when it is contrary to one's own.[156] One of the most consistent applications that he made of this principle was in relation to wealth: God's will is that we give to those in need all that we earn which is above that required to meet our necessities. In other words, self-denial is the converse dimension of works of mercy.[157]

Means of Justifying Grace

Attention has been focused so far on the contribution of the means of grace to growth *within* the Christian life. The question to be considered now is their role in the *initiation* of Christian life. Some historical background will aid in understanding Wesley's convictions on this topic.[158]

Historical Perspectives on Wesley's Pastoral Challenge

In its earliest centuries the majority of initiates to Christianity were adult (or older children) converts. Since they were coming to the church with little background knowledge, they were placed in the catechumenate for a period (often several years long) of training in Christian belief and life. This catechetical training culminated in an intense period of formation during Lent, with baptism of all prepared candidates by the bishop during the Easter vigil. The baptism rite itself included several components: renunciation of sin by the initiate, application of water (expressing forgiveness or cleansing from sin), laying on of hands and/or chrismation (expressing reception of the Holy Spirit), and admission to full communion.

Major changes from these early initiatory practices began in the fourth century. The foundational change was a dramatic increase in baptism of infants. There was more behind this development than simply a growing number of children born to Christian parents. A significant stimulus was the establishment of Christianity as the official religion of the Roman empire, which created connections between baptism and citizenship. Even more important in the West was the broad influence of Augustine's claim that infants required baptism to remove the guilt of Original Sin with which they were born. Under these pressures even nominally Christian parents were likely to desire that their children be baptized as soon as possible.

The emergence of infant baptism as the dominant pattern of Christian initiation significantly impacted the structure and components of the rites. Not only did it rule out a process of catechesis before baptism, it also undermined the gathering of baptisms on a common date. When this was combined with the spread of Christianity into rural areas after its legalization, it became impossible for the bishop to be present at every baptism. The Western church was particularly concerned to preserve an episcopal role in initiation, as an expression that the initiate becomes part of the larger church, not just the local parish. The compromise broadly adopted was to allow local priests to baptize infants soon after birth, but to reserve the imposition of hands or oil (eventually called "confirmation") for the bishop on his next regular visit to the area. While valuing an episcopal connection, Eastern churches have been unwilling to separate the initiatory rites in this fashion. Their alternative concession is to allow priests both to baptize and to chrismate infants, using oil blessed by the bishop.

Once baptism and confirmation were separated in the West, there was a problem of convincing parents of the importance of having their children confirmed; after all, baptism had bestowed forgiveness. The efforts to encourage confirmation gradually led to the theological suggestion that the Gift of the Holy Spirit was not bestowed in infant baptism (at least not in its full sense), but came with confirmation. By the fourteenth century it also became common to restrict communion until confirmation, to precede confirmation with basic catechetical training, and to require as part of the rite a personal affirmation of faith—with the combined effect of further delaying confirmation until an "age of discretion."

True to his Augustinian heritage, Luther retained infant baptism. He was less happy with medieval theological claims about confirmation, or with the requirement of episcopal administration. On the other hand, his stress on faith suggested a need for personal appropriation of one's baptism. This led him to continue the practice of older children giving personal expression of faith to their pastors prior to full participation in the church (i.e., before their first communion). Later Lutherans incorporated a period of catechesis in preparation for this confirmation, a practice given even more emphasis in the Reformed tradition. By contrast, Anabaptists and other believers' churches rejected the validity of any baptism except that of persons personally expressing faith, eliminating the need for a separate rite of confirmation or related restrictions on communion.

The Anglican movement diverged from the medieval developments somewhat less than the continental Reformers. In particular, Cranmer not only endorsed infant baptism and postponed communion until after confirmation, he retained episcopal administration of confirmation. Yet, his interest in confirmation appears to have been more for its component of catechesis than for the rite itself. One indication of this is the rubric which he included in the *Book of Common Prayer* to assure parents who worried about postponing confirmation until after catechism that baptized infants who die before confirmation were certain of salvation. These words of assurance may well have backfired! Through the seventeenth and eighteenth century there was widespread neglect of both catechism and confirmation in Anglicanism. Many apparently assumed that the simple act of their baptism as infants sufficed for their final salvation.

Wesley's Pastoral Response

This sets the context within which Wesley undertook his ministry of inviting the people of England to a life of serious Christian discipleship. The majority of his hearers considered themselves to be Christians, by virtue of their infant baptism. Yet few of them showed evidence of personally appropriating the renunciation of sin and newness of life that was expressed in that baptism. They also exhibited little concern about this lack of appropriation.

Call to Renewed Responsiveness

What Wesley identified as missing in these baptized hearers was ongoing life in the Spirit. Though it was suggested to him many times by members of believers' churches, he never accepted this as evidence that the Spirit was not conveyed through infant baptism. Neither did he give any indication that the problem was the lack of some fuller bestowal of the Spirit reserved specifically for the rite of confirmation. His diagnosis did not focus on an absence of the Spirit's Presence but on his hearers' lack of responsiveness to that Presence. He attributed this lack largely to their presumption that the simple act of baptism (at whatever age) guaranteed salvation. Accordingly, he tried vigorously to awaken them to the realization that the crucial question was not whether one had been baptized, but whether one was continuing to participate *responsibly* in the transformation of life that the *grace* signified in baptism empowers.[159]

It was noted in Chapter Seven that Wesley's initial awakening preaching aimed for immediate assurance of pardon and would often prolong the anxiety of those who had not received it. We also saw that the mature Wesley changed this practice significantly, as he came to appreciate the variability and gradual nature of conversion. Increasingly, the result that Wesley anticipated from awakening sermons was not a "conversion experience," but simply an awareness of one's *need* for conversion. This awareness was precisely the prerequisite for admission into the Methodist society, which he would then encourage.

Methodist Society as Catechumenate

As this suggests, Wesley came to value participation in the Methodist society for its contribution to *kindling* responsive life in the Spirit, not just for nurturing greater growth in that life. Indeed, the mature Wesley would insist that awakening folk to their spiritual need, without joining them into classes for training in the ways of God, was simply begetting children for the murderer.[160] Participation in the society came to serve for newly awakened members like the catechumenate in the Early Church, preparing them for entry into restored relationship with God.[161] As the revival matured it became common for assurance and revitalized spiritual life to come only after participating for a year or more in the foundational levels of the society.[162] This integral role for the society is what made Wesley's approach to evangelism unique. It provided a context for the gradual, individually-variable, and *responsible* appropriation of saving *grace.*

Excursus: The Lord's Supper as a Converting Ordinance[163]

There was one very important way that the life of the awakened in the society differed from that of the catechumen in the Early Church—Wesley encouraged them to partake in communion! This point involves a traditional issue concerning the Lord's Supper that was postponed for treatment until now. The Early Church was careful to restrict participation in the communion service to those fully initiated, for a variety of reasons. The result was that catechumens could not partake. On the other hand, once initiated they were eager to partake regularly. The eucharist was viewed as a sacrament of nurture that was essential to their continuing spiritual transformation.

While the Eastern churches largely maintained an understanding of the eucharist as a regular sacrament of nurture, developments in the West progressively reframed it into an infrequent sacrament of attainment, to be offered only to the "worthy." Two major forces pushed in this direction. One was the increasingly realistic understanding of the Presence of Christ in the sacrament. As this conception grew, both priests and laity became worried about possible sacrilegious treatment of the elements. This eventually led the clergy to withhold the cup from the laity (because easily spilled). Among the laity it spawned a widespread reticence to receive communion at all (fearing the fate described in 1 Cor. 11:30). The ironic result was that the thirteenth-century Western council that formally defined transubstantiation also found it necessary to *mandate* receiving communion at least once a year![164]

The content of this mandate reveals the second force reshaping the understanding of communion in the medieval West: admission to the sacrament was contingent upon one's prior attendance at confession and fulfillment of assigned penance. In other words, the Lord's Supper was becoming more a certification of one's continuing good-standing in the Church than a vital means of nourishing one's spiritual growth. This tone carried over into most Western traditions of the eighteenth century. While they often did away with the confessional, nearly all (including Anglicanism) required some form of certification by one's pastor prior to partaking communion.[165]

True to his initial ecclesiastical exactness, the early Wesley enforced this requirement rigorously during his parish work in Georgia.[166] Back in England, he found an analogous practice among the Moravians, who counseled voluntary abstention from the Lord's Supper unless one had a full assurance of God's pardon (else they would be eating "unworthily"). But in the early years of the revival, at the same time when he was questioning the identification of justification with full assurance, Wesley noticed that some who did not have assurance of faith received it *through* the communion service. He concluded that God offered in the Lord's Supper converting grace as well as confirming grace.[167] But if this is so, then those who feel that they need the grace of God should be encouraged to seek that grace in the Supper, not excluded for being unworthy. Wesley began to do precisely this, offering an "open table" for which the only initial requirement of the recipient was a desire to receive God's grace and to live in faithful response, not some prior fitness or assurance.[168]

Predictably, there were soon attacks that Wesley was offering the grace of communion indiscriminately.[169] The issue at stake here related directly to his orienting concern. On the one hand, he was persuaded of God's gracious prevenience throughout the Way of Salvation—we come to communion in our need, seeking further grace; not in our fitness, seeking certification. On the other hand, Wesley believed that God's grace was responsible—it will not continue to nurture us unless we receive it responsively. The tension of this concern ruled out *preconditions* for access to God's grace, but it leaves a legitimate pastoral role of insuring our *response* to God's grace. Hence, Wesley's practical-theological judgment is evident in his developed model of membership in the Methodist societies (where he offered communion): there was no precondition for entry other than a sense of need, but there were minimum standards of responsiveness expected for renewing membership quarterly.[170]

It is important to note that assurance of faith was *not* one of the minimums required for renewing Methodist membership. Wesley indeed desired this assurance for all of his followers, but this is precisely why he continued to offer the sacramental nurture of the society (along with its support and accountability) to all who were still seeking assurance. He was convinced that they were more likely to suffer loss from missing the Eucharist than from partaking in it "unworthily."[171]

Practical-Theological Implications for Baptism[172]

While Wesley's pastoral attention related to baptism was devoted heavily to awakening new responsiveness in those who were presuming upon their past baptism (infant or otherwise) for salvation, it was not exclusively devoted to this task. For example, his diaries reveal that he also regularly baptized both adults and infants throughout his ministry.[173] It was inevitable that he would ponder the practical-theological implications of his broader pastoral experience for this practice of baptism.

The question of Wesley's understanding of baptism has been another area of major debate in Wesley studies. This debate has focused on the characteristic Western concern about the relative roles of sacramental mediation and receptive faith in regeneration. Those scholars earlier this century who laid great stress on Wesley's "evangelical conversion" typically claimed that this led him to reject any strong notion of baptismal regeneration and that he retained infant baptism only because of its conventional status in Anglicanism.[174] In direct rebuttal, several recent scholars have insisted that Wesley clearly affirmed baptismal regeneration, or baptism as the ordinary means of the new birth, for both adults and infants.[175] In between these stark contrasts, a few brave souls have suggested that Wesley's comments on baptism reveal an intentional creative tension between sacramentalism and evangelicalism.[176] Most have spoken instead of an unresolved ambiguity in Wesley's various comments,[177] and such ambiguity would help account for the ongoing debate and wide diversity of practice among his descendants.[178]

While much of the fervor of this debate might be owed to the agendas of Wesley's later interpreters, its foundation lies in the secondary nature of most of his direct publications on the subject. For example, *Thoughts on Infant Baptism* was a short extract from a four-volume work by William Wall, and "A Treatise on Baptism," was an abridgement of a tract by his father.[179] Aside from some scattered comments and the 1760 sermon on "The New Birth," the other major indicator of Wesley's views is his editorial work in preparing the *Sunday Service.*[180] The differing interpretations of Wesley diverge already on the question of how much weight to place on these various publications. Actually, it would seem reasonable to consider each of them to be reliable indicators of Wesley's convictions *at the time of their publication,* since his editing in each case was significant. The question would then become what practical-theological tensions or development they reveal in his views on baptism. My consideration of this question will begin with his specific comments on adult baptism, because adult convert baptism functioned as the model for framing the theology of baptism in the Early Church and for Wesley.[181]

Adult Baptism as a Means of Responsible Grace

Even though Wesley never included baptism on any of his lists, he surely considered it to be a means of grace. The reason for its omission was that it is not a *repeated* means for the *progressive* nurturing of holiness, as were the other means on the lists. Rather, baptism marked the initiation of the life of holiness.

One of the benefits that Wesley ascribed to adult baptism was forgiveness of sins. However, he specifically identified this as a lower benefit, contrasted with the higher benefit of the regenerating effect of the Holy Spirit "shedding the love of God abroad in our hearts."[182] This relative ranking reveals the therapeutic focus of Wesley's understanding of baptism. The defining purpose of baptism is not to bestow our juridical pardon, but to initiate the graciously-empowered transformation of our lives.

Wesley's various comments on adult baptism also reveal his conviction that the *grace* of baptism is *responsible.* One expression of this conviction is his insistence that, though water baptism is the ordinary way that God conveys the grace of restored pardoning relationship with its regenerating power, the outward sign must be "duly received" to be accompanied by the inward grace.[183] While the grace of baptism is *sufficient* for initiating Christian life, it becomes *efficient* only as we responsively participate. That is why, from early in the revival, Wesley declined to identify the New Birth with baptism in any rigid sense.[184] This concern continued to characterize the mature Wesley, as evidenced by his editing of the *Sunday Service.* He carefully eliminated from the Articles any suggestion that baptism inevitably conveys the benefits of justification and regeneration.[185] Likewise, though he retained the language of regeneration in those parts of the baptismal liturgies *preceding* the actual baptism, he deleted it from prayers *after* the baptism—with the apparent intent of affirming the availability of regeneration in baptism, while protecting against presumption by removing the suggestion of assured reception.[186] Finally, it is possible that Wesley intentionally refocused attention from the water per se to the *act* of baptism as the means by which grace is conveyed. This would have underlined the personal and responsive nature of baptismal grace, on close analogy with his understanding of grace in the Lord's Supper.[187]

To turn the issue around, while the grace of baptism invites our responsive participation, we become more response-able precisely through this participation. That is why Wesley consistently rejected the notion that unbaptized persons who receive the assurance of faith (or "spiritual baptism") do not then need baptism. God has worked in an extraordinary fashion in their case (like with Cornelius), but they should still come to the water for the confirming and strengthening grace that it provides.[188] Wesley's concern here is not that baptism is a juridical necessity for salvation (because it is not), but that it contributes to the therapeutic transformation of our lives.[189] Thus, even after Wesley denied that Quakers would be damned for not observing water baptism, he continued to baptize Quakers who joined his movement.[190]

The other implication of the "responsible" nature of baptismal grace that Wesley stressed should come as no surprise: its benefits remain remissible. Since baptism is not a juridical guarantee of salvation or a source of irresistible grace, it is always possible to neglect the empowering Presence that it conveys and eventually to quench the pardoning relationship that it signifies.[191] While this idea is admittedly suspect in some Western traditions, it resonates strongly with the co-operant nature of baptismal grace affirmed by Eastern Christianity.[192]

Of course, much of Wesley's ministry was based on the assumption that it is also possible to renew the relationship that we have quenched. While he could call this renewal a "new birth," he did not expect or encourage a new baptism in such cases. He never specifically clarified why not.[193] Perhaps it can be understood on analogy with the situation of Prevenient Grace discussed in Chapter Three. While persistent neglect can quench our pardoning relationship with the Divine grace conveyed in baptism, it does not drive the very Presence of that grace from our lives. We have withdrawn from God, but God has not withdrawn from us. Thus, what is needed (and what Wesley labored to create) is a reawakened responsiveness to God's Presence, not a repeated sacramental bestowal of that Presence.

The Benefits of Infant Baptism

Given the emphasis on our responsive participation in baptismal grace in Wesley's theological explication of (adult) baptism, many of his descendants have questioned the retention of infant baptism. They have suggested that alternatives which reserve baptism for a time of personal responsiveness are more appropriate.[194] By contrast, Wesley's own commitment to the practice of infant baptism wavered little—because of the warrant which he saw in Anglican and Early Church practice, and perhaps in Scripture.[195]

This is not to deny that there were changes in Wesley's convictions about the mode of baptism.[196] More important, there was also some change in his identification of the purpose of infant baptism, which is most evident concerning a benefit of infant baptism that has traditionally been affirmed in Western Christianity but denied by the East. I am referring, of course, to remission of the inherited guilt of Original Sin. While the extract *Thoughts Upon Infant Baptism* (1751) did not stress this benefit, it was the leading affirmation of Samuel Wesley's treatise, which John abridged and published in 1758. John retained the basic point, though he removed the characterization of this guilt as "damning."[197] As was noted in Chapter Three, the uncomfortableness that this deletion suggests led Wesley by 1776 to affirm that any inherited guilt of Original Sin was universally cancelled at birth by Prevenient Grace. Most scholars who have noticed this move argue that Wesley never integrated it into his understanding of infant baptism.[198] However, I find it significant that Wesley did not reprint "A Treatise on Baptism" after 1770, while he reprinted *Thoughts Upon Infant Baptism* (which does not mention remission of inherited guilt) in 1780 and 1791. In effect, the mature Wesley editorially joined Eastern Christians in discounting this purpose for infant baptism.

Several scholars have claimed that Wesley also came to reject regeneration as a benefit of infant baptism. They argue that he adopted the Puritan stance that infant baptism provides simply for adoption into God's covenant of salvation and admission into the Church, with its gracious aids. Regeneration would come later when (and if) the person responsively appropriates this covenant relationship with God.[199] Wesley did indeed identify adoption and admission into the Church as benefits of infant baptism.[200] But the claim that he excluded regeneration from these benefits leaves the troubling suggestion that our appropriation of God's covenant is a *precondition* of regenerating grace, rather than a response to this grace.

What evidence is there that Wesley ever excluded regeneration from the benefits of infant baptism? The major warrant cited is his deletion of affirmations of regeneration from the liturgy for infant baptism in the *Sunday Service*.[201] But Wesley retained in this liturgy (as in the adult baptism liturgy) the affirmations of regeneration that *precede* the actual baptism, deleting only affirmations that *follow* the act. As was suggested earlier, his apparent purpose was not to reject the possibility of regeneration, but to avoid the impression of its inevitability—apart from our responsiveness. Of course, this raises precisely the quandary about infant baptism: how can an infant be responsive?[202]

Bernard Holland has suggested that Wesley resolved this quandary by distinguishing between two types of regeneration, an elemental regeneration of baptism and the full regeneration of the New Birth. While baptism bestows a degree of new spiritual vitality, the empowering reception of the Presence of the Holy Spirit comes only with the New Birth. For adults these two may coincide, but they do not for infants (because the second requires responsive reception). Moreover, children all eventually "sin away" their baptismal regeneration and require the fuller regeneration of the New Birth.[203] This solution is more problematic than Holland himself admits.[204] In the first place, it is far from clear that Wesley assumed everyone baptized as an infant would fall away. More important, for those who do fall, Wesley did not attribute the cause to the insufficiency of baptismal grace but to their neglect of that grace. Finally, while Wesley retained language of "infused grace" in "A Treatise on Baptism," his mature understanding of grace as the Presence of the Holy Spirit runs counter to Holland's contrast between baptismal grace and the grace of the New Birth.[205]

On balance, then, it seems best to say that Wesley remained convinced that infant baptism conveyed the regenerating Presence of the Holy Spirit, though he emphasized that the full effectiveness of this *gracious* Presence emerged gradually, as the developing child *responsibly* appropriated it.[206]

Practical-Theological Implications for Confirmation

The mention of one baptized as an infant later appropriating the grace of that baptism naturally calls to mind (in the West) the practice of confirmation. But in his *Sunday Service*, Wesley purposefully removed the rite of confirmation. Consideration of possible practical-theological reasons for this action is important, because it has baffled many of his heirs.[207]

The Importance of Childhood Catechesis

The first point that must be made is that Wesley's deletion of the rite of confirmation was not a rejection of the importance of childhood catechesis.[208] While catechesis had fallen into significant disregard in eighteenth-century Anglicanism this was not the case at the Wesley household where Susanna emphasized religious education of her children, with a specific concern for shaping their character.[209] This made it natural for John to place catechizing children high in the priorities of his pastoral work in Georgia.[210] If his subsequent transformation from parish pastor to traveling evangelist shifted that priority at all, it was only temporarily. Indeed, a growing emphasis on religious education of children can be traced through his revival years.[211]

One indication of this growing emphasis is the proliferation of settings in which he sought to provide such religious education. From nearly the beginning of the revival Wesley was encouraging families to inculcate religion in their children, and preparing materials to aid them in this process.[212] This encouragement grew stronger over time, with the mature Wesley identifying the development of family religion as "the grand desideratum among the Methodists," and directing his preachers to train parents accordingly.[213] He crowned this effort with a series of sermons on the parental duty to provide religious instruction for their children.[214]

Of course, as Wesley quickly recognized, many parents lacked resources to provide any education for their children, let alone religious education. There was widespread illiteracy among the poorer classes, and most had received little religious instruction themselves.[215] As one response to this situation Wesley established several boarding schools. The most well-known of these was Kingswood, opened in 1748 for the children of the colliers. The centrality of religious formation to the purpose of these schools is obvious from the opening ceremonies at Kingswood: John's sermon was on the text "train up a child in the way that he should go," while the hymn that Charles composed for the occasion spoke of the hope to "unite the pair so long disjoin'd, knowledge and vital piety."[216] As John would later instruct a teacher at one of his schools, her task was to "make Christians."[217]

Boarding schools were hardly a sufficient answer to the need for supplementing family religious education. Among other things, few parents are excited about their children being separated for such extended periods of time. The natural alternative was weekly catechesis. Wesley's desire to avoid conflict with the Anglican priests (who were *supposed* to provide this for all children in their parish[218]) appears to have restrained him from taking this step in distinctly Methodist settings for some time. However, by 1756 he was willing to commend one of his preachers for beginning to catechize children in his charge.[219] This practice was destined not only to spread but to develop beyond simply teaching a catechism into an ongoing weekly process of religious education; that is, the prototype of Sunday schools is to be found in Methodism![220] Wesley highly valued these Sunday schools, once characterizing them as "nurseries for Christians."[221]

Wesley's specific procedural recommendations on educating children have drawn the accusation of some later scholars that he had no appreciation of child psychology, a charge mitigated somewhat by comparative treatment with his time.[222] The more serious debate among Wesley's descendants has concerned what relationship he saw between dramatic conversion experiences and the gradual nurture of Christian faith in children. A careful consideration reveals that the mature Wesley appreciated childhood conversion experiences but hardly considered them the norm. Indeed, he encouraged educational nurture of children precisely to help prevent the departure into sin that is presupposed by dramatic conversions.[223]

The Rite of Confirmation

What Wesley objected to, then, was not catechetical training, but the rite of confirmation itself. Some have suggested that his dissatisfaction with this rite stemmed from the impersonal manner in which it was administered in his day.[224] While this may have played a role, there were deeper theological issues. To begin with, Wesley would have balked at the possible implication that reception of the Holy Spirit is *guaranteed* through confirmation. More to the point, he rejected the notion that the Gift of the Holy Spirit is somehow reserved for later bestowal upon folk who were already "partly" Christian.[225] If the intention of confirmation is defined instead as simply renewing or deepening one's responsiveness to the Gift of the Spirit, then Wesley would reject the suggestion that this need is met in any single event; the Way of Salvation is a continual process of deeper responsiveness to the Spirit's Presence, empowered by regular participation in the several means of grace.[226] Finally, after 1746 Wesley would have questioned the Anglican practice of restricting the prerogative of confirmation (i.e., recognition of fully Christian status) to bishops.[227] Thus, his deletion of the rite of confirmation as a required sacramental supplement to baptism was a conscious practical-theological decision.

Communion of Children

Wesley's deletion of confirmation shifted his practice of initiation toward the pattern of Eastern Christianity, but only part way. He did not add a chrismation to the baptism rite for either infants or those of riper years, neither did he extend communion to baptized infants. This latter point is particularly puzzling, since he was aware that his prized Primitive Church had communed baptized infants.[228] Nonetheless, he tended to postpone the invitation to the table. His reason for postponing was obviously not to await confirmation. Nor did he await an assurance of salvation as a prerequisite. What he looked for in children before admitting them to the table was simply some evidence of responsiveness in matters of religion.[229] It was not uncommon for him to discern this in children as young as eight or nine—the same age at which his father had admitted him to communion![230] Indeed, one wonders whether his practice was derived primarily from this precedent. Communing infants from baptism on would actually seem to be more in keeping with his emphasis on God's prevenience in salvation. The question of appropriate responsiveness would then await the child reaching an "age of discretion," and would be handled within the same tension adopted for members of the society.

Means of Prevenient Grace?

It remains to make a few comments on the nascent dimension of present saving grace, Prevenient Grace. The question of whether Wesley identified specific means of Prevenient Grace may seem odd, since he insisted that it was universally available. However, there are three areas in which this possibility must be considered.

The first area is signaled by Wesley's claim (in debate with Moravian quietists) that the Lord's Supper is capable of conveying *preventing* as well as justifying or sanctifying grace.[231] This claim predates Wesley's refined notion of Prevenient Grace, as distinct from the prevenience of grace in general. The specific benefit that it attributes to "preventing grace" is restraint from sin, which is not unique to Prevenient Grace. Thus, it is far from certain that Wesley was intending to affirm here a distinct role for the Lord's Supper in conveying Prevenient Grace. But if he was, a consistent implication would be a totally "open table" for the Lord's Supper; that is, one should not even require baptism as a prerequisite. While rare, such practice has occasionally become evident among Wesley's descendants.[232] This has spawned vigorous debate over whether Wesley himself viewed baptism as an absolute prerequisite for participation in the Lord's Supper. He never explicitly addressed the point. The majority of scholars have argued that he simply assumed it, since the bulk of folk coming to his society were already baptized. And yet, they were not all baptized, nor is it absolutely clear that Wesley required them to be baptized before entering the society or partaking at its table.[233]

While it is debatable whether Wesley ever assumed that the Lord's Supper conveys Prevenient Grace, it is fairly clear that he initially connected Prevenient Grace to baptism—especially infant baptism. Such connection was common in Western sacramental traditions. It was made explicitly in a sermon on Philippians 2:12-13 by William Tilly that Wesley distilled and preached on several occasions between 1732-4.[234] It can still be found in some selections of the *Christian Library*.[235] However, when Wesley published his own sermon on Philippians 2:12-13 in 1785, the connection of Prevenient Grace to baptism was replaced by a reference to "natural conscience."[236] Far from an accident, this was a direct result of his growing emphasis on the universal nature of Prevenient Grace. For the mature Wesley, neither the nascent degrees of regeneration nor the pardon of any inherited guilt for Original Sin are restricted to the baptized. While one might argue that the mature Wesley retained infant baptism to *symbolize* the prevenience of the deeper regenerating work of Divine grace to our human response, he did not view it as a distinctive *means* of Prevenient Grace.[237]

Perhaps a third candidate can fare better as a means that the mature Wesley employed to "enliven" Prevenient Grace in his hearers. In Chapter Three it was argued that Wesley assigned to Prevenient Grace not only the upholding of our partially-restored human faculties but also the initial specific overtures to these faculties. While Prevenient Grace is universal, many have stifled these overtures and fallen "asleep." If the work of God is to proceed in their lives, they must be awakened anew to these overtures and convicted of their need. For Wesley, the chief means to this end was field preaching.[238] Whenever this means was effective, he ushered the awakened person into the society where the full battery of means of grace could nourish and guide their further journey on the Way of Salvation.

CHAPTER 9

The Triumph of Responsible Grace

The previous three chapters have detailed the human dimensions of Wesley's understanding of how God graciously empowers and guides our responsive journey along the Way of Salvation. An eschatological dimension frequently emerged in that discussion. The purpose of this concluding chapter is to bring that eschatological dimension into primary focus.

Eschatology deals with questions of Christian hope or expectation, such as "What is the ultimate goal of God's redemptive work?" "To what degree can we experience this transforming work presently in our lives?" and "What corporate or structural expressions of this redemption should we expect in this age?" The potential for individual experience of present transformation was addressed in the earlier discussion of Christian Perfection, so the other issues will draw most attention here.

My decision to reserve direct consideration of Wesley's eschatology to this final chapter is more debatable than it might appear. This is because there are three relatively distinct discussions currently gathered under the heading of eschatology: (1) clarification of the traditional "last things," such as the intermediate state, resurrection, and judgment; (2) debates over the specific issue of millennialism (expectation of an ideal period of peace and justice *prior* to the new heavens and earth), which blossomed at the beginning of this century; and (3) questions about the relation of the Reign of God to present ecclesial and social-political existence, which have dominated the field most recently.[1] One characteristic claim of this third discussion is that eschatology should function as the overall framework for presenting theology, rather than being confined to its conclusion.[2]

This claim is echoed in some recent analyses of Wesley's theology.[3] As this reflects, the question of Wesley's understanding of the Reign of God and its relation to present reality is attracting increased attention in current scholarship.[4] Unfortunately, this increased attention has largely come at the expense of the other two foci of eschatological discussion. Most of the recent studies deal only in passing with Wesley's millennial views—an issue of heated debate at the turn of the century.[5] Likewise, they devote little attention to the traditional "last things," in contrast to the initial serious investigations of Wesley's eschatology in the early 1960's.[6]

This present situation of studies of Wesley's eschatology is unfortunate because broader scholarship is increasingly recognizing the significant interplay between the three current foci of eschatological concern.[7] My reason for gathering considerations of Wesley's eschatological convictions in this final chapter is to explore this interplay in his case. Far from questioning the present dimension in Wesley's "final hope," my goal is to illumine the dynamics of this dimension.

The Historical Context of Wesley's Eschatology

There is no better example of the interplay between the current distinct areas of eschatological concern than the interrelationship that has existed historically between assumptions about the present expression of the Reign of God, speculation about an earthly millennial reign of Christ, and beliefs about the current situation of deceased believers. The biblical materials leave room for diversity of opinion on each of these topics. For example, while some New Testament passages proclaim the presence of the Reign of God in and through Christ's ministry and resurrection, others emphasize the hope for a future greater realization of this Reign. Again, while Revelations 20 appears to affirm a millennial reign of Christ, this notion is at best tacit within—if not contrary to—other New Testament accounts of the "last days." Finally, while there are some New Testament suggestions that believers enter immediately into a conscious existence in "paradise" at death, other passages present them as "sleeping" until the general resurrection.

The internal diversity on each of these themes allows for a variety of combinations of the three. This potential was quickly realized in the division between early theologians who affirmed a temporary, earthly, millennial reign of Christ (chiliasts) and those who ignored or rejected this possibility (non-chiliasts). Investigation reveals that these alternative views on millennialism correlated with differences on the other two topics under consideration.[8]

Irenaeus is representative of early chiliasts in connecting his affirmation of a millennial reign to both an assessment of the relative lack of the Reign of God in the present age and an insistence that the souls of deceased believers are currently residing in Hades awaiting the resurrection, not already consciously enjoying the benefits of paradise. In fact, the purpose of the millennium for Irenaeus was to fulfill the promises of God's salvific Reign in the created material world and to provide for the further gradual recovery of the Divine Likeness that was necessary before (most) believers could enter God's glorious presence.[9]

By contrast with Irenaeus, Clement of Alexandria is representative of many other early theologians who insisted that believers do enter directly into God's heavenly presence (paradise) at death, where they participate consciously in God's eternal Reign. This being the case, these folk saw no need for a future earthly millennial reign of Christ. Some of these early non-chiliasts (notably, Origen) went much further than denying a future earthly reign of Christ, they spiritualized the very Reign of God—moving it above present historical reality and minimizing any role for the physical creation.[10]

This spiritualizing tendency was not simply an idiosyncrasy. It is related to the fact that early Christianity was shaped by both biblical and Greco-Roman influences. While these two cultural sources had many convergences, they harbored marked differences in matters of eschatology. The central formulation of hope in the Bible—particularly the New Testament—is God's future vindication of all the righteous through resurrection of the dead (body, soul, and spirit), judgment, and restoration of the fallen creation. By contrast, dominant currents in Greek philosophy—particularly the Platonic tradition—portrayed the physical creation (and the human body) as inherently defective, and the ultimate human hope as release from this historical/physical setting into the timeless realm of purely spiritual reality. In extreme forms, early non-chiliasts were basically replacing a biblical eschatology with a Platonic one (a trail previously blazed by Hellenistic Judaism).[11]

Few in the Early Church were content with such a wholesale replacement. Augustine is a good case in point. His earliest eschatological comments—still influenced by his Manichean days—portray a purely spiritual heaven transcending this temporal reality. His later struggle against dualism led him to affirm the importance of our reembodiment. But it did not lead him to embrace Irenaeus' notion of the millennial reign of Christ with the resurrected saints in a glorified physical creation. Part of the reason for this may have been Augustine's more juridical soteriology, which did not place a level of spiritual maturity as prerequisite to entering God's eternal presence.[12] This allowed him to retain the non-chiliasts' assumption that the faithful enter directly into a conscious (disembodied) existence in paradise upon their death. Moreover, Augustine's extension of redemption to the physical was quite limited (not reaching to plants, animals, etc.). While the faithful will be reembodied at the resurrection, it is not for a return to a glorified physical creation. Rather, they will then return to their eternity of heavenly contemplation and praise of God.[13]

Besides the theological factors mentioned, there was clearly also a socio-political factor behind Augustine's rejection of the notion of a temporary earthly millennium.[14] For Irenaeus, who lived in a time of the persecution of the church, Christ's reign in the millennium compensated for the relative absence of the Reign of God in the present. But Augustine framed his eschatology after Christianity's establishment as the religion of the Roman Empire. While he was careful not to identify the Reign of God univocally with either the empire or the church, he was bound to connect the new situation of the church with the promises about this Reign. Indeed, to talk about a future, more adequate, earthly Reign of God in this new context would constitute a challenge to the legitimacy of the Roman Empire—which is why belief in a millennial kingdom was condemned at the Council of Ephesus (431 CE).

The blend of elements seen in Augustine came to dominate eschatology in the Medieval West.[15] The internal tendencies of this blend became ever more evident in the process. When deceased believers enter immediately into the eternal Reign of God in paradise, the role of a future resurrection becomes increasingly moot. When heaven is epitomized in static and ethereal terms, the biblical notion of the new heavens and new earth fades from view. And, when the earthly expression of the Reign of God is closely correlated with existing structures and reality, the *status quo* is underwritten. This led, at a minimum, to adoption of a technical "amillennialism," declaring millennialist positions to be heretical.[16] The more troubling tendency was for the Bible's temporal hope of God's future vindication of the righteous and restoration of creation to be exchanged for a (neo-Platonic) model of the timeless transcendental relationship of Heaven, earthly life, and Hell—a model given classic depiction by Dante in the early fourteenth century.[17]

A serious challenge to this transcendental model arose in the radical wing of the Reformation. This challenge illustrates again the interplay between the different aspects of eschatological concern. One divergence of many Anabaptists from the Medieval model was their emphatic reappropriation of the notion that deceased believers remain in a state of soul sleep. They based this move on arguments about the "natural" meaning of Scripture. It is clear that they also valued how it allowed them to dismiss several ideas that had developed in the Medieval West related to the intermediate state of the dead—particularly claims about purgatory, limbo, a treasury of merits, and worship of the saints. More important for our purposes, their interest in soul sleep was connected to a renewed chiliasm. Given their persecution by the established churches as radicals (because they denied the validity of established religion), Anabaptists were not prone to correlate the Reign of God with present reality. They spurned the Medieval detemporalization of Christian hope, longing for a future time when God would dramatically vindicate the righteous and establish a millennial reign of true Christianity. A few of them even tried to help initiate this millennial reign, with catastrophic results.[18]

Luther joined the Anabaptists in championing soul sleep against the reigning notion of a conscious intermediate state. He would have shared their motivations of seeking the natural meaning of Scripture and undercutting practices related to the merits of the saints. However, he did not share their strongly negative evaluation of the present Reign of God (which he cast in more paradoxical relationship to the present world), and he explicitly rejected their chiliastic fervor. This left some tension in his views which Lutheran scholastics resolved by condemning the notions of soul sleep and a future millennium—in other words, by returning to the Medieval transcendental model.[19]

In contrast to Luther, early Reformed theologians retained the doctrine of the conscious state of the deceased in paradise, defending it against the notion of soul sleep.[20] They also continued the basic Medieval assumption that the Reign of God finds appropriate earthly expression in the present age, rather than a future millennial period.[21] Some ambiguity on this latter point was inevitable, however, precisely because the Reformed tradition emerged in rejection of central late-Medieval claims to this appropriate expression. There was a reformist impulse at the tradition's core. Of course, in places where the Reformed influence was strong enough to effect rapid and fairly complete transformation of the existing situation, this impulse was largely subsumed back into a rather static amillennial eschatology.

But what about where the Reformed community found themselves in the minority, and their agenda unrealized? Such was the circumstance of the Puritans in early seventeenth-century England. Connecting their reformist impulse to their confidence in the sovereignty of God, influential Puritans developed the biblical mention of a "latter-day glory" into an optimistic variety of millennialism. They argued that the final period of this present earthly age (which they discerned as imminent) would witness the incursion of the full Reign of God through the power of the Spirit and the correlated faithful efforts of believers.[22] It is important to recognize the uniqueness of this position. While they retained the assumption that deceased believers enjoy a conscious awareness of God's Reign in paradise, they did not allow this to deflect concern from attaining a fuller expression of that Reign in this world. Likewise, while they looked forward to that fuller expression of God's Reign, they did not assume that it must be preceded by the return of Christ and the resurrection of the saints. To put it in current terms, here lies the emergence of postmillennialism, as distinguished from both the amillennialism of the Medieval church and the magisterial reformers and the premillennialism of Irenaeus and the Anabaptists.

When it first emerged, the postmillennial interest of the Puritans was greeted with skepticism or disdain by mainstream Anglicans. It was viewed as a minor variation of the premillennial errors of the Anabaptists. This makes it all the more surprising that by the end of the seventeenth century the basic theme of postmillennialism—anticipation of a divinely-promised approaching "golden age"—had been widely embraced in Anglican circles, particularly among latitudinarians. The fundamental reason for this change is again one of *zeitgeist*; the optimism of postmillennialism matched cultural and political interests of the emerging Enlightenment age.[23] Indeed, this match was so strong that postmillennial assumptions would come to dominate North Atlantic Christianity by the late eighteenth century.

Responsible Grace's Triumph in Process

This historical background places us in good position to consider Wesley's understanding of doctrines related to "last things." In keeping with the dual sense of the Greek word τελος, the Christian doctrine of "last things" concerns both (1) beliefs about how God's purposes are realized through the *final* events of individual life and the present age, and (2) convictions about the way that these *ultimate* purposes impinge upon and find provisional expressions in our present lives and reality. Wesley scholars agree that both present and future dimensions of eschatology are evident in his thought. There is some disagreement about the relative weight and connection of the two dimensions. A few scholars have expressed the fear that Wesley puts too much emphasis on the present dimension.[24] The more typical concern raised in recent studies is whether he placed too little emphasis on this present dimension, particularly in relation to socio-political aspects of life.[25] Most scholars, however, have commended the creative tension between the present and future dimensions of Christian hope that they discern in Wesley, even if they have struggled to find an adequate designation to capture this tension.[26]

Perhaps the most appropriate designation for Wesley's characteristic emphases is "processive eschatology."[27] This designation implies the value that Wesley placed on the present dimension of God's gracious salvific work. It also reinforces Wesley's conviction that this present dimension is not a static reality; with every responsive attainment that we reach in salvific transformation God presents a new goal that transcends what has been attained. Of course, since we are dealing with a God of *responsible grace,* God also provides the empowerment for this further attainment.

I will consider below how this processive emphasis carries over even to Wesley's depiction of the final triumph of responsible grace. But first it is important to gain greater insight into his assumptions about the present processive triumph of responsible grace. Most investigations of this issue approach it with little consideration of Wesley's millennial views.[28] I have chosen to start with this question because of the interplay between millennialism and the other dimensions of eschatological concern.

Wesley's Millennialism?

As was mentioned earlier, Wesley scholarship has witnessed some debate over his millennial views. This debate has been framed largely in competing claims for Wesley as a premillennialist or a postmillennialist. While there is admittedly enough ambiguity in Wesley's writings to provide grounds for this debate, it has often reflected the theological contexts and agendas of the later scholars more than those of Wesley.[29] It has also suffered from inadequate consideration of development or change in Wesley's views.[30]

A careful consideration of Wesley in his context reveals that there were indeed developments in his millennial assumptions. To set the context, it is important to remember that the Anglican reformation basically carried over the Medieval transcendental model of eschatology, to the point of initially declaring hopes for a millennium to be heretical.[31] This ban on millennial views eventually eased, allowing the emerging Puritan postmillennialism to gain a hearing, along with an occasional echo of Early Church or Anabaptist premillennialism. However, amillennial assumptions would still have dominated Wesley's formal training.

The unquestioned presence of these assumptions remains evident for some time in Wesley's writings. His 1748 series of sermons on the Sermon on the Mount provide a good example. In these sermons he takes it for granted that believers enter God's eternal presence—and the fullness of God's Reign—at death. He allows that this Reign finds incipient expression in believers' lives in this world. However, he makes no mention of a hope for a fuller millennial expression of that Reign. Indeed, he treats Revelation 20:1-6 as depicting the new creation, not a millennial state on this earth. In short, he views the present Church Age as the last of God's dispensations, which will endure until the final consummation.[32]

The first clear instance of Wesley interacting directly with alternative millennial views is his 1755 comments on Revelation 20 in *NT Notes.* As stated earlier, Wesley drew upon Johann Bengel for these comments, and in this case his reliance was nearly total, with the result that he reproduced Bengel's peculiar solution to debates about the imagery in Revelation 20.[33]

It was inevitable that Bengel would wrestle with millennial debates; his Lutheran heritage embraced the amillennial perspective, while his pietist roots conveyed to him both Anabaptist arguments for premillennial readings and early Puritan suggestions of postmillennial views. Bengel tried to resolve the conflict between these positions by proposing that Revelation 20 described *two* millennia. The first millennium (discerned in verses 2, 3, and 7) will be a yet-future time of the flourishing of the church bringing righteousness to this earth, after God overthrows the beast (i.e., the papacy) and binds Satan. It will be succeeded by the second millennium (described in verses 4-6) in which the saints are taken to heaven to reign with Christ, while Satan is loosed again on earth and leads the masses of humanity astray. This second millennium will terminate with the Second Coming of Christ, who will immediately institute the general resurrection, judgment, and the final states.[34]

Despite his mediating intentions, Bengel's proposal actually adopts the fundamental aspect of postmillennialism: the expectation of a future greater expression of the Reign of God on this earth, when a flourishing church effects a period of peace and righteousness without requiring a direct intervention of Christ! This is particularly evident with Bengel's insistence that the binding of Satan that initiates the first millennium will not be obvious from an earthly perspective.[35]

Some have taken Wesley's appropriation of Bengel's exegesis of Revelation 20 to mark a conscious adoption of postmillennialism. Such a judgment misses the tentativeness of Wesley's endorsement, which is particularly evident regarding another dimension of Bengel's interpretation of Revelation. Bengel espoused a "historicist" approach to the book, assuming that it provided a cryptic map of the Church Age, which he attempted to decipher. His method of calculation was complex and went through several revisions; suffice it to say that while he initially set 1742 as the time for the return of Christ, in the books that Wesley relied on he had settled on 1836 as the inception of the *first* millennium. In other words, Bengel's final schedule for Christ's return in judgment was 3836![36] While Wesley retained these chronological suggestions in *NT Notes*, it was with a disclaimer stressing their speculative nature.[37]

Wesley's reserve about Bengel's chronology appears, in part, to reflect the continuing influence of his amillennial training. For example, it is striking that shortly after releasing *NT Notes* Wesley published a tract which highlighted a suggestion of Edmond Halley that an approaching comet might collide with and destroy the earth in 1758.[38] While Wesley's purpose was simply to "awaken" his readers, not endorse an apocalyptic deadline (a practice which he disdained[39]), he betrayed no suggestion that such an imminent end to this age was theologically impossible. Indeed, in a sermon on the Final Judgment preached in 1758 Wesley expressed an explicit expectation that the Second Coming of Christ was imminent (not offset by a millennium of peace!), and related it to a contemporaneous general resurrection and judgment (i.e., without the intervening reign of Christ in premillennialism).[40] The basic amillennial assumptions of his training were still intact.

This is particularly interesting because just after releasing *NT Notes* Wesley had also received a recommendation of a premillennial position from John Fletcher. This was Wesley's first contact with Fletcher, who soon became one of his most trusted colleagues. Fletcher argued that current social struggles would soon climax in the return of Christ to institute an era of peace. This era would later degenerate in renewed rebellion, triggering the final judgment and the end of this world.[41] That Fletcher's argument did not immediately persuade Wesley of premillennialism is evident from a 1763 sermon where Wesley defined the present task of the church as, so far as is possible, overturning the kingdom of Satan and setting up the kingdom of Christ.[42]

The one who is often credited with finally persuading Wesley of the premillennial position is Thomas Hartley. In 1764 Hartley published *Paradise Restored,* which argued for the imminent approach of Christ's glorious reign on earth with his saints.[43] Wesley read the book shortly after publication and wrote Hartley "I cannot but thank you for your strong and reasonable confirmation of that comfortable doctrine, of which I cannot entertain the least doubt as long as I believe the Bible."[44] Hartley's influence likely explains why one of Wesley's rare additions to his sources in the *OT Notes* (published in 1765) was a clarification that the time of peace promised in Isaiah 60:18 would be fulfilled in "the thousand years wherein Christ shall reign upon earth."[45]

Before joining those who conclude on this basis that Wesley's mature position was premillennialism, however, one must consider that he issued two major sermons in the 1780's that explicitly invoked the Puritan idea of a "latter day glory" in describing how the Methodist revival was contributing to the "silent increase" of the Reign of God in the world. This increase was expected to eventuate soon in an era of peace and love, an era that would *culminate* with the return of Christ.[46] A stronger expression of the postmillennialism commended by the Puritans (and essentially endorsed by Bengel) is hard to imagine![47]

What are we to make of this apparent reversal? It is difficult to dismiss the later postmillennial sermons as aberrations; their basic tone resonates with the affirmation of God's present redemptive activity that characterizes the whole of Wesley's thought, even if they extend this affirmation beyond some of his earlier works. In direct contrast, there is little in Wesley that corresponds to the assumption (which has characterized much of modern premillennialism) that present spiritual and social conditions can only worsen until the return of Christ.[48]

This raises the serious possibility that too much has been made of Wesley's interest in Hartley. Examination reveals that Wesley's primary attention was actually devoted not to the exposition of premillennialism in Hartley's *Paradise Restored* but to the appended "Short Defense of the Mystical Writers."[49] More important, I would contend that the basic element which Wesley was endorsing in Hartley's argument for an earthly millennial reign of Christ was Hartley's insistence on a place for all of creation—not just humanity—in God's redemptive work.[50] This was clearly what attracted Wesley about Thomas Burnet's millennial speculations, which he read shortly after.[51] As will be detailed below, a growing insistence on the redemption of all creation runs through Wesley's late writings (1765ff). Since this emphasis was at odds with the residual transcendentalism prominent in current Anglicanism, Wesley readily entertained potential allies. On initial exposure to Hartley's exposition, premillennialism would have appeared to be a strong ally. In time, however, Wesley appears to have realized that many premillennialists confine any salvific benefits for the physical creation to the millennium, anticipating a purely ethereal final state.[52] In his 1785 sermon on "The New Creation" Wesley specifically rejected such a temporary renovation, arguing in detail that the renewed physical creation is God's ultimate goal.[53] With the apparent advantage of premillennialism thus neutralized, the way was cleared for the strong postmillennial expressions noted in contemporaneous late sermons to emerge.

The Kingdom of Grace and the Kingdom of Glory

This emergence of explicit postmillennial sympathies was actually a consistent development of Wesley's central abiding eschatological convictions. For example, a basic assumption of postmillennialism is that the Reign of God is not simply a transcendent contrast to the fallen earthly situation, or a blessing reserved solely for some future era. Rather, God's Reign has an active presence in our current reality through the work of the Spirit in and through believers. This conviction is evident throughout Wesley's writings. Its most detailed articulation is in his 1748 sermon on the Lord's Prayer. In his exposition of the invocation of God's Reign, Wesley posited a distinction between two dimensions of the Kingdom of

God (or the Kingdom of Heaven, which he usually treated as equivalent): one dimension is the "Kingdom of Glory," its eternal fullness in God's Presence; the other dimension is the "Kingdom of Grace," its incipient expression in believers' lives. He stressed that this incipient expression was not simply internal. It is more than assurance of participation in the Kingdom of Glory, it is present happiness and holiness. Those in whom the Kingdom of Grace is present will do God's will here on earth. In that sense, the Kingdom of God begins below and is continued and perfected when we remove from this life.[54] As Charles put the basic point to verse, in the present experience of the Spirit's transforming power we "anticipate our Heaven below."[55]

Of course, affirmation of a present dimension of the Reign of God is not sufficient to designate Wesley a postmillennialist. At most it rules out correlation with extreme forms of premillennialism. As was noted earlier, other sermons in the same series as the one on the Lord's Prayer reflect the amillennial assumptions of the model in which Wesley was trained. As he illustrates, nothing in this model rules out incipient historical expressions of God's Reign. On the other hand, the model's identification of God's perfect Reign with God's eternal transcendence tends to undercut concern for a future realization of God's redemptive purposes for the entire created order. The mature Wesley's growing dissatisfaction with this aspect of the transcendental model will be traced in the final section of this chapter. In essence, his focus of redemptive expectation increasingly shifted from a transcendent Heaven to a future New Creation. Cast in these terms, the believer's present experience of the Spirit's transforming power (i.e., the Kingdom of Grace) is not so much an "anticipation of Heaven above" as a "taste of the powers of the world to come."[56]

To be sure, an insistence on the New Creation could be accommodated in a revised amillennial position. Where postmillennialism finally diverges from the former, as well as from moderate forms of premillennialism, is in its conviction that the incipient presence of the Reign of God in our present world is a *growing* reality, spurred on by the expectation of a penultimate fulfillment of that Reign prior to the New Creation. The discussion of Wesley's understanding of salvation in earlier chapters demonstrated how central the expectation of a growing expression of the Reign of God (Kingdom of Grace) in the individual's life was throughout his writings. His late sermons connecting the Methodist revival with the increase of the Reign of God in the world simply extended this expectation to corporate human life. With this extension, his underlying postmillennial convictions come into full view.

The Reign of Grace in and through the Church

Given his affirmation of God's universal Prevenient Grace, the mature Wesley could identify providential increases in the present Reign of God with secular events like the American and French revolutions.[57] However, his more typical emphasis was on the role of the community of believers in spreading the Reign of God.[58] To develop this role, it would be helpful to sketch Wesley's basic ecclesiological assumptions (readers interested in more technical issues about his views on church government or ministry should consult the available studies[59]).

A good point of entry into Wesley's understanding of the church is recognition of his functional focus—he construed the essence of the church in terms of its contribution to God's redemptive purpose of transforming human life.[60] As he once stated this criterion,

> What is the end of all ecclesiastical order? Is it not to bring souls from the power of Satan to God, and to build them up in his fear and love? Order, then, is so far valuable as it answers these ends: and if it answers them not, it is nothing worth.[61]

Wesley did not consider this functional criterion to be antithetical to episcopal polity. Indeed, he insisted on his preference for and loyalty to Anglicanism to his death.[62] Nonetheless, his utilitarian approach often placed him at odds with the Anglican hierarchy. This meant that his ecclesiological reflection took place in the midst of a struggle to shepherd an "evangelical order" within a church that offered little support for his enterprise.[63] The eventual fruit of this practical-theological venture was a creative synthesis of Anglican and Moravian/pietist emphases: an ecclesiological ideal of small intentional communities integrally linked to the larger church (*ecclesiolae* in *ecclesia*).[64]

The discussion of the means of grace in Chapter Eight should suggest why both elements were crucial to Wesley's ecclesiology. The larger church provides the liturgical worship and sacraments that are indispensable to the empowerment and patterning for Christian life. This role is captured well in the Anglican definition of the church as a place where the pure Word of God is preached and the sacraments duly administered, which explains Wesley's retention of this definition in his Articles of Religion.[65] If he differed at all from the Anglican sense of this point, it would be that he took this simply as a functional definition, not a listing of the marks for determining whether a church was qualified to dispense salvation.[66]

The correlating contribution of the small intentional communities to nurturing Christian life is the support and accountability they provide.

This contribution is captured best in Wesley's characteristic informal definition of the church: the spiritual community of God's people.[67] As this definition suggests, Wesley's mature ecclesiology shifted the focus from the church as institution to the church as community. The value of such a shift continues to draw attention in present ecclesiological discussion.[68]

One further characteristic ecclesiological theme was Wesley's unwillingness to define the church's holiness simply in terms of its relationship to Christ. He insisted that the church must be holy in the fuller sense of nurturing—and expecting—the progressive holiness of each of its members.[69] While this insistence will raise the fear of Donatism among many Western Christians, it is an obvious corollary of *responsible grace.*[70]

Wesley's concern for the internal holiness of the church may raise the additional fear that he would isolate believers from the world, minimizing any impact that they could have in advancing the broader Reign of God, but this overlooks his relational understanding of holiness. We have seen that he defined holiness as essentially love for God and love for others. On such terms, the more we grow in holiness, the more we will give our lives in service to others—both in the church and in the world.[71]

This raises the question of how the community of believers can most appropriately serve humanity at large in advancing the Reign of God. Wesley assumed that it should serve both their spiritual need (through evangelism) and their physical and material needs (through works of mercy). His conviction of the integrity of both types of service grew over time. In the initial stages of the revival he accepted it as obvious that a primary motive for works of mercy was the hope of converting sinners, citing as warrant Jude 7: "what avails it to relieve their temporal wants who are just dropping into eternal fire?"[72] When the later debates with the quietists heated up, however, he found this verse being used to reject all works of mercy as lost labor. His response was to repudiate once-and-for-all the valuation of works of mercy merely as incentives to evangelization. Serving the physical and material needs of others was given integrity in its own right (as a command of God), whether it leads to opportunities for evangelization or not. To neglect such service, Wesley warned, was to endanger one's own salvation.[73]

Wesley's Eschatological Ethics

Wesley's stress on the importance of works of mercy provides a convenient transition to considering his ethical teachings. Once again, the focus of interest will be on basic theological dimensions, not a detailed consideration of specific ethical recommendations. A key issue will be relating

Wesley's ethical convictions to his eschatological vision of spreading the Reign of God in individual lives, social structures, and creation at large.

Personal Ethics

The first area to be considered is personal ethics; i.e., issues related primarily to individual holiness of heart and life.[74] Wesley's most intentional statements of pastoral direction in this area are the General Rules and a series of public tracts, all framed in the midst of the debates with the quietists in the mid-1740's.[75] This context weighted his presentation toward emphasis on the human responsibility to live out God's gracious design for our lives. Such an emphasis could suggest a morose legalism that reduces Christian life to a set of dreary rules, but Wesley would have rejected such a characterization. As shown in Chapter Eight, he understood the General Rules to be character-forming disciplines that nurture Christian holiness. Since he also believed that holiness was integrally related to happiness, he could insist that only a Christian could be truly happy in this life.[76] In other words, as Outler has argued, Wesley was actually a *eudaimonist*, convinced and consistent all his life.[77]

Another fear commonly raised in the area of personal ethics is dualism, or the false opposition of Christian life to the "world." In this case the greatest concern would be sparked by Wesley's occasional warnings against associating too closely with the "sinful world," lest one be infected by its sinful disease.[78] Yet, Wesley's very use of the qualifier "sinful" reflects that he did not identify human life in the world per se as sinful. While one might want to debate specific instances, it seems unwarranted to charge him with a strong ethical dualism (cf. Chapter Three).

One other concern sometimes expressed about a theological emphasis on personal ethics like that found in Wesley is that it fosters an individualistic focus on preserving personal purity, at the expense of caring for others. This concern reflects the fact that there has been a recurrent dichotomy in the history of Western ethics between the axiom of avoiding evil and the axiom of doing good. But here is precisely one of Wesley's greatest strengths. His General Rules specifically connect the injunction to do no harm with the instruction to do good.[79] Moreover, consideration of his use of the phrase "doing good" suggests that he meant by it "being of aid to others."[80] If there is any doubt, the variety of ways in which he and the Methodist people actually ministered to the physical and material needs of others will surely settle it.[81]

Social Ethics[82]

As ethical attention turns to the welfare of others we move into the realm of social ethics. Here the issue is not what forms holiness of character, but what expresses or embodies justice and caring in corporate contexts. In terms of Wesley, the issue is whether James Cone is correct that Wesley's concern for "the warm heart and all that stuff" distracted him from attention to social, political, and economic needs.[83]

As Cone's charge suggests, any adequate analysis of Wesley's social ethics must begin with questions about his understanding of sin and salvation. These questions have been central to recent studies. Several of these studies have argued that while Wesley centered the source of sin in the individual he also perceived the reality of sin's presence and distortion in social and political arenas.[84] Others have suggested that Wesley's emphasis of sanctification involved by analogy transformation of society.[85] Some scholars have been more circumspect, acknowledging that Wesley's awareness of the structural nature of the social problems with which he was trying to grapple was limited, but assessing this as simply a defect of his time, while arguing that his understanding of sin and salvation support a social ethic.[86] Finally, a few scholars have broadened the perspective, highlighting Wesley's "inaugurated eschatology" and his basic conviction of *responsible grace* as foundational to a concern for social and economic issues.[87]

Obviously, the theological foundations of Wesley's social ethics would not even be under discussion if he had not offered ethical direction for the social dimensions of his followers' lives. A brief synopsis of this advice is in order, beginning with his advice on economic issues.[88]

Wesley's economic ethic can be summarized in four points: (1) ultimately everything belongs to God; (2) resources are placed in our care to use as God sees fit; (3) God desires that we use these resources to meet our necessities (i.e., providing shelter and food for ourselves and dependents), and then to help others in need; thus, (4) spending resources on luxuries for ourselves while others remain in need is robbing God![89]

Wesley once paraphrased this ethic—in specific relation to money—in three rules: Gain all you can, save all you can, and give all you can.[90] Some have quoted this maxim as evidence that Wesley epitomized Max Weber's "Protestant Ethic," embracing laissez-faire capitalism.[91] Needless to say, this claim has sparked considerable debate over Wesley's economics.[92] It certainly misrepresents his emphasis in the sermon in question. In discussing the first rule, Wesley's concern was actually to enjoin social responsibility in the manner in which one acquires property, capital, or the means of production; concerning the second rule, he placed primary emphasis on self-denial in use of one's resources, not wasting them on idle expenses or luxuries; then, in the third rule, he renounced accumulation of anything above what meets one's needs, directing its use to meet the needs of our neighbors.[93] In other words, while Adam Smith held that surplus accumulation was the foundation of economic well-being, Wesley viewed it as mortal sin![94] Unfortunately, he found it hard to convince his people of this. They tended to embrace his first two rules and ignore the third! Wesley considered this more than a minor deviation. Through the final decade of his ministry he issued a series of warnings that the increasing wealth of the Methodists correlated directly with a decline in their spiritual growth and in the progress of the revival.[95]

Everything considered so far fits within voluntary Christian charity to those in need. Did Wesley ever focus ethical concern on socio-political changes aimed at alleviating the causes of economic hardship? As mentioned earlier, it is anachronistic to assume that he could have shared our awareness of this dimension of the problem. But this makes the glimpses of such awareness that we do find all the more striking. The strongest example is surely his 1773 *Thoughts on the Present Scarcity of Provisions.* In this tract Wesley traces the current scarcity of food to the waste of grain in distilling, raising too many horses for carriages and French nobility, the monopolizing of farms, general pursuit of luxury by the wealthy, high rents, and high taxes. Among solutions that he proposed were prohibiting distilling, taxing the exportation of horses and use of carriages, banning large farms, repressing luxury, abolishing half of the national debt, and dropping all useless pensions.[96] Admittedly, this sweeping proposal must be tempered by the knowledge that Wesley later read a tract which introduced the principle of inflation to contextualize the present situation, convincing him that things were not really degenerating as he had thought.[97] Even so, some perception of structural contributions to economic situations and a corresponding willingness to support political solutions can be considered characteristic of his mature position.[98]

What was it that deepened Wesley's sensitivity to the corporate/structural dimensions of poverty, moving him beyond his inherited model of self-sufficiency? The basic answer is practical-theological reflection on his involvement in the lives of the poor, including his support of his impoverished sisters.[99] And what made the late Wesley more likely to support political solutions in pursuing ends consistent with the greater Reign of God in the world? I would suggest that it was his contemporaneous growing emphasis on Prevenient Grace. This emphasis would have ruled out any dichotomy between "secular" and "sacred" forms of achieving God's purposes.[100]

The recognition that the mature Wesley showed increased support for some political agendas should not lead to the conclusion that he placed great hope in political action bringing in the millennium. In reality, Wesley remained a political conservative throughout his life—in the technical sense that he considered government's proper primary task to be inhibiting evil more than promoting well-being. His basic reason for this stance was his conviction of universal sinfulness and the subtle ways that even good human aspirations can be twisted to demonic results.[101]

One of the more notorious forms that Wesley's political stance took was initial rejection of the democratic agenda of the American colonists. His stated fear of democracy was that it would degenerate into tyranny because it grounded government in fallible human opinion rather than in God.[102] The apparent implication of this claim is that monarchy is divinely-sanctioned! Indeed, it was common for earlier studies to identify Wesley as a Tory who assumed the divine right of kings and totally rejected democracy.[103] More recent scholarship has argued convincingly that his support of the monarchy was always contingent upon the latter's protection of human rights (particularly from the threat of political anarchists!), and that Wesley was equally attracted to some elements of constitutionalism.[104] Going further, Leon Hynson has argued that one can trace in Wesley a growing willingness to critique the monarchy (or any other governmental system) in terms of how it supported those basic human rights that follow from our creation in the Image of God.[105]

This clearly calls into question the charge that Wesley (particularly the late Wesley) never submitted political laws to a searching criticism of whether they might be bad.[106] The best counterexample to this charge is the topic of slavery. Wesley's encounter with slavery in Georgia made him a vocal opponent of the institution. This opposition was not always easy; for example, his colleague George Whitefield owned slaves and had offered a biblical, humanitarian, and economic rationale for the practice (to make their lives comfortable and to lay the foundation for raising their posterity in the nurture and admonition of the Lord). Wesley's most developed response to such arguments was *Thoughts Upon Slavery*, which systematically contested the various humanitarian and economic justifications of slavery. More important, Wesley drew upon his central mature theological convictions about human equality and Prevenient Grace to provide a theological critique of slavery.[107] Admittedly, the focus of this tract was a voluntary appeal to slave owners, but Wesley's strength of conviction led to increasing support of political moves to abolish slavery in his later years.[108]

Ecological Ethics

The last area of ethics to be considered is ecological ethics. The suggestion that Wesley had an ecological ethic will likely strike readers as anachronistic. Yet, as will be detailed below, he stood out in his contemporary Western setting as a notable exception in affirming God's ultimate purpose of restoring all creation. It would be reasonable to expect him to have encouraged penultimate expressions of this purpose; and indeed he did express a concern that was rare in his day for humane treatment of animals.[109] It is possible to identify the foundations for an ecological ethic drawing on such comments.[110] The more important point is that Wesley's basic theological perspective is conducive to an ecological ethic. In a recent study Douglas Hall has contended that one of the key problems undercutting concern for ecology in Christian circles is a lack of balance between divine sovereignty and human responsibility. Hall then argued that what is needed is a theology that joins a strong doctrine of *grace* with an equally strong place for *responsible* human willing.[111] This, of course, is precisely what Wesley offers.

Responsible Grace's Triumphant Goal

The preceding section should have provided a general sense of Wesley's assumptions about the present provisional expressions of the triumph of responsible grace. It is now time to turn attention to his hopes about the final triumph of that grace, both in individual lives and in creation as a whole. This topic is again best understood against the background of the prevailing eschatological model of his day.

As we noted earlier, neo-Platonic emphases progressively dominated Medieval eschatology. In the process, the biblical hope for future new life in the new heavens and new earth was increasingly replaced by the aspiration of immediate translation at death to a transcendent spiritual heaven (with no place for plants, animals, or even truly physical bodies). In effect, the reality of death was muted (it was simply a transition to "glory"), and the traditional intermediate states blurred into ultimate goals.[112]

A concern to readmit plants and animals to the ultimate hope is evident in some Renaissance figures, and even noticeable (to a lesser degree) in Luther and Calvin. Subsequent Protestant and Catholic theology banished such non-spiritual presences again, however, in the interest of keeping eternal glory focused solely on worship of God. As a result, the model of a transcendent "spiritual" Heaven dominated the major Western Christian traditions, including Anglicanism, through the eighteenth century.[113]

As such, it is not surprising to find Charles Wesley's hymns rather consistently treating death as simply our transition to eternal life with God in glory, and assuring us that this eternal life will continue long after the destruction of the earthly world.[114] What *is* surprising—and will be the focus of the remainder of this chapter—is the degree to which John Wesley came to question this inherited transcendental model of the ultimate hope in his later years.

Death, Immortality, Resurrection

One of the things that strikes many twentieth-century readers as odd is Wesley's fascination with death scenes, particularly those of Christians who expire peacefully, praising God.[115] Equally puzzling is his inclusion of a section of hymns "Describing Death" in his hymnal for Methodist worship. In both cases it is apparent that he considered reflection on death to be beneficial for gaining perspective on this life.[116] While some in our age of "death denial" might view this as a morbid preoccupation, it was a common practice of his time, and it can be argued that it maintains a healthy balance of treating death as both penalty and promise.[117]

The theme of death as promise comes through strongly in many of the hymns just mentioned, such as one that begins "Ah, lovely appearance of death!"[118] The basic point of these hymns, and of John's related sermons, is that death holds nothing for a Christian to fear, indeed it should be welcomed as deliverance from the burdens of life into God's loving care. Of course, while this may have provided comfort to those facing death, it must be admitted that there was often a lurking undertone of condemnation for survivors who mourned the loss of their loved ones too deeply.[119]

In addition to psychological questions, such easy talk of death as promise raises the theological question of whether it has shifted the focus from the biblical hope for resurrection to the Platonic confidence in the immortality of the soul. As originally framed, these notions carried quite different emphases. The doctrine of the immortality of the soul was ultimately an insistence that our spiritual human nature was such that it simply *can* not be destroyed (thus we do not really die). The hope of a future resurrection was based more on a confidence that God *will* not leave us in death (i.e., death is seen as real, but God's grace as more real). It was noted above that some early theologians sided strongly with the emphasis on resurrection, assuming that the deceased await this event in a state of "sleep." Others, assuming a conscious intermediate state, tried to integrate the two notions. The common way of doing this was to argue that the immortality of the soul was not "natural," but a gift of God in anticipation of the universal resurrection.[120]

Wesley never seriously entertained the possibility of soul sleep or the annihilation of the person, contingent upon future resurrection. He refers to the idea only once, rejecting it as a recent invention.[121] While this was in keeping with official Anglican tradition, it is surprising that he showed no more awareness of the precedents among early theologians, the Anabaptists, and even scattered advocates in prior English history.[122] In any case, Wesley took it as obvious that the death of the body could not be the death of our soul.[123] Perhaps sensing the same uneasiness with this claim as the Early Church, he once suggested that this immortality of the soul was not "natural," but a benefit of Prevenient Grace.[124]

To this point Wesley's emphases could fit easily within the transcendental model of his training. However, the atemporal focus of this model could tend to displace interest in the future resurrection of the body. Wesley would have none of this, or the subtle contempt for the body that lay behind it. He consistently affirmed the importance of the resurrection of the body. In fact, in 1732 he abridged and preached a sermon of Benjamin Calamy which argued that the resurrection body was a fresh production of our original body in refined state, not a "new" body (to make this point he had to claim that God would preserve the dust of our body unmixed!).[125] While this literalism would fade slightly, the commitment to bodily resurrection runs steady throughout Wesley's writings.[126]

Intermediate States

I suggested earlier that the Medieval transcendental model tended to blur any distinction between the intermediate situation of believers following death and their ultimate hope. One example of this concerns assumptions about the status between death and resurrection of those sensory abilities that presently rely upon bodily organs. The typical claim of the Medieval model was not only that these abilities would still function in the (disembodied) intermediate state but that they will be *more* acute—leaving one wondering why we need the new body! Wesley adopted this claim of heightened senses in the intermediate state, even while admitting its ambiguities.[127] One way that he tried to resolve the problem was to suggest that our spirit retains an "ethereal body" in its disembodied state.[128] Eventually he simply admitted that he was not sure how it was possible, but it would be the case.[129]

What about the broader transcendental tendency to speak of believers stepping directly from this temporal existence into the fullness of eternal glory? It has already been noted that Charles' hymns reflect this language. John's early sermons do as well (though with some reservation), and remnants of it can be found through the middle period of his ministry.[130] The late Wesley, however, came to reject quite explicitly any equation of the current state of deceased believers with their ultimate hope.[131] While his mature discussions of these issues could use the language of "entering eternity" at death, he immediately clarified that we then enjoy (or suffer) only the *intermediate* expressions of our full destiny, as we await the resurrection, judgment, and the new creation.[132]

The stronger that this emphasis became in Wesley's teaching, the more that he reflected on the nature of these intermediate expressions. This was a topic of considerable discussion in his time, and Wesley interacted with this discussion increasingly over the last few years of his life.[133] One result of this interaction was more explicit differentiation of the intermediate and final states. For example, while Wesley always technically identified Paradise as the intermediate state where deceased believers await resurrection, for some time his descriptions of it quickly blurred into language about the eternal "other world."[134] By contrast, his latest sermons emphasized that, for all of its relative blessedness, Paradise is only the *antechamber* to the full blessedness that God has in store for the saints.[135] In the same way, through most of his ministry Wesley tended to present Hell on Dante's terms, as a contemporaneous realm of eternal torment into which those who die out of pardoning relationship with God immediately descend.[136] Once again, his latest sermons differentiate carefully between the current intermediate state of those awaiting judgment, and the future realm of punishment for the damned, in this case by means of a distinction between *Hades* and Hell.[137]

It should be noted that the late Wesley eventually came to understand *Hades* as a generic term for the realm of all the dead. Paradise then became that subset of *Hades* for the pardoned. Wesley did not mention a specific name for the subset of the reprobate (traditionally, "Tarturus"). More important, he did not allow for any further subsets of the intermediate state beyond these two. Chapter One pointed out that the mature Wesley chose to deal with the problem of God's judgment of the unevangelized by appeal to the universal presence of Prevenient Grace, ruling out Limbo. Likewise, he vigorously rejected the Medieval Western notion of Purgatory. Some of his critical comments in this regard reflect the mistaken assumption that Purgatory provided for gaining forgiveness of sins not repented of in this life. His more fundamental problem with the notion of Purgatory was its assumption of a necessary role for suffering in sanctifying human life.[138]

Wesley's very last sermon presents his most intriguing suggestion about the intermediate state. Whereas his earlier descriptions of Paradise present it in largely static terms as a place where we converse with the saints who have gone before while awaiting the resurrection, this sermon presents the idea that Paradise will be a place where souls of the righteous "ripen" for heaven, getting perpetually holier and happier.[139] This suggestion has a characteristically Eastern Christian tone to it, reminiscent of Irenaeus' description of the purpose of the Millennium. Indeed, Wesley's probable immediate source for the idea was a book consciously drawing on Eastern Orthodox eschatology.[140] Whatever its source, this suggestion fits well with Wesley's conviction about the progressive nature of salvation.

Judgment

Wesley joined the rest of the Christian tradition in connecting judgment to the ultimate hope. He also joined the majority of this tradition in an apparent paradox about that judgment. When one assumed, like Irenaeus, that the deceased await the resurrection in an inert state, then final judgment following the general resurrection truly determines eternal destiny. But when the dominant assumption became instead that the dead pass into conscious intermediate states that are distinct for those who will enjoy eternal salvation and those who will be eternally reprobate, the final judgment appears to be preempted! A common attempt to handle this was to distinguish between particular judgment (at each person's death) and the final judgment.[141] In reality this simply named the problem, and did little to subvert the transcendental impulse to collapse final judgment into particular judgments. Wesley protested this shifting of emphasis to particular judgment, but he also continued to assume that the soul's eternal state is indicated from the moment of death by its intermediate state.[142] If forced to explain the need for final judgment in this event, he likely would have joined the Protestant scholastics in stressing its role for displaying God's glory (*both* justice and mercy) and vindicating righteousness.[143]

When attention turned to the criteria for final judgment there would have been less unanimity between Wesley and Protestant scholastics, particularly Lutheran scholastics. It was noted in Chapter Six that Wesley's initial stronger emphasis on justification by faith was soon tempered by his enduring concern about the role for our responsible appropriation of God's grace. One way that he initially resolved this tension was to agree that admission to eternal salvation was based on faith alone, but to suggest that proportionate reward in heaven was decided by consideration of our active response (i.e., our "works").[144] This notion of variable measures of blessing in heaven carried over into later writings. But the late Wesley also came to insist that initial judgment itself must be based on our works, and that those who deny this are sapping the foundation of inward and outward holiness.[145]

If Wesley's conviction about the co-operant nature of grace led him to place increased emphasis in the matter of judgment on our responsive appropriation of God's offered healing work, it also constrained him to respect the integrity of our possible final rejection of that offer—to our ultimate condemnation. While this possibility is truly grievous, the alternative would ultimately involve either irresistible or indiscriminate salvation, both of which are contradictory to a God of *responsible grace.*[146]

What would this possible state of final rejection of God's healing work in one's life involve? Wesley was well aware of the symbolic function of the term *Gehenna* and other biblical images for damnation.[147] He consistently identified loss of the potential intimate fellowship with God, Christ, and the saints as the essence of the damnation described in these images.[148] Interestingly, this did not render him amenable to the current arguments for annihilationism as an alternative to eternal conscious suffering.[149] While the biblical images may not be literal, Wesley was convinced that they connote at least that actual physical suffering will be involved in the eternal consequences of separation from God.[150]

The New Creation

If the essence of damnation is separation from God, it is only natural that Wesley would identify the essence of heaven as the opportunity to see God, to know God, and to love God.[151] This identification is hardly original to Wesley. It was central to the spiritualized model of heaven common in his day. On this model heaven is a purely spiritual state, where human spirits dwelling in glorified (i.e., spiritualized!) bodies join with all other spiritual beings (no animals!) in continuous worship of the Ultimate Spiritual Being. One of the classic expressions of this model is Richard Baxter's *Saints Everlasting Rest,* which describes heavenly eternal worship of God as "a spiritual rest, suitable for a spiritual nature."[152] Part of the reason that this book became a classic is that Wesley abridged it and republished it repeatedly, circulating it throughout Britain.[153] There can be little doubt that he shared its emphasis on the centrality of worship of God to eternal blessedness.

Through most of his ministry Wesley shared much more than this aspect of the transcendental spiritual view of heaven. In particular, he typically presented heaven as a currently-existing higher reality than this world that is the salvific goal of our lives. Consider, for example, this well-known portion of the Preface to the first volume of *Sermons*:

> I am a spirit come from God and returning to God; just hovering over the great gulf, till a few moments hence I am no more seen—I drop into an unchangeable eternity! I want to know one thing, the way to heaven—how to land safe on that happy shore. God himself has condescended to teach the way: for this very end he came from heaven.[154]

In clear contrast with this quotation, the late Wesley placed increased emphasis on the traditional distinction between three heavens. Only the third heaven is an unchanging reality, being the immediate residence of God. It is into this heaven that saints ascend at death. But (Wesley now insisted) the saints' residence in the third heaven is only temporary, while they await the new creation—that is, the recreation of the (other two) heavens and the earth.[155]

As this change in the use of "heaven" reflects, the late Wesley decisively shifted the focus of his ultimate hope from "heaven above" to the future new creation.[156] Indeed, the new creation became one of the most prominent themes of his late sermons. These sermons leave no doubt that the new creation will be a physical place, though each of its basic elements will be dramatically improved over present conditions. Indeed, they will be even better than the paradise that Adam and Eve knew. There is also no doubt that all creatures will partake in the new creation. The only doubt that Wesley suggests concerns how much more advanced the animals will be in the new creation than now. He speculates, for example, that they will be endowed with reason![157] While this may strike modern readers as pointless speculation, for Wesley it was a quite serious matter of theodicy. He argues that the only satisfactory answer to questions that the present evil in the world raises about the wisdom and goodness of God is for God to restore in salvation even *more* than was present in original creation.[158]

This emphasis on cosmic redemption found in Wesley's late sermons was quite unusual for his time. While there were some contemporary Western sources that would have influenced him, it seems reasonable that his familiarity with this theme in some early Greek theologians also played a role.[159] His sympathy for the general perspective of these early Greek theologians surely played a role in one other suggestion that he offered concerning the nature of our ultimate hope.[160] In 1763 Wesley made the passing comment that growth in grace was so characteristic of the Christian life that the "perfect" would continue to grow to all eternity.[161] Just when one might lay this aside as a quirk, in 1787 Wesley published a translation of Charles Bonnet's *Conjectures Concerning the Nature of Future Happiness*, with a preface commending it as one of the most sensible books on this subject he knew. In this book Bonnet argued that progression in our abilities and maturity is so central to what it means to be human that we will surely continue to progress in the life to come![162]

With his endorsement of Bonnet, one is tempted to say that Wesley finally exchanged the static "rest" of heaven for the progressive "life" of the new creation.[163] More to the point of this study, his mature eschatology had been reshaped in keeping with his larger theological convictions and his orienting concern: the therapeutic *grace* of God was now truly universal (reaching all creation) and truly *responsible* (allowing for continual growth in responsiveness and transformation)!

CONCLUDING REFLECTIONS

I noted in the Introduction that this extended study of Wesley began with the hunch that he might have something to offer contemporary debates concerning the nature and practice of theology. I trust that the preceding chapters have provided some sense of the dynamic connection between theological reflection and Christian life in the world in Wesley's practical-theological activity. For example, we have seen how he tested and reframed doctrinal claims in light of experience (e.g., the role of assurance in salvation and the variable nature of salvation), how theological concerns guided his structuring of the Methodist movement (e.g., the distinctive combination of the means of grace), and how he emphasized the regulative implications of doctrinal convictions for Christian life (e.g., the three offices of Christ and the doctrine of the Trinity).

The Introduction also pointed out that the most serious question concerning Wesley's model of practical-theological activity is whether it sacrifices any appreciable consistency to the demands of the context. Accordingly, a major goal of the preceding chapters has been to demonstrate a dynamic consistency in Wesley's various situation-related theological expressions, reflecting the influence of an abiding orienting concern. In part this meant tracing the connecting thread of individual doctrinal themes through the transitions from the early to the late Wesley—see especially the nature of grace (Chapter Three), justification by faith (Chapter Six), and the purpose of the means of grace (Chapter Eight). At a deeper level it involved pointing out interconnections between doctrinal themes, such as (1) the congruence between his mature views on Prevenient Grace and his understanding of the purpose of infant baptism or the possible salvation of the unevangelized, (2) the role of tempers in his anthropology and his conception of the contribution of the means of grace, or (3) his emphasis on progressive sanctification and his emergent postmillennialism. Throughout it required relating his characteristic theological convictions (and any transitions in them) to his proposed orienting concern of *responsible grace.* To the degree that these efforts are judged successful, Wesley's potential as one possible mentor for current attempts to renew the practice of theology should have been strengthened.

This brings me to the proposal of the orienting concern of "responsible grace" itself. I hope that I have been able to convey a sufficient sense of the dynamic nature of this concern and its permeating presence in Wesley's theology, precisely because I believe that its importance goes *beyond* any unifying function that it might play in Wesley's own thought. I have become increasingly convinced that Wesley's insight into and articulation of this dynamic orienting concern is one of the most instructive contributions that he has to offer to present theological debate. This conviction is based on a judgment that Wesley's orienting "hermeneutical perspective" is distinctively appropriate to, and rooted in, Scripture. It is heightened by the promise that I sense in Wesley's orienting concern for bridging some longstanding ecclesial/theological divides.

As background for this latter claim, I would suggest that the major theological divisions in Christianity are due in part to alternative conceptions of (or *concerns* about) the defining aspect of God's grace. Consider the divisions within Western Christianity. The dominating concern of the Lutheran reformation was to emphasize the unmerited nature of justifying grace, or *free grace*.[1] While the Reformed tradition agreed with this basic Lutheran claim, the more distinctive concern of the Reformed tradition has been to stress God's sovereign disposal of all grace, or *sovereign grace*.[2] A direct reaction to this emphasis emerged within the Reformed tradition—the Arminian insistence on *cooperant grace*.[3] Meanwhile, the radical wing of the Reformation rejected the primarily forensic account of grace in both of the magisterial Protestant traditions, placing defining emphasis on *sanctifying grace*.[4] And the Roman Catholic response to the various Protestant splits, while sharing the greater emphasis on sanctification with the radical wing, was most concerned to defend a claim that the radicals typically denied—that both justifying and sanctifying grace are mediated through the offices and sacraments of the church, or *mediated grace*.[5]

Without rehearsing all the battles, suffice it to say that from the Reformation period on accusations and countercharges have been exchanged between these Western traditions over the implications of each other's characteristic emphasis. What is needed, if these divides are to be bridged theologically, is a conception of grace that can avoid the suggestion of merited salvation while upholding the importance of our transformation in Christ-likeness; or again, a conception that can stress God's gracious sovereignty in a way that actually enhances the place of human responsiveness; or yet again, a conception that can illuminate the vital connections between the pardoning and the transforming dimensions of grace; or finally, a conception that can value the many means through which grace is mediated without rendering use of these means mechanical or presumptuous. I trust that the preceding survey of Wesley's theological convictions makes clear why I believe that his conception of *responsible grace* bears promise in each of these cases.

To the degree that Wesley's conception does help mediate between characteristic Protestant and Roman Catholic theological divisions, it will be of interest to the Eastern Christian traditions.[6] This interest will surely be increased if I have been successful in demonstrating that Wesley's theology presents a creative integration of the juridical and therapeutic emphases that have historically tended to diverge in Eastern and Western Christianity. Wesley was deeply sympathetic with the characteristic Eastern concern for *divinizing grace.*[7] Precisely for this reason, his integral connection of justification to this divinization bears promise for helping to recover a theological wholeness that can contribute to the healing of the long-suffering divide between Eastern and Western Christianity.

The great irony is that any recovery of Wesley as a mentor in the larger Christian community will have to begin at home! Wesley's descendants rather quickly dismissed him as a model for the practice of theological activity, and this dismissal widely led to the loss of the distinctive tension of his concern for responsible grace.[8] As such, my most immediate hope is that this study will serve in some small way to facilitate the recent move among Wesley's modern descendants to reconsider him as a theological mentor.

But this poses what has become for me a crucial question: What would it *mean* to take Wesley as a mentor? Or how would one engage in authentic *Wesleyan* theological activity today? In light of the preceding study, the one thing that it certainly would *not* mean is simple collation and repetition of Wesley's theological pronouncements as a scholastic authority. Rather it would mean—at the very least—to bring theological activity into the service of nurturing contemporary Christian life and witness, just as he did.[9] I believe that it would also mean to bring the orienting concern of *responsible grace* to that situation-related theological activity. In this process it will undoubtedly be necessary to deal with issues that Wesley did not treat, to develop areas of doctrine that he only touched on, to nuance claims that he boldly asserted, and to assert boldly some claims that he played down. It will even mean disagreeing with Wesley at times, out of faithfulness to the Gospel and his own wider vision.[10] Indeed, it could conceivably mean eventually deciding—in responsible dialogue with the Gospel of grace, the broad Christian community, and the wisdom of experience—that there is an even more adequate orienting concern that should guide our practical-theological activity than "responsible grace." But if that day should come, it will be itself a contribution from taking Wesley as a theological mentor.

NOTES

Introduction

1. No one has expressed this judgment more vitriolicly than E.P. Thompson, who described Methodism as "a ritualized form of psychic masturbation" and suggested that it was intelligible only as a social or psychiatric phenomenon, not as a system of thought (*The Making of the English Working Class* [New York: Vintage, 1966], p. 368). More conventional is Paul Johnson's recent characterization of Wesley's form of Christianity as almost totally devoid of intellectual content; i.e., wholly ethical and emotional, containing no doctrinal insights (*A History of Christianity* [New York: Atheneum, 1976], p. 365).

2. For a few examples see Faulkner 1918, p. 38; Schempp 1949, p. 9; Sanders 1954b, p. 591; and Rupert Davies, "The People Called Methodists: 1. Our Doctrines," in *A History of the Methodist Church in Great Britain*, Vol. I, ed. R. Davies, *et al.* (London: Epworth, 1965), p. 147.

3. The reasons for Wesley's failure to complete the final requirement for the B.D. are not totally clear, but relate largely to his disaffection with the perceived hypocrisy of Oxford fellows and dons (cf. Sermon 150, "Hypocrisy in Oxford," *Works*, 4:392-407; and Outler's introduction to the same, *Works*, 4:389-91). It is important to note that the B.D. was taken *after* the M.A. at Oxford, and that the only higher degree was the Doctor of Divinity. On this point, see *The History of the University of Oxford, Vol. V: The Eighteenth Century*, ed. L.S. Sutherland & L.G. Mitchell (Oxford: Clarendon Press, 1986), pp. 469-91.

4. For an analysis of the works Wesley likely read during his undergraduate days at Oxford, see English 1989a. For a fairly complete list of his readings between the years 1725-1735, see Heitzenrater 1972, Appendix IV. For a description of his typical discipline of study during this time, see John Telford, *The Life of Wesley*, 3rd ed. (London: Kelly, 1910), p. 49. For an analysis of his reading through the remainder of his career, see Onva K. Boshears Jr., "John Wesley, the Bookman, A Study in His Reading Interests in the Eighteenth Century" (University of Michigan Ph.D. thesis, 1972). Unfortunately, Frank Baker's anticipated definitive list of Wesley's readings has not yet been published.

5. While it is an overstatement to say that his sermons, taken together, add up to a *Summa Theologica* (Outler 1971a, p. 41), it is also a mistake to assume that Wesley treated only the *ordo salutis.* The practice of restricting treatment of Wesley's theology to the *ordo salutis* began with the first "systematic" treatment of Wesley (Hoon 1936, p. iv) and has carried over into more recent studies like C. Williams 1960, Meredith 1962, and Lessman 1987. The typical assumption behind this restriction is that only Wesley's *distinctive* theological claims should be of interest (cf. Meredith 1962, p. 52). But Wesley's distinctive claims only make sense within the larger doctrinal context

that he shared with his Anglican tradition. Moreover, his orienting concern is sometimes most evident in his decisions about what parts of this larger context to lay aside and how to weave together or balance the parts that he retains. In other words, Wesley's *perspective* on his shared Christian tradition provides as much insight into his theological convictions as do his distinctive doctrinal affirmations.

6. In addition to the contributions of Outler which follow, note Meeks 1985a & 1985b; and Clapper 1989, pp. 169-71.

7. See Outler 1961, p. 5.

8. See Outler 1964a, p. vii; 1974, p. 65; 1977; 1980-2, pp. 6-7; and 1984, p.67.

9. Contrast Outler 1964a, p. 119; with 1985a, p. 48.

10. For a survey of this discussion, see Randy L. Maddox, "The Recovery of Theology as a Practical Discipline," *Theological Studies* 51 (1990):650-72.

11. Maddox 1988. It is important to distinguish the traditional model of theology as a practical discipline from the current specialty-discipline of Practical Theology. For a survey of recent debates over the nature of Practical Theology and how it might relate to a recovered practice of theology per se as practical, see Randy L. Maddox, "Practical Theology: A Discipline in Search of a Definition," *Perspectives in Religious Studies* 18 (1991):159-69.

12. Note how this point is made to the young John by his father in an exchange of letters in 1734, in *Works*, 25:395-409. Compare John's mature perspective on this dialogue in his 1784 Letter to *Gentleman's Magazine*, §6, in *Works* (Jackson), 13:409-10.

13. For one attempt to show some correlations, see Maddox 1994.

14. Peter Slater has argued this at length (in terms of a "central symbol") in *The Dynamics of Religion* (San Francisco, CA: Harper & Row, 1978), pp. 28-46. Stephen Pepper offers an analogous discussion of "root-metaphors" to explain the existence of different schools of philosophy in *World Hypotheses* (Berkeley, CA: University of California Press, 1942), pp. 84-114. H. Paul Santmire has appropriated Pepper's analysis (in terms of a "theological motif") for understanding different Christian theological understandings of creation in *The Travail of Nature* (Philadelphia, PA: Fortress, 1985), pp. 14-15. Finally, James M. Gustafson has discussed the importance of an organizing perspective for providing consistency to theological ethics in *Protestant and Roman Catholic Ethics* (Chicago, IL: University of Chicago, 1978), pp. 139-40.

15. Note Douglas John Hall's admission of the importance of an orienting point of view (the *theologia crucis*) in his recent attempt to recover a more praxis-related and contextual approach to theology; Hall, *Thinking the Faith* (Minneapolis, MN: Augsburg, 1989), pp. 22ff.

16. In an earlier approach to these issues (Maddox 1984 & 1986) I adopted the term "orienting concept" from Gerhard Sauter (cf. Sauter & Alex Stock, *Arbeitsweisen Systematischer Theologie: Eine Anleitung* [Munich: Christian Kaiser, 1976], pp. 151-6). Helpful reader response (e.g., I. Jones 1988, p. 94) convinced me that both the term and the general discussion of its function suggested a more "systematic" reading of Wesley than I intended at that time, and much more so than I would now defend. I have become increasingly convinced of the implicit, meta-conceptual nature of an orienting concern.

17. Cf. Santmire, *Travail of Nature*, p. 15. Note also the defense of Calvin's "root metaphor" in similar terms in Charles Partee, "Calvin's Central Dogma Again," *Sixteenth Century Journal* 18 (1987):191-9.

18. Note here Albert Outler's helpful distinction, referring to Wesley, between doctrinal integrity preserved mechanically (*Augustana Invariata*!) and that preserved organically (1990, p. 35).

19. See Slater, *Dynamic of Religion*, pp. 30, 33.

20. Note in this regard David Kelsey's discussion of how a *discrimen* guides theological criticism of Scripture in *The Uses of Scripture in Recent Theology* (Philadelphia, PA: Fortress, 1975), pp. 159ff. His *discrimen* comes quite close to what I mean by an "orienting concern." He argues that a *discrimen* focuses on the question of the *mode* in which God is present among the faithful (p. 160).

21. Admittedly, Wesley does not appear to have used the specific words "responsible" or "responsibility" in this regard. Few did before the nineteenth century (cf. *Oxford English Dictionary* [2nd ed., 1989], 13:742). His more characteristic language was to speak of a capability for virtue or guilt; e.g., Sermon 67, "On Divine Providence," §15, *Works*, 2:540-1.

22. Wesley revealed some awareness of the problem of exclusive language, and a commitment to inclusive alternatives, when he changed "Christian men" in Anglican Articles XXVII, XXX, and XXXII to simply "Christian" for his edited version (cf. Randy L. Maddox, "Wesley and Inclusive Grammar: A Note for Reflection," *Sacramental Life* 4.4 [1991]:40-43)! Following his precedent, I will edit inclusive language for humanity into quotes of Wesley's works, unless such is deemed misleading.

23. Letter to William Green (25 Oct. 1789), *Letters* (Telford), 8:179. See also *A Letter to the Rev. Dr. Rutherforth* (28 Mar. 1768), §I.3, *Works*, 9:375; *Journal* (1 Sept. 1778), *Journal* (Curnock), 6:209; and Letter to John Mason (13 Jan. 1790), *Letters* (Telford), 8:196.

24. See his Letter to Charles Wesley (31 July 1747), *Works*, 26:254-5.

25. Cf. Outler 1985d, p. 125.

26. Throughout this study the term "Catholic" is used broadly to designate an appreciation for such themes as sacramental spirituality, requisite human growth in holiness, and human participation in salvation—themes that characterized much of pre-Reformation Christianity in both its Eastern and Western forms. "Roman Catholic" will be used to refer to the specific Western Christian tradition that affirms the Roman bishop (Pope) as its leader.

27. A classic example from more recent studies is Schmidt 1962-73. He presents a careful chronological analysis of the developments in Wesley's thought up through his "Protestant" conversion at Aldersgate. Then he switches to a systematic analysis from 1738 on, assuming a theological consistency throughout the remainder of Wesley's life. See also Rattenbury's claim (1928, p. 24) that Wesley's intellectual development after Aldersgate was "slight."

28. The term and basic argument is found in Rattenbury 1938, p. 193. Other examples would be D. Dayton 1985, p. 127; and J.M. Turner 1988, pp. 166-71. Jürgen Weiβbach *negatively* evaluates Wesley's development in similar stages, and there are like suggestions in K. Kim 1992, p. 146.

29. Cf. Heitzenrater 1989, p. 28.

30. E.g., Heitzenrater 1984a, 1:31. Some early uses of this typology portrayed the moves much too dialectically (especially Tuttle 1969, pp. 409-10 [repeated in 1978, p. 334 fn10]). Such uses sparked a strong critique, particularly of emphasis on transition between the middle Wesley and the late Wesley, in J.H. Tyson 1991. Unfortunately Tyson does not dialogue with the most nuanced presentation of these transitions (Heitzenrater 1989, pp. 106-49).

31. Cf. McIntosh 1966, and Rogers 1966 on earlier awareness of justification by faith. On the continuity of Wesley's concern for holiness through the whole of his life, see J.H. Tyson 1991 and Chapters Six & Seven.

32. E.g., see discussions of transitions in Wesley's views concerning the benefits of initial universal revelation (Chapter 1), the role of suffering in God's providence (Chapter 2) the contribution of inherited guilt to human damnation (Chapter 3), the nature of grace as power or pardon (Chapter 4), the imputation of Christ's active righteousness to believers (Chapter 4), the assurance of faith (Chapter 5), the place of works before justification (Chapter 6), the relation of the New Birth to sanctification (Chapter 7), the expectation of entire sanctification shortly after justification (Chapter 7), the purpose of the means of grace (Chapter 8), and the question of millennialism (Chapter 9).

33. I take this image from Outler 1987, p. 139.

34. Maser 1978, p. 12.

35. These include most typically the abridged Articles of Religion included in the *Sunday Service*, the first four volumes of Wesley's *Sermons*, the *NT Notes*, and an edited version of the *Minutes*.

36. Outler 1984, pp. 54-5; and 1985d, p. 353.

37. Throughout this study the designation of a position as characterizing the "mature Wesley" intends that this position reflects Wesley's eventual integration of his deeper appropriation of the emphasis on the graciousness of salvation into his early concern with holiness. Such positions often coalesced prior to 1765, though they remain most characteristic of the late Wesley.

38. Helpful historical surveys of Wesley Studies that would note these dynamics include Baker 1980a; Bence 1981, pp. 10-13; Heitzenrater 1984a, 2:196-207; Källstad 1974, pp. 15-26; Outler 1985a; Rowe 1976; and Schneeberger 1974, pp. 18-29.

39. Compare Richard Denny Urlin, *John Wesley's Place in Church History* (London: Rivington's, 1870), p. 29; to Sanders 1960, p. 493; Crow 1964 & 1966; English 1969; and Baker 1970. See also Knickerbocker 1991.

40. For descriptions of the appeal to and study of patristic material in England just prior to Wesley, see Leslie W. Barnard, "The Use of the Patristic Tradition in the Late Seventeenth and Early Eighteenth Century," in *Scripture, Tradition and Reason*, edited by R. Bauckham & B. Drewery (Edinburgh: T & T Clark, 1988), pp. 174-203; Robert D. Cornwall, "The Search for the Primitive Church: The Use of Early Church Fathers in the High Church Anglican Tradition, 1680-1745," *Anglican and Episcopal History* 59 (1990): 303-29; and Campbell 1991b, pp. 7-21. Campbell distinguishes between polemical, conservative, and programmatic appeals to Christian Antiquity.

41. The most vigorous defense of this claim is Keefer 1982 (synopsis in 1984). The most thorough study of Wesley's conception of and use of early Christian material is Campbell 1991b. Campbell's focus, however, is not on Wesley's "primitivism" per se; it is on how Wesley connects this commitment to Christian tradition with his "evangelical" attempt to renew ideal Christianity (pp. 104, 114-16).

42. Actually, there had once again been early suggestions about the importance of these Greek theologians to Wesley. See especially Alexander Knox, *Remains of Alexander Knox, esq.* (London: Duncan & Malcolm, 1844), Vol. III, p. 483; and Urlin, *Wesley's Place*, pp. 10, 59-86. The one most responsible for recovering this agenda in contemporary Wesley studies is Albert Outler (cf. 1964a, pp. viii-ix; and 1980-2). For a survey of this discussion, see Maddox 1990. More recent contributions are Snyder 1990, Bundy 1991, T. Martin 1991, and McCormick 1991.

43. On the difficulties of historical demonstration of sources see Bundy 1991; and Campbell 1991b, p. 3. In this connection, it is noteworthy that the writings of Macarius found a favorable reception among Pietists and Protestant mystics—cf. Ernst Benz, *Die protestantische Thebais* (Weisbaden: Franz Steiner Verlag, 1963); and Werner Strothmann, ed., *Makarios-Symposium Über das Böse* (Weisbaden: Otto Harrassowitz, 1983). Likewise, many Pietists and mystics placed heavy emphasis on 2 Peter 1:4 (an Eastern Orthodox *locus classicus*); see the survey in Martin Schmidt, "Teilnahme an der göttlichen Natur," in *Weidergeburt und neuer Mensch* (Witten: Luther-Verlag, 1969), pp. 238-98.

44. Naglee 1991 is not likely to supplant Williams, precisely because it does not take into account most recent work in Wesley Studies. There have been a few helpful *popular* studies of Wesley's theology since Williams; of particular note is Harper 1983b. Likewise, two very helpful historical/ biographical studies have recently been released: Richard Heitzenrater, *Wesley and the People Called Methodists* (Nashville, TN: Abingdon, 1994); and Rack 1989.

45. For an initial description of the *Bicentennial Edition*, see Frank Baker, "The Oxford Edition of Wesley's Works and Its Text," in *The Place of Wesley in the Christian Tradition*, ed. Kenneth E. Rowe (Metuchen, NJ: Scarecrow, 1976), pp. 117-33. It could be at least another twenty years before this definitive edition of Wesley's works is complete. This interim situation complicates the matter of noting Wesley references. I have adopted the practice of noting references by a short title and (where applicable) paragraph marker. I then cite the volume and page location from the most critical text currently available. See the Select Bibliography for abbreviations.

46. In addition to the continuing Wesley Historical Society, The Oxford Institute of Methodist Theological Studies began meeting in 1958, the Wesleyan Theological Society was formed in 1965, and a Wesleyan Theology section was organized at the American Academy of Religion in the early 1980's. Chairs of Wesley Studies have also been established at such universities as Duke and Southern Methodist. One of the welcome spinoffs of these developments is the increased scholarly attention that *Charles* Wesley's works are beginning to receive. On the organization of a Charles Wesley Society and the plans for a critical edition of Charles' works, see *PWHS* 47 (1990):128-9. The current standard editions of Charles' works are listed in section I.C of the Reference Bibliography. Secondary studies are listed in section II.C. Berger 1988 provides the most up-to-date survey of the secondary scholarship on Charles Wesley. While my focus in this book is John's theology, I will draw repeatedly on Charles to illuminate both similarities and differences between the brothers.

47. Thus, I question Naglee's claim that Wesley subordinated all other theological concerns to a systematic understanding of eternity and time (1991, pp. 1-2). In essence, Naglee organizes Wesley's theological convictions within a *Heilsgeschichte* (Salvation History) approach. Such is surely possible, but hardly required. Indeed, while my approach broadly resembles Naglee, I find that he deflects attention too much from Wesley's therapeutic understanding of Christian life, towards the (supposedly) *timeless* realities before the creation and after the judgement. Likewise, I dissent from Bryant's attempt (1992a) to develop a standardized four-part system out of a brief comment that Wesley made on "eternal reason." Matthews has shown that interest in the Cambridge Platonists' idea of eternal reason was localized to the early Wesley and never a major theme (1986, p. 16 & Chap. 2). I do not disagree with Bryant's claim that there is an interrelation between Wesley's understanding of God and his anthropology, or between his hamartiology and his soteriology. I simply see

no evidence that Wesley intended in any way to elevate these four elements as a standard "superstructure" for his other doctrinal convictions.

48. Indeed, it is approximated in one of his brief summaries of the Christian worldview: Sermon 122, "Causes of the Inefficacy of Christianity," §6, *Works*, 4:89. The specific pattern was suggested by John Meyendorff, *Byzantine Theology* (New York: Fordham University Press, 1974), p. 128.

Chapter One

1. See especially Noro 1971, L. Wood 1975, Shimuzu 1980, Dreyer 1983, Brantley 1984 & 1990, Matthews 1985 & 1986, O'Malley 1986, Runyon 1988, and Bryant 1992a, pp. 33-84. The most comprehensive and convincing study is Matthews 1986. For a much earlier interest in this topic, see Barber 1923.

2. E.g., *An Earnest Appeal to Men of Reason and Religion*, §32, *Works*, 11:56; Sermon 117, "On the Discoveries of Faith," §1, *Works*, 4:29; and Sermon 119, "Walking by Sight and Walking by Faith," §7, *Works*, 4:51.

3. Cf. Matthews 1986, pp. 259-60; and Bryant 1992a, pp. 41ff.

4. *Works* (Jackson), 13:455-64.

5. Original, London: William Innys, 1728. Abstract in *Survey*, 5:149-96. Browne was influenced by Locke.

6. For example, he disputed Locke's distinction between primary qualities (really in external objects) and secondary qualities (only in the mind); *Thoughts Upon Necessity*, §IV.3, *John Wesley*, pp. 487-8. He also rejected Locke's suggestion that abstract classifications like "species" are products of reasoning rather than derived from experience; *Remarks upon Mr. Locke's 'Essay on Human Understanding'*, *AM* 5 (1782):27ff, *Works* (Jackson), 13:460-1. Note that Wesley prefers to follow Aristotle on this point, seeing genus and species as resident in each particular. For Wesley, reason abstracts from experience what is truly there! In other words, he is a moderate realist.

7. No better example can be given than Peter Browne. See Wesley's extract of *Limits of Human Understanding* in *Survey*, 5:153, 180-2.

8. E.g., Sermon 19, "The Great Privilege of Those that are Born of God," §I.1-10, *Works*, 1:432-4; Sermon 45, "The New Birth," §II.4, *Works*, 2:192; and Sermon 130, "On Living Without God," *Works*, 4:169-76. See also the extended discussion of this topic in Matthews 1986, pp. 247ff. Browne explicitly rejected this idea of special spiritual senses in *Limits of Human Understanding*, pp. 94-6, 111. Wesley edited these rejections out of his abridgement of Browne (cf. *Survey* 5:157-9).

9. This source is stressed in English 1991a, pp. 58-64.

10. The connection to Macarius is stressed in H.-J. Lee 1991, pp. 142-5, 191-2, 205-6. For relevant Macarian homilies that Wesley retained in his abridgement, see Homily 28, §3 (Wesley #16, *Chr. Library*, 1:135) and Homily 44, §1 (Wesley #19, *Chr. Library*, 1:143). This theme of the "spiritual senses" in the Eastern spiritual tradition is just beginning to receive scholarly attention. For a brief overview, see B. Fraigneau-Julien, *Les Sens Spirituels et la Vision de Dieu selon Syméon le Nouveau Théologien* (Paris: Beauchesne, 1985), esp. pp. 27-95. See also: Karl Rahner, "The 'Spiritual Senses' According to Origen," in *Theological Investigations, XVI* (New York: Seabury, 1979), pp. 81-103; Hans Urs von Balthasar, *The Glory of the Lord, I* (New York: Crossroad, 1982), pp. 367-71 (on Macarius in particular, see pp. 269-75, 370); Tomás Spidlík, *The Spirituality of the Christian East* (Kalamazoo, MI: Cistercian Publications, 1986),

pp. 94-5; and Spidlík, *La Spiritualité de l'Orient Chrétien*, Vol. 2, *Le Priere* (Rome: Pontifical Institute of Oriental Studies, 1988), pp. 179-90.

11. An adequate study of these sources is also missing. For an account of medieval writers, see Karl Rahner, "The Doctrine of the 'Spiritual Senses' in the Middle Ages," *Theological Investigations, XVI* (New York: Seabury, 1979), pp. 104-34; M. Olphe-Galliard, "Les sens spirituels dans l'historie de la spiritualité," in *Nos Sens et Dieu*, Charles Baudouin, et al. (Paris: Desclée, 1954), pp. 179-93; and von Balthasar, *Glory of the Lord*, I:371ff. For some investigation of the notion of the "sense of the heart" in the Reformed tradition, see Terrence Erdt, *Jonathan Edwards: Art and the Sense of the Heart* (Amherst, MA: University of Massachusetts, 1980), pp. 1-20. Brantley claims that Wesley retained all of the references to spiritual senses in his abridgement of Edward's *Treatise Concerning Religious Affections* (1990, p. 293). On radical Puritan and early Quaker uses, see Geoffrey Nuttall, *The Holy Spirit in Puritan Faith and Experience* (Oxford: Basil Blackwell, 1947), pp. 38-40, 139-40.

12. See esp. *NT Notes*, Phil. 1:9; and Sermon 62, "The End of Christ's Coming," §III.1, *Works*, 2:481. This aspect of Wesley's "empiricism" has been more commonly known; cf. Hindley 1957.

13. Cf. Sermon 117, "On the Discoveries of Faith," §4, *Works*, 4:30; and Sermon 132, "On Faith," *Works*, 4:188-200. For a recent philosophical defense of such an epistemological role for religious experience, see William P. Alston, *Perceiving God* (Ithaca, NY: Cornell University Press, 1991).

14. For strong denials of any "natural theology" in Wesley, see Lindström 1946, p. 47; C. Williams 1960, pp. 31, 42; J.W. Smith 1964, pp. 79-80; Collins 1986, p. 118; Lessmann 1987, p. 132; and Coppedge 1991, p. 280. For counterarguments that there is at least an implicit "natural theology" in Wesley, see Dunlap 1956, pp. 31-3; H. McDonald 1959, p. 253; Noro 1971, pp. 67-8; and Hendricks 1983.

15. For an articulation (and defense) of this Protestant polarization, see Bruce Demarest, *General Revelation* (Grand Rapids, MI: Zondervan, 1982). Actually, Calvin gives more place to general revelation than Demarest admits, though later Calvinism downplayed this.

16. On the early Greek fathers, see Chrys Saldanha, *Divine Pedagogy: A Patristic View of Non-Christian Religions* (Rome: Editrice Libreria Ateneo Salesiano, 1984). For a contemporary Orthodox discussion, see Dumitru Staniloae, *Orthodoxe Dogmatik* (Zürich: Benziger Verlag, 1985-90), I:19ff.

17. The best evidence of Wesley's difference from typical Western theology here is his abstract of Browne's *Limits of Human Understanding*. When Browne made a distinction between knowledge that we have by our own faculties through the light of nature and that additional knowledge communicated from God, Wesley added a footnote that all "light of nature" so-called flows from Preventing Grace; *Survey*, 5:185.

18. See especially Sermon 106, "On Faith," §2-3, *Works*, 3:492-3. Here Wesley appropriates Fletcher's delineation of four dispensations of the grace of God, distinguished by their progressively greater degrees of revelation.

19. E.g., Sermon 69, "The Imperfection of Human Knowledge," §I.4, *Works*, 2:571. Wesley agreed with Augustine that we have an innate *need* to know God (if we are to be at peace), just no innate knowledge; Sermon 78, "Spiritual Idolatry," §II.2, *Works*, 3:112-13.

20. See Letter to John Burton (10 Oct. 1735), *Works*, 25:439. See also his later evaluation of the materials he read about Native Americans prior to the trip to Georgia as "pure, absolute romance," in *Journal* (18 Jan. 1773), *Works*, 22:358.

21. E.g., Letter to Editor of *Gentleman's Magazine* (20 July 1736), *Works*, 25:464-6 (reprinted in *Journal* [20 July 1736], *Works*, 18:165-7); *Journal* (9 July 1737), *Works*, 18:185; and *Journal* (2 Dec. 1737), 23-8, *Works*, 18:202-4. Cf. J. Ralph Randolph, "John Wesley and the American Indian: A Study in Disillusionment," *MethH* 10.3 (1972):3-11.

22. E.g., *A Farther Appeal to Men of Reason and Religion*, Part II (1745), §III.21, *Works*, 11:268.

23. Sermon 10, "Sermon on the Mount VI," §III.7, *Works*, 1:581.

24. *NT Notes*, John 1:9, Rom. 1:17-19.

25. The document in question is *The Doctrine of Original Sin*, *Works* (Jackson), 9:191-464. On this point, note especially Part I, §II.2-5 (pp. 209-15); and Part II, II.6 (p. 267). See also the homiletical distillation of this work in Sermon 44, "Original Sin," esp. §II.2-3, *Works*, 2:177. For a detailed interrelating of Taylor and Wesley, see A.S. Wood 1992, pp. 29-48.

26. Sermon 106, "On Faith," §I.4, *Works*, 3:494.

27. See the discussion of Prevenient Grace in Chapter Three.

28. On these claims, see Sermon 70, "The Case of Reason Impartially Considered," §II.6 (on Socrates' virtue but lack of hope), *Works*, 2:596; Sermon 119, "Walking by Sight and Walking by Faith," §8-10, *Works*, 4:51-2; and "Thoughts on a Late Publication," §3, *AM* 13 (1790):545-7, *Works* (Jackson), 13:411-13.

29. Recall in this regard that Wesley defined "deism" in his *Dictionary* simply as "denying the Bible;" i.e., ruling out special revelation.

30. Note the methodological claim in his introduction (§24) to the compendium on natural philosophy: "concerning God and Spirits . . . we can neither depend on Reason nor Experiment. Whatsoever [we] know, or can know concerning them, must be drawn from the oracles of God," *Survey*, §1:8 (also in *Works* [Jackson], 13:487).

31. E.g., note his response to such accusations in *A Letter to the Right Reverend the Lord Bishop of London* (11 June 1747), §6, *Works*, 11:337; and *A Second Letter to the Author of 'The Enthusiasm of Methodists and Papists Compared'* (27 Nov. 1751), §20, *Works*, 11:399.

32. See especially, *A Letter to a Person Lately Joined with the People called Quakers* (10 Feb. 1748), *Letters* (Telford), 2:118; *Cautions and Directions Given to the Greatest Professors in the Methodist Societies*, #2, *John Wesley*, p. 300; and Sermon 115, "Dives and Lazarus," §III.7, *Works*, 4:18.

33. *Scripture Hymns*, On Isaiah 8:20, *Poet. Works*, 9:380.

34. This point is quite evident throughout Wesley. Perhaps the most explicit statement is found in the *Compendium of Logic* which Wesley abridged from Henry Aldrich for use at Kingswood school (showing his endorsement): "the principles of divine faith are those, and those only, which are contained in Scriptures" (Bk. II, Chap. 1, IV), *Works* (Jackson), 14:179.

35. See §5 of his famous Preface to the first volume of *Sermons*: "I want to know one thing, the way to heaven. . . . [God] hath written it down in a book," *Works*, 1:105. Note also *NT Notes*, 1 Cor. 2:13.

36. See *A Farther Appeal to Men of Reason and Religion*, Part I, §V.28, *Works*, 11:171-2.

37. See *NT Notes*, 2 Tim. 3:16; and *A Letter to the Right Reverend the Lord Bishop of Gloucester* (26 Nov. 1763), §II.10, *Works*, 11:509.

38. The most relevant example is again from Wesley's abridgement of Browne's *Limits of Human Understanding*, in *Survey*, 5:181-2.

39. "A Clear and Concise Demonstration of the Divine Inspiration of the Holy Scripture," *AM* 12 (1789):211, *Works* (Jackson), 11:484. Scott Jones suggests that Wesley borrowed this demonstration from Richard Baxter (1992, pp. 24, 298-300).

40. See especially his long *Letter to the Reverend Dr. Conyers Middleton* (Jan. 1749) debating the use of Jesus' or the apostles' miracles to prove Scripture, *Letters* (Telford), 2:375-88. The most relevant section was reprinted as *A Plain Account of Genuine Christianity*, see esp. §II.12-III.10, *John Wesley*, pp. 191-4. For helpful discussions of Wesley's "proof" of Scripture, see S. Frost 1938, pp. 66-8; Matthews 1986, p. 110; and Thorsen 1990, pp. 132-3.

41. See the development of this claim in Paul Merritt Bassett, "The Theological Identity of the North American Holiness Movement," in *The Variety of American Evangelicalism*, edited by D.W. Dayton & R.K. Johnston (Downers Grove, IL: Intervarsity, 1991), pp. 72-108; esp. pp. 76-9.

42. On this point, see Luby 1984, p. 301; Abraham 1985a, pp. 122-5; and the exploratory essay: William J. Abraham, "The Epistemological Significance of the Inner Witness of the Holy Spirit," *Faith and Philosophy* 7 (1990):434-50, esp. pp. 443-4.

43. Sermon 85, "On Working Out Our Own Salvation," §1-2, *Works*, 3:199-200.

44. For more details on Wesley's knowledge of and attitude toward other religions, see Maddox 1992b.

45. See *Popery Calmly Considered*, §II.6, *Works* (Jackson), 10:145. This is a distillation of a work by John Williams that Wesley republished: *A Roman Catechism, with a Reply Thereto*, see Q. 25, *Works* (Jackson), 10:100. Wesley specifically referred to the latter work as defining his position in *Journal* (20 Dec. 1768), *Works*, 22:167.

46. See the discussion in Deschner 1960, pp. 51-2. For the background to Wesley's stance, see Dewey Wallace, "'Puritan and Anglican': The Interpretation of Christ's Descent into Hell in Elizabethan Theology," *Archive for Reformation History* 69 (1978):248-86.

47. Cf. Sermon 115, "Dives and Lazarus," §III.1-2, *Works*, 4:16-7; and Sermon 132, "On Faith," §4, *Works*, 4:190.

48. E.g., Letter to 'John Smith' (25 June 1746), §2, *Works*, 26:198; and Sermon 55, "On the Trinity," §18, *Works*, 2:386.

49. See especially, *Minutes* (25 June 1744), *John Wesley*, p. 137; Sermon 91, "On Charity," §I.3, *Works*, 3:295-6; Sermon 127, "On the Wedding Garment," §17, *Works*, 4:147; and Sermon 130, "On Living Without God," §14, *Works*, 4:174. It should be noted that Wesley similarly argued that Christians have no authority to pass sentence on contemporary Jews—Sermon 106, "On Faith," §I.6, *Works*, 3:495 (This is not to deny the general negative tone of most of Wesley's descriptions of contemporary Judaism).

50. A convenient copy of Article XVIII can be found in Oden 1988, p. 118. It had explicitly ruled out salvation based on a response to the "light of nature."

51. The clearest expression of this dilemma is Sermon 91, "On Charity," §I.3, *Works*, 3:295. For the conjoined denial of a pre-existent cause, see Sermon 69, "The Imperfection of Human Knowledge," §III.1-2, *Works*, 2:582-3.

52. This solution was articulated by many of the early Greek fathers (cf. Saldanha, *Divine Pedagogy*). It had also been defended by many Quakers and Anabaptists (against whom Anglican Article XVIII had been framed!). Wesley was aware of the Quaker claim and accepted it; *A Letter to a Person Lately Joined with the People called Quakers* (10 Feb. 1748), §6, *Letters* (Telford), 2:118. For Wesley's own appeal to this criterion, see the 1770 *Minutes*, Q. 28, *Minutes* (Mason), p. 96 (also as "Large Minutes," Q. 77, *Works* [Jackson], 8:337); and Sermon 91, "On Charity," §I.3, *Works*, 3:296.

53. Cf. *NT Notes*, Acts 10:4.

54. Actually, this topic has not been widely discussed by Wesley scholars. For relevant discussions (arranged by increasing affirmation of salvation beyond Christ), see: Marquardt 1977a, p. 112 fn69 (1992, p. 171 fn69); Rogers 1967, pp. 178, 245; Starkey 1962, p. 43; C. Williams 1960, p. 45; Borgen 1972, p. 126; Hurley 1976; Naglee 1991, pp. 594-9; and the discussion in David Lowes Watson, *God Does Not Foreclose: The Universal Promise of Salvation* (Nashville, TN: Abingdon, 1990), pp. 101ff. See also the identification of Wesley as one of the leading defenders of the "wider hope" for the unevangelized in John Sanders, *No Other Name: An Investigation into the Destiny of the Unevangelized* (Grand Rapids, MI: Eerdmans, 1992), pp. 249-51.

55. Cf. *Minutes* (2 Aug. 1745), Q. 8, *John Wesley*, p. 150; and *NT Notes*, Acts 10:35.

56. For a perceptive study of Wesley's mature understanding of foreign missions, see Campbell 1992b. For reflections in relation to contemporary missiological debate, see Mark Royster, "John Wesley's Doctrine of Prevenient Grace in Missiological Perspective" (Asbury Seminary D.Miss. thesis, 1989); LaVerne P. Blowers, "Love Divine All Loves Compelling: Missionary Motives in the Wesleyan Tradition" (Trinity Evangelical Divinity School D.Miss. thesis, 1989); and Theodore R. Doraisamy, *What Hath God Wrought: Motives of Missions in Methodism from Wesley to Thoburn* (Singapore: Methodist Book Room, 1983).

57. See *Journal* (21 Jan. 1746), *Works*, 20:112; and *Journal* (20 May 1768), *Works*, 22:134.

58. He considered it a "useful science" for clergy to study; *An Address to the Clergy*, §II.1, *Works* (Jackson), 10:492. He also *added* it to the curriculum at the Kingswood School in 1781! Compare *A Short Account of the School in Kingswood* (1768), §2, *Works* (Jackson), 13:283; with *A Plain Account of Kingswood School* (1781), §13, *Works* (Jackson), 13:295.

59. Sermon 84, "The Important Question," *Works* 3:182-98. Wesley actually "loads the dice" more toward believing than Pascal, for he argues that the blessings of heaven and sufferings of damnation begin already in this life.

60. Letter to Dr. John Robertson (24 Sept. 1753), *Works*, 26:515-16.

61. This simple argument from design treats nature as an artifact and was radically called into question when modern science discovered some of the natural dynamics (like evolution) that produced apparent design. Indeed, it has been argued by John Hedley Brooke that seventeenth- and eighteenth-century natural theologies like that of Wesley unintentionally facilitated the secularization of science ("Science and the Fortunes of Natural Theology: Some Historical Perspectives," *Zygon* 24 [1989]:3-22). Michael J. Buckley has even suggested that they provoked the emergence of atheism (*At the Origins of Modern Atheism* [New Haven, CT: Yale University Press, 1987])! Wesley's basic agenda could, however, be translated into a post-modern form that focused on the question of whether nature was "intended" rather than whether it was designed—cf. Diogenes Allen, *Christian Belief in a Postmodern World* (Louisville, KY: Westminster/John Knox, 1989).

62. For a schemata of the various editions of this work, see Baker's *Union Catalog*, #220. Wesley was so concerned that his people be familiar with the work that he published a series of extracts between 1781-90 in the *Arminian Magazine*. Interest in *Survey* and Wesley's natural theology was quite high early in the twentieth century; e.g., Barber 1923, Collier 1928, and Eayrs 1926. By contrast, this topic has been largely ignored in recent studies of Wesley's theology. One result is that there has not yet been a critical study of *Survey* to determine Wesley's principles of editing, or what material is original to him (the two-volume first edition is to be included in Volume 17 of *Works* with sources indicated wherever possible).

63. *Survey*, Preface, *Works* (Jackson), 14:300.

64. Among Wesley's acknowledged sources were William Derham's *Physico-Theology* (1713) and *Astro-Theology* (1715), Oliver Goldsmith's *History of the Earth and Animated Nature* (1774), Cotton Mather's *The Christian Philosopher* (1721), Bernard Nieuwentyt's *The Religious Philosopher* (1718), John Ray's *Wisdom of God Manifested in the Works of the Creation* (1691), and William Wollaston's *The Religion of Nature Delineated* (1722). Frank Baker has suggested in a private letter that Wesley actually relied most heavily for his "improving comments" (without acknowledging it) on his former Oxford colleague, James Hervey. Later editions of *Survey* also contained a lengthy abridgement of Charles Bonnet's *Contemplation de la Nature* (1764-5). For a handy survey of this emerging genre, covering many of these sources, see David M. Knight, *Natural Science Books in English, 1600-1900* (New York: Praeger, 1972), Chapter 3. For a discussion of Wesley's early training in this area, see English 1991c.

65. For a few examples, see *Survey*, 1:75, 131-2, 193ff, 217ff, 245ff; 2:112ff; 3:58; and 4:39-48.

66. Note especially the abstract from Matthew Hale appended to *Survey* (5:197-206). The theme of this abstract is repeated in Sermon 78, "Spiritual Idolatry," §I.13-14, *Works*, 3:108-9. See also the discussion in Schofield 1953.

67. See Letter to Samuel Furly (21 May 1762), *Letters* (Telford), 4:181; and Sermon 70, "The Case of Reason Impartially Considered," §II.1-2, *Works*, 2:593-4.

68. *A Plain Account of Genuine Christianity*, §I.13, *John Wesley*, p. 186.

69. The best general expositions of the Wesleyan Quadrilateral are Abraham 1985a, Outler 1985b, and Thorsen 1990. Be careful to distinguish the Wesleyan Quadrilateral, which deals with Wesley's theological method, from the Epworth Quadrilateral, which is a popular British Methodist summary of Wesley's soteriology, formulated by W. B. Fitzgerald in 1903: "all need to be saved, all can be saved, all can know they are saved, all can be saved to the uttermost."

70. For a progressive survey of Outler's use of this term, see Outler 1968, p. 98; 1972, esp. p. 275; and 1985b.

71. Ted Campbell (1991a) has shown clearly the anachronistic character of speaking of the "quadrilateral" in Wesley himself, particularly in regard to tradition. While agreeing with his main point, as the discussion of "tradition" will show, I will retain the four-element pattern heuristically, as conducive for relating Wesley's practice to contemporary concerns.

72. To cite just a few contextual examples: *Journal* (25 Jan. 1738), *Works*, 18:212 fn95; *A Letter to the Author of 'The Enthusiasm of Methodists and Papists Compared'* (1750), §22, *Works*, 11:370; Letter to Samuel Sparrow (28 Dec. 1773), *Letters* (Telford), 6:60; *Advice to the People Called Methodists with Regard to Dress*, §VI.4, *Works* (Jackson), 11:475; Sermon 63, "The General Spread of the Gospel," §7, *Works*, 2:487; "Thoughts on the Consecration of Churches and Burial-Grounds", §8, *Works* (Jackson), 10:511; and Letter to Freeborn Garrettson (24 Jan. 1789), *Letters* (Telford), 8:112.

73. E.g., *A Short History of Methodism*, §6, *Works*, 9:368; Letter to the American Church (10 Sept. 1784), *Letters* (Telford), 7:239; and "Farther Thoughts on Separation from the Church," §1, *Works*, 9:538.

74. E.g., Letter to Dr. John Robertson (24 Sept. 1753), *Works*, 26:519; and *Remarks Upon Mr. Locke's 'Essay on Human Understanding'*, *AM* 5 (1782), *Works* (Jackson), 13:462.

75. E.g., *A Farther Appeal to Men of Reason and Religion*, Part III, §III.28, *Works*, 11:310; *Principles of a Methodist Farther Explained*, §V.7, *Works*, 9:220; *A Plain Account of the People*

Called Methodists, §2, *Works*, 9:254; and Sermon 13, "On Sin in Believers," §III.10, *Works*, 1:325.

76. His monograph on *The Doctrine of Original Sin* (1757) was subtitled: "According to Scripture, Reason, and Experience." See also Sermon 14, "The Repentance of Believers," §I.2, *Works*, 1:336; and *Journal* (17 Dec. 1772), *Works*, 22:356.

77. The best survey of Wesley's understanding and use of Scripture is S. Jones 1992. Also helpful are T. Martin 1991 and Miller 1991. For a specific focus on Wesley's approach to the Old Testament see Casto 1977.

78. E.g., *The Character of a Methodist*, §1, *Works*, 9:33-4; *Journal* (5 June 1766), *Works*, 22:42; *A Plain Account of Christian Perfection*, §10, *Works* (Jackson), 11:373; and Sermon 106, "On Faith," §I.8, *Works*, 3:496.

79. 1766 *Minutes*, Q. 30, *Minutes* (Mason), p. 68 (also as "Large Minutes," Q. 32, *Works* [Jackson], 8:315). He also argues for the need to consult more than Scripture alone in *A Letter to the Reverend Dr. Conyers Middleton* (4-24 Jan. 1749), *Letters* (Telford), 2:325.

80. Note that the Anglican Article VI on Scripture is entitled "Of the *Sufficiency* of the Holy Scripture for Salvation." Its main point is that nothing can be required as essential belief that lacks support in Scripture, not that Scripture alone should be consulted. In this same spirit, Wesley could refer to the Bible as the only *supreme* rule of faith, leaving room for further subordinate rules in tradition, etc., in "Ought We to Separate from the Church of England," §II.4, *Works*, 9:570.

81. Sermon 115, "Dives and Lazarus," §III.7, *Works*, 4:18.

82. Cf. *NT Notes*, James 1:23: "How exactly does the Scripture glass show a [person] the face of his [or her] soul!" The function of Scripture as a guide to piety has been particularly stressed in Ferguson 1984. However, he contrasts this too strongly with other functions.

83. E.g., Letter to John Newton (1 Apr. 1766), *Letters* (Telford), 5:8; and Letter to Joseph Benton (28 Dec. 1770), *Letters* (Telford), 5:215. For demonstrations of how thoroughly Wesley himself was immersed in and used the language of Scripture, see George Lawton, *John Wesley's English: A Study of His Literary Style* (London: Allen and Unwin, 1962), pp. 264ff; Rogal 1979; Rivers 1981, pp. 264-6; and Gallo 1984, p. 153.

84. E.g., *Cautions and Directions Given to the Greatest Professors in the Methodist Societies*, #2, *John Wesley*, p. 300; and Letter to Mary Bishop (26 Dec. 1776), *Letters* (Telford), 6:245.

85. *NT Notes*, Preface, §10.

86. For statements on his own practice, see Letter to William Dodd (5 Feb. 1756), *Letters* (Telford), 3:157-8; and Letter to William Dodd (12 Mar. 1756), *Letters* (Telford), 3:167. On the requirement for clergy to be good textuaries in order to be good divines, see *An Address to the Clergy*, §I.2, *Works* (Jackson), 10:482.

87. His fellowship at Oxford was in Greek. Later, he prided himself on requiring both Greek and Hebrew of the children at Kingswood, and teaching them better than at Oxford! Cf. *A Plain Account of Kingswood School*, §16, *Works* (Jackson), 13:296. For copies of the Greek and Hebrew grammars he abridged for these classes, see *Works* (Jackson), 14:78-160. For a quaint argument that God's choice of Greek for the Christian dispensation makes it a more perfect language than Hebrew, see Letter to Dean D. (1785), *Letters* (Telford), 7:252.

88. For analyses of Wesley's translation of the New Testament, see: George Croft Cell, *John Wesley's New Testament Compared with the Authorized Version* (London: Lutterworth, 1938); Francis Glasson, "Wesley's New Testament Reconsidered," *EpRev* 10.2 (1983):28-34; and Scroggs 1960, pp. 415-17.

89. For an excellent summary of the process of producing these works, see Baker 1989.

90. Cf. Casto 1977, p. 195; and S. Jones 1992, pp. 146ff. For analyses of Charles' biblical interpretation, see Kimbrough 1992 and J.R. Tyson 1992.

91. E.g., Sermon 74, "Of the Church," §I.12, *Works*, 3:50; and Sermon 137, "On Corrupting the Word of God," §I.2, *Works*, 4:247. Note also his scathing criticisms of Jakob Boehme and Baron Swedenborg for their "spiritual" exegesis: "A Specimen of the Divinity and Philosophy of the Highly-Illuminated Jacob Behmen," *AM* 5 (1782):207-11, *Works* (Jackson), 9:514-18; and "Thoughts on the Writings of Baron Swedenborg," §6-7, *AM* 6 (1783):437ff, *Works* (Jackson), 13:427-8. In some contrast with John, Charles relied more heavily on allegorical exegesis in his poetry (cf. Dale 1960, pp. 62-97; and J.R. Tyson 1992, pp. 25-7).

92. Letter to Samuel Furly (10 May 1755), *Works*, 26:557.

93. E.g., Sermon 110, "Free Grace," §20, *Works*, 3:552; *Journal* (23 June 1740), *Works*, 19:155; *A Farther Appeal to Men of Reason and Religion*, Part I, §V.10, *Works*, 11:149; and *Predestination Calmly Considered*, §19, *John Wesley*, p. 434. Interestingly, Wesley apparently considered 1 John the most authentic expression of this "tenor and scope" (cf. *Journal* [9 Nov. 1772], *Works*, 22:352).

94. Note his rejection of resigning the interpretation of Scripture to "unlettered mechanics" in *A Letter to the Rev. Dr. Rutherforth* (28 Mar. 1768), §II.4-6, *Works*, 9:378. Cf. Clemons 1977.

95. See *NT Notes*, Matt. 1:1, 2:6, John 19:24, Acts 15:7, Eph. 4:4. For a collection of Wesley's comments on the differing personalities of the biblical authors emerging in their writings, see Naglee 1991, p. 11. Cf. the discussion in S. Jones 1992, pp. 19-22.

96. There has been vigorous debate recently in conservative Wesleyan circles over whether Wesley was an inerrantist. For arguments that he was, see W. Dayton 1984; McCarthy 1981; and Victor Budgen, "John Wesley and the Biblical Criticism of His Day," *Banner of Truth* (Edinburgh) 154.1 (1976):50-65. For demurs from a strict inerrantist reading, see Abraham 1982; Paul M. Bassett, "The Holiness Movement and the Protestant Principle," *WTJ* 18.1 (1983):7-29; D. Dayton 1985; S. Jones 1992; Shelton 1981; and Thorsen 1990, pp. 132-3. It is true that Wesley explicitly denied that there were any errors in the Bible on at least three occasions: Letter to William Law (6 Jan. 1756), §II.2, *Letters* (Telford), 3:345-6; *A Letter to the Right Reverend the Lord Bishop of Gloucester* (26 Nov. 1763), §II.5, *Works*, 11:504; and *Journal* (24 Aug. 1776), *Journal* (Curnock), 6:117. Likewise, he was prone to harmonizing apparent errors (e.g., *NT Notes*, Matt. 8:28, 21:12; Luke 6:17, 22:24, 22:58, 23:34)—like contemporary inerrantists. However, it is a long way from Wesley's embryonic comments to the intricate theorizing of contemporary inerrancy. The latter's preoccupation with details hardly fits Wesley's typical focus on general themes. More importantly, contemporary inerrancy is predicated on a commitment to total divine control in inspiration, which radically contradicts Wesley's conviction about responsible grace; cf. the insightful discussion in Clark Pinnock, *The Scripture Principle* (San Francisco, CA: Harper and Row, 1984), pp. 101-3. If forced to wager, I would expect a present-day Wesley to come down closer to Pinnock than to the Council on Biblical Inerrancy!

97. A classic exposition of this (typical fundamentalist) view of Scripture as a quarry of facts to be extracted is Charles Hodge, *Systematic Theology* (New York: Scribners, 1874), I:18. By contrast, note Wesley's condemnation of those who searched through his writings for isolated statements and used them out of context;

A Second Letter to the Author of 'The Enthusiasm of the Methodists', §13, *Works*, 11:394. What he would request for his own writings he would surely apply to Scripture!

98. For a few examples of this appeal (scattered through his life) see Sermon 5, "Justification by Faith," §2, *Works*, 1:183; *An Address to the Clergy*, §II.1, *Works* (Jackson), 10:490; Sermon 62, "The End of Christ's Coming," §III.5, *Works*, 2:483; and Sermon 64, "The New Creation," §2, *Works*, 2:501. For background on this principle and a survey of Wesley's uses, see S. Jones 1992, pp. 55-63.

99. E.g., *NT Notes*, Rom. 12:6; *OT Notes*, Preface, §18, I:ix (also in *Works* [Jackson], 14:253); and Sermon 122, "Causes of the Inefficacy of Christianity," §6, *Works*, 4:89.

100. The strongest critique of Wesley, in this regard, is A.W. Martin 1990. See also Scroggs 1960, and W. Thomas 1965, p. 32. By contrast, Oswalt 1977 disregards the potential problems with Wesley's approach to the Old Testament. For one place where Wesley makes explicit his assumption that the Old Testament should be understood as gradually bringing to light Christian truths, see Sermon 67, "On Divine Providence," §4, *Works*, 2:536.

101. Compare this suggestion to the questions of T. Martin 1991, p. 117; and S. Jones 1992, pp. 78, 286-7.

102. Sermon 110, "Free Grace," §25-6, *Works*, 3:555-56. For another example where Wesley's conviction of God's grace *and* justice dictates the interpretation of a particular text, see Sermon 111, "National Sins and Miseries," §1, *Works*, 3:566.

103. E.g., Sermon 12, "The Witness of Our Own Spirit," §6, *Works*, 1:303; Sermon 97, "On Obedience to Pastors," §III.6, *Works*, 3:380; Letter to John Dickens (26 Dec. 1789), *Letters* (Telford), 8:192; and *Serious Thoughts Concerning Godfathers and Godmothers*, §4, *Works* (Jackson), 10:507. For a couple of cases where he leaned a little more towards Zwingli's position, see "Thoughts on the Consecration of Churches and Burial-Grounds," §5, *Works* (Jackson), 10:510; and Sermon 25, "Sermon on the Mount V," §IV.3, *Works*, 1:562-3.

104. E.g., *A Plain Account of the People Called Methodists*, §II.10, *Works*, 9:263.

105. The best available discussion of Wesley's understanding of reason is Matthews 1986, esp. Chapter 2. Also helpful are Thorsen 1990 and L. Wood 1975. Gray 1953 is of significantly less help.

106. Cf. Thorsen 1990, p. 127, 276 fn2. Note that Bishop John Pearson's *An Exposition of the Creed* (which Wesley often recommended and drew on) also places reason second only to Scripture as authoritative for theology (9th ed., [London: Bowyer, 1710], preface).

107. For a clear call for an alternative to both enthusiasm and rationalism, see Sermon 70, "The Case of Reason Impartially Considered," *Works*, 2:587-600. For poignant expressions of his fear about renouncing reason in the name of religion, see *Journal* (15 June 1741), *Works*, 19:200-1; Letter to William Law (6 Jan. 1756), §II.6, *Letters* (Telford), 3:365; and *A Letter to the Rev. Dr. Rutherforth* (28 Mar. 1768), §III.4, *Works*, 9:381. For insightful treatments of Wesley and the Enlightenment, especially on issues of epistemology, see Shimizu 1980, Matthews 1986, and English 1989b.

108. Sermon 70, "The Case of Reason Impartially Considered," §I.2, *Works*, 2:590. Wesley gets this description from Henry Aldrich; cf. *Compendium of Logic*, Book I, Chap. 1, §1, *Works* (Jackson), 14:161. The best example of the influence of the Cambridge Platonists is *An Earnest Appeal to Men of Reason and Religion* (1743), §28, *Works*, 11:55. Rex Matthews has shown that this is a very minor (and primarily early) theme in Wesley (1986, p. 16 & Chap. 2).

109. Among the "poor" uses of reason would be the attempt to rationalize the claims of revelation away. While Wesley is sensitive to this prospect, he is much more

concerned to defend the positive role of reason for regulating Christian belief and life.

110. Cf. *A Letter to the Author of 'The Craftsman'* (8 July 1745), *Works,* 26:149; *NT Notes,* 1 Cor. 14:20; and *A Letter to Rev. Mr. Downes* (17 Nov. 1759), §10, *Works,* 9:359.

111. The phrase is from Letter to Miss March (5 July 1768), *Letters* (Telford), 5:96. See also Sermon 70, "The Case of Reason Impartially Considered," §I.6, *Works,* 2:592. Cf. the discussion in S. Jones 1992, pp. 96-107; and C. Williams 1960, p. 32.

112. He frequently criticized those who engage in complex metaphysical speculation beyond what is revealed in Scripture: e.g., Letter to Joseph Benson (17 Sept. 1788), *Letters* (Telford), 8:89; Sermon 132, "On Faith," §8, *Works,* 4:193; and "Thoughts Upon Jacob Behmen," *AM* 5 (1782), *Works* (Jackson), 9:510.

113. *A Letter to the Rev. Mr. Downes* (17 Nov. 1759), §14, *Works,* 9:361.

114. Cf. Letter to George Stonehouse (27 Nov. 1750), *Works,* 26:446-7; where he argues that the reason that the Holy Spirit perfects our reason is so that we may give a clear *scriptural* defense of our hope (emphasis added).

115. See the discussion of Ramus in Ong 1953.

116. *Works,* 1:104. See also the comments on his sermons in Thorsen 1990, pp. 197-8.

117. Cf. *A Plain Account of the People Called Methodists,* §2, *Works,* 9:254; and Sermon 107, "On God's Vineyard," §III.1, *Works,* 3:511.

118. For a general study of this Anglican "common-sense" tradition, see Henry G. Van Leeuwen, *The Problem of Certainty in English Thought: 1630-1690* (The Hague: Martinus Nijhoff, 1970). Cf. Robert Todd Carroll, *The Common-Sense Philosophy of Religion of Bishop Edward Stillingfleet* (The Hague: Martinus Nijhoff, 1975).

119. Cf. Maddox 1992a, pp. 68-9.

120. Cf. Sermon 55, "On the Trinity," §31, *Works,* 2:376-77; and Letter to Dr. John Robertson (24 Sept. 1753), *Works,* 26:515-56.

121. The best study of Wesley's use of the Anglican standards of doctrine is Baker 1970. The best treatment of his views on Christian antiquity is Campbell 1991b.

122. Note, for example, his revealing comment that he proves his doctrines by "Scripture and reason; and, *if need be,* by antiquity" (emphasis added), in *A Farther Appeal to Men of Reason and Religion,* Part III, §III.28, *Works,* 11:310; and *The Principles of a Methodist Farther Explained,* §V.7, *Works,* 9:220. See likewise his stipulation that both corporate and individual experience be tested by Scripture and reason, in *Advice to the People Called Methodists in Regard to Dress,* §VI.4, *Works* (Jackson), 11:475; and Letter to Elizabeth Ritchie (24 Feb. 1786), *Letters* (Telford), 7:319.

123. E.g., the Preface to his 1771 edition of collected works, *Works* (Jackson), 1:iv.

124. Compare C. Williams 1960, p. 29 to Pucelik 1963, p. 58.

125. Cf. Campbell 1991a, pp. 93-4; Campbell 1992a; and S. Jones 1992, p. 81. For examples of the broader appeal in Wesley's actual usage see S. Jones 1992, pp. 227-32.

126. For examples where these two are explicitly conjoined, see *A Short History of Methodism,* §6, *Works,* 9:368; Sermon 112, "On Laying the Foundation of the New Chapel," §II.1, *Works,* 3:585; and "Farther Thoughts on Separation from the Church," §1, *Works,* 9:538.

127. E.g., "Ought We to Separate From the Church of England?" §II, *Works,* 9:568; Letter to Editor of *Lloyd's Evening Post* (1 Dec. 1760), *Letters* (Telford), 4:115; and *Sunday Service,* p. 2.

128. Cf. his Letter to James Hutton (8 May 1739), *Works,* 25:645. This abridgment can be found in *John Wesley,* pp. 123-33.

129. A few examples of such an appeal include: *An Earnest Appeal to Men of Reason and Religion*, §59, *Works*, 11:68-9; *A Farther Appeal to Men of Reason and Religion*, Part I, §II.4-7, *Works*, 9:111-15; and Sermon 20, "The Lord Our Righteousness," §II.6, *Works*, 1:456. For a discussion of the influence of the *Book of Common Prayer* on Wesley's theology, see K. Wilson 1984, pp. 269-354.

130. Cf. Baker 1970, pp. 140, 213, 324.

131. Appeal to Scripture alone was not sufficient, for the real questions dealt with differing interpretations of Scripture. Wesley's assumption of the superiority of the interpretation of the Early Church is expressed most forcefully in his Letter to Joseph Benson (22 Feb. 1782), *Letters* (Telford), 7:106: "I regard no authorities but those of the Ante-Nicene Fathers; nor any of them in opposition to Scripture."

132. For lists of these writers, see *Plain Account of Genuine Christianity*, §III.11, *John Wesley*, p. 195; and *An Address to the Clergy*, §I.2 & §II.1, *Works* (Jackson), pp. 484, 492. Cf. Campbell 1992a.

133. Sermon 13, "On Sin in Believers," §III.9, *Works*, 1:324. Cf. Letter to Walter Churchey (20 June 1789), *Letters* (Telford), 8:145. A very similar claim can be found in Pearson's *Exposition of the Creed*, Vol. I, p. xix-xx.

134. For recommendations of Pearson's *Exposition of the Creed*, see Letter to Cradock Glascott (13 May 1764), *Letters* (Telford), 4:243; and Letter to Alexander Knox (5 June 1778), *Letters* (Telford), 3:314. He used Pearson in training the assistants; cf. *Journal* (23 Feb. 1749), *Works*, 20:263. Note also his description of Pearson as "as learned and orthodox a divine as ever England bred" in *A Letter to the Right Reverend the Lord Bishop of Gloucester* (26 Nov. 1762), §II.21, *Works*, 11:519.

135. See *Journal* (5 Aug. 1754), *Works*, 20:489; and his objection to the anathemas in the Athanasian Creed in Sermon 55, "On the Trinity," §3, *Works* 2:377. This is probably the reason that Wesley omitted Anglican Article XXI on the "Authority of the General Councils" from his list for the American Methodists. Note, however, that when Wesley "summarized" his own doctrinal commitments in *A Letter to a Roman Catholic* (*John Wesley*, pp. 493-9), it was in terms quite similar to the Nicene-Constantinopolitan creed (cf. the comparison of the two in Geoffrey Wainwright, "Methodism and the Apostolic Faith," in *What Should Methodists Teach?*, edited by M. Douglas Meeks [Nashville: Kingswood Books, 1990], p. 107).

136. See Letter to James Hutton (27 Nov. 1738), *Works*, 25:593; *A Plain Account of Genuine Christianity*, §III.12, *John Wesley*, p. 195; and Sermon 4, "Scriptural Christianity," §I, *Works*, 1:161-5. Note also that he closed his description of the essence of Methodism in *An Earnest Appeal to Men of Reason and Religion* with Charles' poem on "Primitive Christianity," *Works*, 9:90-94. The focus of consideration of the Early Church on its model of Christian life was common in Wesley's Anglican context; cf. Eamon Duffy, "Primitive Christianity Revived: Religious Renewal in Augustan England," in *Renaissance and Renewal in Christian History*, edited by Derek Baker (Oxford: Basil Blackwell, 1977), pp. 287-300; and Campbell 1991b, pp. 55ff, 110.

137. Cf. *Ecclesiastical History*, Preface, §10, *Works* (Jackson), 14:299.

138. E.g., Preface to "The Epistles of the Apostolic Fathers, St. Clement, St. Ignatius, St. Polycarp; and the Martyrdoms of St. Ignatius and St. Polycarp" (in *Chr. Library*, 1:i-iv), *Works* (Jackson), 14:223-4; and *An Address to the Clergy*, §I.2, *Works* (Jackson), 10:484.

139. For some characteristic decrials of the fall of the primitive Church at the time of Constantine, see Sermon 61, "The Mystery of Iniquity," §27, *Works*, 2:463; "Thoughts Upon a Late Phenomenon," §2, *AM* 12 (1789):46-9, *Works*, 9:534; and

Sermon 121, "Prophets and Priests," §8, *Works,* 4:77. See also the summary in Campbell 1991b, pp. 47-51.

140. Cf. Campbell 1991b, p. 105ff.

141. This point has been made by Campbell 1991b, pp. 52, 116. Cf. Keefer 1984, p. 29. For a representative example of the late Wesley, see Sermon 102, "Of Former Times," §18, *Works,* 3:451.

142. Cf. *Journal* (25 Jan. 1738), *Works,* 18:212-13 fn95. See also the discussion in Baker 1970, p. 139.

143. Cf. *A Letter to the Reverend Dr. Conyers Middleton* (4-24 Jan. 1749), *Letters* (Telford), 2:325.

144. Thus, when his followers question why they should submit to Anglican traditions or practices that are not explicitly taught in Scripture, he responds that there may be a thousand rules *subordinate* to Scripture, as long as they do not violate it ("Ought We to Separate from the Church of England," §II.4, *Works,* 9:570).

145. In reacting against some who give tradition too large of a role, Bryant's total subordination of tradition to Scripture (1992a, pp. 36-41) fails to do justice to the reciprocal relationship in Wesley.

146. On Montanus, see Sermon 61, "The Mystery of Iniquity," §24, *Works,* 2:461; Sermon 68, "The Wisdom of God's Counsels," §9, *Works,* 2:555; "The Real Character of Montanus," *AM* 8 (1785):35-6, *Works* (Jackson), 11:485-6; and his editorial addition to his abridgement of Mosheim's *Ecclesiastical History* (1:114), "I have frequently been in doubt, whether he was not one of the wisest and holiest men who was then in the Christian Church! And whether his real fault was not, the bearing a faithful testimony of the general apostasy from Christian holiness." On Novatian, his addition to Mosheim (1:145) was, "I have sometimes wondered. . . . whether he was not himself one of the holiest men who lived in that century: and whether he taught any more, than that *impenitent* sinners ought not to be retained in, or admitted into the Church." See also his Letter to William Dodd (12 Mar. 1756), 9, *Letters* (Telford), 3:170-1. On Pelagius, see Letter to Alexander Coates (7 July 1761), *Letters* (Telford), 4:158; Letter to John Fletcher (16 Aug. 1775), *Letters* (Telford), 6:174-5; and his footnote to Mosheim (1:248), "I doubt whether he was any more an heretic than Castellio or Arminius."

147. There have been some helpful recent studies of Wesley's understanding of the importance of experience (witness of the Spirit) for personal spiritual life (esp. Matthews 1986; and Runyon 1988 & 1990). Thorsen 1989 provides an initial evaluation of the role of experience in Wesley's doctrinal judgments, but a thorough critical study of this topic is still lacking.

148. Cf. Gallo 1984; Abraham 1985, p. 120; and Thorsen 1989, p. 120; and 1990, pp. 45, 101. For an argument that Wesley is actually developing a role of experience implicit in Anglicanism see Miller 1991, pp. 104-8, 170, 227-8.

149. Thus, one can find everything from the "Schleiermacherian" reading of Wesley noted in the early twentieth century, which argued that Wesley appealed to inner spiritual experience for formulating all authentic doctrine (e.g., Eayrs 1926, and Rattenbury 1928, p. 84), to more recent emphatic denials that Wesley understood "experience" as an inner feeling (Baker 1970, p. 24) or used experience for anything more than confirming doctrine (C. Williams 1960, p. 33; Schneeberger 1974, p. 46; R. Davies 1981, p. 70; and Horst 1985, p. 322).

150. The need to distinguish more clearly between these two hampers the generally helpful studies by Thorsen (1989 & 1990 [see esp. p. 211]) and Miller (1991, pp. 211ff).

151. See Sermon 11, "Witness of the Spirit II," §III.6 & §V.2, *Works,* 1:290, 297. Cf. S. Jones 1992, pp. 239-43.

152. Note its use in this regard in Thorsen 1990, pp. 104ff.

153. *The Doctrine of Original Sin,* §II.13, *Works* (Jackson), 9:176.

154. Sermon 44, "Original Sin," *Works,* 2:172-85, esp. §II.2, p. 176. For a perceptive reading of *The Doctrine of Original Sin* that reaches below its inductive rhetoric and reveals its dependence on Wesley's prior (biblical) commitments, see Horst 1985, pp. 287-92. In other words, Wesley's actual practice was not as inductivist as his rhetoric!

155. Cf. Rack 1989, p. 385.

156. E.g., Letter to Charles Wesley (31 July 1747), *Works,* 26:255; and Sermon 13, "On Sin in Believers," §III.7, *Works,* 1:323. Note that in both these cases he argued that his opponent's position was contrary to Scripture *as well as* to experience. In reality, experience had helped him decide the most adequate understanding of Scripture on both issues.

157. Sermon 83, "On Patience," §11-12, *Works,* 3:177-8. Cf. the extract from *A Short View of the Difference Between the Moravian Brethren (So-Called), And the Rev. Mr. John and Charles Wesley, Works* (Jackson), 10:203; Letter to Elizabeth Hardy (26 Dec. 1761), *Letters* (Telford), 4:167; and Letter to Ann Loxdale (12 July 1782), *Letters* (Telford), 7:129. In the last letter he refers to experience as "the strongest of all arguments." One must qualify this by remembering that he was dealing with a case on which he believed that Scripture was silent.

158. Baker 1970, p. 24.

159. Note how often the issues of "how many" have experienced entire sanctification and "how long" they had lived in the experience turn up in his appeals to experience regarding instantaneous sanctification. E.g., *Thoughts on Christian Perfection,* Questions 37 & 38, *John Wesley,* pp. 297-8; Letter to Mrs. Ryan (28 June 1766), *Letters* (Telford), 5:16; Letter to Charles Wesley (9 July 1766), *Letters* (Telford), 5:20; Letter to Charles Wesley (12 Feb. 1767), *Letters* (Telford), 5:41; and Letter to Miss March (30 Nov. 1774), *Letters* (Telford), 6:129. Cf. the Letter to John from Charles Wesley (28 Feb. 1741), *Works,* 26:52.

160. This point is unfortunately missed in John Meyendorff's one passing comment on Wesley's interest in the early Greek fathers' model of theological activity—"Light From the East? 'Doing Theology' in an Eastern Orthodox Perspective," in *Doing Theology in Today's World,* ed. John Woodbridge & Thomas McComiskey (Grand Rapids, MI: Zondervan, 1991), pp. 339-58; here, 344.

161. Tracy 1992 emphasizes the contribution of Wesley's experience of the dire economic needs of many in English society to his characteristic theological convictions.

162. Cf. Owen C. Thomas, "Theology and Experience," *Harvard Theological Review* 78 (1985):179-201, esp. p. 194.

163. This phrase is suggested in Giffin 1988. On the dominance of appeal to Scripture in Wesley's actual theological activity, see S. Jones 1992, p. 212; Miller 1991; and Coppedge 1984.

164. In *Wesley's Standard Sermons,* ed. E.H. Sugden (London: Epworth, 1921), 1:196 fn2.

165. Hoon 1936, p. 343.

166. An explicit example of such assumptions is George Eayrs (1926, pp. 58-9). Eayrs takes at face-value Wesley's Baconian rhetoric that dismisses the heuristic role of theory in experimentation (cf. *Primitive Physick,* Preface, 8, *Works* [Jackson],

14:310). Given modern hermeneutical awareness, most scholars are less willing to affirm that Wesley's inductivist self-understanding is descriptive of his actual practice.

167. For a methodological description and discussion of this phenomenon, see Randy L. Maddox, "Hermeneutic Circle—Vicious or Victorious?" *Philosophy Today* 27 (1983):66-76.

Chapter Two

1. *NT Notes,* 2 Cor. 5:19.

2. Since it is among the areas of his largely "assumed theology," there have been no detailed studies of Wesley's doctrine of God/Father or the Godhead in general. Among the few brief discussions are Cannon 1946, pp. 153-75; Naglee 1991, pp. 99-126; and Collins 1993, pp. 15-34.

3. Cf. Shimuzu 1980, pp. 100ff.

4. Cf. *Survey,* 2:125, "The world around us is the mighty volume wherein God hath declared Himself. . . . The book of nature is written in . . . things which picture out the divine perfections." For a few examples affirming particular attributes, see 2:113, 2:123, 2:210, 3:58, and 3:249-50.

5. Cf. Sermon 69, "The Imperfection of Human Knowledge," §I.1-3, *Works,* 2:569-70.

6. Something affirmed in *NT Notes,* 1 Peter 1:2.

7. Browne discussed analogical knowledge of God in *Limits of Human Understanding,* and *Things Divine and Supernatural Conceived by Analogy with Things Natural and Human* (London: William Innys, 1733). Wesley read and abridged the first volume (in *Survey* 5:149-96). My summary of Browne draws from pp. 153-62 of this abridgment. I believe that Wesley also read the second volume. Twice in 1756 he recommended it to others: *A Letter to the Reverend Mr. Law* (6 Jan. 1756), §II.7, *Letters* (Telford), 3:369; and Letter to Samuel Furly (18 Feb. 1756), *Letters* (Telford), 3:163. Such recommendation seems unlikely if he had not read it himself. For an analysis of Browne's views, see Arthur Robert Winnett, *Peter Browne: Provost, Bishop, Metaphysician* (London: SPCK, 1974).

8. His typical phrase for this was that the author is "speaking after the manner of men." Cf. *NT Notes,* Luke 15:7, Rom. 8:28, Rom. 11:2, Heb. 4:10, 1 Peter 1:2. See also *OT Notes,* Exodus 33:23, where Wesley makes one of his rare insertions to explain the anthropomorphic language of God's hand covering God's backside.

9. See esp. *NT Notes,* Rom. 5:9; and *A Letter to the Reverend Mr. Law* (6 Jan. 1756), §II.2, *Letters* (Telford), 3:346.

10. The best example of this insistence is in *A Farther Appeal to Men of Reason and Religion,* Pt. II, §III.21, *Works,* 11:268. Note that Wesley here is not rejecting the use of analogy to understand what God has revealed, only its ability to comprehend God apart from revelation.

11. Indeed, he says that there is "no analogy or proportion between the mercy of the children of men and that of the most high God" (Sermon 86, "A Call to Backsliders," II.1, *Works,* 3:217). Once again, Wesley's contextual rhetoric must be nuanced! He obviously assumes in the sermon that God's mercy includes all that is good in human mercy, but none of its limitations.

12. See *NT Notes,* Rom. 5:9; *A Letter to the Reverend Mr. Law* (6 Jan. 1756), §II.2, *Letters* (Telford), 3:346; and Letter to Dr. John Robertson (24 Sept. 1753), *Works,* 26:521.

13. Cf. his comment on the biblical statement that God is not the God of the dead—"That is, the term *God* implies such a relation as cannot possibly subsist between him and the dead" (*NT Notes,* Luke 20:38).

14. Cf. Steele 1994, pp. 19-20; and Bryant 1992a, pp. 13-14.

15. On this general theme, see David Berman, "The Repressive Denials of Atheism in Britain in the Seventeenth and Eighteenth Centuries," *Proceedings of the Royal Irish Academy* 82 (1982):211-46. For Wesley's use of "practical Atheism," see Sermon 23, "Sermon on the Mount III," §I.11, *Works*, 1:517 (Outler notes other occurrences of the phrase in the connected footnote).

16. Cf. his few caustic remarks on Hume in: *Journal* (5 March 1769), *Works*, 22:172; *Journal* (5 May 1772), *Works*, 22:321; Sermon 120, "The Unity of the Divine Being," §19, *Works*, 4:69; and Sermon 128, "The Deceitfulness of the Human Heart," §II.7, *Works*, 4:158. For a helpful characterization of the different types of Enlightenment thought, see Henry F. May, *The Enlightenment in America* (New York: Oxford University Press, 1976).

17. E.g., Susan Brooks Thistlethwaite & Mary Potter Engel, eds., *Lift Every Voice: Constructing Christian Theologies from the Underside* (San Francisco, CA: Harper & Row, 1990), p. 77.

18. The *Dictionary* defines "attributes of God" as God's perfections.

19. Browne makes this distinction in *Things Divine and Supernatural*, pp. 248, 258. Wesley used it in Sermon 122, "Causes of the Inefficacy of Christianity," §6, *Works*, 4:89.

20. E.g., Sermon 54, "On Eternity" (1786), *Works*, 2:358-72; Sermon 118, "On the Omnipresence of God" (1788), *Works*, 4:40-47; and Sermon 120, "The Unity of the Divine Being" (1789), *Works*, 4:61-71.

21. Note how he moves from his description of the various divine attributes to a reflection on "true religion" in light of these in Sermon 120, "The Unity of the Divine Being," §16ff, *Works*, 4:66ff. Cf. Outler's introductory comments (*Works*, 4:60).

22. He quotes this article in Sermon 120, "The Unity of the Divine Being," §8, *Works*, 4:63. He also included it in the Articles of Religion for the American Methodists.

23. Note that he includes the "affections" as one aspect of the Image of God in humanity in Sermon 45, "The New Birth," §I.1, *Works*, 2:188. This is particularly the case since Wesley considered love—which God epitomizes—to be the prime affection; cf. Sermon 141 (1730), "The Image of God," §I.2, *Works*, 4:294.

24. Henry Wheeler has noted that it was the American Conference that deleted this phrase in 1784. He also notes that they were returning to the original wording of the Augsburg Confession, the source for the Anglican Article I; Wheeler, *History and Exposition of the Twenty-Five Articles of Religion of the Methodist Episcopal Church* (New York: Eaton and Mains, 1908), pp. 15, 47.

25. *NT Notes*, Luke 15:7. See also his discussion of the analogical nature of ascribing "passions" to God in *NT Notes*, Rom. 5:9; and *A Letter to the Reverend Mr. Law* (6 Jan. 1756), §II.2, *Letters* (Telford), 3:346.

26. *Serious Thoughts on the Perseverance of the Saints*, §14, *Works* (Jackson), 10:289-90.

27. See Sermon 54, "On Eternity," §1, *Works*, 2:358. In §4 (360) he describes present existence as a portion of duration between two eternities. See also Sermon 120, "The Unity of the Divine Being," §2, *Works*, 4:61.

28. E.g., *NT Notes*, Rom. 1:28; 1 Peter 1:2.

29. Here I am disagreeing directly with Naglee (1991, esp. pp. 88-90), who assumes the Greek emphasis on timelessness is more fundamental to Wesley and that his references to "boundless duration" are merely oversimplified analogies used to communicate to his unsophisticated followers.

30. Cf. *Predestination Calmly Considered*, §18, *John Wesley*, p. 433. He admits that the question of how God could know future contingent events is a very difficult one (*NT*

Notes, Acts 15:18). This same tension in understanding Divine Eternity, and the same question about foreknowledge and freedom, are found in the early Greek fathers; cf. Staniloae, *Orthodoxe Dogmatik*, I:159-60, 219.

31. Sermon 118, "On the Omnipresence of God," §III, *Works*, 4:45-7.

32. See Letter to Dr. John Robertson (24 Sept. 1753), *Works*, 26:517. One proposed solution for holding these together was the idea that God possesses "middle knowledge" (i.e., knows all possible contingent worlds, choosing to actualize this one). Wesley was aware of this option and interested enough in it to publish extracts of proponents in the first two volumes of the *Arminian Magazine* (1778-9)—cf. the discussion of these in Bryant 1992a, pp. 129-34. Wesley's lack of more explicit endorsement may reflect awareness of problems with this position. On these problems, see William Hasker, "Providence and Evil: Three Theories," *Religious Studies* 28 (1992):91-105.

33. For a presentation of a "self-limiting" view of God that deals sensitively with the hermeneutical issues and appears congenial to Wesley's basic convictions, see Richard Rice, *God's Foreknowledge and Man's Free Will* (Minneapolis, MN: Bethany House, 1985). Cf. Madron 1965, p. 63.

34. Note his claim that justice and goodness are attributes inseparable from the very idea of God, in *An Earnest Appeal to Men of Reason and Religion*, §15, *Works*, 11:49-50. See also, *NT Notes*, Heb. 2:10.

35. See his criticism of those who deny God's wrath in "Thoughts on the Writings of Baron Swedenborg," §15, *AM* 6 (1783), *Works* (Jackson), 13:434; "Thoughts Upon Jacob Behmen," *AM* 5 (1782), *Works* (Jackson), 9:513; and Letter to Dr. John Robertson (24 Sept. 1753), *Works*, 26:521.

36. Sermon 120, "The Unity of the Divine Being," §7, *Works*, 4:62. See also the claim that God may reward more, but never punish more, than strict justice requires, in *Thoughts upon God's Sovereignty*, §9, *Works* (Jackson), 10:363.

37. *NT Notes*, 1 John 4:8. See also *Predestination Calmly Considered*, §43, *John Wesley*, p. 445; and *Hymns* #136, stanza 7, *Works*, 7:251.

38. See the intertwining of love and justice in Wesley's analysis of the Fall in Sermon 57, "On the Fall of Man," I.3, *Works*, 2:403-4. On contextual variations, see the discussion in *Minutes* (2 Aug. 1745), Qq. 17-18, *John Wesley*, p. 151. See also the discussion of the integral relation of God's love and justice in Hoon 1936, p. 322; and Fuhrman 1963, p. 92.

39. See esp. *Predestination Calmly Considered*, §31 & §43, *John Wesley*, pp. 439, 445. See also *Thoughts Upon Necessity*, §IV.5, *John Wesley*, pp. 490-1: here Wesley is debating whether God could have created us in a way that we had authentic freedom. His main claim is that an omnipotent God can; but more importantly, a God of Love would!

40. See Sermon 34, "The Original, Nature, Properties and Uses of the Law," §III.6-9, *Works*, 2:12-13.

41. Cf. Sermon 120, "The Unity of the Divine Being," §5, *Works*, 4:62.

42. *Predestination Calmly Considered*, §47-50, *John Wesley*, pp. 447-9.

43. At times he debated whether it was simply identical to omniscience (e.g., Sermon 68, "The Wisdom of God's Counsels," §1, *Works*, 2:552; and Sermon 120, "The Unity of the Divine Being," §6, *Works*, 4:62), at other times he listed it among the moral attributes (*NT Notes*, Heb. 2:10).

44. Sermon 67, "On Divine Providence," §14, *Works*, 2:540. Cf. Sermon 68, "The Wisdom of God's Counsels," §4, *Works*, 2:553; and *Predestination Calmly Considered*, §52, *John Wesley*, p. 450.

45. *Thoughts Upon God's Sovereignty, Works* (Jackson), 10:361-3; and *NT Notes*, Rom. 9:21.

46. Sermon 63, "The General Spread of the Gospel," §11, *Works*, 2:489.

47. E.g., *NT Notes*, Rom. 8:28; Sermon 15, "The Great Assize," §II.10, *Works*, 1:365; Sermon 66, "The Signs of the Times," §II.9, *Works*, 2:530; Sermon 118, "On the Omnipresence of God," §II.1, *Works*, 4:43; and Letter to Ann Bolton (18 May 1779), *Letters* (Telford), 6:345.

48. This requires one qualification. Wesley could allow that conversion may begin with an overwhelming power of saving grace, but insisted that this was not common and was always capable of being resisted later (Sermon 63, "The General Work of the Gospel," §12, *Works*, 2:489-90). This is the sense in which one must understand stanza 3 of *Hymns* #381, which begins "Confound, o'erpower me by thy grace" (*Works*, 7:555).

49. Cf. Staniloae, *Orthodox Dogmatik*, 1:203ff; and Wainwright 1987, pp. 10-11. It has also been suggested as an alternative to typical Western Christian conceptions by John Oman, *Grace and Personality* (Cambridge: University Press, 1931), pp. 40-1. Some have compared Wesley with process metaphysics in this context (e.g. Schubert Ogden, "Process Theology and the Wesleyan Witness," *PSTJ* 37.3 [1984]:18-33). There are some similarities, but Wesley would surely question the process commitment to the *metaphysical* (as opposed to *moral*) necessity of Divine noncoercion; cf. David Basinger, *Divine Power in Process Theism* (Albany, NY: SUNY, 1988).

50. Wesley dealt with predestination in a variety of tracts and sermons. The majority of these can be found in *Works* (Jackson), Vol. 10. The most thorough discussion of John's debates over predestination is Coppedge 1987. On Charles, see H. Davies 1992; and J.R. Tyson 1985b.

51. The significance of these various moves has been hotly debated in recent Calvin scholarship. Key to this debate is whether the later Reformed scholastic move of predestination to the locus of God the Father was a distortion of Calvin, sheering the doctrine from its Christological connections and turning it into a wooden supralapsarian decree. On this debate, compare Basil Hall, "Calvin Against the Calvinists," in *John Calvin*, ed. G. E. Duffield (Grand Rapids, MI: Eerdmans, 1966), pp. 19-37; and Richard A. Muller, *Christ and the Decree: Christology and Predestination in Reformed Theology from Calvin to Perkins* (Durham, NC: Labyrinth, 1986). My interest in Calvin's early placement does not relate to the timing or Christological mooring of the electing decrees, but to the implied suggestion that this doctrine is an expression of his basic understanding of the nature of God.

52. This charge can be found already in George Whitefield's claim that Wesley's rejection of predestination in the sermon "Free Grace" makes salvation depend on human *free-will* rather than God's *free-grace*; see his *Letter to the Rev. Mr. John Wesley* (24 Dec. 1740), in *George Whitefield's Journals*, ed. Iain Murray (London: Banner of Truth, 1960), pp. 571-88, here p. 587. More recent examples would include James I. Packer, "Introductory Essay," in John Owen, *The Death of Death in the Death of Christ* (London: Banner of Truth, 1959), pp. 1-25; and Paul K. Jewett, *Election and Predestination* (Grand Rapids, MI: Eerdmans, 1985). Both argue that Arminians (like Wesley) do not appreciate enough humanity's need for God's grace. Ironically, Packer then quotes a hymn to express the inescapable need for this grace—a hymn of Charles Wesley (whom he suggests forgot his Arminianism at this point, p. 8)! Meanwhile Jewett claims that John Wesley's rejection of predestination was fortunately more emotional than critical—he did not see the implications of his Arminian views (p. 17)! One has to wonder *who* is really confused.

53. For examples of this claim, see Walls 1983, pp. 30, 33; Jerry L. Walls, "Can God Save Anyone He Will?" *Scottish Journal of Theology* 38 (1985):155-72; Meeks 1985a, pp. 29-30; Coppedge 1987, pp. 138; and Wainwright 1987, pp. 26-8. See also the parallel comparison of Arminians to Calvinists in Richard Rice, "Divine Foreknowledge and Free-Will Theism," in *The Grace of God, The Will of Man*, pp. 121-39, ed. Clark Pinnock (Grand Rapids, MI: Zondervan, 1989), p. 130.

54. John Knight has argued that Wesley objected to unconditional election *primarily* because of its implication for the doctrine of God prior to 1770, but that in the following years he opposed it *largely* because of its implications for the doctrine of anthropology (1978, p. 21). There may indeed be some shift of emphasis in the later Wesley, but not of essential point. In fact, when he launches the *Arminian Magazine* in 1777, his expressed purpose is not to defend a view of humanity, but to spread the teaching of the "universal love of God" and God's willingness to save all humanity from sin; cf. *AM* 1, Preface, §4, in *Works* (Jackson), 14:279.

55. For just three examples, see his Letter to Susannah Wesley (29 July 1725), *Works*, 25:175; Sermon 110, "Free Grace," §24-5, *Works*, 3:552-6; and *Predestination Calmly Considered*, esp. §36-43, *John Wesley*, pp. 441-5. See also Coppedge 1987, p. 265.

56. *A Letter to the Rev. James Hervey* (15 Oct. 1756), *Letters* (Telford), 3:387.

57. "Address to the Calvinists," stanza 3, *AM* 3 (Aug. 1778):383-4, in *Poetry*, 3:392. For another poem developing these points at length, see "The Horrible Decree," *Poet. Works*, 3:34-8 (reprinted along with several other poems on predestination in *CW Reader*, pp. 294-309).

58. Note in this regard the recent argument of Richard Muller that where Arminius and his predestinarian Reformed opponents differed most fundamentally was in their respective views of God and God's providential action in the creation; Muller, *God, Creation, and Providence in the Thought of Jacob Arminius* (Grand Rapids, MI: Baker, 1991), esp. pp. 13-4, 67-8, 238-41, 281.

59. Sermon 110, "Free Grace," §28, *Works*, 3:557. Note that George Whitefield's chief complaint is that Wesley opposes the Divine sovereignty, in *Letter to the Rev. Mr. John Wesley*, p. 588.

60. Note his claim that the wise person is one who recognizes God as their Father, their friend, and the parent of all good (Sermon 33, "Sermon on the Mount XIII," §II.2, *Works*, 1:692). Cf. Coppedge 1991, pp. 282-3. In this light, Robert Moore's description of Wesley's God as a Monarch jealously guarding all initiative (1979, p. 191) is incomprehensible; Wesley did indeed share a general emphasis on God's transcendence with his age, but was battling against precisely such extremes of that emphasis!

61. Note Wesley's contrast between God's omnipotence and God's love, in relation to human freedom, in *Thoughts Upon Necessity*, §IV.5, *John Wesley*, pp. 473-4. Note also that his deepest objection to predestination was not election to salvation, but unconditional reprobation; *Predestination Calmly Considered*, esp. §19, *John Wesley*, p. 434. Of course, he assumed that any affirmation of unconditional election to salvation necessarily involved reprobation, viewing the attempt to separate these two as mere sophistry, cf. Ibid, §8 (429-30) & §23 (435).

62. See Sermon 63, "The General Spread of the Gospel," §9, *Works*, 2:488; and Sermon 67, "On Divine Providence," §15, *Works*, 2:540-1. In both passages Wesley argues that irresistible grace would obliterate humanity's moral nature, contrary to God's creation design.

63. Note Wesley's description of the purpose of the *Arminian Magazine* in his preface to Volume 1: "Our design is, to publish some of the most remarkable tracts

on the universal love of God, and His willingness to save *all* [persons] from *all* sin, which have been wrote in this and the last century" (§4, *Works* [Jackson], 14:279, emphasis added); cf. Coppedge 1987, p. 272. Whitefield criticized this very connection in *Letter to Rev. Mr. John Wesley*, p. 582.

64. Wesley's longest exposition of the disastrous practical effects of teaching predestination is Sermon 110, "Free Grace," §10-18 (see §11), *Works*, 3:547-50. Compare Whitefield's point-by-point response in his *Letter to the Rev. Mr. John Wesley*, pp. 572ff. See also Wesley's *Predestination Calmly Considered*, 86, *John Wesley*, p. 470; and *Reasons Against a Separation from the Church*, §III.2, *Works*, 9:339-40.

65. This caricature of the predestinarian view comes from Wesley's abridgement (parody?) of *The Doctrine of Absolute Predestination Stated and Asserted* by the Reverend Mr. Augustus Toplady, *Works* (Jackson), 14:190-8.

66. For examples of Article XVII being used against John, see *Journal* (8 May 1747), *Works*, 20:174; and Whitefield's *Letter to the Rev. Mr. John Wesley*, p. 575. For an attempt by John to turn Article XVII to his side, see his *Letter to James Hervey* (15 Oct. 1756), *Letters* (Telford), 3:379; and *Journal* (19 Nov. 1768), *Works*, 22:164-5. For a similar argument by Charles, see his sermon "Justification by Faith," *Early Sermons CW*, p. 46. Admittedly, their arguments get rather strained. However, they do sense correctly that the early Anglican reformation did not emphasize the doctrine of unconditional predestination—cf. O.T. Hargrove, "The Doctrine of Predestination in the English Reformation" (Vanderbilt University Ph.D. thesis, 1966); and P.O.G. White, *Predestination, Policy and Polemic* (New York: Cambridge University Press, 1992).

67. Cf. Oden 1988, p. 117. Wesley also deleted statements on predestination from his edited edition of the Westminster Shorter Catechism (and writings of Joseph Alleine) in *Chr. Library*; cf. J. MacDonald 1906, pp. 2-9; and K. Kim 1992, pp. 168-71.

68. Cf. *NT Notes*, Rom. 8:28-9, Rom. 9 (intro), and 1 Peter 1:2; and his sermon on Romans 8:28-30 (Sermon 58, "On Predestination," §5, *Works*, 2:417). Note also that Wesley defines the "elect" in his *Dictionary* as "all that truly believe in Christ."

69. On the prominence of this instance, see Jaroslav Pelikan, *The Christian Tradition* (Chicago, IL: University of Chicago, 1971-89), 4:223.

70. Preface, §4 & §9, *OT Notes*, 1:iv-v; also in *Works* (Jackson), 14:247, 249.

71. For several examples, see *OT Notes*, Exod. 4:21, 7:13, 8:15, 8:19, 8:32, Deut. 2:30, Psalm 105:25, and Isa. 63:17. Casto 1977 shows that all of these are original to Wesley. See also his *NT Notes*, Rom. 9:18.

72. These variations are traced in detail in Coppedge 1987.

73. The sermon on "Free Grace" can be found in *Works*, 3:544-59. For his most conciliatory statement, see *Journal* (24 Aug. 1743), *Works*, 19:332-3. But then note his renewed questions in Letter to Charles Wesley (8 Aug. 1752), *Works*, 26:498-9. There would be later fluctuations as well, such as in the Letter to Rev. Plenderlieth (23 May 1768), *Letters* (Telford), 5:90.

74. For some representative lists of these elements, see *NT Notes*, Matt. 6:9, Rom. 9:21, 1 Cor. 10:26; and Sermon 120, "The Unity of the Divine Being," §24, *Works*, 4:71.

75. On the dating of creation, see Sermon 71, "Of Good Angels," §I.3, *Works*, 3:8. On the conservation of matter, see Sermon 54, "On Eternity," §7, *Works*, 2:361-3. Note also his assumption that "creation *ex nihilo*" is a tautology, for creation is necessarily "origination," in *A Letter to the Reverend Mr. Law* (6 Jan. 1756), §I.2, *Letters* (Telford), 3:336.

76. The strongest such claims were made in the early twentieth century by partisans of a "scientific" Wesley: Barber 1923, esp. pp. 4, 16-17; and Collier 1928, pp. 148ff. Collier argues that Wesley was an evolutionist in the essential sense, even though he

admits that Wesley did not assume that there had been temporal development between species! Collier's argument has recently been endorsed by Thorsen (1990, pp. 119, 276 fn79).

77. Wesley's most extensive presentation of this notion is in *Survey*, in the form of edited expositions. The first edition had contained a brief reference from John Ray's *The Wisdom of God Manifested in the Works of Creation* (cf. *Survey*, 4:47). He later added an abridgement of Charles Bonnet's *Contemplation de la Nature*, which developed this notion in detail (*Survey*, 4:49ff). Wesley's personal adoption of the notion is evident from its presence in Sermon 56, "God's Approbation of His Works," §I.14, *Works*, 2:396-7; and Sermon 72, "Of Evil Angels," §1, *Works*, 3:16. The standard study of this notion is Arthur O. Lovejoy, *The Great Chain of Being: A Study of the History of an Idea* (Cambridge, MA: Harvard University Press, 1961).

78. Cf. Lovejoy, *Chain of Being*, pp. 242ff (283, on Bonnet); and John C. Greene, *The Death of Man* (Ames, IA: Iowa State University Press, 1959), esp. p. 128 (on Ray).

79. Note his characterization of Georges Buffon's "reverse-evolutionary" blurring of species distinctions as "atheism barefaced" in "Remarks on the Count de Buffon's *Natural History*," *AM* 5 (1782):491ff, *Works* (Jackson), 13:448-55, esp. 453. For a summary of Buffon's position that highlights even its differences from later Darwinian evolution, see J.S. Wilkie, "Buffon, Lamarck, and Darwin: The Originality of Darwin's Theory of Evolution," in *Science and Religious Belief*, ed. C.A. Russell (Milton Keynes: Open University, 1973), pp. 238-81. Thus, while it is tempting, one must not follow Naglee (1991, p. 198) in reading (Darwinian) assumptions of temporal development into such quotations as: "By what degrees does nature raise herself up to man? . . . the ape is this rough draught of man: this rude sketch, an imperfect representation, which nevertheless bears resemblance to him, and is the last creature that serves to display the admirable progression of the works of God" (*Survey*, 4:85-6).

80. Note how he relates this to the fact that God rested from creating on the seventh day in *The Doctrine of Original Sin*, Pt. III, §VII, *Works* (Jackson), 9:335-6. See also the defense of the emphasis on God working through laws of nature in *Survey*, 2:215-16. This was important enough to Wesley that one of his rare additions to his *OT Notes* was an explanation of the Lord planting gardens as "through natural causes, not specific act" (Num. 24:6; cf. Casto 1977, p. 399).

81. Cf. Sermon 26, "Sermon on the Mount VI," §III.7, *Works*, 1:581; and *Serious Thoughts Occasioned by the Late Earthquake in Lisbon*, *Works* (Jackson), 11:6-7.

82. Compare Sermon 56, "God's Approbation of His Works," §I.1, *Works*, 2:388; Sermon 77, "Spiritual Worship," §I.6, *Works*, 3:93; and *Survey*, 3:174-98. On Wesley's ambivalence about Newton, see English 1991b.

83. Compare *Survey*, 3:221-2; with Sermon 64, "The New Creation," §5, *Works*, 2:502.

84. See the discussion in Matthews 1986, pp. 289-91.

85. E.g., Sermon 80, "On Friendship with the World," §7, *Works*, 3:130.

86. See his rejection of the suggestion of Jacob Boehme and William Law that "nature" was a coeternal reality, intermediating between God and creation: *A Letter to the Reverend Mr. Law* (6 Jan. 1756), §I, *Letters* (Telford), 3:333-6; and "Thoughts Upon Jacob Behmen," *AM* 5 (1782), *Works* (Jackson), 9:510. Note also his explicit acceptance of two steps in creation (origination of matter, and formation of that matter) in Sermon 56, "God's Approbation of His Works," §I.1, *Works*, 2:388; and Sermon 57, "On the Fall of Man," §I.6, *Works*, 2:409.

87. The classic example is Sermon 56, "God's Approbation of His Works," *Works*, 2:387-99. One element of this description about which his opinion fluctuated was Thomas Burnet's suggestion that the original creation was uniformly smooth, with

no mountains: compare Sermon 44 (1759), "Original Sin," §I.1, *Works*, 2:174; *OT Notes*, Gen. 7:20 (1765, Wesley's addition, cf. Casto 1977, p. 346); *Journal* (17 Jan. 1770), *Works*, 22:213-4; and Sermon 56 (1782), "God's Approbation of His Works," §I.2, *Works*, 2:389.

88. Cf. *Serious Thoughts Occasioned by the Late Earthquake in Lisbon, Works* (Jackson), 11:10.

89. Cf. *NT Notes*, Luke 10:31; Sermon 69, "The Imperfection of Human Knowledge," §II.1, *Works*, 2:577; and Letter to Ann Bolton (2 Jan. 1781), *Letters* (Telford), 7:45-6.

90. See his discussion of the threefold circle of divine providence (i.e., the human race, so-called Christians, and "real" Christians), in Sermon 67, "On Divine Providence," §16-18, *Works*, 2:541-3; and Sermon 77, "Spiritual Worship," §I.9, *Works*, 3:94. Wesley took this idea from Thomas Crane (cf. Outler's footnote 30 in *Works*, 2:541).

91. E.g., Sermon 71, "Of Good Angels," *Works*, 3:4-15; Sermon 117, "On the Discoveries of Faith," §6, *Works*, 4:31; and the early unpublished Sermon 135, "On Guardian Angels," *Works*, 4:225-35. Cf. Naglee 1991, pp. 202-7. For a related treatment of Charles Wesley's angelology, see Rattenbury 1941, pp. 325ff.

92. See his *last* published sermon: Sermon 132, "On Faith," §11-12, *Works*, 4:195-7.

93. Cf. Sermon 37, "The Nature of Enthusiasm," §27, *Works*, 2:56; Sermon 41, "Wandering Thoughts," §III.1, *Works*, 2:132; Sermon 67, "On Divine Providence," §19-26, *Works*, 2:543-8; and *An Estimate of the Manners of the Present Times*, §13, *Works* (Jackson), 11:159-60. For a collection of brief descriptions of particular providence that Wesley published, see *Works* (Jackson), 11:496-502. See also the discussion in English 1991b, pp. 74-5.

94. Two major occasions on which Wesley took up this defense were in *A Letter to the Reverend Dr. Conyers Middleton* (4-24 Jan. 1749), *Letters* (Telford), 2:312-88; and *A Letter to the Right Reverend the Lord Bishop of Gloucester* (1763), *Works*, 11:467-538 (see esp. §I.6 [474] and §II.7 [506]). For an excellent summary of the exchange between Wesley and Middleton, see Campbell 1986. It must be admitted that Wesley's defenses did not adequately address the kinds of critical questions about miracles being raised by such as David Hume.

95. For a collection of examples, discussion of precedents, and general evaluation of these two practices, see Casto 1977, pp. 138-47.

96. Cf. his complaint about the lack of this element in most histories of England in the Preface (5-9) to his edited *Concise History of England, from the Earliest Times, to the Death of George II* (1776), in *Works* (Jackson), 14:274-5. For studies of how Wesley used historical writings to emphasize providence, see Chandler 1972; Hosman 1970; Seaborn 1986; and Heimo Ertl, *"Dignity in Simplicity." Studien zur Prosaliteratur des englischen Methodismus im 18. Jahrhundert* (Tübingen: Max Niemeyer, 1988), pp. 224ff.

97. Such implications of providence are replete in the prayers Wesley collected and composed for his people; e.g., *A Collection of Forms of Prayer*, Thursday Morning, *Works* (Jackson), 11:224; and *A Collection of Prayers for Families*, Sunday Evening, *Works* (Jackson), 11:240. See also the conclusion to Sermon 67, "On Divine Providence," §27-9, *Works*, 2:548-9.

98. Letter to Miss March (26 Apr. 1777), *Letters* (Telford), 6:263. See also his conclusion that the only thing that we cannot attribute to God's providence is our sin, in Sermon 37, "The Nature of Enthusiasm," §27, *Works*, 2:56.

99. Letter to Mrs. Barton (13 Nov. 1778), *Letters* (Telford), 6:329.

100. The most complete study of this issue in Wesley is D. Wilson 1969, pp. 109ff. See also Bryant 1992a, pp. 85-136.

101. On Satan and devils in general, see Sermon 72, "Of Evil Angels," *Works*, 3:16-29; and Sermon 117, "On the Discoveries of Faith," §6, *Works*, 4:31. For a possible equation of devils with the souls of departed sinners, see Sermon 132, "On Faith," §8-9, *Works*, 4:193-4. For a defense of the diabolic agency of some diseases, see *NT Notes*, Matt. 10:8, Luke 13:11; and Sermon 72, "Of Evil Angels," §II.12-13, *Works*, 3:25-6. For a clear affirmation of God's limitation of diabolic activity, see *A Farther Appeal to Men of Reason and Religion*, Pt. I, §VII.13, *Works*, 11:198. Overall, Wesley's image of Satan appears to owe as much to Milton as to Scripture, cf. Sermon 62, "The End of Christ's Coming," I.8, *Works* 2:476. For a general rejection of dualism see his extract of Humphrey Dittman in Letter to Revd. Samuel Wesley (19 Dec. 1729), *Works*, 25:241; and reprinted in *AM* 3 (1780):604-6.

102. See the discussion in D. Wilson 1969, pp. 134-7. For some examples of the earlier tendency, see Sermon 143, "Public Diversions Denounced," *Works*, 4:319-28; and *Serious Thoughts Occasioned by the Late Earthquake in Lisbon*, *Works* (Jackson), 11:1-13. See also Charles' sermon on the "Cause and Cure of Earthquakes," in *Works* (Jackson), 7:386-99. By the 1760's John was concerned that even "stumbling blocks" not be attributed directly to God, as evidenced by his addition to his source in *OT Notes* on Ezekiel 3:20 (cf. Casto 1977, p. 489). For specific discussions of Wesley's view of war, see Gerdes 1960, Hynson 1976, and Turley 1991.

103. Cf. *Thoughts Upon God's Sovereignty*, *Works* (Jackson), 10:362; and Sermon 67, "On Divine Providence," §15, *Works*, 2:540.

104. As he once put it, "God does [indirectly] produce the action which is sinful; and yet (whether I can account for it or no) the sinfulness of it is not his will or work. He does also produce the nature which is sinful (he supplies the power by which it is produced); and yet (whether I can account for this or no) the sinfulness of it is not his will or work," *The Doctrine of Original Sin*, Pt. III, §VII, *Works* (Jackson), 9:337.

105. Cf. his fear about "imputing evil to the fountain of love and holiness," in Sermon 111, "National Sins and Miseries," §1, *Works*, 3:566.

106. Cf. Sermon 128, "The Deceitfulness of the Human Heart," §4, *Works*, 4:151-2; and Marquardt 1977a, p. 106. See also Charles' conviction that Satan could not have forced Judas to betray Jesus without Judas' free initial agreement, in Hymn on John 13:2, *Poetry*, 2:257.

107. Cf. *The Doctrine of Original Sin*, Pt. II, §I.5, *Works* (Jackson), 9:243; and Sermon 57, "On the Fall of Man," §1, *Works*, 2:401. See also Charles' quaint poem attributing teething-pain to Adam's sin, *Poet. Works*, 7:89-90 (reprint in *CW Reader*, pp. 345-6). Bryant puts a particular stress on the penal explanation of natural evil, drawing on the early sermons (1992a, pp. 110-11).

108. Compare the simplistic appeal to a penal explanation of suffering in the Sermon 140, "The Promise of Understanding," §II.1 (*Works*, 4:285); with the more sophisticated discussion in Sermon 57, "On the Fall of Man," §1 (*Works*, 2:401). Note also his eventual addition of a cure for venereal disease for "innocent sufferers" to *Primitive Physick* (Remedy 466, p. 106; not in the first edition, added in 1770). Cf. discussion in D. Wilson 1969, 138-9.

109. The most disturbing case is his letter to his sister suggesting that the death of her children is a "great instance of the goodness of God" towards her, because it gave her more time to serve God! Letter to Martha Hall (17 Nov. 1742), *Works*, 26:90-1. See also *NT Notes*, Matt. 16:24, and Acts 6:1. Contrast the more careful discussion of the American War for Independence in Sermon 113, "The Late Work of God in North America," *Works*, 3:595-608. See also the Letter to Ann Bolton (18 May 1779), *Letters* (Telford), 6:345. Cf. D. Wilson 1969, pp. 131-3.

110. Sermon 63, The General Spread of the Gospel," §27, *Works*, 2:499.

111. For a few examples, see *The Doctrine of Original Sin*, Preface, §4, *Works* (Jackson), 9:194; Sermon 44, "Original Sin," §III.3, *Works*, 2:184; Sermon 95, "On the Education of Children," §4, *Works*, 3:349; and Sermon 109, "The Trouble and Rest of Good Men," Proem, *Works*, 3:533. I will point out use of this same title for Christ and the Spirit later.

112. Cf. his sermon devoted to this topic: Sermon 60, "The General Deliverance," *Works*, 2:437-50. Andrew Linzey has referred to this sermon as perhaps the best exposition of the view of animal salvation in the Western Christian tradition! Linzey, *Christianity and the Rights of Animals* (London: SPCK, 1987), p. 38. For a survey of the discussion of this issue in eighteenth-century England, see Keith Thomas, *Man and the Natural World* (New York: Pantheon, 1983), pp. 137-42 (mentions Wesley on p. 140).

113. Cf. Panagiotos K. Chrestou, *Partakers of God* (Brookline, MA: Holy Cross Orthodox Press, 1984), pp. 45-6.

114. The key sermons on this theme are: Sermon 59, "God's Love to Fallen Man," *Works*, 2:423-35; and Sermon 60, "The General Deliverance," esp. §III, *Works*, 2:445-50. Note also his criticism of Law's assumption that God's redemption cannot raise things beyond their original situation, *A Letter to the Reverend Mr. Law* (6 Jan. 1756), §II.1, *Letters* (Telford), 3:334. Unfortunately, some of Wesley's descendants have misunderstood this theme, assuming that Wesley was making the Fall part of God's active will; cf. G.F. Hubbartt, "The Theodicy of John Wesley," *AsbSem* 12.2 (1958):15-18.

115. Cf. Coppedge's claim that the integration of the image of God as Father with the existing images of Creator and Judge was central to Wesley's distinctive view of God (1987, pp. 127-9).

116. Sermon 59, "God's Love to Fallen Man," §I.1-3, *Works*, 2:425-7.

117. Sermon 94, "On Family Religion," §III.7, *Works*, 3:341. It does not seem an accident that some of Wesley's clearest statements about God/Father are in materials for families, like his *Collection of Prayers for Families* and *Prayers for Children*, *Works* (Jackson), 11:237ff. Likewise, Charles' major hymns on God/Father are in his *Hymns for the Family* and *Hymns for Children* (cf. Rattenbury 1941, pp. 140, 150).

118. Sermon 26, "Sermon on the Mount VI," §III.4, *Works*, 1:578. I am unaware of any place where Wesley argues that since God is "Father," God must be male (in any sense). At the same time, I have not found an explicit affirmation of the traditional understanding that God transcends human sex distinctions.

119. E.g., *A Plain Account of Genuine Christianity*, §I.3, *John Wesley*, p. 184; Sermon 33, "Sermon on the Mount XIII," §II.2, *Works*, 1:692; and *The Doctrine of Original Sin*, Pt. III, §VI, *Works* (Jackson), 9:332.

120. Consider Wesley's notes on several Old Testament passages that could be interpreted as applying female imagery or metaphors to God. In most cases Wesley simply ignores such implications, following the lead of the commentary sources that he was drawing upon (e.g., Deut. 32:18, Psalm 22:9-16, Psalm 57, Psalm 61, Psalm 123:2, Job 38:29, Job 39, Isa. 42:14, and Isa. 49:15). On Isaiah 46:3 Wesley follows Poole in noting a metaphor of God nurturing tenderly like a "parent" (rather than a "mother"). On Psalm 91:4 Henry had commented "To this (Mother Hen) the great God is pleased to compare his care of his people," but Wesley omitted this comment. The only female image that he notes is in Hosea 11:3 where he retains Henry's comment "He [God] taught them not only as a Father or tutor but, such is the condescension of divine grace, as a mother or nurse."

121. See in this regard Jane Dempsey Douglass, "Calvin's Use of Metaphorical Language for God: God as Enemy and God as Mother," *Princeton Seminary Bulletin* 8 (1987):19-32. She notes that Luther and Calvin demonstrate a greater reticence about female images for God than had been the case in the late Middle Ages. Calvin does honor Scripture's use of such images in his commentaries, but avoids them in his other works. Douglass suggests that the reason for this is that Calvin is consciously avoiding any encouragement of popular religion that was making considerable use of female imagery (via mariology, etc.). Wesley would appear to have inherited this Protestant sensitivity.

Chapter Three

1. As does Gerdes 1958, cf. p. 5.

2. It was noted in Chapter 1, note 146, that Wesley harbored doubts about the condemnation of Pelagius. The secondary literature on Wesley typically bemoans this fact (e.g., Tuttle 1989, p. 140 fn115), and abounds with protestations that he was not really Pelagian. Of course, it is the Western understanding of Pelagius that they differentiate Wesley from. Recent scholarship on Pelagius has produced a more sympathetic "Eastern" reading of him. The best example is Gisbert Greshake, *Gnade als konkrete Freiheit. Eine Untersuchung zur Gnadenlehre des Pelagius* (Mainz: Matthias-Grünewald, 1972). See also, David F. Wright, "Pelagius the Twice-Born," *Churchman* 86 (1972):6-15. If the suggestion of similar "Eastern" tendencies in Wesley is true, then any sympathies that he felt for Pelagius are less surprising.

3. One of the best summaries of the two basic traditions is J. Patout Burns, "The Economy of Salvation: Two Patristic Traditions," *Theological Studies* 37 (1976):598-619. For a related study mentioning variations from these two major positions, see *idem*, "Introduction," *Theological Anthropology* (Philadelphia: Fortress, 1981), pp. 1-22. A helpful more popular summary is Eusebius Stephanou, "The Church Fathers on Divine Indwelling and the Theology of Grace," *Patristic and Byzantine Review* 11 (1992):11-32. For further documentation on the various summaries of Eastern views throughout this book, see Maddox 1990. Studies of early Eastern Christian traditions have recently turned attention to distinctions between native Greek-speaking theologians and early Syriac Christians. While Wesley was not directly familiar with early Christian writings in Syriac, he came in contact with this tradition through the *Homilies* of (Pseudo-) Macarius. Though Macarius wrote in Greek, it has been demonstrated that he was articulating spiritual emphases of Syriac Christianity (see especially Columba Stewart, *Working the Earth of the Heart* [Oxford: Clarendon, 1991]). Wesley also valued an exhortation on the value of repentance in the Christian life that he believed was a translation (via a Greek intermediary) of a Syriac original by St. Ephrem. In this case it is questionable whether the piece was authentic, though its theme resonates with Ephrem's authentic writings. Hoo-Jung Lee (1991) has drawn on this recent scholarly work to argue that Wesley's dependence upon his contacts with Syriac Christianity should be given more emphasis. In particular, Lee argues that Syriac Christianity (epitomized in Macarius) was more amenable to Wesley because it had a deeper recognition of the problem of "Original Sin" than the Greek-speaking theologians (pp. 182ff). I find this specific claim misleading and think that Lee overplays the difference between Syriac Christianity and the main stream of Greek-speaking theologians, a danger warned against by one of the leading scholars of Syriac Christianity—Sebastian Brock (*The Luminous Eye: The Spiritual World Vision of St. Ephrem the Syrian* [Rome: C.I.I.S, 1985], p. 118). There are indeed some

distinctive themes in Macarius' *Homilies,* which Lee has helpfully explicated and which I will note in appropriate contexts. In general, however, I will use the term "Greek theologians" in a broad sense—including Macarius as sharing the major themes of the Eastern Christian traditions.

4. Panagiotos Chrestou traces this reading from the second century theologian Theophilos, but notes as well some exceptions who assume a static creation, such as Gregory of Nyssa (*Partakers of God,* p. 13). Chrestou clearly takes the developmental view as normative for Eastern Christianity (p. 23).

5. Characteristically, one aspect of this desire to be "like God" that was often mentioned was the desire for instantaneous perfection rather than maturation over time! Cf. Chrestou, *Partakers of God,* pp. 23-4.

6. I am not suggesting that Wesley was making a *conscious* integration of Eastern and Western theology. Given his eighteenth-century Anglican setting, he could not have understood it in these terms. He was simply trying to affirm the faith of the Early Church as he understood it and to relate this to the Protestant emphasis on justification by grace—hence the tension noted in Bundy 1991, p. 153.

7. Cf. Sermon 141, "The Image of God," §I.1-4, *Works,* 4:293-5; Sermon 60, "The General Deliverance," §I.2, *Works,* 2:439; and *OT Notes,* Gen. 1:26-8. Robin Scroggs (1960) argues that Wesley's *NT Notes* comment on Rom. 5:21 suggests the contrary, but he reads too much into this one reference (cf. Deschner 1960, p. 65). Indeed, Wesley extended perfection to the entire creation: Sermon 56, "God's Approbation of His Works," §I.2-6, *Works,* 2:389-91.

8. Cf. his reaction to Dr. Taylor's suggestion that Adam was not created perfect in *The Doctrine of Original Sin,* Pt. II, §3, *Works* (Jackson), 9:291-2; and his related comment in Letter to William Dodd (12 Mar. 1756), §3, *Letters* (Telford), 3:168. This alternative can be found in nascent form in Irenaeus, whom Wesley read, but its clearest articulations are in later Eastern thinkers.

9. Thus, I agree with Wynkoop's claim about Wesley's dynamic anthropology, although she misattributes it to original creation (1972, p. 70).

10. Cf. Myrrha Lot-Borodine, *La Déification de L'Homme selon la doctrine des Pères grecs* (Paris: du Cerf, 1970), pp. 200-1.

11. This theme is prevalent throughout the range of Wesley's life. For a few representative examples, see Letter to Richard Morgan (15 Jan. 1734), *Works,* 25:369; *A Farther Appeal to Men of Reason and Religion,* Pt. I, §3, *Works,* 11:106; *A Plain Account of Genuine Christianity,* §II.12, *John Wesley,* p. 191; Sermon 12, "The Witness of Our Spirit," §15, *Works,* 1:309; and Sermon 44, "Original Sin," §III.5, *Works,* 2:185.

12. Note his argument with Law that ideal humanity is seen in redemption rather than creation, *A Letter to the Reverend Mr. Law* (6 Jan. 1756), §I.3, *Letters* (Telford), 3:339. Cf. Blaising 1979, p. 262; and Weiβbach 1970, p. 1.

13. The best general study of Wesley's anthropology is Gerdes 1958. Also helpful are Bryant 1992a, pp. 143-80; Cho 1986; Scanlon 1969; and Weiβbach 1970.

14. Cf. Luby 1984, p. 52.

15. In his *NT Notes* on Rom. 5:21 Wesley had suggested that grace could not reign until after the Fall. Whatever he meant by this, it is clear elsewhere that he viewed creation as an expression of God's grace. E.g., Sermon 1, "Salvation by Faith," §1, *Works,* 1:117; and Letter to 'John Smith' (25 June 1746), 7, *Works,* 26:199.

16. For the threefold analysis see Sermon 45 (1760), "The New Birth," §I.1, *Works,* 2:188 (as Outler notes [#5], Wesley borrowed this typology from Isaac Watts' *Ruin and Recovery of Mankind*). For two examples of the twofold analysis, see Sermon 60 (1781), "The General Deliverance," §I.1, *Works,* 2:439; and Sermon 62 (1781), "The

End of Christ's Coming," §I.3-7, *Works*, 2:474-5. I find little evidence for Bryant's claim (1992a, pp. 143-51) that Wesley's thought shows a temporal development *toward* the threefold analysis (note the dates on the sermons cited). As Bryant himself admits (p. 156), references to the political image are quite rare. More to the point, I do not believe that the possible trinitarian analogy of the threefold analysis was as important to Wesley as Bryant suggests (p. 149). Both John and Charles do call upon Christians to be "transcripts of the Trinity," but I think that this was more a soteriological concern about the recovery of the moral character of God than an anthropological claim about the constituent elements of human nature (see the discussion at the end of Chapter Five). Behind this soteriological concern lies primarily the distinction between the natural Image and the moral Image. None of this, of course, denies Bryant's most basic claim about the relational nature of Wesley's anthropology.

17. Note that Browne had correlated the distinction between human natural and moral attributes with the Image and Likeness of God in, *Things Divine and Supernatural*, pp. 342, 414-5.

18. Sermon 60, "The General Deliverance," §I.1, *Works*, 2:439. Salvation is a renewal of this participation—cf. *NT Notes*, 2 Peter 1:4.

19. This theme is repeatedly emphasized in Eastern Orthodox anthropology. One of the best extended articulations is John D. Zizioulas, *Being as Communion* (Crestwood, NY: St. Vladimir's Press, 1985).

20. Cf. Sermon 60, "The General Deliverance," §I.2, *Works*, 2:439. A "relational" reading of Wesley has been advocated by such scholars as Bryant (1992a, pp. 13-14, 154, but see also p. 288), H.L. Smith (1963, p. 91), J.W. Smith (1964, p. 71), Staples (1963, pp. 246ff), and Wynkoop (1972, pp. 89, 100f). This endorsement of a relational reading of Wesley's anthropology is made with full consciousness of Míguez Bonino's judgment that Wesley's anthropology was incurably individualistic (1981, p. 55; 1983e, p. 254 [24]). I disagree with his claim that Wesley treated human relationships as totally extrinsic to the person. Some recognition of the social determination of human behavior and self-understanding is evident in Wesley's stress on corporate contexts for nurturing holiness. However, I do agree with Míguez Bonino's larger claim that Wesley shared his age's general blindness to the structural and corporate dimensions of sin.

21. Wesley argued that this is the very reason for which God created humans, in *An Earnest Appeal to Men of Reason and Religion*, §46, *Works*, 11:62. See also his description of the spiritual ideal in *The Character of a Methodist*, §5 & §13, *Works*, 9:35, 39.

22. The theme of loving others permeates Wesley's writing. Indeed, he is convinced that one cannot truly love God without also loving other humans; cf. Letter to John Glass (?) (1 Nov. 1757), *Letters* (Telford), 3:237. The implications of this loving in terms of service have been thoroughly discussed in Jennings 1990.

23. Cf. Sermon 60, "The General Deliverance," §I.6, *Works*, 2:444, which assumes that Adam was the protector of animals prior to the Fall. This task of caring for creation was the expression of the "political" Image of God in humanity (cf. Sermon 45, "The New Birth," §I.1, *Works*, 2:188).

24. I would suggest that this is the crucial dimension of the "happiness" that Wesley continually said results from right relationship to God and others; e.g., *NT Notes*, Luke 11:33, John 1:4; and Sermon 7, "The Way to the Kingdom," §I.10, *Works*, 1:223. This suggestion is not totally opposed to that of Holifield (1986, p. 76) that happiness would involve an absence of self-consciousness, for I would not equate self-accep-

tance with self-absorption. Authentic self-acceptance would accompany an orientation of one's love outward to others.

25. This threefold list remained constant throughout his life. It is found in 1730 in Sermon 141, "The Image of God" (§I.1-4, *Works*, 4:293-5) and in the 1782 rewrite of this sermon as Sermon 57, "On the Fall of Man" (§II.6, *Works*, 2:409-10).

26. The best analysis of this aspect of Wesley is Steele 1994 (see also Clapper 1989, pp. 80-3; and Gallo 1984). Steele places Wesley's psychology in a "voluntarist" tradition, where affections and reason are co-determinate of human actions. Steele's analysis raises serious questions about Bryant's claim (1992a, pp. 143ff) that Wesley's early use of "understanding, will, and liberty" was rationalistic, or that Wesley came to see that these were not unique to humanity.

27. In Sermon 62, "The End of Christ's Coming," §I.4 (*Works*, 2:474) Wesley states parenthetically that the affections are only the will exerting itself in various ways. Note as well the apposition (stated or implied) of "will" and "affections" in Sermon 141 (1730), "The Image of God," §I.2, *Works*, 4:294; Sermon 142 (1731), "The Wisdom of Winning Souls," §II.1, *Works* 4:311-3; Letter to John Fletcher (28 Feb. 1766), *Letters* (Telford), 5:5; Sermon 57 (1782), "On the Fall of Man," §II.6, *Works*, 2:409-10; and Sermon 63 (1783), "The General Spread of the Gospel," §11, *Works*, 2:489.

28. Note the description of affections as "dispositions of the soul" in Sermon 30, "Sermon on Mount X," §2, *Works*, 1:651. Also revealing is Wesley's explanation of why those who are entirely sanctified do not sin in terms of having no affection or motive for sin remaining in them, in "Thoughts on Christian Perfection," Q. 5, *John Wesley*, p. 286; and Sermon 83, "On Patience," §10, *Works*, 3:174-6. This use of "affection" was common in Wesley's day, if now obsolete; cf. the fourth meaning listed in *Oxford English Dictionary* (2nd ed., 1989), 1:213. The connections between Wesley's use and that of Jonathan Edwards are developed in Steele 1994. For another articulation contemporary to Wesley, see Francis Hutcheson, *An Essay on the Nature and Conduct of the Passions and Affections* (3rd ed., 1742) Gainesville, FL: Scholars' Facsimilies & Reprints, 1969.

29. Note the description of the pre-Fall Adam as having rational, even, and regular affections in Sermon 141, "The Image of God," §I.2, *Works*, 4:294. The holistic nature of the affections for Wesley is emphasized in Horst 1985, pp. 128-9; and Clapper 1989, esp. p. 163.

30. Note his claim that "From the true love of God and man directly flows every Christian grace, every holy and happy temper. And from these springs uniform holiness of conversation (i.e., action)," in *A Letter to the Rev. Mr. Baily of Cork*, §III.1, *Works*, 9:309.

31. Cf. his insistence that Christian holiness involves a "habitual disposition of the heart" in Sermon 17, "The Circumcision of the Heart," §I.1, *Works*, 1:402-3; and Letter to Richard Morgan, Sr. (15 Jan. 1734), *Works*, 25:369 (Wesley could use "heart" as an equivalent term for the affections; see *Minutes* [26 June 1744], Q. 4, *John Wesley*, p. 140).

32. The clearest expression of this distinction is in the *NT Notes* comment on 1 Thess. 2:17, which contrasts the transient affections of holy grief or joy with "calm, standing temper" of love which constituted the fixed posture of Paul's soul. So far, the studies that are helpfully placing consideration of Wesley's emphasis on the affections back on the scholarly agenda have not observed this distinction sufficiently. Horst rightly recognizes the predominance of the use of the term "temper" but takes it as an inclusive term that simply gathers other terms like affections or

dispositions (1985, p. 124). By contrast, Clapper tends to subsume the term "temper" into that of "affection" (1989, 27-8, 51-3).

33. Note how Wesley can describe the heavenly tempers as providing the "frame" of a Christian's life in *NT Notes,* 2 Peter 3:18. Equally revealing is his comment that God allowed some recreation on the Sabbath because "few minds are of so firm a temper as to be able to preserve a cheerful devotion, a lively gratitude, without it," in Sermon 139 "On the Sabbath," §III.3, *Works,* 4:276. Compare the ninth meaning of "temper" listed in *Oxford English Dictionary* (2nd ed., 1989), 17:744-5 (a quotation from Jonathan Edwards is used as exemplary!); and the equation of temper and character in Hutcheson, *Nature of the Affections,* p. 86.

34. Wesley consistently identified inward holiness with Christian tempers; e.g., *Journal* (13 Sept. 1739), *Works,* 19:97; *An Earnest Appeal to Men of Reason and Religion,* §97, *Works,* 11:88; *A Short Address to the People of Ireland,* §7, *Works,* 9:283; Sermon 30, "Sermon on Mount X," §2, *Works,* 1:651; *NT Notes,* Matt. 23:31, Rom. 5:7; *OT Notes,* Preface, §17, *Works* (Jackson), 14:252; and Sermon 91, "On Charity," §III.12, *Works,* 3:306.

35. Wesley states explicitly that our works proceed from our tempers in *NT Notes,* 2 Cor. 9:6. Thus, one of his common summary phrases for inward and outward holiness is holiness in "tempers, words, and actions"; e.g., *Minutes* (26 June 1744), *John Wesley,* p. 141; *NT Notes,* John 4:24, Gal. 2:20, 5:25, Phil. 1:11; Sermon 85, "On Working Out Our Own Salvation," §I.3, *Works,* 3:203; and Sermon 115, "Dives and Lazarus," §III.7, *Works,* 4:18.

36. Note, for example his argument that when good tempers reign in one's soul they bring liberty from corrupt tempers, in Letter to Joseph Benson (5 Oct. 1770), *Letters* (Telford), 5:203.

37. Cf. *Thoughts Upon Necessity,* §III.9, *John Wesley,* p. 486; and Sermon 60, "The General Deliverance," §I.4, *Works,* 2:440 (Outler notes additional cases in fn22). The first work is a response to several proponents of determinism, most recently Lord Kames (Henry Home); cf. *Journal* (24 May 1774), *Works,* 22:410. One source of Wesley's distinction between "will" and "liberty" is John Locke's *Essay Concerning Human Understanding,* Book II, Chapter 21, which he serialized in the *Arminian Magazine* beginning with *AM* 5 (1782):413 and carrying on through volume 6.

38. Cf. Sermon 57, "On the Fall of Man," §II.6, *Works,* 2:409-10; and Sermon 116, "What is Man?" §11, *Works,* 4:23-4. For possible sources of this conception of liberty see Outler's note (#19) to the second reference, and Bryant 1992a, p. 159. Wesley considered human liberty to be so self-evident that he had nothing but scorn for the philosophical defenses of determinism spawned by the mechanistic logic of modern science; cf. "A Thought on Necessity," §I & §VI.2-3, *Works* (Jackson), 10:474-5, 478-9. In essence, he rejected even "soft-determinism," in favor of "self-determination."

39. E.g., Sermon 8, "The First Fruits of the Spirit," §II.9, *Works,* 1:241; and Sermon 67, "On Divine Providence," §15, *Works,* 2:540-1. The centrality of liberty to Wesley's understanding of humanity has been particularly argued by Hoffman 1968.

40. *NT Notes,* Heb. 9:14. For a study of Wesley's theology that takes conscience as the defining element of his anthropology, see Stuart 1974.

41. Wesley's clearest discussions of conscience are: Sermon 12, "The Witness of Our Own Spirit," §4-6, *Works,* 1:301-2; *Thoughts Upon Necessity,* §IV.5, *John Wesley,* p. 491; and Sermon 105, "On Conscience," *Works,* 3:480-90. For his discussion of God's original inscription of the moral law, see Sermon 34, "The Original, Nature, Properties, and Use of the Law," §I, *Works,* 2:6-8.

42. For these three contexts, see respectively *NT Notes*, 1 Thess. 5:23; Sermon 52, "The Good Steward," §I.2, *Works*, 2:284; and "Some Thoughts on an Expression of St. Paul, in the First Epistle to the Thessalonians, Chapter V, Verse 23," *AM* 9 (1786):543-4, *Works* (Jackson), 11:447-8. When he distinguished spirit from soul in *NT Notes*, he assumed that it was a supernatural gift found only in humans! Cf. on this topic, Gerdes 1958, pp. 61-3.

43. Cf. his *NT Notes* on 1 Thess. 5:23, where he comments that the soul and body make up the whole nature of a human.

44. Cf. Sermon 116, "What is Man," §8, *Works*, 4:22; and Sermon 129, "Heavenly Treasure in Earthen Vessels," §II.1, *Works*, 4:165. Note also Peter Browne's insistence on the interdependence of spirit and body in *Limits of Human Understanding* (Wesley's abridgement, *Survey*, 5:156, 164).

45. It is clear that Wesley did not confine heart to the affections. The most explicit equation of heart and soul is Sermon 51, "The Good Steward," §I.2, *Works*, 2:284. Cf. Gerdes 1958, pp. 67-8. This equation should probably be understood more metaphorically than biologically.

46. For this development, see "Remarks on the Limits of Human Knowledge," *Works* (Jackson), 13:497; Sermon 69, "The Imperfection of Human Knowledge," §I.13, *Works*, 2:576; and Sermon 116, "What is Man," §5, *Works*, 4:21-2.

47. Note the expression of this parallelism included in *Survey*, 1:136-7. That Wesley endorsed this is evident in his "Remarks on the Limits of Human Knowledge" which were appended to *Survey* (cf. *Works* [Jackson], 13:497).

48. Note his insistence that the soul has an "inward" principle of motion, in Sermon 116, "What is Man," §8, *Works*, 4:22. See also the fine discussion of the mind/body problem in Wesley, in Ott 1989.

49. Cf. Strawson 1959, p. 241.

50. E.g., Sermon 51, "The Good Steward," §II.8, *Works*, 2:289-90; Sermon 54, "On Eternity," §6, *Works*, 2:361; and Sermon 116, "What is Man," §10, *Works*, 4:23. Note in the last reference his immediate addition that we will be re-embodied at the resurrection.

51. See Letter to Mary Bishop (17 April 1776), *Letters* (Telford), 6:214; and "Remarks Upon Mr. Locke's *Essay on Human Understanding*," *AM* 5 (1782), *Works* (Jackson), 13:459. In 1786 he suggested that this function is fulfilled by the "soul" (as distinct from "spirit") in "Some Thoughts on an Expression of St. Paul, in the First Epistle of Thessalonians, Chapter V, Verse 23," *AM* 9 (1786):543-4, *Works* (Jackson), 11:447-8.

52. Wesley stresses this in his 1730 Sermon 141, "The Image of God," §II, *Works*, 4:296. In the 1782 rewrite the same point is echoed by a distinction between "dust" and "mortal corruptible dust" (Sermon 57, "On the Fall of Man," §II.1-2. *Works*, 2:405).

53. See respectively: *NT Notes*, 2 Cor. 5:4; Sermon 56, "God's Approbation of His Works," §II.2, *Works*, 2:399; and *NT Notes*, Gal. 5:19.

54. See esp. Henry Diamond Abelove, "The Sexual Politics of Early Wesleyan Methodism," in *Disciplines of Faith*, ed. Jim Obelkevich, *et al.* (London: Routledge & Kegan Paul, 1987), pp. 86-99; John P. Briggs & John Briggs, "Unholy Desires, Inordinate Affections: A Psychodynamic Inquiry into John Wesley's Relationship with Women," *Connecticut Review* 13 (1991):1-18; Hall 1988; and Holifield 1986, p. 134.

55. For arguments that Wesley's "empirical dualism" avoided metaphysical dualism, see Lerch 1941, p. 28; and Gerdes 1958, p. 74.

56. See especially, *NT Notes*, Acts 17:4. Note also the grouping of women with children and slaves, as those lacking the understanding necessary to be given participation in government, in *A Letter to the Reverend Dr. Conyers Middleton* (Jan. 1749), §III.2, *Letters* (Telford), 2:384; *Thoughts Concerning the Origin of Power* (1772), §8-15, *Works* (Jackson), 11:48-50; and *Some Observations on Liberty* (1776), §19, *Works* (Jackson), 11:99. These comments stand in some tension with his encouragement of women to study theology!

57. For his most blatant affirmation of male hierarchy in the family, see the searing letter to his wife where he argues that any act of disobedience to him is also an act of rebellion against God and the King! (Letter to Mrs. Mary Wesley [23 Mar. 1760], *Letters* [Telford], 4:89). For more perspective on this specific relationship, see Kenneth J. Collins, "John Wesley's Relationship with His Wife as Revealed in His Correspondence," *MethH* 32.1 (1993):4-18. Note as well, however, Wesley's strong rejection of physical abuse of wives by their husbands in *Journal* (28 Apr. 1757), *Works*, 21:94-5; and Sermon 94, "On Family Religion," §III.2, *Works*, 3:339. For further discussion of Wesley's views of marriage, see Naglee 1991, pp. 355-99; and Karen Beth Westerfield Tucker, "'Till Death Us Do Part': The Rites of Marriage and Burial Prepared by John Wesley and Their Development in the Methodist Episcopal Church, 1784-1939" (University of Notre Dame Ph.D. thesis, 1992), pp. 138-41. For broader comparative treatment, see Lawrence Stone, *The Family, Sex and Marriage in England 1500-1800* (New York: Harper, 1979).

58. Cf. *NT Notes*, 1 Cor. 11, Eph. 5:22, and 1 Tim. 2:13.

59. See *OT Notes*, Gen. 3:6-8 (I:15), and 5:2 (I:25). Wesley is following Matthew Henry in both cases. His endorsement of this view is evident in its repetition in Sermon 57, "On the Fall of Man," §I.4, *Works*, 2:403.

60. For explicit reliance on Milton, totally overriding the Hebrew text about Adam being there *with* Eve, see Sermon 57, "On the Fall of Man," §I.1-4, *Works*, 2:402-3. Recall that Wesley published *An Extract from Milton's Paradise Lost* (London: Fenwick, 1763). See also Samuel J. Rogal, "The Role of *Paradise Lost* in Works by John and Charles Wesley," *Milton Quarterly* 13 (1979):114-19.

61. Wesley did not develop this possibility in any broad sense. However, he edged toward it on one front as he advanced various justifications for his support of women in ministry. Cf. the analysis of these justifications in Chilcote 1991; E.K. Brown 1983; and Lawson 1963, pp. 176ff.

62. See esp. *The Doctrine of Original Sin*, *Works* (Jackson), 9:191-464; Sermon 44, "Original Sin," *Works*, 2:172-85; Sermon 128, "The Deceitfulness of the Human Heart, *Works*, 4:150-60; and his exclusion of preachers who deny Original Sin from the conference in the 1784 *Minutes*, Q. 20, *Minutes* (Mason), p. 170.

63. Cf. Outler 1985d, p. 171. The best detailed studies of Wesley's understanding of Original Sin and/or inherited depravity are Blaising 1979 and Dorr 1964a (summarized in 1964b).

64. Sermon 26, "Sermon on the Mount VI," §III.13, *Works*, 1:586.

65. Sermon 21, "Sermon on the Mount I," §I.4, *Works*, 1:477. Wesley would have been familiar with this specific therapeutic metaphor from Macarius' Homily 44 (Wesley #19, *Chr. Library*, 1:143-4).

66. E.g., *The Doctrine of Original Sin*, Preface, §4, *Works* (Jackson), 9:194; Sermon 44, "Original Sin," §III.3, *Works*, 2:184; Sermon 54, "On Eternity," §6, *Works*, 2:367; Sermon 95, "On the Education of Children," §4ff, *Works*, 3:349ff; and Sermon 109, "The Trouble and Rest of Good Men," Proem, *Works*, 3:533. This therapeutic

hamartiology is prominent in Charles as well: e.g., "Oxford Sermon on Justification," *Early Sermons CW*, p. 53; *Poetry*, 3:167; and Hymn 105, stanza 2, *Works*, 7:212.

67. Lindström 1946, p. 41.

68. The classic study of this topic is Norman P. Williams, *The Ideas of the Fall and of Original Sin* (London: Longmans, 1927). Williams explicitly distinguishes (and champions, pp. 453ff) a Greek school of thought on this issue from the Latin school that took focus in Augustine.

69. The Council of Orange and Council of Trent attempted to moderate the Augustinian heritage of Western Christianity on this count. Luther and Calvin would reappropriate Augustine's insistence of total depravity.

70. For a convenient summary of the Eastern Orthodox understanding of sin and Original Sin, see Stanley Harakas, *Toward Transfigured Life: The Theoria of Eastern Orthodox Ethics* (Minneapolis, MN: Light and Life, 1983), pp. 81-4. H.-J. Lee's argument (1991, pp. 155, 182ff) that Macarius affirmed "Original Sin" more strongly than early Greek-speaking theologians must be carefully nuanced. Macarius indeed used more striking metaphorical images for human fallenness, and presented it as affecting more dimensions of human life than some Greek-speaking theologians. However, neither he nor other early Syriac theologians affirmed inherited guilt or believed that fallen humanity was totally deprived of the created ability to nurture participation in God. Cf. Arthur Vööbus, "Theological Reflections on Human Nature in Ancient Syrian Traditions," in *The Scope of Grace*, edited by P. Hefner (Philadelphia, PA: Fortress, 1964), pp. 101-119; Hermann Dörries, *Die Theologie des Makarios/Symeon* (Göttingen: Vandenhoeck & Ruprecht, 1978), p. 56; Stewart, *'Working the Earth of the Heart'*, pp. 170-233; and Brock, *Luminous Eye*, pp. 118-22.

71. For discussions of this question, see Blaising 1979, pp. 206-10; Cho 1986, pp. 207-8; Lindström 1946, pp. 28-30; and Rogers 1967, p. 201.

72. Anglican Article IX describes the fault born in our nature as deserving God's wrath (cf. Oden 1988, pp. 114-5). But note that the early sermon which Wesley devotes to Adam's Fall and its impact on later humanity focuses on the corruption of our nature, with no explicit discussion of guilt; Sermon 141 (1730), "The Image of God," esp. §III, *Works*, 4:299.

73. See esp. *Minutes* (25 June 1744), Q. 15, *John Wesley*, p. 138; *The Principles of a Methodist*, §2, *Works*, 9:50; and *The Doctrine of Original Sin*, Pt. II, §III (*Works* [Jackson], 9:313), and Pt. III, §I (Ibid., 316).

74. See Sermon 5 (1746), "Justification by Faith," §I.5-9, *Works*, 1:185-7; and *The Doctrine of Original Sin* (1757), Pt. III, §VI, *Works* (Jackson), 9:332. The decline of this notion is traced below.

75. E.g., *Predestination Calmly Considered*, §34, *John Wesley*, p. 441; and *The Doctrine of Original Sin*, Pt. III, §I, *Works* (Jackson), 9:315.

76. Letter to John Mason (21 Nov. 1776), *Letters* (Telford), 6:239-40. Cf. Sermon 59, "God's Love to Fallen Man," §II.14 (*Works*, 2:434), which rejects the notion that any person will be damned for Adam's sin alone.

77. Wesley changed the description of original sin in Article IX from "fault and corruption" to solely "corruption." He also deleted a paragraph which stated that every person born deserves God's wrath and condemnation (see the parallel comparison in Oden 1988, pp. 114-5). He did, however, leave a phrase about Christ dying for "original guilt" in Article II. This leads Blaising (1979, p. 228 fn132) to doubt that Wesley was intending to deny inherited guilt in this editing.

78. Wesley seems to use "Original Sin" mainly when in dialogue with or responding to someone else who used that term. For example, he used it in *The Doctrine of Original*

Sin responding to Taylor, and in Sermon 44 which distills this treatise. However, his ambivalence about the term is suggested in both works. Cf. *The Doctrine of Original Sin*, Pt. II, §II.11: "From this infection of our nature (call it original sin, or what you please)" (*Works* [Jackson], 9:274); and Sermon 44, "Original Sin," §III.2: "call it 'original sin' or by any other title" (*Works*, 2:183). When simply expositing the reality of human sinfulness in his sermons, he is less likely to use the term "Original Sin" than terms like "inbred sin," "inbred corruption," or "corrupt sinful nature;" cf. Outler's index of passages on "Original Sin" in *Sermons* (*Works* 4:728), the term itself occurs in none of the passages. Likewise, when Wesley referred to Sermon 44 among his pastors, he called it a sermon on "Inbeing Sin" or "Indwelling Sin;" see respectively the 1766 *Minutes*, Q.27, *Minutes* (Mason), p. 58; and the 1780ff editions of "Large Minutes," Q. 56, *Minutes* (Mason), p. 581 (also in *Works* [Jackson], 8:328).

79. Cf. the definition of "Inbeing" in Samuel Johnson, *A Dictionary of the English Language* (London: W. Strahan, 1755), "inherence, inseparableness." The first meaning given in the definitive *Oxford English Dictionary* (2nd. ed., [1989], 7:778) is "The fact of being in; existence in something else; inherence, indwelling, immanence." Note also Wesley's appropriation of the insistence that Original Sin has to do with corruption, not guilt, in his extract of Henry Woolnor in *AM* 6 (1783):431-5 (more on Woolnor below).

80. The following summary draws on Williams, *Ideas of the Fall*; Petro B.T. Bilaniuk, "Traducianism," *New Catholic Encyclopedia* (New York: McGraw-Hill, 1967), 14:230; and Vittorino Grossi, "Traducianism," *Encyclopedia of the Early Church* (New York: Oxford University Press, 1992), p. 849.

81. This theme developed from the comment in Hebrews 7:10 about Levi paying tithes to Melchizedek by virtue of being "in the loins" of Abraham. To understand the focus on Adam, rather than Adam *and* Eve, remember that the current "biology" held that the entire person was in the "seed" planted by the father in the "soil" of the mother's womb. The mother contributed nothing to the nature of the child.

82. Cf. Aquinas, *Summa Theologica*, I-II, qq. 81-83.

83. For examples of this view among early Reformed theologians, see Heinrich Heppe, *Reformed Dogmatics, Set Out and Illustrated from the Sources*, Revised ed. (Grand Rapids, MI: Baker, 1978), pp. 341-2.

84. Cf. Heinrich Schmid, *The Doctrinal Theology of the Evangelical Lutheran Church*, 3rd ed. (Minneapolis, MN: Augsburg, 1899), pp. 166-68, 248-50. The position that they describe is clearly not that of Tertullian.

85. For more information on this and the alternative Greek translations, and their implications, see Meyendorff, *Byzantine Theology*, pp. 144-6.

86. Cf. Heppe, *Reformed Dogmatics*, pp. 227, 331-5 (on Roman 5:12, see p. 347). Calvin represents a transition on this point, and was aware of the more correct translation of Romans 5:12; cf. *Calvin's New Testament Commentaries* (Grand Rapids, MI: Eerdmans, 1960), 8:111-12.

87. For example, it was even appropriated by some later Lutheran scholastics like David Hollaz (cf. Schmid, *Doctrinal Theology*, pp. 239-40).

88. An excellent example of this position which Wesley read and criticized is Chevalier (Andrew Michael) Ramsay's *Philosophical Principles of Natural and Revealed Religion, unfolded in a Geometrical Order* (Glasgow: R. Foulis, 1748-9), 1:347-54 & 2:215ff; cf. Letter to Dr. John Robertson (24 Sept. 1753), *Works*, 26:519 fn13 (Note that Ramsay assumed our previous existence was also embodied; cf. 1:351).

89. For an extended discussion of this point, see Panayiotis Nellas, *Deification in Christ* (Crestwood, NY: St. Vladimir's Seminary Press, 1987), pp. 43ff.

90. Cf. Stephanou, "Divine Indwelling," pp. 14-15.

91. Cf. Article IX, Oden 1988, p. 114. Note how the theme of Adam as the Federal Head of humanity was added by the Westminster Assembly of Divines in their suggested revision of the Thirty-Nine Articles in 1643; E. Tyrrell Green, *The Thirty-Nine Articles and the Age of Reform* (2nd ed., London: Wells, Gardner, Darton & Co., 1912), p. 346.

92. Letter to Dr. John Robertson (24 Sept. 1753), *Works*, 26:519. Wesley was reacting to Ramsay, who had claimed that there were only three possible explanations for how Original Sin is transmitted and then attempted to substantiate his position through a rational critique of the alternatives. Cf. Wesley's comment on Ramsay in *Journal* (14 Sept. 1753), *Works*, 20:474.

93. Probably because of his own disclaimers, few Wesley scholars have traced Wesley's comments on this issue. For one of the few sketchy accounts, see Bryant 1992a, pp. 181-6.

94. Sermon 141, "The Image of God," §II.1-5, *Works*, 4:296-9.

95. A good example is again a homily of Macarius (Homily 5, Wesley #4, *Chr. Library*, 1:99), which says that "As from one Adam the whole race of mankind was spread over the earth,—so one taint in the affections was derived down into the sinful stock of men." One should note, however, Ted Campbell's observation (1991b, p. 62) that Wesley omitted several passages on this theme from his edition of Macarius' *Homilies* (the best example is the opening to #2 [cf. *Chr. Library*, 1:91]). As Campbell suggests, this likely indicates editorial conciseness rather than disagreement.

96. The best example is Sermon 5 (1746), "Justification by Faith," §I.5-9, *Works*, 1:185-7.

97. For the entire dialogue, see Letter to John Wesley (10 July 1755), 18, *Works*, 26:571; Letter to Richard Tompson (25 July 1755), *Works*, 26:575; Letter to John Wesley (15 Aug. 1755), 27, *Works*, 26:580; and Letter to Richard Tompson (2 Feb. 1756), *Letters* (Telford), 3:158-62.

98. Note Wesley's comment on working to finalize the *NT Notes* in *Journal* (23 Sept. 1755), *Works*, 21:31.

99. Cf. Bengel, *Gnomon Novi Testamenti* (Tübingen: Schrammii, 1759), pp. 618-19. Bengel preserved the point of the earlier Western reading of Romans 5:12 by shifting emphasis to Romans 5:14, 19. This is reflected in Wesley's notes on these verses in *NT Notes*. It helps explain how he could defend the point of the traditional Western interpretation of Romans 5:12 two years later in *The Doctrine of Original Sin*, Pt. II, §I.15, *Works* (Jackson), 9:255.

100. For a use of Hebrews 12:9 in Reformed arguments, see Heppe, *Reformed Dogmatics*, p. 229. Bengel contended that propagation of the soul through our parents is not denied in this passage, in the same way as by the mention of spirits it is not denied that our flesh, that is, our nature, is formed by God (*Gnomon Novi Testamenti*, p. 1070).

101. The comment on Hebrews 12:9 in the 1755 edition of *NT Notes* read: "Perhaps these expressions, *fathers of our flesh*, and *Father of spirits*, intimate that our earthly fathers are only the parents of our bodies, our souls not being derived from them, but rather created by the immediate power of God, and infused in the body from age to age" (quoted in a letter reprinted in *Journal* [27 Oct. 1763], *Works*, 21:435).

102. John Taylor, *The Scripture-Doctrine of Original Sin, Proposed to Free and Candid Examination* (3rd ed., London: J. Wilson, 1740). Wesley was aware of Taylor's work from at least 1748 (cf. *Journal* [28 Aug. 1748], *Works*, 20:245). He noted his resolve

to write a response in *Journal* (10 Apr. 1751), *Works,* 20:382. The Preface of his response, *The Doctrine of Original Sin,* is dated 30 Nov. 1756.

103. For the denial of a definitive explanation, see *The Doctrine of Original Sin,* Pt. II, §VII, *Works* (Jackson), 9:335. For defense of elements of the imputed depravity approach, see Pt. II, §II.2 (pp. 262-3); Pt. III, §I (pp. 314-17); and Pt. III, §VI (pp. 332-4). Comments on the "natural generation" explanation can be found in Pt. II, §II.13 (pp. 275-8).

104. Ibid, Pt. II, §III, obj. 3 (p. 294).

105. Cf. Ibid, Pt. II, §I.3 (p. 240) §I.6 (p. 244), §I.8 (p. 247), and §I.18 (p. 258).

106. Note particularly that the homiletical distillation of *The Doctrine of Original Sin* omits Federal Head language, preferring the "natural" explanation that Adam begat in his own image; Sermon 44, "Original Sin," §4, *Works,* 2:173. See also Sermon 45 (1760), "The New Birth," §I.4, *Works,* 2:190.

107. "Thoughts on Christian Perfection" (1759), Q. 23, *John Wesley,* p. 292. Note that Wesley follows a brief repeated disclaimer of the probability of two entirely sanctified persons ever having a child with the argument that even *if* it happened the child would still have Inbeing Sin, because this is entailed by the child's being "in the loins of Adam." Bryant (1992a, p. 185) reads too much into this response. Wesley was not allowing the theoretical possibility of an "immaculate conception," only of a conception by two entirely-sanctified persons. Note that Wesley's final resolution to Tompson's question was that a parent's "spiritual regeneration" cannot be communicated by natural generation; in "On the Origin of the Soul," *AM* 5 (1782):195.

108. Cf. *The Doctrine of Original Sin,* Pt. II, §II.6 *Works* (Jackson), 9:267; Pt. II, §II.16 (p. 282); and especially Pt. III, §VII (pp. 334-9).

109. Woolnor's work was first published in 1641; a third edition was released in London in 1655 with the new title *The Extraction of Man's Soul.* While he mentions no title, it is almost certainly this work that Wesley refers to in *Journal* (27 Jan. 1762), *Works,* 21:350. The original title is given explicitly in *Journal* (7 Nov. 1770), *Works,* 22:258. Wesley notes extracting the book at that time, he published this extract as a series in *AM* 6 (1783). Note the centrality of the First Cause/secondary cause distinction to Woolnor's argument in *Extraction of Man's Soul,* pp. 46-50, 309 (the latter citation extracted by Wesley in *AM* 6 (1783):664-7.

110. This revised form is in current editions. Hebrews was in the third volume of Wesley's revised republication of *NT Notes.* He completed this volume in early 1762 (cf. Baker 1989). Cf. a similar traducian suggestion of creation of all souls at the beginning of world in Schmid, *Doctrinal Theology,* p. 167.

111. He printed the entire letter in his *Journal* (27 Oct. 1763), *Works,* 21:435-6. The letter argues against creationism on the grounds that: (1) it is impossible for God to create souls that are already corrupt; (2) but if God creates pure souls, then God is cruel in holding these persons guilty of Original Sin; or (3) the soul created pure must be polluted by impure body—which the correspondent considered absurd. Compare these arguments to the quote near the bottom of p. 249 in Schmid, *Doctrinal Theology*; and to the same points in Woolnor, *Extraction of Man's Soul,* pp. 39-42 (extracted by Wesley in *AM* 6 [1783]:96-8).

112. He published "On the Origin of the Soul," in *AM* 5 (1782):146-9, 195-7. This piece summarizes themes from Woolnor, but is not an extract. It is Wesley speaking in his own behalf, drawing on Woolnor.

113. Sermon 57, "On the Fall of Man," §II.1-5, *Works,* 2:405-8.

114. Cf. Sermon 76 (1784), "On Perfection," §II.9, *Works*, 3:79-80; Sermon 129 (1790), "Heavenly Treasure in Earthly Vessels," §II.1, *Works*, 4:165; and Sermon 132 (1791), "On Faith," §1, *Works*, 4:188. See also the discussion of Wesley's clarifications about what sin entire sanctification delivers from in Chapter Seven.

115. To see this point, consider Sermon 59 (1782), "God's Love to Fallen Man," §1, *Works*, 2:423. Wesley here carefully attributes rebellion to Adam alone and then notes how the consequence (mischief) of this rebellion fell upon all who were in his loins. They were all "constituted" sinners. That is, they did not themselves sin, but they inherit the corrupting effects of sin. Ironically, a little later in this sermon Wesley gives a passing quotation of Romans 5:12 in explicit Western terms as "in whom all sinned" (I.1, p. 425); however, he immediately adds that subsequent humanity were "made sinners by the disobedience of the one" (pp. 425-6), echoing his earlier point. See also Woolnor, *Extraction of Man's Soul*, p. 187 (extracted by Wesley in *AM* 6 [1783]:492).

116. See esp. Sermon 5 (1746), "Justification by Faith," §I.5, *Works*, 1:185; *NT Notes* (1754), Luke 15:12; and Sermon 45 (1760), "The New Birth," §I.2-4, *Works*, 2:189-90. Compare these to the summary of the Eastern position in Thomas Hopko, *The Spirit of God* (Wilton, CT: Morehouse-Barlow, 1976), p. 14. Given Wesley's affirmation of this general point, it is surprising that he omitted perhaps the clearest expression of it in Macarius' *Homilies* (#12). This probably indicates a judgment that the material in this homily was redundant, not a disagreement with the basic idea.

117. For examples of such descriptions, see *NT Notes*, Rom. 7:8; and Sermon 14, "The Repentance of Believers," §I.20, *Works*, 1:346. The strongest accusations of Wesley in this regard have come from Sugden, *Wesley's Standard Sermons*, 2:459; Flew 1934, p. 335; Rattenbury 1938, p. 203; and Sangster 1943, p. 60.

118. E.g., Bence 1981, pp. 72-3; Blaising 1979, pp. 261-8; Bryant 1992a, p. 174; Bryant 1992b; H.L. Smith 1963, p. 91; and Staples 1963, pp. 248-9, 262ff. Compare, however, the suggestion that Wesley did not have such a relational view, but needs it to bring consistency to his position; in Hannah 1983, and Hynson 1987.

119. Note that Wesley distinguished between "deprive" (to bereave) and "depravation" (corruption) in his *Dictionary*.

120. The distinction between voluntary and involuntary sin is central to Wesley's discussion of Christian perfection and sin in believers. I will discuss it in that connection. For examples of the threefold categorization of sins, see Sermon 7, "The Way to the Kingdom," §II.2, *Works*, 1:226; Sermon 78, "Spiritual Idolatry," §I.5-15, *Works*, 3:105-9; and Sermon 84, "The Important Question," §I.2-4, *Works*, 3:183-5. 1 John 2:16 was one of Wesley's most quoted verses in his sermons (cf. S. Jones 1992, p. 209).

121. E.g., *NT Notes*, Rom. 3:23 & 6:6; *The Doctrine of Original Sin*, Pt. II, §III, *Works* (Jackson), 9:306; and "MS Minutes" (15 Aug. 1758), Q. 6, *John Wesley*, p. 177.

122. Cf. Sermon 5, "Justification by Faith," §I.5, *Works*, 1:185; Sermon 21, "Sermon on the Mount I," §4, *Works*, 1:477; *NT Notes*, Rom. 6:6; and Dorr 1964b, p. 303.

123. For general summaries, see Sermon 141, "The Image of God," §II.2-4, *Works*, 4:298; and Sermon 146, "The One Thing Needful," §I.2-4, *Works*, 4:354. On loss of knowledge, see Sermon 44, "Original Sin," §II.3, *Works*, 2:177. On corruption of the tempers, see *NT Notes*, Rom. 6:6; and Sermon 40, "Christian Perfection," §II.25-7, *Works*, 2:118-9. On loss of liberty, see *NT Notes*, Eph. 2:1. On the blinding of conscience, see Sermon 34, "The Original, Nature, Properties, and Use of the Law," §I.4, *Works*, 2:7.

124. *The Doctrine of Original Sin* abounds with references about the lack of love for God or other humans. On the corrupt relationship to lower animals, see Sermon 60,

"The General Deliverance," §I.6, *Works,* 2:444. For the loss of happiness, see *The Doctrine of Original Sin,* Pt. I, §II.14, *Works* (Jackson), 9:235.

125. For a few examples, see *Advice to the People Called 'Methodists',* §6, *Works,* 9:124-5; Sermon 21, "Sermon on the Mount I," §4, *Works,* 1:477; *NT Notes,* Rom. 6:6; and Letter to John Fletcher (22 Mar. 1771), *Letters* (Telford), 5:231.

126. Note how the affirmation of our total depravity is followed immediately by the promise of God's healing in Sermon 44, "Original Sin," §III, *Works,* 2:183-5.

127. Cf. John Meyendorff, "New Life in Christ: Salvation in Orthodox Theology," *Theological Studies* 50 (1989):481-99; here, 493.

128. Two sections of *The Doctrine of Original Sin* (*Works* [Jackson], 9) are crucial in this regard. In Pt. II, §III (311), he argued that he had a *higher* view of human nature than Taylor who, in denying original sin, ended up making our present sinful situation definitive of our nature. In Pt. II, §VI (332), he argued that admitting the universality of fallenness did not contradict God's justice and goodness, *provided that* all may recover through Christ whatever they had lost; indeed, recover it with unspeakable gain!

129. Jennings 1990, pp. 148-9.

130. On Eastern examples, see Stephanou, "Divine Indwelling," pp. 11-16.

131. Cf. Outler 1977, p. 153.

132. Cf. Dorr 1964b, p. 308.

133. For a few such reminders of God's "preventing grace," see: *A Collection of Forms of Prayer,* Sunday Morning, *Works* (Jackson), 11:204; *A Collection of Prayers for Families,* Monday Morning, *Works* (Jackson), 11:241; *Devotions for Every Day,* Sunday, Gill, p. 72; and *Prayers for Children,* Wednesday Morning, *Works* (Jackson), 11:265. It is likely that only the last text is original to Wesley. However, the others are all appropriated through rather careful editing.

134. This point has been developed by Michael Scanlon (1969, pp. 91ff), who refers to Augustine, Thomas Aquinas, and the Council of Trent (on Trent, see esp. DS 1525 and DS 1553). Outler (1975, p. 34) suggests that Wesley may also have found it in Bellarmine.

135. It is present in Anglican Article X (cf. Oden 1988, p. 115). It can also be found frequently in the *Book of Common Prayer,* and the idea is present in the *Homilies* even though the term is missing (see the insightful surveys of this material in Luby 1984, pp. 83-9; and Rogers 1967, pp. 29-32).

136. This is argued in Luby 1984, pp. 93-4.

137. I will use capitalization to distinguish the specific doctrine of Prevenient Grace from Wesley's broader assumption of the prevenience of *all* grace.

138. C. Williams 1960, p. 44.

139. The most helpful studies of Wesley's general understanding of grace are Luby 1984, and Rakestraw 1985a (summarized in 1984). For a fairly standard summary see Fuhrman 1963.

140. Hillman 1978, esp pp. 27-37 (summarized in 1981). Hillman found 463 uses of grace in the 140 Wesley sermons he consulted: 147 construe grace as pardon (mercy), 176 construe it as power, and 140 invoke both dimensions (1978, p. 28 fn6). This two-dimensional understanding of grace is also found in Charles' hymns (cf. J.R. Tyson 1983, pp. 296ff).

141. See especially his comments in the Preface to his abridgement of Thomas à Kempis' *The Christian Pattern* (1735), §II.13-14, *Works* (Jackson), 14:204-5.

142. The best examples are Sermon 1 (1738), "Salvation by Faith," §1, *Works,* 1:117; and Sermon 6 (1746), "The Righteousness of Faith," §II.8, *Works,* 1:213. The greater

appreciation for the gratuity of salvation involved in this period is also evident by the relatively higher number of references to grace per se (cf. Hillman 1978, pp. 27-8).

143. See especially, *A Letter to the Rev. Mr. Downes* (17 Nov. 1759), §11, *Works*, 9:359-60; and *A Letter to the Rev. Dr. Rutherforth* (28 Mar. 1768), §III.6, *Works*, 9:381. In both he defines grace simply as "the power of God which worketh in us both to will and to do of his good pleasure." Compare Charles' poem "For a Backslider," st. 6: "Pardon less than power I want, than purity within: Holy God, thy nature plant, The antidote of sin" (*Poetry*, 3:257).

144. Sermon 12, "The Witness of Our Spirit," §15-16, *Works*, 1:309-10. See also *A Collection of Prayers for Families*, Friday Morning, *Works* (Jackson), 11:254.

145. Cf. the judgments of Blaising 1979, p. 263; Borgen 1972, pp. 212-3; and Rakestraw 1985a, p. 132. Blaising and Rakestraw draw particular attention to the contribution of early Greek theologians to this understanding of grace (pp. 88ff).

146. E.g., Sermon 110, "Free Grace," §2, *Works*, 3:544; and *NT Notes*, 2 Cor. 8:9, Gal. 1:15, Gal. 2:21, and Eph. 1:6. See also the discussion in Hillman 1978, p. 41. Note the similar equation in Eastern Christian thought described in Vladimir Lossky, *The Mystical Theology of the Eastern Church* (Crestwood, NY: St. Vladimir's Seminary Press, 1976), pp. 212-3.

147. Note particularly Wesley's comment in *NT Notes* on 2 Peter 1:4 (Ye may become partakers of the divine nature) "Being renewed in the image of God, and having communion with him, so as to dwell in God and God in you." Admittedly, Wesley occasionally lapses into quasi-metaphysical language such as God "infusing" a "spark of grace" (Sermon 85, "On Working Out Our Own Salvation," §I.4 & §III.6, *Works*, 3:203, 208). However, even in these contexts his main emphasis is on God's direct work in our lives (cf. Ibid, §I.2, p. 202).

148. E.g., Borgen 1972, p. 123; Dorr 1965; H. Knight 1992, pp. 8-10, 169; and Staples 1963, pp. 253ff.

149. For a dialogue between Protestant, Roman Catholic, and Eastern Orthodox theologians on the subject of grace, see C. Moeller and G. Philips, *The Theology of Grace and the Oecumenical Movement* (London: A.R. Mowbray and Co., 1961). Cf. Stephanou, "Divine Indwelling," pp. 18-20. Calvin was the major Protestant who went beyond the concept of alien righteousness to talk of a seed of virtue (*semen fidei*) implanted in the elect. Later Reformed Orthodoxy equated this with the Scholastic notion of a *habitus*; cf. Otto Gründler, "From Seed to Fruition: Calvin's Notion of the *semen fidei* and Its Aftermath in Reformed Orthodoxy," in *Probing the Reformed Tradition*, pp. 108-15 (Louisville, KY: Westminster/John Knox, 1989).

150. This thesis has been argued persuasively by Craig Blaising (pp. 242ff; esp. 259) and Daniel Luby (pp. 129-30).

151. See, for example, Homily 18 (Wesley #10, 2, *Chr. Library*, 1:115) and Homily 20 (Wesley #12, 8, *Chr. Library*, 1:126). The contribution of Macarius to Wesley's notion of grace has been stressed in Rakestraw 1985a, pp. 98-102; and H.-J. Lee 1991, pp. 190-1.

152. Cf. Luby 1984, pp. 119ff.

153. This point is particularly stressed in Outler 1964a, p. 33; and Wynkoop 1972, p. 155. On the Anglican precedents, see Luby 1984, pp. 80-92.

154. Sermon 19, esp. §II.1 & §III.3, *Works*, 1:435, 442. See also Sermon 90, "An Israelite Indeed," §I.5 (*Works*, 3:284): "Whoever improves the grace he has already received . . . will surely retain it. . . . whereas whoever does not improve this talent cannot possibly retain it."

155. It is cited as a pioneer use in the *Oxford English Dictionary* (2nd ed., 1989), 13:256. This explains why Wesley thought it necessary to provide a definition in his own *Dictionary*, as "acting again."

156. *NT Notes*, Phil. 2:12-13.

157. See Letter to John Mason (21 Nov. 1776), *Letters* (Telford), 6:239; and Sermon 85, "On Working Out Our Own Salvation," §II, *Works*, 3:203-6. The latter passage surveys the progressive aspects of salvation and stresses the prevenience of grace throughout.

158. The most thorough study of Wesley's doctrine of Prevenient Grace is Rogers 1967. It should be supplemented by the insights of J. Smith 1964, Langford 1980-2a, and Blaising 1979.

159. Wesley's *Dictionary* defines an "Arminian" simply as one who believes that redemption is universally available. The rejection of irresistible grace is noted in his *The Question, 'What is an Arminian?' Answered by a Lover of Free Grace*, *Works* (Jackson), 10:358-61. Wesley's own classic statement of the universality of grace (including Prevenient Grace) is Sermon 110, "Free Grace," *Works*, 3:544-59. Defense of this theme was also central to his publication of the *Arminian Magazine*; cf. Preface to Volume One, §4, *Works* (Jackson), 14:279. For his most irenic expression of the ultimate resistibility of grace (including Prevenient Grace), see *Journal* (24 Aug. 1743), *Works*, 19:332.

160. Note that he designates the universal forgiveness of inherited guilt as the earliest benefit of Christ, followed by partial restoration of our faculties, etc., in *Minutes* (25 June 1744), Q. 16, *John Wesley*, p. 139. These benefits he will later identify with Prevenient Grace; cf. Rogers 1967, pp. 204-5.

161. Note that he attributes to Prevenient Grace our first wish to please God, the first dawn of light concerning God's will, and the first slight, transient conviction of having sinned against God; in Sermon 85, "On Working Out Our Own Salvation," §II.1, *Works*, 3:203.

162. See *Predestination Calmly Considered*, §47, *John Wesley*, p. 230; and his abridgement of Browne's *Limits of Human Understanding*, where he footnotes Browne's claim that we have some knowledge of divine things by the light of nature with the qualification that all "light of nature" so-called flows from preventing grace (*Survey*, 5:185).

163. Wesley placed particular emphasis on this aspect. Cf. Sermon 34, "The Original, Nature, Properties, and Use of the Law," §I.4, *Works*, 2:7; *NT Notes*, John 1:9, Rom. 3:14; Sermon 43, "The Scripture Way of Salvation," §I.2, *Works*, 2:156-7; Sermon 105, "On Conscience," §I.4-5, *Works*, 3:481-2; and Sermon 129, "Heavenly Treasure in Earthly Vessels," §I.1, *Works*, 4:163. See also the discussion in Rogers 1967, pp. 182ff.

164. This is not to say that the Spirit cannot use special revelation to awaken our sense of sinfulness, only that the availability of special revelation is not a prerequisite of Prevenient Grace. Neither should it suggest that the benefits of Prevenient Grace are "natural"; recall that Wesley grounded even initial revelation in Christ's redemption (cf. Chapter One).

165. Cf. *Predestination Calmly Considered*, §46-7, *John Wesley*, pp. 229-30; and Sermon 116, "What is Man," §11, *Works*, 4:23-4. Note also the stanza in the Hymn "Universal Redemption" which Wesley appended to his sermon *Free Grace*: "A power to Choose, a will to obey, freely [God's] grace restores" (*Works*, 3:560).

166. E.g., *Advice to the People Called 'Methodists'*, §6, *Works* 9:124-5; and Letter to John Fletcher (28 Feb. 1766), *Letters* (Telford), 5:5.

167. See *Minutes* (16 June 1747), Q. 10, *John Wesley*, p. 167. Note also the suggestion that there is "an actual seed or spark" of spiritual life restored in all persons because of Christ, in the earlier *Minutes* (25 June 1744), Q. 16, *John Wesley*, p. 139. Of course, such works would not "merit" salvation, because the power to do them comes through grace.

168. I take this to be the legitimate point of the occasional (potentially misleading) suggestion that Wesley considered Prevenient Grace to be irresistible (e.g., Luby 1984, p. 107; and Collins 1989, p. 24).

169. Sermon 43, "The Scripture Way of Salvation," §I.2, *Works*, 2:156-7. The need for a distinction between the continuing benefits and the specific overtures of Prevenient Grace was first noted by James Smith (1964). It was further clarified by Donal Dorr (1964b, pp. 312-14).

170. Wesley appears to be groping for this distinction in his correspondence with 'John Smith' (25 June 1746), when he argues that even though our faculties are God's gifts they still need a distinct power of God to enable them to produce saving faith (§7, *Works*, 26:199-200). He is hampered at this point by the typical Western distinction between God's "natural" and "supernatural" work (cf. Smith's prior letter to Wesley [26 Feb. 1746], 6, *Works*, 26:187).

171. In Sermon 9, "The Spirit of Bondage and of Adoption," §I (*Works*, 1: 251-5), Wesley graphically describes a person who has shut out the overtures of God. Their spiritual senses are now asleep, but can be awakened.

172. Langford 1980-2a, pp. 55-8.

173. Explicit articulations of this position are rare. Langford detects its major implications in Umphrey Lee's claim (1936, 124-5, 315) that, for Wesley, the "natural man" is a logical abstraction.

174. Cf. Cushman 1947.

175. For a cogent critique of Cushman, see Wainwright 1987, pp. 17-20. Robert Moore's suggestion that Wesley had a "Theology of Passivity" would be open to the same criticisms (1979, pp. 129ff).

176. Langford's representative of the first emphasis is Cannon (cf. 1946, pp. 115-16). He cites Colin Williams as representative of the second (cf. 1960, pp. 41-3). It is unclear, but Williams may actually consider the grace which ignites our restored faculties to be another aspect of Prevenient Grace.

177. Langford 1980-2a, p. 59.

178. This point has been argued strongly by Albert Outler (cf. 1961, p. 10; 1969, p. 57; and 1974, p. 71 fn17). For an expression of this English tradition, see Peter Heylyn, *Historia Quinqu-Articularis: or, a Declaration of the Judgement of the Western Churches, and more particularly of the Church of England in the Five Controverted Points, reproached in these last times by the name of Arminianism* (London: Thomas Johnson, 1660). The earliest extensive discussion of Wesley's "Arminianism" was Pask 1939 (conclusions summarized in 1960 essay). The issues are given independent up-to-date review in Eaton 1988 and McGonigle 1994 (who presents the evidence for Wesley's reading of Arminius). Briefer discussions can be found in Keefer 1986 & 1987; and McGonigle 1988. Ultimately, the question of how "Arminian" Wesley was is related to the question of how "Calvinist" Arminius was! On this question see the differentiation of an "authentic" Calvin from both high Calvinism and Arminianism, with suggestions of some of Wesley's affinities to this authentic Calvin, in Clifford 1990, esp. pp. 125, 132-4, 161, 189.

179. For a survey of the doctrine in prior Anglican theologians, see Rogers 1967, pp. 32-58. For specific mention of early Greek precedents, see Eaton 1988, pp. 227ff; Outler 1980-2, p. 15; and Rogers 1967, p. 29 fn1.

180. Blaising 1979, pp. 263-70. Note as well the defense of the Eastern notion of synergism against Western misconceptions that it underplays grace in John Breck, "The New Testament Concept of Election," in *Salvation in Christ: A Lutheran-Orthodox Dialogue*, edited by J. Meyendorff & R. Tobias (Minneapolis, MN: Augsburg/Fortress, 1992), pp. 151-8.

181. On this point, note two analogies that Wesley suggested to describe the situation of our debilitated faculties: a prenatal child, who has senses but cannot yet sense reality (Sermon 45, "The New Birth," §II.4, *Works*, 2: 192); and a toad supposedly imprisoned within a tree, with the same general results (Sermon 130, "On Living Without God," *Works*, 4:169-76). As with all analogies, these are ambiguous and can suggest various readings. Rex Matthews rightly rejects any interpretation which implies that Wesley assumed our human faculties retain their power latently, needing only the removal of external obstacles. However, his alternative sometimes suggests that Prevenient Grace implants new capacities in humans. It would seem better to talk of the gracious reempowerment of our existing debilitated faculties. Cf. Matthews 1986, pp. 282-3, 303-5.

182. For an example of Wesley responding to this accusation, see *Some Remarks on Mr. Hill's 'Review of all the Doctrines Taught by Mr. John Wesley'*, §7, pt. 5, *Works* (Jackson), 10:379.

183. Cf. Cell 1935, pp. 256-7, 270. Others basically agreeing with Cell would be Hildebrandt (1951, p. 173) and Ireson (1973, pp. 281, 413).

184. Cf. Cannon 1946, pp. 113-17; Lindström 1946, p. 215; Sanders 1960, p. 495; Weißbach 1970, pp. 71-5; Stuart 1974, p. 113; Rakestraw 1984, p. 199; etc.

185. See respectively: Starkey 1962, p. 116; Marquardt 1977b; Outler 1969, p. 59; Meredith 1962, p. 125; and Coppedge 1987, p. 266.

186. See Cell 1935, p. 257.

187. Cannon's language about human "initiative" in salvation (1946, p. 116) comes close to this misunderstanding. Others who describe Wesley as a synergist are typically quite careful to assign the initiative and power of salvation to God (e.g., C. Williams 1960, p. 72; and Bence 1981, pp. 129-30).

188. "Synergism" is most properly defined in terms of Philip Melanchthon's insistence on co-operant grace, not semi-Pelagian suggestions of inherent human power and human initiative; cf. the definition in *Oxford Dictionary of the Christian Church* (2nd ed., 1974).

189. *Works* 3:199-209.

190. For Wesley's recommendation of Tilly's sermon, see Letter to Richard Morgan, Jr. (30 Sept. 1735), *Works*, 25:438. He prepared an extract of this sermon for his own use. For a summary of Tilly's basic claims, see Rogers 1966, p. 139. Wesley retained Macarius' Homily 15 on this passage in his abridgement (Wesley #7, *Chr. Library*, 1:108-10).

191. This is particularly the case in comparison to Macarius, who can give the impression that humans must first turn to God in our own power, and only then does co-operative grace begin (a point missed in H.-J. Lee 1991, p. 184). Ted Campbell has shown that Wesley carefully edited out any such suggestions in his edition of Macarius' *Homilies* (1991b, pp. 62-3).

192. For a few examples of this frequent point, see Sermon 14, "The Repentance of Believers," §II.6, *Works*, 1:350; Sermon 25, "Sermon on the Mount V," §IV.13,

Works, 1:570; Sermon 33, "Sermon on the Mount XIII," §III.10, *Works* 1:697; and "A Thought on Necessity," §V.6-VI.1, *Works* (Jackson), 10:478.

193. See in this regard the argument of J. Knight (1968) that Wesley showed a relative switch of emphasis from our dependence on grace to our ability to work out salvation during the last twenty years of his ministry. Knight worries that Wesley is already beginning the undervaluing of grace that characterized the Methodist traditions after his death. He notes in passing that increased struggles with antinomianism may have played a part. Indeed! If Knight did not assume that theologians are supposed to preserve unchanging ideally-balanced formulations, then this context-sensitive move on Wesley's part would not be so disturbing.

194 .The choice of Luby (1984, p. 103).

195. Cf. Sermon 146, "The One Thing Needful," §I.5, *Works,* 4:355. In this 1734 sermon Wesley first details how sin has enslaved our human faculties, and then says "The one work *we* have to do is to return from the gates of death to perfect soundness" (emphasis added). In §III.1 he adds that Christ has "given us light," so now we must press toward the mark of salvation. There is a clearer affirmation of our spiritual inability in Sermon 17, "The Circumcision of the Heart" (I.3, *Works,* 1:403), but one cannot be sure that this was in the 1733 original or strengthened in the 1748 rewrite, since the manuscript is missing. For a helpful summary of Wesley's early gospel of "moral rectitude," including the question of the role of baptism in this early soteriology, see Outler 1975, pp. 35.

196. A move *toward* this use of "natural" is evident in Sermon 9 (1746), "The Spirit of Bondage and of Adoption," §I, *Works,* 1:251-5. As Outler notes in his introduction (p. 248), the distinction that Wesley makes here between "natural," "legal," and "evangelical" persons was drawn from the Reformed theologian Thomas Boston, though its roots go back to Augustine. Wesley's use of "natural man" in this sermon is actually ambiguous. It does not appear to be a state of total deprivation of spiritual sense and ability, but persons who have shut up their soul against God's overtures (hence the definition of "natural man" in Cushman 1947, p. 113; and Collins 1989, pp. 24-5). However, Charles' 1742 sermon "Awake Thou That Sleepest" had already identified this notion (and the related verse - Eph. 5:14) with the state "into which the sin of Adam hath cast all who spring from his loins" (§I.1, in *Works,* 1:142). Likewise, John moved increasingly to equating "natural" and "fallen" during this period; cf. *NT Notes,* 1 Cor. 2:14, Rom. 7:5; Sermon 19, "The Great Privilege of Those That are Born of God," §II.8, *Works,* 1:439; Sermon 44, "Original Sin," §II.2-3 & §III.5, *Works,* 2:177, 185; and Sermon 45, "The New Birth," §II.4, *Works,* 2:192.

197. E.g., Sermon 85, "On Working Out Our Own Salvation," §III.3-4, *Works,* 3:207.

198. This was first suggested by U. Lee 1936, p. 124. It has been echoed by many since him.

199. A suggestion apparent in Dorr 1964b, p. 314.

200. It must be admitted that there is an occasion or two where the late Wesley seems to waver between assigning our ability to sense our need for God to creation or assigning it to restoration (e.g., Sermon 129, "Heavenly Treasure in Earthly Vessels," §I.1, *Works,* 4:163). However, his typical insistence on restoration remains, even here (e.g., Sermon 105, "On Conscience," §I.5, *Works,* 3:482).

201. Donal Dorr has raised this question from a Roman Catholic perspective (1964b, pp. 317-20), reaching a conclusion similar to the one here suggested. See also my earlier discussion in Maddox 1987a, pp. 9-12.

202. Sermon 1, "Salvation by Faith," §1-3, *Works,* 1:117-8.

Chapter Four

1. For a few examples of the explicit connection of these two aspects, see *A Farther Appeal to Men of Reason and Religion*, Pt. I, §I.6, *Works*, 11: 107-8; Sermon 12, "The Witness of Our Spirit," §15, *Works*, 1:309; Sermon 29, "Sermon on the Mount IX," §21, *Works*, 1:643; and Sermon 57, "On the Fall of Man," §II.8, *Works*, 2:410.

2. Sermon 123, "On Knowing Christ After the Flesh," *Works*, 4:98-106, esp. §9 (102).

3. For the precedent in Browne's *Limits of Human Understanding*, see Wesley's abridgement, *Survey*, 5:186. On Wesley himself, see Campbell 1991b, pp. 80-1.

4. There is no better evidence of this than Wesley's most compact summary of his Christological commitments—in *A Letter to a Roman Catholic*, §7 (*John Wesley*, pp. 494-5). His opening line is: "I believe that Jesus of Nazareth was the Saviour of the world." He then proceeds to summarize the work of Christ in terms of the three offices, before finally affirming the traditional language about Christ's two natures.

5. Cf. the discussion of the Christological debates in William Placher, *A History of Christian Theology* (Philadelphia, PA: Westminster, 1983), pp. 68-87.

6. *On the Incarnation of the Lord*, §54. See also Clement of Alexandria, *Exhortation to the Greeks*, 1.8.4.

7. Cf. Renshaw 1965, p. 249.

8. *A Letter to the Reverend Mr. Law* (6 Jan. 1756), §II.3, *Letters* (Telford), 3:351-7. Note also his claim that if Adam had not fallen we would not have loved the Son for the most important reason. We might have loved the Son's glory, but not for "bearing our sins in his own body on the tree," in Sermon 59, "God's Love to Fallen Man," §I.3, *Works*, 2:427.

9. The study in question is Deschner 1960. For the central problem he discerned in Wesley's Christology, see pp. 12, 14-5. For his own reflection on the neo-Orthodox context of the book, see 1985, p. ix.

10. See especially Deschner 1960, pp. 105-7, 183. For a critical dialogue with Deschner's revisions, see H. Knight 1992, pp. 57-60, 68-9. See also the related critique in Gallaway 1988, esp. pp. 106ff.

11. Deschner limited his study to the "standard" sermons and the *NT Notes*. In the original study he recognized that Wesley's attempt to hold justification and sanctification together was what constitutes his distinctive place in Protestantism (1960, p. 185). In reflecting on the book more recently he admitted that he would now need to take more seriously the Eastern theme of *theosis* in understanding Wesley (1985, p. ix).

12. See the series of letters exchanged between Wesley and Law in *Works*, 25:540-50.

13. Sermon 59, "God's Love to Fallen Man," §I.2-3, *Works*, 2:426-7.

14. Letter to Mary Bishop (7 Feb. 1778), *Letters* (Telford), 6:297-8.

15. There is much on John's understanding of the Atonement in Deschner 1960. The other extended study—combining John and Charles—is Renshaw 1965. There is helpful material as well in Lindström 1946, pp. 55-75; and Gallaway 1988. For Charles in particular, see J.R. Tyson 1983.

16. Gustaf Aulén has named this classical conception the Christus Victor model of the Atonement; cf. *Christus Victor: An Historical Study of the Three Main Types of the Idea of the Atonement* (New York: Macmillan, 1931). This work is still one of the best places to start in studying different models of the Atonement. Aulén's agenda is to reclaim the Christus Victor model for Western theology, partly by arguing that it is

implicit in Luther! Two other helpful recent treatments of the various models I will be discussing are Gilbert Greshake, "Der Wandel der Erlösungsvorstellungen in der Theologiegeschichte," in *Erlösung und Emancipatie*, ed. L. Scheffczyk (Freiburg: Herder, 1973), pp. 61-101; and Paul S. Fiddes, *Past Event and Present Salvation* (Louisville, KY: Westminster/John Knox, 1989). For more on early Greek authors in particular, see Frances M. Young, *The Use of Sacrificial Ideas in Greek Christian Writers From the New Testament to John Chrysostom* (Cambridge, MA: The Philadelphia Patristics Foundation, 1979).

17. See in this regard Sermon 146, "The One Thing Needful," §II.3, *Works*, 4:356. After a graphic description of our sin-diseased nature and the need to be healed in §I, Wesley notes that Christ's incarnation and death were to restore us to health by releasing us from bondage, but goes into no further details.

18. See *NT Notes*, Luke 2:43 & John 1:14. I hasten to add that Charles invokes this theme more often, particularly in hymns related to Christmas. E.g., "Hymn for Christmas Day" (*Hymns and Sacred Poems*, 1739), *Poet. Works*, 1:184; *Hymns for the Nativity*, #5 & #8, *Poet. Works*, 4:110, 114; and "Hymn on Luke 1:35," *Poetry*, 2:76. See also the discussion in J.R. Tyson 1985a, pp. 17, 20.

19. Cf. *NT Notes*, Col. 2:15 & 1 Tim 2:6. The paucity of references to the ransom image has been noted in C. Williams 1960, p. 87; and Lindström 1946, p. 71. For a valiant effort to locate this image in Wesley, see Renshaw 1965, pp. 98-100. Deschner refers to the military metaphor in Wesley (1960, p. 116) but is dealing more with Christ's present and future work as King than with the explanation of Christ's death.

20. This point is developed in Selleck 1983, p. 225.

21. Cf. Sermon 146, "The One Thing Needful," §I.3-4, *Works*, 4:354.

22. Note the similar objections to the theme of Christ triumphing over the principalities and powers in Pearson, *Exposition of the Creed*, pp. 247ff.

23. *NT Notes*, 1 Peter 2:24.

24. He devoted three major sermons to the topic in his first collection of *Sermons*: Sermon 34, "The Original, Nature, Properties, and Use of the Law," *Works*, 2:4-19; Sermon 35, "The Law Established through Faith I," *Works*, 2:20-32; and Sermon 36, "The Law Established through Faith II," *Works*, 2:33-43.

25. This point is central to J.H. Tyson 1991.

26. Cf. Sermon 34, "The Original, Nature, Properties, and Use of the Law," §III.6-9, *Works*, 2:12-13.

27. *NT Notes*, Rom. 7:12.

28. The "Platonic" tone of this view of the law is clear (cf. Collins 1986). However, his Plato is mediated through the Christian tradition. The Moral Law is not a self-existing Ideal, it is an aspect of the nature of the eternal God.

29. *NT Notes*, Rom. 7:12.

30. See esp. Sermon 7, "The Way to the Kingdom," §I.10-12, *Works*, 1:223-4. Outler notes that at least 30 sermons contain this correlation, in *Works*, 1:35 fn28.

31. On the Adamic law, its loss, and its partial reinscription (which I will mention shortly), see Sermon 34, "The Original, Nature, Properties, and Use of the Law," §I, *Works*, 2:6-7; Sermon 105, "On Conscience," §I.4-5, *Works*, 3:481-2; and *Farther Thoughts on Christian Perfection*, Q. 1, *Works* (Jackson), 11:414-5.

32. Cf. Letter to John Hosmer (7 June 1761), *Letters* (Telford), 4:155; and Letter to Miss March (31 May 1771), *Letters* (Telford), 5:255.

33. Note the centrality of Prevenient Grace to the discussion of Wesley's political and social ethics in Hynson 1984, pp. 70ff; and Marquardt 1977a, pp. 104ff (1992, pp. 89ff).

34. Cf. *NT Notes,* Rom. 3:14, Gal. 3:19. Note in the latter passage that he characterizes the ceremonial law as a *punishment* imposed on Israel! For a somewhat milder characterization, see *NT Notes,* 1 Tim. 1:8.

35. See *Farther Thoughts on Christian Perfection,* Q. 4, *Works* (Jackson), 11:415-16; and Letter to John Hosmer (7 June 1761), *Letters* (Telford), 4:155.

36. Sermon 34, "The Original, Nature, Properties, and Use of the Law," §II.3, *Works,* 2:9.

37. *NT Notes,* Rom. 10:4, Matt. 5:17.

38. See Sermon 25, "Sermon on the Mount V," §I.1-4, *Works,* 1:551-3; and *NT Notes,* Rom. 3:20, Gal. 5:1, Gal. 5:13.

39. Twelve of the original forty-four sermons were a series on the Sermon on the Mount—now Sermons 21-33, *Works,* 1:466-698. See also his equation of Christ's law with the Sermon on the Mount in his "Letter to an Evangelical Layman" (20 Dec. 1751), §3, *Works,* 26:482.

40. Note Wesley's clarifying footnote to his *Farther Thoughts on Christian Perfection,* Q. 1, *Works* (Jackson), 11:415. See also the discussion in Deschner 1960, p. 98; and Lindström 1946, pp. 80-1.

41. Cf. *The Character of a Methodist,* §13, *Works,* 9:39; Sermon 10, "The Witness of the Spirit I," §I.8, *Works* 1:274; Sermon 24, "Sermon on the Mount IV," §III.2, *Works,* 1:542; and Sermon 120, "The Unity of the Divine Being," §17, *Works,* 4:67. Note also his (unfortunate) distinction between a Jew and a Christian as between one who obeys God out of fear and one who obeys God out of love; *Minutes* (13 May 1746), Q. 11, *John Wesley,* p. 157. This misses the clear teaching in Jewish Scripture that keeping the Torah is in response to God's grace.

42. On the objective basis, note that Wesley equates "preaching the love of God" with "preaching the life, death, resurrection, and the intercession of Christ," in Letter "To an Evangelical Layman" (20 Dec. 1751), §2, *Works,* 26:482. On the subjective assurance, see Sermon 11, "The Witness of the Spirit II," §III.5, *Works,* 1:290.

43. See: Extract from *A Short View of the Difference Between the Moravian Brethren, (so-called) and the Rev. Mr. John and Charles Wesley, Works* (Jackson), 10:202-3; and *A Second Dialogue between an Antinomian and His Friend, Works* (Jackson), 10:281.

44. Note in this regard Wesley's addition to his sources in the *OT Notes* comment (3:2385-6) on the promise in Ezekiel 36:28 that God will place the Holy Spirit within us: "Observe: then, and not before, are these promises to be fulfilled to the house of Israel." The promises in question deal with observing God's commandments and keeping God's statutes. See also his *NT Notes* comments on Rom. 4:15 & 6:14.

45. On these points, see esp. Sermon 25, "Sermon on the Mount V," §II.2-3, *Works,* 1:554; Sermon 35, "The Law Established through Faith I," *Works,* 2:20-32; and Sermon 36, "The Law Established through Faith II," *Works,* 2:33-43.

46. Note Wesley's description of contrasting law and faith as a "dangerous way of speaking" in *A Second Dialogue between an Antinomian and His Friend, Works* (Jackson), 10:284. Hence, the theological care he took to moderate the law/gospel contrast in his edited republication of Jonathan Edwards' *Faithful Narrative* (summarized in Steele 1994, pp. 190-2). In his disagreements with the Moravians he explicitly worried that false teaching would lead to false living; *Journal* (3 Sept. 1741), *Works,* 19:212. Hulley concludes that the law/gospel relation was the ethical debate in which Wesley most consistently engaged (1988, pp. 53ff). See also D. Dayton 1991b.

47. See in this regard Tore Meistad's enlightening comparison of Wesley's exposition of the Sermon on the Mount with that of Luther (and comments on later

Lutheran developments); Meistad 1989 (conclusions summarized in 1987). Cf. Pinomaa 1968.

48. Sermon 34, "The Original, Nature, Properties, and Use of the Law," §IV, *Works*, 2:15-19. See also the discussion in Lindström 1946, pp. 81ff.

49. Cf. Meistad 1989, p. 413.

50. For an example of Wesley responding to the charge that he had given up the doctrine of the Atonement, see *An Answer to Mr. Rowland Hill's Tract, entitled 'Imposture Detected'*, §I.7, *Works*, 9:406. Hill equated Atonement per se with the Substitutionary Justification explanation of the Atonement, which Wesley did reject.

51. These variations are not always distinguished. Aulén, for example, groups them together as the "objective" approach, though he notes some of the nuances between them. Fiddes does stress the difference between Anselm and Calvin, but follows a common course of lumping together the Penalty Satisfaction and Substitutionary Justification accounts as "penal substitution."

52. It is a caricature of Anselm to charge that he believed that Christ had to die to placate a wrathful God, enticing God to be merciful. One of his most fundamental principles was that God is impassible, so Christ's death could not change God! Rather, it maintained both Divine mercy and honor simultaneously.

53. For a characteristic focus on God as Sustainer of the Good, see *Summa Theologica*, II, q. 109, a. 7. On the preferability of satisfaction of penalty over mere pardon, see *Summa Theologica*, III, q. 46, aa. 1-2. For more on the atonement per se, see *Summa Theologica*, III. qq. 47-9; and Philip L. Quinn, "Aquinas on Atonement," in *Trinity, Incarnation, and Atonement*, edited by Ronald Feenstra and Cornelius Plantinga, Jr. (Notre Dame, IN: University of Notre Dame, 1989), pp. 153-77.

54. Since the individualistic and egalitarian turn in modern philosophy, Westerners have found it easier to appreciate the need for order to be preserved through law than the obligation not to offend sovereign honor.

55. That is, passive obedience deals roughly with the same claims as the Penalty Satisfaction approach, *except* that its efficacy is often limited to only the elect, particularly in the Reformed tradition.

56. *The Principles of a Methodist*, §3, *Works*, 9:51. All three elements are evident as well in his extended quotation on justification from Anna Maria Van Schurman in his Letter to William Law (6 Jan. 1756), *Letters* (Telford), 3:353-6.

57. Cf. *NT Notes*, 2 Peter 1:1.

58. Cf. *NT Notes*, Rom. 3:25.

59. Discussions of the Anglican standards can be found in Lindström 1946, pp. 60-4; and Renshaw 1965, pp. 41-3.

60. Cf. Deschner 1960, pp. 156-7.

61. One of the earliest instances of this tension is vividly portrayed in Wesley's discussion with Zinzendorf, recorded in *Journal* (3 Sept. 1741), *Works*, 19:211-15. Note especially Zinzendorf's complaint that Wesley wants to teach inherent righteousness instead of imputed (p. 212). For an argument that Calvin did not himself let the theme of substitution undercut the place of subsequent sanctification, see Trevor Hart, "Humankind in Christ and Christ in Humankind: Salvation as Participation in Our Substitute in the Theology of John Calvin," *Scottish Journal of Theology* 42 (1991):67-84.

62. See *A Letter to the Rev. James Hervey* (15 Oct. 1756), *Letters* (Telford), 3:371-88. For brief accounts of the exchange between Hervey and Wesley, see Coppedge 1987, pp. 145-55; and Gunter 1989, pp. 244-5. It is also interesting to note that Wesley

edited or deleted references to the imputed active righteousness of Christ in his reprint from William Beveridge in *Chr. Library*; cf. K. Kim 1992, pp. 133-5.

63. See Sermon 20, "The Lord Our Righteousness," *Works*, 1:449-65 (esp. §I.4 [453] and §II.5 [455-6]). Albert Outler dates the late Wesley from this sermon. For other major pieces dealing with this issue, see *Thoughts on the Imputed Righteousness of Christ*, *Works* (Jackson), 10:312-15; *A Blow at the Root; or Christ Stabbed in the House of His Friends*, *Works* (Jackson), 10:364-9; and Sermon 127, "On the Wedding Garment," *Works*, 4:140-8. See also the discussion in Deschner 1960, pp. 152-7.

64. See respectively: *Thoughts on the Imputed Righteousness of Christ*, §14, *Works* (Jackson), 10:315; and Sermon 20, "The Lord Our Righteousness," §II.19, *Works*, 1:462. Note also the identical concern about imputed active righteousness in Staniloae, *Orthodoxe Dogmatik*, I:233. By contrast, note the complaint—from a Reformed perspective—that Wesley undervalues how trust in the completeness of Christ's work can motivate Christian life in K. Kim 1992, p. 104.

65. Sermon 20, "The Lord Our Righteousness," §II.12, *Works*, 1:458.

66. On these points, see *NT Notes*, 1 Cor. 15:47; *Predestination Calmly Considered*, §36-7, *John Wesley*, pp. 441-2; Extract from *A Short View of the Difference Between the Moravian Brethren (So Called), And the Rev. Mr. John and Charles Wesley*, *Works* (Jackson), 10:202; and *A Second Dialogue between an Antinomian and His Friend*, *Works* (Jackson), 10:277. See also the discussion in Renshaw 1965, pp. 93ff.

67. Note how he makes this move in his *NT Notes* comments on Rom. 3:25: (Whom God hath set forth a propitiation)—To appease an offended God. But if, as some teach, God never was offended, there was no need for this propitiation. And, if so, Christ died in vain. (To declare his righteousness)—To demonstrate not only his clemency, but his justice; even that vindictive justice whose essential character and principal office is, to punish sin. . . .

68. Cf. *NT Notes*, Rom. 3:26.

69. Note his rejection of the idea that the law itself is something which can be offended or must be satisfied, in *Some Remarks on Mr. Hill's 'Review of all the Doctrines Taught by Mr. John Wesley'*, §12, Sec. V, *Works* (Jackson), 10:388; and *A Letter to the Rev. James Hervey* (15 Oct. 1756), *Letters* (Telford), 3:372. See also the discussion in C. Williams 1960, p. 84.

70. See in this regard Deschner's argument that Wesley's limitation of Christ's satisfaction to only God's condemning justice (as distinguished from positive justice) ultimately means that God's justice abdicates and God's mercy justifies (1960, pp. 168, 175).

71. Cf. the insightful critique of the penal substitution theory in Fiddes, *Present Salvation*, pp. 98-104 (remember, Fiddes lumps together what I am calling the Penalty Satisfaction and Substitutionary Justification views).

72. *Journal* (27 July 1749), *Works*, 20:292-3. See also Letter to Dr. John Robertson (24 Sept. 1753), *Works*, 26:522. Such troublesome language about Christ pacifying an angry God is even more prevalent in Charles' hymns! For a discussion of this, see J.R. Tyson 1983, pp. 325-46.

73. Cf. *NT Notes*, Rom. 3:25-6, 4:5; Letter to Mary Bishop (7 Feb. 1778), *Letters* (Telford), 6:298; and a stanza from the hymn "Universal Salvation" which Wesley circulated with his sermon *Free Grace*: "Their misery called for all thy grace, but justice stopped the way. Mercy the fatal bar removed, Thy only Son it gave" (*Works*, 3:560).

74. See Renshaw 1965, pp. 83-6.

75. See Letter "To an Evangelical Layman" (20 Dec. 1751), §2, *Works*, 26:482.

76. Cf. the excerpt of Abelard's comments on Romans 3:19-29 in *A Scholastic Miscellany,* edited by Eugene Fairweather (Philadelphia, PA: Westminster, 1956), pp. 276-84 (esp. p. 283).

77. Wesley himself never mentioned Abelard explicitly. If he accepted the common assumption that Abelard was like the Socinians in reducing Christ to a mere man, he would have adamantly rejected him. Nonetheless, some comparisons exist. One of the few reflections on Wesley's similarities (and differences) with Abelard is Cell 1935, pp. 318-24.

78. Two of the best examples are *NT Notes* comments on passages which focus on this theme. In Luke 15:32 he develops an extended allegory between the parable of the Prodigal Son and the return of a guilty sinner to God. His account climaxes in the exclamation "Behold with wonder and pleasure the gracious reception they find from divine, injured goodness." Concerning the exhortation to come boldly to the throne of God in Hebrews 5:16, Wesley notes that this is the throne of our "reconciled Father," and that "grace erected it, and reigns there."

79. There are many other passages in Charles' hymns with this theme as well. To cite just two particularly appropriate examples: "Away with our Fears! The Godhead appears in Christ Reconcil'd, the Father of Mercies in Jesus the Child." (*Hymns for the Nativity,* #8, *Poet. Works,* 4:113); and "Thou didst Thy Son bestow Thy truth of grace to prove, and Jesus did by dying show sincerity of Love. . . . " (Hymn on John 3:17, *Poetry,* 2:222). See also the comparisons of Charles' hymns on Christ's passion with those of Isaac Watts in Marshall & Todd 1982, pp. 70-1.

80. Hymn #27, *Works,* 7:114.

81. Hymn #193, *Works,* 7:322-3.

82. On the typical identification of Christ and God in Charles' hymns, see Rattenbury 1941, p. 151.

83. Sermon 103, "What is Man?" esp. §II.7, *Works,* 3:460.

84. This is best seen in Wesley's consistent rejection of Socinianism on the grounds that it values Christ's death only as an "example" for humanity and not as a ransom from the penalty of sin—e.g., Letter to Mary Pendarves (19 June 1731), *Works,* 25:288; Letter to George Whitefield (27 Apr. 1741), *Works,* 26:60; and Letter to John Robertson (24 Sept. 1753), *Works,* 26:522.

85. This model is relatively less well-known than the others, being often omitted from standard discussions of the Atonement. For a sympathetic exposition, see H. Orton Wiley, *Christian Theology* (Kansas City, MO: Beacon Hill, 1952), 2:252-9.

86. On this point Grotius is actually on close terms with Anselm, who also rejected the idea of Christ being a penalty substitute. The purpose of Christ's satisfaction of God's honor, for Anselm, was to offset the need for punishment (cf. Fiddes, *Present Salvation,* p. 97).

87. On his general awareness of Grotius, note Wesley's recommendation of an English translation of his works in Letter to Joseph Benson (22 Oct. 1777), *Letters* (Telford), 6:285. Outler identifies as a likely dependence on Grotius the mention of Christ as Representative in Sermon 5, "Justification by Faith," *Works,* 1:186 fn22.

88. E.g., William Pope, Richard Watson, John Miley, and H. Orton Wiley. By contrast, note the dismissal of this suggestion in Cannon 1946, p. 209.

89. Note his claim that God's pardoning love (seen in Christ) is the source of all Christian obedience, in *An Earnest Appeal to Men of Reason and Religion,* §61, *Works,* 11:70.

90. Hymn #194, st. 5, *Works,* 7:325.

91. Note the connection of God's great mercy and Christ's satisfaction of justice in *The Principles of a Methodist*, §3, *Works*, 9:51.

92. Eastern Orthodoxy is critical of the West for limiting Christ's atonement to only the forensic aspect of pardon. Instead, they highlight the dimension of restoring human nature (cf. Staniloae, *Orthodoxe Dogmatik*, 2:102). By his connection of pardon and restored empowering relationship, Wesley merges these two concerns.

93. Note that the most central critique made of Deschner's reading of Wesley's Christology is that he orients it almost totally toward the past; e.g., H. Knight 1992, pp. 57-61, 68ff; and Gallaway 1988, p. 198.

94. Letter to Charles Wesley (28 Dec. 1774), *Letters* (Telford), 6:134.

95. Most early theologians distinguished Christ's work into only regal and priestly roles. Eusebius provides one of the few threefold analyses. Calvin is the one who developed this notion extensively. His formula then became standard in both Reformed and Lutheran Orthodoxy, and common in many Roman Catholic treatments. Wesley would have known it from several Anglican sources—in particular, his favorite doctrinal summary, Pearson's *Exposition of the Creed* (pp. 93ff). The three-fold office is less common in Eastern Orthodox analysis, but see Staniloae, *Orthodoxe Dogmatik*, 2:89ff.

96. E.g., *Minutes* (9 Aug. 1745), Q. 15, *John Wesley*, p. 150; and "MS Minutes" (23 May 1753), Q. 4, *Minutes* (Mason), p. 718. A further sign of the importance of this theme to Wesley is that one of his few additions to Bengelius' comments on Revelations in the *NT Notes* was an explication of Christ as Prophet, Priest, and King (Rev. 5:6).

97. Deschner 1960, p. 205.

98. Cf. Deschner 1960, pp. 74, 165 (note, however, that Deschner chooses to treat Priest last—as foundational). Collins 1993 opts for the traditional order (pp. 44ff). For an example of Wesley beginning the triad with Priest see Sermon 36, "The Law Established through Faith II," §II.6, *Works*, 2:37-8. See also his summary of how Christ is the power and wisdom of God—with his cross, his death, his life, his kingdom (*NT Notes*, 1 Cor. 1:24).

99. See esp., *NT Notes*, Matt. 1:16; and Sermon 36, "The Law Established through Faith II," §II.6, *Works*, 2:37.

100. He uses the language of Christ as intercessor in his summary of his Christology in *A Letter to a Roman Catholic*, §7, *John Wesley*, p. 494. He also allowed the imagery to filter through in the devotional guides and hymns that he provided for his people; e.g., *Devotions for Every Day*, Thursday, Gill, p. 81; and Hymn #194, st. 4, *Works*, 7:324. For the comparison to the *Book of Common Prayer*, see Selleck 1983, p. 225.

101. Sermon 62, "The End of Christ's Coming," §III.1-2, *Works*, 2:480-1. This sermon describes the work of Christ entirely in terms of its present dimensions, moving from our restoration to our renewal in holiness and eventual resurrection from death (Christ's work as King).

102. For specific reflections on this issue, see *Thoughts on Christian Perfection*, Q. 5, *John Wesley*, p. 285; *Farther Thoughts on Christian Perfection*, Q. 9, *Works* (Jackson), 11:417; Letter to Dorothy Furly (15 Sept. 1762), *Letters* (Telford), 4:189; and *Journal* (25 July 1761), *Works*, 21:338.

103. Cf. *NT Notes*, Heb. 7:25.

104. Cf. *NT Notes*, Matt. 1:16; and *A Letter to a Roman Catholic*, §7, *John Wesley*, p. 494.

105. Sermon 23, "Sermon on the Mount III," §IV, *Works*, 1:533. Note also his description of the Sermon on the Mount as "the noblest compendium of religion

which is to be found even in the oracles of God," in *Journal* (17 Oct, 1771), *Works,* 22:293.

106. Cf. *NT Notes,* John 9:5. See also Gallaway's comments on how Jesus is held up as a model of virtues in *Hymns* (1988, p. 162).

107. E.g., Deschner 1960, p. 102.

108. *NT Notes,* Matt. 5:17.

109. Sermon 36, "The Law Established through Faith II," §II.6, *Works,* 2:38. For shorter accounts of Christ's Kingship that align with this, see *NT Notes,* Matt. 1:16, Phil. 3:8; *A Letter to a Roman Catholic,* §7, *John Wesley,* p. 494; and Sermon 62, "The End of Christ's Coming," §III.2-4, *Works,* 2:481-2.

110. The frequency of King imagery in *Hymns* is discussed in Gallaway 1988, pp. 244, 297 fn9. For a representative hymn, see #186, st. 8, *Works,* 7:315.

111. Sermon 48, "Self-Denial," §I.13, *Works,* 2:245. See also Sermon 61, "The Mystery of Iniquity," §11, *Works,* 2:455.

112. See Robert Murray, *Symbols of Church and Kingdom: A Study in Early Syrian Tradition* (New York: Cambridge University Press, 1975), pp. 199-203.

113. See especially Homily 44 of Macarius (Wesley #19, *Chr. Library,* 1:142-5).

114. For its frequency in *Hymns,* see Gallaway 1988, p. 242. For a collection and analysis of the image in Charles, see J.R. Tyson 1983, pp. 464-76.

115. *NT Notes,* 1 Cor. 15:24.

116. Note in this regard Sermon 142, "The Wisdom of Winning Souls," §II.1, *Works* 4:311-3, where (the early) Wesley defines winning souls in terms of regulating one's understanding and affections. The idea of doctrine as grammar has been developed in George Lindbeck, *The Nature of Doctrine* (Philadelphia, PA: Westminster, 1984). For an insightful reading of Wesley's teachings on faith and affections in light of Lindbeck, see Horst 1985.

117. Note Sermon 36, "The Law Established Through Faith II," §III.1, *Works,* 2:41. Wesley argues here that merely preaching Christ in all his offices is vain unless authentic Christian obedience results.

118. Cf. "MS Minutes" (23 May 1753): "The most effectual way of preaching Christ is to preach him in all his offices, and to declare his law as well as gospel to believers and unbelievers" (in *Minutes* [Mason], p. 718).

119. See esp. *NT Notes,* Phil. 3:8; and the discussion in Fuhrman 1963, p. 160.

120. Gallaway 1988, pp. 97ff.

121. *A Letter to a Roman Catholic,* §7, *John Wesley,* pp. 494-5. For comparison to the Ecumenical Creed, see Wainwright, "Methodism and the Apostolic Faith."

122. For recognition of this agenda in Calvin, see François Wendel, *Calvin* (New York: Harper, 1963), p. 259. See also Heppe, *Reformed Dogmatics,* pp. 449-51; and Schmid, *Doctrinal Theology,* p. 336.

123. The label of practical Monophysite is Outler's (*Works* 1:470 note f). The suspicion of Docetism is raised by Scroggs 1960, p. 420.

124. Cf. Deschner 1960, p. 17.

125. *The Character of a Methodist,* 1, *Works,* 9:34. For other examples of criticism of these two, see *NT Notes,* John 10:30; Sermon 123, "On Knowing Christ After the Flesh," §4-5, *Works,* 4:99-100; and his *Dictionary* definitions of them.

126. Sermon 77, "Spiritual Worship," *Works,* 3:89-102. In this sermon he tries to show that Christ was divine, and can thus be worshipped, because Scripture assigns to him the very tasks of God. He also once made reference to the argument that Jesus *claimed* to be God, so either he was that, or else he was the vilest of men (*NT Notes,* John 10:30).

127. Cf. *Journal* (5 April 1768), *Works*, 22:124.

128. As Scroggs notes (1960, p. 420), Wesley's Jesus is preeminently the Jesus of John's Gospel, which is easy to *mis*read in docetic terms. Wesley does indeed miss the clearest affirmations of Jesus' humanity in the Gospel of John! He assumes from John 1:1 that John was writing to counteract some who were doubting Jesus' deity! Moreover, he translated I John 4:3 as "every spirit which confesseth not Jesus Christ who is come in the flesh is not of God" (*NT Notes*). Note that the epistle's original main point (you must confess that Jesus came in the flesh) has become a subordinate clause!

129. One should note, however, the alternative interpretation of this passage in Clapper 1989, p. 55.

130. Noted in Campbell 1991b, p. 81.

131. The Article in question is #2 (cf. Oden 1988, p. 112). For the suggestion that Christ's human nature was a direct creation, see *NT Notes*, Eph. 1:3.

132. Deschner 1960, p. 167.

133. I noted earlier Wesley's concern about this expressed in Sermon 123, "On Knowing Christ After the Flesh," *Works*, 4:98-106. Thus, it is not at all surprising that he should change references to Christ as "our Best Friend" to "our Lord" in his transformation of Robert Nelson's *The Great Duty of Frequenting the Christian Sacrifice* into his Sermon 101, "The Duty of Constant Communion" (cf. *Works*, 3:429).

134. *NT Notes*, John 2:4.

135. See the discussion in Deschner 1960, pp. 28-9. Note also that Wesley rejected the suggestions that Christ's humanity had a preexistence like his divinity (Sermon 62, "The End of Christ's Coming," §II.2, *Works*, 2:478); or that Christ was the union of a human person with the divinity of the Father ("Thoughts on the Writings of Baron Swedenborg," §12, *AM* 6 [1783] *Works* [Jackson], 13:431).

136. But compare Sermon 85, "On Working Out Our Own Salvation," §4 (*Works*, 3:201): "[Christ] 'emptied himself' of that divine fullness, veiled his fullness from the eyes of [humans] and angels, 'taking'—and by that very act emptying himself—'the form of a servant, being made in the likeness of man,' a real man like other men." This comes close to affirming *kenosis*, though the word "veiled" still occurs and it is not clear what all Wesley is including in the divine "fullness"—is it the divine attributes, or only the divine glory? Charles comes closer to a kenotic Christology in some of his hymns, but he also ultimately wants to affirm a "latent Godhead" in Jesus (*Hymns for the Nativity*, #5, *Poet. Works*, 4:109). Cf. the discussion in Quantrille 1989, p. 49.

137. *NT Notes*, Matt. 17:2.

138. Deschner 1960, pp. 32-7.

139. E.g., *NT Notes*, Luke 4:30, John 8:59.

140. Deschner 1960, pp. 31-2.

141. Cf. his insistence that in Christ dwelled not only the divine powers, but the divine nature, the very substance of God; in *NT Notes*, Col. 1:9.

142. Cf. Deschner 1960, p. 167: "In Wesley there is a definite tendency to suggest that the one who suffers and dies is God."

143. Note Wesley's introductory sermon to the series on the Sermon on the Mount, where he stresses that the one teaching in the sermon is "the Lord of Heaven and Earth," "the Great Lawgiver," etc.; Sermon 21, "Sermon on the Mount I," §2, *Works*, 1:470.

144. Note the conclusion to his sermon dedicated to defending the full deity of Christ: "As there is but one God in heaven above and in the earth beneath, so there

is only one happiness for created spirits, either in heaven or earth"; Sermon 77, "Spiritual Worship," §III.1, *Works*, 3:97.

145. These points have been raised repeatedly by José Míguez Bonino (e.g., 1981, p. 56; and 1983b, p. 212 [8]).

Chapter Five

1. Thomas Jackson included in his edition of Wesley's *Works* two sermons on the Holy Spirit that he had found among Wesley's papers: "On the Holy Spirit" (7:508-20), and "On Grieving the Holy Spirit" (7:485-92). These were actually abridgements that Wesley made of other authors' sermons for his use. The first was by John Gambold and the second by William Tilly (cf. *Works*, 4:524, 531). One can assume that these sermons are at least amenable to Wesley (cf. *Works*, 4:x), but should not use them as primary sources for his pneumatology.

2. His most extended consideration of these issues was in response to a tract on "The Office and Operations of the Holy Spirit" by Bishop William Warburton (meant to counteract perceived Methodist "enthusiasm"). In the Preamble of his response Wesley contended that the topic of the tract is connected with "the whole of real religion"; *A Letter to the Right Reverend the Lord Bishop of Gloucester* (26 Nov. 1762), *Works*, 11:467.

3. There is some precedent for this equation in the Anglican standards, but not as clear as it is in Wesley; cf. Luby 1984, pp. 82-91. The two major secondary studies of Wesley's understanding of the Holy Spirit are Starkey 1962 and Lessmann 1987. Kellett 1975 actually discusses Wesley's doctrine of the Holy Spirit very little. His real agenda is to argue that Wesley helped recover a place for religious experience in the context of an eighteenth-century Anglicanism that was too anti-enthusiastic (cf. pp. 184-6, 191-2). For helpful shorter studies see Cannon 1968, Outler 1988, Staples 1986, and Starkey 1980.

4. Sermon 12, "The Witness of Our Spirit," §15, *Works*, 1:309.

5. Cf. the unanimous opinions of Lessmann (1987, pp. 11-12), Luby (1984, p. 117), Rakestraw (1985a, p. 142), and Starkey (1962, p. 37).

6. *Instructions for Children*, p. 10.

7. Sermon 51, "The Good Steward," §I.8, *Works*, 2:286.

8. *A Letter to a Roman Catholic*, §8, *John Wesley*, p. 495.

9. For his passing endorsement of two traditional proofs for the full deity of the Holy Spirit, see his *NT Notes* comments on Acts 5:4 (the parallelism in the Ananias and Sapphira story) and 1 Cor. 2:11 (only the Spirit of God knows the things of God). There was a prolonged demonstration of the divinity of the Spirit in Pearson's *Exposition of the Creed*, which Wesley recommended.

10. Cf. *NT Notes*, John 15:26.

11. Luby 1984, p. 130. In light of this inherently personal nature of grace, one of the arguments against using some qualification of "grace" for designating Wesley's orienting concern (such as I have offered) is blunted. I have in mind Manfred Marquardt's argument that the major category of love is more adequate than that of grace because love reflects Wesley's move from legal to personal categories in interpreting the relation of God to persons (recorded in Robert Burtner, "John Wesley in Switzerland," *QR* 4.1 [1984]:22-30, p. 25). I agree that Wesley is best interpreted in terms of personal categories, *like grace*!

12. Cf. Staniloae, *Orthodoxe Dogmatik*, 2:241-4.

13. Sermon 127, "On the Wedding Garment," §19, *Works*, 4:148.

14. As Wesley put it in *A Letter to a Roman Catholic*, the Spirit is "not only perfectly holy in himself, but the immediate cause of all holiness in us" (§8, *John Wesley*, p. 495). He may have appropriated this specific characterization from the sermon "On Grieving the Holy Spirit" by William Tilly which he had abridged; cf. *Works* (Jackson), 7:486.

15. E.g., *A Farther Appeal to Men of Reason and Religion*, Pt. I, §V.13, *Works*, 11:153; and Sermon 57, "On the Fall of Man," §II.8, *Works*, 2:410.

16. A homily of Macarius is again exemplary: #20 (Wesley #12, *Chr. Library*, 1:126).

17. Note the designation of the Spirit as the "Physician of souls" in his abridgement of Austin's *Devotions for Every Day* (Gill, p. 90).

18. *Advice to the People Called 'Methodists'*, §6, *Works*, 9:124. Cf. Starkey 1962, p. 17.

19. Cf. *Oxford English Dictionary* (2nd ed., 1989), 7:1037. Wesley's use would fit their definition 4.b of "inspire": "to actuate or influence; animate; affect, rouse, or control by an infused, animating, or exalting influence." Note that Wesley equates "inspire" with infusing new vitality and virtue in Christian lives in *A Farther Appeal to Men of Reason and Religion*, Pt. I, §V.28, *Works*, 11:171.

20. Wesley retains the Collect, with its prayer for God to "cleanse the thoughts of our hearts by the inspiration of the Holy Spirit" in his *Sunday Service*, p. 125.

21. Cf. *A Farther Appeal to Men of Reason and Religion*, Pt. I, §V.28, *Works*, 11:171; Wesley argues for the word "inspiration" on the basis that it is biblical, it has a near relation to "spirit," and it is not as "strong" as the alternative word "influence"!

22. Sermon 19, "The Great Privilege of Those that are Born of God," §III.2-3, *Works*, 1:442.

23. William P. Alston, "The Indwelling of the Holy Spirit," in *Divine Nature and Human Language* (Ithaca, NY: Cornell University Press, 1989), pp. 223-52.

24. *A Letter to a Roman Catholic*, §8, *John Wesley*, p. 495. Wesley is actually presenting here a summary of the comments on the Holy Spirit in Pearson's *Exposition of the Creed* (pp. 326ff); cf. *A Farther Appeal to Men of Reason and Religion*, Pt. I, §V.23, *Works*, 11:163-5.

25. *NT Notes*, John 16:8.

26. E.g., *A Farther Appeal to Men of Reason and Religion*, Pt. I, §V.22-3, *Works*, 11:163-5; Sermon 4, "Scriptural Christianity," §5, *Works*, 1:161; and *A Letter to the Right Reverend the Lord Bishop of Gloucester* (26 Nov 1762), §I.1ff, *Works*, 11:468ff.

27. I agree with Lessmann (1987, pp. 97-8) that it would not be faithful to Wesley to split up the Spirit's work in terms of the arenas of the individual, the Church, and the world. Much of the Spirit's work in both individual lives and the world as a whole is through the Church! That is why I am investigating dimensions of the Spirit's work, rather than arenas of that work.

28. *NT Notes*, John 16:8. It must be admitted that Wesley comments in the same work on 1 Corinthians 12:3 that "None have the Holy Spirit but Christians : all Christians have this Spirit." This is best understood in the sense that only Christians have the deeper participation of the Spirit's Presence, not that the Spirit has no Presence among non-believers.

29. The specific studies of Wesley's doctrine of the Witness of the Spirit (or Assurance) are Yates 1952, Benner 1966, Noll 1975, and S. Martin 1990. They concentrate more on issues of historical precedent for Wesley's views than on analyzing the distinctive texture of his understanding. They must be supplemented by the recent studies of Wesley's understanding of grace, faith, and assurance drawn on below. On Charles' convictions in this regard, see Townsend 1979 (but note that

Townsend is unsympathetic with Charles' Arminian theology and emphasis on religious experience; cf. p. 266!).

30. Lessmann 1987, p. 47.

31. Cf. his *Journal* entry for 12 Aug. 1771: "The very thing which Mr. Stinstra calls fanaticism is no other than heart-religion; in other words, 'righteousness, and peace, and joy in the Holy Ghost.' These must be *felt*, or they have no being. All, therefore, who condemn inward feelings in the gross, leave no place either for joy, peace, or love in religion; and consequently reduce it to a dry dead carcass" (*Works*, 22:287).

32. *Minutes* (13 May 1746), Q. 1, *John Wesley*, p. 159.

33. Chapter 6, "Great Expectations: Aldersgate and the Evidences of Genuine Christianity," in Heitzenrater 1989, pp. 106-49 (reprinted in *Aldersgate Reconsidered*, ed. R.L. Maddox [Nashville, TN: Kingswood Books, 1990], pp. 49-91). For some earlier recognition of these transitions, see Yates 1952, pp. 72ff; C. Williams 1960, pp. 102-14; and Starkey 1962, pp. 67-70. For arguments against any significant change in Wesley (which I find less than convincing), see Benner 1966, pp. 226-34; and J.H. Tyson 1991, pp. 42-67. Townsend argues that Charles did not follow John in eventually recognizing the legitimacy of degrees of assurance (1979, p. 190).

34. Letter to Susanna Wesley (18 June 1725), *Works*, 25:169-70. As this might suggest, Wesley was in the practice at this time of gauging his spiritual state several times a day; cf. Heitzenrater 1984, 1:51-60.

35. As Luther put it, "Faith is a living, daring confidence in God's grace, so sure and certain that a man would stake his life on it a thousand times," *Works of Luther* (Philadelphia, PA: A.J. Holman, 1932), 6:452. On Calvin's identification of faith with certainty, see M. Charles Bell, *Calvin and Scottish Theology: The Doctrine of Assurance* (Edinburgh: Handsel Press, 1985), p. 8.

36. Cf. Matthews 1986, pp. 240.

37. A position that Wesley tries to defend in a Letter to Susanna Wesley (29 July 1725), *Works*, 25:175.

38. See esp. Letter from Samuel Wesley, Sr. (1 Sept. 1725), *Works*, 25:181.

39. Cf. Letter to "John Smith," (22 Mar. 1748), 6, *Works*, 26:289.

40. Matthews 1986, p. 241.

41. The basic assumption of Yates 1952. See the critique of Yates in Benner 1966, pp. 201-2; and Stoeffler 1976b, pp. 193-4.

42. Both Luther and Calvin connect assurance with the Holy Spirit. As such, one can show parallels between them and Wesley, even though there was little direct dependence (on convergence with Luther, see Hildebrandt 1951, pp. 41ff; with Calvin, see Stoeffler 1964, pp. 133ff). This heritage had to reach Wesley through the Moravians, however, for later magisterial Protestantism had departed from their founders' understandings of the witness of the Spirit. Lutheran Scholasticism largely limited it to validating the truth of Scripture (cf. Gillian Evans, Alister McGrath, & Allan Galloway, *The Science of Theology* [Grand Rapids, MI: Eerdmans, 1986], p. 172), while Reformed Scholasticism tended to lay more stress on the rational basis for assurance than on the Spirit's witness (cf. Bell, *Calvin and Scottish Theology*; and R.T. Kendall, *Calvin and English Calvinism to 1649* [Oxford: Oxford University Press, 1979]).

43. On the precedence for Wesley's understanding in the Anglican standards, see Yates 1952, p. 197; Noll 1975; and Selleck 1983, pp. 251-2.

44. This point is stressed in H.-J. Lee 1991, pp. 190-1. For evidence of Wesley reading Macarius, see his Diary (30 July 1736), *Works*, 18:405. For discussion of this

theme in Macarius, see Dörries, *Theologie des Makarios/Symeon*, p. 205. On the general Eastern emphasis, see Spidlík, *Spirituality of the Christian East*, pp. 72-3.

45. Cf. *Journal* (29 Jan. 1738), *Works*, 18:216. As Heitzenrater notes, Wesley's evaluation here reflects some "hindsight" from his contacts with Böhler (1989, p. 121).

46. See *Journal* (6 June 1738), *Works*, 18:254.

47. Especially important was the preaching of Christian David; cf. *Journal* (10 Aug. 1738), *Works*, 18:270-81.

48. Cf. Sermon 110 (1739), "Free Grace," §14, *Works*, 3:549; *The Principles of a Methodist* (1740), §9, 25-7, *Works*, 9:53, 60-3; *Hymns and Sacred Poems* (1740), Preface, 7, *Works* (Jackson), 14:325; Sermon 2 (1741), "The Almost Christian," *Works*, 1:131-41; and *An Earnest Appeal to Men of Reason and Religion* (1743), §23, *Works*, 11:53.

49. E.g., Letter to Arthur Bedford (28 Sept. 1738), §1-4, *Works*, 25:562-4; *Journal* (14 Oct. 1738), *Works*, 19:19; Letter to Samuel Wesley, Jr. (30 Oct. 1738), *Works*, 25:575-8; *Journal* (16 Dec. 1738), *Works*, 19:27-8; and *Journal* (4 Jan. 1739), *Works*, 19:29-31. Note that the *Journal* extracts here were not published until 1742.

50. *Journal* (4 Feb. 1738), *Works*, 18:228.

51. Note Wesley's apparent affirmation of precisely this tension in the Letter to Charles Wesley (27 June 1766), *Letters* (Telford), 5:16.

52. Trace the course of the debates in: *Minutes* (25 June 1744), Qq. 5-10, *John Wesley*, p. 137; *Minutes* (2 Aug. 1745), Qq. 1-4, *John Wesley*, p. 149; and *Minutes* (16 June 1747), Qq. 1-11, *John Wesley*, p. 165-7.

53. Letter to Charles Wesley (31 July 1747), *Works*, 26:254-5.

54. E.g., *A Second Letter to the Author of 'The Enthusiasm of Methodists and Papists Compared'*, §20, *Works*, 11:398-9; and *A Letter to the Rev. Dr. Rutherforth* (28 Mar. 1768), §I.4, *Works*, 9:375-6.

55. See Sermon 86, "A Call to Backsliders," esp. §2, *Works*, 3:211-16; and Sermon 89, "The More Excellent Way," esp. §7, *Works*, 3:263-77. See also two striking personal letters of encouragement: Letter to Miss March (11 Nov. 1760), *Letters* (Telford), 4:109; and Letter to Alexander Knox (11 July 1778), *Letters* (Telford), 6:315.

56. Cf. Sermon 106, "On Faith," *Works*, 3:492-501, esp. §I.10, p. 497; Sermon 117, "On The Discoveries of Faith," §12-13, *Works*, 4:35; and the comment that no one who fears God and really strives to please God is in a state of damnation, in "MS Minutes" (15 Aug. 1758), Q. 2, *John Wesley*, p. 177. For a dialogue over these issues, see Kenneth J. Collins, "Other Thoughts on Aldersgate: Has the Conversionist Paradigm Collapsed?" *MethH* 30 (1991):10-25; Randy L. Maddox, "Continuing the Conversation," *MethH* 30 (1992):235-41; and Kenneth J. Collins, "A Reply to Randy Maddox," *MethH* 31 (1992):51-4.

57. Note the footnotes added to the Preface of *Hymns and Sacred Poems* (1740) when it was reprinted as part of the *Plain Account of Christian Perfection* in 1766, *Works* (Jackson), 11:379-80; and the footnotes he added in 1774 to his earlier evaluation of his spiritual state just prior to Aldersgate, in *Journal* (29 Jan. 1738), *Works*, 18:214-16, notes h, i, j, k.

58. Cf. Letter to Dorothy Furly, (21 Oct. 1757), *Letters* (Telford), 3:230; and Letter to Mary Cooke (30 Oct. 1785), *Letters* (Telford), 7:298.

59. A comment to Melville Horne in 1788, recorded in Robert Southey, *The Life of Wesley* (New York: W.B. Gilley, 1820), 1:258.

60. Matthews 1986, pp. 240ff (summarized in 1985, p. 406).

61. Cf. Sermon 1 (1738), "Salvation by Faith," §I.5, *Works*, 1:121; and *The Principles of a Methodist* (1740), §9, *Works*, 9:53.

62. For some of the earliest examples, see *An Earnest Appeal to Men of Reason and Religion* (1743), §6, *Works*, 11:46; Sermon 4 (1744), "Scriptural Christianity," §I.1, *Works*, 1:161; Letter to "John Smith" (28 Sept. 1745), §15, *Works*, 26:159; and Sermon 5 (1746), "Justification by Faith," §IV.2, *Works*, 1:194.

63. Matthews 1986, pp. 244-5. By "objective" I mean simply the conviction that it is not self-generated; cf. Clapper 1989, p. 126.

64. Note his claim that "a consciousness of pardon cannot be the condition of pardon," in Letter to Joseph Benson (21 May 1781), *Letters* (Telford), 7:61. Wesley had tried to protect against a psychologizing of assurance earlier by arguing that it was a direct gift of the Holy Spirit, not a product of human faith; Letter to Rev. Arthur Bedford (28 Sept. 1738), §3, *Works*, 25:563.

65. See esp. Letter to Samuel Walker (19 Sept. 1757), §1, *Letters* (Telford), 3:222; and Sermon 43, "The Scripture Way of Salvation," §II.3, *Works*, 2:162.

66. See esp.: *An Earnest Appeal to Men of Reason and Religion*, §6-9, *Works*, 11:46-8; *A Plain Account of Genuine Christianity*, §II.7, *John Wesley*, p. 189; and *NT Notes*, Gal. 2:20.

67. It is astounding that Wesley can be misread on this point. However, James Packer has recently criticized Wesley for changing faith from a matter of trust (*fiducia*) to a matter of volition—i.e. choosing to do something out of one's own power ("Arminianisms," in *Through Christ's Word*, edited by W.R. Godfrey & J.L. Boyd [Phillipsburg, NJ: Presbyterian and Reformed, 1985], pp. 121-48; here, p. 133). There is no such move in Wesley! Indeed, the move to emphasizing faith as spiritual experience was precisely to highlight our human dependance on God's gracious prevenience!

68. Luby 1984. Note especially his connection of the cooperant nature of grace with its perceptibility (pp. 105, 145-7).

69. The identity of "John Smith" remains uncertain. There were twelve letters between him and Wesley, beginning in May 1745 and ending in March 1748. They can be found scattered in *Works*, 26:138-294. For a good summary and analysis of their dialogue, see Matthews 1986, pp. 340-57.

70. Letter to "John Smith" (30 Dec. 1745), §13, *Works*, 26:181. Note also Charles' charge that a denial of the perceptibility of the inspiration of the Spirit is a denial of the Spirit's work per se, in Sermon 3, "Awake, Thou that Sleepest," §III.8, *Works*, 1:155.

71. Cf. *A Letter to the Rev. Mr. Downes* (17 Nov. 1759), §11, *Works*, 9:359-60.

72. E.g., *A Farther Appeal to Men of Reason and Religion*, Pt. I, §I.6 & §V.2, *Works*, 11:108, 140. Cf. Matthews 1985, p. 414.

73. E.g., Letter to Philothea Briggs (23 July 1772), *Letters* (Telford), 5:331.

74. E.g., *NT Notes*, Phil. 1:9; *An Earnest Appeal to Men of Reason and Religion*, §6 & §32, *Works*, 11:46, 56; and Sermon 43, "The Scripture Way of Salvation," §II.1, *Works*, 2:160. See also the discussion in Chapter One.

75. Cf. Luby 1984, pp. 154ff.

76. His basic understanding is laid out in three major sermons: Sermon 10, "The Witness of the Spirit I," *Works*, 1:269-84; Sermon 11, "The Witness of the Spirit II," *Works*, 1:285-98; and Sermon 12, "The Witness of Our Own Spirit," *Works*, 1:300-13.

77. E.g., *NT Notes*, 1 Thess. 1:5, Heb. 6:11, 1 John 4:7; and Sermon 11, "The Witness of the Spirit II," §III.5, *Works*, 1:290. Scott Jones notes that this is the second most frequently quoted verse in Wesley's sermons (1992, p. 209).

78. See esp. Sermon 11, "The Witness of the Spirit II," §II.4 & §V.1, *Works*, 1:287, 296. For an extended exposition of the witness of the Spirit as a renewed consciousness of relationship with God, see Staples 1963, pp. 296ff.

79. Note Wesley's claim that this knowledge is not communicated by a chain of reasoning, but by a kind of *intuition*, a direct view; in Sermon 62, "The End of Christ's Coming," §III.1, *Works*, 2:481. Cf. Luby 1984, p. 152. In this light, it is very interesting that William Alston has argued that the most conceivable manner that God could share Godself with humanity would be by allowing such a direct awareness of God's love ("Indwelling of the Holy Spirit," p. 250)!

80. For a summary of the eighteenth-century Anglican emphasis on present virtues, see Chamberlain 1993, pp. 668-70. Townsend has argued that Charles differed from John on this point, assuming that the witness of the Spirit ratified the witness of conscience, rather than vice-versa (1979, p. 153).

81. Cf. Runyon 1990; and Wesley's pastoral admonition against looking *inward* too much and *upward* too little in Letter to Mary Bishop (16 Feb. 1771), *Letters* (Telford), 5:222.

82. Compare Sermon 10, "The Witness of the Spirit I," §I.7 (*Works*, 1: 274), with Sermon 11, "The Witness of the Spirit II," §II.2 (*Works*, 1:287). As Outler notes (*Works*, 1:287, note b) Wesley was never enslaved to precise quotation, but this change seems more than accidental.

83. Sermon 10, "The Witness of the Spirit I," §I.11, *Works*, 1:275-6.

84. Sermon 11, "The Witness of the Spirit II," §V.3, *Works*, 1:297-8. Less than a year before this sermon was written John had sent Charles a despondent letter in which he claimed never to have had any witness of the Spirit (27 June 1766, *Letters* [Telford], 5:16). Of course, this letter must be read in light of John's tendency to magnify moments of despondency and then forget them (cf. his 1780 comment that he does not remember having felt one quarter of an hour of lowness of spirits since he was born! [Sermon 77, "Spiritual Worship," §III.2, *Works*, 3:98]). Note also his explicit claim to have experienced the witness of the Spirit in the present sermon §III.6, *Works*, 1:290.

85. E.g., Sermon 11, "The Witness of the Spirit II," §II.4 & §V.4, *Works*, 1:287, 298.

86. Sermon 11, "The Witness of the Spirit II," §III.8 & §IV.4 *Works*, 1:292, 294. Note in this regard Yates' criticism of Wesley for maintaining that the direct witness of the Spirit must be antecedent to the indirect witness (i.e, a clean conscience and fruit) (1952, pp. 135-6). Yates' fear is that Wesley does not anchor our assurance adequately in an "objective" base. Wesley's fear would be that Yates is adopting works-righteousness!

87. This point permeates Wesley's works. For a few examples, see *The Character of a Methodist*, §13, *Works*, 9:39; *An Earnest Appeal to Men of Reason and Religion*, §61, *Works*, 11:70; *A Farther Appeal to Men of Reason and Religion*, Pt. I, §I.3, *Works*, 11:106; Sermon 10, "The Witness of the Spirit I," §I.8, *Works*, 1:274; and Sermon 120, "The Unity of the Divine Being," §17, *Works*, 4:67. Of course, since the mature Wesley assumes a universal presence of initial restoring grace, he can also assume some ability to respond to God prior to the witness of the Spirit. This assumption lies behind his exhortation of one with the faith of a servant to work righteousness while crying out for the witness of the Spirit; Sermon 106, "On Faith," §II.4, *Works*, 3:500.

88. Note his comment about God withdrawing the witness of the Spirit only if we give occasion, in Letter to Miss J.C. (30 Jan. 1762), *Letters* (Telford), 4:170.

89. E.g., *Journal* (6 Oct. 1738), *Works*, 19:15; *A Second Letter to the Author of 'Enthusiasm of Methodists and Papists Compared'*, §20, *Works*, 11:398-9; and *NT Notes*, Heb. 6:11.

90. Criticism of this aspect of Wesley's understanding of the witness of the Spirit has been forcefully raised in Luby 1984, pp. 232, 301; and Lodahl 1988.

91. Cf. *A Letter to the Rev. Dr. Rutherforth* (28 Mar. 1768), §III.1, *Letters* (Telford), 9:381. Here Wesley has to admit that while we experience the fruits of the Spirit's inspiration inwardly, we must turn to the Bible to determine whence they come!

92. On this point, see Stephen Toulmin, *Cosmopolis: The Hidden Agenda of Modernity* (New York: Free Press, 1990).

93. See Abraham, "Inner Witness of the Spirit," esp. pp. 447-8.

94. While Wesley would not purposefully exclude any of the fruit mentioned in Galatians 5, his characteristic summaries show a marked tendency to focus on love, joy, and peace. A good example is *Journal* (4 Jan. 1739), *Works,* 19:30.

95. For a few examples of Wesley's appropriation of virtue categories, see *An Earnest Appeal to Men of Reason and Religion,* §3, *Works,* 11:45; *Minutes* (2 Aug. 1745), Q. 1, *John Wesley,* p. 152; *A Short Address to the People of Ireland* (1749), §7, *Works,* 9:283; and Sermon 17, "The Circumcision of the Heart," §I.1, *Works,* 1:402-3. With the growing dominance of the "decisionist psychology" championed by many Enlightenment thinkers, later Wesley scholars have often misunderstood (or ignored) this aspect of Wesley. It has been recovered by recent studies, in particular: Heitzenrater 1994, Horst 1985, Lovin 1985, and Steele 1994.

96. Note his identification of true Christian religion with holy tempers in Sermon 30, "Sermon on Mount X," §2, *Works,* 1:651; *NT Notes,* Matt. 23:31; Sermon 84, "The Important Question," §III.2, *Works,* 3:189; and Sermon 91, "On Charity," §III.12, *Works,* 3:306. Cf. Horst 1985, p. 129; and Clapper 1989, pp. 85, 164-5.

97. For one of the clearest examples, see *Journal* (13 Sept. 1739), *Works,* 19:97.

98. Cf. *NT Notes,* 1 Thess. 2:17; and Sermon 100, "On Pleasing All Men," §II.1, *Works,* 3:422. See also the discussion in Clapper 1989, p. 28; and Horst 1985, pp. 138-46.

99. Cf. Horst 1985, pp. 147-78.

100. See esp. *Advice to the People Called 'Methodists',* §6, *Works* 9:124; and *A Farther Appeal to Men of Reason and Religion,* Pt. I, §I.6, *Works,* 11: 107-8.

101. Cf. *Minutes* (16 June 1747), Q. 10, *John Wesley,* p. 167; and Sermon 83, "On Patience," §3, *Works,* 3:171.

102. Note his claim that when God enables us to live in conformity to Christ, God does not destroy any of our affections, but makes them more vigorous, in Sermon 63, "The General Spread of the Gospel," §11, *Works,* 2:489.

103. Geoffrey Wainwright has suggested use of the notion of *habitus* to designate the continuing effect of the Holy Spirit on individual character (1987, p. 21; 1988a, p. 908). This is possible given his apparent definition which avoids overseparation of the Spirit and grace. However, the term *habitus* has been subjected to such a range of meanings in Roman Catholic theology (many suggestive of "created grace") that it seems wiser simply to use Wesley's language of abiding tempers. On *habitus,* see the characteristically broad definition in *Sacramentum Mundi* (New York: Herder, 1969), 3:1-3.

104. *NT Notes,* 2 Peter 3:18.

105. See esp. *A Farther Appeal to Men of Reason and Religion,* Pt. 1, §V.23, *Works,* 11:163-5; and his interview with Bishop Butler (16-18 Aug. 1739) in *Works,* 19:471-4.

106. For a good survey of these outbreaks and Wesley's general concern to avoid real "enthusiasm," see Gunter 1989, pp. 118-37. See also the discussion of Wesley's attempt to control enthusiasm in W.S. Johnson 1988.

107. *A Letter to a Person Lately Joined with the People Called Quakers* (10 Feb. 1748), §2, *Letters* (Telford), 2:117.

108. Sermon 37, "The Nature of Enthusiasm," §20ff, *Works,* 2:53ff. Note also his insistence that the ordinary operations of the Spirit do not overpower our natural

faculties, in Letter to the Editor of *London Magazine* (12 Dec. 1760), *Letters* (Telford), 4:123.

109. Letter to Elizabeth Ritchie (24 Feb. 1786), *Letters* (Telford), 7:319.

110. The best evidence that this is the focal distinction between "ordinary" and "extraordinary" is that it is the criterion he quotes from a tract accusing him of emphasizing extraordinary operations of the Spirit, a charge he then seeks to disprove by showing that he emphasizes only operations of the Spirit available to "all Christians!" See *A Farther Appeal to Men of Reason and Religion*, Pt. I, §V.4, *Works*, 11:141-2: "a distinction is to be made between those passages of Scripture about the blessed Spirit that peculiarly belong to the primitive church, and those that relate to Christians of all ages" (Richard Smalbroke). Note also his distinction between "ordinary" prophets who were trained in schools and "extraordinary" prophets which God called from time to time, in Sermon 121, "Prophets and Priests," §6, *Works*, 4:76-7.

111. Cf., *A Farther Appeal to Men of Reason and Religion*, Pt. I, §V.22-3, *Works*, 11:163-5; Sermon 4, "Scriptural Christianity," §5, *Works*, 1:161; and *A Letter to the Right Reverend the Lord Bishop of Gloucester* (26 Nov 1762), §I.1ff, *Works*, 11:468ff.

112. Note that he defines "prophet" as a foreteller, and "evangelist" as one who preaches the gospel immediately before or after an apostle! *NT Notes*, Eph. 4:11. He develops a different distinction between evangelists and pastors, in an attempt to justify his lay preachers, in Sermon 121, "Prophets and Priests," §7, *Works*, 4:77.

113. E.g., *NT Notes*, 1 Peter 4:10; and Sermon 89, "The More Excellent Way," §1-3, *Works*, 3:263-4.

114. The most ambitious example is Fadiey Lovsky, *Wesley: Apôstre des Foules, Pasteur des Pauvres* (Lausanne: Foi et Victoire, 1977).

115. It includes: Wisdom, insight, counsel, power, knowledge, fear of the Lord, and piety (the last found in the Septuagint and Vulgate, but not the original Hebrew of Isaiah 11:2).

116. He did leave a reference to the seven-fold gifts by Poole in his *OT Notes* comment on Isaiah 11:2. In *NT Notes*, Acts 2:38 he is quick to clarify that the "gift of the Holy Spirit" is not the power of speaking in tongues but "the constant fruits of faith." This point is also involved in his very distinction between extraordinary gifts and ordinary fruit. For a reference by Charles to the seven-fold gifts as what was bestowed on believers at Pentecost, see his hymn "On the Descent of the Holy Ghost at Pentecost," *Poet. Works*, 1:165.

117. Note the sermon "On the Holy Spirit" by John Gambold that he abridged for his own use during his Oxford years which describes "the particular extraordinary gifts vouchsafed to the first ages for the edification of the Church," *Works* (Jackson), 7:514.

118. James Clark, *Montanus Redivivus: or, Montanism revived, in the Principles and Discipline of the Methodists*, (Dublin: Aunders, 1760), originally a 1756 sermon which Wesley was informed of and to which he responded.

119. See Letter to James Clark (3 July 1756), *Letters* (Telford), 3:180-3; and Letter to James Clark (18 Sept. 1756), *Letters* (Telford), 3:200-4.

120. Sermon 4, "Scriptural Christianity," §3, *Works*, 1:160.

121. Cf. Sermon 113 (1778), "The Late Work of God in North America," *Works*, 3:595-608; Sermon 63 (1783), "The General Spread of the Gospel," §17-27, *Works*, 2:493-8; and Sermon 66 (1787), "The Signs of the Times," §II.1, *Works*, 2:525.

122. Note Wesley's *NT Notes* qualification of the command for women to be silent in church in 1 Cor. 14:34: "unless they are under an extraordinary impulse of the

Spirit"! See also his letter to Mary Bosanquet (13 June 1771), *Letters* (Telford), 5:257. On lay male preachers, see *A Letter to a Clergyman* (4 May 1748), *Works*, 9:248-51.

123. See esp. Sermon 89 (1787), "The More Excellent Way," §2, *Works*, 3: 263-4; and Sermon 121 (1789), "Prophets and Priests," §8, *Works*, 4:77.

124. See *Journal* (15 Aug. 1750), *Works*, 20:356-7. Note that the book Wesley is referring to here was written by one who had come under the influence of the "French Prophets."

125. Cf. Snyder 1989, p. 215-6.

126. Howard A. Snyder (with Daniel V. Runyon), *The Divided Flame: Wesleyans and the Charismatic Renewal* (Grand Rapids, MI: Zondervan, 1986), pp. 54-64. The Pentecostal movement would differ from the Charismatic on the last point, for it has tended to institutionalize itself separately, rather than remaining in tension with its parent institutional setting.

127. The definitive study of these connections for Pentecostalism is Donald W. Dayton, *Theological Roots of Pentecostalism* (Grand Rapids, MI: Zondervan, 1987). See also Daniel Brandt-Bessire, *Aux Sources de la Spiritualité Pentecôtiste* (Geneva: Labor et Fides, 1986). On the Charismatic movement, see Lucinda Schmieder, *Geisttaufe: Ein Beitrag zur neueren Glaubensgeschichte* (Paderborn: Ferdinand Schöningh, 1982); and Snyder, *Divided Flame.*

128. Note his comments after attending a meeting of some of the French Prophets in *Journal* (22 June 1739), *Works*, 19:72-3; his denial that he views extravagant behavior as necessarily a sign of the Spirit in *A Letter to Rev. Dr. Rutherforth* (28 Mar. 1768), §III.12, *Works*, 9:381; and his criticism of George Bell (who led a faction out of the Wesleyan Methodists) that Bell valued extraordinary gifts more than the ordinary grace of God, in *Journal* (24 Nov. 1762), *Works*, 21:398-9; and Letter to Ann Bolton (5 Dec. 1772), *Letters* (Telford), 5:349.

129. Cf. *NT Notes*, Acts 2:38, 1 Cor. 14:27; and *A Letter to the Reverend Dr. Conyers Middleton* (4 Jan. 1749), Sec. IV, §VI, *Letters* (Telford), 2:363-8.

130. See the discussion of this issue in connection with entire sanctification in Chapter Seven. One might also check the responses of Methodism to the Charismatic movement in its midst: R. William Davies & Ross Pert, *Methodism and the Charismatic Movement* (London: Dent, 1973); and *Guidelines: The United Methodist Church and the Charismatic Renewal* (Nashville, TN: Discipleship Resources, 1976).

131. Cf. Snyder, *Divided Flame*, pp. 64-5.

132. Cf. A.S. Wood 1977.

133. There are occasional short treatments of Wesley's understanding of the Trinity in general studies of his soteriology (e.g., C. Williams 1960, pp. 93-7). The only focused treatments are Pillow 1986 and Wainwright 1990 (much the better of the two). Charles' understanding of the Trinity has received more thorough attention in Quantrille 1989 (see also Bryant 1990). Jonathan Sinclair Carey's "Wesley, Methodism and the Unitarians" (*Faith and Freedom* 45 [1992]:102-12) is actually a puzzlement over why New England Congregationalists and Unitarians paid so little attention to Methodism, which might have balanced their rationalism.

134. The best example is William Warburton's *The Doctrine of Grace: or, the Office and Operation of the Holy Spirit vindicated from the insults of infidelity and the abuse of fanaticism* (1762), to which Wesley replied in *A Letter to the Right Reverend the Lord Bishop of Gloucester* (26 Nov. 1762), *Works*, 11:467-538. See also his reply to Thomas Dockwray's *The Operations of the Holy Spirit Imperceptible, and How Men may Know when they are under the Guidance and Influence of the Spirit* (1743) in *A Farther Appeal to Men of Reason and Religion*, Pt. I, §V, *Works*, 11:138-76.

135. The best recent overall survey and analysis of the doctrine of the Holy Spirit is Yves M. J. Congar, *I Believe in the Holy Spirit,* 3 vols. (New York: Seabury, 1983). On Roman Catholicism, see 1:151ff. On Protestantism see also Alasdair I. C. Heron, *The Holy Spirit* (Philadelphia, PA: Westminster, 1983), pp. 99-117.

136. On Cannon's (Protestant) reading, Wesley treats the Spirit as only the continuing inspiration of Christ (1946, p. 214). I agree with Lessmann (1987, p. 134) that this is too narrow a reading of Wesley's convictions about the Spirit.

137. Surveyed in Nuttall, *Holy Spirit in Puritan Faith.*

138. The most vigorous Eastern critique of the *filioque* can be found in Vladimir Lossky, "The Procession of the Holy Spirit in Orthodox Trinitarian Doctrine," in *In the Image and Likeness of God* (Crestwood, NY: St. Vladimir's Seminary Press, 1974), pp. 71-96. See also Staniloae, *Orthodoxe Dogmatik,* 1:283. For a survey of recent debate on the issue, see Congar, *Holy Spirit,* Vol. 3.

139. Cf. Anglican Article V (Wesley #IV) in Oden 1988, p. 113. Wesley also retains the phrase in *A Collection of Forms of Prayer,* Sunday Morning, *Works* (Jackson), 11:203. The clearest reference in his own words is in *NT Notes,* John 15:26. One might note, however, David Tripp's argument that Wesley is here more concerned to distinguish the temporal missions and eternal procession of the Spirit than to affirm the *filioque,* in "The Ecumenical Creed—A Time for Initiative," *Doxology* 8 (1991):37-44, p. 43.

140. The coordination of Pneumatology and Christology in Wesley is often noted, e.g.: Outler 1988, p. 8; Stuart 1974, p. 167; and A.S. Wood 1977, p. 26.

141. Cf. *A Letter to a Roman Catholic,* §8, *John Wesley,* p. 495. Concerning Wesley's dependence on Pearson, see note 24 above. Pearson had included discussion of the *filioque* (*Exposition of the Creed,* pp. 323ff), though he argued that East and West really differ only in expression, not fundamental commitments (p. 325).

142. For analysis of Anglican awareness of and attitudes to contemporary Eastern Orthodoxy just prior to Wesley, see Christopher Knight, "'People so Beset with Saints': Anglican Attitudes to Orthodoxy, 1555-1725," *Sobornost* 10.2 (1988):25-36.

143. Donald Dayton has argued thus (1986, p. 139), as has David Tripp ("Ecumenical Creed"). William Cannon's argument to the contrary (1968, pp. 441-2) appears to reverse the positions of East and West!

144. See in this regard Charles' verse on the witness of the Spirit: "Come quickly from above and bring the Father down, infuse the perfect love, make all the Godhead known," in *Hymns of Petition and Thanksgiving for the Promise of the Father,* #11, st. 5, *Poet. Works,* 4:178-9.

145. For general reflections on these differences, see Congar, *Holy Spirit,* 3:xvff; and Heron, *Holy Spirit,* pp. 83-6, 90-4.

146. See *Survey,* 5:187-93. Another good example that would have influenced Wesley is Pearson, *Exposition of the Creed,* pp. 32ff, then p. 321. For an analysis of this typical Western pattern, see Karl Rahner, *The Trinity* (New York: Herder, 1970).

147. *A Letter to a Roman Catholic,* §6, *John Wesley,* p. 494. He proceeds in §7 to affirm that the Son is truly God, and in §8 to affirm the same of the Spirit. He never explicitly uses the Trinitarian language of three persons in one essence but the implicit trinitarian claim is clear.

148. See his comments about his abstract of Browne's discussion of the Trinity, which he had sent, in his Letter to Miss March (3 Aug. 1771), *Letters* (Telford), 5:270. Whether Browne discards the distinctness of the "persons" as easily as Wesley charges is debatable; cf. *Survey,* 5:188.

149. *NT Notes,* John 8:19.

150. Cf. Wainwright 1990, p. 40.

151. For an insightful Eastern Orthodox development of the connections between a communal view of God and a communal anthropology, see Zizioulas, *Being as Communion.* For argument of a parallel in Wesley, see Bryant 1992a, pp. 13-14.

152. Cf. Staples 1986, p. 92; and Starkey 1962, pp. 30-1.

153. *NT Notes,* 1 John 5:8. Wesley followed Bengelius in arguing that this verse was authentic (see also Sermon 55, "On the Trinity," 5, *Works,* 2:378-9).

154. Note his use of an equation of "power" and "nature" to unite the Father and the Son in *NT Notes,* John 10:30. He stresses that one thereby preserves the plurality of persons and unity of nature.

155. Cf. Pillow 1986, p. 7; and Starkey 1962, p. 31. For a similar claim about Charles, see Quantrille 1989, pp. 122-9.

156. Sermon 55, "On the Trinity," §17, *Works,* 2:384.

157. Sermon 55, "On the Trinity," §3, *Works,* 2:376-7. For a possible explanation of this distinction, see Maddox 1992a, p. 72. Note also his willingness to admit that there are occasional instances of true piety among those with erroneous understandings of the Trinity, in his preface to "An Extract from the Life of Mr. Thomas Firmin," *AM* 9 (1786), *Works* (Jackson), 14:293.

158. Outler notes (*Works,* 2:373) at least 23 recorded instances of Wesley preaching on the text of his written sermon on the Trinity, which presumably would have been on the same topic.

159. See the analysis in Tripp 1990, p. 59. For a few examples, see *NT Notes,* Matt. 6:13, Luke 4:18, and Acts 10:48.

160. See Letter to Mary Bishop (17 April 1776), *Letters* (Telford), 6:213. *Hymns on the Trinity* can be found in *Poet. Works,* 7:201-346.

161. Cf. Sermon 55, "On the Trinity," §17, *Works,* 2:384. Note also that the work on the Trinity that Wesley particularly valued (William Jones, *The Catholic Doctrine of the Trinity,* 1754) had been written to reject the Arian suggestions of Samuel Clarke; cf. Letter to Mary Bishop (17 Apr. 1776), *Letters* (Telford), 6:213. Cf. the discussion in Wainwright 1990.

162. On the formative role of doctrinal convictions, see Maddox 1992a, pp. 73-4.

163. In this, I am rejecting Stuart's claim that the doctrine of the Trinity is primarily an expression of the formative influence of Wesley's experience on his theology (1974, p. 3). Wesley drew on the Trinity more to norm experience than vice-versa.

164. Hymn #7, *Works,* 7:88. Recall also the discussion of the reflexive nature of God-knowledge in Chapter Two.

165. For Wesley's use of "practical atheism," see Sermon 23, "Sermon on the Mount III," §I.11, *Works,* 1:517. On the general idea of practical unitarianism, see H. Richard Niebuhr, "Theological Unitarianisms," *Theology Today* 40 (1983-4):150-7; and Nikos A. Nissiotis, "The Importance of the Doctrine of the Trinity for Church Life and Theology," in *The Orthodox Ethos,* pp. 32-69, edited by A.J. Philippou (Oxford: Holywell Press, 1964), pp. 35-7. Concern about such practical unitarianism may be reflected in Wesley's criticism of Thomas Maxfield for praying to the Son of God only, or more than to God/Father; cf. *Journal* (29 Oct. 1762), *Works,* 21:397.

166. E.g., Sermon 29, "Sermon on the Mount IX," §29, *Works,* 1:649; Sermon 76, "On Perfection," §III.7, *Works,* 3:85; Sermon 120, "The Unity of the Divine Being," §24, *Works,* 4:71; *A Collection of Forms of Prayer,* Thursday Evening, *Works* (Jackson), 11:226; and *Devotions for Every Day,* Office for a Family, Gill, p. 94. Of course, Wesley recognized that all three "Persons" were ultimately involved in every action of God; cf. Sermon 77, "Spiritual Worship," *Works,* 3:89-102; and *NT Notes,* John 16:13.

167. Since John valued Charles' hymns so highly for drawing out the implications of the Trinity, consider one of them as an example of this creative tension: "Father in whom we live, in whom we are, and move; the glory, power, and praise receive of thy creating love. . . . Incarnate Deity, let all the ransomed race render in thanks their lives to thee, for thy redeeming grace. . . . Spirit of Holiness, let all thy saints adore thy sacred energy, and bless thy heart-renewing power." *Hymns for Those Who Seek and Those Who have Redemption in the Blood of Jesus Christ* (1747), #34, st. 1-3, *Poet. Works,* 4:254-5. See also the comments on Wesley's trinitarian ethics in Hynson 1984, pp. 109-10.

Chapter Six

1. E.g., Gustafson 1968, pp. 79-82; and Dicker 1971, p. 94. Contrast the rebuttal in Gallaway 1988, pp. 44-5.

2. Particularly helpful surveys and analyses of the issues arising in the "Western" reading of Wesley's soteriology are Cannon 1946, Lindström 1946, and C. Williams 1960.

3. Outler 1976, pp. 29-30. For a very similar evaluation of Charles' soteriology, see J.R. Tyson 1986, pp. 57-70; and Brian Frost, *Living in the Tension Between East and West* (London: New World Publications, 1984), pp. 38ff.

4. In this regard, see the perceptive comments of Jaroslav Pelikan on the differences between East and West in "Orthodox Theology in the West: The Reformation," in *The Legacy of St. Vladimir,* ed. John Breck, et al. (Crestwood, NY: St. Vladimir's Seminary Press, 1990), pp. 159-65. Recall as well the references in Chapter 3, note 3.

5. Cf. the discussion of the emergence of the doctrine of infused grace and the Lutheran critique of it in Reinhold Seeburg, *The History of Doctrine* (Grand Rapids, MI: Baker, 1977), 2:114-23, 160-1, 202, 240-1, and 433-4.

6. One of the most developed Eastern discussions of justification is Staniloae, *Orthodoxe Dogmatik,* 1:233ff. Note as well, however, his emphasis (against the West) that justification is only one aspect of salvation, in Ibid., 2:253-79. See also the graphic contrast of East and West in Meyendorff, *Byzantine Theology,* p. 146.

7. Note the echoes of this charge in even sympathetic treatments like Jouko Martikainen, "Man's Salvation: Deification or Justification?" *Sobornost* 7.3 (1976):180-92; and William G. Rusch, "How the Eastern Fathers Understood What the Western Church Meant by Justification," in *Justification by Faith,* edited by H.G. Anderson, et al. (Minneapolis, MN: Augsburg, 1985), pp. 131-42. For more positive Lutheran readings see Tuomo Mannermaa, *Der im Glauben Gegenwärtige Christus: Rechtfertigung und Vergottung zum ökumenischen Dialog* (Hannover: Luther Verlagshaus, 1989); and Simo Peura and Antti Raunio, eds., *Luther und Theosis: Vergöttlichung als Thema der abendländischen Theologie* (Helsinki: Luther-Agricola Gesellschaft, 1990). For a provocative attempt to champion Calvin as one who broke out of the Western paradigm by emphasizing participation in Christ as the essence of salvation, see Hart, "Humankind in Christ and Christ in Humankind."

8. Cf. Lossky, *Mystical Theology,* pp. 197ff.

9. Sermon 43, "The Scripture Way of Salvation," §I.1, *Works,* 2:156. Outler notes that this sermon has the most extensive history of oral preaching behind it of any of the written sermons (1985d, p. 155); thus he recommends it as the best single essay by which to judge Wesley's soteriology (1964a, p. 271).

10. "Thoughts Concerning Gospel Ministers," *AM* 7 (1784): 550-3, *Works* (Jackson), 10:455-6.

11. *Minutes* (13 May 1746), Q. 3, *John Wesley*, p. 159.

12. E.g., *NT Notes*, Titus 3:5; and Sermon 20, "The Lord Our Righteousness," §II.17, *Works*, 1:461. Note also Charles' variation in his poem on 1 Cor. 2:12: "God to man hath freely given. . . . Forgiveness, holiness, and heaven" (*Poetry*, 2:460).

13. See respectively: *Hymns and Sacred Poems* (1740), Preface, §4, *Works* (Jackson), 14:323; *Plain Account of the People Called Methodists*, §I.2, *Works*, 9:255; and *NT Notes*, 1 Peter 1:9.

14. *Journal* (24 May 1738), 14, *Works*, 18:250.

15. For a survey of the various ways that Aldersgate has been interpreted, including some who argue that Wesley's initial claim was only for his justification, not full therapeutic deliverance from sin, see Maddox, "Aldersgate: A Tradition History," in *Aldersgate Reconsidered*, pp. 133-46.

16. See his extended account of the events leading up to Aldersgate, including the claims of Böhler (§11), in *Journal* (24 May 1738), *Works*, 18:242-50.

17. Ibid, §13 (p. 249). Wesley's description of "opening up" to these verses suggests his occasional practice of bibliomancy; if so, he would have taken these verses as divinely intended for him. 2 Peter 1:4 was a common text used by early Greek writers to stress the therapeutic recovery of the Image of God. Wesley understands it this way too in his *NT Notes*, so it was almost certainly this emphasis that struck him that morning. I emphasize the verb "be" because Wesley's *Journal* translation follows the King James Version at this point. In his own translation later in the *NT Notes* he renders this as a promise that we may *become* partakers of the divine nature. This translation reflects Wesley's later rejection of the expectation of instantaneous entire sanctification!

18. Ibid. Wesley understood redemption (like salvation) to include more than forgiveness; it involves renewal of the person in Christ-likeness.

19. It is important to note that it was indeed Luther's "Preface" to the Epistle of Romans that was read that night, not his later *Commentary on Romans*; cf. John T. McNeill, "Luther at Aldersgate," *LQHR* 164 [sixth series, 8] (1939):200-17. The theme of God's grace empowering our recovery of Christ-likeness is central to the early part of this Preface; cf. *Works of Martin Luther*, 6:449-51.

20. *Journal* (6 June 1738), *Works*, 18:254.

21. The best analysis of this developing distinction is Heitzenrater 1989, pp. 106-49.

22. See in this regard the 1765 *Minutes*, Q. 26, *Minutes* (Mason), pp. 51-2. "In 1729, my brother and I read the Bible; saw inward and outward holiness therein; followed after it, and incited others so to do. In 1737 we saw, 'This holiness comes by faith.' In 1738 we saw, 'We must be justified before we are sanctified.' But still holiness was our point, inward and outward holiness."

23. To cite just three examples from the different periods of his theological work: Sermon 101 (1735), "The Trouble and Rest of Good Men," Proem, *Works*, 3:533; *Plain Account of Genuine Christianity* (1749), §III.10, *John Wesley*, p. 195; and Sermon 69 (1784), "The Imperfection of Human Knowledge," §II.8, *Works*, 2:581. Note also the affirmation of therapeutic nature of Wesley's understanding of salvation in D. Dayton 1986, p. 142 [251]; and Lindström 1946, p. 43. Obviously, I find incredible the claim of Blake Neff (1982, pp. 82-3) that Wesley avoided healing terminology for sanctification. The literary method of Neff's study is quite suspect.

24. *The Doctrine of Original Sin*, Preface, §4, *Works* (Jackson), 11:194; and Sermon 44, "Original Sin," §III.3, *Works*, 2:184. For one of the best examples of the same emphasis in Charles see *Poetry*, 3:167.

25. *A Farther Appeal to Men of Reason and Religion*, §Pt. I, 3, *Works*, 11:106 (emphasis added). For a few other examples from various periods see: Letter to Richard Morgan, Sen. (15 Jan. 1734), *Works*, 25:369; Sermon 12 (1746), "The Witness of Our Spirit," §16, *Works*, 1:310; Sermon 44 (1759), "Original Sin," §III.5, *Works*, 2:185; and Sermon 62 (1781), "The End of Christ's Coming," §III.5, *Works*, 2:482.

26. Cf. *Oxford English Dictionary* (2nd ed., 1989), 3:868.

27. For the emphasis that true religion must find expression in actual love of God and others, see *An Earnest Appeal to Men of Reason and Religion*, §2-3, *Works*, 11:45; and Sermon 120, "The Unity of the Divine Being," §16, *Works*, 4:66-7. For a call to recover a more caring relationship to brute creation, see Sermon 60, "The General Deliverance," §1 & §III.10, *Works*, 2:437, 449; Sermon 95, "On the Education of Children," §25, *Works*, 3:360; and the letter he includes in his *Journal* (16 July 1756), *Works*, 21:68-9.

28. The strong connection between our holiness and our happiness can be found throughout Wesley's works. Outler finds it in at least thirty sermons (1984, p. 35 fn28). For particularly clear examples from both ends of his career, see his Letter to Mary Pendarves (19 July 1731), *Works*, 25:293; and Sermon 60 (1782), "The General Deliverance," §I.2, *Works*, 2:439.

29. Outler 1971b, p. 10.

30. Cf. the discussions of deification of the flesh in Timothy Ware, *The Orthodox Church* (New York: Penquin, 1984), p. 238; and Georgios I. Mantzaridis, *The Deification of Man* (Crestwood, NY: St. Vladimir's Seminary Press, 1984).

31. Baker's *Union Catalog* lists three pages (76-8) of editions and republications. See also George S. Rousseau, "John Wesley's *Primitive Physick* (1747)," *Harvard Library Bulletin* 16 (1968):242-56. Wesley had earlier published the much briefer *A Collection of Receits for the Use of the Poor* (Bristol: Farley, 1745; description in Green, *Bibliography*, pp. 38-9).

32. For helpful comparative analyses of Wesley's remedies, see: Eunice Bonow Bardell, "*Primitive Physick*: John Wesley's Receipts," *Pharmacy in History* 21 (1979):111-21; Clifford W. Callaway, "John Wesley's *Primitive Physick*: An Essay in Appreciation," *Proceedings of the Mayo Clinic* 49 (1974):318-24; John Cule, "The Rev. John Wesley, M.A., 1703-1791: 'The Naked Empiricist' and Orthodox Medicine," *Journal of the History of Medicine and Allied Sciences* 45 (1990):41-63; A. Wesley Hill, *John Wesley Among the Physicians* (London: Epworth, 1958); Lester S. King, *The Medical World of the Eighteenth Century* (Chicago, IL: University of Chicago, 1958), pp. 34-39; and Samuel J. Rogal, "Pills for the Poor: John Wesley's *Primitive Physick*," *Yale Journal of Biology and Medicine* 51 (1978):81-90. For his specific interest in electricity, see *The Desideratum; or, Electricity Made Plain and Useful* (London: W. Flexney, 1760; reprint, Nashville, TN: United Methodist Publishing House, 1992); *Journal* (4 Jan. 1768), *Works*, 22:117; and Samuel J. Rogal, "Electricity: John Wesley's 'Curious and Important Subject'," *Eighteenth-Century Life* 13 (1989):79-90.

33. *Primitive Physick*, Preface, §8-14, *Works* (Jackson), 14:310-12. Cf. Letter to 'John Smith' (25 March 1747), §11, *Works*, 26:235. Wesley's derogatory comments on "professional" physicians helps explain the fervor of the response from the physician William Hawes: *An Examination of the Revd. Mr. John Wesley's Primitive Physick* (London, 1776).

34. Cf. *Primitive Physick*, Preface, §1-3, *Works* (Jackson), 14:307-8.

35. Cf. Letter to Alexander Knox (26 Oct. 1778), *Letters* (Telford), 6:328; and Letter to Lady Maxwell (5 July 1765), *Letters* (Telford), 4:309.

36. See *Primitive Physick*, Preface, §16, *Works* (Jackson), 14:314-16; and the helpful secondary studies of Philip Ott. Wesley's primary source for this emphasis was George Cheyne, whose *Essay of Health and Long Life* (1724) he read the year of its publication (cf. Letter to Susanna Wesley [1 Nov. 1724], *Works*, 25:151). He also republished extracts dealing with this theme from Samuel Tissot and William Cadogan (cf. the prefaces reprinted in *Works* [Jackson], 14:254-9, 265-9).

37. For a couple of the numerous examples of Wesley's report of directly answered prayers for healing, see *Journal* (12 Nov. 1746), *Works*, 20:145; and *Journal* (22 Sept.-3 Oct. 1756), *Works*, 21:78. On the importance of prayer in support of medical treatments, see *Advices with Respect to Health*, Preface, §9, *Works* (Jackson), 14:258; and Letter to Robert Carr Brackenbury (13 Feb. 1784), *Letters* (Telford), 7:209. Implicit in the latter type of prayer is Wesley's admonition (quoting Ecclesiasticus 38:1-2), "Honor the physician, for God hath appointed him," *Journal* (30 Sept. 1786), *Journal* (Curnock), 7:212.

38. One source of this insistence was another book by George Cheyne, *Natural Method of Curing the Diseases of the Body and the Disorders of the Mind Depending on the Body* (1742), which Wesley again read shortly after publication (*Journal* [12 Mar. 1742], *Works*, 19:256-7). See also the *Journal* account where he argues that this interconnection means that no one can be a complete physician who is not a Christian, or willing to draw upon the help of Christian ministers; *Journal* (12 May 1759), *Works*, 21:191.

39. *Primitive Physick*, Preface, §16, VI, *Works* (Jackson), 14:316.

40. See again the Letter to Alexander Knox (26 Oct. 1778), *Letters* (Telford), 6:327. For a clear recognition that there are much greater limits to our physical healing than our spiritual healing *in this life*, see Sermon 62, "The End of Christ's Coming," §III.1-4, *Works*, 2:480-82.

41. For two of the strongest statements, see Sermon 1, "Salvation by Faith," §1-3, *Works*, 1:117-8; and *A Farther Appeal to Men of Reason and Religion*, Pt. I, §I.6, *Works*, 11:107-8. See also his interchange with William Law over whether Law recognized the necessity of grace to enable obedient living (series of letters in *Works*, 25:540-50).

42. E.g., Wesley's strong statement of resistible grace in Sermon 110, "Free Grace" (§22, *Works*, 3:554) was written in 1739! See the discussion of the co-operant nature of grace in Chapter Three.

43. *Works*, 3:199-209.

44. Cf. Sermon 127, "On The Wedding Garment," §19, *Works*, 4:148.

45. Sermon 63, "The General Spread of the Gospel," §12, *Works*, 2:490; and Sermon 85, "On Working Out Our Own Salvation," §III.7, *Works*, 3:208. Compare Wesley's biting criticism of Augustine in Sermon 68, "The Wisdom of God's Counsels," §9, *Works*, 2:556.

46. Cf. the discussion in C. FitzSimons Allison, *The Rise of Moralism* (Wilton, CT: Morehouse Barlow, 1966); Cannon 1946, pp. 32-43, 85-88; Outler 1984, p. 187 fn38; and Clifford 1990.

47. Robert Tuttle has argued that Wesley's views on these issues went through the phases of a dialectic: thesis (pre-1738)—faith initiated by inward and outward works; antithesis (1738-64)—faith initiated solely by God's grace; and synthesis (post-1764)—faith initiated by grace and confirmed by works (Tuttle 1969, pp. 409-10; 1978, p. 334 fn10). Such a sharp distinction is rightly criticized by J.H. Tyson 1991. However, I find the more nuanced transitional readings of Fujimoto 1986 and

Gunter 1989 (pp. 67-117) to be warranted. Further documentation for the following summary can be found in their works.

48. See esp. his retrospective reflections in *Journal* (25 Jan. 1738), *Works*, 18:212 fn95.

49. The best example is his 1733 Sermon 17, "The Circumcision of the Heart," §I.3, *Works*, 1:403.

50. Note his 1738 publication of *The Doctrine of Salvation, Faith, and Good Works*, an abstract from the *Homilies* (*John Wesley*, pp. 123-33). For other appeals to various Anglican standards in defense of Justification by Faith, see *A Farther Appeal to Men of Reason and Religion*, Pt. I, §II.4, *Works*, 11:111; and *A Letter to the Rev. Mr. Horne* (1761), §I.6-10, *Works*, 11:445-9. For the classification of justification by faith as the fundamental doctrine of Anglicanism, see his feisty 1741 Sermon 150, "Hypocrisy in Oxford," §I.5, *Works*, 4:395.

51. See esp. *Journal* (13 Sept. 1739), *Works*, 19:96; *The Principles of a Methodist*, §2, *Works*, 9:50-1; Sermon 5, "Justification by Faith," §III.2, *Works*, 1:191; Sermon 110, "Free Grace," §3, *Works*, 3:545; and Sermon 150, "Hypocrisy in Oxford," §I.7, *Works*, 4:396-7.

52. Cf. *Journal* (31 Dec. 1739), *Works*, 19:132-3; and Letter to Count Zinzendorf and the Church at Herrnhut (5-8 Aug. 1740), *Works*, 26:27. Note also his dismay over Luther's comments on "good works" in his 1531 *Commentary on the Epistle to the Galatians* (Luther at his most polemical!), in *Journal* (15 June 1741), *Works*, 19:201.

53. Cf. *Minutes* (25 June 1744), Q. 3, *John Wesley*, p. 137; *Minutes* (1 Aug. 1745), Q. 2, *John Wesley*, p. 148; and *A Farther Appeal to Men of Reason and Religion*, Pt. I, §II.11, *Works*, 11:117.

54. Some modern interpreters have agreed that Wesley was hereby totally abandoning the Protestant view of justification by faith. The strongest such claims are in Koerber 1967 (a Roman Catholic scholar, who approves of the change); George Tavard, *Justification: An Ecumenical Study* (New York: Paulist, 1983), pp. 84-92 (a Lutheran who laments the change); and K. Kim 1992, pp. 32, 42 (a Reformed scholar who also laments it). For arguments that Wesley remained within a broadly Protestant view, see Lindström 1946, pp. 93-8; C. Williams 1960, pp. 57ff; and Blaising 1979, pp. 275, 309-10 fn214. See also the discussion of repentance in Chapter Seven.

55. Compare *An Earnest Appeal to Men of Reason and Religion*, §9, *Works*, 11:47-8; with Letter to Richard Hart (11 July 1763), *Letters* (Telford), 4:220.

56. For progressive steps in this direction, see *Minutes* (1745), Qq. 7-8, *John Wesley*, pp. 149-50; *NT Notes*, Acts 10:4; *Minutes* (1770), Q. 23, *Minutes* (Mason), p. 96 (also as "Large Minutes," Q. 77, *Works* [Jackson], 8:337); and his deletion of Anglican Article XIII from the Articles of Religion (Oden 1988, p. 116). See also Maddox 1992b.

57. Cf. *Some Remarks on Mr. Hill's "Review of all the Doctrines Taught by Mr. John Wesley"*, §7, pt. 5, *Works* (Jackson), 10:379; and "Thoughts on Salvation by Faith," *AM* 2 (1779):119-23, *Works* (Jackson), 11:492-6.

58. Note that in his manifesto on "Salvation by Faith" (where he had initially rejected any good works *prior* to faith) he makes a central point that his affirmation of justification by faith is not opposed to good works and holiness but productive of them; Sermon 1, §III.1, *Works*, 1:125.

59. Cf. Letter to Mary Bishop (18 Oct. 1778), *Letters* (Telford), 6:326; and Sermon 99, "The Reward of Righteousness," §I.3, *Works*, 3:430.

60. Cf. *NT Notes*, Eph. 2:5; and his Preface to the reprint of *The Whole Duty of Man* in *Chr. Library* (1751), 21:5, *Works* (Jackson), 14:231. Cf. the comparison of Wesley's

disavowal of meritorious works and Marx's distinction between authentic and alienated works in Runyon 1981, pp. 22ff; and Míguez Bonino 1983e, p. 249 [20-1].

61. Cf. *A Blow at the Root: or, Christ Stabbed in the House of His Friends, John Wesley*, pp. 378-83; and *Thoughts on the Imputed Righteousness of Christ, Works* (Jackson), 10:312-15. See also the survey of this debate in Lawson 1974, pp. 243-338.

62. E.g., *Minutes* (25 June 1744), Qq. 11-13, *John Wesley*, p. 138; Letter to Dorothy Furly (19 Oct. 1759), *Letters* (Telford), 4:71; and Sermon 43, "The Scripture Way of Salvation," §III.5, *Works*, 2:164.

63. Cf. Fujimoto 1986, p. 4.

64. E.g., Letter from 'John Smith,' (May 1745), §1, *Works*, 26:143.

65. Two of the latest strong responses are: Letter to John Newton (14 May 1765), *Letters* (Telford), 4:298; and *Some Remarks on 'A Defense of the Preface to the Edinburgh Edition of Aspasio Vindicated'* (1766), §3, *Works* (Jackson), 10:349.

66. Note his conclusion that one need not affirm justification by faith to be a Christian, they need only fear God and work righteousness; in *Journal* (1 Dec. 1767), *Works*, 22:114. After this point, affirmations of the doctrine of justification by faith are more muted and tied directly to his concern for holiness; e.g. Sermon 127, "On the Wedding Garment," §18, *Works*, 4:147-8.

67. Cf. *The Principles of a Methodist*, §5-7, *Works*, 9:51-2; *A Letter to the Rev. Mr. Horne* (1761), §I.8, *Works*, 11:448; and *Some Remarks on Mr. Hill's 'Review of all the Doctrines Taught by Mr. John Wesley'*, §12, sec. XVII, *Works* (Jackson), 10:393.

68. E.g., *A Farther Appeal to Men of Reason and Religion*, Pt. I, §I.6, *Works*, 11:108.

69. For further arguments to this effect, see Pucelik 1963, pp. 27-9; and Klaiber 1991.

70. See esp. *A Letter to the Rev. Mr. Horne* (1761), §II.3, *Works*, 11:453. See also the comparison of this theme to Eastern Orthodoxy in Wainwright 1987, pp. 10-11.

71. *Minutes* (1770), Q. 23, *Minutes* (Mason), p. 96 (also as "Large Minutes," Q. 77, *Works* [Jackson], 8:337).

72. See Wesley's own comments to this effect in his 1790 (!) Sermon 127, "On the Wedding Garment," §18, *Works*, 4:147-8.

73. Outler 1976, p. 14. See also the similar judgment in Crow 1964 (summarized in 1966).

74. See esp. *Predestination Calmly Considered*, §68-79, *John Wesley*, pp. 458-68; and his frequent comments to this effect on biblical passages in *NT Notes* (e.g., Matt. 18:34, John 6:70, and 1 Cor. 9:27). For Charles' agreement, see *Scripture Hymns* (1742), 3 John 11, *Poet. Works*, 13:215. Note how difficult it is to appreciate Wesley's point from a Reformed perspective in Alan P.F. Sell, *The Great Debate: Calvinism, Arminianism and Salvation* (Grand Rapids, MI: Baker, 1982), p. 75.

75. For suggestions of the possibility of an irremissible state, see *Journal* (24 Aug. 1743), *Works*, 19:333; and Letter to Thomas Olivers (24 Mar. 1757), *Letters* (Telford), 3:213. For later rejections of such a state, see Letter to Elizabeth Hardy (26 Dec. 1761), *Letters* (Telford), 4:167; *Farther Thoughts Upon Christian Perfection* (1763), Q. 30, *Works* (Jackson), 11:426; and Letter to Charles Wesley (27 Jan. 1767), *Letters* (Telford), 5:38.

76. Cf. Staniloae, *Orthodoxe Dogmatik*, 2:260ff. Recall the suggestion that the very desire for instant perfection is the essence of sin in Chrestou, *Partakers of God*, pp. 23-4.

77. Of the Western traditions, Lutheranism has been most uncomfortable with any talk of gradual growth or progress in the Christian life; cf. Gilbert Meilaender,

"The Place of Ethics in the Theological Task," *Currents in Theology and Mission* 6 (1979):196-203.

78. E.g., *The Principles of a Methodist*, §18 & §25, *Works*, 9:57, 60.

79. Note especially *A Letter to the Author of 'The Enthusiasm of Methodists and Papists Compared'* (1750), §19, *Works*, 11:368-9.

80. See his *Dictionary* definition and *NT Notes*, Matt 18:3, Acts 3:19.

81. See the comment on God creating in six days, rather than instantaneously, that Wesley retained in *OT Notes*, Genesis 1:2. Cf. Letter to Dr. John Robertson (24 Sept. 1753), *Works*, 26:518; and Naglee 1991, p. 161.

82. Cf. *Hymns and Sacred Poems* (1740), Preface, §9, *Works* (Jackson), 14:326; *A Farther Appeal to Men of Reason and Religion*, Pt. I, §I.4, *Works*, 11:107; *Minutes* (26 June 1744), Q.2, *John Wesley*, p. 140; and Sermon 85, "On Working Out Our Own Salvation," §II.1, *Works*, 3:203-4.

83. E.g., Sermon 40, "Christian Perfection," §II.1, *Works*, 2:105; Letter to Joseph Benson (16 March 1771), *Letters* (Telford), 5:229; and *Journal* (5 June 1772), *Works*, 22:337.

84. Cf. Sermon 40, "Christian Perfection," §I.9, *Works*, 2:104-5; *NT Notes*, Luke 2:52; and Sermon 106, "On Faith," §II.5, *Works*, 3:501.

85. *Farther Thoughts Upon Christian Perfection*, Q. 29, *Works* (Jackson), 11:426. But compare the discussion of Glorification in Chapter Seven.

86. E.g., *NT Notes*, 2 Peter 3:18.

87. Cf. Letter to John Trembath (17 Aug. 1760), *Letters* (Telford), 4:103; and Letter to Elizabeth Ritchie (19 Jan. 1782), *Letters* (Telford), 7:103. Note as well, however, his pastoral sensitivity in recognizing that our growth in grace may not always be immediately evident, in Letter to Philothea Briggs (23 July 1772), *Letters* (Telford), 5:331.

88. Note his description of the step-by-step process of falling into sin in Sermon 19, "The Great Privilege of Those That are Born of God," §II.7-9, *Works*, 1:439-40. I am not as convinced as Wainwright (1988a, pp. 902-3) that Wesley sees the ins and outs of Christian life too instantaneously.

89. Cf. *A Farther Appeal to Men of Reason and Religion*, Pt. I, §I.5, *Works*, 11:107.

90. Cf. "Thoughts on Christian Perfection," Q. 28, *John Wesley*, p. 294; *A Plain Account of Christian Perfection*, §26, *Works* (Jackson), 11:442-3; and (using the circumstance/substance distinction) *Minutes* (1768), Q. 23, *Minutes* (Mason), pp. 80-1 (also as "Large Minutes," Q. 56, *Works* [Jackson], 8:328-9).

91. This distinction was added to his *NT Notes* comment on Acts 5:31 in the third edition (1760-2).

92. E.g., Letter to Charles Wesley (27 Jan. 1767), *Letters* (Telford), 5:39; and Letter to Ann Loxdale (12 July 1782), *Letters* (Telford), 7:129. The emphasis is in the original.

93. Cf. Hillman 1978, p. 388; and the related argument in Robert R. Drovdahl, "Myth of Becoming, Myth of Being," *Christian Education Journal* 13 (1992): 25-32.

94. On justification, see *Hymns and Sacred Poems* (1740) Preface, §9, *Works* (Jackson), 14:326; and Letter to 'John Smith' (30 Dec. 1745), §12, *Works*, 26:180. On sanctification see note 84 above.

95. Cf. *Journal* (15 Sept. 1762), *Works*, 21:389; *Minutes* (1768), Q. 23, *Minutes* (Mason), p. 81 (also as "Large Minutes," Q. 56, *Works* [Jackson], 8:329); Letter to John Mason (10 Jan 1774), *Letters* (Telford), 6:66; and Letter to Freeborn Garrettson (26 June 1785), *Letters* (Telford), 7:276.

96. Sermon 106, "On Faith," §I.12, *Works*, 3:497-8. Recall the discussion of this topic in Chapter Five.

97. See the classic expression of this integral connection in Sermon 85, "On Working Out Our Own Salvation," §II.1, *Works*, 3:204.

98. E.g., Letter to 'John Smith' (30 Dec. 1745), §12, *Works*, 26:180; and Sermon 43, "The Scripture Way of Salvation," §III.18, *Works*, 2:168-9.

99. Note in this regard Holland 1971. While Holland's use of terms is not always faithful to Wesley (cf. Heitzenrater 1989, p. 254 fn195) he does capture the general transition in John's model of conversion. See also Maddox, "Continuing the Conversation."

100. The language of a "twice-born" model of conversion was popularized by William James in *The Varieties of Religious Experience* (New York: Modern Library, 1902). He contrasted the former with a "once-born" model. James' own discussion of these models intertwined two significantly different comparisons. At times he appears to suggest that the contrast is one between the "sick soul" who needs a significant spiritual renewal and the "healthy soul" who does not. More often he makes clear that all religious persons have undergone spiritual renewal, and that the difference is between those for whom this transformation was gradual (once-born) and those for whom it involved a dramatic and memorable reorientation (twice-born). His basic argument is that these differences are a function of variant personality features and that both types of conversion can be effective in producing saintly persons. To make clear that I am rejecting James' first apparent comparison, I will refer to the "gradualist" model, rather than the "once-born" model.

101. Note the claim at the 1753 conference that ninety-nine out of a hundred would know the exact time when they were justified as long as they had received clear scriptural preaching; "MS Minutes" (22 May 1753), *Minutes* (Mason), p. 718. See also Wesley's elderly reflections on this period in the comment to Melville Horne recorded in Southey, *Life of Wesley*, 1:258.

102. Letter to Mary Cooke (30 Oct. 1785), *Letters* (Telford), 7:298. This advice is particularly striking in light of the controversy of John Fletcher with Walter Shirley and Howell Harris over whether the Spirit's work was in effusions (baptisms) of power or "imperceptible dews;" cf. Fraser 1988, p. 366. Unfortunately, this aspect of the mature Wesley is missed by Chamberlain 1993, p.675.

103. E.g., Sermon 69, "The Imperfection of Human Knowledge," §III.5, *Works*, 2:584; and Letter to Miss March (31 May 1771), *Letters* (Telford), 5:255.

Chapter Seven

1. A pioneering example of this approach that Wesley was familiar with is William Perkins' *A Golden Chaine, or the Description of Theology; Containing the Order of the Causes of Salvation and Damnation* (London: J. Legatt, 1591). The tendency to sequence the "steps" of salvation was evident in both Lutheran and Reformed scholasticism. For a compendium of the Lutheran discussion, see Schmid, *Doctrinal Theology*, pp. 407-99. The classic presentation of the Reformed scholastic *ordo salutis* is Abraham Kuyper's *The Work of the Holy Spirit* (1888; English reprint, Grand Rapids, MI: Eerdmans, 1979). I will interact most with the Reformed version of the *ordo salutis*, since that is the one Wesley disputed with the most. Though Kuyper postdates Wesley, I will draw on his work as a reliable summary of the central claims of this group.

2. E.g., Horst 1985, p. 78; Runyon 1985, p. 11; Gallaway 1988, p. 26; Heitzenrater 1989, p. 109; Meistad 1989, pp. 30-1; and Naglee 1991, pp. 274ff.

3. Actually, Wesley would probably have seen little difference between "way" and "order." He could as easily talk of the "order" in which we might encounter God's work in our life (e.g., Sermon 16, "The Means of Grace," V.1-2, *Works,* 1:393-4 [but note V.3, p. 395!]) and the "golden chain" of pardon, holiness, and heaven (Sermon 42, "Satan's Devices," II.4, *Works,* 2:149-50). One should not make too much of such uses however, because "*ordo salutis*" became common as a technical term in Protestant Scholasticism only in the latter part of the eighteenth century.

4. Kuyper, *Holy Spirit,* p. 297. Note his insistence that preparatory grace ends when regenerating grace begins (p. 290), and his use of "successive stages" (p. 295). Recall as well that Perkins titled his book *A Golden Chaine,* and included a schematic chart to show the sequential order of the events in the chain.

5. The best (or worst!) example is his Preface to *An Abstract of the Life and Death of the Reverend Learned and Pious Mr. Thomas Halyburton* (1739), §2, *Works* (Jackson), 14:212. Note also the tight structure of the borrowed typology of the natural, legal, and evangelical states in Sermon 9 (1746), "The Spirit of Bondage and Adoption," *Works,* 1:249-66.

6. I would point again especially to Sermon 85, "On Working Out Our Own Salvation," §II.1, *Works,* 3:203-4. Note also Craig Gallaway's comments on the structure of the 1780 *Hymns* (1988, pp. 88-9). While admitting that some tensions remain, I do not believe that the late Wesley was as constrained by the framework of the *ordo salutis* as is charged in Míguez Bonino 1983e, p. 250 (20); and James Gustafson, *Christ and the Moral Life* (Chicago, IL: University of Chicago, 1968), p. 82.

7. Cf. Sermon 1, "Salvation by Faith," §3, *Works,* 1:118; and Sermon 43, "The Scripture Way of Salvation," §I.8, *Works,* 2:160. See also the similar judgment of Lindström (1946, pp. 110-1).

8. They would *assume* that there will be subsequent growth, but insist that our salvation is not in any way contingent upon it; cf. Kuyper, *Holy Spirit,* pp. 349-50.

9. 1770 *Minutes,* Q. 28, *Minutes* (Mason), p. 96 (also as "Large Minutes," Q. 77, *Works* [Jackson], 8:338).

10. One of the earliest such projects was Hoon 1936. The most influential examples have been Lindström 1946 and C. Williams 1960. The most ambitious recent example is Collins 1984b & 1989. Readers should compare the present approach to these works.

11. Particularly Horst 1985.

12. Cf. Kuyper, *Holy Spirit,* pp. 283-95. Lutheran scholastics would be more prone to see repentance as one aspect of the regenerating process, prior to justifying faith; cf. Schmid, *Doctrinal Theology,* pp. 458ff.

13. *The Doctrine of Original Sin,* Pt. II, §III, *Works* (Jackson), 9:308. See also his *Dictionary* definition and *NT Notes,* John 3:7.

14. Cf. Rattenbury 1941, p. 261; Townsend 1979, p. 236; and J.R. Tyson 1986, p. 219.

15. Cf. Sermon 43, "The Scripture Way of Salvation," §I.4, *Works,* 2:158; Sermon 45, "The New Birth," §IV.3, *Works,* 2:198; and *The Doctrine of Original Sin,* Pt. II, §III, *Works* (Jackson), 9:310; Sermon 107, "On God's Vineyard," §I.6-7, *Works,* 3:506-7.

16. See *The Principles of a Methodist,* §29 (*Works,* 9:64), where Wesley quotes approvingly a summary of his position as distinguishing between two degrees of regeneration. It is puzzling that Borgen would deny this distinction (1972, pp. 148-9).

17. Note that in the quotation in *The Principles of a Methodist,* §29 (*Works,* 9:64) Wesley adds parenthetically that there may be *more* than two degrees of regeneration! Note also his connection of Prevenient Grace with a degree of (new) life in Letter

to John Mason (21 Nov. 1776), *Letters* (Telford), 6:239; and Sermon 85, "On Working Out Our Own Salvation," §II.1, *Works*, 3:203-4.

18. For an explicit Reformed denial of regeneration being co-operant, see Kuyper, *Holy Spirit*, pp. 306, 318.

19. *The Doctrine of Original Sin*, Pt. II, §III, *Works* (Jackson), 9:306. Note in this regard his criticism of William Law for recommending the spiritual exercise of "the presence of God" to the unawakened; Sermon 79, "On Dissipation," §19, *Works*, 3:123.

20. Cf. Sermon 9, "The Spirit of Bondage and Adoption," §II.1, *Works*, 1:255; and Sermon 16, "The Means of Grace," §V.1, *Works*, 1:393.

21. Cf. *The Doctrine of Original Sin*, Pt. II, §III, *Works* (Jackson), 9:306; *Hymns and Sacred Poems* (1740), Preface, §10, *Works* (Jackson), 14:326; and *NT Notes*, Rom. 4:5.

22. On this topic see Holland 1973; and Outler 1984, pp. 200-1.

23. Cf. *Minutes* (13 May 1746), Qq. 2-3, *John Wesley*, p. 156; Sermon 17, "The Circumcision of the Heart," §II.1-7, *Works*, 1:409-12; and Letter to Joseph Cownley (21 Apr. 1750), *Works*, 26:418.

24. The most strident such work is William Sargant, *Battle for the Mind: A Physiology of Conversion and Brain-Washing* (Garden City, NY: Doubleday, 1957), pp. 92ff. For a cogent rebuttal to Sargant see Ian Ramage, *Battle for the Free Mind* (London: George Allen & Unwin, 1967).

25. Downes 1960, pp. 180-1, 251; D. Wilson 1963, p. 14; Ramage, *Battle for the Free Mind*, pp. 118-24.

26. E.g., Sermon 110 (1739), "Free Grace," 11, *Works*, 3:548.

27. See again Wesley's comment to Melville Horne quoted in Southey, *Life of Wesley*, 1:295.

28. Cf. *Journal* (8 June 1762), *Works*, 21:368-8; *Journal* (8 Oct. 1770), *Works*, 22:255; *Journal* (17 Jan. 1772), *Works*, 22:304-5; and *Journal* (29 Sept. 1774), *Works*, 22:429.

29. Note the interest in "the first wish to please God, the first dawn of light concerning His will, and the first slight, transient conviction of having sinned" in Sermon 85, "On Working Out Our Own Salvation," §II.1, *Works*, 3:203.

30. Cf. Letter to James Hutton and the Fetter Lane Society (30 Apr. 1739), *Works*, 25:640; and *Journal* (15 June 1739), *Works*, 19:70. There were also a few localized outbreaks later; e.g., *Journal* (5 Aug. 1759), *Works*, 21:233.

31. E.g., *Journal* (12 Mar. 1743), *Works*, 19:317; *A Farther Appeal to Men of Reason and Religion*, §III.4 & §VII.13, *Works*, 11:122-3, 197-8; and *Journal* (25 Nov. 1759), *Works*, 21:234. Cf. the discussions in D. Wilson 1969, pp. 92-103; and Ramage, *Battle for the Free Mind*, pp. 140-78.

32. Cf. *Minutes* (2 Aug. 1745), Q. 18, *John Wesley*, p. 151; Sermon 35 (1750), "The Law Established Through Faith I," §I.3, *Works*, 2:22-3; and Letter to Joseph Cownley (21 Apr. 1750), *Works*, 26:418.

33. The earliest clear articulation of this point is his Letter "To an Evangelical Layman" (20 Dec. 1751), esp. §3, *Works*, 26:482. For more on the third use of the law see Chapter Four.

34. On the mature Wesley's contextual hermeneutic of law and gospel, see D. Watson 1984, p. 39. For a related claim regarding Wesley's contextual variation on definitions of sin, see J.R. Tyson 1989.

35. The most striking example is in *A Word to a Condemned Malefactor*, §3, which begins: "Oh repent, repent! Know yourself; see and feel what a sinner you are" (*Works* [Jackson], 11:180). See also Sermon 7, "The Way to the Kingdom," §II.1, *Works*, 1:225 (listing of other examples in note 55).

36. Some scholars conflate these overlapping distinctions (e.g., Collins 1989, p. 34) The best evidence that Wesley was dealing with two distinct issues is that he specifically mentions the contrast between self-knowledge and change of heart *within* his treatment of repentance after conversion in Sermon 14, "The Repentance of Believers," §I.1, *Works*, 1:336. Likewise, it is clear in this sermon that Wesley understands believers to be repenting of more than their remaining inward sin, they repent also for the sins that cleave to their actions (and omissions)!

37. A major accuser in this regard was Thomas Church. See particularly Wesley's response to Church in *Principles of a Methodist Farther Explained*, §II.2, *Works*, 9:178. For the Reformed scholastic view of this theme see Kuyper, *Holy Spirit*, pp. 338-40, 349.

38. Cf. Sermon 21, "Sermon on the Mount I," §I.4, *Works*, 1:477; Sermon 5, "Justification by Faith," §IV.2, *Works*, 1:194; and Sermon 7, "The Way to the Kingdom," §II.1, *Works*, 1:225. Note that Wesley deleted Jeremy Taylor's descriptions of repentance as the rigorous transformation of life from his 1752 reprint of Taylor in the *Chr. Library* (cf. K. Kim 1992, pp. 119-21). See also Blaising 1979, p. 275; and Outler's description of this redefinition of repentance as a landmark in the development of Wesley's soteriology (1974, p. 74).

39. Cf. the comments building on the reference to a "first repentance" in Sermon 7, "The Way to the Kingdom," §II.7, *Works*, 1:229; and Sermon 21, "Sermon on the Mount I," §I.10-11, *Works*, 1:480-1. Note also that Wesley once differentiated between these two aspects as "legal repentance" and "evangelical repentance" (*NT Notes*, Matt. 3:8). Here he is reflecting a typology of conversion used in Sermon 9, "The Spirit of Bondage and Adoption" (*Works*, 1:249-66) which contrasted the "legal man," who is convinced of sin but not of God's gracious pardon, with the "evangelical man," who is conscious of being freed from the guilt and power of sin.

40. Cf. Lawson 1974.

41. Note Wesley's explicit mention of this assumption at the beginning of Sermon 14, "The Repentance of Believers," *Works*, 1:335 (and see Outler's note 1). Cf. the discussion of this point in Kuyper, *Holy Spirit*, pp. 349-52 (he equates conversion and repentance). With Luther's emphasis on *simul justus et peccator* the Lutheran tradition has always assumed that there is continual repentance in the Christian life.

42. Compare *Collection of Forms of Prayer for Every Day of the Week*, Preface, *Works* (Jackson), 14:271-2; and *The Christian's Pattern* (Thomas à Kempis), Preface, §II.9-14, *Works* (Jackson), 14:202-5; to Letter to Ann Granville (3 Oct. 1731), *Works*, 25:318.

43. E.g., Sermon 40, "Christian Perfection," §II.6, *Works*, 2:107; Sermon 18, "The Marks of the New Birth," §I.5, *Works*, 1:420; Letter to William Dodd (12 Mar. 1756), §5-9, *Letters* (Telford), 3:169-70; and *NT Notes*, 1 John 2:1 (the verse on which this distinction is usually based, Wesley slides by it!).

44. Sermon 1, "Salvation by Faith," §II.6, *Works*, 1:124.

45. Note Whitefield's rejection of the suggestion that true believers do not struggle with sinful desires in a series of letters to Wesley in *Works*, 26:11, 31-2, 66.

46. This distinction is first made in Sermon 40 (1741), "Christian Perfection," §II.21, *Works*, 2:117. Further clarification can be traced through *Minutes* (25 June 1744), Qq. 7-9, *John Wesley*, p. 138; *Minutes* (26 June 1744), Q. 4, *John Wesley*, p. 140; *Minutes* (2 Aug. 1745), Q. 1, *John Wesley*, p. 152; and Sermon 8 (1746), "The First Fruits of the Spirit," §II.5, *Works*, 1:239. There is an apparent exception to this distinction in Sermon 18, "The Marks of the New Birth," §I.4-6 (*Works*, 1:419-21); however, while this sermon was published in 1748, note that Outler traces its oral roots back to 1739 (p. 416).

47. Cf. Sermon 13 (1763), "On Sin in Believers," *Works*, 1:317-34. On the perfectionist controversy see Fraser 1988, pp. 237-92; and Gunter 1989, pp. 215ff.

48. The passage most at issue is Sermon 40, "Christian Perfection," §II:2-20 (*Works*, 2:105-16), which is devoted to a protracted argument that even babes in Christ are "so far perfect as not to commit sin." Wesley's concern is to reject the *necessity* of sin (cf. §II.14, p. 112). However, he does not explicitly mention the possibility of falling. Note how central this possibility is to his response to accusations, in Letter to William Dodd (12 Mar. 1756), §4-9, *Letters* (Telford), 3:168-70.

49. This connection is explicit from at least 1746; cf. Sermon 8, "The First-Fruits of the Spirit," §II.4, *Works*, 1:238.

50. Sermon 13 (1763), "On Sin in Believers," §IV.13, *Works*, 1:332.

51. Cf. *Minutes* (25 June 1744), Q. 7, *John Wesley*, p. 138.

52. The clearest case in point is the Letter to William Dodd (12 Mar. 1756), §8-9, *Letters* (Telford), 3:170-1.

53. Sermon 43, "The Scripture Way of Salvation," *Works*, 2:155-69. See also Sermon 14 (1767), "The Repentance of Believers," §I.11, *Works*, 1:341.

54. Cf. Sermon 14, "The Repentance of Believers," *Works*, 1:335-52 (esp. §2 & §I.1); and Sermon 43, "The Scripture Way of Salvation," §I.5-6, *Works*, 2:158-9.

55. See "Thoughts on Christian Perfection," Q. 6, *John Wesley*, p. 287; *Journal* (24 July 1761), *Works*, 21:336-7; and Sermon 76, "On Perfection," §I.3, *Works*, 3:73. Roman Catholic scholars have seen a parallel here to the distinction between mortal sins, venial sins, and imperfections (e.g., McNulty 1963, p. 87; and Pucelik 1963, pp. 22-26). While he may have misunderstood the comparison, Wesley disavowed it in *Some Remarks on Mr. Hill's Review of All the Doctrines Taught by the Mr. John Wesley*, §25, *Works* (Jackson), 10:408; and (much stronger) *Some Remarks on Mr. Hill's Farrago Double-Distilled*, §50, *Works* (Jackson), 10:444.

56. In addition to general surveys of Wesley's soteriology noted earlier, helpful studies of his understanding of justification are Brockwell 1983, Langford 1980-2a, Outler 1977, H.O. Thomas 1990, and D. Watson 1986a. See also the attempt to align Wesley squarely with the Reformers in Cannon 1946.

57. E.g., *Minutes* (25 June 1744), Q. 1, *John Wesley*, p. 137; *NT Notes*, Rom. 3:24; and Sermon 43, "The Scripture Way of Salvation," §I.3, *Works*, 2:157.

58. In the 1738 Sermon 1, "Salvation by Faith," he includes both deliverance from the guilt and the power of sin under "justification" in the broad sense (§II.7, *Works*, 1:124). He was clearly distinguishing the two within a year: *Journal* (13 Sept. 1739), *Works*, 19:96. Note also his strong rejection of the Moravian's identification of entire sanctification with justification in his extract from *A Short View of the Differences Between the Moravian Brethren, (So Called) And the Rev. Mr. John and Charles Wesley*, *Works* (Jackson), 10:203.

59. The following summary is heavily dependant upon Outler 1976 & 1977.

60. This charge is technically incorrect because Trent clearly understood the righteousness of believers to be a result of God's gracious action in their lives, not a product of their inherent abilities. This is not to deny that there were significant differences between Trent and Protestants on how God's grace is conveyed and how humans co-operate with it. For Perkins' arguments see *Golden Chaine*.

61. See the discussions of this issue in Henry McAdoo, *The Spirit of Anglicanism* (New York: Scribners, 1965); and Allison, *Rise of Moralism*. However, note also the critique of Allison in Outler 1977, p. 155; and Chamberlain 1993, p. 659.

62. See the reference in Outler 1977 (p. 155) to a Latin fragment discovered by Richard Heitzenrater.

63. Sermon 5, "Justification by Faith," §II.4, *Works*, 1:188-9.

64. Sermon 5, "Justification by Faith," §II.5, *Works*, 1:189; and Sermon 20, "The Lord Our Righteousness," §II.5, *Works*, 1:455. Cf. Borgen 1972, p. 130. Wesley, of course, did not himself use these scholastic labels.

65. Cf. Lindström 1946, p. 76.

66. *Minutes* (25 June 1744), Q. 16, *John Wesley*, p. 139. See also *A Blow at the Root: or, Christ Stabbed in the House of His Friends*, §10, *John Wesley*, p. 381.

67. Outler 1976, p. 31.

68. Note Staniloae's claim (*Orthodoxe Dogmatik*, 2:267-8) that the West typically worries only about the forgiveness of the *Erbsunde* (the depravity resulting from the Fall), not its "cancelling" (*aufheben*) by restored participation! This would not apply to Wesley. One might note in this regard as well Jürgen Moltmann's recent call for Protestant soteriology to develop a more integral connection between justification and the New Birth—and his explicit dialogue with Wesley in such an attempt—in *The Spirit of Life* (Minneapolis, MN: Fortress, 1992), pp. 163-71.

69. Indeed, Wesley deleted the three references to Adoption in the Westminster Smaller Catechism in his abridgement for the *Chr. Library*; cf. J. MacDonald 1906, pp. 9-10; and K. Kim 1992, pp. 78-9 (but note that I suggest a different reason for this than Kim).

70 .See esp. Sermon 1, "Salvation by Faith," §II.1-5, *Works*, 1:121-3; and Sermon 4, "Scriptural Christianity," §I.1, *Works*, 1:161.

71. *An Earnest Appeal to Men of Reason and Religion*, §29, *Works*, 11:55.

72. Note Luby's argument that Wesley understood grace to have a dual effect of transforming our way of perceiving and empowering a new way of living (1984, p. 199). For a similar claim in Eastern Orthodox soteriology see Hopko, *Spirit of God*, p. 59.

73. Cf. Schmid, *Doctrinal Theology*, pp. 459, 488.

74. Cf. Kuyper, *Holy Spirit*, pp. 446-7; and Jonathan H. Rainbow, "Double Grace: John Calvin's View of the Relationship of Justification and Sanctification," *Ex Auditu* 5 (1989):99-105.

75. Cf. *A Farther Appeal to Men of Reason and Religion*, Pt. I, §VI.1, *Works*, 11:176; and *NT Notes*, Rom. 4:5.

76. See his *Journal* (24 June 1741), *Works*, 19:202-3; and the pugnacious sermon completed the same day (but never formally presented), Sermon 150, "Hypocrisy in Oxford," §I.7, *Works*, 4:396-7 (note that he defines Anglicanism as a Reformed Church in §I.5, p. 395).

77. See Letter to Several Preachers and Friends (10 July 1771), *Letters* (Telford), 5:264. Clifford has argued that Wesley's most proximate source for reclaiming the idea of two-fold justification was likely Richard Baxter, the reference to Bull being after-the-fact (1990, p. 59). The distinction is found in Baxter's *Saint's Everlasting Rest* which Wesley abridged in the *Chr. Library*. J.H. Tyson 1991 has emphasized some differences between the way Bull understood the distinction and Wesley. Chamberlain's criticism of Methodism (1993, p. 672) overlooks Wesley's reappropriation of this theme.

78. E.g., *Journal* (13 Sept. 1739), *Works*, 19:96; Sermon 5, "Justification by Faith," §II.1, *Works*, 1:187; Sermon 43, "The Scripture Way of Salvation," §I.4, *Works*, 2:158; and Sermon 85, "On Working Out Our Own Salvation," §II.1, *Works*, 3:204.

79. Cf. Sermon 19, "The Great Privilege of Those That are Born of God," §2, *Works*, 1:431-2; and Sermon 45, "The New Birth," §1 & §IV.3, *Works*, 2:187, 198.

80. E.g., *NT Notes*, Rom. 6:18, Heb. 8:12.

81. Note Horst's discussion of the situational dynamics of Wesley's use of the doctrine of two-fold justification (1985, p. 97).

82. Cf. *Minutes* (25 June 1744), Q. 1, *John Wesley*, p. 137; and *A Farther Appeal to Men of Reason and Religion*, Pt. I, §I.4, *Works*, 11:107.

83. Sermon 25, "Sermon on the Mount V," §III.9, *Works*, 1:559-60; and Sermon 20, "The Lord Our Righteousness," §II.12, *Works*, 1:458.

84. Letter to James Hervey (15 Oct. 1756), *Letters* (Telford), 3:374.

85. Note his *NT Notes* comment on 1 Peter 1:2 that while salvation is a free gift, it is such a gift that the final issue depends on our future obedience to the Heavenly call.

86. Cf. his appeal to Anglican teachings in this regard in *Farther Appeal to Men of Reason and Religion*, Pt. I, §I.2 & §II.4, *Works*, 11:106 & 111; and the discussion of this point in Lindström 1946, pp. 198ff.

87. See 1770 *Minutes*, Q. 28, *Minutes* (Mason), pp. 95-6 (also in "Large Minutes," Q. 77, *Works* [Jackson], 8:337); and Letter to Several Preachers and Friends (10 July 1771), *Letters* (Telford), 5:264.

88. On the Methodist split, see Gunter 1989, pp. 250ff. For Wesley scholarship, note that Colin Williams treats these *Minutes* under the subheading "The Problem of 1770" (1960, p. 61).

89. Cf. the similar judgments of Lindström 1946, pp. 210-13; Fujimoto 1986, p. 6; and J.H. Tyson 1991.

90. See the evaluations of Lindström 1955, p. 188; and C. Williams 1960, p. 100. Eastern Orthodox theologians would argue that Roman Catholics too ultimately make justification the dominant element of salvation; cf. Staniloae, *Orthodoxe Dogmatik*, 2:253ff.

91. Míguez Bonino 1983b, p. 208 [4]. This integration of justification into sanctification sounds remarkably like the position articulated by Eastern Orthodox theologians in *Salvation in Christ: A Lutheran-Orthodox Dialogue*, edited by John Meyendorff & Robert Tobias (Minneapolis, MN: Augsburg/ Fortress, 1992), see esp. pp. 19, 48-9.

92. Sermon 107 (1787), "On God's Vineyard," §I.8, *Works*, 3:507.

93. Compare Schmid, *Doctrinal Theology*, p. 410; with Kuyper, *Holy Spirit*, p. 378. But also note Heppe, *Reformed Dogmatics*, pp. 526, 543; Heppe treats justification and faith more as simply contemporaneous.

94. See the classic summary in Sermon 5, "Justification by Faith," §IV.2, *Works*, 1:194.

95. Cf. Sermon 5, "Justification by Faith," §IV.4-6, *Works*, 1:195-6.

96. *Minutes* (25 June 1744), Q. 4, *John Wesley*, p. 137.

97. The reader may want to compare the positive discussion of this distinction in C. Williams 1960, pp. 64ff.

98. Sermon 14, "The Repentance of Believers," §II.6, *Works*, 1:349-50.

99. Letter to 'John Smith' (30 Dec. 1745), *Works*, 26:183.

100. For a few of the many examples, see: *The Character of a Methodist*, §5 & §13, *Works*, 9:35, 39; *The Principles of a Methodist*, §9, *Works*, 9:53; "Minutes" (13 May 1746), Q. 6, *John Wesley*, p. 160; *An Earnest Appeal to Men of Reason and Religion*, §61, *Works*, 11:70; Sermon 10, "The Witness of the Spirit I," §I.8, *Works*, 1:274; Sermon 36, "The Law Established Through Faith," §III.3, *Works*, 2:41-2; and Sermon 120, "The Unity of the Divine Being," §17, *Works*, 4:67.

101. See Letter to Dr. John Robertson (24 Sept. 1753), *Works*, 26:518; and the comparison of Wesley to Edwards in H. Knight 1988.

102. Sermon 36, "The Law Established Through Faith II," §II.1, *Works*, 2:38.

103. Sermon 91, "On Charity," §III.11, *Works*, 3:306.

104. E.g., Sermon 10, "Witness of the Spirit I," §II.7, *Works*, 1:280.

105. Sermon 35, "The Law Established through Faith," §II.6, *Works*, 2:27-8. See also Sermon 33, "Sermon on the Mount XIII," §III.5, *Works*, 1:695-6.

106. Note Outler's claim and the list of examples in *Works*, 1:139 fn58. For the following discussion see also Schneeberger 1974, pp. 126-7; and Turner 1985, p. 55.

107. Cf. *Minutes* (25 June 1744), Q. 14, *John Wesley*, p. 138; *NT Notes*, James 2:14; and *A Letter to the Rev. Mr. Horne* (1761), §II.8, *Works*, 11:456.

108. Cf. Staniloae, *Orthodoxe Dogmatik*, 2:279-88.

109. The standard study of Wesley's overall understanding of sanctification is Lindström 1946. Other helpful theological studies include Dieter 1987, Hulley 1990, Langford 1980-2b, D.M. Moore 1985, Walters 1972, and A.S. Wood 1986. Fraser 1988 provides the best historical study of Wesley in the context of struggles over the doctrine in early British Methodism. For American Methodist developments, see Peters 1956. For traditional American Holiness readings, see Cox 1964 and Moyer 1992. For innovative reinterpretations in the Holiness tradition, see Staples 1963 and Wynkoop 1972.

110. Cf. *Minutes* (17 June 1747), Q. 2, *John Wesley*, p. 168. For some clarifications of Wesley's changing nomenclature, see D.M. Moore 1985.

111. Lindström 1946, p. 123.

112. Rom. 7:24. Note that the middle Wesley interpreted this verse as Paul impersonating an "awakened man" who is aware of sin but does not yet enjoy the empowering grace of God to conquer it; cf. his *NT Notes* comment and Sermon 9, "Spirit of Bondage and Adoption," II.9-10, *Works*, 1:258-60.

113. Remember that our very ability to welcome these overtures is owed to the nascent rejuvenation of Prevenient Grace.

114. Cf. Letter to Thomas Olivers (24 Mar. 1757), *Letters* (Telford), 3:212; Letter to Sarah Crosby (14 Feb. 1761), *Letters* (Telford), 4:133; Sermon 14, "The Repentance of Believers" (1767), §I.20, *Works*, 1:346; Letter to Samuel Bardsley (3 Apr. 1772), *Letters* (Telford), 5:315; and Letter to Mrs. Barton (8 Oct. 1774), *Letters* (Telford), 6:116. There are even more examples of such language in Charles' hymns.

115. Wesley listed this very suggestion among the "deviant" teachings of the lay preacher Thomas Maxfield (Letter to Thomas Maxfield [2 Nov. 1762], *Letters* [Telford], 4:192). He confronted it again, in a form that he judged less virulent, with his close associates Joseph Benson and John Fletcher; cf. Letter to Joseph Benson (28 Dec. 1770), *Letters* (Telford), 5:215; Ibid (9 Mar. 1771), 5:228; Ibid (16 Mar. 1771), 5:229; and Letter to John Fletcher (22 Mar. 1775), *Letters* (Telford), 6:146.

116. The Holiness branch of the Methodist family tended to follow Fletcher in equating entire sanctification with the baptism of the Holy Spirit. Realization of the exegetical difficulties of this position (initiated by McGonigle 1973) spawned vigorous debate over the topic among Holiness scholars and a growing awareness that Wesley did not agree with Fletcher. For a brief bibliographical survey of this debate and an analysis of the interchange between Wesley and Fletcher, see Dayton, *Roots of Pentecostalism*, pp. 48-54, 184-5. The clearest evidence of Wesley's rejection of Fletcher's proposal has recently been unearthed and discussed in Fraser 1988, pp. 382-6, 490-2.

117. Cf. Sermon 40 (1741), "Christian Perfection," §II.1-2, *Works*, 2:105; *NT Notes* (1754), 1 Cor. 2:6, Col. 4:12; Sermon 13 (1763), "On Sin in Believers," V.1, *Works*, 1:332-3; Sermon 83 (1784), "On Patience," §10, *Works*, 3:175; and Sermon 107

(1787), "On God's Vineyard," §I.7, *Works*, 3:507. For early Greek precedents, see Spidlík, *Spirituality of Christian East*, pp. 68-70.

118. Sermon 43, "The Scripture Way of Salvation," §I.7 & §III.11, *Works*, 2:159, 166. For a study of this theme in Macarius see Dörries, *Theologie des Makarios*, pp. 118ff. For emphasis on the convergence between Wesley and the Alexandrian tradition on the portrayal of Christian life as gradual development of the virtues, see Bundy 1991.

119. For some examples of this complaint which specifically contrast with the threefold exhortation of the General Rules to external holiness, see: *Journal* (13 Sept. 1739), *Works*, 19:87; *An Earnest Appeal to Men of Reason and Religion*, §47-8, *Works*, 11:62-3; and Sermon 22, "Sermon on the Mount II," §II.4, *Works*, 1:496-7 (note Outler's list of other examples in fn45).

120. *Journal* (13 Sept. 1739), *Works*, 19:97. Contra Bryant (1992a, p. 167), Wesley uses this language for sanctification and Christian perfection long before 1757.

121. *The Nature, Design, and General Rules of the United Societies*, §4-6, *Works*, 9:70-3.

122. Cf. *An Earnest Appeal to Men of Reason and Religion*, §97, *Works*, 11:88; Sermon 30, "Sermon on Mount X," §2, *Works*, 1:651; and *NT Notes*, 2 Cor. 9:6.

123. Sermon 91, "On Charity," §III.12, *Works*, 3:306. Cf. Letter to Richard Morgan, Sr. (15 Jan. 1734), *Works*, 25:369; *Journal* (13 Sept. 1739), *Works*, 19:97; Letter to 'John Smith' (30 Dec. 1745), *Works*, 26:179; and *NT Notes*, Matt. 23:31. On the contribution of the *Book of Common Prayer* to this theme in Wesley, see Selleck 1983, p. 296.

124. Sermon 83, "On Patience," §10, *Works*, 3:174-5. See also discussions in Lindström 1946, pp. 161ff; Schneeberger 1974, pp. 96-100; and Cubie 1985.

125. *A Letter to the Rev. Mr. Baily of Cork*, §III.1, *Works*, 9:309. Cf. *An Earnest Appeal to Men of Reason and Religion*, §3, *Works*, 11:45; *A Plain Account of Genuine Christianity*, §I.7-9, *John Wesley*, p. 185; *NT Notes*, 1 Thess. 2:17; and Sermon 92, "On Zeal," §II.5, *Works*, 3:313.

126. Sermon 100, "On Pleasing All Men," §II.1, *Works*, 3:422.

127. Cf. Sermon 17, "The Circumcision of the Heart," §I.1, *Works*, 1:402-3. Wesley commended this sermon for articulating his understanding of sanctification throughout his life; cf. Letter to John Newton (14 May 1765), *Letters* (Telford), 4:299.

128. See especially Lovin 1985; Hulley 1988, p. 2; Steele 1994; and Heitzenrater 1994. Somewhat more cautious is Hauerwas 1975, 1985. Note as well the argument that a virtue ethic is particularly appropriate to Orthodox ethics in Vigen Guroian, *Incarnate Love: Essays in Orthodox Ethics* (Notre Dame, IN: University of Notre Dame Press, 1987).

129. Compare *The Doctrine of Original Sin*, Pt. II, III, *Works* (Jackson), 9:292; and Pt. III, §VIII, *Works* (Jackson), 9:343-4.

130. Letter to Dr. John Robertson (24 Sept. 1753), *Works*, 26:517-8.

131. E.g., *Minutes* (2 Aug. 1745), Q. 1, *John Wesley*, p. 152.

132. Note his equation of "growing in grace" with growth in every Christian temper in *NT Notes*, 2 Peter 3:18.

133. Letter to Robert Carr Brackenbury (15 Sept. 1790), *Letters* (Telford), 8:238.

134. The fourth edition (1777) is in *Works* (Jackson), 11:366-446. For the specific claim to consistency see 27, p. 443.

135. Chronological consideration of Wesley's emphases regarding Christian Perfection is a recent agenda. Lindström's study, for all of its strengths, played down any changes or tensions after 1738 (cf. 1946, p. 16). Sangster (1943, pp. 82-5) had previously suggested the need to consider later fluctuations in Wesley's assumptions about the attainment of Christian Perfection, but the first study to sketch any of these

was Walters 1972. More detailed contributions have been made by D.M. Moore 1985; Fraser 1988; and Gunter 1989, pp. 202ff. The following summary is informed by these studies.

136. Two brief helpful summaries of influences on Wesley's understanding of Christian Perfection are Outler 1984, pp. 83-5; and D.M. Moore 1985, pp. 29-34. Both highlight the influence of early Greek theologians.

137. Cf. Outler 1961, pp. 12-13; 1964a, p. 31; 1980-2, p. 16; and Turner 1988, pp. 166-7.

138. E.g., Sermon (1733), "The Circumcision of the Heart," esp. §I.1, *Works*, 1:403; *Collection of Forms of Prayer for Every Day of the Week* (1733), Preface, *Works* (Jackson), 14:271-2; and *The Christian's Pattern* (1735), Preface, §II.9-14, *Works* (Jackson), 14:202-5.

139. E.g., Sermon 136 (1727), "On Mourning for the Dead," §5, *Works*, 4:239; Letter to Ann Granville (Oct. 1731), *Works*, 25:318; and Sermon 109 (1735), "The Trouble and Rest of Good Men," Proem. & §II.4, *Works*, 3:534, 539.

140. Note his connection between holiness and the distinguishing mark of one in a state of acceptance by God in Sermon 17 (1733), "The Circumcision of the Heart," §3 & §I.1, *Works*, 1:402-3.

141. Cf. Sermon 1, "Salvation by Faith," §II.6, *Works*, 1:124.

142. *Hymns and Sacred Poems* (1740), Preface, §7-9, *Works* (Jackson), 14:324-6. There is no explicit concession of infirmities in this work.

143. The next two paragraphs summarize Sermon 40, "Christian Perfection," *Works*, 2:99-121. The major points of this sermon were repeated in the Preface to the 1742 *Hymns and Sacred Poems*, *Works* (Jackson), 14:328-30; and in *The Principles of a Methodist* (1742), §12, *Works*, 9:53-5.

144. Note that Wesley appended a qualifying footnote to this and several other claims in the 1740 Preface when he reprinted it in the *Plain Account of Christian Perfection* (*Works* [Jackson], 11:379-80). For a sympathetic study of the pastoral concern evident in these footnotes, see Walters 1973.

145. Recall the later suggestion that new believers are given a power to keep down all inward sin in *Minutes* (25 June 1744), Q. 7, *John Wesley*, p. 138.

146. To cite just a few examples: *Minutes* (26 June 1744), Qq. 2-7, *John Wesley*, pp. 140-1; *Hymns and Sacred Poems* (2nd edition, 1745), Preface, *Works* (Jackson), 14:328-30; and Sermon 13 (1763), "On Sin in Believers," *Works*, 1:317-34. Again there is the apparent exception (suggesting that the New Birth frees also from inward sin) in Sermon 18, "The Marks of the New Birth," §I.4 (*Works*, 1:419), but its oral roots go back to 1739 (p. 416).

147. Cf. Sermon 40, "Christian Perfection," §II.14, *Works*, 2:112; and Charles' hymn #132 in *Hymns and Sacred Psalms* (1749), *Poet. Works*, 5:328.

148. E.g., *Minutes* (17 June 1747), Qq. 2-3, *John Wesley*, p. 167-8; and Sermon 40, "Christian Perfection," §II.27-28, *Works*, 2:119-20. Note also his deletion of material in the Westminster Shorter Catechism that delayed perfection until after death in his abridgement for *Chr. Library*, in J. MacDonald 1906, pp. 10, 22. Fraser collects the evidence of Methodists claiming entire sanctification during this period, while noting that Wesley did not publish it at the time (1988, p. 199).

149. He deleted a suggestion by Michael de Molinos that "perfection can be reached in two to six months" from his 1754 abridged reprint in *Chr. Library*; cf. Tuttle 1989, p. 136.

150. On the impossibility of sinning after entire sanctification, see *Journal* (24 Aug. 1743), *Works*, 19:333; *Minutes* (26 June 1744), *John Wesley*, p. 141; and Letter to

Thomas Olivers (24 Mar. 1757), *Letters* (Telford), 3:213. The last reference specifically ties this expectation to Wesley's reticence about accepting claimed attainment too soon. Thus the rigor with which Wesley examined Sarah Ryan's claims to entire sanctification noted in Fraser 1988, pp. 231-2, 474-80.

151. Note especially *Journal* (2 Dec. 1744), *Works*, 20:44; the recommended response in *Minutes* (26 June 1744), Qq. 9-10, *John Wesley*, p. 141; Letter to 'John Smith' (25 June 1746), §8, *Works* 26:202; and *Minutes* (17 June 1747), Qq. 14-15, *John Wesley*, p. 171.

152. Sermon 42 (1750), "On Satan's Devices," esp. §5 & §II.5-7, *Works*, 2:140, 150-1.

153. Note Wesley's response to this charge, probably made by Bishop Gibson of London, in *Farther Appeal to Men of Reason and Religion*, Pt. 1, §III.5-6, *Works*, 11:125-7.

154. This is precisely his conclusion to Sermon 40, "Christian Perfection," §II.30, *Works*, 2:121. See the similar suggestion of Fujimoto (1986, p. 211 fn118). The reader should note, however, Fraser's argument—drawing on differences between the manuscript and published minutes of the 1744-5 conferences—that the middle Wesley stressed present attainment more in private setting (especially band meetings) than he did in public (1988, pp. 57-61).

155. E.g., Letter to Dorothy Furly (6 Sept. 1757), *Letters* (Telford), 3:221.

156. This was a key topic of the 1758 Conference; cf. *Journal* (9 Aug. 1758), *Works*, 21:165; and "MS Minutes" (15 Aug. 1758), *John Wesley*, p. 177. It was again the topic in 1759, Wesley's summary from that Conference being published as "Thoughts on Christian Perfection" in 1760 (*John Wesley*, pp. 283-98). Note as well the comments on the 1761 conference in Gunter 1989, p. 211.

157. E.g., Letter to Miss March (27 June 1760), *Letters* (Telford), 4:100; and *Farther Thoughts Upon Christian Perfection* (1763), Q. 25, *Works* (Jackson), 11:423. The phrase "cut short the work" apparently entered Methodist circles through Charles, who found it integral to his 1738 "conversion" and later related it to entire sanctification; cf. the discussion in Fraser 1988, pp. 90ff.

158. E.g., *Journal* (23 June 1761), *Works*, 21:331; and *Journal* (6 Aug. 1762), *Works*, 21:384.

159. *Farther Thoughts Upon Christian Perfection* (1763), Q. 24, *Works* (Jackson), 11:423; and *Journal* (8 Sept. 1765), *Works*, 22:20. Compare *Journal* (14 June 1742), *Works*, 19:278.

160. Cf. *Journal* (15 Sept. 1762), *Works*, 21:389.

161. Wesley had argued this interpretation of developments already in 1745! *Minutes* (2 Aug. 1745), Q. 15, *John Wesley*, pp. 150-1.

162. This claim is developed in Fraser 1988, pp. 278-82.

163. Cf. Letter to William Dodd (12 Mar. 1756), §4, *Letters* (Telford), 3:168.

164. E.g., Letter to Charles Wesley (9 July 1766), *Letters* (Telford), 5:20; and *An Extract From the Journal of Elizabeth Harper*, Preface, §1, *Works* (Jackson), 14:261.

165. Compare Letter to Thomas Olivers (24 Mar. 1757), *Letters* (Telford), 3:213; to Letter to Elizabeth Hardy (26 Dec. 1761), *Letters* (Telford), 4:167; *Farther Thoughts Upon Christian Perfection*, Q. 30, *Works* (Jackson), 11:426; and Letter to Charles Wesley (27 Jan. 1767), *Letters* (Telford), 5:38. This change is also evidently behind Wesley's deletion of the final paragraph in his 1759 "Thoughts on Christian Perfection," Q. 5 (*John Wesley*, p. 286), which had said that no motive (affection) remained in the entirely sanctified to induce them to sin, from his 1766 reprint of this material in *A Plain Account of Christian Perfection*, §19, (*Works* [Jackson], 11:396.

166. Compare *Journal* (6 June 1763), *Works*, 21:415; to Letter to Thomas Olivers (24 Mar. 1757), *Letters* (Telford), 3:213.

167. Compare Letter to Mrs. Bennis (29 Mar. 1766), *Letters* (Telford), 5:6; to the earlier reticence in *Minutes* (17 June 1747), *John Wesley*, pp. 170-1 (it is noteworthy that Wesley quietly omitted this cautionary statement from his 1766 quotation of the 1747 *Minutes* in *A Plain Account of Christian Perfection*, §17, *Works* [Jackson], 11:391!). For a transition between these two positions see "Thoughts on Christian Perfection" (1760), Qq. 17-20, *John Wesley*, pp. 289-90. Charles came to consider all testifying to be prideful; cf. his later poems on Job 9:20 (*Poet. Works*, 9:238), Matthew 8:4 (*Poetry*, 2:20), and 1 John 1:8 (*Poetry*, 2:472).

168. Published in 1760 as "Thoughts on Christian Perfection," Q. 6, *John Wesley*, p. 287. This is the earliest instance which I have found of this extended definition. There is an abbreviated use of the distinction in 1749 in relation to the bands (thus, not exclusively about entire sanctification) in *A Plain Account of the People Called Methodists*, §VII.1, *Works*, 9:254. For suggestions on the earlier history of this distinction and possible sources of Wesley's phrasing (since he had read many of them), see Outler 1984, p. 315; and McGonigle 1994.

169. Sermon 40, "Christian Perfection," §I.7, *Works*, 2:103.

170. Thus I disagree with Outler's equation of inward and involuntary sin (1984, p. 320 fn16).

171. Sermon 1, "Salvation by Faith," §II.6, *Works*, 1:124.

172. See Sermon 40, "Christian Perfection," §I.7, *Works*, 2:103. The context makes clear that "known sins" means sins revealed by God to be such. For the assumption that Christians would know all essential for salvation see §I.4, p. 102.

173. Letter to William Dodd (12 Mar. 1756), §7, *Letters* (Telford), 3:169-70.

174. Cf. Sermon 40 (1741), "Christian Perfection," §II.6, *Works*, 2:107; and Sermon 9, "The Spirit of Bondage and Adoption," §IV.1, *Works*, 1:264.

175. See respectively the first meaning listed for "wilful" in the *Oxford English Dictionary* (2nd ed., 1989), 20:339; and Sermon 9, "The Spirit of Bondage and Adoption," IV.1 (*Works*, 1:264), where Wesley's suggestion of our accountability for our unwilling sins is in the context of arguing that sincerity is not enough.

176. For formal examples, see Sermon 41, "Wandering Thoughts," §III.6, *Works*, 2:131; and Sermon 76, "On Perfection," §II.9, *Works*, 3:79. The most detailed examples are in pastoral letters: Letter to John Hosmer (7 June 1761), *Letters* (Telford), 4:155; Letter to Miss March (31 May 1771), *Letters* (Telford), 5:255; and Letter to Mrs. Bennis (16 June 1772), *Letters* (Telford), 5:322.

177. Cf. Letter to John Hosmer (7 June 1761), *Letters* (Telford), 4:155. See also the chart comparing Adamic perfection and Christian perfection in Lindström 1946, pp. 153-4.

178. There had been a few scattered instances of such claims in earlier years, such as *Journal* (2 Dec. 1744), *Works*, 20:44. Compare the frequency that now follows: 2 Aug. 1759 (21:221), 18 Jan. 1760 (21:239), 12 Mar. 1760 (21:247), etc. This led Wesley to conclude Extract 12 of his *Journal*, which covered 6 May 1760 to 28 Oct. 1762, focussing on these claims, with the observation that his "Pentecost" (of leading people into Christian Perfection) had finally come (*Works*, 21:392)! See also survey of claims in Fraser 1988, pp. 243ff.

179. For a summary of the claims of Maxfield and Bell and the turmoil they caused, see Fraser 1988, pp. 267-92; and Gunter 1989, pp. 215-21. See also Wesley's major Letter to Thomas Maxfield (2 Nov. 1762), *Letters* (Telford), 4:192-4; and his *Cautions and Directions, Given to the Greatest Professors in the Methodist Societies*, *John Wesley*, pp. 299-305. For one of the earliest evidences of some suggesting that entire sanctifica-

tion is necessary for salvation, see Letter to Elizabeth Hardy (5 Apr. 1758), *Letters* (Telford), 4:10.

180. See esp. Letter to Thomas Maxfield (26 Jan. 1763), *Letters* (Telford), 4:201; and the concern about antinomianism in Letter to Thomas Maxfield (2 Nov. 1762), 2, *Letters* (Telford), 4:193.

181. The best example is his 1764 summary of his views published in *Plain Account of Christian Perfection*, §26, *Works* (Jackson), 11:441-3. Rejection of any idea of angelic perfection was central to the publication of three sermons: "Wandering Thoughts" (1760), "On Sin in Believers" (1763), and "The Repentance of Believers" (1768). See also the insistence of the continuing need for Christ's atonement in "Thoughts on Christian Perfection," Q. 5, *John Wesley*, pp. 285-6; and *Farther Thoughts Upon Christian Perfection*, Q. 9, *Works* (Jackson), 11:417.

182. The strongest expression is surely Sermon 89, "The More Excellent Way," §8, *Works*, 3:266. Wesley had been clear on this point for some time; cf. Sermon 42, "On Satan's Devices" (1750), §II.3, *Works*, 2:149; and Letter to Thomas Olivers (24 Mar. 1757), *Letters* (Telford), 3:213. Compare however the 1740 edition of Sermon 40, "Christian Perfection," §II.2 (*Works*, 2:105), which had stated that only those who enjoy Christian Perfection are "properly Christians." As Outler notes (fn57), Wesley revised this in the 1750 edition to read that only these are "perfect Christians."

183. Recall the reservations about talking about a "state" of sanctification apart from emphasis on daily responsible living in the 1770 *Minutes*, Q. 28. *Minutes* (Mason), p. 96 (also in "Large Minutes," Q. 77, *Works* [Jackson], 8:338). Cf. D.M. Moore 1985, p. 48; and Fraser 1988, pp. 321-36.

184. See Sermon 43, "The Scripture Way of Salvation," §III.12 & §III.18, *Works*, 2:167, 169.

185. For the development in Charles' views see J.R. Tyson 1986 & Fraser 1988, pp. 77-148, 302-313. On the differences between the brothers in particular see J.R. Tyson 1986, pp. 227-301; and his collection of relevant hymns in *CW Reader*, pp. 360-97. See also three letters from John to Charles: (9 July 1766), *Letters* (Telford), 5:20; (27 Jan. 1767), *Letters* (Telford), 5:38-9; and (12 Feb. 1767), *Letters* (Telford), 5:41.

186. Hymn on Matthew 9:17, *Poetry*, 2:23.

187. In this regard, there is one intriguing letter in which John seems to suggest that *he* puts most emphasis on the gradual work of sanctification and Charles presses the instantaneous (Letter to Charles Wesley [27 June 1766], *Letters* [Telford], 5:16). Scholars disagree on how to explain this letter, but all agree that the reverse was the case. Peters (1956, p. 183) attributes the letter to depression. J.R. Tyson thinks John was trying to persuade (indeed, shame) Charles to put more emphasis on the instantaneous (1986, pp. 292-4; note slightly revised suggestion in *CW Reader*, p. 388).

188. See Letter to Charles Wesley (27 Jan. 1767), §3, *Letters* (Telford), 5:39.

189. See the 1784 Sermon 76, "On Perfection," §II, *Works*, 3:76-87.

190. To note a few late examples: *Journal* (30 May 1787), *Journal* (Curnock), 7:283; *Journal* (7 Oct. 1789), *Journal* (Curnock), 8:16; and *Journal* (29 Mar. 1790), *Journal* (Curnock), 8:55.

191. E.g., Sermon 40 (1741), "Christian Perfection," §II.1-2, *Works*, 2:105; *NT Notes* (1754), 1 Cor. 2:6, Col. 4:12; Sermon 13 (1763), "On Sin in Believers," §V.1, *Works*, 1:332-3; Sermon 83 (1784), "On Patience," §10, *Works*, 3:175; and Sermon 107 (1787), "On God's Vineyard," §I.7, *Works*, 3:507.

192. Sermon 83, "On Patience," §14, *Works*, 3:179.

193. For appreciative Eastern Orthodox comparisons of Wesley's understanding of sanctification to *theosis* see: Charles Ashanin, *Essays on Orthodox Christianity and*

Church History (Indianapolis, IN: Broad Ripple, 1990), pp. 90-1; David C. Ford, "Saint Makarios of Egypt and John Wesley: Variations on the Theme of Sanctification," *Greek Orthodox Theological Review* 33 (1988):285-312; Harakas, *Transfigured Life*, pp. 183-4; and (more critical) Harold Jonathan Mayo, "John Wesley and the Christian East: On the Subject of Christian Perfection" (St. Vladimir's Orthodox Theological Seminary Master's thesis, 1980). One might also compare with Wesley the discussion of "perfection" in Christian life in Staniloae, *Orthodoxe Dogmatik*, 2:263, 275.

194. Note the concern about any claims to "perfection" in Christian life within both Protestant Scholastic traditions: Schmid, *Doctrinal Theology*, pp. 486-91; and Kuyper, *Holy Spirit*, p. 474. For some valiant attempts to relate Wesley's perspective to Luther, see P. Watson 1963 & Scott 1939; on Calvin, see Marshall 1962 & Wainwright 1988a; and for Roman Catholic studies, see Dorr 1965 & Pucelik 1963.

195. "Brief Thoughts on Christian Perfection" (1767), *Works* (Jackson), 11:446. Similar descriptions abound in his writings, from as early as *Minutes* (26 June 1744), Q. 6, *John Wesley*, p. 141.

196. Sermon 83, "On Patience," §10, *Works*, 3:176.

197. The least nuanced example is Sermon 14, "The Repentance of Believers," §I.20, *Works*, 1:346. For evidence of ambiguity about such language, see *Journal* (18 Nov. 1763), *Works*, 21:439. This language is even more common in Charles' hymns. The best example is in *Hymns for Those Who Seek and Those Who Have Redemption in the Blood of Jesus Christ*, #9, st. 2, *Poet. Works*, 4:219. Note that John omitted this stanza when he included the remainder of the hymn in the 1780 *Hymns* (#374, *Works*, 7:545-7).

198. Cf. Homily 26 (Wesley #14 - *Chr. Library*, p. 110).

199. Indeed, the most common criticism of Wesley's doctrine of Christian Perfection among his Methodist descendants has been that it is based on an inadequate view of sin as some "thing" easily destroyed; e.g., Flew 1934, pp. 327-39; Rattenbury 1941, pp. 299-306; Lindström 1946, p. 148; C. Williams 1960, p. 88; W. Thomas 1965, pp. 36-48; Hillman 1978, pp. 393ff; Wakefield 1978, p. 170; Duque Zúñiga 1983, pp. 267-8; and Lessmann 1987, p. 141.

200. Letter to Joseph Benson (5 Oct. 1770), *Letters* (Telford), 5:203-4. Note also the definition of Christian Perfection as "love filling the heart, expelling pride, anger, desire, self-will . . . ," in *Farther Thoughts Upon Christian Perfection*, Q. 12, *Works* (Jackson), 11:418; an expansion of the same point in "MS Minutes" (15 Aug. 1758), Q. 6, *John Wesley*, p. 177.

201. U. Lee 1936, p. 185. It is not clear that Lee was using "affection" in the dispositional sense that Wesley intended it.

202. This theme runs from Sermon 40 (1741), "Christian Perfection" (*Works*, 2:99-121), to Sermon 129 (1790), "Heavenly Treasure in Earthly Vessels" (*Works*, 4:162-7).

203. Note his comment that the term "sinless perfection" is not worth disputing about in *Farther Thoughts Upon Christian Perfection*, Q. 11, *Works* (Jackson), 11:418.

204. His earliest defenses of the possibility draw mainly on Scripture; e.g., *Minutes* (17 June 1747), Qq. 4-10, *John Wesley*, pp. 168-70 (See discussion in Miller 1991, esp. pp. 261ff). An influential example from Christian tradition would have been Macarius' Homily 18, 2 (Wesley #10, *Chr. Library*, p. 98).

205. Note the description of Christian Perfection in terms of taking on the disposition of Christ in Sermon 76, "On Perfection," §I.5, *Works*, 3:74.

206. See Sermon 40, "Christian Perfection," §II.14, *Works*, 2:112; and Charles' hymn #132 in *Hymns and Sacred Psalms* (1749), *Poet. Works*, 5:328. Cf. Outler 1964a, p. 253; and Bence 1981, p. 150.

207. E.g., Sermon 83, "On Patience," §11-12, *Works*, 3:176-8; and Sermon 43, "The Scripture Way of Salvation," §III.18, *Works*, 2:168. See also two letters spanning the debates over this issue: Letter to Thomas Olivers (24 Mar. 1757), *Letters* (Telford), 3:213; and Letter to Sarah Rutter (5 Dec. 1789), *Letters* (Telford), 8:190.

208. Cf. "Thoughts on Christian Perfection," Qq. 37-8, *John Wesley*, pp. 297-8; and Letter to Charles Wesley (12 Feb. 1767), *Letters* (Telford), 5:41.

209. *Minutes* (26 June 1744), *John Wesley*, p. 141.

210. Cf. "Thoughts on Christian Perfection" (1760), Q. 26, *John Wesley*, p. 293; Sermon 43, "The Scripture Way of Salvation" (1765), §III.17, *Works*, 2:168; *Farther Thoughts Upon Christian Perfection* (1766), Qq. 16, 20-21, *Works* (Jackson), 11:420-2; and Letter to Hannah Ball (19 June 1774), *Letters* (Telford), 6:93.

211. For references to at least one of Wesley's preachers disputing the existence of this distinct Witness, see Letter to Mrs. Bennis (29 March 1766), *Letters* (Telford), 5:6; and Letter to Mrs. Bennis (24 July 1769), *Letters* (Telford), 5:142. For recent criticisms see Starkey 1980, p. 75; and Staples 1986, pp. 103ff.

212. Compare "Thoughts on Christian Perfection" (1760), Q. 26, *John Wesley*, p. 293; to *Farther Thoughts Upon Christian Perfection* (1766), Qq. 16 & 18, *Works* (Jackson), 11:420.

213. E.g., Lindström 1946, p. 105; Bence 1981, pp. 14ff; Fujimoto 1986, pp. 221-2; and A.S. Wood 1986, p. 5.

214. Sermon 42, "On Satan's Devices," §II.7, *Works*, 2:151.

215. E.g., Sermon 40, "Christian Perfection," §I.9, *Works*, 2:104-5; Sermon 106, "On Faith," §II.5, *Works*, 3:501; and *Journal* (6 May 1785), *Journal* (Curnock), 7:75.

216. To show just how central this is in his advice to his pastors I will list several examples: *Minutes* (1768), Q. 28, *Minutes* (Mason), p. 81 (also as "Large Minutes," Q. 56, *Works* [Jackson], 8:329); Letter to Thomas Wride (12 Nov. 1773), *Letters* (Telford), 6:54; Letter to John Mason (10 Jan. 1774), *Letters* (Telford), 6:66; Letter to Francis Wolfe (10 July 1774), *Letters* (Telford), 6:97; Letter to Thomas Rankin (21 July 1774), *Letters* (Telford), 6:103; Letter to Samuel Bardsley (1 Feb. 1775), *Letters* (Telford), 6:137; Letter to John Valton (20 Nov. 1775), *Letters* (Telford), 6:190; and Letter to Freeborn Garrettson (26 June 1785), *Letters* (Telford), 7:276. The point also comes through repeatedly in the *Journal*; cf. (28 May 1761), *Works*, 21:326; (15 Sept. 1762), *Works*, 21:389; (30 Sept. 1765), *Works*, 22:23; (19 Mar. 1774), *Works*, 22:400; (4 Aug. 1775), *Works*, 22:460; (14 Aug. 1776), *Journal* (Curnock), 6:120; (21 May 1783), *Journal* (Curnock), 6:411-12; and (3 May 1784), *Journal* (Curnock), 6:502.

217. *The Character of a Methodist*, *Works*, 9:32; and Sermon 40, "Christian Perfection," *Works*, 2:99.

218. Wesley never claimed entire sanctification explicitly. Indeed he once said he had not yet arrived (Letter to the Editor of *Lloyd's Evening Post* [5 Mar. 1767], *Letters* [Telford], 5:43-4). This apparent lack of claim is particularly problematic for those in the Holiness Movement and several have tried to locate references that they believe are Wesley's account of his entire sanctification. The most common suggestions are *Journal* (23-5 Dec. 1744), *Works*, 20:46-7; and *Journal* (28 Oct. 1762), *Works*, 21:392 (for examples, see Roy Nicholson, "John Wesley's Personal Experience of Christian Perfection," *AsbSem* 6.1 [1952]:65-89; George Turner, *The More Excellent Way* [Winona Lake, IN: Light and Life Press, 1952], p. 171; and E.W. Lawrence, "John Wesley's Experience of Heart Holiness," *Wesleyan Methodist* [3 Feb. 1960]:8-9, 72-3). For

instances of identification of Aldersgate as Wesley's entire sanctification, see Carl F. Eltzoltz, *John Wesley's Conversion and Sanctification* (Cincinnati: Jennings & Graham, 1908) and the discussion in W. Stephen Gunter, "Aldersgate, the Holiness Movement, and Experiential Religion," in *Aldersgate Reconsidered*, pp. 121-31. For suggestive attempts to explain instead why he could not claim it—even though they believe he had attained it, see Bence 1981, p. 62 fn4; S. Martin 1990, pp. 21-2; and Peters 1956, pp. 201ff.

219. Cf. Sermon 58, "On Predestination," §10, *Works*, 2:418-19; and Sermon 127, "On the Wedding Garment," §6, *Works*, 4:143.

220. Cf. *Farther Appeal to Men of Reason and Religion*, Pt. I, §I.2 & §II.4, *Works*, 11:106 & 111; *A Letter to the Rev. Mr. Horne* (1761), §II.6, *Works*, 11:455; Letter to Thomas Olivers (24 Mar. 1757), *Letters* (Telford), 3:213; and Lindström 1946, p. 126. Charles shared this idea as seen in one of his last hymns "Preparation for Death," *CW Reader*, p. 371.

221. Cf. Letter to Elizabeth Hardy (5 Apr. 1758), *Letters* (Telford), 4:10-13.

222. *Minutes* (2 Aug. 1745), Q. 2, *John Wesley*, p. 152; and "Brief Thoughts on Christian Perfection," *Works* (Jackson), 11:446.

223. See Sermon 132, "On Faith," §5, *Works*, 4:190-1; and Letter to James Hervey (15 Oct. 1756), *Letters* (Telford), 3:380.

224. *Farther Thoughts Upon Christian Perfection*, Q. 29, *Works* (Jackson), 11:426. See also *Conjectures Concerning the Nature of Future Happiness* (Dublin: Dugdale, 1787) which Wesley translated and abridged from Charles Bonnet. In it Bonnet affirmed that progression in our development as persons will continue in the life to come (pp. 23-4).

Chapter Eight

1. H. Knight 1992, p. 2.

2. Cf. *The Christian's Pattern*, Preface, §II.13, *Works* (Jackson), 14:204; Sermon 149, "On Love," §4, *Works*, 4:381; *Journal* (25 June 1740), *Works*, 19:157; *The Nature, Design, and General Rules of the United Societies*, §4-6, *Works*, 9:70-3; "Directions given to the Band Societies," §III, *Works*, 9:79; *Minutes* (2 Aug. 1745), Q. 11, *John Wesley*, p. 153; Sermon 16, "The Means of Grace," §II.1, *Works*, 1:381; *NT Notes*, Matt. 12:7, Acts 2:42, Eph. 6:18; "Large Minutes," Q. 48, *Works* (Jackson), 8:322-3; Sermon 92, "On Zeal," §II.5, *Works*, 3:313; Sermon 85, "On Working Out Our Own Salvation," §II.4, *Works*, 3:205-6; and Sermon 98, "On Visiting the Sick," §1, *Works*, 3:385.

3. H. Knight 1992 is the most detailed and insightful study of Wesley's understanding of the full range of the means of grace. For other helpful studies of this general topic, see Collins 1985, Harper 1983a, W.P. Jones 1987, McCulloh 1964, Trickett 1989; and Wakefield 1991. One should also consult studies of Wesley's general sacramentology such as Borgen 1972 & 1988, Parris 1963, Reist 1971, Sanders 1954a, Staples 1991, and Wainwright 1988.

4. For a helpful discussion of this issue and the various Western differences on the Eucharist, see Alasdair I.C. Heron, *Table and Tradition: Toward an Ecumenical Understanding of the Eucharist* (Philadelphia, PA: Westminster, 1983).

5. Note how the second prayer in Zwingli's eucharistic liturgy contrasts the flesh with the power of the Spirit through the Word, in *Prayers of the Eucharist: Early and Reformed*, ed. R.C.D. Jasper & G.J. Cuming (London: Collins, 1975), p. 118.

6. See Heron, *Table and Tradition*, p. 128.

7. E.g., *Journal* (1 May 1741), *Works*, 19:191.

8. Sermon 16, "The Means of Grace," §IV.3 & §V.4, *Works,* 1:391, 396.

9. *A Farther Appeal to Men of Reason and Religion,* Pt. I, V.28, *Works,* 11:171-2. See also the discussion of uncreated grace in Chapter Three and of the Spirit's inspiration in Chapter Five.

10. See esp. Sermon 16, "The Means of Grace," §II.1, *Works,* 1:381; and *Instructions for Children,* p. 10.

11. For details on these developments see Joseph Martos, *Doors to the Sacred: A Historical Introduction to Sacraments in the Catholic Church* (Garden City, NY: Doubleday, 1981).

12. For Anglican precedents to Wesley's conception of the means of grace, see Selleck 1983, pp. 307-10. He followed his Anglican tradition in limiting "sacraments" in the technical sense to baptism and eucharist. This is best seen in *Popery Calmly Considered,* §IV.1, *Works* (Jackson), 10:149 (distilling *A Roman Catechism, with a Reply Thereto,* Q. 52, *Works* [Jackson], 10:113)—on these two works see Chapter 1, note 45. For mention of Eastern Orthodoxy's relative lack of concern for delimiting the means of grace, see Casimir Kucharek, *The Sacramental Mysteries: A Byzantine Approach* (Allendale, NJ: Alleluia Press, 1976), p. 334.

13. H. Knight 1992, pp. 11, 35ff. Cf. the related suggestion in Selleck 1983 that Wesley used the Book of Common Prayer to keep Methodism from degenerating into a self-centered individualism.

14. See respectively: Letter to 'John Smith' (25 June 1746), §9, *Works,* 26:203; and Letter to Gilbert Boyce (22 May 1750), *Works,* 26:425. Cf. John Bowmer, "Early Methodism and the Quakers," *RelLife* 23 (1954):418-29 (deals only with the negative side).

15. See Sermon 16, "The Means of Grace," §V.4, *Works,* 1:395.

16. The point of this claim, as originally developed, was not that the sacraments are effective apart from faithful participation of the recipient, but that their effectiveness is not hampered by the possible moral unworthiness of the officiant! It was an argument against the Donatists that God could minister grace through imperfect clergy.

17. Their key reference is Wesley's acknowledgment at this point that constant use of the means of grace does not in itself justify him before God; *Journal* (29 Jan. 1738), *Works,* 18:214.

18. Cf. *Journal* (7 Nov. 1739), *Works,* 19:121; and *Journal* (31 Dec. 1739), *Works,* 19:132-3.

19. "Low-church" readings of Wesley's understanding of the sacraments are less common in recent Wesley scholarship than before, the clearest examples would be Parris 1963, esp. pp. 97-100; A.S. Wood 1967, p. 247; and Reist 1971. The most vigorous argument for Wesley's sacramental understanding of Christian life remains Rattenbury 1948 (but see also K. Wilson 1984, esp. pp. 291ff). The most influential expositions of the creative balance in Wesley's position are Sanders 1954a & 1966; and Borgen 1972 (digested in 1988). Note Borgen's responses to both Rattenbury (p. 18) and the portrayal of Aldersgate as a rejection of sacramental emphasis on Wesley's part (pp. 271-3).

20. For similar claims see W.P. Jones 1987, p. 14; and H. Knight 1992, p. 104.

21. E.g., Sermon 16, "The Means of Grace," §V.4, *Works,* 1:396; and *Popery Calmly Considered,* §IV.2, *Works* (Jackson), 10:149 (distilling *A Roman Catechism, with a Reply Thereto,* Q. 54, *Works* [Jackson], 10:113). As Luby argues (1984, pp. 250-4) Wesley is misunderstanding authentic Roman Catholic teaching, which concurs with his major point. He clearly accepted the real point of *ex opere operato,* which is that sacraments

are not rendered ineffective by an unworthy minister—cf. Sermon 32, "Sermon on the Mount XII," §8, *Works,* 1:682-3; *OT Notes,* 1 Samuel 2:17 (original to Wesley); Letter to Mary Bishop (18 Oct. 1778), *Letters* (Telford), 6:327; and Sermon 104, "On Attending the Church Service," §27-30, *Works,* 3:475-7. As such, his deletion of Anglican Article XXVI, "Of the Unworthiness of the Ministers, Which Hinders not the Effect of the Sacrament," likely reflects more an unwillingness to provide any excuse for ministerial immorality than a view of the effectiveness of the sacraments (cf. Oden 1988, p. 120).

22. E.g., Sermon 45, "The New Birth," §IV.4, *Works,* 2:200-1; and Letter to Dr. John Robertson (24 Sept. 1753), *Works,* 26:523.

23. For a few of the best known examples, see Letter to Count Zinzendorf and the Church at Herrnhut (5-8 Aug. 1740), *Works,* 26:27; Sermon 16, "The Means of Grace," *Works,* 1:378-97; Letter to William Law (6 Jan. 1756), *Letters* (Telford), 3:366; and *Cautions and Directions Given to the Greatest Professors in the Methodist Societies* (1762), §II, *John Wesley,* p. 300.

24. Cf. Sermon 16, "The Means of Grace," §II.1, *Works,* 1:381; and Sermon 74, "Of the Church," §I.12, *Works,* 3:49-50. For a convenient quotation of the relevant portion of the Anglican catechism, see Borgen 1972, pp. 49-50.

25. Cf. *NT Notes,* Acts 22:16; Letter to William Law (6 Jan. 1756), §II.4, *Letters* (Telford), 3:357; Letter to Mr. Potter (4 Nov. 1758), *Letters* (Telford), 4:38; and Sermon 74, "Of the Church," §I.12, *Works,* 3:49-50.

26. E.g., *NT Notes,* Mark 16:16; and *Journal* (5 Feb. 1760), *Works,* 21:240.

27. Technically, the basic ability to respond would be upheld by Prevenient Grace, while the specific response would be evoked by the empowering Presence of the Holy Spirit in baptism (see Chapter Three).

28. For more on the following account, see Kucharek, *Sacramental Mysteries,* pp. 335-70; and Hans Schwarz, *Divine Communication Word and Sacrament in Biblical, Historical, and Contemporary Perspective* (Philadelphia, PA: Fortress, 1985), pp. 101-11.

29. E.g., Hopko, *Spirit of God,* pp. 33-57; Mantzaridis, *Deification of Man,* pp. 41-60; Stephanou, "Divine Indwelling," p. 16; and Gennadios Limouris, "The Sanctifying Grace of the Holy Spirit," in *Come Holy Spirit: Renew the Whole Creation,* ed. G. Limouris (Brookline, MA: Holy Cross, 1990), pp. 181-94.

30. The following is informed by John Meyendorff, "Notes on the Orthodox Understanding of the Eucharist," in *The Sacraments: An Ecumenical Dilemma,* edited by Hans Küng (New York: Paulist, 1966), pp. 51-58; John H. McKenna, *Eucharist and Holy Spirit: The Eucharistic Epiclesis in 20th Century Theology* (London: SPCK, 1975), pp. 15-89; and Alexander Schmemann, *The Eucharist* (Crestwood, NY: St. Vladimir's Seminary Press, 1988), pp. 213-27.

31. For comparing the liturgies about to be discussed, see the handy collection in Jasper & Cuming, *Prayers of the Eucharist.* The relevant passages in the 1549 and 1552 Anglican liturgies are near the bottom of pp. 156 & 163. See also R.T. Beckwith, "The Anglican Eucharist: From the Reformation to the Restoration," in *The Study of Liturgy,* ed. Cheslyn Jones, *et al.* (Revised edition, New York: Oxford University Press, 1992), pp. 309-18.

32. The best examples are *Hymns on the Lord's Supper,* #72 (Rattenbury, p. 217) & #16 (Rattenbury, p. 200). It is significant that there was little precedent in Brevint for this insertion! Cf. the discussion in Rattenbury 1928, p. 183; Rattenbury 1948, pp. 50-1 [45-6]; Bowmer 1951, p. 86; Hodges & Allchin 1966, p. 39; Borgen 1972, pp. 74-5; and Nichols 1988a, p. 19.

33. Cf. *Sunday Service,* pp. 135-6.

34. For affirmation of the role of the other "Persons" in the eucharist, see *Hymns on the Lord's Supper*, #58, st. 4 (Rattenbury, p. 213); #66 (p. 216); #75 (p. 218); and #150 (p. 243).

35. Cf. "The Christian Sacrament and Sacrifice," §III.7, Rattenbury, p. 181. Charles' verse is in hymn #75, st. 4 (p. 218). See also Sermon 101, "The Duty of Constant Communion," §I.2-3, *Works*, 3:429.

36. Note especially his claim that the means of grace are less than nothing apart from their end of fostering true religion, in Sermon 16, "The Means of Grace," §II.2, *Works*, 1:381. Cf. Hillman's comparison of Wesley and Calvin in this regard (1978, pp. 437-8).

37. "The Christian Sacrament and Sacrifice," §II.1, Rattenbury, p. 176. Note that Brevint developed this theme (V, pp. 184-6) more as an assurance that the blessings of life which we have today through the eucharist will be crowned by eternal life than as a guarantee of salvation (hence Wesley could retain it).

38. See the discussion of the co-operant nature of salvation in Chapter Six.

39. Cf. Sermon 16 (1746), "The Means of Grace," §II.1, *Works*, 1:381; Letter to William Law (6 Jan. 1756), *Letters* (Telford), 3:357; Sermon 74 (1785), "Of the Church," §I.12, *Works*, 3:49-50; and the 1787 change of Robert Nelson's *The Great Duty of Frequenting the Christian Sacrifice* in Sermon 101, "The Duty of Constant Communion" that is described in Borgen 1972, p. 222 fn22.

40. Note the changes in Anglican Article XXV (Oden 1988, p. 119) and Article XXVII (Oden 1988, p. 121); and the discussion in Borgen 1972, pp. 222-3.

41. *Devotions for Every Day*, Tuesday, Gill, p. 77.

42. While Borgen 1972 is the most complete study of Wesley on the sacraments, his dependence on the conceptuality of the *ordo salutis* (cf. p. 47) results in relative neglect of this question of how the sacraments actually *nurture* Christian character! Attention to the latter question is the strength of H. Knight 1992.

43. Cf. Letter to Mrs. Mary Pendarves (19 July 1731), *Works*, 25:293-4.

44. Cf. *The Character of a Methodist*, §4-5, §13, *Works*, 9:35, 39; *Journal* (7 Nov. 1739), *Works*, 19:121; *Journal* (31 Dec. 1739), *Works*, 19:132-3; and Letter to Count Zinzendorf and the Church at Herrnhut (5-8 Aug. 1740), *Works*, 26:27.

45. Cf. *Minutes* (2 Aug. 1745), Q. 11, *John Wesley*, p. 153; Sermon 16 (1746), "The Means of Grace," §III.1, *Works*, 1:385; and his mature advice to one with the "faith of a servant" in Sermon 106 (1788), "On Faith," §II.4, *Works*, 3:500.

46. Cf. Sermon 101, "The Duty of Constant Communion," *Works*, 3:428-39. Though Wesley lists obedience to Divine command as an initial reason for receiving the Lord's Supper as often as possible (§I.1), he proceeds immediately to stress the gracious benefits that we receive through it (§I.2).

47. Letter to Mrs. Woodhouse (17 May 1766), *Letters* (Telford), 5:12. See also his retention of the commendation of holy exercises to nourish grace in his edited catechism published as well in 1766, *Christian Instructions*, p. 4.

48. E.g., D. Watson 1986b, pp. 225, 238; and S. Johnson 1987, p. 25.

49. Analysis of how Methodists widely reduced the reason for receiving the Lord's Supper to a matter of obedience can be found in John Bowmer, *The Lord's Supper in Methodism 1791-1960* (London: Epworth, 1961); and Paul Sanders, "The Sacraments in Early American Methodism," *Church History* 26 (1957):355-71 (a synopsis of Sanders 1954a). For a similar move in Holiness circles, see Donald Wood, "A Matter of Obedience: John Wesley on the Lord's Supper," *Preacher's Magazine* 56.1 (1980):33-4.

50. Cf. Sermon 16, "The Means of Grace," §II.1, *Works*, 1:381.

51. This point emerged clearly in William Hasker's response (pp. 60-2) to Albert Truesdale, "Christian Holiness and the Problem of Systemic Evil," *WTJ* 19.1 (1984):39-59. For appeal to the means of grace to address this issue, see H. Knight 1992, p. 85.

52. For specific studies of the Wesleys' understanding of the Lord's Supper (in addition to the general studies of sacramentology listed in note 2 above), see Bowmer 1951, George 1964b, Grislis 1963, S. Johnson 1987, Nichols 1988b, Rattenbury 1948, and Sanders 1966. The prominence of *Hymns on the Lord's Supper* to this topic makes the combined consideration of the brothers inescapable.

53. Cf. the comparison of various lists in Borgen 1972, p. 106.

54. See Sermon 10, "Sermon on the Mount VI," §III.11, *Works*, 1:585; and Sermon 85, "On Working Out Our Own Salvation," §II.4, *Works*, 3:205. Note also the argument that the Lord's Supper is the most glorious means of grace that Wesley retained in "The Christian Sacrament and Sacrifice," §IV.6, Rattenbury, p. 183.

55. The uniqueness (and count) of Wesley's frequency of communion is defended in Bowmer 1951, pp. 3-17. Cf. H. Davies 1961, p. 63. For some qualifications of these claims, see Rack 1989, pp. 19-20, 403. For examples of daily communion in holy seasons, see *Journal* (25 Dec. 1774), *Works*, 22: 441; and *Journal* (30 Mar. 1777), *Journal* (Curnock), 6:142.

56. Cf. *Sunday Service*, p. ii; and Sermon 101, "The Duty of Constant Communion," *Works*, 3:428-39. As Outler notes (p. 427), this sermon is drawn from Robert Nelson's *The Great Duty of Frequenting the Christian Sacrifice*, but is revised to the point that it can be considered true to Wesley.

57. This development is traced in Bowmer 1951, pp. 62-81. Ironically, it is in his attempts to justify his restriction of administering sacraments from his lay-preachers that Wesley comes the closest to discounting the need for the sacraments—cf. "Ought We to Separate from the Church of England" (1755), §III.1, *Works*, 9:572; and Letter to Nicholas Norton (3 Sept. 1756), *Letters* (Telford), 3:186.

58 .Cf. Rattenbury 1948, p. 152 [139]; Nichols 1988a, p. 21; and Nichols 1988b.

59. Wesley retained the Anglican Articles relating to the eucharist essentially unchanged in the Articles of Religion, with the exception of Article XXIX which conflicted with his affirmation of the eucharist as a converting ordinance (cf. Oden 1988, pp. 121-2). He also retained the "Order for the Administration of the Lord's Supper" in the *Sunday Service* (pp. 125-39) with very few changes (cf. Bowmer 1951, pp. 206-15). He republished *Hymns on the Lord's Supper* nine times during his life, and published the Brevint extract separately three times.

60. Cf. Bowmer 1951, p. 166; Grislis 1963, p. 103; and Borgen 1972, pp. 27-8.

61. See "The Christian Sacrament and Sacrifice," §VI.2, Rattenbury, pp. 186-7; *A Roman Catechism, with a Reply Thereto* (by John Williams), Q. 70, *Works* (Jackson), 10:120; and *NT Notes*, Matt. 26:26-8, Mark 14:24, Luke 22:19.

62. Note the dialogue over the adequacy of this modern notion in Bowmer 1951, p. 178; George 1964b, pp. 150-4; and Borgen 1972, pp. 86-8. Contrast the questionable claim in Hildebrandt 1967 that *Hymns on the Lord's Supper* is closer to the Roman Catholic understanding of sacrifice.

63. *Hymns on the Lord's Supper*, #92, st. 1, Rattenbury, p. 223. Cf. "The Christian Sacrament and Sacrifice," §III-IV, Rattenbury, pp. 179-84. Note also that Wesley retained Anglican Article XXVIII unchanged in the Articles of Religion (Oden 1988, p. 121).

64. E.g., "The Christian Sacrament and Sacrifice," §VI.5, Rattenbury, pp. 183; and *Hymns on the Lord's Supper*, #116, st. 5, Rattenbury, p. 232.

65. Actually, the extract from Brevint retained language suggesting the ubiquity of Christ (§VI.5, Rattenbury, pp. 183). This led Hildebrandt to suggest correlations between Wesley and Luther (1951, pp. 148-9). Borgen has shown that Wesley clearly denied the ubiquity of the human nature of the risen Christ (1972, pp. 59-66). His rejection of the change of substance in the elements is evident in the retention of Anglican Article XXVIII in the Articles of Religion (Oden 1988, p. 121); and *Popery Calmly Considered,* §IV.5, *Works* (Jackson), 10:151 (distilling *A Roman Catechism, with a Reply Thereto,* Q. 63, *Works* [Jackson], 10:118).

66. Cf. *Hymns on the Lord's Supper,* #57, st. 4, Rattenbury, p. 213: "Sure and real is the grace, the manner is unknown." For criticism of such practices as "adoring the Host," see *Popery Calmly Considered,* §IV.6, *Works* (Jackson), 10:152 (distilling *A Roman Catechism, with a Reply Thereto,* Q. 72, *Works* [Jackson], 10:121).

67. Cf. Anglican Article XXVIII (Wesley XVIII), Oden 1988, p. 121. For discussion of the different versions of the Anglican Articles, see Green, *Thirty-Nine Articles,* pp. 218-9.

68. See William R. Crockett, "Holy Communion," in *The Study of Anglicanism,* ed. S. Sykes and J. Booty (London: SPCK, 1988), pp. 272-85.

69. See the affirmations of "receptionism," "virtualism," or a Calvinist "spiritual Presence" position in Rattenbury 1948, p. 59 [54]; George 1964a, pp. 183-4; Sanders 1966, p. 165; and Staples 1991, p. 224 (but note also Borgen's enigmatic qualification of such identifications [1972, pp. 67-8]).

70. Wesley had written his mother on 26 Jan. 1732, including a friend's argument that any affirmation of Christ's human nature in the Lord's Supper would lead inevitably to either con- or trans-substantiation, defending instead a receptionist position. Susanna's response was that she too understood by the real presence of Christ that "the divine nature of Christ is then eminently present to impart (by the operation of his Holy Spirit) the benefits of his death to worthy receivers" (Letter from Mrs. Susanna Wesley [21 Feb. 1732], *Works,* 25:326). Unfortunately, Wesley's initial letter is lost, so the reasonable inference that the reference to the Holy Spirit in parentheses is Susanna's addition cannot be verified.

71. See his response to his mother's letter (which also allows more reconstruction of the suggestion in the lost letter), Letter to Mrs. Susanna Wesley (28 Feb. 1732), *Works,* 25:328.

72. This seems a much more adequate way to put it than Borgen's claim (1972, pp. 75, 211) that "God dispenses his grace, whenever he wills." Cf. the critique of Borgen in H. Knight 1992, pp. 131ff.

73. Cf. "The Christian Sacrament and Sacrifice," §III.3, Rattenbury, p. 180; *Hymns on the Lord's Supper,* #40, Rattenbury, p. 208; and Sermon 16, "The Means of Grace," §III.11, *Works,* 1:585 (which recommends the Lord's Supper for those desiring an *increase* in the grace of God).

74. Note the direct connection of these three dimensions in "The Christian Sacrament and Sacrifice," §II.1, Rattenbury, p. 176.

75. E.g., Geoffrey Wainwright, *Eucharist and Eschatology* (New York: Oxford University Press, 1981), p. 56. See also Rattenbury 1948, pp. 61-78; Bowmer 1951, p. 184; George 1964b, p. 150; Sanders 1966, pp. 163, 167; and S. Johnson 1987, p. 35 (but contrast Borgen 1972, pp. 18-19, 231). Compare this theme to the emphasis on Eucharist as the sacrament of the Kingdom in Schmemann, *Eucharist,* pp. 27-48.

76. John's understanding of Christ as King was treated in Chapter Four. His emphasis on how the hope of entire sanctification encourages growth toward that goal was noted in Chapter Seven. For the specific context of the eucharist as pledge,

note this theme in *Hymns on the Lord's Supper*, #96, #102, #110 (st. 3), and #112 (st. 3), Rattenbury, pp. 225-30.

77. Note the guided confession using the ten commandments and the later prayer of confession in *Sunday Service*, p. 125-7, 132. The importance of this liturgical component to Wesley's understanding of Christian holiness has been stressed by H. Knight 1992, pp. 138-9; and Paul Merritt Bassett, "Wesleyan Words in the Nineteenth-Century World: 'Sin,' A Case Study," *EvJl* 8 (1990):15-40, esp. pp. 25-7.

78. The closing prayer is in *Sunday Service*, pp. 137-8. Note the extended section on this theme that Wesley retained in "The Christian Sacrament and Sacrifice," §VII-VIII, Rattenbury, pp. 188-93. See also *Hymns on the Lord's Supper*, #139, st. 1, (Rattenbury, p. 239): "God of all-redeeming grace, By Thy pardoning love compell'd, Up to Thee our souls we raise, Up to Thee our bodies yield."

79. Wesley's liturgical spirituality is a focus of Brockwell 1990; Gordon 1991; H. Knight 1992, pp. 92-5; Selleck 1983; and K. Wilson 1984. For specific consideration of the *Sunday Service*, see also George 1984; Wade 1981, pp. 1-86; and J. White 1984.

80. *A Farther Appeal to Men of Reason and Religion*, Pt. I, §III.4, *Works*, 11:122; *A Word to a Methodist*, §3, *Works*, 9:244; *Reasons Against a Separation from the Church of England*, §III.2, *Works*, 9:389; 1766 *Minutes*, Q. 28, *Minutes* (Mason), p. 59 (also as "Large Minutes," Q. 45, *Works* [Jackson], 8:321-2); and Sermon 84, "The Important Question," §III.1, *Works*, 3:189.

81. For just a few examples: *Journal* (23 Dec. 1744), *Works*, 20:46; *Journal* (1 Oct. 1749), *Works*, 20:306; and *Journal* (13 Nov. 1763), *Works*, 21:438. See also Selleck 1983, pp. 63-143.

82. Cf. Sermon 39, "Catholic Spirit," §I.11, *Works*, 2:86; and *Journal* (5 June 1766), *Works*, 22:42-3. For reflection on his claims to primitive warrant, see Campbell 1991b, pp. 94-101; and Tews 1978.

83. For the range of evaluations of developed Methodist worship, compare H. Davies 1961, pp. 184ff to Bishop 1975.

84. In this regard it is important to note that when Wesley occasionally boasted about the superiority of Methodist worship to that in the parish churches, his focus was on the Methodist officiants' greater seriousness and conformity of life to their confession; he assumed the same general components of worship in both. Cf. Letter to a Friend (20 Sept. 1757), *Letters* (Telford), 3:226-8.

85. Daily corporate morning and evening prayers had declined drastically in eighteenth-century Anglicanism, even as the private discipline required of priests (cf. Norman Sykes, *Church and State in England in the Eighteenth Century* [New York: Farrar, Straus and Giroux, 1975], pp. 246-8). By contrast, Wesley regularly read the assigned prayer service—as a leader at churches or society gatherings when possible, and privately when not (cf. Selleck 1983, pp. 186-200). He desired this practice by his followers, but also recognized the many difficulties. His compromise was to provide formal prayers for Sunday, the litanies for Wednesday and Friday, and to encourage corporate times of extemporaneous prayer on the other days (*Sunday Service*, p. ii, 4).

86. Cf. Wade 1981, p. 86; and Wainwright 1986. One may note that in the 1754 *NT Notes* (Matt. 12:8) Wesley admitted that Sunday was not the Sabbath, while he inserted a speculation into the 1765 *OT Notes* (Exodus 20:8, cf. Casto 1977, p. 373) that Sunday was the *original* Sabbath, which the Israelites had changed and Jesus was simply restoring by his resurrection.

87. Cf. H. Davies 1961, p. 29; and Bishop 1975, p. 16.

88. Compare "MS Journal" (2 Jan. 1737), *Works*, 18:460; to *Journal* (1 Apr. 1738), *Works*, 18:233.

89. See respectively: Letter to Mary Bishop (18 Oct. 1778), *Letters* (Telford), 6:326; *Reasons Against a Separation from the Church of England*, §III.2, *Works*, 9:389; and 1766 *Minutes*, Q. 28, *Minutes* (Mason), p. 59 (also as "Large Minutes," Q. 45, *Works* [Jackson], 8:321-2).

90. Cf. Casto 1977, pp. 128-37; and Wesley F. Smith, "John Wesley's Lectionary," *LQHR* 183 (new series, 27) (1958):298-304.

91. Casto 1977, p. 137.

92. E.g., see the *Journal* comments for November 1 in 1756 (*Works*, 21:81), 1766 (*Works*, 22:66), 1767 (*Works*, 22:107-8), 1788 (*Journal* [Curnock], 7:445), and 1789 (*Journal* [Curnock], 8:21). This makes it all-the-more striking that he removed All Saints Day from the calendar in *Sunday Service*! For more on Wesley's interest in the saints, see Laurence Hull Stookey, "The Wesleys and the Saints," *Liturgy* 5 (1985-6):77-81; and Geoffrey Wainwright, "Wesley and the Communion of Saints," *One in Christ* 27 (1991):332-45.

93. Gill, pp. 92-3.

94. Note the emphasis on the saints as examples in Hulley 1988, p. 3. See also the criticism of intercessory prayer to saints in *Popery Calmly Considered*, §III.3, *Works* (Jackson), 10:146 (distilling *A Roman Catechism, with a Reply Thereto*, Qq. 34-37, *Works* [Jackson], 10:104-5).

95. Charleston, SC: Timothy, 1737 (reprint ed., Nashville, TN: United Methodist Publishing House, 1992).

96. Cf. Baker 1970, p. 51; and Rack 1989, p. 122.

97. Cf. Beckerlegge 1983, pp. 62ff; and Bishop 1975, pp. 135-48. See also Gallaway's stress on hymns as a "means of grace" (1988, p. 200).

98. For characterization of Charles' poetry as "romantic," see Noll 1974, and Brantley 1987. Contrast Dale 1960, pp. 11, 127-54; Routley 1968, p. 30; Welch 1971, pp. 102-3; Marshall & Todd 1982, pp. 79-87; and J.R. Tyson 1986, pp. 23-5.

99. Cf. Letter to a Friend (20 Sept. 1757), *Letters* (Telford), 3:227); *Journal* (29 Aug. 1762), *Works*, 21:387; *Journal* (9 Aug. 1768), *Works*, 22:152; *Journal* (22 Oct. 1768), *Works*, 22:161-2; *Journal* (29 Mar. 1782), *Journal* (Curnock), 6:346. See also the discussion in Routley 1968, pp. 6-19; Samuel J. Rogal, "John Wesley and the Organ: the Superfluous Pipes," *Church Music* 74.2 (1974):27-31; Wade 1981, pp. 12-15, 67; and Bufford W. Coe, "John Wesley and Church Music," *Sacramental Life* 6.4 (1993):5-12.

100. For example, in addition to *Hymns on the Lord's Supper*, some popular collections that were reprinted throughout Wesley's life are *Hymns for the Nativity of Our Lord* (1745, facsimile reprint: Madison, NJ: Charles Wesley Society, 1991), *Hymns for Our Lord's Resurrection* (1746, facsimile reprint: Madison, NJ: Charles Wesley Society, 1992)), and *Hymns for Ascension-Day* (1746).

101. The major studies of Wesley's understanding and practice of preaching are William Doughty, *John Wesley: Preacher* (London: Epworth, 1955); and Outler 1984. Wesley's specific "awakening sermons" were for his field-preaching.

102. 1753 *Minutes*, Q. 48, *Minutes* (Mason), p. 558 (also as "Large Minutes," Q.36, *Works* [Jackson], 8:317). See also his abridged essay for his preachers: *Directions Concerning Pronunciation and Gesture* (Bristol: Farley, 1749).

103. See the discussion of preaching Christ in all three offices in Chapter Four. Note in this regard the mature Wesley's complaint about "gospel sermons" that say nothing about good tempers and good works, in Letter to Mary Bishop (18 Oct.

1778), *Letters* (Telford), 6:326. But he equally condemned those who offer too little gospel in their sermons; cf. *Journal* (2 Aug. 1767), *Works,* 22:96-7.

104. For general studies of the place of communal support as a means of grace see K. Wilson 1984, pp. 355-453; and Nelson 1987.

105. Cf. *Journal* (1 May 1738), *Works,* 18:236-7; *The Nature, Design, and General Rules of the United Societies* (1743), *Works,* 9:69-73; and *A Plain Account of the People Called Methodists* (1749), §I, *Works,* 9:254-9. One should also note that the mature Wesley came to include earlier expressions of such support groups in tracing the origins of Methodism; *A Short History of the People Called Methodists* (1781), §9, *Works,* 9:430.

106. See the description of the societies (and classes) as "spiritual helps" in Sermon 107, "On God's Vineyard," §II-III, *Works,* 3:508-12.

107. See respectively, *Hymns and Sacred Poems* (1939), Preface, §4-5, *Works* (Jackson), 14:321; and Sermon 24, "Sermon on the Mount IV," §I.1, *Works,* 1:533-4.

108. *Hymns,* #489, st. 3-4, *Works,* 7:677.

109. The best studies of the love feast are Baker 1957, and R. Johnson 1979. On primitive precedent, see Campbell 1991b, pp. 97-8.

110. Note his description of the design of the love-feast for free and familiar conversation in *Journal* (19 July 1761), *Works,* 21:336.

111. Cf. *Hymns,* #507, st. 1, *Works,* 7:698. In retrospect, the elevation of the role of testimonies set up the love feast for a distorting impact of decisionistic revivalism, leading to its demise; cf. Baker 1957, pp. 56-7.

112. See the discussion in Rack 1989, pp. 411-2. The love feast in question is noted in *Journal* (1 Jan. 1739), *Works,* 19:29. Wesley traces the watch-night service back to developments at Kingswood in *A Plain Account of the People Called Methodists,* III.1, *Works,* 9:264. The service which he describes there is likely noted in *Journal* (12 Mar. 1742), *Works,* 19:257. Naturally, he also mentioned parallels to early Christian vigils (cf. Campbell 1991b, p. 98).

113. See Section IV, "For Believers Watching," in *Hymns, Works,* 7:450-66. Of particular note are: #296, st. 1 (450); #299, st. 1-2 (454); #305, st. 3 (461); and #309 (465).

114. E.g., *Journal* (24 Sept. 1779), *Journal* (Curnock), 6:255; *Journal* (1 Mar. 1782), *Journal* (Curnock), 6:343; *Journal* (31 Dec. 1784), *Journal* (Curnock), 7:42; and *Journal* (10 July 1789), *Journal* (Curnock), 7:517.

115. Cf. the careful textual history in Marion A. Jackson "An Analysis of the Source of John Wesley's *Directions for Renewing Our Covenant with God,*" *MethH* 30 (1992):176-84.

116. Cf. *Journal* (6 Aug. 1755), *Works,* 21:23; and *A Short History of the People Called Methodists,* §58, *Works,* 9:461.

117. Note Wesley's description of a Covenant Service providing some with a sense of pardon, some a sense of full salvation, and many a fresh manifestation of God's grace healing their backslidings, in *Journal* (1 Jan. 1775), *Works,* 22:441. In 1779 Wesley extracted the relevant portion of Alleine and published it separately as *Directions for Renewing Our Covenant with God.* A ready copy of the liturgy for the service can be found in *The United Methodist Book of Worship* (Nashville, TN: United Methodist Publishing House, 1992), pp. 291-4. The preliminary directions are reprinted in Tripp 1969, pp. 177-88. See also *Hymns,* #518 (*Works,* 7:710-11), which is the traditional hymn for the covenant service (cf. *Journal* [12 July 1778], *Journal* [Curnock], 6:203). The centrality of confession to the service is emphasized in Wagley 1991.

118. R. Davies 1961, p. 67. See also the reflections in Tripp 1969, and Bishop 1975, pp. 94ff.

119. Note the direct connection Wesley makes between fellowship and spiritual direction in *A Plain Account of the People Called Methodists*, §I.11, *Works*, 9:259.

120. E.g., *Journal* (17 Aug. 1751), *Works*, 20:357; Letter to William Church (13 Oct. 1778), *Letters* (Telford), 6:324; Letter to Adam Clarke (3 Jan. 1787), *Letters* (Telford), 7:362; and Sermon 122, "Causes of the Inefficacy of Christianity," §7, *Works*, 4:90.

121. E.g., *Journal* (21 Aug. 1774), *Works*, 22:426; "Thoughts on Methodism," *AM* 10 (1787):100ff, *Works* (Jackson), 13:258-61; and Sermon 107, "On God's Vineyard," *Works*, 3:503-17. See also the quotation attributed to Wesley in *A History of the Methodist Church in Great Britain*, ed. R. Davies *et al.* (London: Epworth, 1988) 4:194. The most extended (but dated) study of Wesley's understanding of Christian discipline is Russell 1951. For a brief up-to-date study see Trickett 1989.

122. The best summary of Methodist discipline is Sermon 107, "On God's Vineyard," §III, *Works*, 3:511-2. See also the study of Wesley's use of disciplinary measures in C. White 1991. The official form of the General Rules is in *A Plain Account of the People Called Methodists*, §I.8, *Works*, 9:257. Note that the original form of the first rule was to "avoid evil of every kind." The focus on known sin in "On God's Vineyard" (1787) reflects Wesley's mature thought. Accounts of the use of tickets (as well as some pictures) can be found in D. Watson 1985, pp. 104-5, 208-11.

123. On the issue of Wesley's legalism and some of its sources, see McNulty 1963, pp. 100-3; Collins 1984a; and Hatton 1990. Note the late Wesley's hesitant qualification of this rigor in terms of "two orders of Christian life" in Sermon 89, "The More Excellent Way," *Works*, 3:263-77.

124. See esp. 1766 *Minutes*, Q. 28, *Minutes* (Mason), pp. 60-2 (also as "Large Minutes," Q. 27, *Works* [Jackson], 8:310-13).

125. Cf. *Journal* (25 June 1745), *Works*, 20:34; and Letter to John Valton (18 Jan. 1782), *Letters* (Telford), 7:101. Wesley's concern that discipline be potentially redemptive is the likely reason for the deletion of Anglican Article XXXIII, which enjoins avoidance of the excommunicated, from his Articles of Religion (cf. Oden 1988, p. 123).

126. For similar assessments of the General Rules as character-forming, in response to God's grace, see Nausner 1989 and D. Watson 1990, p. 37.

127. Cf. Sermon 23, "Sermon on the Mount III," §I.4, *Works*, 1:512; and Sermon 97, "On Obedience to Pastors," §III.6, *Works*, 3:380.

128. Cf. Letter to Charles Wesley (25 Mar. 1772), *Letters* (Telford), 5:314; *A Farther Appeal to Men of Reason and Religion*, Pt. II, §II.34-5, *Works*, 11:246-7; and "Large Minutes," Q. 26, pt. 11, *Works* (Jackson), 8:310. For analyses of Wesley's own practice as a spiritual director, see Harper 1985, Selleck 1990, and Tracy 1988. See also discussions of his model of pastoral care in Outler 1971b, and Selleck 1984.

129. For Wesley's description of these various levels, see *Rules of the Band Societies* (1738), *Works*, 9:77-8; *Directions Given to the Band Societies* (1744), *Works*, 9:79; *Minutes* (28 June 1744), Qq. 1-5, *John Wesley*, p. 143-4; and *A Plain Account of the People Called Methodists*, §II-VIII, *Works*, 9:260-70. Note also the discussions in Dean 1985, pp. 148ff; H. Knight 1992, pp. 98-103; Selleck 1990; Snyder 1989, pp. 203-8; D. Watson 1985, pp. 93-121; and D. Watson 1986b, pp. 230-37.

130. For arguments that accountability was the most important purpose (among several) of the various substructures, see Dean 1985, p. 298; D. Watson 1985 p. 116; and Snyder 1989, pp. 203-8.

131. Note David Watson's assessment of the development of classes alongside of the bands as a response to the growing number of Methodists coming from the working class (1986b, p. 229).

132. Note Dean's description of each level as the "spark plug" of the level below it (1985, pp. 201-10).

133. I say "some" assurance because the mature Wesley came to value the bands as much for nurturing incipient assurance as for maintaining it. According to Dean (1985, p. 164) no more than one fourth of Methodists were in a band at any one time.

134. See Sermon 49, "The Cure of Evil-Speaking," §III.1, *Works*, 2:260; and Sermon 65, "The Duty of Reproving Our Neighbor," *Works*, 2:511-20.

135. For a discussion of some precedents that may have influenced Wesley's creation of the Penitent bands, see Campbell 1991b, p. 87.

136. Note his encouragement of regular attendance at the select society in Letter to Mrs Marston (11 Aug. 1770), *Letters* (Telford), 5:196; Ibid (26 Aug. 1770), *Letters* (Telford), 5:198; and Letter to Mrs. Pawson (16 Nov. 1789), *Letters* (Telford), 8:184.

137. See *A Plain Account of the People Called Methodists*, §VIII.2, *Works*, 9:270. Cf. Dean 1985, p. 185.

138. Note how this goal is explicit in *Minutes* (28 June 1744), Q. 5, *John Wesley*, p. 144. Cf. the discussion of this goal in Walsh 1990. For a more general comment on the select societies providing leadership to the larger group, see Letter to Mrs. Clark (1 June 1782), *Letters* (Telford), 7:158.

139. For a study of the early Wesley's devotional practices, see Harper 1981. The best surveys of the devotional pattern that he recommended to his Methodist people are George 1963, Dearing 1966, and Harper 1983a.

140. Letter to John Trembath (17 Aug. 1760), *Letters* (Telford), 4:103.

141. Note, for example his comment that meditating on Scripture will bring us the mind of Christ, "and in consequence of this, while you joyfully experience all the holy tempers described in this book, you will likewise be outwardly holy as He that hath called you is holy in all manner of conversation"; *OT Notes*, Preface, 17, *Works* (Jackson), 14:252. See also H. Knight 1992, p. 151.

142. Note the rebuttals to such suggestion of doubt in Selleck 1983, p. 189; and Casto 1977, p. 133.

143. E.g., Letter to Margaret Lewen (June 1764), *Letters* (Telford), 4:247; and *OT Notes*, Preface, §18, *Works* (Jackson), 14:253. See also the helpful discussions in Harper 1983a, pp. 28-35; and M. Robert Mulholland, Jr., *Shaped by the Word* (Nashville, TN: The Upper Room, 1985), pp. 119-28.

144. Cf. Letter to George Holder (8 Nov. 1790), *Letters* (Telford), 8:247; and his prescription of encouraging more reading of spiritual literature in places where the work of God seems to stand still, in 1768 *Minutes*, Q. 23, *Minutes* (Mason), p. 79 (abridged as "Large Minutes," Q. 56, *Works* [Jackson], 8:328).

145. Letter to Miss March (29 Mar. 1760), *Letters* (Telford), 4:90. See also *Journal* (4 Sept. 1772), *Works*, 22:348.

146. *NT Notes*, Matt 6:8.

147. For example, note the reflection questions organized into *A Collection of Forms of Prayer*, *Works* (Jackson), 11:203-37. See also the discussion in Gill 1951.

148. Note how Wesley places works of mercy in a circle more closely related to holy tempers and love than works of piety, in Sermon 92, "On Zeal," §II.5, *Works*, 3:313. See also his defense of works of mercy as means of grace in Sermon 98, "On Visiting the Sick," §1, *Works*, 3:385.

149. Cf. *Advice to the People Called Methodists*, §3, *Works*, 9:124; Sermon 23, "Sermon on the Mount III," §I.1, *Works*, 1:510; *NT Notes*, 1 Cor. 13:4, Gal. 5:14; Sermon 36, "The Law Established Through Faith II," §III.3, *Works*, 2:41-2; Sermon 90, "An Israelite Indeed," §2, *Works*, 3:279; and Sermon 91, "On Charity," §I.3, *Works*, 3:295. See also Marquardt 1977a, pp. 127-30 [107-9].

150. E.g., Letter to John Glass (1 Nov. 1757), *Letters* (Telford), 3:237; *NT Notes*, 1 John 3:23; and the warning that works of mercy are necessary to salvation in Sermon 98, "On Visiting the Sick," §2, *Works*, 3:386. As Henry Knight explains (1992, p. 4) this means that in cases of conflict works of mercy would take precedence over works of piety!

151. Note in this regard that Wesley retained and emphasized the collection of alms for the poor in society communion services; cf. *Sunday Service*, p. 130; "The Christian Sacrament and Sacrifice," §VIII, Rattenbury, pp. 192-3; and Bowmer 1951, pp. 98-9.

152. Sermon 92, "On Zeal," §II.5, *Works*, 3:313.

153. Cf. Sermon 27, "Sermon on the Mount VII," *Works*, 1:592-611; 1768 *Minutes*, Q. 23, a. 8, *Minutes* (Mason), p. 80 (also as "Large Minutes," Q. 56, *Works* [Jackson], 8:328); Harper 1983a, pp. 47-52; and Baker 1970, pp. 30-1.

154. Cf. Sermon 143 (1732), "Public Diversions Denounced," *Works*, 4:319-28; *Advice to the People Call'd Methodists, with Regard to Dress* (1780), *Works* (Jackson), 11:466-77; Sermon 78 (1781), "Spiritual Idolatry," §II.6, *Works*, 3:114; and Sermon 88 (1786), "On Dress," *Works*, 3:248-61. See also the discussion in McNulty 1963.

155. Note his criticism of undue austerity in Sermon 27, "Sermon on the Mount VII," §IV.4, *Works*, 1:609. *An Extract of the Life of Madam Guion*, Preface, §8, *Works* (Jackson), 14:277. Here Charles tended to differ from John, speaking of the "sad necessity of pain" for growth in holiness (*Scripture Hymns*, On Matthew 20:22, *Poet. Works*, 10:336). Cf. the comparison of the two brothers in Hodges & Allchin 1966, p. 29; and J.R. Tyson 1986, pp. 261-8.

156. See Sermon 48, "Self-denial," *Works*, 2:238-50.

157. This correlation is explicit in Sermon 28, "Sermon on the Mount VIII," §25-6, *Works*, 1:628-9; Sermon 50, "The Use of Money," §III.3, *Works*, 2:277; Sermon 88 (1786), "On Dress," §14, *Works*, 3:254; and a letter reprinted with commendation by Wesley in *Journal* (20 Nov. 1767), *Works*, 22:112-3. For one of the quaintest examples of how Wesley lived this correlation himself, see his Letter to Officer of Excise Tax (Sept. 1776), *Letters* (Telford), 6:230. Cf. Charles Wallace, "Simple and Recollected: John Wesley's Life-style," *RelLife* 46 (1977):188-212.

158. The following summary is indebted to Martos, *Doors to the Sacred*, pp. 163-229; Kucharek, *Sacramental Mysteries*, pp. 73-155; David R. Holeton, "Initiation," in *Study of Anglicanism*, pp. 261-72; J.D.C. Fisher, *Christian Initiation: Baptism in the Medieval West* (London: SPCK, 1965); and Nathan D. Mitchell, "Dissolution of the Rite of Christian Initiation," in *Made, Not Born* (Notre Dame, IN: University of Notre Dame, 1976), pp. 50-82.

159. See esp. *A Farther Appeal to Men of Reason and Religion*, Pt. I, §I.5, *Works*, 11:107; Sermon 18, "The Marks of the New Birth," §IV.2-5, *Works*, 1:428-30; and Sermon 45, "The New Birth," §IV.4, *Works*, 2:200.

160. Cf. *Journal* (25 Aug. 1753), *Works*, 21:424; and *Journal* (22 Mar. 1782), *Journal* (Curnock), 6:345.

161. Wesley draws this parallel in *A Plain Account of the People Called Methodists*, §I.10, *Works*, 9:258. Cf. H. Knight 1992, pp. 181-2; and Henderson 1980.

162. For specific emphasis on the role of the class meeting, see Dean 1985, pp. 301-3; H. Knight 1992, pp. 99-100, 181; William B. Lewis, "The Methodist Class Meeting," in *Spiritual Renewal for Methodism*, pp. 21-37, ed. Samuel Emerick (Nashville, TN: Evangelistic Materials, 1958), pp. 24-5; and George Hunter III, *To Spread the Power* (Nashville, TN: Abingdon, 1987), pp. 56-9. For a general agreement on the dynamics of conversion within the society, but questioning whether the class meeting itself was a frequent site, see Thomas R. Albin, "An Empirical Study of Early Methodist Spirituality," in *Wesleyan Theology Today*, pp. 275-90, ed. T. Runyon (Nashville, TN: Kingswood, 1985), pp. 278-9.

163. For discussions of Wesley's position on the Lord's Supper as a converting ordinance, see esp. Bowmer 1951, pp. 110-19; Grislis 1963, p. 102; Bowmer 1964; Borgen 1972, pp. 197-8; Harper 1983a, pp. 41-2; and Selleck 1983, pp. 119-36. For some suggestions of historical precedents, see Benedicta Ward, "A Converting Ordinance: Some Reflections on the Hymns of Charles Wesley in Light of Medieval Biblical Commentaries," *Fairacre Chronicle* 21.1 (1988):13-25 (and in *Signs and Wonders* [Brookfield, VT: Variorum Ashgate Publishers, 1992]).

164. Cf. the Fourth Lateran Council (1215 C.E.), Canons I & XXI (a convenient copy can be found in John H. Leith, ed., *Creed of the Churches* [Atlanta, GA: John Knox, 1973], pp. 57-9).

165. Note the prefatory rubric to the Lord's Supper in the 1549 *Book of Common Prayer* (a convenient copy in Bard Thompson, ed., *Liturgies of the Western Church* [Cleveland, OH: World Publishing, 1961], p. 245).

166. Indeed, this rigor contributed to the growing dissatisfaction of the colonists with his ministry; cf. the *Journal* and diary accounts for 3 July 1737 and following (*Works*, 18:183ff).

167. On these changes, see *Journal* (29 May 1737), *Works*, 18:182; *Journal* (7 Nov. 1739), *Works*, 19:121; and *Journal* (27-28 June 1740), *Works*, 19:159.

168. Wesley was familiar with this basic claim from Robert Nelson's *The Great Duty of Frequenting the Christian Sacrifice*, which he abridged for his own purposes in 1732 and published in a further reduced form as Sermon 101, "The Duty of Constant Communion" (see §II.7-10, *Works*, 3:433-4). One might also note how his receptionist understanding of the Presence of Christ fit this move, since fear of sacrilegious treatment of the elements would not arise with nearly the same force as in the medieval model.

169. Note how this question is raised in *The Principles of a Methodist Farther Explained*, §II.7, *Works*, 9:183-4.

170. See the discussion of Wesley's progression of this specific issue in Bowmer 1951, pp. 110-19. Cf. D. Watson 1990.

171. Note that Wesley dropped the opening rubric requiring advance notification of intention to commune from the liturgy for the Lord's Supper in *Sunday Service* (p. 125), and deleted Anglican Article XXIX, which affirms the condemnation of those who partake unworthily, from his Articles of Religion (Oden 1988, p. 122). See also *Journal* (8 Sept. 1760), *Works*, 21:275; and *Journal* (16 June 1764), *Works*, 21:472.

172. Given the debates over Wesley's understanding of baptism, no single secondary source can be recommended as definitive. A good place to start would be comparative reading of Holland 1970, Borgen 1989, Hohenstein 1990, and Felton 1992 (pp. 13-45).

173. Earlier studies that rely only on the published *Journals* have missed this point, because Wesley rarely included these mentions in the published form. Holland has brought them to our attention (1970, pp. 101-2). To take just one month as an

example, in July 1740 Wesley lists seven adult baptisms, 2 infant baptisms, and there are two other possible references to child baptism; cf. Diary, July 5, 9, 13, 24 & 30, *Works*, 19:423-8.

174. See esp. Cannon 1946, pp. 127-9. Cf. English 1967a; and Reist 1971, pp. 48-9.

175. E.g., Borgen 1972, pp. 133; Naglee 1987, pp. 105, 120-30; Hohenstein 1990, pp. 27ff; and Felton 1992, pp. 34ff.

176. E.g., C. Williams 1960, pp. 116, 121; and K. Wilson 1984, p. 417.

177. E.g., Lindström 1946, pp. 107ff; Sanders 1954, p. 600; H. Davies 1961, pp. 205-6; Starkey 1962, p. 91; and Parris 1963, pp. 59, 97-100.

178. For British Methodism, see Holland 1969 & 1970, pp. 5-8; for German Methodism, see Lessmann 1987, p. 139; for American Methodism, see Hohenstein 1990, and Felton 1992; and for the American holiness movement, see Staples 1991, pp. 161ff; and Stan Ingersol, "Christian Baptism and the Early Nazarenes: The Sources that Shaped a Pluralistic Baptismal Tradition," *WTJ* 25.2 (1990):24-38.

179. "A Treatise on Baptism" was included in *A Preservative Against Unsettled Notions in Religion* (Bristol: Farley, 1758). The abridgement was originally prepared in 1756 from Samuel Wesley's *The Pious Communicant Rightly Prepar'd* . . . (London: Charles Harper, 1700).

180. For good surveys of the changes in the *Sunday Service* from the *Book of Common Prayer*, see English 1967b, and Hohenstein 1990, pp. 40ff.

181. Note how "A Treatise on Baptism" builds the definition of baptism in §I-II around an adult model (with a few passing concessions to infant baptism), and then taking up the topic of the specific legitimacy of infant baptism in §IV (*John Wesley*, pp. 318-32). The primacy of adult baptism for understanding Wesley is also emphasized in H. Knight 1990.

182. Cf. *Journal* (25 Jan. 1739), *Works* 19:32; and *Journal* (2 Oct 1758), *Works*, 21:166.

183. Cf. *NT Notes*, Eph. 5:26; *Journal* (2 Feb. 1760), *Works*, 21:240; and the hymn to be sung at the baptism of adults, *Hymns*, #464, *Works*, 7:646-7.

184. E.g., *Journal* (13 Sept. 1739), *Works*, 19:97; *NT Notes*, Col. 2:12; Letter to Mr. Potter (4 Nov. 1758), *Letters* (Telford), 4:38; and Sermon 45, "The New Birth," §IV.1-2, *Works*, 2:196-7.

185. Cf. his substitution of "justification" for "baptism" in the title of Anglican Article XVI (Oden 1988, pp. 116-7); and his elimination of the description of baptism as an "instrument" in Anglican Article XXVII (Oden 1988, p. 121).

186. This point is detailed in Hohenstein 1990, pp. 46-52, 67. See similar suggestions of Wesley's intent in Baker 1970, p. 53; J. White 1984, p. 20 [12-13]; and Felton 1992, p. 37.

187. The possible evidence of this move is Wesley's deletion of the word "therein" from the blessing of the font in both the infant and adult baptism rituals (cf. the discussion in Hohenstein 1990, p. 55).

188. Cf. *NT Notes*, Acts 10:47; and Sermon 74 (1785), "Of the Church," §I.12, *Works*, 3:49-50.

189. Note the concession of baptism not being absolutely essential for salvation in *NT Notes*, John 3:5.

190. E.g., *Journal* (15 Oct. 1756), *Works*, 21:79.

191. E.g., *A Farther Appeal to Men of Reason and Religion*, Pt. I, §I.5, *Works*, 11:107; Sermon 18, "The Marks of the New Birth," §IV.2-5, *Works* 1:428-30; *NT Notes*, Mark 16:16; and Sermon 45, "The New Birth," §IV.4, *Works*, 2:200.

192. Contrast English's description of the limitations of Wesley's understanding of baptism from a Western perspective (1967a, p. 191) with the emphasis on the

co-operant nature of baptismal grace in Eastern Orthodoxy in Mantzaridis, *Deification*, pp. 41-6; and Meyendorff, *Byzantine Theology*, p. 194.

193. See the worry of Wainwright 1988b, p. 13. Compare my following suggestion to Wesley's comment about sinning away the "washing of the Holy Ghost" in *Journal* (24 May 1738), *Works*, 18:242-3.

194. For one of the most thoughtful examples, see Geoffrey Wainwright, "The Need for a Methodist Service for the Admission of Infants to the Catechumenate," *LQHR* 191 (new series, 37) (1968):51-60.

195. Note his appeals to this warrant in *Thoughts Upon Infant Baptism*, pp. 10-19; and "A Treatise on Baptism," §IV.7-9, *John Wesley*, pp. 326-9. If anything, Charles' support for infant baptism was even stronger than John's, as evidenced by his indictment of those who forbid it in a poem on Mark 10:14, *Poetry*, 2:60.

196. These changes are discussed in Baker 1970, p. 156; Campbell 1991, pp. 29-30; and Felton 1992, pp. 18-20.

197. Cf. "A Treatise on Baptism," §II.1, *John Wesley*, p. 321-2. Note Galliers' comparative analysis about John deleting the adjective "damning" from the description of the guilt of original sin (1960, p. 122). This would correspond to Wesley's contemporaneous qualification that no one will die eternally merely due to inherited sin in *The Doctrine of Original Sin*, Pt. II, §I, *Works* (Jackson), 9:315.

198. E.g., Sanders 1954, pp. 601-2; Naglee 1987, pp. 136-8 ; and Felton 1992, pp. 26-7.

199. E.g., Sanders 1954, p. 603; Galliers 1960, p. 157; Stoeffler 1962, p. 10; English 1967a, pp. 151, 175-87; Cho 1972, p. 68; Stoeffler 1976a, pp. 313-4; and Selleck 1983, pp. 199-200. Note also the explicit rejection of this option in Borgen 1989, p. 98.

200. These are the focus of *Thoughts upon Infant Baptism*, and specifically identified in "A Treatise on Baptism," §II.2-3, *John Wesley*, p. 322.

201. The changes in the *Sunday Service* have been particularly stressed by English (1967a&b). Some of the changes that English notes come in the 1786 edition, about which there is question whether they should be attributed to Wesley or to Coke (cf. Hohenstein 1990, pp. 57ff).

202. Note that Wesley strongly rejected the suggestion that the sponsors of the infant being baptized fulfill the role of responsiveness in the infant's place in *Serious Thoughts Concerning Godfathers and Godmothers*, §6, *Works* (Jackson), 10:508.

203. Holland 1970, esp. pp. 56-9. See also Felton 1992, pp. 42, 173.

204. Note the concession in Holland 1970, p. 77. Compare the strong critiques of Holland in Borgen 1972, pp. 173-81; Hohenstein 1990, p. 29; and H. Knight 1992, pp. 179ff.

205. For the mention of a principle of grace being "infused" in baptism, see "A Treatise on Baptism," §II.4, *John Wesley*, p. 323 (but note even here its connection to the unquenched Presence of the Holy Spirit).

206. See this basic claim, though in language of created grace rather than the uncreated Presence of the Spirit, in Cushman 1964, p. 86; Dorr 1964a, p. 197; and Naglee 1987, p. 121. Charles' confidence that infant baptism conveys the regenerating Presence of the Spirit is evident in such hymns as "On Micah 7:20," *Poet. Works*, 10:100; and "On Matthew 19:13," *Poet. Works*, 10:322.

207. That this deletion was not incidental is shown by earlier negative comments on confirmation in "Ought We to Separate from the Church of England," §II.4, *Works*, 9:572; and *Popery Calmly Considered*, §IV.4, *Works* (Jackson), 10:150-1 (distilling *A Roman Catechism, with a Reply Thereto*, Q. 58, *Works* [Jackson], 10:116). Cf. the bafflement over the deletion in J. White 1984, p. 20 [13].

208. Naglee's attempt to argue that Wesley implicitly supported confirmation suffers from failing to make the distinction between catechesis and the rite of confirmation (1987, esp. pp. 174, 205).

209. Note the letter from his mother describing her typical practice, in *Journal* (1 Aug. 1742), *Works*, 19:286-91. Wesley reprinted an extract (with a closing paragraph not in the earlier citation) over forty years later in Sermon 96, "On Obedience to Parents," §I.10, *Works*, 3:367-8. For background on the general decline of catechesis, see Michel Dujarier, *A History of the Catechumenate* (New York: Sadlier, 1979).

210. See *Journal* (26 Feb. 1737), *Works*, 18:176; and *A Short History of the People Called Methodists*, §7, *Works*, 9:430.

211. The best recent studies of Wesley's understanding and practice of religious education are Towns 1970, Tracy 1982, and Willhauck 1992.

212. Wesley published *Instructions for Children* in 1745 (Preface in *Works* [Jackson], 14:217-8). The first half of this catechism appears to be loosely dependent upon Claude Fleury's *Grand Catéchisme historique* (1683), the second half is an abridged translation of Pierre Poiret's *Les Principes Solides de la Religion et de la Vie Chrétienne, appliqués a l 'Education des enfans* (1705). Note Wesley's favorable comparison of this volume to the Anglican catechism in Letter to Mary Bishop (15 Mar. 1777), *Letters* (Telford), 6:258; and his general estimate of it in *A Short Account of the Life and Death of the Rev. John Fletcher* (1786), Chapter VIII, §12, *Works* (Jackson), 11:339. Wesley then prepared his own *Lessons for Children* in installments between 1746 and 1754 (Preface in *Works* [Jackson], 14:216-17). He also released a first collection of Charles' *Hymns for Children* in 1746. Further collections of hymns for children were published in 1763 and 1787; along with *Hymns for the Use of Families* in 1767.

213. Cf. *Journal* (16 Nov. 1766), *Works*, 22:68; 1766 *Minutes*, Q. 28, *Minutes* (Mason), p. 63 (also as "Large Minutes," Q. 13, *Works* [Jackson], 8:302-6); and 1766 *Minutes*, Q. 30, *Minutes* (Mason), p. 69 (also as "Large Minutes," Q. 33, *Works* [Jackson], 8:315-6). As one might expect, some parents objected to Wesley presuming to advise them on raising children when he had none of his own; cf. *Journal* (5 Oct. 1766), *Works*, 22:63; and *Journal* (30 Mar. 1768), *Works*, 22:124.

214. Cf. Sermon 94, "On Family Religion," *Works*, 3:334-46; Sermon 95, "On the Education of Children," *Works*, 3:347-60; and Sermon 96, "On Obedience to Parents," *Works*, 3:361-72. See also "A Thought on the Manner of Educating Children," *AM* 6 (1783):380-3, *Works* (Jackson), 13:474-7.

215. Cf. Rack 1989, p. 9.

216. See *Journal* (24 June 1748), *Works*, 20:229; and *Hymns for Children* (1763), #40, st. 5, *Poet. Works*, 6:408. For descriptions of the regime and curriculum at Kingswood, see *A Short Account of the School in Kingswood*, *Works* (Jackson), 13:283-9; "A Plain Account of Kingswood School," *AM* 4 (1781):381ff, *Works* (Jackson), 13:289-301; and Arthur G. Ives, *Kingswood School in Wesley's Day and Since* (London: Epworth, 1970).

217. Letter to Mary Bishop (21 May 1781), *Letters* (Telford), 7:62-3.

218. On the actual general neglect of this duty, see Sykes, *Church and State*, pp. 243-6.

219. *Journal* (11 Apr. 1756), *Works*, 21:49. Wesley's deletion of the catechism in the *Book of Common Prayer* from his *Sunday Service* reflects his judgment that his own edited catechism was a better resource, not a depreciation of catechesis per se. Note his favorable comparison of *Instructions for Children* to the Anglican catechism in Letter to Mary Bishop (15 Mar. 1777), *Letters* (Telford), 6:258; and his general estimate of it in *A Short Account of the Life and Death of the Rev. John Fletcher* (1786), Chapter VIII, §12, *Works* (Jackson), 11:339.

220. The earliest example may be a Sunday class that Hannah Ball started in 1769, mentioned in a letter that she wrote to Wesley on 16 December 1770 (*Letters* [Telford], 5:218). This would antedate Robert Raines; cf. discussion in Willhauck 1992, pp. 232-4.

221. *Journal* (18 July 1784), *Journal* (Curnock), 7:3. See also Letter to Richard Rotta (17 Jan. 1787), *Letters* (Telford), 7:364; Letter to Alexander Suter (24 Nov. 1787), *Letters* (Telford), 8:23-4; and Letter to Walter Churchey (25 May 1789), *Letters* (Telford), 8:238.

222. The strongest such criticisms of Wesley are probably John O. Gross, *John Wesley: Christian Educator* (Nashville: The Board of Education, The Methodist Church, 1954), pp. 9-12; and John Wesley Prince, *Wesley on Religious Education* (New York: Methodist Book Concern, 1926), pp. 143-5. For a helpful comparative treatment, see Willhauck 1992.

223. See the discussion of this issue in Willhauck 1992, esp. pp. 164-9, 234-6, 263-7. One might note as well Charles' hymnic prayers that his children should quickly and naturally embrace Christian life; *CW Poetry*, 1:287-92.

224. For example, Wesley's own confirmation was likely in a group of eight hundred (Baker 1970, p. 10). Cf. the detailed study of confirmation practice in this time in Sykes, *Church and State*, pp. 115-37, 429-36.

225. Recall his rejection of this idea in relation to the debates over entire sanctification as the "baptism of the Holy Spirit" discussed in Chapter Seven.

226. Cf. Borgen 1989, p. 102; and Hohenstein 1990, pp. 62, 65.

227. His reading of a book by Peter King in 1746 convinced him that presbyters and bishops were identical in the Primitive Church; cf. *Journal* (20 Jan. 1746), *Works*, 20:112. In this light, it is ironic that one of Wesley's few quotations from the Office of Confirmation in the *Book of Common Prayer* was to persuade a bishop that the emphasis which he was placing on the work of the Holy Spirit in people's lives was in keeping with the teaching of the Anglican church; *A Letter to the Right Reverend the Lord Bishop of Gloucester*, §II.22, *Works*, 11:522.

228. As Campbell points out (1991b, p. 96), Wesley left references to this practice in his edited historical works. The Eastern churches have continued this practice to the present. It lasted into the thirteenth century in the Western church; cf. Martos, *Doors to the Sacred*, p. 182.

229. Cf. *Journal* (5 Sept. 1773), *Works*, 22:388; *Journal* (12 Sept. 1773), *Works*, 22:389; and *Journal* (2 Oct. 1784), *Journal* (Curnock), 7:23. See also Josselyn 1988.

230. Cf. Bowmer 1971, p. 21. Wesley was also aware of the Moravian practice of communing children from around this age; cf. "MS Journal" (31 July 1737), *Works*, 18:532.

231. *Journal* (28 June 1740), *Works*, 19:159.

232. Cf. the defense of this practice in James Porter, *A Compendium of Methodism* (New York: Carlton & Porter, 1851), pp. 290-1.

233. For some varying emphases in this debate, see Bowmer 1964; English 1967a, p. 150; Selleck 1983, pp. 121-2; Felton 1992, p. 24; Wainwright 1987, p. 45; and Wainwright 1988b, pp. 13-15.

234. See the relevant quotations in Rogers 1967, p. 129 (and his comments on p. 103 fn1).

235. See especially a passage in the excerpt from William Beveridge's *Private Thoughts Upon Religion* found in *Chr. Library*, 48:74-5.

236. Cf. Sermon 85, "On Working Out Our Own Salvation," §III.4, *Works*, 3:207. See also the discussion of Wesley's changing views on this connection in Rogers 1967, pp. 204-5; and Fujimoto 1986, p. 256.

237. Cf. the reflections on the relation of infant baptism and Prevenient Grace in Borgen 1972, p. 127; Wainwright 1983, p. 175; and Staples 1991, p. 179.

238. Cf. *Journal* (4 Sept. 1763), *Works*, 21:427; *Journal* (30 Sept. 1767), *Works*, 22:106; 1768 *Minutes*, Q. 23, a. 2, *Minutes* (Mason), p. 79; *Journal* (6 Sept. 1772), *Works*, 22:348; and *Journal* (15 Mar. 1784), *Journal* (Curnock), 6:484-5.

Chapter Nine

1. For recent texts representing each of these discussions, see Joseph Ratzinger, *Eschatology: Death and Eternal Life* (Washington, DC: Catholic University of America Press, 1988); Stanley J. Grenz, *The Millennial Maze* (Downer's Grove, IL: Intervarsity, 1992); and Howard Snyder, *Models of the Kingdom* (Nashville, TN: Abingdon, 1991).

2. The classic articulation of this claim is Jürgen Moltmann, *Theology of Hope* (London: SCM, 1967), pp. 15ff.

3. See especially Runyon 1981, pp. 10-11; Bence 1981, pp. 245-7; and H.-J. Lee 1991, pp. 83ff.

4. In addition to Runyon, Bence, and H.-J Lee, see Cubie 1986 and Hynson 1988.

5. The main protagonists were West 1894 and Rall 1920. Further details on this debate will be given below.

6. I.e., Strawson 1959, and Downes 1960. The only recent studies to comment on most of these topics are Naglee 1991, pp. 451ff; and Collins 1993, pp. 189-203.

7. I have in mind such studies as Brian Hebblethwaite, *The Christian Hope* (Grand Rapids, MI: Eerdmans, 1984); Colleen McDannell & Bernhard Lang, *Heaven: A History* (New Haven, CT: Yale University Press, 1988); and Zachary Hayes, *Visions of a Future: A Study of Christian Eschatology* (Wilmington, DE: Michael Glazier, 1989).

8. This thesis is detailed in Charles E. Hill, *Regnum Caelorum: Patterns of Future Hope in Early Christianity* (Oxford: Clarendon, 1992). Another helpful study of early Christian eschatology is Brian E. Daley, *The Hope of the Early Church: A Handbook of Patristic Eschatology* (New York: Cambridge University Press, 1991).

9. On Irenaeus see Daley, *Hope of Early Church*, pp. 28-32; Hebblethwaite, *Christian Hope*, pp. 44-8; Hill, *Regnum Caelorum*, p. 17; and McDannell & Lang, *Heaven*, pp. 47-53. Other early chiliasts include Justin Martyr and Tertullian.

10. On this spiritualizing tendency, epitomized in Origen, see Hebblethwaite, *Christian Hope*, pp. 48ff.

11. See McDannell & Lang, *Heaven*, p. 14.

12. Note the argument of Jacques Le Goff that purgatory came to fill the role in the West from Augustine on that the millennium played for many Greek theologians: preparing believers for final glory. The key difference is that purgatory addressed a juridical need, not a therapeutic one! Le Goff, *The Birth of Purgatory* (Chicago, IL: University of Chicago, 1984), pp. 5, 61ff, 82-3.

13. On Augustine, see Daley, *Hope of Early Church*, pp. 131-50; Hebblethwaite, *Christian Hope*, pp. 54-6; and McDannell & Lang, *Heaven*, pp. 61-7.

14. For an argument that socio-political factors are heavily determinative of differing millennial views, see Stanley Gundry, "Hermeneutics or Zeitgeist as the Determining Factor in the History of Eschatologies," *Journal of the Evangelical Theological Society* 20 (1977):45-55.

15. Major elements of this blend also came to characterize Eastern Christian eschatology. However, the Orthodox have been notably uncomfortable with too much emphasis on an immediate transition into God's glorious presence. Cf. Constantine N. Tsirpanlis, *Introduction to Eastern Patristic Thought and Orthodox Theology* (Collegeville, MN: Liturgical Press, 1991), pp. 205-11.

16. See the descriptions of Medieval eschatology, and condemned millennial movements, in Hebblethwaite, *Christian Hope*, pp. 61-7; and McDannell & Lang, *Heaven*, p. 84.

17. One of the best studies of this Medieval model is C.S. Lewis, *The Discarded Image* (Cambridge: University Press, 1964). See also Le Goff, *Birth of Purgatory*, pp. 2-4, 334-55.

18. See the discussion of Anabaptists in George Williams, *The Radical Reformation* (Philadelphia, PA: Westminster, 1962); Hebblethwaite, *Christian Hope*, pp. 87ff; and Hill, *Regnum Caelorum*, p. 180. For specific consideration of soul sleep, see Williams, pp. 20-4, 104-6, 580-92.

19. On Luther, see Paul Althaus, *The Theology of Martin Luther* (Philadelphia, PA: Fortress, 1966), pp. 410-17. For later scholastics, see Schmid, *Doctrinal Theology*, pp. 633-4, 650, 657-8.

20. Calvin devoted an entire treatise to the topic, *Psychypannychia* (1545). See also Heppe, *Reformed Dogmatics*, pp. 695-6.

21. Cf. Heppe, *Reformed Dogmatics*, p. 701.

22. See Peter Toon, "The Latter Day Glory," in *Puritan Eschatology*, ed. P. Toon (London: James Clarke, 1970), pp. 23-41; and Hill, *Regnum Caelorum*, pp. 132-9.

23. Cf. the dialogue between Bernard Capp, "The Millennium and Eschatology in England," *Past and Present* 57 (1972):156-62; Bryan W. Ball, *A Great Expectation: Eschatological Thought in English Protestantism to 1660* (Leiden: E.J. Brill, 1975); and Margaret C. Jacob, "Millenarianism and Science in the Late Seventeenth Century," *Journal of the History of Ideas* 37 (1976):335-41.

24. E.g., Lerch 1941, p. 118; Schempp 1949, p. 131; and Schneeberger 1974, pp. 139ff.

25. E.g., C. Williams 1960, p. 87; and Villa-Vicencio 1989, p. 99.

26. In a desire to stress the present dimension some scholars initially talked of Wesley's "realized eschatology," though they made very clear that any present realization was at best partial, awaiting its fulfillment (e.g., Bowmer 1951, pp. 184-5; Downes 1960, p. 14; C. Williams 1960, pp. 192-4; Fuhrman 1963, pp. 445-7; and Mercer 1967, pp. 58-9). To capture the tension more adequately Downes (1960, p. 17) suggested the term "anticipated eschatology." Recent scholars have tended to opt instead for the designation "inaugurated eschatology" (e.g., Logan 1985, p. 363; S. Johnson 1987, p. 45 fn57; Hynson 1988, p. 50; and Meistad 1989, p. 48), or simply to emphasize the "already/not yet tension" in Wesley's eschatology (e.g., Snyder 1980, p. 87; Rakestraw 1985a, p. 235; Naglee 1991, p. 501; and H.-J. Lee 1991, pp. 96-7).

27. This designation has been suggested and defended by Clarence Bence (cf. 1979 & 1981, pp. 7, 105 fn4). Note how essentially the same language is used to describe Eastern Orthodox eschatology in Tsirpanlis, *Eastern Patristic Thought*, pp. 177-9.

28. Cf. Downes 1960, pp. 168-9; and Bence 1979, p. 53 & 1981, p. 200.

29. The debate began when Nathaniel West (1894) advanced an argument that Wesley was a premillennialist, as an implicit critique of the optimism of emerging Methodist liberalism. This claim was vigorously countered by H.F. Rall (1920), a

leading Methodist liberal, who argued for a postmillennial (or possibly amillennial) reading of Wesley. Most subsequent scholars have joined Rall in aligning Wesley with postmillennialism; e.g., Mercer 1967, p. 60 (1970, p. 127 fn120); Snyder 1980, p. 87; Rakestraw 1985a, p. 234; and Cubie 1986, p. 361. For a more detailed survey of the debate, see K. Brown 1989.

30. The one study that has attempted to provide such a temporal account (with mixed results) is Naglee 1991, p. 574-81. See also the correlation of Wesley's apocalyptic interest to current events in Fraser 1988, pp. 70-4.

31. Article XLI of the original forty-two Edwardian articles (1553), rejected millennial teachings as heretical and Jewish. This article was dropped in 1563. Cf. Charles Hardwick, *A History of the Articles of Religion* (London: George Bell, 1895), pp. 348-9.

32. See especially Sermon 22, "Sermon on the Mount II," §I.13, *Works*, 1:494-5; Sermon 25, "Sermon on the Mount V," §II.4, *Works*, 1:555; and Sermon 26, "Sermon on the Mount VI," §III.8-10, *Works*, 1:581-4. The same general perspective is evident in Charles' hymns of the time. Note, for example, how he equates the millennial year with eternity in *Hymns*, #45, st. 2 (*Works*, 7:137); or with the renewal of the universe in *Hymns*, #60, st. 3 (*Works*, 7:156)

33. Wesley's notes drew both from the comments on Revelations in *Gnomon Novi Testamenti* and Bengel's lengthy German commentary, *Erklärte Offenbarung Johannis und vielmehr Jesu Christi* (Stuttgart: Erhardt, 1740).

34. The most handy summary of Bengel's views is Wesley's abridged translation in *NT Notes*, Rev. 20:2-4. For a more detailed secondary study, see Gottfried Mälzer, *Johann Albrecht Bengel* (Stuttgart: Calwer Verlag, 1970), pp. 311-35. It is interesting how often this distinction between the two millennia is overlooked or dismissed in debates about Wesley's millennial views. A particularly astonishing example is West 1894, p. 22.

35. Note the comment on the imprisonment and loosing of Satan being transacted in the "invisible world" in *NT Notes*, Rev. 20:5.

36. Bengel's final timetable is given in *Gnomon Novi Testamenti*, p. 1332. The basics of his approach are summarized in *NT Notes*. For a good analysis of his method of calculation and the changes in his chronology, see Mälzer, *Bengel*, pp. 220-52, 311-35.

37. See his prefatory note to the book of Revelations in *NT Notes*. This disclaimer grew more explicit over time; cf. his reflections when editing the *NT Notes* for the second edition in *Journal* (6 Dec. 1762), *Works*, 21:400; Letter to Christopher Hopper (3 June 1788), *Letters* (Telford), 8:63; and Letter to Walter Churchey (26 June 1788), *Letters* (Telford), 8:67.

38. The tract in question is *Serious Thoughts Occasioned by the Late Earthquake at Lisbon* (1755), *Works* (Jackson), 11:1-13. Note also Wesley's later response to the charge that he was here endorsing an apocalyptic deadline: *Some Remarks on Mr. Hill's 'Farrago Double-Distilled'*, §20, *Works* (Jackson), 10:424-5.

39. For example, one of the "enthusiastic" excesses that Wesley criticized in George Bell was Bell's prediction that the world would end on 28 February 1763; cf. *Journal* (7 Jan. 1763) and (28 Feb. 1763), *Works*, 21:402, 407.

40. Sermon 15, "The Great Assize," *Works*, 1:355-75. The imminent expectation is evident in §IV.5 (374). Note that the mention of a possible thousand year period after Christ's return concerns the length of time that it may take to complete universal judgment (§II.2, p. 360), not a period of triumphant reign. See also the evidence for Wesley's apocalyptic interest during this time in Fraser 1988, p. 70.

41. Fletcher's first Methodist contact was one of the 1755 meetings when Wesley made reference to impending revolutions in eschatological terms. He wrote to Wesley soon after (29 Nov. 1755) to share his own understandings. His letter was published after Wesley's death in *AM* 16 (1793):370-6, 409-16. A handy excerpt can be found in *Works*, 26:613-6.

42. Sermon 52, "The Reformation of Manners," §2, *Works*, 2:302. Note also that Wesley retained Bengel's insistence that the inception of the coming millennium of peace would not be obvious from an earthly perspective in his carefully revised 1762 reissue of *NT Notes*.

43. The full title was *Paradise Restored: or, A Testimony to the Doctrine of the Blessed Millennium, with some considerations of its approaching Advent from the Signs of the Times. To which is added, A Short Defense of the Mystical Writers.* (London: Richardson, 1764).

44. Letter to Thomas Hartley (27 Mar. 1764), *Letters* (Telford), 4:234.

45. See *OT Notes*, Isaiah 60:18; and Casto 1977, p. 484.

46 .Cf. Sermon 63 (1783), "The General Spread of the Gospel," §13-27, *Works* 2:490-9; and Sermon 66 (1787), "The Signs of the Times," §II.1-4, *Works*, 2:525-7. The respective specific uses of "latter-day glory" are §16 (493) and §II.1 (525).

47. The comparison to Bengel is particularly noteworthy, because he ascribes the inception of the first millennium to a new work of the Spirit or God's grace leading to a heightened holiness or obedience of God's people, precisely the elements that Wesley highlights about his Methodist movement! Cf. Mälzer, *Bengel*, p. 324.

48. Admittedly, this assumption is most characteristic of early dispensational premillennialism, which postdates Wesley. However, he discerned the general assumption in his time and devoted one of his late sermons to arguing that current conditions were better, not worse, than any time in the history of the Church (Sermon 102, "Of Former Things," *Works*, 3:442-53).

49. This appendix was a response to Bishop Warburton's tract on the doctrine of grace, which Wesley had also responded to in a 1763 public letter. Wesley's *Journal* comments on reading Hartley deal solely with this appended section, and his subsequent letter to Hartley is dominated by a discussion of differences in their respective responses to Warburton—cf. *Journal* (5 Feb. 1764), *Works*, 21:442-3; and Letter to Thomas Hartley (27 Mar. 1764), *Letters* (Telford), 4:234.

50. This point is central to Hartley's first chapter, *Paradise Restored*, pp. 1-73 (esp. p. 38).

51. I am referring to Thomas Burnet's *The Sacred Theory of the Earth* (London, 1719). For a discussion of the millenarian nature of this work, see Jacob, "Millenarianism and Science." Wesley's comments upon reading this book highlight Burnet's suggestions about the renovation of the physical creation (*Journal* [17 Jan. 1770], *Works*, 22:213-4).

52. An intriguing case in point is the article "Of the Renovation of All Things," which was published in *AM* 7 (1784):154-5, 209-11. This article insists on the need for the renovation of the physical creation, but only as an *intermediate state*, with the final state being purely ethereal! The source of the article is not listed; it may well be Hartley! It is doubtful that it is original to Wesley because of its reliance on Irenaeus and the vigor with which Wesley would reject the intermediate status of the renovated creation the next year.

53. Sermon 64, "The New Creation" *Works*, 2:500-10.

54. Sermon 26, "Sermon on the Mount VI," §III.8-10, *Works*, 1:581-4. This distinction is prominent in *NT Notes* (e.g., Matt. 3:2, 5:3, 6:10, 6:33, 11:11, 13:24; Luke 11:52, 17:21; and Rom. 14:17) and remains evident in some of Wesley's latest sermons; e.g.,

Sermon 108, "On Riches," §4, *Works*, 3:520; and Sermon 117, "On the Discoveries of Faith," §12, *Works*, 4:34.

55. In his hymn "For the Anniversary Day of One's Conversion" in *Hymns and Sacred Psalms* (1740), included in *Hymns*, #1, st. 9, *Works*, 7:81. Cf. *Hymns*, #20, st. 3, *Works*, 7:104; *Hymns*, #77, st. 2, *Works*, 7:176; and *Hymns*, #211, *Works*, 7:344-5.

56. For several examples of Wesley invoking this phrase from Hebrews 6:5, see *Journal* (17 Nov. 1743), *Works*, 20:4; *Journal* (3 Jan. 1747), *Works*, 20:152; *A Plain Account of the People Called Methodists* (1749), §I.2, *Works*, 9:255; Letter to Cradock Glascott (13 May 1764), *Letters* (Telford), 4:242; Letter to Mary Stokes (17 Mar. 1771), *Letters* (Telford), 5:230; and Sermon 64 (1785), "The New Creation," §2, *Works*, 2:501.

57. E.g., Sermon 113, "The Late Work of God in North America," §II.15, *Works*, 3:607; and Letter to Thomas Morrell (4 Feb. 1790), *Letters* (Telford), 8:199.

58. This is quite clear in Sermon 52, "The Reformation of Manners," §2, *Works*, 2:302. See also the discussion in Deschner 1960, p. 126-7; Bence 1979, p. 52; Hynson 1988, p. 47; Eli 1993; and Snyder, *Models of the Kingdom*, p. 61.

59. The major studies of Wesley's ecclesiology are Bence 1984, Berg 1984, Kissack 1964 (pp. 1-62), Míguez Bonino 1983c, Outler 1964b, Snyder 1980 & 1989, Stoeffler 1976a, Wainwright 1983, and R. Williams 1964. For general studies of his views on ministry, see Bowmer 1975, Collins 1988, Lawson 1963, Nygren 1962, Score 1963, and Shipley 1960. The specific topic of women in ministry is treated in Chilcote 1991, E.K. Brown 1983, and Lawson 1963 (pp. 176ff). On the correlated topic of the role of laity, see Garlow 1979 and Snyder 1980, p. 155.

60. Cf. Outler 1964b, p. 19. The centrality of mission to Wesley's understanding of the church and ministry—indeed of Christianity itself—has been a special emphasis of Schmidt (1953, p. 456; 1958; 1972, p. 145; and 1976, p. 88).

61. Letter to "John Smith" (25 June 1746), §10, *Works*, 26:206.

62. The best studies of Wesley's relation to Anglicanism are Baker 1960 & 1970. For a helpful study of the Enlightenment influences and resulting ecclesiological tensions of a position like that of Wesley, see Daniel Mark Cere, "Ecclesiology and Enlightenment Social Theory: The Reconstruction of Ecclesiology in the Tradition of Anglican Religious Liberalism from John Hales to Thomas Arnold," Concordia University (Montreal) Ph.D. thesis, 1990.

63. For characterizations of Methodism as an order or society within the Church of England, see Outler 1964b, p. 13; W.P. Jones 1987, pp. 11-12; and R. Davies 1989, pp. 2-3.

64. Cf. Hildebrandt 1951, p. 73; C. Williams 1960, p. 149; Stoeffler 1976a; Snyder 1980, pp. 114-23; D. Watson 1985, pp. 80-1; and Snyder 1989, p. 221. The term "ecclesia *pro* ecclesia" is suggested by R. Williams 1964, p. 211. Note the same basic idea applied to Macarius in Dörries, *Theologie des Makarios*, p. 458.

65. Anglican Article XIX (cf. Oden 1988, p. 118). See Wesley's discussion of this article in *An Earnest Appeal to Men of Reason and Religion*, §78, *Works*, 11:78; and Sermon 74, "Of the Church," §18-9, *Works*, 3:53. Cf. Baker 1960, p. 213; and Berg 1984, p. 321.

66. Relate this point to Staniloae's argument that their juridical view of salvation prevents Western Christians from properly appreciating the Church's role in salvation; Staniloae, *Orthodoxe Dogmatik*, 2:153.

67. See esp. *NT Notes*, Acts 5:11, 10:31; and Sermon 74," Of the Church," 5, *Works*, 3:47-8. Cf. Cannon 1968, p. 443; Verhalen 1969, p. 45; Outler 1980-2, p. 16; Bence 1984, p. 301; Dean 1985, pp. 93-6; and Snyder 1989, p. 211.

68. Consider, for example, Avery Dulles' argument that contemporary Roman Catholic ecclesiology needs to develop an understanding of the church as a Com-

munity of Disciples; in *A Church to Believe In* (New York: Crossroad, 1987), pp. 1-18. Actually, Wesley's ecclesial descendants have as much to relearn on this account as anyone. One attempt to help them do so is Howard Snyder, *Liberating the Church: The Ecology of Church and Kingdom* (Downer's Grove, IL: Intervarsity, 1983).

69. See esp. *Letter to a Roman Catholic*, §9, *John Wesley*, p. 495; *NT Notes*, Eph. 5:26-7; Letter to the Editor of the *London Chronicle* (19 Feb. 1761), *Letters* (Telford), 4:137; and Sermon 74, "Of the Church," §III.28, *Works*, 3:55-6.

70. Recall Wesley's defense of Novatian noted in Chapter 1, note 146. It is revealing to see the same basic claim that Wesley made being advanced in Staniloae, *Orthodoxe Dogmatik*, 2:212-3.

71. Note the way this is expressed in *Hymns*, #512, st. 3-4, *Works*, 7:704.

72. Sermon 110 (1739), "Free Grace," §18, *Works*, 3:551.

73. Cf. Sermon 24 (1748), "Sermon on the Mount IV," §III.7, *Works*, 1:545-6. The same basic point can be found nearly forty years later in Sermon 98 (1786), "On Visiting the Sick," §2, §II.4, *Works*, 3:385-6, 391.

74. The most complete study of Wesley's views on personal ethics is McNulty 1963. On the specific topic of Wesley's views on alcohol, see Ivan Burnett, Jr., "Methodist Origins: John Wesley and Alcohol," *MethH* 13.4 (1975):3-17.

75. See *The Nature, Design, and General Rules of the United Societies*, §4, *Works*, 9:70-1; and the tracts collected in *Works* (Jackson), 11:164-202.

76. Cf. Letter to Mrs. Mary Pendarves (19 July 1731), *Works*, 25:293; Letter to William Wogan (28 Mar. 1737), *Works*, 25:500; *A Short Address to the People of Ireland* (1749), §8, *Works* (Jackson), 9:174-5; and Sermon 77 (1780), "Spiritual Worship," §III.5, *Works*, 3:99.

77. Outler 1975, p. 81. See also Hoffman 1968, p. 158.

78. See esp. Sermon 80, "On Friendship with the World," §17, *Works*, 3:134-5; and Sermon 81, "In What Sense Are We to Leave the World," *Works*, 3:142-55. Lest one think that Wesley wanted Christians to abandon the sinful world to its disease, compare Sermon 52, "The Reformation of Manners," *Works*, 2:301-23.

79. See *The Nature, Design, and General Rules of the United Societies*, §4-5, *Works*, 9:70-2. This point was emphasized by Christopher P. Momany in a presentation at the 1992 Wesleyan Theological Society entitled "Wesley's General Rules: A Paradigm for Postmodern Ethics" (slated for publication in *WTJ* 28.1 [1993]).

80. Note his response to the question of why he meddled with medical applications of electricity: "For the same reason as I published the *Primitive Physick*—to do as much good as I can." Letter to the Editor of the *London Magazine* (12 Dec. 1760), *Letters* (Telford), 4:123.

81. Wesley surveys most of these in *A Plain Account of the People Called Methodists*, §XII-XV, *Works*, 9:275-80. For helpful secondary summaries, see Marquardt 1977a, pp. 25-8 [27-9]; Jennings 1990, pp. 58-66; and (with an interesting comparison to the present Latin American situation) Dorothy F. Quijada, "Juan Wesley y su Ministerio Integral," *Boletin Teólogico* 24.46 (1992):107-45.

82. Helpful summaries of the various studies on Wesley's social and political ethics can be found in Schneeberger 1974, pp. 25-29; and Keefer 1990.

83. James Cone, *Black Theology of Liberation* (Philadelphia, PA: Lippincott, 1970), p. 72.

84. Cf. Etchegoyen 1985, p. 250 [162]; Meistad 1989, p. 442; J.R. Tyson 1989, p. 78, 83-6; and Villa-Vicencio 1989, pp. 97-8.

85. E.g., Madron 1965, p. 27; Madron 1981; and Duque Zúñiga 1983, p. 272. Contrast Theodore R. Weber, "Breaking the Power of Canceled Sin: Possibilities and

Limits of a Wesleyan Social Theology," *QR* 11.1 (1991):4-21 (who argues that Wesley did not develop this analogy, but we must). It must be noted here that it is misleading in this regard simply to quote Wesley's claim that there is "no holiness but social holiness" (e.g., Arias 1985, p. 76 [230]; Etchegoyen 1985, p. 253 [164]; and Hulley 1987, p. 73). This claim related to the corporate nature of discipleship, not social transformation.

86. Cf. Marquardt 1977a, p. 165 [134-5]; Míguez Bonino 1981, pp. 58-9 & 1983d, p. 68; and Villa-Vicencio 1982, pp. 88-9. For a strong reservation about this agenda, arguing that Wesley was not even a good model for his own time, see Hall 1987. Then note the claim that the later nineteenth-century holiness movement actually provided more theological grounding for the turn to the poor than Wesley himself in D. Dayton 1991a & 1994.

87. See esp. Schneeberger 1974, p. 163; Marquardt 1977a, pp. 104-21 [89-101]; Meistad 1989, pp. 426ff; and Jennings 1990, pp. 139-56 (esp. p. 146). They see more of these themes present in Wesley than does Villa-Vicencio (1989, pp. 97-101).

88. The best studies of this are Marquardt 1977a and Jennings 1990. For some related reflections on Charles, see Kimbrough 1993.

89. This stance is first articulated in Sermon 28 (1748), "Sermon on the Mount VIII," §11, 25-6, *Works*, 1:618-9, 628-9. Note Wesley's continuing praise of this sermon in *Journal* (1 Sept. 1778), *Journal* (Curnock), 6:209. For a few other articulations of this point, see *OT Notes* (1765), Deut. 5:19 (Wesley's addition, per Casto 1977, p. 404); Sermon 51 (1768), "The Good Steward," §I.1, *Works*, 2:283; and Sermon 126 (1790), "On Worldly Folly," §II.4, *Works*, 4:136. The best short evaluation is Ball-Kilbourne 1984.

90. Sermon 50, "The Use of Money," *Works*, 2:266-80.

91. E.g., Ernst Cahn, "John Wesley als Vorkämpfer einer christlichen Sozialethik," *Die Christliche Welt* 46 (1932):208-12; Robert Kingdon, "Laissez-Faire or Government Control: A Problem for John Wesley," *Church History* 26 (1957):342-54; Bernard Semmel, *The Methodist Revolution* (New York: Basic Books, 1972), pp. 75ff; and Sturm 1982, p. 137.

92. For direct critiques of the Weber thesis, see Yuki Kishida, "John Wesley's Ethics and Max Weber," *WQR* 4 (1967):43-58; Charles Elliott, "The Ideology of Economic Growth: A Case Study," in *Land, Labour and Population in the Industrial Revolution*, eds. E.L. Jones & G.E. Mingay (New York: Barnes & Noble, 1967), pp. 75-99; Marquardt 1977a, pp. 43-4 [41-2]; and Madron 1981, p. 109. For counterarguments that Wesley was actually a nascent socialist, see W.H. Meredith, "John Wesley, Christian Socialist," *Methodist Review* 83 (1901):426-39; Kathleen Walker MacArthur, *The Economic Ethics of John Wesley* (New York: Abingdon/Cokesbury, 1936); P. Watson 1964, p. 57 fn75; and Robert Hughes, "Wesleyan Roots of Christian Socialism," *The Ecumenist* 13 (1975):49-53. Concerning this proposal, it is true that Wesley valued the ideal of community of goods described in Acts, but he supported only voluntary means for effecting this, not social-political coercion, as evidenced by his retention (with slight revisions) of Anglican Article XXXVIII, which denied the claim of some Anabaptist groups to common title of all wealth (Oden 1988, p. 126). See the fine study of this issue in Walsh 1990, esp. pp. 45-6.

93. The best exposition of "The Use of Money" is Outler 1985c (unfortunately not published). Also helpful is Clarence Haywood's comparison of Wesley to the traditional Aquinian ethic of a just price in "Was John Wesley a Political Economist?" *Church History* 33 (1964):314-21. Contrast the caricature of Wesley's position on this theme in H. Richard Niebuhr, *The Social Sources of Denominationalism* (New York:

Meridian, 1957), pp. 68-9, 91. Jennings' reticence about this theme (1990, pp. 165ff) must be understood in light of such caricatures.

94. Cf. Outler 1984, pp. 92-3. Jennings' suggestion (1990, pp. 97-117) that Wesley rejected the very idea of private property seems less defensible.

95. Cf. Sermon 87 (1781), "The Danger of Riches," *Works,* 3:228-46; Sermon 61 (1783), "The Mystery of Iniquity," §34, *Works,* 2:468; Sermon 68 (1784), "The Wisdom of God's Counsels," §16-8, *Works,* 2:560-3; "Thoughts on Methodism," *AM* (1786):101ff, *Works* (Jackson), 13:258-61; Sermon 108 (1788), "On Riches," *Works,* 3:519-28; Sermon 122 (1789), "Causes of the Inefficacy of Christianity," §9, §17-18, *Works,* 4:91, 95-6; Sermon 125 (1789), "On a Single Eye," *Works,* 4:120-30; Sermon 126 (1790), "On Worldly Folly," *Works,* 4:132-8; and Sermon 131 (1790), "The Danger of Increasing Riches," *Works,* 4:178-86. See also the discussion in Jennings 1990, pp. 118ff.

96. See *Thoughts on the Present Scarcity of Provisions, Works* (Jackson), 11:53-9 (Wesley admitted that few of these proposals would be adopted).

97. Wesley mentions reading this (unidentified) tract in *Journal* (2 Sept. 1776), *Journal* (Curnock), 6:125-6. In 1778 he drew upon it to revise his earlier estimate of the situation, in *A Serious Address to the People of England, with Regard to the State of the Nation, Works* (Jackson), 11:140-9.

98. The strongest claim to this effect is Black 1984, pp. 165-7.

99. The specific impact of Wesley's support of his sisters is developed in Couture 1991, esp. pp. 130-1. For general discussion of the contribution of his involvement with the poor, see Marquardt 1977a, pp. 28ff [30ff]; and Jennings 1990, pp. 53ff.

100. Note the claims about Wesley rejecting any dichotomy between secular and sacred in Hall 1963, p. 124; Meistad 1987; and Meistad 1989, p. 76.

101. Cf. Madron 1965, pp. 95, 104. In addition to this study by Madron, good treatments of Wesley's political ethics are Hynson 1973, 1983, & 1984.

102. Note especially his Letter to Editor of the *Gentleman's Magazine* (24 Dec. 1785), *Letters* (Telford), 7:305; and *Thoughts Concerning the Origin of Power, Works* (Jackson), 11:46-53. For several tracts related to the American colonies, see *Works* (Jackson), 11:80-140.

103. One of the latest examples is Lynwood M. Holland & Ronald F. Howell, "John Wesley's Concept of Religious and Political Authority," *Journal of Church and State* 6 (1964):296-313.

104. E.g., Cooper 1962, p. 116; Hynson 1973; and Rakestraw 1985b. Cf. the argument of Harry Howard that the "Toryism" of Wesley's Day was one which supported a constitutional monarchy rather than divine right of kings, in "John Wesley: Tory or Democrat?" *MethH* 31 (1992):38-46.

105. Hynson 1983, pp. 58-60. Cf. Black 1984, p. 157; and Hempton 1993. Note how this move would fit Wesley's increased emphasis on Prevenient Grace (a connection made in Meistad 1989, pp. 410-11; and Hynson 1985). One right to which Wesley drew particular attention was freedom of conscience in matters of religion; cf. *Thoughts Upon Liberty,* 16, *Works* (Jackson), 11:37; and Hynson 1972.

106. This charge is raised in Schneeberger 1977, p. 48. For a contrasting collection of Wesley's protests against unjust situations and laws, see Jennings 1990, pp. 71-96.

107. *Thoughts Upon Slavery* can be found in *Works* (Jackson), 11:59-79; and W.T. Smith 1986. For secondary studies of Wesley on slavery, see Madron 1964; Marquardt 1977a, pp. 78ff [70ff]; Phipps 1981; Brendlinger 1982; and W.T. Smith 1986. It is significant that rather than try to contradict those specific scriptures which seemed to condone slavery, Wesley used the broad scriptural theme of equal human dignity

to critique the practice (compare his *NT Notes* comment on 1 Cor. 7:17-22 with that on 1 Tim. 1:10).

108. Wesley's last known letter was an encouragement of William Wilberforce in his political fight against slavery (Letter to William Wilberforce [24 Feb. 1791], *Letters* [Telford], 8:265). He had earlier included a letter by Thomas Walker requesting petitions against the slave trade be sent to Parliament in *AM* 11 (1788):263-4.

109. See Sermon 60, "The General Deliverance," §1 & §III.10, *Works*, 2:437, 449; Sermon 95, "On the Education of Children," §25, *Works*, 3:360; and the letter he includes in his *Journal* (16 July 1756), *Works*, 21:68-9.

110. See the attempt to do so in Rakestraw 1986.

111. Douglas John Hall, *Imaging God: Dominion as Stewardship* (Grand Rapids, MI: Eerdmans, 1986), pp. 42-53.

112. On this general characterization, see McDannel & Lang, *Heaven*, esp. p. 84. For an insightful study of how this move is evidenced in changing understandings of death, see Philippe Ariès, *The Hour of Our Deaths* (New York: Alfred Knopf, 1991). In specific connection to intermediate states, see Le Goff, *Birth of Purgatory*.

113. Cf. McDannel & Lang, *Heaven*, pp. 142-5, 152-4, 172. Note that there is no discussion of the new creation in either Heppe, *Reformed Dogmatics*; or Schmid, *Doctrinal Theology*.

114. For several examples, see *Hymns for Children*, #8, *Poet. Works*, 6:378-9; *Hymns and Sacred Psalms*, #174, *Poet. Works*, 5:382; Poem on Luke 16:4, *CW Poetry*, 2:156; *Hymns*, #50, st. 3, *Works*, 7:142; *Hymns*, #51 st. 1 & 5, *Works*, 7:143-4; *Hymns*, #67, st. 2, *Works*, 7:165; *Hymns*, #69, st. 2, *Works*, 7:167; and *Hymns*, #72, st. 2, *Works*, 7:171.

115. See esp. Letter to Miss March (5 July 1768), *Letters* (Telford), 5:96; and Sermon 114 (1785), "On the Death of John Fletcher," 3:611-29.

116. The section of *Hymns* on "Describing Death" includes ##39-52, *Works*, 7:129-45. Note #42, st. 2 (p. 133) "How then ought I on earth to live?"

117. Compare the judgments of Strawson 1959, p. 243; and Holifield 1986, pp. 86-7. Cf. Beckerlegge's note in *Works*, 7:137. To put Wesley in his context, see Ariès, *Hour of our Deaths*, pp. 300-12.

118. *Hymns*, #47, *Works*, 7:138-9. See also *Hymns*, ##48-51, *Works*, 7:139-44; and Wesley's entry on his mother's death in *Journal* (20 June 1742), *Works*, 19:282-3.

119. These undertones are strongest in some early manuscript sermons: Sermon 133, "Death and Deliverance," *Works*, 4:206-14; and Sermon 136, "On Mourning for the Dead," *Works*, 4:237-43.

120. Note this argument from Gregory of Nyssa in Pelikan, *Christian Tradition*, 1:51.

121. Sermon 51, "The Good Steward," §II.10, *Works*, 2:290-1.

122. The doctrine of soul sleep or soul death was rejected as unscriptural in Article XL of the original forty-two Edwardian articles of 1553 (dropped in 1563); cf. Hardwick, *Articles of Religion*, pp. 348-9. For a survey of the scattered interest in the doctrine leading up to Wesley's time, see Norman T. Burns, *Christian Mortalism from Tyndale to Milton* (Cambridge, MA: Harvard University Press, 1972). It is important, that while many early Syriac writers affirmed soul sleep, Macarius did not (see Daley, *Hope of Early Church*, p. 118).

123. Cf. Sermon 51, "The Good Steward," §II.6-8, *Works*, 2:288-90; Sermon 116, "What is Man," §10, *Works*, 4:23; and Sermon 124, "Human Life a Dream," §7, *Works*, 4:112-3.

124. See *Minutes* (25 June 1744), Q. 16 (*John Wesley*, p. 139) where Wesley relates not only the removal of the guilt of Original Sin, but the provision for immortal

bodies following resurrection, and the present life of the soul to the universal benefit of Christ's atonement (what he will later term Prevenient Grace).

125. This sermon "On the Resurrection of the Dead" was included as an admitted abridgement in *Works* (Jackson), 7:474-85. This claim was common in Protestant scholasticism and post-Restoration England; cf. Heppe, *Reformed Dogmatics*, p. 700; Schmid, *Doctrinal Theology*, p. 640; and Philip C. Almond, "The Contours of Hell in English Thought, 1660-1750," *Religion* 22 (1992):297-311, here, p. 301.

126. See especially Sermon 15 (1758), "The Great Assize," §I.1, *Works*, 1:358; and his translation of Charles Bonnet's *Conjectures Concerning the Nature of Future Happiness* (Dublin: Dugdale, 1787), pp. 19ff (note Wesley's commendatory preface, reprinted in *Works* [Jackson], 14:307).

127. Cf. Sermon 51, "The Good Steward," §II.6-8, *Works*, 2:288-90; Sermon 116, "What is Man," §10, *Works*, 4:23; Sermon 124, "Human Life a Dream," §7, *Works*, 4:112-3.

128. See the references and attending discussion in Chapter 3, note 42.

129. See his last sermon, Sermon 132, "On Faith," §2, *Works*, 4:188-9.

130. The clearest example is the Sermon 133 (1725), "Death and Deliverance," §4, *Works*, 4:208, but note the hints of reservation in §13 (211). Traces remain as late as Sermon 43 (1765), "The Scripture Way of Salvation," §I.1, *Works*, 2:156.

131. Cf. Sermon 115 (1788), "Dives and Lazarus," §I.3, *Works*, 4:7.

132. E.g., Sermon 84, "The Important Question," §II.4-5, *Works*, 3:186-7; and Sermon 117, "On the Discoveries of Faith," §8-9, *Works*, 4:32-3.

133. For a sense of the discussion of this topic in Wesley's day, see Ezra Abbot's bibliography, entries 2462-2599, in William R. Alger, *Critical History of the Doctrine of a Future Life* (10th ed. New York: W.J. Widdleton, 1878), pp. 879-84. Wesley's interest is reflected in his request that Archibald Campbell's *The Doctrines of a Middle State between Death and Resurrection* (London, 1721) be read to him in the final month of his life (noted in Outler 1984, page 89 fn85). Wesley refers to Campbell in his last sermon—Sermon 132, "On Faith," §4, *Works*, 4:190.

134. The clearest example is Sermon 109 (1735), "The Trouble and Rest of Good Men" (*Works*, 3:533-41), compare §I.3 (537) to §II.6 (540). This same ambiguity is present in the hymns (##65-77) gathered in the section "Describing Heaven" in *Hymns* (*Works*, 7:161-76).

135. E.g., Sermon 115 (1789), "Dives and Lazarus," §I.3, *Works*, 4:7; and Sermon 132 (1791), "On Faith," §5, *Works*, 4:190-1.

136. Note how fleeting any distinction between the intermediate state of the unreconciled and Hell as a final state of damnation is in Sermon 72 (1782), "Of Hell," *Works*, 3:31-44.

137. Cf. Sermon 115 (1788), "Dives and Lazarus," §I.3, *Works*, 4:8; Sermon 117 (1788), "On the Discoveries of Faith," §9, *Works*, 4:33; and Sermon 132 (1791), "On Faith," §4, *Works*, 4:189. This distinction is not found in earlier sermons.

138. Cf. *NT Notes*, 1 Cor. 3:13; Letter to William Law (6 Jan. 1756), §II.7, *Letters* (Telford), 3:370; *The Advantage of the Members of the Church of England over Those of the Church of Rome*, §13, *Works* (Jackson), 10:137; *Popery, Calmly Considered*, §II.5, *Works* (Jackson), 10:144 (distillation of *A Roman Catechism, with a Reply Thereto* [by John Williams], Q. 20, *Works* [Jackson], 10:98); and Sermon 115, "Dives and Lazarus," §I.5, *Works*, 4:8-9. Note that he kept Anglican Article XXII which rejects the Roman Catholic notion of purgatory as not scriptural in the Articles of Religion (Oden 1988, p. 119). Remember in this regard John's disagreement with Charles over the role of suffering in sanctification (cf. Chapter 8, note 155).

139. Sermon 132, "On Faith," §5-6, *Works*, 4:190-2

140. In the previous paragraph Wesley had referred to Archibald Campbell, whose *The Doctrines of a Middle State between Death and Resurrection* he was having read to him at the time. Outler notes (1987, p. 190 fn10) that Campbell had been involved in dialogues with the Eastern Orthodox and that his book reflects characteristic Eastern Orthodox eschatology.

141. Cf. Schmid, *Doctrinal Theology*, pp. 644.

142. Cf. *NT Notes*, Heb. 9:27; and Sermon 51 (1768), "The Good Steward," §III.1, *Works*, 2:292-3.

143. Compare Sermon 15, "The Great Assize," esp. §II.10, *Works*, 1:364; to Heppe, *Reformed Dogmatics*, p. 706; and Schmid, *Doctrinal Theology*, pp. 644-5.

144. E.g., *NT Notes*, Rom. 9:21, 1 Cor. 3:8.

145. E.g., Sermon 89, "The More Excellent Way," §8, *Works*, 3:266; and *Journal* (22 Mar. 1774), *Works*, 22:400.

146. For attempts to argue that universalism might be a consistent development of Wesley's emphasis on grace, while recognizing that Wesley does not himself teach this, see Rattenbury 1941, p. 133; Deschner 1960, pp. 139-40; and Downes 1960, pp. 174-6.

147. Cf. *NT Notes*, Matt. 5:22; and Sermon 15, "The Great Assize," §III.1, *Works*, 1:366-7, which strings together various biblical images with language of the devouring "dogs of hell"—pride, malice, despair, and so on.

148. See Letter to William Law (6 Jan. 1756), §II.7, *Letters* (Telford), 3:368-70; Sermon 73, "Of Hell," §I.4, *Works*, 3:35; and the only hymn on Hell in *Hymns* (#78, *Works*, 7:176-7).

149. Wesley's rejection of this possibility can be found in *A Letter to a Roman Catholic*, §10, *John Wesley*, pp. 495-6; *Journal* (8 Aug. 1773), *Works*, 22:385; and Sermon 54, "On Eternity," §15, *Works*, 2:367. He does not identify the source that he is rejecting, but among those raising this alternative were Capel Berrow (suggested in *Works*, 22:385 fn71) and William Whiston (whose work on cosmology Wesley had read). For a discussion of Whiston and other contemporary examples, see Daniel P. Walker, *The Decline of Hell: Seventeenth Century Discussions of Eternal Torment* (Chicago, IL: University of Chicago, 1964); and Almond, "Contours of Hell."

150. Note particularly: Sermon 73, "Of Hell," §II.1-4, *Works*, 3:36-7; *Instructions for Children*, pp. 12-3; and his complaint that Swedenborg's account of Hell removes all terror from it, in *Journal* (22 Apr. 1779), *Journal* (Curnock), 6:231; and "Thoughts on the Writings of Baron Swedenborg," §27, *AM* 6 (1783):437ff, *Works* (Jackson), 13:442. But consider as well the argument that Wesley's descriptions of Hell were low-keyed for his day, in Strawson 1959, p. 247; Downes 1960, pp. 180ff; D. Wilson 1963; and Outler 1986, p. 30.

151 .Letter to Mary Bishop (17 April 1776), *Letters* (Telford), 5:213-14.

152. Baxter, *Saints Everlasting Rest* (1649), p. 49. Cf. McDannel & Lang, *Heaven*, p. 172.

153. The first republication was in 1754 as volume 37 of the *Christian Library* (the passage in question is retained on p. 65). It was reissued separately five times during Wesley's life, and numerous times thereafter (see Baker, *Union Catalog*, #131.ix).

154. *Sermons* (1746), Preface, §5, *Works*, 1:105. Note as well his comment that the "world to come" is so styled, not because it does not yet exist, but because it is not yet visible in *NT Notes*, Eph. 1:21.

155. See Letter to Mary Bishop (17 April 1776), *Letters* (Telford), 5:213-14; and Sermon 64 (1785), "The New Creation," §5-6, *Works*, 2:502. The other two heavens

would be the sub-lunar (i.e., the earth's atmosphere) and the celestial (the realm of the stars and other planets).

156. Note, for example, how he defines the "eternal world" as a future state to commence after the present in Sermon 119 (1788), "Walking by Sight and Walking by Faith," §8, *Works,* 4:52. Cf. H.-J. Lee 1991, p. 83.

157. See esp. Sermon 60, "The General Deliverance," §III, *Works,* 2:445-50; and Sermon 64, "The New Creation," *Works,* 2:500-10.

158. See Sermon 63, "The General Spread of the Gospel," §27, *Works,* 2:499; and Wesley's preface to his extracts from John Hilldrop's *Free Thoughts on Brute Creation* in *AM* 6 (1783):33, *Works* (Jackson), 14:290. This same concern may explain why the first examples of identification of the new creation as the ultimate hope in Charles' hymns are in cases responding to major earthquakes and other theodicy-inspiring events; e.g., three hymns responding to the great Lisbon earthquake, *Hymns,* #59, st. 3, *Works,* 7:154; *Hymns,* #60, st. 3, *Works,* 7:156; and *Hymns,* #63, st. 6-7, pp. 159-60.

159. One contemporary source arguing that all creation will participate in final salvation that Wesley acknowledged drawing on, by excerpting and serializing in the *Arminian Magazine,* was John Hilldrop's *Free Thoughts on Brute Creation* (cf. *AM* 6 [1783]:33ff). McDannel & Lang (*Heaven,* pp. 181ff) discern this theme in Swedenborg as well—a source Wesley would not be likely to acknowledge. For comparison of Wesley (as an exemplary exception in the West) to the more common theme of cosmic redemption in Patristic and later Eastern Orthodox eschatology, see James A. Nash, *Loving Nature: Ecological Integrity and Christian Responsibility* (Nashville, TN: Abingdon, 1991), p. 125. Note also the comments on Wesley's views about animal redemption in Chapter 2, note 112.

160. Note that Irenaeus suggests the possibility of continued growth even after judgment (cf. Daley, *Hope of Early Church,* p. 31.

161. *Farther Thoughts Upon Christian Perfection,* Q. 29, *Works* (Jackson), 11:426.

162. See Charles Bonnet, *Conjectures Concerning the Nature of Future Happiness* (Dublin: Dugdale, 1787), esp. pp. 23-4 (Wesley's commendatory preface is reprinted in *Works* [Jackson], 14:307).

163. Note the listing of the theme of heaven involving continual spiritual progress as a modern theme in the Western Christian understanding of heaven in McDannel & Lang, *Heaven,* pp. 181ff.

Concluding Reflections

1. Note how Paul Althaus organizes his discussion of Luther's soteriology under the heading of "The Freedom of the Gracious God" in *Theology of Luther,* pp. 274ff. See also the discussion in Gerhard O. Forde, "Justification by Faith Alone: The Article By Which the Church Stands or Falls?" *Dialog* 27 (1988):260-7, esp. p. 265.

2. It is no accident that a classic survey of the doctrine of grace in the Reformed tradition by Abraham Booth is titled *The Reign of Grace* (reprint ed.; Swengel, Pa: Reiner Publications, 1976). For an argument that the sovereignty of God (and God's grace) is central to Ulrich Zwingli's theology, see W.P. Stevens, *Zwingli: An Introduction to His Thought* (New York: Oxford University Press, 1992). For the same claim about Calvin, see A. Mitchell Hunter, *The Teaching of Calvin* (London: James Clarke, 1950), pp. 49-51; and H. Henry Meeter, *The Basic Ideas of Calvinism,* 6th ed. (Grand Rapids, Mich: Baker, 1990), pp. 15-22. Finally, note Jonathan Edwards' description of the absolute sovereignty of God as "my chosen light, my chosen doctrine," in *The Works of Jonathan Edwards* (Edinburgh: Banner of Truth, 1974), 1:xlviii.

3. Note the discussion of the cooperant nature of grace for Arminius in Carl Bangs, *Arminius* (Nashville, TN: Abingdon, 1971), pp. 340ff.

4. This point is argued well in Alvin J. Beachy, *The Concept of Grace in the Radical Reformation* (Nieuwkoop: B. de Graaf, 1977).

5. See in this regard Richard P. McBrien, "Roman Catholicism, *E Pluribus Unum*," in *Religion and America*, ed. Mary Douglas and Steven Tipton (Boston, MA: Beacon, 1982), pp. 179-89; and Thomas F. O'Meara, "Grace as a Theological Structure in the *Summa theologica* of Thomas Aquinas," *Recherches de Théologie ancienne et médiévale* 55 (1988):130-53.

6. Note the suggestion that what Eastern Orthodoxy itself has to offer is a mediation between Protestantism and Roman Catholicism in Panagiotis I. Bratsiotis, "The Fundamental Principles and Main Characteristics of the Orthodox Church," in *The Orthodox Ethos*, ed. A.J. Philippou (Oxford: Holywell Press, 1964), pp. 23-31. For a recent appreciative Eastern Orthodox analysis of a possible model in the West (who shares strong similarities to Wesley!), see Nicholas Lossky, *Lancelot Andrewes the Preacher (1555-1626), The Origins of the Mystical Theology of the Church of England* (Oxford: Clarendon, 1991).

7. Note the characterization of the theme of divinization as central to all areas of Eastern Orthodox theology in Petro B.T. Bilaniuk, "The Mystery of *Theosis* or Divinization," in *The Heritage of the Early Church*, ed. by P.B.T. Bilaniuk (Rome: Pontifical Institute for Oriental Studies, 1973), pp. 337-59.

8. This process has been well documented on both side of the Atlantic. The most important studies of British Methodist theology are Dunlap 1956; and William Strawson, "Methodist Theology 1850-1950," in *A History of the Methodist Church in Great Britain*, eds. R. Davies, *et al.* (London: Epworth, 1983), 3:182-231. The most significant analyses of North American Methodism are Robert Eugene Chiles, *Theological Transition in American Methodism: 1790-1935* (New York: Abingdon, 1965; reprint ed., Lanham, MD: University Press of America, 1983); Langford 1983; Leland Scott II, "Methodist Theology in America in the Nineteenth Century," *RelLife* 25 (1955):87-98; and David Clark Shipley, "The Development of Theology in American Methodism in the Nineteenth Century," *LQHR* 184 (sixth series, 28) (1959):249-64.

9. Relate this to the legitimate worry that the current interest in Wesley may serve (consciously or not) as a means to ignore the problems and perplexities of our present context, expressed in Míguez Bonino 1983d, pp. 65-6; and Villa-Vicencio 1989, p. 93.

10. Cf. Meeks 1985a, p. 21; and Outler 1974, pp. 64-5.

SELECTED BIBLIOGRAPHY

Preface

A brief characterization of this bibliography is in order. It seeks to provide a fairly comprehensive listing of significant recent studies of John Wesley's theology. Biographical and other works are included only if they have an appreciable component dealing with Wesley's theology. From works published prior to 1960, only those of the most continuing significance are included. Of course, many other earlier works and biographical studies have been cited in the endnotes when relevant.

I have included all types of serious scholarly material, including unpublished dissertations (unless they were adequately summarized in published articles or issued later as books). Readers who wish to consult any of these dissertations should know that most can be purchased from University Microfilms (Ann Arbor, MI), and that almost all are available through a Research Library Interloan Network (RLIN) library.

The abbreviations adopted for primary Wesley materials are noted in the Bibliography. They follow standards recently suggested. The abbreviations used throughout the Bibliography and endnotes for journals and series are listed below.

Abbreviations

AM	*Arminian Magazine* (London)
AsbSem	*The Asbury Seminarian*
AsbThJ	*The Asbury Theological Journal*
BGEmK	Beiträge zur Geschichte der Evangelish-methodistischen Kirche
ChQ	*Church Quarterly*
DrG	*The Drew Gateway*
DukeDivSB	*The Duke Divinity School Bulletin*
DukeDivSR	*The Duke Divinity School Review*
EpRev	*The Epworth Review*
EvJl	*Evangelical Journal*
LQHR	*The London Quarterly and Holburn Review*
MethH	*Methodist History*
PSTJ	*The Perkins School of Theology Journal*
PWHS	*Proceedings of the Wesley Historical Society*
QR	*Quarterly Review*
RelLife	*Religion in Life*
TFor	*Teologisk Forum*
WQR	*Wesleyan Quarterly Review*
WTJ	*Wesleyan Theological Journal*

I. PRIMARY WORKS

A. Bibliographies

Baker, Frank, ed. *A Union Catalog of the Publications of John and Charles Wesley.* Durham, NC: The Divinity School, Duke University, 1966; Second (revised) ed., Stone Mountain, GA: George Zimmermann, 1991.

Green, Richard. *The Works of John and Charles Wesley: A Bibliography.* 2nd ed. London: Methodist Publishing House, 1906; reprint ed., New York: AMS Press, 1976.

B. Select Editions and Compends of John Wesley's Works

The Bicentennial Edition of the Works of John Wesley. 35 volumes projected. Editor in Chief, Frank Baker. Nashville, TN: Abingdon, 1984ff. (Volumes 7, 11, 25, and 26 originally appeared as the *Oxford Edition of The Works of John Wesley.* Oxford: Clarendon, 1975-83). Abbreviation: *Works.*

Vol. 1: *Sermons I.* Ed. Albert C. Outler, 1984.
Vol. 2: *Sermons II.* Ed. Albert C. Outler, 1985.
Vol. 3: *Sermons III.* Ed. Albert C. Outler, 1986.
Vol. 4: *Sermons IV.* Ed. Albert C. Outler, 1987.
Vol. 7: *A Collection of Hymns for the Use of the People Called Methodists.* Eds. Franz Hildebrandt & Oliver Beckerlegge, 1983.
Vol. 9: *The Methodist Societies I: History, Nature and Design.* Ed. Rupert E. Davies, 1989.
Vol. 11: *The Appeals to Men of Reason and Religion and Certain Related Open Letters.* Ed. Gerald R. Cragg, 1975.
Vol. 18: *Journals and Diaries I, 1735-38.* Eds. W. Reginald Ward & Richard P. Heitzenrater, 1988.
Vol. 19: *Journals and Diaries II, 1738-43.* Eds. W. Reginald Ward & Richard P. Heitzenrater, 1990.
Vol. 20: *Journals and Diaries III, 1743-54.* Eds. W. Reginald Ward & Richard P. Heitzenrater, 1991.
Vol. 21: *Journals and Diaries IV, 1755-65.* Eds. W. Reginald Ward & Richard P. Heitzenrater, 1992.
Vol. 22: *Journals and Diaries V, 1765-75.* Eds. W. Reginald Ward & Richard P. Heitzenrater, 1993.
Vol. 25: *Letters I, 1721-39.* Ed. Frank Baker, 1980.
Vol. 26: *Letters II, 1740-55.* Ed. Frank Baker, 1982.

Christian Instructions: Extracted From a Late French Author. Bristol: William Pine, 1766.

A Christian Library: Consisting of Extracts from and Abridgments of the Choicest Pieces of Practical Divinity Which have been Published in the English Tongue. 50 vols. Bristol: Farley, 1749-55; reprint ed., 30 vols., London: Cordeux, 1819-27. Abbreviation: *Chr. Library.*

"The Christian Sacrament and Sacrifice." (Extracted from Dr. Brevint). In J. Ernest Rattenbury. *The Eucharistic Hymns of John and Charles Wesley,* pp. 176-93. London: Epworth, 1948 (and *Poet. Works,* 3:185-214).

A Collection of Forms of Prayer for Every Day of the Week. 3rd ed. London: Hutton, 1738; reprint ed., Nashville, TN: United Methodist Publishing House, 1992. Abbreviation: *Forms of Prayer.*

The Complete English Dictionary. 3rd ed. London: Hawes, 1777.

A Concise Ecclesiastical History, From the Birth of Christ to the Beginning of the Present Century. 4 vols. (Extracted from John Laurence Mosheim). London: Paramore, 1781. Abbreviation: *Ecclesiastical History.*

Devotions for Every Day in the Week and the Great Festivals. (An abridgement of John Austin's *Devotions in the Antient Way of Offices, with Psalms, Hymns, and Prayers for Every Day of the Week, and Every Holiday in the Year*). *Chr. Library,* (1755) Vol. 42, pp. 73-236, (1826) Vol. 25, pp. 243-480. Reprinted in abridged form in *John Wesley's Prayers,* pp. 71-100. Ed. Frederick C. Gill. London: Epworth, 1951. Abbreviation: *Devotions for Every Day.*

Explanatory Notes Upon the New Testament. 2 vols. London: Bowyer, 1755; reprint ed., Peabody, MA: Hendrickson, 1986. Abbreviation: *NT Notes.*

Explanatory Notes upon the Old Testament. 3 vols. Bristol: Pine, 1765; reprint ed., Salem, OH: Schmul, 1975. Abbreviation: *OT Notes.*

Instructions for Children. 8th edition. Bristol: William Pine, 1767.

John Wesley. Ed. Albert C. Outler. A Library of Protestant Thought Series. New York: Oxford University Press, 1964. Abbreviation: *John Wesley.*

The Journal of the Rev. John Wesley, A.M. 8 vols. Ed. Nehemiah Curnock. London: Epworth, 1909-16. Abbreviation: *Journal* (Curnock).

The Letters of the Rev. John Wesley, A.M. 8 vols. Ed. John Telford. London: Epworth, 1931. Abbreviation: *Letters* (Telford).

Minutes of the Methodist Conferences, from the First, held in London, by the Late Rev. John Wesley, A.M., in the Year 1744. Volume I. London: John Mason, 1862. Abbreviation: *Minutes* (Mason).

Primitive Physick: Or an Easy and Natural Method of Curing Most Diseases. 22nd ed. Philadelphia: Hall, 1791; reprint ed., Nashville, TN: United Methodist Publishing House, 1992.

The Sunday Service of the Methodists in North America London: Strahan, 1784; reprint ed., Nashville, TN: United Methodist Publishing House, 1992. Abbreviation: *Sunday Service.*

A Survey of the Wisdom of God in the Creation, or A Compendium of Natural Philosophy. 3 volumes. 2nd edition. Bristol: William Pine, 1770; 5 volumes. 5th edition (corrected 4th ed.). London: Maxwell & Wilson, 1809. Abbreviation: *Survey.*

Thoughts Upon Infant-Baptism, Extracted from a Late Author (William Wall). Bristol: Farley, 1751.

The Works of John Wesley. 14 vols. 3rd ed. Ed. Thomas Jackson. London: Wesleyan Methodist Book Room, 1872; reprint ed., Grand Rapids, MI: Baker, 1979. Abbreviation: *Works* (Jackson).

C. Select Editions and Compends of Charles Wesley's Works

"Awake, Thou That Sleepest." In *Works,* 1:142-58.

"The Cause and Cure of Earthquakes." In *Works* (Jackson), 7:386-399.

Charles Wesley: A Reader. Ed. John R. Tyson. New York: Oxford University Press, 1989. Abbreviation: *CW Reader.*

Charles Wesley's Earliest Evangelical Sermons: Six Manuscript Sermons Hitherto Unpublished. Eds. Thomas A. Albin & Oliver A. Beckerlegge. England: Wesley Historical Society, 1987. Abbreviation: *Early Sermons CW.*

Hymns on the Lord's Supper. In J. Ernest Rattenbury. *The Eucharistic Hymns of John and Charles Wesley,* pp. 195-249. London: Epworth, 1948 (and *Poet. Works,* 3:215-341).

The Journal of Charles Wesley, M.A. 2 vols. Ed. Thomas Jackson. London: John Mason, 1849; Kansas City, MO: Beacon Hill, 1980. Abbreviation: *Journal CW.*

The Poetical Works of John and Charles Wesley. 13 vols. Ed. Grant Osborn. London: Wesleyan Methodist Conference Office, 1868-72. Abbreviation: *Poet. Works.*

Sermons of the Late Rev. Charles Wesley. London: Baldwin, Craddock & Joy, 1816. (See Heitzenrater 1989, pp. 150-61 on these sermons). Abbreviation: *Sermons CW.*

The Unpublished Poetry of Charles Wesley. 3 vols. Eds. S T Kimbrough, Jr. & Oliver A. Beckerlegge. Nashville, TN: Kingswood, 1988-92. Abbreviation: *Poetry.*

II. SECONDARY WORKS

A. Bibliographies

Field, Clive D. "Bibliography: John Wesley - Theology." In *A History of the Methodist Church in Great Britain,* Vol. IV, pp. 703-23. Ed. Rupert Davies, *et al.* London: Epworth Press, 1988 (See yearly supplements in *PWHS* from 1986ff [volume 46ff]).

Jarboe, Betty. *John and Charles Wesley: A Bibliography.* Metuchen, NJ: Scarecrow, 1987.

B. Books, Dissertations, and Articles on John Wesley

Abraham, William James

1982 "Inspiration in the Classical Wesleyan Tradition." In *A Celebration of Ministry: Essays in Honor of Frank Bateman Stanger,* pp. 33-47. Ed. Kenneth C. Kinghorn. Wilmore, KY: Francis Asbury.

1985 "The Wesleyan Quadrilateral." In *Wesleyan Theology Today,* pp. 119-26. Ed. Theodore H. Runyon. Nashville, TN: Kingswood.

Arias, Mortimer

1983 "Las comunidades de base y la tradición wesleyana." In *La Tradición Protestante en la Teología Latinoamericana,* pp. 103-25. Ed. José Duque. San Jose, Costa Rica: DEI.
English: "Methodist Societies in the Eighteenth Century and Christian Base Communities in the Twentieth Century." In *Wesleyan Theology Today,* pp. 227-39. Ed. Theodore H. Runyon. Nashville, TN: Kingswood, 1985.

1985 "As Mediaçôes Distorcionantes Na Transmissáo do Legado Original de Wesley." In *Luta pela vida e evangelizaçáo: A tradiçâo metodista na teologia latino-americana,* pp. 22-33. J. Míguez-Bonino, *et al.* Sâo Paulo: Ediçôes Paulinas, 1985.
English: "Distortions in the Transmission of the Original Legacy of Wesley." in *Faith Born in the Struggle for Life,* pp. 229-43. Ed. Dow Kirkpatrick. Grand Rapids, MI: Eerdmans, 1988.

Arnett, William Melvin

1954 "John Wesley: Man of One Book." Drew University Ph.D. thesis.

1973 "A Study in John Wesley's Explanatory Notes upon the Old Testament." *WTJ* 8:14-32.

1979a "John Wesley and the Law." *AsbSem* 34:22-31.

1979b "The Role of the Holy Spirit in Entire Sanctification in the Writings of John Wesley." *WTJ* 14.2:15-30.

Assmann, Hugo

1985 "Basta a 'Santidade Social'? Hipótese de um católico romano sobre a fidelidade metodista." In *Luta pela vida e evangelização: A tradição metodista*

na teologia latino-americana, pp. 189-202. J. Míguez-Bonino, *et al.* São Paulo: Edições Paulinas.
English: "Is 'Social Holiness' Enough?A Catholic Reading." in *Faith Born in the Struggle for Life*, pp. 26-37. Ed. Dow Kirkpatrick. Grand Rapids, MI: Eerdmans, 1988.

Baker, Frank
1957 *Methodism and the Love Feast.* London: Epworth.
1960 "John Wesley's Churchmanship." *LQHR* 185 (sixth series, 29):210-15, 269-74.
1966 "The Doctrines in the *Discipline*: A Study of the Forgotten Theological Presuppositions of American Methodism." *DukeDivSR* 31: 39-55; reprint, *From Wesley to Asbury*, pp. 162-82. Durham, NC: Duke University Press, 1976.
1970 *John Wesley and the Church of England.* Nashville, TN: Abingdon.
1980a "Unfolding John Wesley: A Survey of Twenty Years' Studies in Wesley's Thought." *QR* 1.1:44-58
1980b "Introduction." *Works*, 25:1-140.
1987 "John Wesley and Practical Divinity." *WTJ* 22.1:7-15.
1989 "John Wesley, Biblical Commentator." *Bulletin of the John Rylands University Library of Manchester* 71.1 (1989):110-20.

Ball-Kilbourne, Gary L.
1984 "The Christian as Steward in John Wesley's Theological Ethics." *QR* 4.1:43-54.

Barber, Frank Louis
1923 *The Philosophy of John Wesley.* Toronto: N.p.

Beach, Waldo & Niebuhr, H. Richard
1955 "John Wesley." In *Christian Ethics*, pp. 353-65. New York: Roland Press.

Beckerlegge, Oliver Aveyard
1983 "Introduction, §6-7." *Works*, 7:55-69.

Bence, Clarence Luther
1979 "Processive Eschatology: A Wesleyan Alternative." *WTJ* 14.1:45-59.
1981 "John Wesley's Teleological Hermeneutic." Emory University Ph.D. thesis.
1984 "Salvation and the Church: The Ecclesiology of John Wesley." In *The Church*, pp. 297-317. Eds. Melvin Dieter and Daniel Berg. Anderson, IN: Warner.

Benner, Forest T.
1966 "The Immediate Antecedents of the Wesleyan Doctrine of the Witness of the Spirit." Temple University Ph.D. thesis.

Berg, Daniel
1984 "The Marks of the Church in the Theology of John Wesley." In *The Church*, pp. 319-31. Eds. Melvin Dieter and Daniel Berg. Anderson, IN: Warner

Berger, Teresa
1989 *Theologie in Hymnen? Zum Verhältnis von Theologie und Doxologie am Beispiel der "Collection of Hymns for the Use of the People Called Methodists"*. Altenberge: Telos Verlag.
1992 "'Theologie, die man singen kann . . . ' Christologische Titel im methodistischen Gesangbuch von 1780." *Una Sancta* 47:123-9.

Bishop, John
1975 *Methodist Worship in Relation to Free Church Worship.* New York: Scholars Studies.

Black, Robert Edwin
1984 "The Social Dimensions of John Wesley's Ministry as Related to His Personal Piety." Union Seminary of Virginia Ph.D. thesis.

Blaising, Craig Alan
1979 "John Wesley's Doctrine of Original Sin." Dallas Theological Seminary Th.D. thesis.

Blankenship, Paul Freeman
1964 "The Significance of John Wesley's Abridgement of the Thirty-Nine Articles as Seen from His Deletions." *MethH* 2.3:35-47.

Bolster, George Reed
1952 "Wesley's Doctrine of Sanctification." *Evangelical Quarterly* 24: 144-55.

Borgen, Ole Edvard
1972 *John Wesley on the Sacraments: A Theological Study.* Nashville, TN: Abingdon; reprint ed., Grand Rapids, MI: Zondervan, 1985.
1988 "John Wesley: Sacramental Theology - No Ends without the Means." In *John Wesley: Contemporary Perspectives,* pp. 67-82. Ed. John Stacey. London: Epworth. Reprints with slight variations in *Context: Essays in Honour of Peder Borgen,* pp. 35-44. Eds. P.W. Bøckmann & R. Kristiansen. Trondheim, Norway: Tapir, 1988; and *AsbThJ* 46 (1991):63-85.
1989 "Baptism, Confirmation, and Church Membership in the Methodist Church Before the Union of 1968: A Historical and Theological Study." *MethH* 27:89-109, 163-81.

Bouyer, Louis
1965 "John Wesley and Methodism." In *Orthodox Spirituality & Protestant and Anglican Spirituality,* pp. 187-93. New York: Desclee.

Bowmer, John Coates
1951 *The Sacrament of the Lord's Supper in Early Methodism.* London: Dacre Press.
1959 "John Wesley's Philosophy of Suffering." *LQHR* 184 (sixth series, 28):60-6.
1964 "A Converting Ordinance and The Open Table." *PWHS* 34:109-13.
1975 *Pastor and People: A Study of Church and Ministry in Wesleyan Methodism.* London: Epworth.

Brantley, Richard Estes
1984 *Locke, Wesley, and the Method of English Romanticism.* Gainesville, FL: University Presses of Florida.
1990 "The Common Ground of Wesley and Edwards." *Harvard Theological Review* 83:271-303. Reprint in *Coordinates of Anglo-American Romanticism,* pp. 7-42. Gainesville, FL: University Presses of Florida, 1993.

Brendlinger, Irv A.
1982 "A Study of the Views of Major Eighteenth Century Evangelicals on Slavery and Race, with Special Reference to John Wesley." University of Edinburgh Ph.D. thesis.

Brightman, Robert Sheffield
1969 "Gregory of Nyssa and John Wesley in Theological Dialogue on the Christian Life." Boston University Ph.D. thesis.

Brockwell, Charles Wilbur, Jr.
1983 "John Wesley's Doctrine of Justification." *WTJ* 18.2:18-32.
1990 "Wesleyan Spirituality: A Methodist/Anglican Nexus." *Midstream* 29:140-52.

Brown, Earl Kent

1983 *Women in Mr. Wesley's Methodism.* Lewiston, NY: Edwin Mellen.

1985 "Feminist Theology and the Women of Mr. Wesley's Methodism." In *Wesleyan Theology Today*, pp. 143-50. Ed. Theodore H. Runyon. Nashville, TN: Kingswood.

Brown, Kenneth O.

1989 "John Wesley - Post or Premillennialist?" *MethH* 28:33-41.

Bryant, Barry Edward

1992a "John Wesley's Doctrine of Sin." King's College, University of London Ph.D. thesis.

1992b *John Wesley on the Origin of Evil.* Wesley Fellowship Occasional Paper #7. Derbys, England: Moorley's Bookshop.

Bundy, David

1991 "Christian Virtue: John Wesley and the Alexandrian Tradition." *WTJ* 26.1:139-63.

Burrows, Aelred

1988 "Wesley the Catholic." In *John Wesley: Contemporary Perspectives*, pp. 54-66. Ed. John Stacey. London: Epworth.

Byrne, Brendan

1986 "Ignatius Loyola and John Wesley: Experience and Strategies of Conversion." *Colloquium: the Australian and New Zealand Theological Review* 19.1:54-66.

Campbell, Ted Allen

1986 "John Wesley and Conyers Middleton on Divine Intervention in History." *Church History* 55:39-49.

1991a "The 'Wesleyan Quadrilateral': The Story of a Modern Methodist Myth," *MethH* 29:87-95; reprint, in *Doctrine and Theology in the United Methodist Church*, pp. 154-61. Ed. Thomas Langford. Nashville, TN: Kingswood, 1991.

1991b *John Wesley and Christian Antiquity: Religious Vision and Cultural Change.* Nashville, TN: Kingswood.

1992a "Christian Tradition, John Wesley, and Evangelicalism." *Anglican Theological Review* 74:54-67.

1992b "John Wesley on the Mission of the Church." In *The Mission of the Church in Methodist Perspective*, pp. 45-62. Edited by Alan Padgett. Lewiston, NY: Edwin Mellen.

Cannon, William Ragsdale

1946 *The Theology of John Wesley, with Special Reference to the Doctrine of Justification.* New York: Abingdon-Cokesbury; reprint ed., Lanham, MD: University Press of America, 1984.

1959 "Perfection." *LQHR* 184 (sixth series, 28):213-17.

1961 "John Wesley's Doctrine of Sanctification and Perfection." *Mennonite Quarterly Review* 35:91-5.

1968 "The Holy Spirit in Vatican II and in the Writings of Wesley." *RelLife* 37:440-53.

Casto, Robert Michael

1977 "Exegetical Method in John Wesley's *Explanatory Notes upon the Old Testament*: A Description of His Approach, Uses of Sources, and Practice." Duke University Ph.D. thesis.

Cell, George Croft
1935 *The Rediscovery of John Wesley*. New York: Henry Holt; reprint ed., Lanham, MD: University Press of America, 1983
Chamberlain, Jeffrey S.
1993 "Moralism, Justification, and the Controversy over Methodism." *Journal of Ecclesiastical History* 44:652-78.
Chandler, Douglas R.
1972 "John Wesley and the Uses of the Past." In *The 1972 Willson Lectures*, pp. 27-37. Washington, DC: Wesley Theological Seminary.
Chilcote, Paul Wesley
1991 *John Wesley and the Women Preachers of Early Methodism.* Metuchen, NJ: Scarecrow.
Cho, John Chongnahm
1972 "John Wesley's View on Baptism." *WTJ* 7:60-73.
1986 "Adam's Fall and God's Grace: John Wesley's Theological Anthropology." *Evangelical Review of Theology* 10:202-13.
Clapper, Gregory Scott
1984 "'True Religion' and the Affections: A Study of John Wesley's Abridgement of Jonathan Edwards' *Treatise on Religious Affections.*" *WTJ* 19.2:77-89.
1989 *John Wesley on Religious Affections: His Views on Experience and Emotion and Their Role in the Christian Life and Theology.* Metuchen, NJ: Scarecrow.
1990 "*Orthokardia*: The Practical Theology of John Wesley's Heart Religion." *QR* 10.1:49-66.
Clemons, James Thomas
1977 "John Wesley - Biblical Literalist?" *RelLife* 46:332-42; reprint, *EpRev* 6.3 (1979):61-9.
Clifford, Alan Charles
1990 *Atonement and Justification: English Evangelical Theology, 1640-1790.* Oxford: Clarendon.
Collier, Frank Wilbur
1924 *Back to Wesley.* New York: Methodist Book Concern.
1928 *John Wesley Among the Scientists.* New York: Abingdon.
Collins, Kenneth Joseph
1984a "John Wesley's Theology of the Law." Drew University Ph.D. thesis.
1984b "A Hermeneutical Model for the Wesleyan *Ordo Salutis.*" *WTJ* 19.2: 23-37.
1985 "John Wesley and the Means of Grace." *AsbSem* 40.2:23-31; reprint: *DrG* 56.3 (1986):26-33.
1986 "Wesley's Platonic Conception of the Moral Law." *WTJ* 21:116-28.
1987 "John Wesley and Liberation Theology." *AsbThJ* 42.1:85-90.
1988 "John Wesley's Concept of the Ministerial Office." *WTJ* 23:107-21.
1989 *Wesley on Salvation: A Study in the Standard Sermons.* Grand Rapids, MI: Zondervan.
1990 "The Influence of Early German Pietism on John Wesley." *Covenant Quarterly* 48:23-42.
1993 *A Faithful Witness: John Wesley's Homiletical Theology.* Wilmore, KY: Wesley Heritage Press.
Cooper, Alan Lamar
1962 "John Wesley: A Study in Theology and Ethics." Columbia University Ph.D. thesis.

Coppedge, Allan

1984 "John Wesley and the Issue of Authority in Theological Pluralism." *WTJ* 19.2:62-76.

1987 *John Wesley in Theological Debate.* Wilmore, KY: Wesley Heritage Press.

1991 "How Wesleyans Do Theology." In *Doing Theology in Today's World*, pp. 267-89. Edited by John Woodbridge & Thomas McComiskey. Grand Rapids, MI: Zondervan.

Couture, Pamela D.

1991 "Sexuality, Economics, and the Wesleyan Alternative." In *Blessed are the Poor? Women's Poverty, Family Policy, and Practical Theology*, pp. 119-34. Nashville, TN: Abingdon.

Cox, Leo George

1964 *John Wesley's Concept of Perfection.* Kansas City, MO: Beacon Hill.

Cragg, Gerald Robertson

1975 "Introduction." *Works*, 11:1-36.

Crow, Earl Pickett

1964 "John Wesley's Conflict with Antinomianism in Relation to the Moravians and Calvinists." University of Manchester Ph.D. thesis.

1966 "Wesley and Antinomianism." *DukeDivSR* 31:1-19.

Cubie, David Livingstone

1965 "John Wesley's Concept of Perfect Love: A Motif Analysis." Boston University Ph.D. thesis.

1984 "Separation or Unity? Sanctification and Love in Wesley's Doctrine of the Church." In *The Church*, pp. 333-95. Eds. Melvin Dieter & Daniel Berg. Anderson, IN: Warner.

1985 "Wesley's Theology of Love." *WTJ* 20.1:122-54.

1986 "Eschatology from a Theological and Historical Perspective." In *The Spirit and the New Age*, pp. 357-414. Eds. R.L. Shelton & A.R.G. Deasley. Anderson, IN: Warner.

Cushman, Robert Earl

1947 "Salvation for All: John Wesley and Calvinism." In *Methodism*, pp. 103-15. Ed. W.K. Anderson. New York: Methodist Publishing House; reprint, *Faith Seeking Understanding*, pp. 63-74. Durham, NC: Duke University Press, 1981.

1964 "Baptism and the Family of God." In *The Doctrine of the Church*, pp. 79-102. Ed. Dow Kirkpatrick. New York: Abingdon.

1988 "Orthodoxy and Wesley's Experimental Divinity." *QR* 8.2:71-89.

1989 *John Wesley's Experimental Divinity: Studies in Methodist Doctrinal Standards.* Nashville: Kingswood.

Davies, Horton

1961 *Worship and Theology in England.* Vol. III: *From Watts and Wesley to Maurice, 1690-1850.* Princeton, NJ: Princeton University Press.

Davies, Rupert Eric

1961 "The History and Theology of the Methodist Covenant Service." *Theology* 64:62-68.

1981 "Justification, Sanctification, and the Liberation of the Person." In *Sanctification and Liberation*, pp. 64-82. Ed. Theodore H. Runyon. Nashville, TN: Abingdon.

1989 "Introduction." *Works*, 9:1-29.

Dayton, Donald W.

1985 "The Use of Scripture in the Wesleyan Tradition." In *The Use of the Bible in Theology*, pp. 121-36. Ed. Robert K. Johnston. Atlanta, GA: John Knox.

1986 "Pneumatological Issues in the Holiness Movement." In *Spirit of Truth: Ecumenical Perspectives on the Holy Spirit*, pp. 131-57. Eds. Th. Stylianopoulos and S. Mark Heim. Brookline, MA: Holy Cross Orthodox Press (= *Greek Orthodox Theological Review* 31.3-4 [1986]); reprint, *The Spirit and the New Age*, pp. 237-71. Eds. R. L. Shelton & A.R.G. Deasley. Anderson, IN: Warner, 1986.

1991a "The Wesleyan Option for the Poor." *WTJ* 26.1:7-22.

1991b "Law and Gospel in the Wesleyan Tradition." *Grace Theological Journal* 12 (1991):233-43.

1994 "'Good News for the Poor': The Methodist Experience After Wesley." In *The Portion of the Poor*. Ed. M. Douglas Meeks. Nashville, TN: Kingswood.

Dayton, Wilber T.

1984 "Infallibility, Wesley, and British Methodism." In *Inerrancy and the Church*, pp. 223-54. Chicago, IL: Moody.

Dean, William Walter

1985 "Disciplined Fellowship: The Rise and Decline of Cell Groups in British Methodism." University of Iowa Ph.D. Thesis.

Dearing, Trevor

1966 *Wesleyan and Tractarian Worship: An Ecumenical Study*. London: Epworth.

Deschner, John William

1960 *Wesley's Christology: An Interpretation*. Dallas, TX: Southern Methodist University Press.

1985 "Foreword." *Wesley's Christology: An Interpretation*, reprint edition, pp. ix-xx. Dallas, TX: Southern Methodist University Press.

Dicker, Gordon Stanley

1971 "The Concept 'Simul Justus et Peccator' in Relation to the Thought of Luther, Wesley and Bonhoeffer, and its Significance for a Doctrine of the Christian Life." Union Seminary Th.D. thesis.

Dieter, Melvin Easterday

1987 "The Wesleyan Perspective." In *Five Views on Sanctification*, pp. 11-46. Melvin Dieter, *et al.* Grand Rapids, MI: Zondervan.

1988 "Wesleyan Theology." In *John Wesley: Contemporary Perspectives*, pp. 162-75. Ed. John Stacey. London: Epworth.

Dorr, Donal J.

1964a "The Wesleyan Doctrine of Sin and Salvation." St. Patrick's College (Maynooth) D.D. thesis.

1964b "Total Corruption and the Wesleyan Tradition." *Irish Theological Quarterly* 31:303-21.

1965 "Wesley's Teaching on the Nature of Holiness." *LQHR* 190 (sixth series, 34):234-9.

Downes, James Cyril Thomas

1960 "Eschatological Doctrines in the Writings of John and Charles Wesley." Edinburgh University Ph.D. thesis.

Dreyer, Frederick

1983 "Faith and Experience in the Thought of John Wesley." *American Historical Review* 88:12-30.

1987 "Evangelical Thought: John Wesley and Jonathan Edwards." *Albion* 19:177-92.

1989 "Edmund Burke and John Wesley: The Legacy of Locke." In *Religion, Secularization and Political Thought*, pp. 111-29. Edited by James E. Crimmins. London: Routledge.

Dunlap, Elden Dale

1956 "Methodist Theology in Great Britain in the Nineteenth Century." Yale University Ph.D. thesis.

Duque Zúñiga, José

1983 "Perfección cristiana y ética social." In *La Tradición Protestante en la Teología Latinoamericana*, pp. 257-76. Ed. José Duque. San José, Costa Rica: DEI.

Eaton, David Eugene

1988 "Arminianism in the Theology of John Wesley." Drew University Ph.D. thesis.

Eayrs, George

1926 *John Wesley, Christian Philosopher and Church Founder.* London: Epworth.

Eichen, Erich von

1934 *Rechtfertigung und Heiligung bei Wesley dargestellt unter Vergleichung mit den Anschauungen Luthers und des Luthertums.* Heidelberg: By Author. (Published version of first half of University of Heidelberg Ph.D. thesis).

Eli, Richard George

1993 *Social Holiness: John Wesley's Thinking on Christian Community and Its Relationship to the Social Order.* New York: Peter Lang.

English, John Cammel

1967a "The Heart Renewed: John Wesley's Doctrine of Christian Initiation." *WQR* 4:115-92. Also issued as monograph under same title by Wesleyan College, Macon, GA, 1967.

1967b "The Sacrament of Baptism According to the Sunday Service of 1784." *MethH* 5.2:10-15.

1969 "John Wesley and the Anglican Moderates of the Seventeenth Century." *Anglican Theological Review* 51:203-20.

1989a "John Wesley's Studies as an Undergraduate." *PWHS* 47:29-37.

1989b "John Wesley and the English Enlightenment: An 'Appeal to Men of Reason and Religion'." *Studies on Voltaire and the Eighteenth Century* 263:400-03.

1991a "John Wesley's Indebtedness to John Norris." *Church History* 60:55-69.

1991b "John Wesley and Isaac Newton's 'System of the World'." *PWHS* 4 8:69-86.

1991c "John Wesley's Scientific Education," *MethH* 30.1:42-51.

Etchegoyen, Aldo

1985 "Teologia do Pecado e Estruturas de Opressão." In *Luta pela vida e evangelização: A tradição metodista na teologia latino-americana*, pp. 243-55. J. Míguez-Bonino, *et al.* São Paulo: Edições Paulinas.
English: "Theology of Sin and Structures of Oppression." In *Faith Born in the Struggle for Life*, pp. 156-66. Ed. Dow Kirkpatrick. Grand Rapids, MI: Eerdmans, 1988.

Faulkner, John Alfred

1918 *Wesley as Sociologist, Theologian, Churchman.* New York: Methodist Book Concern.

Felton, Gayle Carlton

1992 *This Gift of Water: The Practice and Theology of Baptism Among Methodists in America.* Nashville, TN: Abingdon.

Ferguson, Duncan S.
1984 "John Wesley on Scripture: The Hermeneutics of Pietism." *MethH* 22:234-45.

Flew, R. [Robert] Newton
1934 *The Idea of Perfection in Christian Theology.* London: Oxford University Press.

Fraser, M. Robert
1988 "Strains in the Understandings of Christian Perfection in Early British Methodism." Vanderbilt University Ph.D. thesis.

Frost, Stanley Brice
1938 *Die Authoritätslehre in den Werken John Wesleys.* Munich: Ernest Reinhardt. English translation by author: *The Doctrine of Authority in the Works of John Wesley.* London: N.p.

Fuhrman, Eldon Ralph
1963 "The Concept of Grace in the Theology of John Wesley." University of Iowa Ph.D. thesis.

Fujimoto, Mitsuru Samuel
1986 "John Wesley's Doctrine of Good Works." Drew University Ph.D. thesis.

Gallaway, Craig B.
1988 "The Presence of Christ with the Worshipping Community: A Study in the Hymns of John and Charles Wesley." Emory University Ph.D. thesis.

Galliers, Brian James Newby
1960 "Baptism in the Writings of John Wesley." *PWHS* 32:121-4, 153-7.

Gallo, Bruno
1984 "Bibbia ed Entusiasmo: John Wesley e la Retorica Delle Emozioni." *Bergomum* 78:141-59.

Garlow, James Lester
1979 "John Wesley's Understanding of the Laity as Demonstrated By His Use of the Lay Preachers." Drew University Ph.D. thesis.

George, Alfred Raymond
1963 "Private Devotion in the Methodist Tradition." *Studia Liturgica* 2:223-36.
1964a "The Real Presence and the Lord's Supper." *PWHS* 34:181-7.
1964b "The Lord's Supper." In *The Doctrine of the Church,* pp. 140-60. Ed. Dow Kirkpatrick. New York: Abingdon.
1984 "The Sunday Service 1784." *Doxology* 1:5-13.

Gerdes, Egon Walter
1958 "John Wesleys Lehre von der Gottesebendbildlichkeit des Menschen." Keil University Ph.D. thesis.
1960 "John Wesley's Attitude Toward War." Emory University Ph.D. thesis.

Giffin, John
1988 "Scriptural Standards in Religion: John Wesley's Letters to William Law and James Hervey." *Studia Biblica et Theologica* 16:143-68.

Gill, Frederick Cyril
1951 "Introduction." *John Wesley's Prayers,* pp. 9-17. Ed. F.C. Gill. London: Epworth.

Gordon, James M.
1991 "John and Charles Wesley." In *Evangelical Spirituality,* pp. 11-40. London: SPCK.

Gray, Wallace Gale

1953 "The Place of Reason in the Theology of John Wesley." Vanderbilt University Ph.D. thesis.

Greve, Lionel

1976 "Freedom and Discipline in the Theology of John Calvin, William Perkins, and John Wesley: An Examination of the Origin and Nature of Pietism." Hartford Seminary Ph.D. thesis.

Grislis, Egil

1963 "The Wesleyan Doctrine of the Last Supper." *DukeDivSB* 28:99-110.

Gunter, W. Stephen

1989 *The Limits of "Love Divine": John Wesley's Response to Antinomianism and Enthusiasm.* Nashville, TN: Kingswood.

Hall, Thor

1963 "The Christian's Life: Wesley's Alternative to Luther and Calvin." *DukeDivSB* 28:111-26. Slightly revised reprint in *Context: Essays in Honour of Peder Borgen,* pp. 45-60. Eds. P.W. Bøckmann & R. Kristiansen. Trondheim, Norway: Tapir, 1988.

1987 "Tradition Criticism: A New View of Wesley." In *Inaugurating the Leroy A. Martin Distinguished Professorship of Religious Studies,* pp. 6-23. The University of Tennessee at Chattanooga.

1988 "Wesley Og Hans Kvinner." *TFor* 2.2:43-66.

Hannah, Vern A.

1983 "Original Sin and Sanctification: A Problem for Wesleyans." *WTJ* 18.2:47-53.

Harper, J. Steven

1981 "The Devotional Life of John Wesley: 1703-38." Duke University Ph.D. thesis.

1983a *Devotional Life in the Wesleyan Tradition.* Nashville, TN: Upper Room.

1983b *John Wesley's Message for Today.* Grand Rapids, MI: Zondervan.

1985 "John Wesley: Spiritual Guide." *WTJ* 20.2:91-6.

1988 "Wesley's Sermons As Spiritual Formation Documents." *MethH* 26:131-38.

Hatton, Peter

1990 "John Wesley, Jeremy Taylor, Seneca and Control." *EpRev* 17.3:69-83.

Hauerwas, Stanley Martin

1975 *Character and the Christian Life: A Study in Theological Ethics.* San Antonio, TX: Trinity University Press.

1985 "Characterizing Perfection: Second Thoughts on Character and Sanctification." In *Wesleyan Theology Today,* pp. 251-63. Ed. Theodore H. Runyon. Nashville, TN: Kingswood.

Heitzenrater, Richard Paul

1972 "John Wesley and the Oxford Methodists." Duke University Ph.D. thesis.

1984a *The Elusive Mr. Wesley.* 2 vols. Nashville, TN: Abingdon.

1984b "The Present State of Wesley Studies." *MethH* 22:221-33.

1987 "Plain Truth: Sermons as Standards of Doctrine." *DrG* 57.3:16-30. (Reprint: 1989, pp. 174-88).

1988b "Wesley and His Diary." In *John Wesley: Contemporary Perspectives,* pp. 11-22. Ed. John Stacey. London: Epworth.

1989 *Mirror and Memory: Reflections on Early Methodism.* Nashville, TN: Kingswood.

1994 "The Imitatio Christi and the Great Commandment: Virtue and Obligation in Wesley's Ministry with the Poor." In *The Portion of the Poor.* Ed. M. Douglas Meeks. Nashville, TN: Kingswood.

Hempton, David Neil

1993 "John Wesley and England's 'Ancien Régime'." In *Modern Religious Belief,* pp. 36-55. Ed. Stuart Mews. London: Epworth.

Henderson, David Michael

1980 "John Wesley's Instructional Groups." Indiana University Ph.D. thesis.

Hendricks, Melvin Elton

1983 "John Wesley and Natural Theology." *WTJ* 18.2:7-17.

Henry, Granville C., Jr.

1960 "John Wesley's Doctrine of Free Will." *LQHR* 185 (sixth series, 29): 200-4.

Hildebrandt, Franz

1951 *From Luther to Wesley.* London: Lutterworth.

1956 *Christianity According to the Wesleys.* London: Epworth; reprint, Durham, NC: Labyrinth Press, 1993.

1967 *I Offered Christ.* Philadelphia, PA: Fortress.

1983 "Introduction, I" *Works,* 7:1-22.

Hillman, Robert John

1978 "Grace in the Preaching of Calvin and Wesley: A Comparative Study." Fuller Theological Seminary Ph.D. thesis.

1981 "Grace in the Preaching of Calvin and Wesley." In *Dig or Die: Papers Given at the World Methodist Historical Society Conference, 8/10-15/1980,* pp. 279-89. Eds. J. Udy & E. Clancey. Sydney, Australia: World Methodist Historical Society.

Hindley, John Clifford

1957 "The Philosophy of Enthusiasm: A Study in the Origins of 'Experimental Theology'." *LQHR* 182 (sixth series, 26):99-109, 199-210.

Hodges, Herbert Arthur & Allchin, A. M. [Archibald Macdonald]

1966 "Introduction." *A Rapture of Praise: Hymns of John and Charles Wesley,* pp. 19-50. London: Hodder and Stoughton.

Hoffman, Thomas G.

1968 "The Moral Philosophy of John Wesley: The Development of His Moral Dynamic." Temple University Ph.D. thesis.

Hohenstein, Charles R.

1990 "The Revisions of the Rites of Baptism in the Methodist Episcopal Church, 1784-1939." University of Notre Dame Ph.D. thesis.

Holifield, Elmer Brooks

1986 *Health and Medicine in the Methodist Tradition.* New York: Crossroad.

Holland, Bernard George

1969 "The Background to the 1967 Methodist Service for Infant Baptism." *ChQ* 2:43-54.

1970 *Baptism in Early Methodism.* London: Epworth.

1971 "The Conversions of John and Charles Wesley and Their Place in Methodist Tradition." *PWHS* 38:45-53, 65-71.

1973 "'A Species of Madness': The Effect of John Wesley's Early Preaching." *PWHS* 39:77-85.

Hoon, Paul Waitman

1936 "The Soteriology of John Wesley." Edinburgh University Ph.D. thesis.

Horst, Mark Lewis

1985 "Christian Understanding and the Life of Faith in John Wesley's Thought." Yale University Ph.D. thesis.

1987 "Experimenting with Christian Wholeness: Method in Wesley's Theology." *QR* 7.2:11-23.

Hosman, Glenn Burton

1970 "The Problem of Church and State in the Thought of John Wesley as Reflecting His Understanding of Providence and His View of History." Drew University Ph.D. thesis.

Hulley, Leonard D.

1987 *Wesley: A Plain Man for Plain People.* Westville, South Africa: Methodist Church of South Africa.

1988 *To Be and To Do: Exploring Wesley's Thought on Ethical Behaviour.* Pretoria: University of South Africa.

1990 "An Interpretation of John Wesley's Doctrine of Perfect Love." *Theologia Evangelica* 23.1:21-29.

Hurley, Michael

1968 "Introduction" In *John Wesley's Letter to a Roman Catholic*, pp. 22-47. Nashville, TN: Abingdon.

1976 "Salvation Today and Wesley Today." In *The Place of Wesley in the Christian Tradition*, pp. 94-116. Ed. Kenneth E. Rowe. Metuchen, NJ: Scarecrow.

Hynson, Leon Orville

1972 "John Wesley's Concept of Liberty of Conscience." *WTJ* 7:36-46.

1973 "John Wesley and Political Reality." *MethH* 12.1:37-42.

1976 "War, The State, and the Christian Citizen in Wesley's Thought." *RelLife* 45:204-19.

1979 "John Wesley and the 'Unitas Fratrum': A Theological Analysis." *MethH* 18.1:26-59.

1983 "Human Liberty as Divine Right: A Study in the Political Maturation of John Wesley." *Journal of Church and State* 25:57-85.

1984 *To Reform the Nation: Theological Foundations of Wesley's Ethics.* Grand Rapids, MI: Zondervan.

1985 "Implications of Wesley's Ethical Method and Political Thought." In *Wesleyan Theology Today*, pp. 373-88. Ed. Theodore H. Runyon. Nashville, TN: Kingswood.

1987 "Original Sin as Privation: An Inquiry into a Theology of Sin and Sanctification." *WTJ* 22.2:65-83.

1988 "John Wesley's Theology of the Kingdom of God." *WTJ* 23:46-57.

Ireson, Roger William

1973 "The Doctrine of Faith in John Wesley and the Protestant Tradition: A Comparative Study." University of Manchester Ph.D. thesis.

Jennings, Theodore Wesley, Jr.

1990 *Good News to the Poor: John Wesley's Evangelical Economics.* Nashville, TN: Abingdon.

Johnson, Richard O.

1979 "The Development of the Love Feast in Early American Methodism." *MethH* 18:67-83.

Johnson, Susanne

1987 "John Wesley on the Duty of Constant Communion: The Eucharist as a Means of Grace for Today." In *Wesleyan Spirituality in Contemporary Theological Education*, pp. 25-46. Nashville, TN: General Board of Higher Education and Ministry, United Methodist Church.

Johnson, W. Stanley

1988 "John Wesley's Concept of Enthusiasm." *Kardia* 3:27-38.

Jones, Ivor H.

1988 "Grace, von Balthasar and the Wesleys." *Freedom and Grace*, pp. 86-102. Eds. I.H. Jones & K.B. Wilson. London: Epworth Press.

Jones, Scott Jameson

1992 "John Wesley's Conception and Use of Scripture." Southern Methodist University Ph.D. thesis (forthcoming - Nashville, TN: Kingswood).

Jones, W. Paul

1987 "The Wesleyan Means of Grace." In *Wesleyan Spirituality in Contemporary Theological Education*, pp. 11-15. Nashville, TN: General Board of Higher Education and Ministry, United Methodist Church.

Josselyn, Lynne

1988 "The Comparative Eucharistic Views of John Wesley and John Nevin with an emphasis on Christian Nurture and the Admission of Children to the Lord's Table." *New Mercersburg Review* 4:18-35.

Källstad, Thorvald

1974 *John Wesley and the Bible: A Psychological Study*. Bjärnum, Sweden: Bjärnums Tryckeri.

1988 "John Wesley Och Mystiken." *TFor* 2.2:7-42.

1989 *Innerlighetens religion: John Wesley väg från pliktreligion via mystik till levande Kristus-tro.* Delsbo, Sweden: Bokförlaget Åsak, Sahlin & Dahlström AB.

Keefer, Luke L., Jr.

1982 "John Wesley: Disciple of Early Christianity." Temple University Ph.D. thesis.

1984 "John Wesley: Disciple of Early Christianity." *WTJ* 19.1:26-32.

1986 "John Wesley and English Arminianism." *EvJl* 4:15-28.

1987 "Characteristics of Wesley's Arminianism." *WTJ* 22.1:87-99.

1990 "John Wesley, The Methodists, and Social Reform in England." *WTJ* 25.1:7-20.

Kellett, Norman Lawrence

1975 "John Wesley and the Restoration of the Doctrine of the Holy Spirit to the Church of England in the 18th Century." Brandeis University Ph.D. thesis.

Kim, Hong Ki

1991 "The Theology of Social Sanctification Examined in the Thought of John Wesley and in Minjung Theology: A Comparative Study." Drew University Ph.D. thesis.

Kim, Kwang Yul

1992 "A Tension Between the Desire to Follow the Example of Jesus' Life and the Desire to Trust in His Redemptive Work: The Theology of John Wesley Reflected in his *Christian Library*." Westminster Theological Seminary Ph.D. thesis.

Kissack, Reginald

1964 *Church or No Church? A Study of the Development of the Concept of Church in British Methodism.* London: Epworth.

Klaiber, Walter

1991 "Aus Glauben, damit aus Gnaden: Der Grundsatz paulinischer Soteriologie und die Gnadenlehre John Wesleys." *Zeitschrift für Theologie und Kirche* 88:313-38.

Knickerbocker, Waldo E., Jr.

1991 "Arminian Anglicanism and John and Charles Wesley." *Memphis Theological Seminary Journal* 29:79-97.

Knight, Henry Hawthorne, III

1988 "The Relation of Love to Gratitude in the Theologies of Edwards and Wesley." *EvJl* 6:3-12.

1989 "The Significance of Baptism for Christian Life: Wesley's Pattern of Christian Initiation." *Worship* 63:133-42.

1990 "The Baptismal Shaping of Christian Lives: Wesley's Class Meetings and Service of Covenant Renewal." *Doxology* 7:17-22.

1992 *The Presence of God in the Christian Life: John Wesley and the Means of Grace.* Metuchen, NJ: Scarecrow.

Knight, John Allen

1968 "Aspects of Wesley's Theology After 1770." *MethH* 6.3:33-42.

Koerber, Carolo (Charles) J.

1967 *The Theology of Conversion According to John Wesley.* Rome: Neo-Eboraci.

Langford, Thomas Anderson

1980-2a "John Wesley's Doctrine of Justification by Faith." *Bulletin of the United Church of Canada Committee on Archives and History* 29:47-62.

1980-2b "John Wesley's Doctrine of Sanctification." *Bulletin of the United Church of Canada Committee on Archives and History* 29:63-73.

1983 *Practical Divinity: Theology in the Wesleyan Tradition.* Nashville, TN: Abingdon.

1985 "Constructive Theology in the Wesleyan Tradition." In *Wesleyan Theology Today*, pp. 56-61. Ed. Theodore H. Runyon. Nashville, TN: Kingswood.

1988 "Is There Such a Thing as Wesleyan Theology?" *EpRev* 15.2:67-72.

Lawson, Albert Brown

1963 *John Wesley and the Christian Ministry.* London: SPCK.

1974 "John Wesley and Some Anglican Evangelicals of the Eighteenth Century. A Study in Cooperation and Separatism; With Special Reference to the Calvinistic Controversies." Sheffield University Ph.D. thesis.

Leger, J. Augustin

1914 "Wesley's Place in Catholic Thought." *Constructive Quarterly* 2:329-60.

Lee, Umphrey

1936 John Wesley and Modern Religion. Nashville, TN: Abingdon-Cokesbury.

Lee, Hoo-Jung

1991 "The Doctrine of New Creation in the Theology of John Wesley." Emory University Ph.D. thesis.

Lelièvre, Matthieu

1924 *La Théologie de Wesley.* Paris: Publications Méthodistes.

Lerch, David

1941 *Heil und Heiligung bei John Wesley.* Zürich: Christliche Vereinsbuchhandlung.

Lessmann, Thomas

1987 *Rolle und Bedeutung des Heiligen Geistes in der Theologie John Wesleys.* BGEmK 30. Ed. Studiengemeinschaft für Geschichte der Evangelisch-methodistischen Kirche. Stuttgart: Christliches Verlagshaus.

Leupp, Roderick Thomas

1985 "The Art of God: Light and Darkness in the Thought of John Wesley." Drew University Ph.D. thesis.

Lindström, Harald Gustaf

1946 *Wesley and Sanctification.* Stockholm: Nya Bokförlags Aktiebolaget; reprint with Foreword by Timothy Smith, Wilmore, KY: Francis Asbury.

1955 "The Message of John Wesley and the Modern Man." *DrG* 25.4:186-95.

Lodahl, Michael E.

1988 "'The Witness of the Spirit': Questions of Clarification for Wesley's Doctrine of Assurance." *WTJ* 23:188-97

Logan, James Cecil

1985 "Toward a Wesleyan Social Ethic." In *Wesleyan Theology Today*, pp. 361-72. Ed. Theodore H. Runyon. Nashville, TN: Kingswood.

Lovin, Robin W.

1985 "The Physics of True Virtue." In *Wesleyan Theology Today*, pp. 264-72. Ed. Theodore H. Runyon. Nashville, TN: Kingswood.

Luby, Daniel Joseph

1984 "The Perceptibility of Grace in the Theology of John Wesley. A Roman Catholic Consideration." Pontificia Studiorum Universitas A.S. Thomas Aquinas in Urbe Ph.D. thesis.

McCarthy, Daryl

1981 "Early Wesleyan Views of Scripture." *WTJ* 16.2:95-105.

McCormack, James T.

1986 "The Forgotten Notes of John Wesley." *Irish Biblical Studies* 8:22-42.

McCormick, Kelly Steve

1983 "John Wesley's Use of John Chrysostom on the Christian Life: Faith Filled with the Energy of Love." Drew University Ph.D. thesis.

1991 "Theosis in Chrysostom and Wesley: An Eastern Paradigm on Faith and Love." *WTJ* 26.1:38-103.

McCulloh, Gerald O.

1964 "The Discipline of Life in Early Methodism through Preaching and Other Means of Grace." In *The Doctrine of the Church*, pp. 161-81. Ed. Dow Kirkpatrick. New York: Abingdon.

McDonald, Hugh Dermot

1959 *Ideas of Revelation*, chapter IX. London: Macmillan.

MacDonald, James Alexander

1906 *Wesley's Revision of the Shorter Catechism.* Edinburgh: George A. Morton.

McEldowney, James Edward

1943 "John Wesley's Theology in its Historical Setting." University of Chicago Ph.D. thesis.

McGonigle, Herbert

1973 "Pneumatological Nomenclature in Early Methodism." *WTJ* 8:61-72.

1988 *The Arminianism of John Wesley.* Wesley Fellowship Occasional Paper #3. Derbys, England: Moorley's Bookshop.

1994 "John Wesley—Evangelical Arminian." Keele University Ph.D. thesis.

McIntosh, Lawrence D.
1966 "The Nature and Design of Christianity in John Wesley's Early Theology." Drew University Ph.D. thesis.

McNulty, Frank John
1963 "The Moral Teachings of John Wesley." Catholic University of America S.T.D. thesis.

Maddox, Randy Lynn
1984 "Responsible Grace: The Systematic Perspective of Wesleyan Theology." *WTJ* 19.2:7-22.
1986 "Responsible Grace: The Systematic Nature of Wesley's Theology Reconsidered." *QR* 6.1:24-34.
1987a "Karl Rahner's Supernatural Existential: A Wesleyan Parallel?" *EvJl* 5:3-14.
1987b "Wesleyan Theology and the Christian Feminist Critique." *WTJ* 22: 101-11.
1988 "John Wesley - Practical Theologian?" *WTJ* 23:122-47.
1990 "John Wesley and Eastern Orthodoxy: Influences, Convergences, and Differences." *AsbThJ* 45.2:29-53.
1992a "Opinion, Religion, and 'Catholic Spirit': John Wesley on Theological Integrity." *AsbThJ* 47.1:63-87.
1992b "Wesley as Theological Mentor: The Question of Truth or Salvation Through Other Religions." *WTJ* 27:7-29.
1994 "Wesleyan Resources for a Contemporary Theology *of* the Poor." *AsbThJ* 49.1:35-47.

Madron, Thomas William
1964 "John Wesley on Race: A Christian View of Equality." *MethH* 2.4: 24-34.
1965 "The Political Thought of John Wesley." Tulane University Ph.D. thesis.
1981 "John Wesley on Economics." In *Sanctification and Liberation*, pp. 102-15. Ed. Theodore Runyon. Nashville, TN: Abingdon.
1991 "No Justice Without Love." *Christian Social Action* 4.6:13-16.

Marquardt, Manfred
1977a *Praxis und Prinzipien der Sozialethik John Wesleys.* Göttingen: Vandenhoeck & Ruprecht. English Translation: *John Wesley's Social Ethics: Praxis and Principles.* Nashville, TN: Abingdon, 1992.
1977b "John Wesleys Synergismus." In *Die Einheit der Kirche: Dimensionen ihrer Heiligkeit, Katholizität und Apostolizität*, pp. 96-102. Ed. Lorenz Hein. Wiesbaden: Franz Steiner.
1988 "Gewissheit und Anfechtung bei Martin Luther und John Wesley." *Theologie für die Praxis* 14.1:14-28.

Marshall, I. [Ian] Howard
1962 "Sanctification in the Teaching of John Wesley and John Calvin." *Evangelical Quarterly* 34:75-82.

Martin, A.W., Jr.
1990 "'Then As Now': Wesley's Notes as a Model for United Methodists Today." *QR* 10.2:25-47.

Martin, Sydney
1990 *John Wesley and the Witness of the Spirit.* Wesley Fellowship Occasional Paper #5. Derbys, England: Moorley's Bookshop.

Martin, Troy W.
1991 "John Wesley's Exegetical Orientation: East or West?" *WTJ* 26.1:104-38.

Maser, Frederick Ernest
1978 "The Unknown John Wesley." *DrG* 49.2:1-28.
Massa, Mark S.
1983 "The Catholic Wesley: A Revisionist Prolegomenon." *MethH* 22:38-53.
Matsumoto, Hiroaki
1967 "John Wesley's Understanding of Man." *WQR* 4:83-102; reprint, *Japanese Contributions to the Study of John Wesley*, pp. 79-98. Ed. Clifford Edwards. Macon, GA: Wesleyan College, 1967.
Matthews, Rex Dale
1985 "'With the Eyes of Faith': Spiritual Experience and the Knowledge of God in the Theology of John Wesley." In *Wesleyan Theology Today*, pp. 406-15. Ed. Theodore Runyon. Nashville, TN: Kingswood.
1986 "Religion and Reason Joined: A Study in the Theology of John Wesley." Harvard University Th.D. thesis.
Meeks, Merrill Douglas
1985a "The Future of the Methodist Theological Traditions." In *The Future of the Methodist Theological Traditions*, pp. 13-33. Ed. M. Douglas Meeks. Nashville, TN: Abingdon.
1985b "John Wesley's Heritage and the Future of Systematic Theology." In *Wesleyan Theology Today*, pp. 38-46. Ed. Theodore H. Runyon. Nashville, TN: Kingswood.
Meistad, Tore
1987 "Martin Luther and John Wesley on the Sermon on the Mount." In *Context: Essays in Honour of Peder Borgen*, pp. 137-51. Eds. P.W. Bøckmann & R. Kristiansen. Trondheim, Norway: Tapir.
1989 "To Be a Christian in the World: Martin Luther's and John Wesley's Interpretation of the Sermon on the Mount." University of Trondheim (Norway) Ph.D thesis.
Mercer, Jerry Lee
1967 "The Destiny of Man in John Wesley's Eschatology." *WTJ* 2:56-65.
1970 "A Study of the Concept of Man in the Sermons of John Wesley." Claremont University Ph.D. thesis.
Meredith, Lawrence
1962 "Essential Doctrine in the Theology of John Wesley, With Special Attention to the Methodist Standards of Doctrine." Harvard University Th.D. thesis.
Michalson, Carl
1982 "The Hermeneutics of Holiness in Wesley." In *God's Word for Today*, pp. 31-52. Eds. Wayne McCown and James Earl Massey. Anderson, IN: Warner.
Míguez Bonino, José
1981 "Wesley's Doctrine of Sanctification From a Liberationist Perspective." In *Sanctification and Liberation*, pp. 49-63. Ed. Theodore Runyon. Nashville, TN: Abingdon.
1983a "¿Conservar el Metodismo? En busca de un genuino ecumenismo." In *La Tradición Protestante en la Teología Latinoamericana*, pp. 329-41. Ed. José Duque. San José, Costa Rica: DEI.
1983b "Conversión, hombre nuevo y compromiso." In *La Tradición Protestante en la Teología Latinoamericana*, pp. 207-18. Ed. José Duque. San José, Costa Rica: DEI.
English: *International Review of Missions* 72 (1983):324-32; and *Faith Born in*

the Struggle for Life, pp. 3-14. Ed. Dow Kirkpatrick. Grand Rapids, MI: Eerdmans, 1988.

1983c "La eclesiología Wesleyana." In *La Tradición Protestante en la Teología Latinoamericana*, pp. 277-86. Ed. José Duque. San José, Costa Rica: DEI.

1983d "¿Fue el Metodismo un movimiento liberador?" In *La Tradición Protestante en la Teología Latinoamericana*, pp. 63-73. Ed. José Duque. San José, Costa Rica: DEI.

1983e "Justificatión, sanctficación y plenitud." In *La Tradición Protestante en la Teología Latinoamericana*, pp. 243-55. Ed. José Duque. San José, Costa Rica: DEI.
English:*Faith Born in the Struggle for Life*, pp. 15-25. Ed. Dow Kirkpatrick. Grand Rapids, MI: Eerdmans, 1988.

Miller, Richard A.
1991 "Scriptural Authority and Christian Perfection: John Wesley and the Anglican Tradition." Drew University Ph.D. thesis.

Monk, Robert Clarence
1966 *John Wesley: His Puritan Heritage.* Nashville, TN: Abingdon.

Moore, D. Marselle
1985 "Development in Wesley's Thought on Sanctification and Perfection." *WTJ* 20.2:29-53.

Moore, Robert Louis
1979 *John Wesley and Authority: A Psychological Perspective.* Missoula, MT: Scholars Press.

Moyer, Bruce Eugene
1992 "The Doctrine of Christian Perfection: A Comparative Study of John Wesley and the Modern American Holiness Movement." Marquette University Ph.D. thesis.

Mullen, Wilbur H.
1978 "John Wesley's Method of Biblical Interpretation." *RelLife* 47:99-108.

Naglee, David Ingersoll
1987 *From Font to Faith: John Wesley on Infant Baptism and the Nurture of Children.* New York: Peter Lang.
1991 *From Everlasting to Everlasting: John Wesley on Eternity and Time.* 2 vols. New York: Peter Lang.

Nausner, Helmut
1973 "John Wesley - ein Reformator? Christliche Vollkommenheit als Lebensthema." In *Was bedeutet uns Heute die Reformation?*, pp. 99-127. Ed. Rudolf Zinnhobler. Linz: Oberösterreichischer Landesverlag.
1989 "The Meaning of Wesley's General Rules; An Interpretation." *AsbThJ* 44.2:43-60.

Neff, Blake J.
1982 "John Wesley and John Fletcher on Entire Sanctification: A Metaphoric Cluster Analysis." Bowling Green State University Ph.D. thesis.

Nelson, James D.
1987 "Christian Conference." In *Wesleyan Spirituality in Contemporary Theological Education*, pp. 47-53. Nashville, TN: General Board of Higher Education and Ministry, United Methodist Church.

Newton, John Anthony
1964 *Methodism and the Puritans.* London: Dr. William's Library Trust.

1970 "Perfection and Spirituality in the Methodist Tradition." *ChQ* 3:95-103.

1972 "The Ecumenical Wesley." *Ecumenical Review* 24:160-75.

1984 "The Theology of the Wesleys." In *The Methodist Heritage*, pp. 1-10. Ed. D. Milbank. London: Southlands College.

1988 "John Wesley's Theology in Historical Perspective." *Journal of the Lincolnshire Methodist History Society* 4.1:28-38.

Noll, Mark Allan

1975 "John Wesley and the Doctrine of Assurance." *Bibliotheca Sacra* 132:161-77.

Noro, Yoshio

1967a "The Character of John Wesley's Faith." *WQR* 4:10-26; reprint, *Japanese Contributions to the Study of John Wesley*, pp. 6-22. Ed. Clifford Edwards. Macon, GA: Wesleyan College, 1967.

1967b "Wesley's Understanding of Christian Perfection." *WQR* 4:27-42; reprint, *Japanese Contributions to the Study of John Wesley*, pp. 23-38. Ed. Clifford Edwards. Macon, GA: Wesleyan College, 1967.

1971 "Wesley's Theological Epistemology" *The Iliff Review* 28:59-76.

Nygren, Ellis Herbert

1962 "John Wesley's Changing Concept of the Ministry." *RelLife* 31:264-74.

Oden, Thomas Clark

1988 *Doctrinal Standards in the Wesleyan Tradition.* Grand Rapids, MI: Zondervan.

O'Malley, J. [John] Steven

1986 "Recovering the Vision of Holiness: Wesley's Epistemic Basis." *AsbThJ* 41:3-17.

Ong, Walter Jackson

1953 "Peter Ramus and the Naming of Methodism." *Journal of the History of Ideas* 14:235-48; reprint in *Faith and Contexts*, Vol. II, pp. 38-51. Atlanta, GA: Scholars Press, 1992.

Orcibal, Jean

1951 "Les spirituels français et espagnols chez John Wesley et ses contemporains." *Revue de L'Historie des Religions* 139:50-109.

1965 "The Theological Originality of John Wesley and Continental Spirituality." In *A History of the Methodist Church in Great Britain*, Vol. I:83-111. Eds. R.E. Davies and E.G. Rupp. London: Epworth.

Oswalt, John Newell

1977 "Wesley's Use of the Old Testament in His Doctrinal Teachings." *WTJ* 12:39-53.

Ott, Philip Wesley

1980a "John Wesley on Health: A Word for Sensible Regimen." *MethH* 18: 193-304.

1980b "John Wesley and the Non-Naturals." *Preventive Medicine* 9:578-84.

1989 "John Wesley on Mind and Body: Toward an Understanding of Health as Wholeness." *MethH* 27:61-72.

1991 "John Wesley on Health as Wholeness." *Journal of Religion and Health* 30:43-57.

Outler, Albert Cook

1961 "Towards a Re-appraisal of John Wesley as a Theologian." *PSTJ* 14: 5-14; reprint: 1991, pp. 40-54.

1964a "Introduction." *John Wesley*, pp. 1-33. New York: Oxford University Press.

1964b "Do Methodists Have A Doctrine of the Church?" In *The Doctrine of the Church*, pp. 11-28. Ed. Dow Kirkpatrick. Nashville, TN: Abingdon; reprint: 1991, pp. 212-26.

1968 "Theologische Akzente." In *Der Methodismus*, pp. 84-102. Ed. C.E. Sommer. Stuttgart: Evangelisches Verlagswerk.

1969 "Methodism's Theological Heritage: A Study in Perspective." In *Methodism's Destiny in an Ecumenical Age*, pp. 44-70. Ed. Paul M. Minus, Jr. Nashville, TN: Abingdon; reprint: 1991, pp. 190-209.

1971a *Evangelism in the Wesleyan Spirit.* Nashville, TN: Tidings.

1971b "Pastoral Care in the Wesleyan Spirit." *PSTJ* 25:4-11; reprint: 1991, pp. 176-88.

1972 "Introduction of the Disciplinary Statement." *Daily Christian Advocate* (April 19, 1972): 218-21; reprint, *Doctrine and Theology in the United Methodist Church*, pp. 20-5. Ed. Thomas Langford. Nashville, TN: Kingswood, 1991.

1974 "John Wesley as Theologian Then and Now." *MethH* 12.4:63-82; reprint: 1991, pp. 56-74.

1975 *Theology in the Wesleyan Spirit.* Nashville, TN: Discipleship Resources.

1976 "The Place of Wesley in the Christian Tradition." In *The Place of Wesley in the Christian Tradition*, pp. 11-38. Ed. Kenneth E. Rowe. Metuchen, NJ: Scarecrow; reprint: 1991, pp. 76-95.

1977 "John Wesley: Folk Theologian." *Theology Today* 34:150-60; reprint: 1991, pp. 112-24.

1980-2 "John Wesley's Interests in the Early Fathers of the Church." *Bulletin of the United Church of Canada Committee on Archives and History* 29:5-17; reprint, 1991, pp. 98-110.

1983 "The Rediscovery of John Wesley Through His Faith and Doctrine." *Historical Bulletin* (World Methodist Historical Society) 12:4-10.

1984 "Introduction." *Works*, 1:1-100. (And assorted introductions and notes throughout).

1985a "A New Future for 'Wesley Studies': An Agenda for 'Phase III'." In *The Future of the Methodist Theological Traditions*, pp. 34-52. Ed. M. Douglas Meeks. Nashville, TN: Abingdon; reprint: 1991, pp. 126-42.

1985b "The Wesleyan Quadrilateral in Wesley." *WTJ* 20.1:7-18; reprint: 1991, pp. 22-37.

1985c "How to Run a Conservative Revolution and Get No Thanks for It." Unpublished paper presented at The John Wesley Theological Institute (Illinois).

1985d Introductions and notes throughout: *Works*, vol. 2.

1986 Introductions and notes throughout: *Works*, vol. 3.

1987 Introductions and notes throughout: *Works*, vol. 4.

1988 "A Focus on the Holy Spirit: Spirit and Spirituality in John Wesley." *QR* 8.2:3-18; reprint: 1991, pp. 160-73.

1989 "Pietism and Enlightenment: Alternatives to Tradition." In *Christian Spirituality III*, pp. 240-56. Edited by Louis Dupré & Don Saliers. New York: Crossroad.

1990 "Methodists in Search of Consensus." In *What Should Methodists Teach?*, pp. 23-38. Ed. M. Douglas Meeks. Nashville, TN: Kingswood.

1991 *The Wesleyan Theological Heritage: Essays of Albert D. Outler.* Edited by Thomas C. Oden & Leicester R. Longden. Grand Rapids, MI: Zondervan.

Parris, John Roland
1963 *John Wesley's Doctrine of the Sacraments.* London: Epworth.
Pask, Alfred Henry Speedie
1939 "The Influence of Arminius upon the Theology of John Wesley." University of Edinburgh Ph.D. thesis.
1960 "The Influence of Arminius on John Wesley." *LQHR* 185 (sixth series, 29):258-61.
Peters, John Leland
1956 *Christian Perfection and American Methodism.* Nashville, TN: Pierce & Washabaugh; reprint ed., Grand Rapids, MI: Zondervan, 1985.
Phipps, William E.
1981 "John Wesley on Slavery." *QR* 1.3:23-31.
Piette, Maximin
1937 *John Wesley in the Evolution of Protestantism.* New York: Sheed and Ward.
Pillow, Thomas Wright
1986 "John Wesley's Doctrine of the Trinity." *The Cumberland Seminarian* 24:1-10.
Pinomaa, Lennart
1968 "Tro - lag - helgelse hos Luther, Calvin och John Wesley." *Norsk Teologisk Tidsskrift* 69:107-18.
Pucelik, Thomas M.
1963 "Christian Perfection According to John Wesley." Rome: Officium Libri Catholici.
Rack, Henry Derman
1989 *Reasonable Enthusiast.* Philadelphia, PA: Trinity Press International; revised reprint, Nashville, TN: Abingdon, 1993.
Rakestraw, Robert Vincent
1984 "John Wesley as a Theologian of Grace." *Journal of the Evangelical Theological Society* 27:193-203.
1985a "The Concept of Grace in the Ethics of John Wesley." Drew University Ph.D. thesis.
1985b "Human Rights and Liberties in the Political Ethics of John Wesley." *EvJl* 3:63-78.
1986 "The Contribution of John Wesley Toward An Ethic of Nature." *DrG* 56.3:14-25.
Rall, Harris Franklin
1920 "Was John Wesley a Premillenialist?" In *Modern Premillenialism and the Christian Hope,* pp. 245-53. New York: Abingdon; reprint, *Was Wesley a Pre-millenialist?* New York: Methodist Book House, 1921.
Rattenbury, J. [John] Ernest
1928 *Wesley's Legacy to the World.* London: Epworth.
1938 *The Conversion of the Wesleys.* London: Epworth.
1948 *The Eucharistic Hymns of John and Charles Wesley.* London: Epworth; reprint (updated grammar), Cleveland, OH: OSL Publications, 1990.
Ravindrathas, Paramanathan
1987 "Wesley og Økumenikk." *TFor* 1.2:6-19.
Reist, Irwin W.
1971 "John Wesley's View of the Sacraments: A Study in the Historical Development of a Doctrine." *WTJ* 6:41-54.

1972 "John Wesley's View of Man: A Study in Free Grace Versus Free Will." *WTJ* 7:25-35.

1975 "John Wesley and George Whitefield: A Study in the Integrity of Two Theologies of Grace." *Evangelical Quarterly* 47:26-40.

Renders, Helmut

1990 *John Wesley als Apologet: Systematisch-theologische Hintergründe und Praxis wesleyanischer Apologetik und ihre missionarische Bedeutung.* BGEmK 38. Ed. Studiengemeinschaft für Geschichte der Evangelisch-methodistischen Kirche. Stuttgart: Christliches Verlagshaus.

Renshaw, John Rutherford

1965 "The Atonement in the Theology of John and Charles Wesley." Boston University Ph.D. thesis.

Rivers, Isabel

1981 "John Wesley and the Language of Scripture, Reason, and Experience." *Prose Studies* 4:252-84; slightly revised reprint as "John Wesley and the Language of Scripture, Reason, and Tradition." In *Reason, Grace, and Sentiment*, Vol. I, pp. 205-53. New York: Cambridge University Press, 1991.

Rogal, Samuel J.

1979 "Scripture Quotation in Wesley's *Earnest Appeal*." *Research Studies* 47 (1979):181-8.

1983 *John and Charles Wesley.* Boston, MA: Twayne Publishers.

1988 "John Wesley's Journal: Prescriptions for the Social, Spiritual, and Intellectual Ills of Britain's Middle Class." *Andrews University Seminary Studies* 26:33-42.

Rogers, Charles Allen

1966 "John Wesley and William Tilly." *PWHS* 35:137-41.

1967 "The Concept of Prevenient Grace in the Theology of John Wesley." Duke University Ph.D. thesis.

Routley, Erik Reginald

1968 *The Musical Wesleys.* New York: Oxford University Press.

Rowe, Kenneth E.

1976 "The Search for the Historical Wesley." In *The Place of Wesley in the Christian Tradition*, pp. 11-38. Ed. Kenneth E. Rowe. Metuchen, NJ: Scarecrow.

Runyon, Theodore H.

1981 "Wesley and the Theologies of Liberation." In *Sanctification and Liberation: Liberation Theologies in the Light of the Wesleyan Tradition*, pp. 9-48. Ed. Theodore H. Runyon. Nashville, TN: Abingdon.

1985 "What is Methodism's Theological Contribution Today?" In *Wesleyan Theology Today*, pp. 7-13. Ed. Theodore H. Runyon. Nashville, TN: Kingswood.

1988 "A New Look at 'Experience'." *DrG* 57.3:44-55; abbreviated reprint, *International Journal for Philosophy of Religion* 31 (1992):187-94.

1989 "Wesley and 'Right Experience'." *Papers of the Canadian Methodist Historical Society*, Vol. 7, pp. 55-65.

1990 "The Importance of Experience for Faith." In *Aldersgate Reconsidered*, pp. 93-107. Ed. Randy Maddox. Nashville, TN: Kingswood.

Rupp, E. [Ernest] Gordon

1952a "Methodism in Relation to Protestant Tradition." In *Proceedings of the Eighth Ecumenical Methodist Conference*, pp. 93-106. London: Epworth; issued as separate essay by Epworth in 1951.

1952b *Principalities and Powers.* London: Epworth.
1971 "Paul and Wesley." In *De Dertiende Apostel en het Elfde Gebod*, pp. 102-10. Eds. G.C. Berkouwer & H.A. Oberman. Kampen: J.H. Kok.
1983 *John Wesley und Martin Luther.* BGEmK 16. Ed. Studiengemeinschaft für Geschichte der Evangelisch-methodistischen Kirche. Stuttgart: Christliches Verlagshaus.
1986 *Religion in England, 1688-1791.* Oxford: Clarendon.

Russell, Bernard Curry
1951 "The Theory and Practice of Christian Discipline According to John Wesley: Its Theological Bases and its Modern Relevance." Drew University Ph.D. thesis.

Sanders, Paul Samuel
1954a "An Appraisal of John Wesley's Sacramentalism in the Evolution of Early American Methodism." Union Theological Seminary (NY) Ph.D. thesis.
1954b "John Wesley and Baptismal Regeneration." *RelLife* 23:591-603.
1960 "What God Hath Joined Together?" *RelLife* 29:491-500.
1966 "Wesley's Eucharistic Faith and Practice." *Anglican Theological Review* 48: 157-74. Reprints: *Work/Worship* 17.1 (1967):1-13; as a booklet - *Wesley's Eucharistic Faith and Practice* (Flanders, NJ: Work/Worship, 1967); *Doxology* 5 (1988):21-34.

Sangster, William Edwin
1943 *The Path to Perfection. An Examination and Restatement of John Wesley's Doctrine of Christian Perfection.* London: Epworth.

Scanlon, Michael Joseph
1969 "The Christian Anthropology of John Wesley." Catholic University of America S.T.D. thesis.

Schempp, Johannes
1949 *Seelsorge und Seelenführung bei John Wesley.* Stuttgart: Christliches Verlagshaus.

Schmidt, Martin
1953 "Die ökumenische Bedeutung John Wesleys." *Theologische Literaturzeitung* 78:449-60.
1958 *The Young Wesley: Missionary and Theologian of Missions.* London: Epworth.
1962 *John Wesley: A Theological Biography.* Vol. I. New York: Abingdon.
1972 *John Wesley: A Theological Biography.* Vol. II.1. New York: Abingdon.
1973 *John Wesley: A Theological Biography.* Vol. II.2. New York: Abingdon.
1976 "Wesley's Place in Church History." In *The Place of Wesley in the Christian Tradition*, pp. 67-93. Ed. Kenneth E. Rowe. Metuchen, NJ: Scarecrow.

Schneeberger, Vilém D.
1974 *Theologische Wurzeln des Sozialen Akzents bei John Wesley.* Zürich: Gotthelf.
1977 "Der Begriff der christlichen Freiheit bei John Wesley." *Communio Viatorum* 20:47-61.

Schofield, Robert Edwin
1953 "John Wesley and Science in 18th Century England." *Isis* 44:331-40.

Score, John Nelson Russell II
1963 "A Study of the Concept of Ministry in the Thought of John Wesley." Duke University Ph.D. thesis.

Scott, Percy

1939 *John Wesleys Lehre von der Heiligung verglichen mit einem lutherisch-pietistichen Beispiel.* Berlin: Alfred Töpelmann.

Scroggs, Robin Jerome

1960 "John Wesley as a Biblical Scholar." *Journal of Bible and Religion* 28:415-22.

Seaborn, Joseph William

1986 "Wesley's Views of the Uses of History." *WTJ* 21:129-36.

Selleck, J. [Jerald] Brian

1983 "The Book of Common Prayer in the Theology of John Wesley." Drew University Ph.D. thesis.

1984 "An Historical Consideration of Worship and the Cure of Souls." *DrG* 54.2:25-51.

1990 "John Wesley and Spiritual Formation." *Doxology* 7:6-16.

Shelton, Raymond Larry

1981 "John Wesley's Approach to Scripture in Historical Perspective." *WTJ* 16.1:23-50.

Shimizu, Mitsuo

1980 "Epistemology in the Thought of John Wesley." Drew University Ph.D. thesis.

Shipley, David Clark

1960 "The Ministry in Methodism in the Eighteenth Century." In *The Ministry in the Methodist Heritage*, pp. 11-31. Ed. Gerald McCulloh. Nashville, TN: Department of Ministerial Education.

Slaatte, Howard Alexander

1963 *Fire in the Brand: An Introduction to the Creative Work and Theology of John Wesley.* New York: Exposition Press; reprint ed., Lanham, MD: University Press of America, 1983.

Smith, Harmon Lee

1963 "Wesley's Doctrine of Justification: Beginning and Process." *DrG* 28.2:88-98; reprint, *LQHR* 189 (sixth series, 33) (1964):120-8.

Smith, James Weldon

1964 "Some Notes on Wesley's Doctrine of Prevenient Grace." *RelLife* 34:68-80.

Smith, Robert Doyle

1990 "John Wesley and Jonathan Edwards on Religious Experience: A Comparative Analysis." *WTJ* 25.1:130-46.

Smith, Timothy Lawrence

1985 "John Wesley and the Wholeness of Scripture." *Interpretation* 39:246-62.

Smith, Warren Thomas

1986 *John Wesley and Slavery.* Nashville, TN: Abingdon.

Snyder, Howard Albert

1980 *The Radical Wesley and Patterns of Church Renewal.* Downers Grove, IL: Intervarsity.

1989 *Signs of the Spirit: How God Reshapes the Church.* Grand Rapids, MI: Zondervan.

1990 "John Wesley and Macarius the Egyptian." *AsbThJ* 45.2:55-9.

Staples, Rob Lyndal

1963 "John Wesley's Doctrine of Christian Perfection: A Reinterpretation." Pacific School of Religion Ph.D. thesis.

1972 "Sanctification and Selfhood: A Phenomenological Analysis of the Wesleyan Message." *WTJ* 7.1:3-16.

1986 "John Wesley's Doctrine of the Holy Spirit." *WTJ* 21:91-115; reprint, *The Spirit and the New Age*, pp. 199-236. Eds. R.L. Shelton and A.R.G. Deasley. Anderson, IN: Warner.

1991 *Outward Sign and Inward Grace: The Place of Sacraments in Wesleyan Spirituality.* Kansas City, MO: Beacon Hill.

Starkey, Lycurgus Monroe, Jr.

1962 *The Work of the Holy Spirit: A Study in Wesleyan Theology.* New York: Abingdon.

1980 "The Holy Spirit and the Wesleyan Witness." *RelLife* 49:72-80.

Steele, Richard Bruce

1994 *"Gracious Affections" and "True Virtue" according to Jonathan Edwards and John Wesley.* Metuchen, NJ: Scarecrow.

Stoeffler, F. [Fred] Ernest

1962 "Infant Baptism: Entry into Covenant." *The Christian Advocate* 4.11 (May 24):10-11.

1964 "The Wesleyan Concept of Religious Certainty: Its Pre-History and Significance." *LQHR* 189 (sixth series, 33):128-39.

1976a "Tradition and Renewal in the Ecclesiology of John Wesley." In *Traditio—Krisis—Renovatio aus theologischer Sicht*, pp. 298-316. Eds. B. Jaspert & R. Mohr. Marburg: Elwert.

1976b "Pietism, The Wesleys, and Methodist Beginnings in America." In *Continental Pietism and Early American Christianity*, pp. 184-221. Ed. F.E. Stoeffler. Grand Rapids, MI: Eerdmans.

Strawson, William

1959 "Wesley's Doctrine of the Last Things." *LQHR* 184 (sixth series, 28):240-9.

Streiff, Patrick Philipp

1985 "Der ökumenische Geist im frühen Methodismus." *Pietismus und Neuzeit* 11:59-77.

Stuart, William James

1974 "Theology and Experience: A Reappraisal of Wesley's Theology." University of Zürich Ph.D. thesis.

Sturm, Roy Albert

1982 *Sociological Reflections on John Wesley and Methodism.* Indianapolis, IN: Central Publishing.

Sweetland, William Ernest

1955 "A Critical Study of John Wesley as Practical Thinker and Reformer." Michigan State University Ph.D. thesis.

Tamez, Elsa

1983 "El Wesley de los pobres." In *La Tradición Protestante en la Teología Latinoamericana*, pp. 219-36. Ed. José Duque. San José, Costa Rica: DEI.
English: "Wesley as Read by the Poor." In *The Future of the Methodist Theological Traditions*, pp. 67-84. Ed. M. Douglas Meeks. Nashville, TN: Abingdon, 1985.

Tews, Jane Alison

1978 "The Origin and Outcome of the Liturgies of John Wesley." Claremont School of Theology D.Min. thesis.

Thomas, Howe Octavius Jr.

1988 "John Wesley's Awareness and Application of the Method of Distinguishing Between Theological Essentials and Theological Opinions." *MethH* 26:84-97.

1990 "John Wesley's and Rudolf Bultmann's Understanding of Justification by Faith Compared and Contrasted." University of Bristol Ph.D. thesis.

Thomas, Wilhelm

1965 *Heiligung im Neuen Testament und bei John Wesley*. Zürich: Christliche Vereinsbuchhandlung.

Thorsen, Donald A. D.

1989 "Experimental Method in the Practical Theology of John Wesley." *WTJ* 24:117-41.

1990 *The Wesleyan Quadrilateral*. Grand Rapids, MI: Zondervan.

Todd, John Murray

1958 *John Wesley and the Catholic Church*. London: Hoddard & Stoughton.

Towns, Elmer L.

1970 "John Wesley and Religious Education." *Religious Education* 65:318-28.

Tracy, Wesley D.

1982 "Christian Education in the Wesleyan Mode. *WTJ* 17.1:30-53.

1988 "John Wesley, Spiritual Director: Spiritual Guidance in Wesley's Letters." *WTJ* 23:148-62.

1992 "Economic Policies and Judicial Oppression as Formative Influences on the Theology of John Wesley." *WTJ* 27:30-56.

Trickett, David

1989 "Spiritual Vision and Discipline in the Early Wesleyan Movement." In *Christian Spirituality III*, pp. 354-71. Edited by Louis Dupré & Don Saliers. New York: Crossroad.

Tripp, David Howard

1969 *The Renewal of the Covenant in the Methodist Tradition*. London: Epworth.

1990 "'Observe the Gradation!' John Wesley's Notes on the New Testament." *QR* 10.2:49-64.

Turley, Briane K.

1991 "John Wesley and War." *MethH* 29:96-111.

Turner, John Munsey

1985 *Conflict and Reconciliation: Studies in Methodism and Ecumenism in England, 1740-1982*. London: Epworth.

1986 "John Wesley: Theologian for the People." *Journal of United Reform Church History Society* 3:320-8.

1988 "Victorian Values - Or Whatever Happened to John Wesley's Scriptural Holiness?" *PWHS* 46:165-84.

Tuttle, Robert Gregory, Jr.

1969 "The Influence of Roman Catholic Mystics on John Wesley." University of Bristol Ph.D. thesis.

1978 *John Wesley: His Life and Theology*. Grand Rapids, MI: Zondervan.

1989 *Mysticism in the Wesleyan Tradition*. Grand Rapids, MI: Zondervan.

Tyson, John Horton

1991 "The Interdependence of Law and Grace in John Wesley's Teaching and Preaching." University of Edinburgh Ph.D. thesis.

Tyson, John Rodger

1982 "John Wesley and William Law: A Reappraisal." *WTJ* 17.2:58-78.

1988 "Essential Doctrines and Real Religion: Theological Method in Wesley's *Sermons on Several Occasions*." *WTJ* 23:163-79.

1989 "Sin, Self, and Society: John Wesley's Hamartiology Reconsidered." *AsbThJ* 44.2:77-89.

Verhalen, Philippo (Philip) A.

1969 *The Proclamation of the Word in the Writings of John Wesley.* Rome: Pontificia Universitas Gregoriana.

Villa-Vicencio, Charles M. L.

1982 "The Origins and Witness of Methodism." In *Denominationalism—Its Sources and Implications,* pp. 64-94. Edited by W.S. Vorster. Pretoria: University of South Africa.

1989 "Towards a Liberating Wesleyan Social Ethic for South Africa Today." *Journal of Theology for Southern Africa* 68:92-102.

Wade, William Nash

1981 "A History of Public Worship in the Methodist Episcopal Church and Methodist Episcopal Church, South from 1784 to 1905." University of Notre Dame Ph.D. thesis.

Wagley, Laurence A.

1991 "The Wesleyan Revival and Forgiveness of Sin." *Liturgy* 9.4:87-93.

Wainwright, Geoffrey

1983 "Ekklesiologische Ansätze bei Luther und bei Wesley." In *Ökumenische Erchließung Martin Luthers,* pp. 173-83. Edited by P. Manns and H. Meyer. Paderborn: Bonifatius-Druckerei.

1986 "Der Sonntag zwischen Schöpfung, Erlösung und Vollendung." In *Der Sonntag,* pp. 163-74. Edited by A. Altermatt and T. Schnitker. Würzburg: Echter Verlag.

1987 *Geoffrey Wainwright on Wesley and Calvin: Sources for Theology, Liturgy and Spirituality.* Melbourne: Uniting Church Press.

1988a "Perfect Salvation in the Teaching of Wesley and Calvin." *Reformed World* 40:898-909.

1988b "The Sacraments in Wesleyan Perspective." *Doxology* 5:5-20.

1990 "Why Wesley was a Trinitarian." *DrG* 59.2:26-43.

Wakefield, Gordon Stevens

1978 "La Littérature du Désert chez John Wesley." *Irénikon* 51:155-70.

1991 "Traditions of Spiritual Guidance: John Wesley and the Methodist System." *The Way* 31:69-91.

Walls, Jerry L.

1981 "John Wesley's Critique of Martin Luther." *MethH* 20:29-41.

1983 "The Free Will Defense, Calvinism, Wesley, and the Goodness of God." *Christian Scholar's Review* 13:19-33.

Walsh, John

1990 "John Wesley and The Community of Goods." In *Protestant Evangelicalism* (Studies in Church History, Subsidia 7), pp. 25-50. Edited by Keith Robbins. Oxford: Blackwell.

Walters, Orville S.

1972 "The Concept of Attainment in John Wesley's Christian Perfection." *MethH* 10.3:12-29.

1973 "John Wesley's Footnotes to Christian Perfection." *MethH* 12.1:19-36.

Ward, W. [William] Reginald

1988 "Introduction." *Works,* 18:1-119.

Watson, David Lowes

1984 "Christ Our Righteousness: The Center of Wesley's Evangelistic Message." *PSTJ* 37:34-47.

1985 *The Early Methodist Class Meeting: Its Origins and Significance.* Nashville, TN: Discipleship Resources.

1986a "Justification by Faith and Wesley's Evangelistic Message." *WTJ* 21: 7-23.

1986b "Methodist Spirituality." In *Protestant Spiritual Traditions,* pp. 217-73. Ed. Frank Senn. New York: Paulist.

1990 "Aldersgate Street and the General Rules: The Form and the Power of Methodist Discipleship." In *Aldersgate Reconsidered,* pp. 33-47. Ed. R.L. Maddox. Nashville, TN: Kingswood.

Watson, Philip Saville

1963 "Wesley and Luther on Christian Perfection." *Ecumenical Review* 15:291-302.

1964 *The Message of the Wesleys: A Reader of Instruction and Devotion.* New York: Macmillan; reprint ed., Grand Rapids, MI: Zondervan, 1984.

1983 *Das Autorität der Bibel bei Luther und Wesley.* BGEmK 14. Ed. Studiengemeinschaft für Geschichte der Evangelisch-methodistischen Kirche. Stuttgart: Christliches Verlagshaus.

Weiβbach, Jürgen

1970 *Die Neue Mensch im theologischen Denken John Wesleys.* BGEmK 2. Ed. Studiengemeinschaft für Geschichte der Evangelisch-methodistischen Kirche. Stuttgart: Christliches Verlagshaus.

West, Nathaniel

1894 *John Wesley and Premillenialism.* New York: Hunt and Eaton; abridged, edited reprint, "John Wesley a Premillenarian." *Christian Workers Magazine* 17 (1916):96-101.

Weyer, Michel

1987 *Die Bedeutung von Wesleys Lehrpredigten für Die Methodisten.* BGEmK 26. Ed. Studiengemeinschaft für Geschichte der Evangelisch-methodistischen Kirche. Stuttgart: Christliches Verlagshaus.

White, Charles Edward

1991 "John Wesley's Use of Church Discipline." *MethH* 29:112-18.

White, James Floyd

1984 "Introduction." *John Wesley's Sunday Service of the Methodists in North America,* pp. 9-21. Nashville, TN: United Methodist Publishing House & United Methodist Board of Higher Education and Ministry.

Willhauck, Susan Etheridge

1992 "John Wesley's View of Children: Foundations for Contemporary Christian Education." Catholic University of America Ph.D. thesis.

Williams, Colin Wilbur

1960 *John Wesley's Theology Today.* Nashville, TN: Abingdon.

Williams, Ronald Gordon

1964 "John Wesley's Doctrine of the Church." Boston University Th.D. thesis.

Wilson, Charles Randall

1977 "The Relevance of John Wesley's Distinctive Correlation of Love and Law." *WTJ* 12:54-9.

Wilson, David Dunn

1963 "The Importance of Hell for John Wesley." *PWHS* 34:12-16.

1968 "The Influence of Mysticism on John Wesley." Leeds University Ph.D. thesis.

1969 *Many Waters Cannot Quench: A Study of the Sufferings of Eighteenth-century Methodism and their Significance for John Wesley and the First Methodists.* London: Epworth.

Wilson, Kenneth Alexander

1984 "The Devotional Relationship and Interaction Between the Spirituality of John Wesley, the Methodist Societies, and the Book of Common Prayer." Queens University of Belfast Ph.D. thesis.

Wood, A. [Arthur] Skevington

1967 *The Burning Heart: John Wesley - Evangelist.* Exeter: Paternoster; reprint ed., Minneapolis, MN: Bethany House, 1978.

1975 "The Contribution of John Wesley to the Theology of Grace." In *Grace Unlimited,* pp. 209-22. Ed. Clark Pinnock. Minneapolis, MN: Bethany Fellowship.

1977 "John Wesley, Theologian of the Spirit." *Theological Renewal* 6 (June/July 1977):26-34; reprint, *Evangelical Review of Theology* 4 (1980):176-88.

1986 *Love Excluding Sin: Wesley's Doctrine of Sanctification.* Wesley Fellowship Occasional Paper #1. Derbys, England: Moorley's Bookshop.

1992 *Revelation and Reason: Wesleyan Responses to Eighteenth-Century Rationalism.* Bulkington: The Wesley Fellowship.

Wood, Lawrence Willard

1975 "Wesley's Epistemology." *WTJ* 10:48-59.

Wynkoop, Mildred Bangs

1971 "A Hermeneutical Approach to John Wesley." *WTJ* 6:13-22.

1972 *A Theology of Love: The Dynamic of Wesleyanism.* Kansas City, MO: Beacon Hill.

1979 "Theological Roots of the Wesleyan Understanding of the Holy Spirit." *WTJ* 14.1:77-98.

Yates, Arthur Staley

1952 *The Doctrine of Assurance with Special Reference to John Wesley.* London: Epworth.

Young, Frances

1985 "Grace and Demand: The Heart of Preaching." *EpRev* 12.2:46-55.

C. Books, Dissertations, and Articles on Charles Wesley

Baker, Frank

1988 *Charles Wesley's Verse: An Introduction.* London: Epworth; revised reprint of "Introduction" to *Representative Verse of Charles Wesley.* Ed. Frank Baker. London: Epworth, 1962.

Berger, Teresa

1988 "Charles Wesley und sein Leidgut: eine Literaturübersicht." *Theologische Revue* 84:441-50; enlarged English translation, "Charles Wesley: A Literary Overview." In *Charles Wesley: Poet and Theologian,* pp. 21-29. Edited by S T Kimbrough, Jr. Nashville, TN: Kingswood, 1992.

1989 *Theologie in Hymnen? Zum Verhältnis von Theologie und Doxologie am Beispiel der "Collection of Hymns for the Use of the People Called Methodists".* Altenberge: Telos Verlag.

1992 "'Theologie, die man singen kann . . . ' Christologische Titel im methodistischen Gesangbuch von 1780." *Una Sancta* 47:123-9.

Brantley, Richard
1987 "Charles Wesley's Experimental Art." *Eighteenth-Century Life* 11:1-11.
Bryant, Barry Edward
1990 "Trinity and Hymnody: The Doctrine of the Trinity in the Hymns of Charles Wesley." *WTJ* 25.2:64-73.
Dale, James
1960 "The Theological and Literary Qualities of the Poetry of Charles Wesley in Relation to the Standards of His Age." Cambridge University Ph.D. thesis.
Davies, Horton
1992 "Charles Wesley and the Calvinist Tradition." In *Charles Wesley: Poet and Theologian*, pp. 186-203. Edited by S T Kimbrough, Jr. Nashville, TN: Kingswood.
Downes, James Cyril Thomas
1960 "Eschatological Doctrines in the Writings of John and Charles Wesley." Edinburgh University Ph.D. thesis.
Gallaway, Craig B.
1988 "The Presence of Christ with the Worshipping Community: A Study in the Hymns of John and Charles Wesley." Emory University Ph.D. thesis.
Holland, Bernard George
1971 "The Conversions of John and Charles Wesley and Their Place in Methodist Tradition." *PWHS* 38:45-53, 65-71.
Houghton, Edward
1992 *The Handmaid of Piety and other papers on Charles Wesley's Hymns.* York: Quack Books in association with the Wesley Fellowship.
Kimbrough, S T, Jr.
1992 "Charles Wesley and Biblical Interpretation." In *Charles Wesley: Poet and Theologian*, pp. 106-36. Edited by S T Kimbrough, Jr. Nashville, TN: Kingswood.
1993 *A Song for the Poor: Hymns by Charles Wesley.* New York: Board of Global Ministry, United Methodist Church.
Langford, Thomas
1992 "Charles Wesley as Theologian." In *Charles Wesley: Poet and Theologian*, pp. 97-105. Edited by S T Kimbrough, Jr. Nashville, TN: Kingswood.
Marshall, Madeleine & Todd, Janet
1982 *English Congregational Hymns in the Eighteenth Century*, pp. 60-88. Lexington, KY: University of Kentucky.
Nichols, Kathryn
1988a "Charles Wesley's Eucharistic Hymns: Their Relationship to the *Book of Common Prayer*." *The Hymn* 39.2:13-21.
1988b "The Theology of Christ's Sacrifice and Presence in Charles Wesley's *Hymns on the Lord's Supper*." *The Hymn* 39.4:19-29.
Noll, Mark Allan
1974 Romanticism and the Hymns of Charles Wesley." *Evangelical Quarterly* 46:195-223
Quantrille, Wilma Jean
1989 "The Triune God in the Hymns of Charles Wesley." Drew University Ph.D. thesis.
Rattenbury, J. [John] Ernest
1941 *The Evangelical Doctrines of Charles Wesley's Hymns.* London: Epworth.

1948 *The Eucharistic Hymns of John and Charles Wesley*. London: Epworth; reprint (updated grammar), Cleveland, OH: OSL Publications, 1990.

Renshaw, John Rutherford

1965 "The Atonement in the Theology of John and Charles Wesley." Boston University Ph.D. thesis.

Rogal, Samuel J.

1983 *John and Charles Wesley*. Boston, MA: Twayne Publishers.

Routley, Erik Reginald

1968 *The Musical Wesleys*. New York: Oxford University Press.

Townsend, James Arthur

1979 "Feelings Related to Assurance in Charles Wesley's Hymns." Fuller Theological Seminary Ph.D. thesis.

Tyson, John Roger

1983 "Charles Wesley's Theology of the Cross: An Examination of the Theology and Method of Charles Wesley as Seen in His Doctrine of the Atonement." Drew University Ph.D. thesis.

1985a "Charles Wesley's Theology of Redemption." *WTJ* 20.2:7-28.

1985b "God's Everlasting Love: Charles Wesley and the Predestinarian Controversy." *EvJl* 3:47-62.

1986 *Charles Wesley on Sanctification*. Grand Rapids, MI: Zondervan.

1992 "Transfiguration of Scripture: Charles Wesley's Poetic Hermeneutic." *AsbThJ* 47.2:17-41.

Welch, Barbara Ann

1971 "Charles Wesley and the Celebrations of Evangelical Experience." University of Michigan Ph.D.

INDEX OF SELECTED NAMES

(Includes first occurrence for all short titles)

Abraham, William, 265n42, 267n69, 269n96, 273n148, 318n93

Allison, C. FitzSimons, 326n46, 334n61

Almond, Philip, 371n125

Alston, William, 263n13

Althaus, Paul, 363n19

Aulén, Gustaf, 303n16

Baker, Frank, 24, 46, 260n38, 260n39, 261n45, 269n89, 271n121, 272n130, 273n142, 273n149, 352n96, 353n109, 353n111, 356n153, 358n186, 359n196, 366n62, 366n65

Barber, Frank, 262n1, 266n62, 280n76

Bassett, Paul, 265n41, 269n96, 351n77

Beckerlegge, Oliver, 352n97, 370n117

Bence, Clarence, 260n38, 296n118, 301n187, 344n213, 362n3, 363n27-8, 366n58-9, 366n67

Bengel, Johann, 37, 79, 254n99, 364n33-4, 365n42, 365n47

Benner, Forest, 313n29, 314n33, 314n41

Bishop, John, 351n83, 351n87, 352n97, 354n118

Black, Robert, 369n98, 369n105

Blaising, Craig, 90, 286n12, 291n63, 292n71, 292n77, 296n118, 298n145, 298n150, 299n158, 327n54, 333n38

Borgen, Ole, 266n54, 298n145, 298n148, 331n16, 345n3, 346n19, 348n40, 348n42, 349n53, 349n60, 349n62, 350n65, 350n69, 350n72, 350n75, 357n163, 357n172, 358n175, 359n199, 359n204, 361n226, 362n237

Bowmer, John, 346n14, 348n49, 349n52, 349n55, 349n57, 349n60, 349n62, 350n75, 356n151, 357n163, 357n170, 361n230, 361n233, 363n26, 366n59

Brantley, Richard, 262n1, 352n98

Brock, Sebastian, 285n3

Brockwell, Charles, 334n56, 351n79

Browne, Peter, 27, 31, 49-50, 51, 94, 138, 262n8, 263n17, 287n17, 290n44, 299n162

Bryant, Barry, 261n47, 262n1, 262n3, 273n145, 276n14, 277n32, 282n100, 283n107, 286n13, 287n16, 287n20, 288n26, 289n38, 294n93, 295n107, 296n118, 320n133, 322n155, 338n120

Bundy, David, 260n42, 261n43, 338n118

Burns, J. Patout, 285n3

Campbell, Ted, 260n40-1, 261n43, 266n56, 267n71, 271n121, 271n125, 272n132, 272n139-41, 282n94, 294n95, 301n191, 303n3, 311n130, 351n82, 353n109, 353n112, 359n196, 361n228

Cannon, William, 91, 275n2, 300n176, 301n187, 308n88, 312n3, 321n143, 323n2, 326n46, 334n56, 358n174, 366n67

Carey, Jonathan, 320n133

Casto, Robert, 268n77, 269n90, 282n95, 352n90-1, 355n142

Cell, George, 91, 308n77

Chamberlain, Jeffrey, 317n80, 330n102, 334n61, 335n77

Cho, John Chongnahm, 286n13, 292n71, 359n199

Chrestou, Panagiotos, 284n113

Clapper, Gregory, 258n6, 288n26, 288n29, 289n32, 311n129, 316n63, 318n96, 318n98
Clifford, Alan, 300n178, 326n46, 335n77
Collier, Frank, 266n62, 280n76
Collins, Kenneth, 263n14, 275n2, 291n57, 300n168, 302n196, 304n28, 307n98, 315n56, 331n10, 333n36, 345n3, 354n123, 362n6, 366n59
Congar, Yves, 321n135
Coppedge, Allan, 263n14, 274n163, 278n50, 279n53, 279n60, 280n63, 280n72, 284n115, 301n185, 306n62
Cubie, David, 338n124, 362n4, 364n29
Cushman, Robert, 89, 302n196, 359n206
Dale, James, 269n91, 352n98
Daley, Brian, 362n8
Davies, Horton, 278n50, 349n55, 351n83, 351n87, 358n177
Davies, Rupert, 211, 257n2, 273n149, 366n63
Dayton, Donald, 259n28, 269n96, 305n46, 320n127, 321n143, 324n23, 337n116, 368n86
Dean, William, 354n129-30, 355n132-3, 355n137, 357n162, 366n67
Deschner, John, 96, 110, 113, 116, 117, 265n46, 286n7, 303n15, 303n19, 304n40, 306n60, 307n63, 307n70, 309n93, 309n98, 310n107, 310n124, 311n135, 311n142, 366n58, 372n146
Dörries, Hermann, 292n70
Dorr, Donal, 291n63, 297n132, 298n148, 300n169, 302n199, 302n201, 343n194, 359n206
Downes, James, 332n25, 362n6, 363n26, 363n28, 372n146, 372n150
Dunlap, Elden, 263n14, 374n8
Duque Zúñiga, José, 343n199, 367n85
Eaton, David, 300n178, 301n179
Eayrs, George, 266n62, 273n149, 274n166
English, John, 260n39, 262n9, 267n64, 270n107, 281n82, 282n93, 358n174, 358n180, 358n192, 359n199, 359n201, 361n233
Etchegoyen, Aldo, 367n84, 368n85
Felton, Gayle, 357n172, 358n175, 358n178, 358n186, 359n196, 359n198, 359n203, 361n233
Ferguson, Duncan, 268n82
Fiddes, Paul, 304n16
Flew, R. Newton, 296n117, 343n199
Fraser, M. Robert, 334n47, 336n109, 337n116, 339n135, 339n148, 340n150, 340n154, 340n157, 340n162, 341n178-9, 342n183, 342n185, 364n30, 364n40
Frost, Stanley, 265n40
Fuhrman, Eldon, 277n38, 297n139, 310n119, 363n26
Fujimoto, Mitsuru, 326n47, 328n63, 336n89, 340n154, 344n213, 362n236
Gallaway, Craig, 114, 303n10, 303n15, 309n93, 310n106, 310n114, 323n1, 330n2, 352n97
Galliers, Brian, 359n197, 359n199
Gallo, Bruno, 268n83, 273n148, 288n26
George, A. Raymond, 349n52, 349n62, 350n69, 350n75, 351n79, 355n139
Gerdes, Egon, 283n102, 285n1, 286n13, 290n42, 290n45, 290n55
Grislis, Egil, 349n52, 349n60, 357n163
Gunter, W. Stephen, 306n62, 318n106, 327n47, 334n47, 336n88, 339n135, 340n156, 341n179, 345n218
Guroian, Vigen, 338n128
Gustafson, James, 258n14, 323n1, 331n6
Hall, Thor, 368n86, 369n100
Harakas, Stanley, 292n70
Harper, J. Steven, 261n44, 345n3, 354n128, 355n139, 355n143, 356n153, 357n163
Hauerwas, Stanley, 338n128
Hebblethwaite, Brian, 362n7
Heitzenrater, Richard, 124, 257n4, 259n29-30, 260n38, 261n44, 318n95, 324n21, 330n99, 330n2, 334n62, 338n128
Heppe, Heinrich, 293n83
Heron, Alasdair, 321n135, 345n4
Hildebrandt, Franz, 301n183, 314n42, 349n62, 350n65, 366n64
Hill, Charles, 362n8

Hillman, Robert, 84-5, 298n142 298n146, 329n93, 343n199, 348n36
Hoffman, Thomas, 289n39, 367n77
Hohenstein, Charles, 357n172, 358n175, 358n178, 358n180, 358n186-7, 359n201, 359n204, 361n226
Holifield, E. Brooks, 287n24, 290n54, 370n117
Holland, Bernard, 224-5, 330n99, 332n22, 357n172-3, 358n178
Hoon, Paul, 47, 257n5, 277n38, 331n10
Hopko, Thomas, 296n116
Horst, Mark, 273n149, 274n154, 288n29, 288n32, 310n116, 318n95-6, 318n98-9, 330n2, 331n11, 336n81
Hulley, Leonard, 305n46, 337n109, 338n128, 352n94, 368n85
Hynson, Leon, 246, 283n102, 296n118, 304n33, 323n167, 362n4, 363n26, 366n58, 369n101, 369n104
Jacob, Margaret, 363n23
Jennings, Theodore, 83, 287n22, 367n81, 368n87-8, 369n93-5, 369n99, 369n106
Johnson, Susanne, 349n52, 350n75, 363n26
Jones, Scott, 264n39, 268n77, 269n90, 269n95-6, 270n98, 270n101, 271n111, 271n125, 274n151, 274n163
Jones, W. Paul, 345n3, 346n20, 366n63
Keefer, Luke, 260n41, 273n141, 300n178, 367n82
Kellett, Norman, 312n3
Kim, Kwang Yul, 259n28, 280n67, 307n62, 307n64, 327n54, 335n69
Kimbrough, S T, 269n90, 368n88
Knight, David, 267n64
Knight, Henry, 192, 194, 298n148, 303n10, 309n93, 337n101, 345n3, 346n20, 348n42, 349n51, 350n72, 351n77, 351n79, 354n129, 355n141, 356n150, 356n161, 357n162, 358n181, 359n204
Knight, John, 279n54, 302n193
Koerber, Carolo, 327n54
Kucharek, Casimir, 346n12
Kuyper, Abraham, 330n1
Langford, Thomas, 88-90, 299n158, 334n56, 337n109, 374n8
Lawson, Albert, 291n61, 328n61, 333n40, 366n59
Lee, Umphrey, 300n173, 302n198, 343n201
Lee, Hoo-Jung, 262n10, 285n3, 292n70, 298n151, 301n191, 314n44, 362n3, 363n26, 373n156
Le Goff, Jacques, 362n12
Lerch, David, 290n55, 363n24
Lessmann, Thomas, 124, 257n5, 263n14, 312n3, 312n5, 313n27, 343n199, 358n178
Lindström, Harald, 176, 263n14, 292n67, 292n71, 301n184, 303n15, 304n19, 305n40, 306n48, 306n59, 323n2, 324n23, 327n54, 331n10, 335n65, 336n86, 336n89-90, 337n109, 338n124, 338n135, 341n177, 343n199, 344n213, 358n177
Lossky, Vladimir, 298n146
Lovin, Robin, 318n95, 338n128
Luby, Daniel, 128, 265n42, 286n14, 297n135-6, 297n139, 297n150, 297n152-3, 300n168, 302n194, 312n3, 312n5, 312n11, 316n75, 317n79, 317n90, 335n72
McDannell, Colleen, 362n7
McGonigle, Herbert, 300n178, 337n116, 341n168
McNulty, Frank, 334n55, 354n123, 356n154
Macarius, 28, 86, 91, 113, 125, 178, 188, 261n43, 263n10, 285n3, 291n65, 292n70, 294n95, 296n116, 301n191, 313n16, 343n204, 366n64, 370n122
Maddox, Randy, 258n10-2, 258n16, 259n22, 260n42, 265n44, 271n119, 275n167, 285n3, 302n201, 315n56, 322n157, 322n162, 324n15, 327n56
Madron, Thomas, 277n33, 367n85, 368n92, 369n101, 369n107
Mälzer, Gottfried, 364n34
Mantzaridis, Georgios, 325n30
Marquardt, Manfred, 266n54, 301n185, 304n33, 312n11, 367n81, 368n86-8, 368n92, 369n99, 369n107

Martin, Troy W., 260n42, 268n77, 270n101
Martos, Joseph, 346n11
Matthews, Rex, 127, 261n47, 262n1, 262n3, 265n40, 270n105, 270n107-8, 273n147, 281n84, 301n181, 314n36, 314n40, 316n69, 316n72
Meeks, M. Douglas, 258n6, 279n53, 374n10
Meistad, Tore, 305n47, 306n49, 330n2, 363n26, 367n84, 368n87, 369n100, 369n105
Mercer, Jerry, 363n26, 364n29
Meredith, Lawrence, 257n5, 301n185
Meyendorff, John, 262n48
Míguez Bonino, José, 172, 287n20, 312n145, 328n60, 331n6, 366n59, 368n86, 374n9
Miller, Richard, 268n77, 273n148, 273n150, 274n163
Montanus, 44, 134-5, 273n146
Moore, D. Marselle, 337n109-10, 339n135-6, 342n183
Moore, Robert, 279n60, 300n175
Naglee, David, 261n44, 261n47, 266n54, 269n95, 275n2, 276n29, 282n91, 291n57, 330n2, 358n175, 359n198, 359n206, 360n208, 362n6, 363n26, 364n30
Neff, Blake J., 324n23
Nichols, Kathryn, 349n52, 349n58
Noll, Mark, 313n29, 314n43, 352n98
Noro, Yoshio, 262n1, 263n14
Novatian, 44, 273n146, 367n70
Nuttall, Geoffrey, 263n11
Outler, Albert, 15-6, 21, 24, 36, 142, 146, 151, 168, 243, 257n5, 259n18, 259n25, 260n33, 260n38, 260n42, 267n69, 291n63, 297n131, 297n134, 298n153, 300n178, 301n179, 301n185, 302n195, 310n123, 312n3, 321n140, 323n9, 326n46, 332n22, 333n38, 334n56, 334n59, 334n61, 337n106, 339n136-7, 341n168, 341n170, 352n101, 354n128, 366n59-60, 366n63, 366n67, 368n93, 369n94, 372n150, 374n10
Parris, John, 345n3, 346n19, 358n177
Pearson, John, 43, 270n106, 272n133, 272n134, 304n22, 309n95, 312n9, 313n24, 321n141, 321n146
Pelagius, 44, 273n146, 285n2
Pelikan, Jaroslav, 280n69
Perkins, William, 330n1
Peters, John, 337n109, 342n187, 345n218
Pillow, Thomas, 320n133, 322n155
Pucelik, Thomas, 271n124, 328n69, 334n55, 343n194
Quantrille, Wilma, 311n136, 320n133, 322n155
Rack, Henry, 274n155, 349n55, 352n96, 353n112, 360n215
Rakestraw, Robert, 297n139, 298n145, 298n151, 301n184, 312n5, 363n26, 364n29, 369n104, 370n110
Rattenbury, J. Ernest, 259n27-8 273n149, 282n91, 296n117, 308n82, 331n14, 343n199, 346n19, 349n52, 349n58, 350n69, 350n75, 372n146
Reist, Irwin, 345n3, 346n19, 358n174
Renshaw, John, 106, 303n15, 304n19, 306n59, 307n66
Rogal, Samuel, 268n83, 291n60, 325n32, 353n99
Rogers, Charles, 260n31, 266n54, 292n71, 297n135, 299n158, 299n160, 299n163, 301n179, 361n234, 362n236
Runyon, Theodore, 262n1, 273n147, 317n81, 328n60, 330n2, 362n3
Saldanha, Chrys, 263n16
Sanders, Paul, 257n2, 260n39, 301n184, 345n3, 346n19, 348n49, 349n52, 350n69, 350n75, 358n177, 359n198-9
Sangster, William, 296n117, 338n135
Scanlon, Michael, 286n13, 297n134
Schempp, Johannes, 257n2, 363n24
Schmemann, Alexander, 347n30
Schmid, Heinrich, 293n84
Schmidt, Martin, 259n27, 261n43, 366n60
Schneeberger, Vilém, 260n38, 273n149, 337n106, 338n124, 363n24, 367n82, 368n87, 369n106
Scroggs, Robin, 268n88, 270n100, 286n7, 310n123, 311n128

Selleck, J. Brian, 304n20, 309n100, 314n43, 338n123, 346n13, 351n79, 351n85, 354n128-9, 355n142, 357n163, 359n199, 361n233
Shimizu, Mitsuo, 262n1, 270n107, 275n3
Smith, Harmon, 287n20, 296n118
Smith, James, 263n14, 287n20, 299n158, 300n169
Snyder, Howard, 135-6, 320n125-7, 320n131, 354n129-30, 362n1, 363n26, 364n29, 366n58-9, 366n64, 366n67, 367n68
Southey, Robert, 315n59
Spidlík, Tomás, 262n10
Staniloae, Dumitru, 263n16
Staples, Rob, 287n20, 296n118, 298n148, 312n3, 316n78, 322n152, 337n109, 344n211, 345n3, 350n69, 358n178, 362n237
Starkey, Lycurgus, 266n54, 301n185, 312n3, 312n5, 314n33, 322n152, 322n155, 344n211, 358n177
Steele, Richard, 276n14, 288n26, 288n28, 305n46, 318n95, 338n128
Stephanou, Eusebius, 285n3
Stewart, Columba, 285n3
Stoeffler, F. Ernest, 314n41-2, 359n199, 366n59, 366n64
Strawson, William, 290n49, 362n6, 370n117, 372n150, 374n8
Stuart, William, 289n40, 301n184, 321n140, 322n163
Sugden, Edward, 47, 274n164, 296n117
Sykes, Norman, 351n85
Thomas, Wilhelm, 270n100, 343n199
Thompson, Bard, 357n165
Thorsen, Donald, 265n40, 267n69, 269n96, 270n105-6, 271n116, 273n147-8, 273n150, 274n152, 281n76
Townsend, James, 313n29, 314n33, 317n80, 331n14
Tracy, Wesley, 274n161, 354n128, 360n211
Trickett, David, 345n3, 354n121
Tripp, David, 321n139, 321n143, 322n159, 354n118
Tsirpanlis, Constantine, 363n15
Turner, John, 259n28, 337n106, 339n137
Tuttle, Robert, 259n30, 326n47
Tyson, John H., 259n30, 260n31, 304n25, 314n33, 326n47, 335n77, 336n89
Tyson, John R., 269n90-1, 278n50, 297n140, 303n15, 304n18, 307n72, 310n114, 323n3, 331n14, 332n34, 342n185, 342n187, 352n98, 356n155, 367n84
Villa-Vicencio, Charles, 363n25, 367n84, 368n86-7, 374n9
Wade, William, 351n79, 351n86, 352n99
Wainwright, Geoffrey, 272n135, 278n49, 279n53, 300n175, 310n121, 318n103, 320n133, 321n150, 322n161, 328n70, 343n194, 345n3, 350n75, 351n86, 352n92, 359n193-4, 361n233, 362n237, 366n59
Wakefield, Gordon, 343n199, 345n3
Walters, Orville, 337n109, 339n135, 339n144
Watson, David L. , 266n54, 332n34, 334n56, 354n122, 354n126, 354n129-30, 355n131, 357n170, 366n64
Watson, Philip, 343n194, 368n92
Weiβbach, Jürgen, 259n28, 286n12-3, 301n184
Wesley, Charles, 31, 56, 106-7, 113, 159, 160, 186, 240, 247, 261n46, 269n90-1, 278n50, 280n66, 282n91, 283n102, 283n106-7, 284n117, 292n66, 297n140, 298n143, 303n15, 304n18, 307n72, 308n79, 308n82, 311n136, 313n29, 314n33, 316n70, 317n80, 319n116, 320n133, 321n144, 322n155, 323n167, 323n3, 324n12, 325n24, 328n74, 337n114, 339n147, 340n157, 341n167, 342n187, 343n197, 344n206, 345n220, 348n35, 349n52, 352n98, 352n100, 356n155, 357n163, 359n195, 359n206, 361n223, 366n32, 368n88, 373n158
Wheeler, Henry, 276n24
White, James, 351n79, 358n186, 359n207
Whitefield, George, 278n52

Willhauck, Susan, 360n211, 361n220, 361n222-3

Williams, Colin, 24, 84, 257n5, 263n14, 266n54, 271n111, 271n124, 273n149, 300n176, 301n187, 304n19, 307n69, 314n33, 320n133, 323n1, 327n54, 331n10, 336n88, 336n90, 336n97, 343n199, 358n176, 363n25-6, 366n64

Williams, Norman, 292n68

Wilson, David, 282n100, 283n102, 283n108-9, 332n25, 332n31, 372n150

Wilson, Kenneth, 272n129, 346n19, 351n79, 353n104, 358n176

Wood, A. Skevington, 320n132, 321n140, 344n213, 346n19

Wood, Lawrence, 262n1, 270n105

Wynkoop, Mildred Bangs, 286n9, 287n20, 298n153, 337n109

Yates, Arthur, 313n29, 314n33, 314n41, 314n43, 317n86

Zizioulas, John, 287n19

INDEX OF SELECTED SUBJECTS

(See also the detailed Table of Contents)

Affections, 51-2, 69, 81-2, 88, 113, 115-6, 132, 145-6, 164, 180, 184, 188, 201,276n23, 288n26-9, 288n32

Aldersgate, 125-7, 144-5, 155, 196, 257n27, 324n15, 345n218

Animal salvation, 82, 146, 246-7, 252-3, 284n112

Assurance, 128, 130 (and see Witness of the Spirit)

Authority of Scripture, 32, 36-40, 41, 43, 45-6, 133, 269n96

Awakening, 88, 101, 112, 160-1

Baptism of the Holy Spirit, 177, 136, 227, 337n116

Consistency, 17-21, 58, 81, 118, 151, 180, 187, 199, 239, 254

Deification, (see Theosis)

Early/Middle/Late Wesley, 20, 75, 78-81, 85, 92-3, 103-4, 124-6, 127, 144-5, 148-51, 160-1, 163-5, 169, 180-7, 195-6, 200-1, 236-8, 245-6, 249, 252-3, 260n32, 326n47

Eastern Christian emphases, 23, 28, 55, 62, 65-8, 73-4, 77-8, 82-4, 86, 95-7, 112-5, 120, 121, 137-9, 142-3, 146, 152, 178, 180, 187, 194, 197-8, 217, 219, 223, 224, 250, 253, 262n10, 265n52, 274n160, 277n30, 285n3, 292n70, 296n116, 298n146, 301n180, 307n64, 309n92, 315n44, 322n151, 322n165, 335n68, 335n72, 336n90, 336n91, 337n108, 338n118, 338n128, 343n193, 350n75, 361n228, 362n12, 363n15, 363n27, 366n66, 366n70, 374n6, 374n7 (see also Macarius)

Emotion, 69, 124, 130, 131-2, 136, 208

Faith and Works, 175-6, 148-51, 242-3, 251

Faith of a Servant, 127, 154, 155, 161, 173, 220-1, 317n87

Grace, 84-7, 119-20, 297n139

Habit, 69-70, 132, 163, 179, 212, 318n103

Imputed righteousness, 103-4, 150, 166-8, 171

Inclusive grammar, 259n22

Inherited guilt, 74-5, 87

Inspiration, 31-2, 38, 121-2, 128-9

Law/Gospel, 100, 112, 114, 161, 209, 305n46

Liberty, 69-70, 71, 82, 88, 184, 289n38-9

"Mature" Wesley, 260n37

Ordo Salutis, 157-8, 257n5, 313n3, 348n42

Orienting Concern, 16-7, 39, 83, 113-4, 124, 149, 171-2, 186-7, 220, 253, 255-6, 258n16

Prevenient Grace, 29, 75, 84, 99, 123, 132, 159-61, 224, 228-9, 241, 245-6, 249, 347n27, 369n105

"Responsible Grace", 19, 55, 83, 86, 87-90, 100, 104, 130, 140, 148, 149-51, 156, 172, 196, 201, 218, 222, 235, 242, 253, 255-6, 312n11

Sin , 73-83, 163-5, 184-5, 244

Spiritual Senses, 27-8, 31, 128-9, 262n10, 263n11

Tempers, 37, 69-70, 81-2, 88, 98, 132-3, 145-6, 147, 152, 164, 178-9, 181-2, 187-8, 201, 212, 215, 288n30, 288n32, 338n132, 355n141, 355n148

Theosis, 66, 122, 132, 197, 303n11, 343n193

Uncreated Grace, 86, 90, 193, 195, 198, 204

Virtue (or character), 122, 129-30, 132, 179, 200-1, 243-4, 310n106, 317n80, 318n95, 338n118, 338n128

Wesley & Eastern Christianity, 23, 28-9, 42-3, 55, 62, 66-8, 73-5, 78, 81, 82, 84-5, 86, 90, 91, 96, 97-8, 115, 117, 120, 122, 137-9, 145, 146, 152, 176, 194, 198-200, 223, 224, 227, 250, 253, 260n42, 322n151, 328n70, 343n193, 343n136, 366n66, 366n70, 373n159 (Wesley's "synthesis" of East and West: 23, 67, 82, 85, 96, 114, 119, 142, 153-4, 256, 286n6, 336n91)

Wesley & Saints, 60, 207-8, 352n92

Wesley's "Arminianism," 84, 87, 90, 278n52, 299n159, 300n178

Wesley's Practical Theology, 16-7, 42, 44, 46, 47, 51, 78, 84, 92, 98, 112-4, 126, 139-40, 143, 155, 158, 162, 163, 166ff, 186, 199, 206-7, 220, 225-7, 241, 245, 254

Witness of the Spirit, 32, 35, 45, 124-31, 168, 173-4, 189